Semantics, Culture, and Cognition

SEMANTICS, CULTURE, AND COGNITION

Universal Human Concepts in Culture-Specific Configurations

ANNA WIERZBICKA

New York   Oxford
OXFORD UNIVERSITY PRESS
1992

Oxford University Press

Oxford   New York   Toronto
Delhi   Bombay   Calcutta   Madras   Karachi
Kuala Lumpur   Singapore   Hong Kong   Tokyo
Nairobi   Dar es Salaam   Cape Town
Melbourne   Auckland

and associated companies in
Berlin   Ibadan

Copyright © 1992 by Anna Wierzbicka

Published by Oxford University Press, Inc.
200 Madison Avenue, New York, NY 10016

Oxford is a registered trademark of Oxford University Press

Library of Congress Cataloging-in-Publication Data
Wierzbicka, Anna.
Semantics, culture, and cognition : universal human concepts in
culture-specific configurations / Anna Wierzbicka.
p.   cm.   Includes bibliographical references and index.
ISBN 0-19-507325-8. — ISBN 0-19-507326-6 (pbk.)
1. Universals (Linguistics)   2. Semantics.
3. Language and culture.   4. Intercultural communication.
5. Psycholinguistics.
I. Title.
P204.W54   1992
401'.43—dc20   91-22152

1 3 5 7 9 8 6 4 2

Printed in the United States of America
on acid-free paper

ACKNOWLEDGEMENTS

Research for this book was supported by a grant from the Australian Research Council, which enabled me to obtain valuable research assistance throughout this project. I would like to express my gratitude to Jean Harkins, Lisette Frigo, and Tim Curnow, who at different times have worked as my research assistants. I owe a special debt of gratitude to Jean Harkins, who was associated with this project longer than anyone else and with whom I had countless invaluable discussions. I would also like to thank those colleagues who at various stages discussed the contents of the book with me and offered valuable comments, criticisms, and suggestions: Felix Ameka, Jura Apresjan, Andrzej Bogusławski, Bob Dixon, Cliff Goddard, Igor Mel'čuk, and Tim Shopen. Thanks are also due to Ellalene Seymour for her expert and patient typing of successive drafts.

Some portions of this book first appeared, in different form, as articles in journals. I thank the publishers for permission to include revised and expanded versions of the following publications:

Soul and mind: Linguistic evidence for ethnopsychology and cultural history, *American Anthropologist*, vol. 91, 1989.
Human emotions: Universal or culture-specific? *American Anthropologist*, vol. 88, 1986.
Prototypes in semantics and pragmatics: Explicating attitudinal meanings in terms of prototypes, *Linguistics*, vol. 27, 1989.
Kinship semantics: Lexical universals as a key to psychological reality, *Anthropological Linguistics*, vol. 29, 1987.
Semantics and the interpretation of cultures: The meaning of 'alternate generations' devices in Australian languages, *Man*, vol. 21, 1986.
Does language reflect culture? Evidence from Australian English, *Language in Society*, vol. 15, 1986.

CONTENTS

VI LANGUAGE AS A MIRROR OF CULTURE
AND 'NATIONAL CHARACTER'

Semantics, Culture, and Cognition

Introduction

1. Are Languages 'Essentially the Same' or 'Essentially Different'? Universalism and Cultural Relativism

Language is a tool for expressing meaning. We think, we feel, we perceive—and we want to express our thoughts, our feelings, our perceptions. Usually we want to express them because we want to share them with other people, but this is not always the case.[1] We also need language to record our thoughts and to organise them. We write diaries, we write notes to ourselves, we make entries in our desk calendars, and so on. We also swear and exclaim—sometimes even when there is no one to hear us. The common denominator of all these different uses of language is not communication but meaning.[2]

But if language is a tool for expressing meaning, then meaning, at least to some extent, must be independent of language and transferable from one language to another. Yet this essential separateness—and separability—of meaning from language has sometimes been denied. For example, the eighteenth-century German thinker Johann Gottfried Herder maintained that thinking is essentially identical with speaking and therefore differs from language to language and from nation to nation. "The human spirit thinks with words", he maintained (1877–1913, v.21:19). "What is thinking? Inward language. . . . [T]alking is thinking aloud" (v.21:88). Consequently, "every nation speaks . . . according to the way it thinks and thinks according to the way it speaks". Thoughts cannot be transferred from one language to another because every thought depends on the language in which it has been formulated.

Profound semantic differences between languages were also emphasised by Wilhelm von Humboldt, who saw different languages as bearers of different cognitive perspectives, different worldviews. He wrote:

> [E]ach language . . . contains a characteristic worldview. As individual sound mediates between object and person, so the whole of language mediates between human beings and the internal and external nature that affects them. . . . The same act which enables him [man] to spin language out of himself enables him to spin himself into language, and each language draws a circle around the people to whom it adheres which it is possible for the individual to escape only by stepping into a different one. (1903–36, v.7:60)

3

Similar ideas were forcefully put forward by Edward Sapir, who wrote in a famous passage:

> Language is a guide to 'social reality'. Though language is not ordinarily thought of as of essential interest to the students of social science, it powerfully conditions all our thinking about social problems and processes. Human beings do not live in the objective world alone, nor alone in the world of social activity as ordinarily understood, but are very much at the mercy of the particular language which has become the medium of expression for their society. It is quite an illusion to imagine that one adjusts to reality essentially without the use of language and that language is merely an incidental means of solving specific problems of communication or reflection. The fact of the matter is that the 'real world' is to a large extent unconsciously built up on the language habits of the group. No two languages are ever sufficiently similar to be considered as representing the same social reality. The worlds in which different societies live are distinct worlds, not merely the same world with different labels attached. (1949:162)

Similarly, Whorf wrote:

> [Language] is not merely a reproducing instrument for voicing ideas but rather is itself the shaper of ideas, the program and guide for the individual's mental activity, for his analysis of impressions, for his synthesis of his mental stock in trade. . . . We dissect nature along lines laid down by our native languages. The categories and types that we isolate from the world of phenomena we do not find there because they stare every observer in the face; on the contrary, the world is presented in a kaleidoscopic flux of impressions which has to be organized by our minds—and this means largely by the linguistic systems in our minds. We cut nature up, organize it into concepts, and ascribe significances as we do, largely because we are parties to an agreement to organize it in this way—an agreement that holds throughout our speech community and is codified in the patterns of our language. The agreement is, of course, an implicit and unstated one, *but its terms are absolutely obligatory;* we cannot talk at all except by subscribing to the organization and classification of data which the agreement decrees. (1956:213–14)

Other students of language—for example, Noam Chomsky—regard languages as differing from one another almost exclusively in form. Thus, Chomsky sees the lexicon of a language not as a unique system of categorisation imposed on external reality, nor as a 'shaper of ideas', but essentially as a set of labels to be attached to concepts which are language-independent and are determined not culturally but biologically.

> Language and thought are awakened in the mind, and follow a largely predetermined course, much like other biological properties. . . . Human knowledge and understanding in these areas . . . is not derived by induction. . . . Rather, it grows in the mind, on the basis of our biological nature, triggered by appropriate experience, and *in a limited way* shaped by experience that settles options left open by the innate structure of the mind. (1987:25; emphasis added)

Much depends, ·of course, on the intended interpretation of phrases as "in a limited way". Humboldt (1903–36, v.4:2), too (unlike Herder), used qualifying phrases of this kind. For example, he wrote that "thinking is not merely dependent on language in general but, *up to a certain degree,* on each specific language" (emphasis added). But to what degree?

According to Chomsky, to a very low degree indeed. Chomsky (1987:18) recalls, in this connection, 'Plato's problem' as formulated by Bertrand Russell: "How comes it that human beings, whose contacts with the world are brief and personal and limited, are nevertheless able to know as much as they do know?" He comments: "[A]cquisition of lexical items also poses Plato's problem in a very sharp form, and we must assume . . . that the conceptual resources of the lexicon are largely fixed by the language faculty *with only minor variation possible*" (1987:48; emphasis added). Humboldt's view of the proportions between the universal and the culture-specific aspects of languages in general, and of their lexicons in particular, was entirely different:

> To be sure, a midpoint, around which all languages revolve, can be sought and really found, and this midpoint should always be kept in mind in the comparative study of languages, both in the grammar and lexicon. For in both there is a number of things which can be determined completely *a priori,* and which can be separated from the conditions of a particular language. On the other hand, there is *a far greater* number of concepts, and also grammatical peculiarities, which are so inextricably woven into the individuality of their language that they can neither be kept suspended between all languages on the mere thread of inner perception nor can they be carried over into another language without alteration. (1903–36, v.4:21–23; emphasis added)

In fact, Humboldt goes so far as to suggest that there are very few words in any language which do have exact equivalents in other languages.

A hundred and fifty years separate Chomsky's reflections from Humboldt's, and it might be expected, in view of this fact, that they would be based on a much firmer empirical basis. This, however, is not the case. If anything, the opposite is true. For example, Humboldt wrote:

> When, for example, in Sanskrit the elephant is sometimes called the twice-drinker, otherwise the double-toothed one, otherwise still the one-provided-with-a-hand, many different concepts are designated, even though the same object is meant. For language does not represent objects but rather the concepts which, in the process of speech, have been formed by the mind independent of those objects. (1903–36, v.7:89–90)

This is an interesting example pointing, convincingly, to some language-specific conceptualisations of certain aspects of reality. By contrast, Chomsky's examples, intended to illustrate the supposedly innate and culture-independent character of most concepts, seem at times somewhat fanciful.

Chomsky (1987:22) maintains that "there is no clear alternative to the assumption that acquisition of vocabulary is guided by a rich and invariant conceptual system, which is prior to any experience". Except for the adjective "rich", this assertion can be seen as essentially consistent with Humboldt's view. But then Chomsky goes on to say:

> Many have found this conclusion completely unacceptable, even absurd: it certainly departs radically from traditional views. Some, for example Hilary Putnam, have argued that it is entirely implausible to suppose that we have 'an innate stock of notions' including *carburetor, bureaucrat,* etc. If he was correct about this, it would not be particularly to the point, since the problem arises in a most serious way in connection with simple words such as 'table', 'person', 'chase', 'persuade', etc. But Putnam's argument for the examples he mentions is not compelling. (1987: 33)

The idea that even concepts such as *carburetor* or *bureaucrat* may be innate and universal was presumably not intended to be taken literally,[3] but the idea that "simple words" such as *table, chase,* or *persuade* stand for such concepts apparently *was* so intended. And yet it would have been enough to discuss the matter thoroughly with one or two bilingual persons to find out that words of this kind do not have exact equivalents in other languages, and therefore cannot stand for concepts which are innate and universal.

For example, in Polish (my own native language) *table* has not one counterpart but two: *stół* and *stolik,* both of which differ in some respects from *table* (and from one another). For example, a coffee table or a telephone table would have to be described in Polish as *stolik,* whereas a dining table would have to be called *stół.* The verb *chase,* too, has two different counterparts in Polish, *ścigać* and *gonić,* both of which differ in some respects from *chase.* (Roughly speaking, *ścigać* implies an intention to move faster than the target, where *gonić* implies an intention to catch.) As for *persuade,* it has only one equivalent in Polish, *przekonać,* but in this case the Polish word has two different equivalents in English, *persuade* and *convince,* both differing in some respects from each other (cf. Wierzbicka 1987b) and from the Polish word.

The idea that English words such as *table, chase,* and *persuade* are just English 'labels' for innate and universal human concepts suggests that Chomsky's thoughts on the subject of lexical universals are based on speculative reflection rather than on any empirical investigations. Speculation of this kind has been occurring for centuries. It is time for it to be replaced by systematic empirical investigations, on a broad cross-linguistic and cross-cultural basis.

2. What Is Universal in Language and Thought?

There seems hardly any need to argue at length against the two most extreme views concerning the relationship between meaning and language: the view that meanings cannot be transferred *at all* from one language to another, and the view that meanings can be *fully* transferred.

On the one hand, it is obviously the common experience of mankind that translation *is* possible. In particular, the Gospels or parts of the Gospels have been translated into more than one thousand languages, and if they haven't been translated into *all* the languages of the world it is not because of any inherent linguistic difficulties. On the other hand, it is almost equally a truism to say that a translator is necessarily a betrayer: *traduttore traditore*, say the Italians, and no bona fide translator would disagree with this judgement. Even more importantly, it is a common conviction of bilingual and bicultural people all over the world that they lead a 'double life', and that the meanings they express in one language differ from those expressed in the other (cf. Hunt and Banaji 1988; Green 1989; cf. also Wierzbicka 1985c).

The real question, then, is not *whether* meaning can be transferred from one language to another but *to what extent* it can be so transferred; not *whether* meaning is language-independent but *to what extent* it is. Or, to put it differently, to what extent languages are shaped by 'human nature' and to what extent they are shaped by culture.

In particular, we should ask whether there really are some meanings which can be expressed in separate words (or perhaps separate morphemes) in all the different languages of the world. Are there, say, some words in English which would have exact semantic equivalents in all languages and which could therefore be regarded as 'labels' for innate universal human concepts?

The task of comparing all the words of all known human languages on an item-by-item basis is a daunting and, presumably, impossible one. The only realistic prospect must be a different one: to form a number of alternative hypotheses and to test them.

One hypothesis, advanced by Swadesh (1955), took as its premise the idea that universal human concepts are probably determined by the universal conditions of human life, above all by the universal features of the human environment. All human beings know from experience the sun, the moon, the stars; all human beings know rain, wind, water, and fire. Moreover, all human beings are familiar with their own bodies. It was assumed, then, that concepts which might have equivalents in all languages should be looked for among words for natural phenomena such as the sun, the moon, rain, water, or fire, and among words for parts of the human body such as ears, eyes, hands, or legs.

The more this search for universal human concepts based on nature proceeded, however, the more obvious it became that it was doomed to failure. Certainly, all human beings have heads, eyes, ears, and hands; and all human beings know the sky above their heads and the ground under their feet. But they don't think about these things in the same way. And language doesn't reflect the world directly: it reflects human conceptualisation, human interpretation of the world. As a result, words referring to parts of the body, and words referring to the world around us, can be as language-specific as those referring to customs, rituals, and beliefs.

For example, the Eastern Aztecs in Central America don't have a special word for the side of the body—they only distinguish between the thorax and the abdomen—so that when a Bible translator wants to say that Jesus was pierced in the side, he must decide whether he was pierced in the side below the ribs or between the ribs, because there is no general word for 'side' (Nida and Taber 1969). Many languages use the same word for 'hand' and 'arm' (for example, Slavonic languages, Irish, Greek, Hausa, Tibeto-Burman, Australian languages).

What holds for body parts holds also for the features of our physical environment. For example, not all languages have a general word for wind. They may distinguish several kinds of wind, such as 'zephyrs', 'tornadoes', 'hot winds off the desert', and 'freezing winds', without having a general word for 'wind' (cf. Nida and Taber 1969). Not all languages have a general word for 'cloud'. For example, Polish distinguishes lexically between grey or greyish clouds which suggest rain (*chmura*) and light white clouds which don't (*obłok*). Not all languages have a general word for the sun. For example, in the Australian Aboriginal language Nyawaygi, there is one word for 'sun low in the sky in the morning and in the evening' and another for 'hot sun, when overhead'. In the same language there is no general word for 'moon', but there is one word for 'full moon' and another for 'new moon' (cf. Dixon 1980:104).

The native classification of animals and plants differs notoriously from language to language. For example, in the Australian Aboriginal language Nunggubuyu (Heath 1978) the word for 'bird' includes fruit-bats and some flying insects such as grasshoppers. In the Australian Aboriginal language Warlpiri (Hale, Laughren, and Nash 1983–86) there is no general word for animals. Edible animals are distinguished from non-edible ones, the word for edible animals being the same as the word for meat. Similarly, there is no general word for 'plant', but rather for edible and non-edible plants.

The names of species, too, are language-specific, to some degree. For example, Japanese doesn't distinguish lexically between mice and rats, calling them both with one word (*nezumi*), which, of course, has no equivalent in English. Australian Aboriginal languages don't have a word for 'kangaroo', because they distinguish lexically between different species which in English can all be called, indiscriminately, *kangaroo*. And so on. (For a further discussion, see Wierzbicka 1990c.)

It is clear, then, that if we are to find truly universal human concepts, we must look for them not in the world around us but in our own minds.

The idea that universal human concepts are to be found in the inner world of human thought goes back at least as far as the seventeenth century, to the great rationalist thinkers of that century: Leibniz, Descartes, Pascal. In particular, Leibniz believed that every human being is born with a set of innate ideas which become activated and developed by experience but which latently exist in our minds from the beginning. These innate ideas are so clear to us that no explanation can make them any clearer. On the contrary, we interpret all our experience through them.

Leibniz (1903:430) called those ideas with which, he believed, every human being was born "the alphabet of human thoughts". All complex thoughts—all meanings—arise through different combinations of simple ideas, just as written sentences and written words arise through different combinations of letters from the alphabet. He wrote:

> Although the number of ideas which can be conceived is infinite, it is possible that the number of those which can be conceived by themselves is very small; because

an infinite number of anything can be expressed by combining very few elements. On the contrary, it is not only possible but probable, because nature usually tends to achieve as much as possible with as little as possible, that is, to operate in the simplest manner. . . . The alphabet of human thoughts is the catalogue of those concepts which can be understood by themselves, and by whose combination all our other ideas are formed. (1903:430)

Complex meanings codified in separate words may differ from language to language because each language may choose a separate word for a different combination of simple ideas. But 'simple ideas', on which human speech and human thought are based, are presumably the same for all people on earth.[4]

The task of discovering the ultimate simples (the 'atoms of human thought') was seen by Leibniz as difficult and time-consuming, but by no means impossible. It had to be pursued by trial and error, that is, by sustained, systematic attempts to define as many words as possible, so that one could identify on an empirical basis those concepts which serve as the building blocks from which all others are constructed. The basic guideline in this search was the requirement that the set of simple concepts should contain only those which are truly necessary for defining all the others. Whatever *can* be defined is conceptually complex and *should* be defined; whatever *cannot* be defined (without circularity and without going from simple to complex and from clear to obscure) should *not* be defined. Only in this way can the true alphabet of human thoughts be discovered. "Reducenda omnia alia ad ea quae sunt absolute necessaria ad sententias animi exprimendas" (Leibniz 1903:281): 'All other [expressions] should be reduced to those which are absolutely necessary for expressing the thoughts in our minds.' If we do not discover this alphabet of necessary concepts which cannot be made clearer by any definitions ("quae nullis definitionibus clariores reddere possunt", 1903:435), we can never successfully elucidate meanings conveyed in language, because without this basic tool we will only be able to translate unknowns into other unknowns.

Leibniz (1903:430) illustrates the need for analysing all complex meanings into components which are self-explanatory with the following comparison. "Suppose I make you a gift of a large sum of money saying that you can collect it from Titius; Titius sends you to Caius; and Caius, to Maevius; if you continue to be sent like this from one person to another you will never receive anything." Definitions and other semantic formulae which send one from one unknown to another are like this. It is only by decomposing complex meanings into components which can be regarded as self-explanatory that any true understanding can ever be achieved.

A program similar to Leibniz' was proposed in the 1960s by Andrzej Bogusławski (1966; 1970), who saw in it a possible basis for linguistic semantics. I adopted this program in my own work, and in 1972, on the basis of empirical investigation of several semantic domains in a few European languages, I proposed in my book *Semantic primitives* a first hypothetical list of such elementary human concepts. It included fourteen elements: *I, you, someone, something, this, want, don't want, think, imagine, feel, part, world, say,* and *become.*

Since that time, semantic investigations based on the Leibnizian assumptions have been pursued on a wider empirical basis, extending to a number of non-Indo-

European languages (for example, to the African Tano-Congo language Ewe in the work of Felix Ameka, to Chinese in the work of Hilary Chappell, and to Australian Aboriginal languages in the work of Nicholas Evans, Cliff Goddard, Jean Harkins, Joyce Hudson and David Wilkins). This expansion has prompted the idea that the search for the 'alphabet of human thoughts' should be linked—directly and explicitly—with the search for lexical universals, that is, for concepts which have been lexicalised (as separate words or morphemes) in all the languages of the world.

As the empirical basis of the work expanded, and as the theoretical analysis continued over the years, the list of primes originally postulated was revised and expanded. My current hypothesis is that of the fourteen primes posited in 1972 ten are truly valid: *I, you, someone, something, this, say, want, don't want,* (or: *no*), *feel,* and *think.* In addition, I would now strongly postulate as valid the following three: *know, where,* and *good.* Other elements which are currently being investigated as possible candidates include *when, can, like, the same, kind of, after, do, happen, bad, all, because, if,* and *two.* Four older candidates, *part, become, imagine,* and *world,* are at present regarded as problematic but have not been definitely abandoned. (See Wierzbicka 1989a and b and 1991c; Goddard 1989a and b; Bogusławski 1975, 1989, and 1990; Wierzbicka and Goddard, eds., forthcoming.)

The 'list' of hypothetical semantic primitives proposed here is in fact not just a list, but a mini-language, with its own grammatical categories and its own syntax. Thus, the elements 'I', 'you', 'someone', and 'something' form something like a nominal class; the elements 'this' and 'the same' (or 'other') can be regarded as an analogue of determiners; 'good' and 'bad' as an analogue of adjectives; 'think', 'say', 'want', and 'know' as an analogue of verbs; and so on. I presume that the 'sentences' in the mini-language have the form of simple clauses, such as the following ones:

> I think this
> I want this
> you do this
> this happened
> this person did something bad
> something bad happened because of this

The whole problem of the 'grammar of human thoughts' is of course as important as that of the lexicon of human thoughts. For reasons of space, however, it cannot be discussed here. (For some discussion, see the introduction to Wierzbicka 1988a; see also Wierzbicka 1991c and in press e.)

I believe that the final identification of the universal set of semantic primitives (that is, of the 'alphabet of human thoughts') is an urgent task of linguistic semantics, with vital consequences not only for linguistics but also for cognitive science and for cultural anthropology, as a universal and 'culture-free' analytical framework is indispensable for a rigorous analysis and comparison of meanings encoded and conveyed in language.

3. Semantic Primitives and Lexical Universals

3.1 The Search for the Primitives

If there is a universal set of human concepts, is it possible to discover what they really are? And if one were faced with several alternative lists of candidates for such concepts, could one determine in a non-arbitrary way which list is most likely to be true?

The spectre of alternative lists, all equally plausible, has often been raised by students of language and thought. Curiously, however, fears of this kind are usually expressed by theorists who have never tried to engage in an empirical search for universal human concepts. Those who have engaged in such a search know that it may be easy to propose some candidates but that it is exceedingly difficult to justify them, and that the danger of several equally plausible lists is (at least at this stage) a myth.

The challenge consists not in *proposing* a list of candidates (although even this has been attempted very seldom, and by very few scholars) but in justifying it.

Chomsky (1987:23), for example, writes: "However surprising the conclusion may be that nature has provided us with an innate stock of concepts, and that the child's task is to discover their labels, the empirical facts appear to leave open few other possibilities." This is correct, I believe; I have been trying to establish it for twenty years. But it is not clear what kind of "empirical facts" Chomsky has in mind. If his "empirical criteria" lead him to the conclusion that English words such as *table, chase,* or *persuade* (not to mention *bureaucrat* or *carburetor*) stand for innate, universal human concepts, then whatever those criteria are they can hardly have much in common with those employed in this book.

In the research presented here, there are two independent avenues of empirical evidence: (1) the role a given concept plays in defining other concepts and (2) the range of languages in which a given concept has been lexicalised. For example, the concept realised in English by the verb *say* is useful for defining, among other things, hundreds of English verbs of speech, such as *ask, demand, apologise, curse, scold, persuade,* and *criticise* (cf. Wierzbicka 1987a). By contrast, words such as *chase* or *persuade* are not similarly useful in defining other words. Furthermore, the concept realised in English as *say* is known to have its exact semantic equivalents in hundreds of other languages, and in fact there is no known human language which wouldn't have a word expressing this concept. By contrast, English words such as *chase* or *persuade* are highly language-specific, and it is questionable whether they have exact semantic equivalents in *any* other language, let alone in *every* other language.

The combination of these two independent criteria—defining power and universality—provides a powerful empirical check on the range of hypotheses which could be put forward on the basis of mere speculation and gives the program of research defined in this way a strongly empirical character.

When the great seventeenth-century thinkers (above all, Descartes) first formulated the idea that there is an innate stock of human concepts, they offered two criteria for their identification: (1) these concepts must be intuitively clear and self-explanatory; and (2) they must be impossible to define. For example, it was claimed, it is impossible to define the concept of 'thinking' (in particular, the concept of *cogito* 'I think'), and any attempt to do so can only lead to greater obscurity and confusion. Furthermore, there is no need to define this concept, because its meaning is intuitively clear to us.

However, Descartes' two criteria have proved insufficient as operational guidelines: it is not always clear whether a concept can or cannot be further defined (without circularity and without increased obscurity), and whether a concept is, or isn't, as clear and self-explanatory as any human concept can be.

Leibniz added to Descartes' two criteria a third, which has proved much more helpful as an operational guideline: (3) the requirement that the ultimate 'simples' in the alphabet of human thought should be not only clear and indefinable but also demonstrably active as 'building blocks' in the construction of other concepts. It is this third criterion which made Leibniz engage in extensive lexicographic experimentation: to see which concepts have a potential for defining other concepts one has to try them out in vast numbers of tentative definitions.

In recent linguistic work, we have added two further criteria to the three inherited from the seventeenth century: (4) the requirement that candidates for the status of innate and universal human concepts should 'prove themselves' in extensive descriptive work involving many different languages of the world (genetically and culturally distant from one another) and (5) the requirement that the concepts which have 'proved themselves' as building blocks in definitions should also prove themselves as lexical universals, that is, as concepts which have their own 'names' in all the languages of the world. Of the candidates considered by Leibniz, some (for example, 'I' and 'this') have proved themselves in this respect; others (for example, 'perceive') have not.

It should be noted that the criterion of 'universal words' (or morphemes) is entirely independent of the criterion of 'versatile building blocks', and that there are very few human concepts which can be suspected of satisfying both: in all probability, no more than three dozen. I say 'words' for simplicity's sake. In fact, I mean lexical equivalents of any kind, possibly smaller or larger than words. For example, Japanese has, loosely speaking, two items corresponding to the English word *want*—the adjective *hoshii* and the bound morpheme *tai*—and it is not clear at this stage which of them should be regarded as the semantic equivalent of *want*. Similarly, in Chichewa the equivalent of the English word *good* is a bound morpheme (Hill 1987:99), but this fact doesn't discredit the concept 'good' as a possible lexical universal.

According to Robert Bugenhagen (personal communication; hereafter p.c.), in the Mangap-mbula language of New Guinea, the same verb, *so,* is used for both 'saying' and 'wanting'. This would contradict the claim that both 'say' and 'want' are lexical universals, if the language had no other resources to convey these notions. This, however, is not the case: the verb *so* can be analysed as meaning, essentially, 'say' (not 'say/want'), and there is another lexeme in the language which means only 'want': *lele-pa,* lit., 'insides-for'. This lexeme comprises two recognisable words, but it can be regarded as one lexical item, embodying the universal semantic primitive 'want'.

The possibility of hypothetical semantic primitives' being realised as lexical units larger than words can be illustrated from English. For example, the elements referred to earlier as *part* and *place* (or *where*) are really expressed in English more fully as (*X*) *is a part of* (*Y*) and (*X*) *is in place* (*P*). ('Being somewhere' or 'being a part of something' is not analysable into 'being' and 'somewhere' or 'being', 'part', and 'of'.)

Humboldt (1903–36, v.4:21–23) claimed, as we have seen, that all languages revolve, both in grammar and in lexicon, around a small number of universal concepts, which are determined completely a priori and that these concepts "can be sought and really found". But he didn't say *how* they can be found or how one can even start looking for them.

I believe the answer to the basic question of how to start lies in Leibniz' idea of 'building blocks' which have to prove themselves in definitions. A plausible set of indefinables which can 'generate' all other words (and all the grammatical meanings) of a language can be tentatively established on the basis of any human language (Latin, English, or whatever). But before accepting such a set as a likely 'alphabet of human thoughts' we would first have to verify its applicability to other languages. The criterion of 'universal words' quickly exposes some weak points of any tentative set of indefinables and points to the need for revisions. This leads to an amended set of candidates, which can in turn be checked against the requirement of 'universal words'. The process of adjustments and readjustments may be a long one, but it is a task for decades, not centuries or millennia. Above all, it can be seen as a realistic and realisable goal, not a golden dream to be relegated to the realm of Utopia.

3.2 The Problem of Polysemy

Unlike the search for indefinables, the search for lexical universals may seem to be a purely empirical task: laborious, to be sure, but relatively straightforward. In fact, however, the presence or absence of a word for a given concept cannot be established by any mechanical, checklist method. The search is empirical, but it also necessarily has an analytic dimension. Above all, there is the problem of polysemy. I have postulated 'you' and 'I' as universal semantic primitives, but what I mean by 'you' is 'you SG' ('thou') rather than 'you PL' or 'you SG/PL'. Yet one doesn't have to look further than modern English to find a language which doesn't seem to have a word for 'thou'. To maintain the claim that 'thou' is a lexical universal we would have to posit polysemy for the word *you:* (1) you SG, (2) you PL. Initially, this seems an unattractive solution, but I think there are good reasons for accepting it. Polysemy is a fact of life, and basic, everyday words are particularly likely to be polysemous (cf. Zipf 1949). For example, *say* is polysemous between the abstract sense, which ignores the physical medium of expression (for example, "What did he say in his letter?"; "The fool said in his heart: there is no God"), and the more specific sense, which refers to oral speech only. *Know* is polysemous between the two senses which are distinguished in French as *savoir* and *connaître* or in German as *wissen* and *kennen* (cf. "I know that this is not true" vs. "I know this man").

It goes without saying that polysemy must never be postulated lightly, and that it has always to be justified on language-internal grounds, but to reject polysemy in a dogmatic and a priori fashion is just as foolish as to postulate it without justification. In the case of the English word *you*, I think its polysemy can be justified on the basis of the distinction between the forms *yourself* and *yourselves;* the choice between *yourself* and *yourselves* is determined by the choice between *you* SG and *you* PL ("you must defend yourself" vs. "you must defend yourselves").

3.3 Semantic Equivalence Versus Pragmatic Equivalence

If there are scholars who, like the ordinary monolingual person, believe that most words in one language have exact semantic equivalents in other languages, there are also those who believe that *no* words in one language can have exact equivalents in many other languages, let alone in all the languages of the world. For example, they say, there are languages which have no personal pronouns, no words for 'you' or 'I'. Japanese is sometimes cited as an example of this. This, however, is a fallacy, not a fact. The truth of the matter is that, for cultural reasons, Japanese speakers try to avoid *the use* of personal pronouns (cf. Barnlund 1975). It is polite not to refer overtly to 'you' and 'I' in Japanese, and the language has developed a wealth of devices which allow its speakers to avoid such overt reference, without producing any misunderstandings. For example, there are certain verbs in Japanese (so-called honorific verbs) which are never used with respect to the speaker, and there are 'humble', self-deprecating verbs which are never used with respect to the addressee; the use of such verbs often sufficiently identifies the person spoken about as to make an overt reference to 'you' and 'I' unnecessary. But the words for 'you' and 'I' do exist and *can* be used when it is necessary or desired.

It is also true that many languages, especially South-East Asian languages, have developed a number of elaborate substitutes for 'you' and 'I', and that in many circumstances it is more appropriate to use some such substitute than the barest, the most basic pronoun. For example, in a polite conversation in Thai, the use of the basic words for 'you' and 'I' would sound outrageously crude and inappropriate. Instead, various self-deprecating expressions would be used for 'I' and various deferential expressions for 'you'. Many of the expressions which stand for 'I' refer to the speaker's hair, crown of the head, top of the head, and the like, and many of the expressions which stand for 'you' refer to the addressee's feet, soles of the feet, or even to the dust underneath his feet, the idea being that the speaker is putting the most valued and respected part of his own body, the head, at the same level as the lowest, the least honorable part of the addressee's body (cf. Cooke 1968). But this does not mean that Thai has no personal pronouns, no basic words for 'you' and 'I'.

A language may not make a distinction which would correspond to that between the words 'he' and 'she', and in fact many languages, for example, Turkish, have just one word for 'he' and 'she', undifferentiated for sex. But no known language fails to make a distinction between the speaker and the addressee, i.e., between 'you' and 'I'.

This does not mean that the range of use of the words for 'you' and 'I' is the same in all languages. For example, in Thai, the word *chán*, which Thai-English dictionaries gloss as 'I', has a range of use incomparably more narrow than its English equivalent. When used by women, it is restricted to intimates, and it signals a high degree of informality and closeness; when used by men, it signals superiority, rudeness, disrespect (Treerat 1986; Cooke 1968). But since there are no invariant semantic components which could be always attributed to *chán*, other than 'I', the heavy restrictions on its use must be attributed to cultural rather than semantic factors. In a society where references to oneself are in many situations expected to be accompanied by expressions of humility or inferiority, a bare 'I' becomes pragmatically marked, and it must be interpreted as either very intimate or very rude. But this pragmatic markedness should not be confused with demonstrable semantic complexity.

Similarly, in Japanese there are many different words corresponding to the English word *you*, none of which has the same range of use as the English word *you*. Nonetheless I would claim that one of these words, *kimi*, can be regarded as a semantic equivalent of *you*. Originally, *kimi* meant 'ruler, sovereign', and presumably conveyed deference or respect, but in current usage no constant and identifiable attitude can be ascribed to this word. "Women use *kimi* only with intimates or those of inferior status, but men use it when speaking to strangers and in any situation" (Russell 1981:120). This range of use is different from that of *you*, but it can make perfect sense if we assume that in terms of meaning, *kimi* is identical with *you* SG, and that in Japan women are expected to show respect to people of equal or higher status with whom they are not intimate.

The foregoing discussion notwithstanding, the search proposed here is aimed at real semantic universals, not at approximations. For example, the suggestion that the Gidabal dialect of the Bandjalang language in Australia doesn't have an exact semantic equivalent for the English word *this*, because the nearest Gidabal equivalent, *gaya*, implies 'visibility' as well as 'thisness' (Brown 1985:287), represents potentially a serious counter-example to the claim that 'this' is a lexical universal. What matters here is not so much that the Gidabal word *gaya* has a range of use somewhat different from that of the English word *this*, but that this difference in use appears to be due to a specifiable semantic difference: 'this' (in English) vs. 'this, which I can see' (in Gidabal).

Closer inspection, however, suggests that this particular counter-example is more apparent than real. Crowley's (1978:72) authoritative study of Bandjalang makes it clear that the so-called visible demonstrative is in fact unmarked, and that there is another, marked 'invisible' demonstrative. The closest Bandjalang equivalent of *this* doesn't mean 'this, which I can see'; it means simply 'this' (cf. also Holmer 1971).

Differences in the range of use can often be explained in terms of factors other than the semantic. But the presence of a *specifiable semantic* difference could not be reconciled with the claim that two lexical items have the same meaning. Experience shows, however, that reports concerning alleged semantic differences cannot be accepted at face value.

3.4 Why Aim at a Minimal Set of Primitives?

One last aspect of the search for a plausible set of universal semantic primitives which must be touched on concerns the size of this set. As George Miller (1978) asked, why should we necessarily pursue a *minimal* set of hypothetical primitives?

Miller's own answer (that the fewer items we posit the smaller the chance of error; 1978:76) makes sense, but I don't think it covers the most important point, namely that only a minimal set of primitives can enable us to account for *all* the semantic relations which give structure to the lexicon. If a single semantic 'molecule' is left unanalysed and is allowed to pass for a semantic 'atom', the relations between this 'molecule' and many other lexical items will be necessarily left unexplained.

A good illustration of the disadvantages of having a large metalexicon is provided by Longman's ambitious *Dictionary of contemporary English* (LDOCE 1978), an innovative dictionary operating with a 'controlled' vocabulary of two thousand words in terms of which all the other words included in the dictionary are defined. Because of the huge number of undefined words, the relations between words such as, say, *request, demand, order,* and *command* are not explained at all (since all these words are included in the set of two thousand). Moreover, the words outside the set of the 'basic' two thousand cannot be satisfactorily defined either, because the large semantic chunks such as 'request' or 'demand', operating as indefinables, are too big to be of much use in defining words such as *urge, persuade,* or *appeal* (which are not in the basic set). To capture the differences and the similarities among all such verbs we need 'small', fine-grained semantic components (such as 'want', 'think', or 'say'), not bulky ones (such as 'request' or 'demand').

If such fine-grained components are necessary for semantic comparisons within one language, they are ten times more necessary for semantic comparisons across language boundaries. For example, if we want to compare speech act verbs from different languages, we can do so only if we present their meanings as configurations of a small number of simple components such as 'want', 'think', or 'know', not as configurations of a larger number of components some of which would necessarily be quite complex. The point is that relatively complex concepts are usually language-specific. Only very few and very simple concepts have any chance of belonging to the shared lexical core of all languages. For cross-linguistic semantic research we must rely on the shared concepts. The problem before us is how to find *any* such concepts. Only the trimmest possible set of hypothetical indefinables established within any one language may have any chance at all of having a matching set of *semantic* equivalents in all other languages of the earth. (I stress the word *semantic* to prevent confusion with *absolute* equivalents, which we cannot expect to find at all; see section 3.3.)

4. Natural Semantic Metalanguage

Needless to say, the reader has the right to remain sceptical with respect to all the main tenets advanced here and to say, I don't know whether there are any 'universal words', and even if there were such words, I don't know whether there are any indefinable words in terms of which all the other words could be defined, and even if there were such words, I don't know whether they could ever be identified; furthermore, even if there is a set of indefinables and defining concepts, and even if there is a set of universal words, I don't know whether the former would necessarily correspond to the latter: that is, I don't know whether there is a set of concepts which would meet both of these criteria at the same time.

In response to such scepticism, however, I would reply that if there were no such set it would have to be invented: meanings *cannot* be rigorously described and compared without some kind of culture-free semantic metalanguage.

To explain any meanings we need a set of presumed indefinables; and to explain meanings across language and culture boundaries we need a set of presumed universals. We can understand ourselves to the extent to which we can rely on some concepts which are self-explanatory ("si nihil per se concipitur, nihil omnino concipietur", Leibniz 1903:430; that is, 'if nothing can be understood by itself nothing at all can ever be understood'), and we can understand other languages and other cultures to the extent to which we can rely on shared concepts. To be able to elucidate the meanings encoded in other languages we need a 'natural' semantic metalanguage, which would be maximally universal and maximally self-explanatory.

In modern linguistic literature, attempts have often been made to represent meaning in terms of various artificial symbols, features, markers, and the like. I believe that such attempts are fundamentally misconceived because any artificial symbols have to be explained, and to explain them we need some other symbols, and so on—until we reach the level of symbols which are self-explanatory. (It is again the story of Titius, Caius, and Maevius.) Artificial languages are never self-explanatory; an artificial 'Featurese' or 'Markerese' can never lead us to true understanding, because, as Lewis (1970:169–70) put it, "we can know the Markerese translation of an English sentence without knowing the first thing about the meaning of the English sentence". And within natural language, there is also only a small minority of words which can be plausibly regarded as self-explanatory.

Jerry Fodor, one of the main promoters of the use of artificial symbols in semantic analysis, responded to Lewis' remarks in the following way:

> It is . . . true that 'we can know the Markerese translation of an English sentence without knowing the first thing about the meaning of the English sentence'. . . . But, of course, this will hold for absolutely any semantic theory whatever so long as it is formulated in a symbolic system; and, of course, there is no alternative to so formulating one's theories. We're *all* in Sweeney's boat; we've all gotta use words when we talk. Since words are not, as it were, self-illuminating like globes on a Christmas tree, there is no way in which a semantic theory can guarantee that a given individual will find its formulae intelligible. (1975:120–21)

I believe, with Descartes and Leibniz, that there *are* words which are "self-illuminating like globes on a Christmas tree". But even if there were no such absolutely self-illuminating words, surely it would have to be conceded that some words are more so than others. For example, *person* is more "self-illuminating" than *animate, this* is more so than *deictic, think* more so than *cognition, do* more so than *agency, say* more so than *locutionary,* and so on.

Similarly, even if there were no absolutely 'universal words' there can be little doubt that some words are 'more universal' than others. Whether or not words such as *person, this, think, say, want,* or *do* are absolutely universal, they do have their semantic equivalents in countless languages of the world, and they do differ in this respect from words such as *animate, deictic, cognition, agency, deontic,* or *locutionary.* Whether or not we can find a set of concepts which would be truly clear, truly simple, and truly universal, if we want to be able to understand, and to explain, what people say, and what they mean, we must establish a set of words which would be maximally clear, maximally simple, and maximally universal. If we couldn't *discover* an 'alphabet of human thoughts', we would have to *construct* it.

I believe the best strategy for trying to discover such an 'alphabet' (if there is one) is to try to construct it; or rather, to construct a number of successive approximations of such an alphabet and to test them in wide-ranging cross-cultural semantic analysis. The natural semantic metalanguage employed and tested in this and other works by myself and colleagues is based on this assumption.[5]

Any postulated set of universal semantic primitives will readily attract a barrage of counter-examples. The challenge consists in continuing the search until a set is found which will not collapse under their weight. But the evidence cannot be even looked for until there is a hypothetical set of primitives to be tested.

Abstract speculation about semantic primitives can be useful in that it can help to identify some plausible candidates. But a set of plausible candidates constitutes only the starting point of the search. "In any case, a great deal of detailed lexical analysis would be required in order to determine which concepts should be taken as cognitive atoms for building all the others" (Miller 1978:76). This echoes Leibniz' view:

> Les premiers termes indéfinibles ne se peuvent aisement reconnoistre de nous, que comme les nombres premiers: qu'on ne sçauroit discerner jusqu'icy qu'en essayant la division [par tous les autres qui sont moindres]. (1903:187)

> The primary terms, the indefinables, cannot be easily recognised by us except in the way that the prime numbers are: we can only recognise them as such if we try to divide them [by all the smaller ones].

5. The Limits of Translatability

I believe that the past two decades of extensive and wide-ranging lexicographic experimentation conducted by colleagues and me confirm my initial hypothesis (Wierzbicka 1972a) that the stock of elementary human concepts is very restricted, and that in all probability it includes fewer than three dozen elements. It is possible that the set of 'universal words' is somewhat larger. For example, Berlin and Kay (1969) have produced evidence suggesting that all, or nearly all, languages may have words for two basic colours, black and white (or, perhaps, dark and light); these words are not indefinable (cf. Wierzbicka 1980:42–44), but they are perhaps universal. I have argued (in Wierzbicka 1987b; see also chapter 9) that all languages appear to have words for mother and father, which are not indefinable, but which still may be universal. Nonetheless, there can be little doubt that most of the lexicon of any language is, to a greater or lesser degree, language-specific—despite Chomsky's (1987:48) dogmatic assertion that "the conceptual resources of the lexicon are largely fixed by the language faculty, with only minor variation possible". If by "conceptual resources" he means the innate 'alphabet of human thoughts', then there is no evidence suggesting that there is in this area any cross-linguistic variation whatsoever; if, however, this means the vocabulary as a whole (as Chomsky apparently intends), then cross-linguistic and cross-cultural variation are not minor but colossal, as Leibniz, Humboldt, Sapir, Whorf, Weisgerber, and many other scholars of the past clearly saw, and as fresh empirical evidence constantly confirms. Furthermore, fresh empirical evidence constantly confirms the basic insight that lexical variation reflects cultural differences among different speech communities and thus provides priceless clues to the study of culture and society.

To quote Locke:

> A moderate skill in different languages will easily satisfy one of the truth of this, it being so obvious to observe great store of words in one language which have not any that answer them in another. Which plainly shows that those of one country, by their customs and manner of life, have found occasion to make several complex ideas, and given names to them, which others never collected into specific ideas. This could not have happened if these species were the steady workmanship of nature, and not collections made and abstracted by the mind, in order to naming [*sic*], and for the convenience of communication. The terms of our law, which are not empty sounds, will hardly find words that answer them in the Spanish or Italian, no scanty languages; much less, I think, could any one translate them into the Caribbee or Westoe tongues; and the *versura* of the Romans, or *corban* of the Jews, have no words in other languages to answer them; the reason whereof is plain, from what has been said. Nay, if we look a little more nearly into this matter, and exactly compare different languages, we shall find that, though they have words which in translations and dictionaries are supposed to answer one another, yet there is scarce one of ten amongst the names of complex ideas, especially of mixed modes, that stands for the same precise idea which the word does that in dictionaries it is rendered by. . . . These are too sensible proofs to be doubted; and we shall find this much more so in the names of more abstract and compounded ideas, such as are the greatest part of those which make up moral discourses: whose names, when men come curiously to compare with those they are translated into, in other languages, they will find very few of them exactly to correspond in the whole extent of their significations. (1959, v.2:48–49)

The experience of bilingual people all over the world echoes Locke's remarks. But monolingual popular opinion often dismisses, or ignores, the evidence of bilingual witnesses and the insight of keen observers such as Locke and follows speculations which are totally at variance with empirical evidence, as a recent discussion of the concept encapsulated in the Russian word *glasnost'* illustrates:

> Linguists call the belief that words determine thought "linguistic relativism"—or the Whorfian hypothesis. . . . Most linguists aren't crazy about the Whorfian hy-

pothesis. It suffers from circular logic, since the only way we English-speakers can talk about supposedly untranslatable concepts is to put them into English. The appeal of linguistic relativism in our time . . . may involve what the philosopher Karl Popper calls "the myth of the framework": our desire to believe that people who differ from us are beyond the reach of rational discussion, shut off in an imprisoning framework of words and concepts utterly alien to our own. . . . But, fortunately, détente, freedom, and *glasnost'* are concepts available to all of us. It is not the barriers of language that keep us from applying them. (*The New Yorker,* March 30, 1987, editorial comments)

This passage is conspicuous for its naivety, wishful thinking, and ethnocentrism, betraying a lack of any deep familiarity with languages and cultures other than the writer's own. Empirical study of different languages of the world shows that their lexicons are full of concepts "utterly alien to our own". For example, the Russian words *duša* (roughly 'soul') and *sud'ba* (roughly 'fate'), studied in the first two chapters of this book, are truly alien to speakers of English. I believe the meaning of these concepts, which are essential to the understanding of Russian culture and Russian national character, *can* be explained in English, and in the two chapters in question I attempt to do so. But no understanding of such crucial and culture-specific concepts will ever be achieved if it is not grasped at the outset that they *are* "alien to our own".

But if every language provides its own set of lexicalised concepts, every language suggests its own categorisation and its own interpretation of the world—consequently, every language is indeed a different "guide to reality" (cf. Sapir 1949:162). If most linguists seem nonetheless "not crazy about the Whorfian hypothesis", as *The New Yorker* put it, the reason is not that they have any evidence to the contrary, but that, until recently, tools were lacking which would have made possible a rigorous comparison of conceptual systems embodied in the lexicons of different languages (and, for that matter, in their grammars; cf. Wierzbicka 1988a). But the availability of a natural semantic metalanguage, based on presumed lexical universals, makes such a rigorous comparison possible.

Anyone who has undertaken such comparison (as I have in the present book and elsewhere) must conclude, I think, that the lexicons of different languages do indeed suggest different conceptual universes, and that not everything that can be said in one language can be said (without additions and subtractions) in another, and that it is not just a matter of certain things' being *easier* to say in one language than in another. On the other hand, there are good reasons to believe that every language has words available for the basic human concepts, and that everything that can be expressed at all can be expressed by combining those basic concepts in the right way. In this sense—but only in this sense—anything that can be said in one language can be translated, without a change of meaning, into other languages. Complex and culture-specific concepts such as those encapsulated in the Russian words *duša, sud'ba,* or *glasnost'* can be defined in terms of the basic concepts, and the definitions *can* be translated into the English version of the metalanguage, as they can be translated into its Japanese, Chinese, Pitjantjatjara, or Ewe versions. Each such version can be regarded as a *natural* semantic metalanguage, intelligible, in principle, to native speakers of the language in question. Nonetheless, each such version represents a standardised and non-idiomatic *metalanguage* rather than a natural language in all its richness and idiosyncrasy. This difference between a natural language and a natural semantic metalanguage derived from natural language defines the limits of precise translatability.

As pointed out by Grace (1987:14), modern linguistic literature tends to treat the "intertranslatability postulate" as a kind of unquestionable assumption. For example, Grace quotes Lenneberg's (1953:67) statement "A basic maxim in linguistics is that anything can be expressed in any language" (cf. also Carroll 1953:47; Osgood and Sebeok 1954:13; Searle 1969:19; Katz 1976:37). Grace rejects this basic assumption and argues instead that a language is shaped by culture, and that "what can be said . . . may be quite different from one language-culture system to another" (cf. also Pawley 1987).

I agree with Grace on all of these crucial points. I think, however, that he goes too far when he claims that "what is said cannot in any satisfactory way be separated from the way in which it is said" (1987:10), or that the worlds of meaning associated with different language-culture systems are incommensurable because there is no "common measure" (1987:7). The universal alphabet of human thoughts offers such a common measure and makes different semantic universes associated with different languages commensurable.

It is true that in natural language, what can be said cannot be fully separated from the way in which it is said, but in natural semantic metalanguage, the 'what' *can* be separated from the 'how'. For this reason, the use of the natural semantic metalanguage enables us to compare meanings across language and culture boundaries. In particular, it enables us to show how highly culture-dependent most meanings are.

If every language, has, so to speak, some 'one-element words' from the 'alphabet of human thoughts', expressing those basic concepts, every language has also a vast repertoire of complex concepts ('many-element words'), which constitute culture-specific configurations of the elementary building blocks and provide clues to culture-specific ways of thinking.

I do not claim, needless to say, that the *absence* of a word from a language proves the absence of the corresponding concept, or the inability to form this concept. But the *presence* of a word proves the presence of the concept, and, moreover, its salience in a given culture; compare Humboldt:

> From the mass of indeterminate and, as it were, formless thought a word pulls out a certain number of features, connects them, gives them form and colour through the choice of sounds, through a connection with other related words, and through the addition of accidental secondary modifications. (1903–36, v.4:248)

The natural semantic metalanguage employed here facilitates explanations not only of the meanings of words but also of syntactic and morphological constructions. In fact this book is by no means restricted to lexical analysis. Grammatical constructions, too, encode meanings (cf. Wierzbicka 1988a), and these meanings, too, differ from language to language and are culturally revealing (cf., in particular, chapters 9, 10, 11, and 12).

Languages are the best mirror of the human mind (Leibniz 1949:368), and it is through them, I believe, that we can identify the 'alphabet of human thoughts', that is, the basic conceptual framework with which human beings operate. At the same time, languages are the best mirror of human cultures, and it is through the vocabulary of human languages that we can discover and identify the culture-specific conceptual configurations characteristic of different peoples of the world.

In his famous introduction to the *Handbook of American Indian languages,* Boas wrote:

> [L]anguage seems to be one of the most instructive fields of inquiry in an investigation of the formation of the fundamental ethnic ideas. . . . Judging the importance of linguistic studies from this point of view, it seems well worth while to subject the whole range of linguistic concepts to a searching analysis, and to seek in the peculiarities of the grouping of ideas in different languages an important characteristic in the history of the mental development of the various branches of mankind. (1911:70–71)

The reference to "the history of the mental development of the various branches of mankind" belongs to the epoch when Boas wrote his introduction, but the view that "fundamental ethnic ideas" are reflected in language and can be revealed through a searching linguistic analysis defines a program which linguistics has not yet fulfilled and which should finally be given the place it deserves on the agenda of linguistic research. Boas' reference to the "peculiarities of the *grouping* of ideas in different languages" (emphasis added) corresponds even in form with the version of this program developed in this book and outlined in its subtitle: "Universal human concepts in culture-specific configurations".

6. Is Human Thinking 'Fuzzy'?

The assurances of universalists notwithstanding, not everything that can be said in Russian can be said in English, or vice versa. ("Inye mysli na inom jazyke ne mysljatsja", 'some thoughts cannot be thought in some languages', wrote the émigré-Russian poet Tsvetaeva, 1972:151.) Everything, however, can be translated into the natural semantic metalanguage, in its Russian, English, Pitjantjatjara, or any other natural-language-based versions. The concomitant claim is, of course, that every word (other than the members of the basic 'alphabet') can be defined.

The traditional assumption that words can be defined, however, has recently fallen on bad times. Many linguists, philosophers, and psychologists have come to doubt the definability of words and, moreover, are trying to present their pessimism and despair on this score as a new and superior wisdom. For example, Lyons (1981:56) starts his discussion of the problem with the lines from *Hamlet:*

> To define true madness
> What is't but to be nothing else but mad?
> (II, 2)

and then, after reflecting on the meaning of concrete words such as *table* and *chair*, he comments (1981:56): "the whole question of definition is far more complex— and a good deal more interesting—than most people realise. Madness it may be to define not only 'madness', but any word at all".

And he concludes: "[W]e have come finally to the view that most everyday words—words denoting natural and cultural kinds—are necessarily somewhat inde-terminate in meaning, and, therefore, for theoretically interesting reasons, undefin-able" (1981:73–74).

The most influential example of a 'fuzzy' and 'indefinable' concept offered in the literature is no doubt that of 'game', first introduced by Wittgenstein (1953:31– 32) in a famous passage of his *Philosophical investigations* and endlessly repeated by other writers: linguists, philosophers, psychologists, and others. Concepts, Witt-genstein argued, are mutually related by "family resemblance". They cannot be given accurate definitions in terms of discrete semantic components; it is impossible to capture the semantic invariant of a concept such as, for example, 'game', because all that different instances share is a vague "family resemblance", not a specifiable set of components.

Wittgenstein's idea of "family resemblance" has played a colossal role in the development of what is called "prototype semantics" and has acquired the status of an almost unchallengeable dogma in the current literature on meaning (cf., for example, Jackendoff 1983; Baker and Hacker 1980; Lakoff 1986).

The new slogan "against definitions" is now proclaimed even in the titles of some scholarly publications (cf., for example, Fodor et al. 1980). A new climate of opinion has emerged in which anyone who tries to define anything at all runs the danger of being seen as an old-fashioned figure, out of touch with his or her times and intellectual currents. To be with it, a semanticist is expected to talk not about definitions but about family resemblances, prototypes, and the fuzziness of human thought (cf. Wierzbicka 1990a).

The 'modern' view on the subject is, it is assumed, that words can't be defined because the meaning encoded in human language is essentially 'fuzzy', as is human thinking in general. It is sometimes acknowledged that, for 'practical reasons', definitions may be necessary, but this 'practical task' is regarded as pedestrian, and it is left to lexicographers.

Theoreticians, it is implied, have higher things to attend to. Remarkably, no-body seems to believe that dictionary definitions are good, but to try to improve on them, or to develop methods for doing so, is seen as being neither necessary nor possible; in any case, it is not something that theorists of language and thought should be expected to take an interest in. The task was not deemed unworthy by Leibniz, Spinoza, Hume, or Sapir, but it *is* below the dignity of most language theorists in the second half of the twentieth century.

In this new climate of opinion even those language theorists who do not claim that thinking is 'fuzzy' nonetheless assert confidently that words cannot be ade-quately defined and present this discovery as 'good news', or at least as something that there is no reason to worry about. For example, Chomsky writes: "Anyone who has attempted to define a word precisely knows that this is an extremely difficult matter, involving intricate and complex properties. Ordinary dictionary definitions do not come close to characterizing the meaning of words" (1987:21). That much is certainly true and uncontroversial. But Chomsky continues:

> The speed and precision of vocabulary acquisition leaves no real alternative to the conclusion that the child somehow has the concepts prior to experience with language, and is basically learning labels for concepts that are already part of his or her conceptual apparatus. This is why dictionary definitions can be sufficient for their purpose though they are so imprecise; the rough approximation suffices, because the basic principles of word meaning (whatever they are) are known to the dictionary user, as they are to the language learner, independently of any instruction or experience. (1987:21)

But imagine a child (or an immigrant) trying to find out what the word *insinuate* means, and finding in a dictionary (*Webster's* 1965) the information that it means "to suggest or hint indirectly"; *to hint* means "to suggest", a *hint* is "a suggestion, an indirect allusion", and *to suggest* is "hint, insinuate". Will this language learner— helped by his or her "conceptual apparatus"—know what the word *insinuate* means and how to use it?

Consider the following set of dictionary definitions (*Concise Oxford* 1964):

reprove	=	rebuke, chide
rebuke	=	reprove, reprimand, censure authoritatively
reprimand	=	official(ly) rebuke
censure	=	blame, criticise unfavourably, reprove
criticise	=	discuss critically, censure

Can any language learner find out from such 'definitions' (again, helped by his or her 'conceptual apparatus') what the verbs in question mean and how they differ from one another?

When it comes to key concepts in distant cultures—such as, for example, *amae* in Japanese, or *liget* in Ilongot, or *toska* in Russian (see chapter 4)—the idea that they might be accessible to outsiders 'without instruction or experience' must seem even more fanciful, and the suggestion that they don't need adequate definitions, even more unhelpful.

Of course, it may be argued that Chomsky is talking about children's acquisition of their first language, not about the understanding of other languages and other cultures. But children acquiring the basic vocabulary of their native language don't need dictionaries at all. It is above all second language learners who need dictionaries, and they need good ones, not bad ones.

What is most striking in Chomsky's remarks are the absence of any cross-cultural perspective whatsoever and the complete disregard for the fact that words differ in meaning across language and culture boundaries. For any language and culture learner, a good dictionary is a tool of prime importance, and it is an odd view for a linguist to take that there is no need to try to improve on the existing dictionaries, however bad they may be, because one can always rely on one's innate conceptual apparatus!

To anyone seriously trying to learn another language and to understand another culture, the 'discovery' that words cannot be defined ("for theoretically interesting reasons") can hardly be anything but very bad news. Fortunately, this 'news' is not true. As Armstrong et al. (1983:268) point out, "the only good answer [to the question, 'why do so many doubt the validity of the definitional view?'] is that the definitional theory is difficult to work out in the required detail. No one has succeeded in finding the supposed simplest categories (the features)."

But very few semanticists have actually tried to find the "simplest categories", and among those who did, most looked in the wrong direction, looking indeed for *features* instead of looking for *words*. But, as I have argued earlier, what is needed is not some artificial Featurese or Markerese, but a natural semantic metalanguage, derived from natural language and therefore intuitively intelligible. The reason why "definitions haven't been forthcoming" is that very few linguists have tried to provide them or to develop a coherent theoretical foundation on which adequate definitions could be based.

Serious lexicographic research, based on rigorous theoretical foundations, is just beginning. The success of this research will depend on (among other things) sustained efforts to establish the basic stock of human concepts—universal semantic primitives—out of which thoughts and complex concepts are constructed and in terms of which all complex concepts, in any language, can be explained. It will also depend on a critical re-examination of the fashionable prejudice that human thinking is 'fuzzy' and that meanings cannot be analysed in an accurate and rigorous way.

It is of course entirely possible, and even likely, that in addition to a universal set of elementary concepts there are also certain universal principles of semantic structure, which facilitate the acquisition of meaning. But if there are such principles, they can be discovered only through systematic lexicographical research, on a broad cross-linguistic and cross-cultural basis. This is another reason why linguists should engage in such research, instead of continuing to treat it as unnecessary or unimportant.

7. 'God's Truth' and 'Human Understanding'

It is impossible for a human being to study anything—be it cultures, language, animals, or stones—from a totally extra-cultural point of view. As scholars, we remain within a certain culture, and we are inevitably guided by certain principles and certain ideals which we know are not necessarily shared by the entire human race.

We must also rely on certain initial concepts: we cannot start our inquiry in a complete conceptual vacuum. It is important, however, that as we proceed, we try to distinguish what in our conceptual apparatus is determined by the specific features of the culture to which we happen to belong, and what can be, with some justification, regarded as simply *human*.

In the past, Western science and philosophy were motivated to a large extent by a desire to find the truth (objective, culture-independent truth, 'God's truth').[6] At the same time, however, it was, and often still is, profoundly ethnocentric. For example, many psychologists (and even many anthropologists) rely uncritically on concepts such as 'mind', 'anger', 'fear', or 'depression', regarding them as essential aspects of 'human nature', and apparently without ever suspecting that these concepts are culture-specific. (See chapters 1, 2, 3, and 4.)

In anthropology, concepts such as 'lineal', 'collateral', 'generation', 'descending', and 'ascending' are routinely used for the description of kinship vocabulary, and they are often claimed to be not only convenient descriptive tools but parts of the 'meaning' intended by the Eskimos, the Tahitians, or the Zulus. (See chapters 9 and 10.) Philosophers often rely uncritically on concepts such as 'freedom', 'courage', 'justice', or 'promise' without even suspecting that these concepts, too, may be creations of one particular culture (their own). (Cf., for example, Searle 1969; see also chapters 5 and 6.) Even linguists can sometimes assert that some 'simple words' from their native language (for example *table, chair,* and *persuade*) stand for innate and universal human concepts.

But it is not enough to be aware of the dangers of ethnocentrism. Cultural relativism, too, presents dangers to any pursuit of truth, and to scholarly inquiry into language, thought, and culture. Discussing Nietzsche's cultural relativism, Bloom points out that

> at the center of his [Nietzsche's] every thought was the question "how is it possible to do what I am doing?" He tried to apply to his own thought the teachings of cultural relativism. This practically nobody else does. For example, Freud says that men are motivated by desire for sex and power, but he did not apply those motives to explain his own science or his own scientific activity. (1987:204)

Trying to explore both the universal and the culture-specific aspects of meaning we should beware of using concepts provided by our own culture as culture-free analytical tools, but we should also be aware that we do need *some* culture-free analytical tools. We, too, must ask ourselves, "How is it possible to do what I am doing?"

As human beings, we cannot place ourselves outside all cultures. This does not mean, however, that if we want to study cultures other than our own all we can do is to describe them through the prism of our own culture, and therefore to distort them. We *can* find a point of view which is universal and culture-independent, but we must look for such a point of view not *outside* all human cultures (because we cannot place ourselves outside them) but *within* our own culture, or within any other culture with which we are intimately familiar. To achieve this, we must learn to separate *within* a culture its idiosyncratic aspects from its universal aspects. We must learn to find 'human nature' within every particular culture. This is necessary not only for the purpose of studying 'human nature' but also for the purpose of studying the idiosyncratic aspects of any culture that may interest us. To study different cultures in their culture-specific features we need a universal perspective, and we need a culture-independent analytical framework. We can find such a framework in universal human concepts, that is, in concepts which are inherent in *any* human language.

If we proceed in this way, we can study any human culture without the danger of distorting it by applying to it a framework alien to it, and we can aim at both describing it 'truthfully' and at understanding it.

We cannot understand a distant culture 'in its own terms' without understanding it at the same time in our own terms. What we need for real 'human understanding' is to find terms which would be both 'theirs' and 'ours'. We need to find *shared* terms, that is, universal human concepts.

It is interesting to note that even Whorf (1956:36) appears to have recognised the existence of 'a common stock of concepts' (he calls them "conceptions"). "The very existence of such a common stock of conceptions, possibly possessing a yet un-studied arrangement of its own", he wrote, "does not yet seem to be greatly appreci-ated; yet to me it seems to be a necessary concomitant of the communicability of ideas by language; it holds the principle of this communicability, and is in a sense the universal language to which the various specific languages give an entrance."

There is no conflict between a search for truth, 'God's truth', and a search for understanding, 'human understanding'. The truth about 'human understanding' is, I believe, that it is based on a universal, and presumably innate, 'alphabet of human thoughts', and it is this 'alphabet of human thoughts' which offers us a key to the understanding of other peoples and other cultures.

I

LINGUISTIC EVIDENCE FOR ETHNOPSYCHOLOGY AND ETHNOPHILOSOPHY

1

Soul, Mind, and Heart

1. The Russian *Duša* Versus the English *Soul*

The word *duša* (roughly, 'soul') is—alongside *sud'ba* (roughly, 'fate/destiny') and *toska* ('a painful feeling')—one of the leitmotifs of Russian literature and Russian conversation (see also chapter 12). Its range of use is extremely wide and its frequency extremely high. In English translations of Russian novels, *duša* is sometimes translated as *soul*, but in most cases, it is either omitted or replaced with either *heart* or *mind*.[1] To some extent, this can be explained in purely cultural terms: Anglo-Saxon culture doesn't encourage much talk about 'souls', and English prose doesn't seem to tolerate as many references to people's souls as typical Russian prose would. If the translator of a Russian novel does try to render *duša* as *soul* wherever possible (rather than simply omit it), the high frequency of the word *soul* gives the English prose a slightly odd flavour. This can be illustrated with the following passage from Robert Chandler's translation (Grossman 1985) of Vasily Grossman's (1980) novel *Žizn' i sud'ba* (*Life and fate*):

> I'm used to looking into people's eyes for symptoms of diseases—glaucoma, cataract. Now I can no longer look at people's eyes like that; what I see now is the reflection of the soul. A good soul, Vityenka! A sad, good-natured soul, defeated by violence, but at the same time triumphant over violence. A strong soul, Vitya! . . . Sometimes I think that it's not so much me visiting the sick, as the other way around—that the people are a kind doctor who is healing my soul. (1985:87)

Even if a translator is eager always to render *duša* as *soul*, no matter how often it is used, and in this way to violate Anglo-Saxon cultural conventions in order to remain faithful to the spirit of the original, often it is felt to be simply not possible, because the range of contexts where *duša* can be used in Russian is much wider than the range of contexts where *soul* can acceptably be used in English. In other words, often *duša* cannot be translated as *soul* not just because the frequency of *soul* would become too high for Anglo-Saxon cultural tastes but for intrinsic linguistic reasons (which is not to say that those intrinsic linguistic reasons are not, ultimately, culturally determined as well). Some examples:

> . . . on povtoril to že uže ot vsej duši. (Tolstoy 1953:733)

31

. . . he repeated the words from the bottom of his heart. [lit., 'from his whole soul'] (Tolstoy 1929–37, 10:273)

Ja . . . ot vsej duši rešilsja zabyt' vse, čto bylo meždu nami. (Tolstoy 1953:467)

I . . . resolved with my whole soul to forget everything that had come between us. (Tolstoy 1929–37, 9:486)

. . . javljajutsja tysjači komplikacij, kotoryx ona teper', otdyxaja dušoj posle vsex stradanij i ispytanij, ne vidit i ne xočet videt'. (Tolstoy 1953:681)

. . . thousands of complications appear which at present, while resting [lit., 'with (her) soul'] after all the sufferings and trials, she neither sees nor wishes to see. (Tolstoy 1929–37, 10:219)

Mne stalo legče na duše. (Grossman 1980:49)

I actually felt relieved. (Grossman 1985:85)

?I felt relieved in my soul.

Ej stanovilos' spokojnej, legče na duše. (Grossman 1980:41)

She always felt calmer for these conversations. (Grossman 1985:74)

?She felt calmer, relieved in her soul.

. . . ot ètogo na duše na veselej, a užas oxvatyvaet. (Grossman 1980:53)

. . . rather than feeling happier, I am seized with horror. (Grossman 1985:92)

?rather than feeling happier [lit., more cheerful in my soul], I am seized with horror.

In the last three examples, the word *duša* appears in the phrase *na duše*, lit., 'on (the) soul', which is most commonly used to refer to feelings and moods. This contrasts with the phrase *v duše*, literally 'in (the) soul', which tends to be used to refer to other aspects of inner life, and in particular to secret thoughts (compare the examples from *War and peace* adduced later). But from the way these two phrases *na duše* and *v duše* are used in Russian it is clear that they are not 'idioms' of any kind (as might be suggested) but applications of the same concept which is encoded in the noun *duša* used with other prepositions, or without any prepositions. The following examples from Tolstoy's diaries illustrate this:

Mučitel'no tjaželo na duše. Znaju, čto èto k dobru duše, no tjaželo. Kogda sprošu sebja: čto že mne nužno—ujti ot vsex. Kuda? K Bogu, umeret'. Prestupno želaju smerti. (Tolstoy 1985, v.22:284)

'My heart (duša) is heavy. I know that this is good for my soul (duša) but it is hard. I ask myself: what do I need—(I know:) to get away from everybody. Where to? To God, to die. It is criminal of me, but I want to die.'

Zdorovie nexorošo. Na duše uže ne tak xorošo, kak bylo. Tolstoj zabiraet silu nado *mnoj*. Da vret on. Ja, Ja, tol'ko i est' Ja, a on, Tolstoj, mečta, i gadkaja, i glupaja. (Tolstoy 1985, v.22:303)

'My health is not good. "On the soul" it is not as good as before. "Tolstoy" is winning over me. But he is lying. I, I, that's all there is, and he, "Tolstoy", is a dream, a loathsome, stupid dream.'

Clearly, the phrase *na duše*, 'on the soul', can refer not only to feelings and moods but, in general, to the current state of a person's *duša*.

The high frequency and the wide scope of use of the Russian *duša* distinguish it not only from the English *soul* but also from its closest lexical equivalents in other European languages, in particular from the French *âme* and from the German *Seele*. In fact, one could probably arrange European languages on a scale, with Russian and English at the opposite ends and with French and German in between.

To illustrate this general proposition, let me mention here one somewhat crude but characteristic statistic: of fifty occurrences of *duša* in Tolstoy's *War and peace* which I have counted, only twenty-six have been rendered as *Seele* in German (Tolstoy n.d.), and only eighteen have been rendered as *âme* in French (Tolstoy 1945).

Individual counts of this kind, however, can be misleading, as the frequency of the literal equivalents of *duša* depends of course on the translator's attitude. In the English translation of *War and peace* by Louise Maude and Aylmer Maude (Tolstoy 1930–31), most instances of *duša* have in fact been rendered as *soul*, often producing rather bizarre English sentences. The results of such overly literal translations are interesting because they highlight the wide scope of the use of *duša* in Russian. For example:

A strange feeling of exasperation and yet of respect for this man's self-possession mingled at that moment in Rostov's soul. (Tolstoy 1930–31, v.1:318)

He is such a lofty, heavenly soul. . . . (Tolstoy 1930–31, v.1:433)

'It can't be helped! It happens to everyone!' said the son with a bold, free and easy tone, while in his soul he regarded himself as a worthless scoundrel whose whole life could not atone for his crime. (Tolstoy 1930–31, v.1:452)

Pierre listened with swelling heart, gazing at the mason's face with shining eyes, not interrupting or questioning him, but believing with his soul what the stranger said. (Tolstoy 1930–31, v.1:465)

With my whole soul I wish to be what you would have me be. . . . (Tolstoy 1930–31, v.1:468)

Not a trace of his former doubts remained in his soul. (Tolstoy 1930–31, v.1:469)

Terrible doubts rose in his soul. (Tolstoy 1930–31, v.1:552)

Pierre in his secret soul agreed with the steward . . . but he insisted, though reluctantly, on what he thought right. (Tolstoy 1930–31, v.1:504)

The impression of relatively high frequency of *duša* in Russian is confirmed by word counts such as Zasorina's (1977) or Šteinfeldt's (1974). According to Zasorina's data, the word *duša* occurs as many as 377 times in a corpus based on one million words of running text, and if we add to this the occurrences of the adjective *duševnyj* and the adverb *duševno*, the figure rises to 450. According to Kučera and Francis (1967), the corresponding figure for the English *soul* is 73. It is also instructive to compare these figures with the figures for the Russian word *telo* and the English word *body*. Thus, in Russian, the 450 occurrences of *duša* correspond to 311 occurrences of *telo*, whereas in English, the 73 occurrences of *soul* correspond to 291 occurrences of *body*. In other words, in the English corpus there is roughly speaking 1 occurrence of *soul* to 4 occurrences of *body*, whereas in the Russian corpus there are as many as 6 occurrences of *duša* (that is, 6 times more) to 4 occurrences of *telo*.

I believe that differences in the scope of use of *duša* in Russian and of the normal use of *soul* in English reflect differences in the underlying semantic structure and that these reflect, in turn, significant differences in the cultural outlook, or in what is sometimes called ethnopsychology. In what follows, I will explore the differences between the Russian *duša* and the English *soul*, and their cultural implications, in some detail.

2. The Need for a Semantic Metalanguage

The word *soul* stands for a concept which has often been said to be philosophically important (like *truth, knowledge,* or *good;* cf. Peursen 1966:1), but its meaning has not been elucidated in the philosophical literature. Some philosophers treat this word simply as a more elegant and somewhat stylised substitute for the word *mind*, as Kenny (1973) does in the title of his book: *The anatomy of the soul: historical essays in the philosophy of mind*. Others feel that *soul* should not be simply identified with *mind* but declare that the relationship between these two concepts simply cannot be clarified, because both concepts are too elusive for that. For example, Teichman writes:

> The claim that the Soul exists seems to be a bigger claim, and a more controversial claim, than the claim that the mind exists. . . . Although they are different, the notions overlap. It is not possible to give a simple yes-or-no answer to the question as to whether the mind and the Soul are identical. In some contexts 'mind' means much the same as 'Soul' and in other contexts it does not. Generally speaking, however, *Soul* incorporates more than *mind*. (1974:3)

In my view, however, it is entirely possible to give a simple yes-or-no answer: no, they are not identical. Rigourous semantic analysis does allow us to clarify these elusive concepts and to spell out their relationship in a clear and precise way. But to do this, one needs a suitable methodological framework; above all, one needs a culture-independent semantic metalanguage.

In what follows, I will try to explicate concepts such as the English *soul, mind,* and *heart,* or the Russian *duša,* relying as far as possible on the proposed universal semantic primitives. In addition, the proposed explications will also contain some words—such as *see*—which are probably not elementary but which are reasonably close to the level of primitives and which I have discussed in other publications[2] (see, in particular, Wierzbicka 1980).

3. *Soul*

We can begin with what seems reasonably clear: the word *soul* can only refer to persons, not to things, and it doesn't normally refer to a person as a whole but only to one part of a person; the part to which it refers is not a part of the body, and it cannot be seen. As a first approximation, therefore, we could propose the following explication:

> *soul*
> a part of a person
> one cannot see it

But the phrasing 'a part of a person' seems to suggest that there are other parts, which are seen as being on a par with the soul. In fact, however, the concept 'soul' evokes just one other 'part', which is in some sense on the same level: the body. In other words, the concepts 'soul' and 'body' seem to reflect a dual, rather than a multiple, structure. For this reason, it may be more accurate to phrase the relevant component as 'one of the two parts of a person' rather than simply 'a part of a person'. This idea of dual structure fits in well with the idea of 'invisibility': in the folk philosophy reflected in the word *soul* a person has two parts: one which can be seen (the body) and one which cannot be seen (the soul). This leads us to the following amended formula:

> *soul*
> one of two parts of a person
> one cannot see it

However, there are at least two other aspects of the concept 'soul' which are missing from this formula: one referring to the 'transcendental', other-worldly nature of this (hypothetical) entity, and another referring to its moral character, that is, to its links with the idea of 'good'. To account for the 'transcendental' character of *soul* we could simply add to the explication the component 'it is not part of this world'. But in fact the 'transcendental' character of 'soul' seems to have some positive aspect as well: souls are not seen as part of 'this' world because they are seen as belonging to another, spiritual world (of things that can't be seen), that is, to a world that material things are not part of and that has some links with an immaterial good being or beings (God and perhaps other good spirits). To account for this, it seems more appropriate to explicate the 'transcendental' character of 'soul' along the following lines:

> it is part of another world
> good beings are part of that world
> things are not part of that world

The link between 'soul' and a spiritual world of good beings also explains the fact that the soul is the source of values in a human being as well. This can perhaps be represented as follows: 'because of this part a person can be a good person'. This leads us to the following definition:

> soul₁
>
> one of two parts of a person
> one cannot see it
> it is part of another world
> good beings are part of that world
> things are not part of that world
> because of this part a person can be a good person

For example, the reflection of the soul in someone's eyes is a reflection of that hypothetical invisible entity which is at the root of all good in a person and which belongs to a spiritual world different from the world of which material things are a part.

It might be suggested that the link of the concept 'soul' with values should be represented in terms of 'good' and 'bad', rather than simply 'good': 'because of this part, a person can be good or bad'. Linguistic evidence, however, seems to suggest that the link in question is perceived in terms of 'good' alone, that is, in terms of a person's capacity (or incapacity) for good. For example, one can call someone 'a kind soul', or 'a good soul', but not 'a cruel soul', 'a bad soul', or 'an evil soul'. *Soul* is analogous in this respect to *heart* (which will be discussed in more detail later): one can say that someone 'has a good/kind/warm/loving heart' but not that he or she 'has a bad/evil/vicious/hating heart'. Expressions such as 'heartless', 'a heart of stone', or 'cold heart' suggest a lack of warmth, love, or compassion, rather than wickedness or viciousness.

Furthermore, just as a 'heartfelt emotion' has to be a 'good emotion' (for example, gratitude or admiration rather than envy or contempt), so a 'soulful expression' could refer only to a 'good' face, never to a vicious, evil-looking face, distorted by hatred, anger, or jealousy.

Needless to say, the idea that entities of this kind (other-worldly and potentially good) exist at all belongs to a certain philosophy of the human person, a philosophy to which not everybody would want to subscribe. Nonetheless, it should be acknowledged that this view is a part of the folk philosophy of the speakers of English, a folk philosophy embodied in English (and no doubt due to the Christian tradition).

The existence of 'souls' has often been denied, of course, as, for example, in the following quotes:

> My mind is incapable of conceiving such a thing as a soul. I may be in error, and man may have a soul; but I simply do not believe it. (Thomas A. Edison, "Do we live again?", quoted in Stevenson 1946:1888)

> Nobody knows how the idea of a soul or the supernatural started. It probably had its origin in the natural laziness of mankind. (John B. Watson, "Behaviorism", quoted in Stevenson 1946:1888)

But to deny the existence of 'souls' one has to know what this word stands for in the shared semantic universe of the speakers of English. Since the existence of 'souls' is often denied, the meaning of the word *soul* must include something—some supernatural or transcendental reference—which would explain some people's need to voice such denials.

It is interesting to note that in older English the meaning of *soul* was different from what it is now and reflected a different folk philosophy. The existence of *soul* in that older meaning could not be so readily denied because that older *soul* was open to introspection (rather like *mind* is in contemporary English). For example, Hamlet's mother says:

> O Hamlet, speak no more;
> Thou turn'st mine eyes into my very soul;
> And there I see such black and grained spots,
> As will not leave their tint.
> (SHAKESPEARE, *Hamlet*, III, 4)

In that older meaning (which has survived in most people's passive knowledge of English, and to a varying degree in a stylistically marked active use) *soul* refers to an entity which has both a religious and a phenomenological (psychological) dimension. The meaning in question (*soul₂*) can be portrayed as follows:[3]

> *soul₂*
> one of two parts of a person
> one cannot see it
> it is part of another world
> good beings are part of that world
> things are not part of that world
> other people can't know what things happen in that part of a person
> sometimes the person doesn't know what these things are
> these things can be good or bad
> because of this part, a person can be a good person

Other people can't know what is happening in a person's *soul₂*. The 'owner' of the soul can know these things but doesn't always: sometimes one has to make an effort to drag these things to the surface of one's consciousness, and often people prefer not to make that effort (as Hamlet's mother indicates).

It appears that the same meaning of *soul* which we find in Shakespeare is also present in texts such as hymns still sung in churches, for example:

> Praise, my soul, the King of Heaven!
> To his feet thy tribute bring.
> (Henry Francis Lyle)

It is noteworthy that the word *mind* can never be used in such exhortations whether religious or irreligious:

> *Praise, my mind, the King of Heaven!
> *Think about it, my mind!

Consider also the following contrast:

> Confession is good for your soul (?mind).
> Chess is good for your mind (?soul).

Contrasts of this kind highlight, I think, both the transcendental and the moral implications of *soul$_2$* (and their absence from *mind*).

One gets the impression that in modern English this older sense of *soul* is often employed as a conscious stylisation, or as a kind of rhetorical figure. Consider, for example, the title of a recently published book, Bloom's *The closing of the American mind: how higher education has failed democracy and impoverished the souls of today's students*. The author is a professor at the University of Chicago, but also a translator of Plato and Rousseau. The word *soul* hints here, perhaps somewhat metaphorically, at 'spiritual riches', which are opposed to an education oriented toward the world of material things and material success (cf. Bowler 1987).

Such an archaic and perhaps metaphorical use of *soul* should, I think, be distinguished from an equally marked modern use which appears to be philosophically and religiously neutral. This third sense of *soul* occurs more often in translations—not only from Russian but also from German and French—than in original English discourse. For example, the following is from an English translation of Thomas Mann's *The magic mountain:*

> [I]f he had been able to believe in work as a positive value, a self-justifying principle, believe in it in the very depth of his soul, even without being himself conscious of doing so. . . . (1976:34)

In this use, *soul* seems to make no reference to 'another world', and to focus primarily on the psychological and moral aspects of a person's existence. Like *soul$_2$*, however, it hints at a 'deep' stratum of a person's personality, of which the person is not immediately aware. Since the use in question is rather marginal in modern English, and is encountered mostly in translations, I will call it *soul$_m$* (for marginal).

> *soul$_m$*
> a part of a person
> one cannot see it
> other people can't know what things happen in that part
> sometimes the person doesn't know what these things are
> these things can be good or bad

As this explication suggests, the psychological use of *soul* does not seem to imply a body-soul dichotomy, has no 'transcendental' implications, and does not refer to a moral 'core' of a person (because it doesn't contain the component 'because of this part a person can be a good person'). Rather, it is seen as a substratum of hidden psychological processes, unknowable to outsiders, and not necessarily clear to the 'insider'. Nonetheless, for all its psychological orientation, *soul$_m$* does seem to refer to values, to the notions of 'good' and 'bad'. It is different in this respect from *mind*, which has come to occupy a place of great importance in modern English, and, presumably, in the underlying folk philosophy of the human person. Before taking a closer look at the concept of 'mind', however, let us consider the use of the Russian word *duša* as a counterpart of the English *soul*.

4. Duša

As noted earlier, *soul* can always be translated into Russian as *duša*—whereas the reverse is not true. Common Russian prayers "za upokoj duši . . .", 'for the eternal rest of the soul of so-and-so . . . ', appear to use the word *duša* in exactly the same (Christian) sense in which the word *soul* is used in analogous English prayers. Materialist ideology denies the existence of *duša* in this sense, and, for example, in Soviet kindergartens children were often taught rhymes such as the following:

> . . . no nauka dokazala
> čto duši ne suščestvuet
> 'but science has proved
> that soul doesn't exist'

On the other hand, in Soviet literature, loyal Communists and party officials who would never seriously use words such as *grex* 'sin' or *satana* 'satan' often do use the word *duša*—apparently not in opposition to *telo* 'body' but in reference to moral and psychological aspects of a person's personality. For example:

Za čto pridralis' k mal'čiku? Ved' on čestno skazal, a oni emu lomajut dušu, trebujut soznanija v tom, čego ne soveršal. (Rybakov 1987, pt.1:10)

'Why do they victimise that boy? He said honestly what he thought and they are trying to break his spirit [*duša*], demanding that he confess to something that he didn't do.'

I vse ego usilija na protjaženii ètix let svodilis' k tomu, čtoby vosstanovit' v leningradskix kommunistax čuvstvo vnutrennego dostoinstva, snjat' nanesennuju im duševnuju travmu. (Rybakov 1987, pt.3:123)

'And all his [Kirov's] efforts during these years were directed towards restoring a sense of inner dignity to the communists of Leningrad, to removing their spiritual trauma.'

The same author has no hesitation in attributing the words *duša* and *duševno* to Stalin (in an internal monologue):

I vse ravno on [Stalin] rožden ne dlja poeziji, poet ne možet byt' borcom—poezija razmjagčaet dušu. (Rybakov 1987, pt.3:48)

'And in any case he [Stalin] was not born for poetry. A poet cannot be a man of action—poetry softens the soul.'

It seems to me that to give a coherent account of all such facts we have to postulate two different, though related, meanings of the word *duša:* a religious or quasi-religious meaning corresponding to the meaning of *soul*₁ explicated earlier, and a second meaning, which will be discussed in more detail later and which has no exact equivalent in English. This second meaning of *duša* has an entirely different status from that of *soul*ₘ in English: it is extremely common and it is deeply rooted in the common Russian 'ethnography of speaking' (cf. Hymes 1962) and 'ethnography of thinking'. It is much closer in status to the 'psychological' meaning of the German word *Seele*. But, as pointed out earlier, the psychological use of *duša* has a much greater scope than that of *Seele* (not to mention *soul*ₘ), and the underlying concept ('duša') has to be regarded as different, and unique. Before exploring this concept in more detail, however, let us look now at the English concept of 'mind'.

5. *Mind*

The idea that *mind* is a folk concept reflected in the English language rather than an objective and universally valid category of human thought may seem surprising, if not impertinent. It is relatively easy to see that concepts such as those encoded in the Japanese words *kokoro* or *ki* (Lock 1984), in the Samoan word *loto* (Gerber 1985), or in the Ilongot word *rinawa* (Rosaldo 1980) are culture-specific. It is harder to realise, however, that the same applies to the concept encoded in the English word *mind*. Titles of scholarly articles, books, and chapters, such as "A folk model of the mind" (D'Andrade 1987) or "Western conceptions of the mind from the Greek to the nineteenth century" (Murphy and Murphy 1969), reflect, I think, this error of perspective. They illustrate the familiar problem of the reification of essentially Western ethnopsychological categories that are then taken as the conceptual foundation of scientific inquiry (Lutz 1985b:67; see also Needham 1972:222–23 and Schieffelin 1985).

A less familiar aspect of this problem to which I would like to draw attention is that it is usually *English*—rather than 'Western'—ethnopsychological categories that are taken as the conceptual foundation of scientific inquiry, and that *English* ethnopsychological categories are often mistaken for 'Western' ethnopsychological categories and constructs. The concept of 'mind' is, I think, a case in point, and a particularly striking one, in view of the colossal role it plays not only in psychology, psychiatry, and anthropology but, above all, in philosophy.

D'Andrade (1987) compares the "Western model of the mind" with a non-Western (Ifaluk) "model of the mind", without taking note of the fact that the very concept of 'mind' is an English folk construct, with no equivalent in Ifaluk. What he is really comparing are the English and the Ifaluk models of 'person' (for which both of these languages do have a word), and his comparison is interesting and instructive, but the subject of that comparison is not quite what he says it is. Consider, for example, the following (D'Andrade 1987:143): "The model used on Ifaluk also differs from the present Western model in considering the mind to be located in the gut, which includes the stomach and the abdominal region. Thus, thoughts, feelings, desires, hunger, pain, and sexual sensations are all experienced in the gut." This is like saying that 'in the Russian model the mind is located in the soul'. The point is that neither Ifaluk nor Russian has any (lexicalised) folk concept of the 'mind'. On the other hand, they both do have the concept of 'person', and also the concepts of 'think' and 'want', which appear to be universal conceptual primitives (although being embedded in different semantic and cultural systems they cannot, of course, be exact pragmatic equivalents).

D'Andrade's description of the "Western folk model of the mind" is not really focussed on the folk concept 'mind' either. It is true that English has common verbs for perceptions, belief, knowledge, feelings, desires, and wishes, and this fact does throw light on the English folk model of the person but not on the folk concept of 'mind'. The very fact that a phrase such as 'a good mind' has nothing to do with feelings, perceptions, or desires demonstrates that. Feelings and wishes have something to do with 'a good heart' but not with 'a good mind', whereas perceptions have nothing to do with either.

When anthropological literature refers, as it often does (cf., for example, Johnson 1985; Shweder and Bourne 1984; Hsu 1985), to the concepts of 'person' or 'self' ('I'), in a cross-cultural perspective, this is in my view justified, despite the wide variation in the folk philosophies of person and self, because the words *person* (*someone*) and *I* seem to have semantic equivalents in all languages of the world, and so can be reasonably regarded as conceptual universals. But this is not true of the English concept 'mind' (just as it is not true of the French concept 'esprit', or of the Japanese concept 'ki'). It is a concept specific to Anglo-Saxon culture, which has no exact semantic equivalents in other European languages, let alone in other, geographically and culturally more distant, languages of the world.

It is interesting to consider from this point of view the claim often made in the anthropological and philosophical literature about the 'Cartesian' split between body and mind, dominating Western ethnopsychology and ethnophilosophy as a whole. Dualism is, no doubt, a characteristic feature of the traditional 'Western' folk philosophy in so far as Western culture has been, traditionally, a Christian culture, and Christianity does distinguish 'soul' from 'body' and does allow for their separation (although it promises the resurrection of the body as well as the immortality of the soul; cf., for example, Phillpotts 1920). But this traditional Western dualism is related to the distinction between body and soul, not between body and mind.

A different kind of dualism which can be said to have emerged in Western culture is the sharp distinction between two 'parts' of a living human person, a material and an immaterial one, viewed as inseparable, that is to say, between the body and something other than the body but inextricably linked with the body. But as soon as we identify that other 'something' as *mind,* we are exchanging a universal, scientific perspective for an anglocentric one; we are adopting the point of view of a particular folk psychology in the belief that we are discussing folk psychologies from a culture-independent point of view.

Philosophical discussions often seem to be quite confused on this point because of their failure to take into account semantic differences between words such as *soul, âme,* and *Seele,* and between the older and the more recent meanings of these words. For example, Teichman (1974:2) writes, "some philosophers, for example Leibniz and Teilhard de Chardin, have believed that every created thing, whether animate or not, has or is a Soul or mind". She does raise the question "how we know, if we do know, that all these opinions about the nature of the mind are indeed opinions about the *mind*", but she totally ignores the linguistic aspect of the problem, that is to say, the fact that *mind* is an English word, without exact equivalents in French, German, or Latin. Consequently, she concludes that "there must be some description of the mind to which we can all assent", forgetting that, for example, Teilhard de Chardin was talking about *âme,* not about *mind.*

It is important to point out in this connection that the so-called Cartesian distinction between body and mind is in fact different from the distinction which was drawn by Descartes himself. Descartes opposed 'body', *corps,* to *âme* (cf. Descartes 1952), and the concept of 'âme' as used by Descartes was no doubt derived from the folk concept encoded in the French word *âme* as it was used in seventeenth-century French. It was certainly different from that encoded in the modern English word *mind.*

For example, Murphy and Murphy (1969:144) in their anthology of "Western psychology" introduce excerpts from Descartes' work "Les passions de l'âme", with the following sentence: "Let us let Descartes have his say on the mind-body interaction", thus identifying Descartes' *âme* with the English *mind.* In the excerpts themselves the word *âme* is sometimes translated as *soul* and sometimes as *mind,* but the concluding comments are again framed in terms of *mind* (1969:148): "Descartes' mind-body dualism began to run into rougher and rougher water as physical and biological science progressed."

If one translates Descartes' word *âme* as *mind,* and then uncritically bases one's interpretation of Descartes' thought on this translation, one is likely to distort that thought—just as one is likely to distort Freud's thought if one translates his word *Seele* as *mind* and assumes that this is an adequate translation (cf. Oeing-Hanhoff 1984:84–85 and Barrett 1987:20).

In the case of Freud's work, it has been claimed that the identification of *Seele* with *mind* has led to a very serious misinterpretation of his teachings. Thus, Bettelheim writes:

> Of all the mistranslations of Freud's phraseology, none has hampered our understanding of his humanist views more than the elimination of his references to the soul (*die Seele*). Freud evokes the image of the soul quite frequently—especially in crucial passages where he is attempting to provide a broad view of his system. . . . Unfortunately, even in these crucial passages the translations make us believe that he is talking about our mind, our intellect. (1983:70)

In my view, Bettelheim underestimates the objective difficulty of translating Freud's *Seele* into English and dismisses too lightly the differences between the German word *Seele* and the English word *soul,* although he does mention in passing (1983:76) that "in common American usage the word *soul* has been more or less restricted to the sphere of religion" and that "this was not the case in Freud's Vienna and it is not the case in German-speaking countries today". Nonetheless I believe he is right in finding the rendering of *Seele* as *mind* "totally inadmissible" (Brull's words; Brull 1975:275).

Phillpotts (1920:725) reflects the common assumption: "The English word 'soul' (and its equivalents in cognate European languages) in its primary meaning designates an entity conceived as the cause or vehicle of the bodily life and physical activities of the individual person". Clearly, the assumption is that *soul* and its "equivalents in cognate European languages" mean the same.

In the case of Descartes, no doubt less harm is done by identifying the word *âme* with the English word *mind,* because of Descartes' emphasis on conscious thinking as the most important non-bodily aspect of our humanity. Yet to imply that he saw human beings as composed of a body and a mind is misleading.

It should be added that the identification of concepts such as *âme* or *Seele* with the English concept of *mind* has sometimes been defended on the grounds that "*Mind* in English became an all-inclusive term to designate 'that which is not material'" (MacLeod 1975:121). In my view, this is an illusion. *Mind* has become not so much an all-inclusive term as the dominant term for a non-material half of a human being. But it is not the same half that either Descartes or Freud was talking about.

It is therefore misleading to present the conceptual dualism opposing *body* to *mind* as a characteristic feature of 'Western culture' as a whole. Linguistic evidence shows that this dualism—in that form—is a characteristic feature of Anglo-Saxon culture, not necessarily of Western culture in general.

It is certainly not a feature of Russian culture, which opposes *telo,* 'body', to a characteristically Russian concept of *duša₂*, not to anything like the English *mind.* In fact, Russian, like German and French, doesn't have a word for *mind.* The fact that the French word *esprit* and the German *Geist* translate both *mind* and *spirit,* shows that they are not exact semantic equivalents of either of these words. The closest Russian counterparts of *mind* are the related words *um* and *razum,* but *um* and *razum,* like the English *intellect* and *reason,* or the German *Verstand* and *Vernunft,* are viewed as 'mental faculties' (exercised in mental activities), rather than as 'entities' or pseudo-entities like *soul, heart,* or *mind.* For example, babies have neither *um* nor *razum,* as they don't have an *intellect* or a *reason,* whereas they do have a *mind.* Adjectives derived from these nouns point in the same direction: *umnyj* means something like 'clever', *razumnyj* something like 'rational'. The fact that in many contexts *um* translates *cleverness* and *intelligence* further highlights the lack of correspondence between *um* and *mind.*

One can only agree with Johnson (1985:98): "In the Western world, particularly, questions about the body were methodically dissociated from questions of the mind and/or soul. Although most commonly described as 'Cartesian', such dissociation derived support from other philosophical, theological, and folk traditions in the West." It is harder, however, to accept Johnson's further statement: "Mind/body distinctions enjoyed a relative ascendancy in the Western world as describing methodically and philosophically different forms of reality. As repeatedly noted, the Western emphasis on dualism left its imprint on science, psychology, and ordinary 'ways of thinking' (see Ryle 1949)." First, the 'ordinary ways of thinking' reflected in the English language are different from those reflected in French, German, or

Italian. Second, even if we restrict our attention to the English-speaking world, what exactly enjoyed a relative ascendancy in that world? The question is important for the correct understanding of European cultural history. I believe, however, that to answer it we need conceptual tools more precise and more reliable than change-able and unanalysed folk constructs such as *mind* and *soul*.

6. A Brief Look at the Changes in the Folk Concepts 'Soul' and 'Mind'

The older stratum of English (reflected, for example, in Shakespeare's plays) in-cludes, as we have seen, the word *soul*, which combines transcendental (religious), psychological (phenomenological), and moral aspects. According to the folk theory reflected in this concept, a human being has two 'parts': a material one, which can be seen (the body), and an immaterial one, which cannot be seen (the soul), and the immaterial part is not a part of 'this world' (with the implications that it belongs to 'another world' and that it can perhaps be separated from the body). Clearly, this is a Christian *soul*, but a Christian soul which is also seen as an inner 'place', where events occur which are inaccessible to outsiders but which are in principle accessi-ble to introspection. These events have a moral dimension and are subject to a person's will.

In the same stratum of English there was also the word *mind*, which appears to have meant something rather different from what *mind* means in present-day En-glish. To begin with, it didn't seem to focus on the intellectual and the rational, on thinking and knowing, in the way the modern *mind* does. For example, when Mary Baker Eddy wrote, "God is Mind, and God is infinite; hence all is mind" (*Science and Health*, p.492, quoted in Stevenson 1946:1306), she seemed to mean something closer to the present-day *spirit* than to the present-day *mind*.

Second, the older English *mind* was clearly linked with emotions, whereas in present-day English emotions are normally linked with *heart*, not with *mind*. Hence, the archaic nature of the following quotes:

> The mind that would be happy, must be great.
> (YOUNG, "Night thoughts",
> Night IX, 1.1378, quoted in
> Stevenson 1946:1309)

> Vain, very vain, my weary search to find
> That bliss which only centres in the mind.
> (GOLDSMITH, "The traveller", 1.423,
> quoted in Stevenson 1946:1307)

> The flash and outbreak of a fiery mind
> A savageness in unreclaimed blood.
> (SHAKESPEARE, *Hamlet*, II, 1,
> quoted in Stevenson 1946:1312)

Present-day *minds* are usually not described as "happy" or "fiery". Rather, they are described as 'inquisitive', 'inquiring' (seeking knowledge), 'brilliant' (good at thinking), 'keen' (active in thinking and seeking to know), and so on.

Third, the older English *mind* seemed to be linked with values, whereas the modern one is morally neutral. Consequently, the innumerable references to a 'noble mind', 'ignoble mind', 'innocent mind', or 'generous mind' in older English literature sound a little strange and archaic to the modern ear; for example, "The sweet converse of an innocent mind" (Keats, "Sonnet: To solitude", quoted in Stevenson 1946:1309).

Thus, the older *mind* had both a spiritual and a psychological dimension, but it did not have the predominantly intellectual orientation which it has now, with thinking and knowing dominating any other non-bodily aspects of a person's inner life. It is true that the current concept of 'mind' doesn't exclude emotions and moral impulses quite as clearly as *reason* and *intellect* do. Nonetheless, the current *mind* focusses on thinking and knowing, not on feeling, wanting, or any other non-bodily processes. To say that someone has 'a good mind' suggests clearly that a person can *think* well, rather than that he or she has some other 'good' qualities. It is as unambiguous in its intellectual implications as a 'good heart' is in its emotional and moral ones.

I suggest the following explication of the modern *mind:*

> mind
> one of two parts of a person
> one cannot see it
> because of this part, a person can think and know

Thus, several interesting things appear to have happened in the history of *mind:* it shed its spiritual connotations, lost its links with values and emotions, and became a concept focussed on the intellect, more or less to the exclusion of any other aspects of a person's 'inner' life.

Parallel to these changes in the meaning of *mind,* and to the changes in the meaning of *soul* which were considered earlier, a certain compartmentalisation seems to have developed in the folk theory of the person: emotions have been relegated to the 'heart', moral choices have become restricted to *character* or *conscience,* and any other-worldly concerns have been relegated to the *soul* (in the new, narrowly religious sense of the word). It has often been pointed out that in Western culture a split occurred between intelligence and emotions and that these two aspects of human personality have come to be seen as opposing each other (cf., for example, Lutz 1985a:84; Cunningham and Tickner 1981; Johnson 1985:125–27). It is important to add, however, that this separation of 'thinking' from 'feeling' was accompanied by another split: that between the psychological and the moral aspect of the human person. At the time when the human person was seen as composed, essentially, of a body and a soul, the *soul* was both psychological and moral (as well as transcendental); at the time when the human person is seen as composed, essentially, of a body and a mind, that mind is seen as purely psychological (with the emphasis on the intellect, not on the emotions).

Furthermore, the more narrow scope of the modern *mind* in comparison with the older *soul* seems to be accompanied by, so to speak, a lesser depth, as the modern emphasis on the intellect, on thinking and knowing, is also an emphasis on the rational and the conscious. Hamlet's mother didn't want to know what was hidden in the depths of her soul. It would be harder, however, to refer (in everyday English) to 'the depths of one's (own) mind' and to express a desire not to know what was hidden there. The *soul* used to be seen as 'deep' and hard to know in its deeper strata. But the modern *mind* doesn't seem to be seen as similarly 'deep' and stratified and endowed with an inscrutable 'bottom'. One can still thank somebody 'from the bottom of one's heart', but one cannot believe something 'at the bottom of one's mind'.

As pointed out by Cunningham and Tickner (1981:238), "It was Jung's belief that Western man, in pursuit of reason, had cut himself off from his instincts and feelings which issue from the unconscious". The explications of *soul* and *mind* proposed here tally well, I think, with that belief, as the explication of the older English concept of *soul* includes the component 'sometimes the person doesn't know what these things are (i.e. the things which happen in one's soul)', whereas the explication of the modern English concept of *mind* doesn't include such a component.

In fact, even other people's *minds* don't seem to us as inscrutable as their *souls* used to seem to our ancestors. The problem of the 'unknowability of other minds' is much discussed by philosophers, but in ordinary language this unknowability doesn't seem to be implied by the use of the word *mind*. In fact, modern psychology and the more recent cognitive science seem to be predicated on the assumption that what is called the 'human mind' *can* be studied. For this reason, I have not included in the explication of *mind* the component 'other people can't know what these things are'. The *soul* used to be a very comprehensive concept, combining religious, psychological, and moral aspects, seen as one and jointly opposed to the material body. In the course of its history, however, *soul* lost ground and became restricted to the purely religious sphere.

A concomitant change affected *mind,* which won in its competition with *soul* as a word referring to the psychological aspect of the human person and as the dominant counterpart of the *body* in modern Anglo-Saxon thinking. This victory of *mind* over *soul,* combined with the shift in the meaning of *mind,* witnesses the birth of a new kind of dualism in English 'ordinary ways of thinking', a dualism devoid of religious and moral connotations and reflecting the supreme value placed in modern Anglo-Saxon culture on rational thinking and knowing, rather than on other aspects of the human person. To put it rather crudely, a human being used to be thought of as composed of a body and a transcendental, moral, emotional, 'inscrutable' soul and has now come to be thought of as composed instead of a body and an intellect.

This folk view embodied in modern English does indeed come close to Descartes' formula, summing up a human being as a "res cogitans" (cf. Vendler 1972), a 'thing which thinks'. But for Descartes this was only the most extreme, the most provocative formulation of his philosophy of the person. Normally, he opposed body (*corps*) to *âme,* that is to say, to something closer to the Shakespearean *soul* than to the modern English *mind*. Gilbert Ryle's (1949) sarcastic formula "the ghost in the machine" is helpful here, because it reminds us that Descartes' distinction between *corps* and *âme* was something rather different from the modern Anglo-Saxon folk distinction between *body* and *mind*.

This is, then, what the 'ascendancy of mind' in the English-speaking world means—according to the testimony of the English language. What exactly has happened in the other parts of the Western world is a matter for further investigation. A semantic study of the words *Seele, esprit, âme,* and their closest counterparts in other European languages should, I think, prove very revealing from the point of view of 'Völker-psychologie' and cultural history. This chapter, however, concentrates mainly on the Russian *duša,* and on the lexical contrasts between English and Russian, though I will return briefly to the contrast between *duša* and *Seele* in a later section.

As pointed out earlier, the Russian *duša* is a kind of psychological substratum, which—unlike the English *mind*—focusses mainly on values and emotions. This raises the question of the relationship between *duša* and *heart*.

7. *Heart* and *Serdce*

'Heart' is seen in English as the organ of emotions, as the corresponding Russian word *serdce* (also a name of the body part) is in Russian. It goes without saying that both *heart* and *serdce* as the names of an imaginary organ of emotions are semantically distinct from the same words used as the names of a part of the body. Nonetheless, it appears that the emotional *heart* (or *serdce*) is perceived as more closely related to the body than either *soul* or *mind*. To account for this relationship between the emotional and the physical senses of the word *heart* (and *serdce*) we can perhaps add an imaginary component to the explication of the emotional sense, along the following lines (cf. Mel'čuk et al. 1984:70):

> *heart/serdce*
> a part of a person
> one can imagine that it is a part of the person's body
> [in the middle of the upper half of the body
> one can hear its movements]

Before sketching a full definition of this concept, however, it should be pointed out that neither *heart* nor *serdce* is viewed as a seat of *all* emotions but only of emotions which are seen as either 'good' or 'bad'. Thus, one can say

> His heart was full of joy/bitterness/sadness.

but hardly

> ?His heart was full of surprise/amazement/interest.

Surprise, amazement, or interest can be 'felt', but they cannot be felt 'in one's heart'. The reason is, I believe, that they make no reference to the concepts 'good' and 'bad'.

It should be pointed out, however, that although from an egocentric point of view a *heart* can feel both 'good' and 'bad' things (for example, both joy and sorrow), in an allocentric perspective a *heart* can contain only 'good things' (for example, admiration or gratitude) but not 'bad things' (for example, hatred, jealousy, or contempt). As pointed out earlier, a person can be *kind-hearted* or *warm-hearted*, but not *evil-hearted* or *vicious-hearted*. This suggests that a heart is seen as not only an organ of feelings (good and bad) but also an organ of empathy and benevolence (good feelings for others).

This leads us to the following explication of *heart*:

> *heart*
> a part of a person
> one cannot see it
> one can imagine that it is a part of a person's body
> [in the middle of the upper half of the body
> one can hear its movements]
> because of this part, a person can feel good things and bad things
> because of this part, a person can feel good things towards other people

In this case, the phrasing 'a part of a person' seems preferable to 'one of two parts of a person', because *heart* is not contrasted with the body in the way *soul* or *mind* is and does not evoke a dualistic view of human personality in the way *soul* and *mind* do.

The Russian concept of 'serdce' seems to correspond exactly to that encapsulated in the English word *heart*. It is all the more interesting, therefore, to note that Russian has two words, not one, which can refer to a hypothetical organ of emotions and that the meaning of these words is different. In English, feelings are linked with a person's *heart*, but in Russian they are linked either with a person's *serdce* ('heart') or with a person's *duša*. If we equate the religious sense of *duša* with that of the English *soul*, we shall have to posit for Russian another entity, *duša₂*, with no equivalent in English.

8. *Duša₂*

In Russian, one can be said to feel love in one's *duša*. For example:

> Ja vas ljubil . . . ljubov' ešče, byt' možet
> v duše moej ugasla ne sovsem. (Pushkin)
>
> 'I loved you once . . . that love perhaps
> has not yet died in my soul (*duša*).'

Even more typically, however, love is linked with *serdce*, 'heart'. For example, a popular song includes the following line:

> Spasibo serdce čto ty umeeš' tak ljubit'.
> 'Thank you, heart, that you can love so much.'

Other feelings, too, can be linked with either one's *duša* or with one's *heart*. The constraint that only good or bad feelings can be felt in one's heart applies to *duša*, too: for example, one cannot feel surprise in one's *duša* any more than one can feel it in one's *serdce* or in one's *heart*. Otherwise, however, good and bad emotions can in principle be said to be felt either in one's *duša* or in one's *serdce*. For example:

Pejže s gorja, gde že kružka,
serdcu budet veselej. (Pushkin)

'Drown your sorrows, pass the cup
Let the heart grow merry.'

. . . ot ètogo na duše ne veselej, a užas oxvatyvaet. (Grossman 1980:53)

'. . . rather than feeling happier [lit., in my soul], I am seized with horror.'
(Grossman 1985:92)

Spasibo ot vsego serdca. (Tsvetaeva 1969:67)

'Thank you with all my heart.'

Celuju vas i ot vsej duši blagodarju. (Tsvetaeva 1972:508)

'I kiss you and thank you with all my soul (*duša*).'

It is interesting to note that both *duša* and *serdce* as the organ of emotion are often contrasted in Russian with *golova*, 'head', as the organ of thinking. For example:

Golova ustaet dumat', duša čuvstvovat'. (Tsvetaeva 1972:104)

'The head grows weary of thinking, the soul of feeling.'

U menja—za gody i gody (1917–1927)—otupel ne um, a duša. Udivitelnoe nab-
ljudenie: imenno na čuvstva nužno vremja, a ne na mysl'. (Tsvetaeva 1969:56)

'Over the years it was not my mind (*um*) but my soul (*duša*) that grew dull. An amazing observation: You need time to have feelings, not thoughts.'

This might seem to suggest that in the context of emotions *duša* is simply an equivalent of *serdce*. In fact, nothing could be further from the truth. There are many emotions which can be said to be felt either in one's *duša* or in one's *serdce*, but the interpretation of the emotion in question is in each case different.

To begin with, not all emotions which can be linked with one's *serdce* can be linked with one's *duša*. For example, good feelings that a person may have for a dog or a cat would normally not be linked with one's *duša*, though they could easily be linked with a person's *serdce*. It is instructive to consider in this connection the following two passages from Tsvetaeva's letters, where *serdce* as an organ of emotions is explicitly contrasted with *duša* as an organ of emotions. In the first example, Tsvetaeva is writing about her ten-year-old son, Mur (cf. also chapter 4):

Menee vsego razvit—duševno: ne znaet toski, sovsem ne ponimaet. Lob—serdce—
i potom uže—duša: normal'naja duša desjatiletnego rebenka, t.e.—začatok. (K

serdcu—otnošu ljubov' k roditeljam, žalost' k životnym, vse èlementarnoe—k duše—vse bespričinno bolevoe.) Xudožestvenen. Otmečaet krasivoe—v prirode i vezde. No—ne pronzën. (Pronzën = duša. Ibo duša = bol' + vse drugoe.) (Tsvetaeva 1969:131)

'Least of all is he developed spiritually (*duševno*): he is a stranger to yearning (*toska*), he simply doesn't understand it. The head—the heart—and then the soul (*duša*): the normal soul of a ten year old child, i.e. an embryo. (I regard love for one's parents and pity for animals as pertaining to the heart; everything elementary, all pain without a cause belongs to the soul.) He is artistic. He notices beauty in nature and everywhere else. But he's not pierced by it. (To be pierced means to have a soul. For soul is pain plus everything else.)'

In this second example, Tsvetaeva is urging her friend Anna Teskova to join her for a holiday:

Vam nužno vzjat' kakoj-to duševnyj otpusk—u sem'i. Ne prodyšavšis' duša ssyxaetsja, znaju èto po sebe. Sem'ja ved'—serdce. Serdce razrastaetsja v uščerb duši, duše sovsem net mesta, otsjuda estestvennoe želanie—umeret', ne ne byt', a smoč' byt'. (Tsvetaeva 1969:46)

'You need to take a sort of spiritual (*duševnyj*) holiday—from the family. The soul that doesn't breathe freely dries up—I know it from experience. The family is a thing of the heart after all. The heart expands at the expense of the soul. There's no place for the soul at all—hence the natural desire to die. Not to not be—but to be able to be.'

To some extent, statements of this kind should no doubt be regarded as personal and idiosyncratic. One can hardly accept a poet's personal 'definitions' of key concepts such as *duša* as objectively valid explications of the Russian words in question. Nonetheless, the general thrust of these definitions must accord fairly well with other speakers' intuitions, since it corresponds quite well with the observable range of the word's use.

The conclusion seems to be this: *duša* is seen in Russian as an organ of deeper, purer, and more morally and spiritually coloured feelings than *serdce*. But the word *organ* might suggest one part among many. This implication would be consistent with the meaning of *serdce*, but not with that of *duša*. *Duša* is seen not as one part among many but as one of just two parts: that is, it is a person minus the person's body (the invisible half). But it is also viewed as an internal spiritual theatre, as a place where events happen of a kind that could never happen in the world of inanimate things (*oduševlennyj*, lit., 'having a soul', is also a word for 'animate'). These events are unknowable to outsiders ("čužaja duša potëmki", the proverb says, 'another person's *duša* is unfathomable'). Feelings occupy a prominent place among these events, and these feelings, too, are hidden to outsiders (unlike other, more superficial feelings, which can be associated with observable bodily symptoms).

The hidden nature of feelings associated with *duša* is no doubt linked with their 'deeper', more spiritual nature. Superficial, externally observable feelings can occur in animals as well as in people. For example, an animal, too, can be afraid, startled, or enraged. But the feelings linked with *duša* have to be 'deeper' in two different ways: they cannot be externally observable, and they have to be of a kind that only persons (rather than animals) could experience. This suggests that they should be linked with values.

This leads us to the following definition of *duša₂* (the first approximation), as distinct from the purely religious meaning (*duša₁*), which is the same as *soul₁* defined in section 3 previously.

> *duša₂*
> one of two parts of a person
> one cannot see it
> because of this part, things can happen in a person
>   that cannot happen in anything other than a person
> these things can be good or bad
> because of this part, a person can feel things
>   that nothing other than a person can feel
> other people can't know what these things are
> because of this part a person can be a good person

The idea of 'things happening' in a Russian *duša* is, I think, important, because it suggests, correctly, a dynamic inner world, which can be likened to a stage rather than to an entity. The proverb "čužaja duša potëmki", 'another person's soul is unfathomable', refers not so much to the unknowable quality of another person's *duša* as to the mysterious processes which go on there (above all, emotional, but morally coloured, processes).

It should be stressed, however, that although the Russian *duša* is seen above all as a moral and emotional core of a person, it does not totally exclude other functions of a person's inner life, such as thinking and knowing, as long as those other functions are somehow linked to values and to a person's hidden inner world.

In particular, the word *duša* can refer to a person's inner knowledge. For example:

Čelovek—v duše—znal, čto vybrosivšis' iz okna—upadet v verx. (Tsvetaeva 1972:613)

'You knew in your soul that if you threw yourself out of a window you would fall on your feet.'

The knowledge in question, however, cannot be purely factual or rational: it must be related to values.

Similarly, *duša* can refer to inner speech. This use of *duša* is sometimes rendered in English by means of the word *heart,* but frequently it is simply deleted. For example:

On v duše uprekal Ljudmilu. . . . (Grossman 1980:40)

'In his heart he reproached Ljudmila. . . .' (Grossman 1985:72)

But again, although one can *reproach, blame,* or *praise* someone in one's *duša,* mathematical or logical problems can only be solved in a person's *golova* ('head'), not in a person's *duša.*

Human will, too, is included in the domain of *duša*, whereas in English it is usually linked with *character* rather than with *soul*. For example, Grossman's (1980:37) expression "duševnaja sila" 'spiritual strength' (where *duševnaja* is an adjective derived from *duša*) is translated by Chandler as "strength of character" (Grossman 1985:18).

The wide scope of the concept *duša* is also clearly illustrated in the following sentence from Pasternak's novel *Doktor Živago:*

V Jurinoj duše vse bylo sdvinuto i pereputano, i vse rezko samobytno—vzgljady, navyki i predraspoloženija. (Pasternak 1959:78)

Once again, in a context such as this, *duša* cannot be rendered in English as *soul*. In Max Hayward and Manya Harari's translation of the novel it is rendered as *mind:*

Everything in Yura's mind was mixed up together and misplaced and everything was sharply his own—his views, his habits and his inclinations. (Pasternak 1958:67)

Interestingly, there are cases where the word *duša* is used to refer to a person's mental life as a whole. English usually uses in such cases the noun *mind,* or the adjective *mental,* or no word at all. For example, the English expression *mentally ill* has its counterpart in the Russian phrase *duševnobol'nye* (and in German, in *Seelenkrank*), which seems to imply that in the Russian (and in the German) cultural tradition people viewed in English as *mentally ill* are perhaps viewed in a less clinical and more person-oriented perspective—as people whose inner world is impaired, rather than as people whose intellectual faculties are—and this inner world seems to have spiritual and emotional dimensions, as well as purely intellectual ones. This view would be more in keeping with an older cultural tradition, going back to antiquity (cf. Pigeaud 1981).

Thus, the Russian *duša* is used very widely and can refer to virtually all aspects of a person's personality: feelings, thoughts, will, knowledge, inner speech, ability to think. Given the richness and the scope of this word it is not surprising that in the opposition of *telo* (body) and *duša,* it is the *duša* which is commonly seen as the more important one and which tends to be identified with the person as a whole. For example:

Ja èto moja duša—osoznanie ee. (Tsvetaeva 1972:124)

'I am my soul—my perception of it.'

Ja o svoej duše govorju, o glavnoj, o trebovatel'noj, o negodujuščej sebe. (Tsvetaeva 1972:104)

'I am talking about my soul, about my essential, demanding, indignant self.'

Èto byli plečo i noga, a vse ostal'noe—bolee ili menee ona sama, ee duša ili suščnost', strojno složennaja v očertanija i otzyvčivo rvuščajasja v buduščee. (Pasternak 1959:34)

'Everything between her shoulder and her foot was vaguely herself—her soul or essence neatly fitting into the outline of her body and impatiently straining towards the future.' (Pasternak 1958:32)

The tremendous value which the Russian culture places on the inner world called *duša* is reflected in the fact that *duša* is used in Russian as a symbol of pricelessness. For example:

Ona dušu otdast za lišnee pjat' svečej. (Tsvetaeva 1972:113)

'She would give her soul for an additional 5 candles.'

Ja by—dušu otdala—za takuju njanju i za takogo kota. (Tsvetaeva 1972:614)

'I would give my soul for such a nanny and for such a cat.'

Čto dlja vas sdelat'? Ja by polžizni, ja by pravyj glaz, ja by dušu . . . (Tsvetaeva 1972:96)

'What could I do for you? I would [give] half my life, I would [give] my right eye, I would [give] my soul. . . .'

Of course, this use of *duša* as a symbol of pricelessness may in fact be related to *duša₁* ('soul') rather than to *duša₂*. But in Russian, the psychological *duša₂* is closely related to the religious *duša₁*, much more closely than the English *mind* is related to the English *soul*. Thus, in addition to the components

> one of two parts of a person
> one cannot see it

which *soul, mind, duša₁*, and *duša₂* all share, *duša₂* shares also with *duša₁* (and with *soul₁*) the component

> because of this part, a person can be a good person

a component which the morally neutral *mind* doesn't have. In addition, the personal 'spiritual' component of *duša₂*:

> because of this part, things can happen in a person
> that cannot happen in anything other than a person

sets 'duša' apart from the material world and in contrast to it; this corresponds, in a way, with the contrast between 'this world' and 'the world of spirit', hinted at in the definition of *duša₁* (and of *soul₁*):

> it is part of another world
> good beings are part of that world
> things are not part of that world

It should be added that in Russian the words for *soul* (*duša₁*, Adj. *duševnyj*) and for *spirit* (*dux*, Adj. *duxovnyj*) are cognate and are felt to be synchronically related. *Duša₂* not only is formally identical with *duša₁* but also is cognate, and is felt to be cognate, with *dux*. *Mind* is of course not formally related to either *soul* or *spirit* and is semantically further from them than *duša₂* is from *duša₁* or from *dux*.[4]

One final point which should be made in the present context is this: Although the Russian word *duša* can be used in two different senses, a religious and a psychological one, it seems nonetheless clear that it can also be used in a third sense, which combines the psychological meaning with the religious one. This combined sense is particularly clear in sentences referring to religious experiences, or to religiously inspired moral efforts, as in the following examples:

> Polnaja vostorgom duša ego žaždala svobody, mesta, široty. . . . 'Oblej zemlju slezami radosti tvoeja i ljubi sii slezy tvoi. . . .' prozvenelo v duše ego. . . . Kak budto niti oto vsex ètix besčislennyx mirov božiix sošlis' razom v duše ego, i ona vsja trepetala, 'soprikasajas' miram inym'. . . . I nikogda, nikogda ne mog zabyt' Aleša vo vsju žizn' svoju potom ètoj minuty. 'Kto-to posetil moju dušu v tot čas'— govoril on potom s tverdoju veroj v svoi slova. (Dostoevsky 1958:452)

> '[He did not stop on the steps either, but went quickly down;] his soul overflowing with rapture, yearned for freedom, space, openness. (. .) "Water the earth with the tears of your joy and love those tears . . ." echoed in his soul. . . . There seemed to be threads from all those innumerable worlds of God, linking his soul to them, and it was trembling all over "in contact with other worlds". . . . And never, never, all his life long, could Alyosha forget that minute. "Someone visited my soul in that hour", he used to say afterwards, with implicit faith in his words.' (Dostoevsky 1974:378)

> Duševnoe sostajanie xorošo, spokoen i bol'šej čast'ju dobr. (Tolstoy 1985, v.22:135)

> 'My inner state [lit., 'the state of the soul'] is good, I am calm and, on the whole, good [i.e., morally good].'

> Zdorovie nexorošo. Duševnoe sostajanie xorošee, gotov k smerti. (Tolstoy 1985, v.22:108)

> 'My health is not good. My inner state [lit., 'the state of the soul'] is good, I am ready for death.'

It would be counter-intuitive to say that in these sentences there are some instances of *duša₁* (and *duševnyj₁*) interspersed with some instances of *duša₂* (and *duševnyj₂*). Rather, it appears that we are dealing here with a complex *duša₃* (and *duševnyj₃*)—emotional, moral, and transcendental at the same time. In these passages, Tolstoy and Dostoevsky seem to identify their (or their hero's) psychological *duša*, suffering, rejoicing, and striving after good and after God, with their transcendental *duša*, destined to leave the body and to be united with God.

If *duša* does indeed have these three distinct senses—one religious, one psychological, and one combined—we would have to acknowledge that in actual use it is by no means always clear which sense is intended. Since, however, in some contexts religious connotations are clearly excluded, it appears that for present-day Russian an account in terms of three distinct (though not always distinguishable) senses offers the most satisfactory description. (In addition, there are also a host of idiomatic expressions involving *duša,* but these cannot be discussed in this chapter.)

9. The Russian *Duša* and the German *Seele*

As pointed out earlier, *duša* in the psychological sense can often be translated into German as *Seele:* that is, it can be rendered by the same word which also translates the religious/transcendental *duša*$_1$. In philosophical psychology, too, the use of *Seele* in German (cf., for example, Bettelheim 1983) seems to parallel the use of *duša* in Russian (cf., for example, Frank 1964). Furthermore, in German, as with the Russian word, *Seele* can sometimes be used in a 'combined' sense, psychological and religious at the same time. All these facts raise the problem of what exactly is the relationship between *duša*$_2$ and *Seele (Seele*$_2$)? Perhaps *duša*$_2$ is not a characteristically Russian concept, after all, but one which has an exact equivalent in German?

I have said, however, that although *duša*$_2$ can often be translated into German as *Seele,* often it cannot. For example, in Strenge's German translation of *War and peace* (Tolstoy n.d.), no fewer and no more than about half the instances of *duša*$_2$ have been translated as *Seele.* Moreover, in original German literature *Seele* is encountered far more rarely than *duša* is in Russian literature (outside religious contexts). To interpret facts of this kind it is important to establish in what kinds of contexts *duša* is not, or tends not to be, translated as *Seele.* An examination of such contexts suggests that *Seele* seems to be reserved for 'deep' emotions, emotions which have to be dragged to the surface of one's consciousness, whereas the Russian *duša* can also be used with respect to 'superficial' ones, those of which the person is fully aware. In particular, the expression *v duše* 'in the soul' is often used to indicate a contrast between what one privately thinks and what one says to others, for example:

> Jura v duše podivilsja političeskoj oborotlivosti Vadima. (Rybakov 1987, pt.2:138)
>
> 'In his heart (*duša*), Jura was startled by Vadim's political agility (but he didn't show it).'
>
> On naxal, cinik, v duše smeetsja nad temi, kogo obiraet. (Rybakov 1987, pt.2:72)
>
> 'He's a shameless cynic, who secretly (in his *duša*) laughs at those he's swindling.'
>
> Prixoditsja terpet' moi notacji, xotja v duše on preziraet menja, kak plebeja i xama. (Rybakov 1987, pt.2:71)
>
> 'He just has to endure my reproofs though in his heart (*duša*) he despises me as a plebeian.'

In German, *Seele* cannot be used like that.

Furthermore, in Russian *duša* can be used with reference to certain passing moods, whereas in German *Seele* is reserved for inner states 'deeper' than the level of 'mood'. For example:

> Čital Djemka 'Živuju vodu'i ne mog razobrat': to li kniga takaja nud' i mut', to li èto na duše u nego. (Solzhenitsyn 1968a, v.1:136)

> 'Djomka las "Das Wasser des Lebens" und konnte einfach nicht dahinterkommen: Lag es nun an dem Buch oder an seiner eigenen Stimmung, dass er es so dumm und langweilig fand?' (Solzhenitsyn 1971:112)

> 'Djomka was reading "The living water", and he couldn't decide: was the book so dull and boring or was it something "on" his soul.'

> Tak opredelenno oni splanirovali—i na duše u Pavla Nikolaeviča prosvetlelo. (Solzhenitsyn 1968a, v.1:199)

> 'Nun hatten sie einen festen Plan entworfen, ihm wurde es wieder wohler ums Herz.' (Solzhenitsyn 1971:161)

> 'Now they had made up a definite plan—and Pavel Nikolaevitch felt more cheerful "on his soul".'

This semantic contrast between *duša* and *Seele* is reflected in the syntax of the two words: *duša* can take not only the preposition *v* 'in', which suggests 'depth', but also the preposition *na* 'on', which suggests 'surface', but *Seele* (unlike *Herz* 'heart') cannot take the corresponding preposition *auf:*

> Mne stalo legče na duše.
>
> to-me it-become lighter on soul
>
> Ich fühlte mich erleichtert (*auf der Seele).
>
> 'I felt relieved.'

Furthermore, the link of *Seele* with 'deeper' experiences, experiences of which one is not fully aware, is supported by the observation that the verb *wissen* 'know' is incompatible with *Seele*, whereas the corresponding Russian verb *znat'* is compatible with *duša;* compare the example from Tsvetaeva (1972:613) quoted earlier:

> Čelovek—v duše—znal . . .
>
> ?'Man wusste in seiner Seele . . .'
>
> 'You knew in your soul . . .'

Similarly, other verbs suggesting consciousness, such as *glauben* 'to believe' or *überzeugt sein* 'to be convinced', are less compatible with *Seele* than their counterparts are with *duša*.

It is also significant that *Seele* can hardly be used in German with reference to conscious expressive acts such as thanks or congratulations, or to fully conscious emotional attitudes such as sympathy or compassion:

Celuju vas i ot vsej duši blagodarju. (Tsvetaeva 1972:508)

?'Ich küsse Sie und danke Ihnen von ganzer Seele.'

'I kiss you and thank you with all my heart.'

. . . ot duši pozdravljaju (Tsvetaeva 1972:453)

?'Ich kongratuliere Ihnen von ganzer Seele.'

'I congratulate you with all my heart.'

Da, ja ot vsej duši žaleju ego. (Tolstoy 1964, v.1–2:327)

'Von ganzem Herze (?von ganzer Seele) beklage ich ihn.' (Tolstoy n.d.:375)

'Yes, I pity him with all my heart.'

Facts of this kind suggest that the German *Seele* is as inscrutable as the Shake-spearean *soul*. If it no longer includes the metaphysical component 'it is not a part of this world', and is to that extent closer to *duša*, it does include the component 'sometimes the person doesn't know what these things are' (which the Russian *duša* clearly doesn't include), and to that extent it is closer to the older English *soul*.

The emotions and the thoughts that one has in one's *duša* and the feelings that one has 'on' one's *duša* are hidden to outsiders, but there is no implication that they may be hidden to the 'insider' as well. Furthermore, there are many expressions in Russian which point to a widely felt need to express those 'hidden' inner states to somebody, to exteriorise them. These expressions include *izlit' dušu*, lit., 'to pour out one's soul (*duša*)'; *otvesti dušu*, 'to relieve one's soul (*duša*)'; *otkryt' dušu*, lit., 'to open one's soul (*duša*)'; *duša naraspašku*, lit., 'a wide-open soul (*duša*)', that is, 'a communicative, sincere, frank person'; *razgovorivat' po dušam'*, 'to talk from soul to soul', that is, very intimately; and so on. What these expressions suggest is that although other people cannot know what goes on in a person's *duša* without being told, there is an expectation that normally people would want, and need, to tell someone what goes on in there. The German *Seele* has no such implications of a need for exteriorisation. To account for this difference, we could phrase the relevant components in the following way:

> *Seele* – other people cannot know what these things are
> *duša* – other people cannot know what these things are if the person doesn't say it

It might even be justified to add to *duša* one further component:

> a person would want someone to know what these things are

Thus, although both *Seele* and *duša* refer to things that are hidden and personal, in the case of *duša* these hidden things are much less hidden and are much more readily exteriorised than in the case of *Seele*.

It is interesting to note here what Bettelheim says about the concept of *Seele* as used by Freud (Bettelheim translates *Seele* as *soul*):

> By 'soul' or 'psyche' Freud means that which is most valuable in man while he is alive. Freud was a passionate man. For him, the soul is the seat both of the mind and of the passions, and we remain largely unconscious of the soul. In important respects, it is deeply hidden, hardly accessible even to careful investigation. It is intangible, but it nevertheless exercises a powerful influence on our lives. It is what makes us human. (Bettelheim 1983:77)

This whole emphasis on the hidden and subconscious character of *Seele* highlights the nature of this concept in ordinary German. As Bettelheim emphasises, Freud always relied on everyday German words and didn't want to change their meaning in any way.

But the Russian *duša,* although kindred to *Seele* in several aspects, is not similarly exclusively linked with the subconscious: it spans the conscious and the subconscious. This means that the Russian *duša* is much more comprehensive than the German *Seele:* it can include all the inner experiences (as long as they are morally coloured), and not only the 'deeper' and more inscrutable ones. This explains, I think, the wider scope of *duša* and its greater importance in Russian discourse.

It is also interesting to note that the readiness to open and to 'pour out' one's *duša* is seen in Russian culture as something good, and that the 'hiding' of one's *duša* is seen as something bad, as this passage from one of Tolstoy's (1984, v.19:28) letters indicates: "Turgenev's influence on our literature was extremely good and fruitful. He didn't use his talent (his ability to represent well) for hiding his soul (*duša*), as others have done and are doing, but for putting it all inside out."

If Russians freely 'open their souls' to other people, how do they show *special* intimacy, one might ask, of the kind that one would be more likely to share with one's best friends rather than with strangers? According to the testimony of the Russian language, special intimacy belongs not to the soul as such but to the hidden recesses 'behind the soul'. The most relevant word here is *zaduševnost',* literally 'behind-the-soulness'. This is a concept which, according to Jarintzov,

> is lovable to a Russian mind, but which would be ridiculous in translation, because the conception itself is strange to the English. The word means 'one behind the soul' (*zaduševnyj*)—or a quality which dwells in the deepest recesses of one's spirit. . . . We call our best-beloved friend a 'behind-the-soul' one. But I understand that the best friends among the English people seldom like to share between them what is 'behind their souls', so there is no wonder that the English speech lacks the described definition [i.e., concept]. (Jarintzov 1916:99)

It is possible that the greater readiness of the Russian *duša* to 'pour itself out' is linked not only with the fact that it is more comprehensive and not restricted to the 'innermost' personal states (like the German *Seele*) but also with the fact that *duša* seems to suggest actual or potential good feelings toward other people, whereas *Seele* doesn't seem to have such implications.

As evidence for this conjecture I could mention the following facts (commonly mentioned in Russian dictionaries). First, the adjective *duševnyj* implies not only 'sincerity', 'frankness', 'openness', and the like, but also 'serdečnost'', that is, an affectionate quality. Second, a similar implication of friendliness or affection is present in the expression *govorit' po dušam*, lit., 'to talk from soul to soul'. Third, the expression *duša-čelovek* 'a soul-human being' implies a good, friendly, tender person. Fourth, the word *duša* or its diminutives can be used as terms of endearment, as *darling* is in English. In modern German, the word *Herz* 'heart' can be used like that, but *Seele* cannot. All this suggests that *duša* may also include a component referring to a person's 'good feelings toward other people'.

If *duša* implies potential good feelings toward other people, this might contribute to its implications of openness and communicativeness: it is perhaps easier to 'open' our inner self to other people if we feel 'good feelings' toward them. But whether or not there is a link between 'openness' and 'good feelings', a reference to 'good feelings' may in any case be justified for *duša*.

The German *Seele* doesn't seem to have such implications, as witness expressions such as *seelische Grausamkeit* 'mental cruelty', which could never be translated into Russian as **duševnaja žestokost'*, since the notions of *duša* and *duševnyj* seem incompatible with notions such as cruelty.

This brings us to the following, expanded version of the definition of *duša₂* (note the new components (g) and (i)):

duša₂

(a) one of two parts of a person
(b) one cannot see it
(c) because of this part, things can happen in a person that cannot happen in anything other than a person
(d) these things can be good or bad
(e) because of this part, a person can feel things that nothing other than a person can feel
(f) other people can't know what these things are if the person doesn't say it
(g) a person would want someone to know what these things are
(h) because of this part, a person can be a good person
(i) because of this part a person can feel something good toward other people

10. 'Res Cogitans', 'Res Sentiens'

The ethnotheory embodied in the English language opposes the body to an (imaginary) entity centred around thinking and knowing. It clearly reflects, therefore, the much discussed rationalistic, intellectual, and scientific orientation of mainstream Western culture. The ethnotheory embodied in the Russian language opposes the body to an (imaginary) entity of a rather different kind: subjective, unpredictable, spontaneous ("things happen"), emotional, spiritual, and moral; an entity which is hidden and yet ready to reveal itself in intimate and cordial personal relations and one which is personal and interpersonal at the same time. "Čelovek v drugix ljudjax i est' *duša* čeloveka", 'you in others, that's what your soul (*duša*) is', Pasternak (1959:82) says.

Of course the English lexicon, too, allows the speaker to view the human person as an emotional, communicative, moral, and spiritual being, by supplying words (and concepts) such as *heart, spirit, conscience, character,* and *personality.* But the basic dualistic model embodied in the English lexicon (body versus mind) ignores those aspects of the human person and focusses on the intellectual and rational aspect. By contrast, the basic dualistic model embodied in the Russian lexicon focusses on the emotional, the spontaneous, and the moral, not on the intellectual and the rational.

In English, a person (especially a woman) can be called 'a good soul', but this is a somewhat disparaging and patronising kind of praise. Socrates described the 'soul' (*psyche*) as "that in us which has knowledge and goodness" (Phillpotts 1920:741). In English thinking, the ideas of 'knowledge and goodness' have become separated, and assigned, separately, to 'mind' and 'soul'. As a result, a person described as 'a good soul' is most unlikely to be also 'a brilliant mind'. In Russian thinking, no similar gulf has emerged between 'knowledge' and 'goodness', and the Russian *duša* could still be described as 'that in us which has wisdom and goodness'—provided, however, that one could add immediately, 'and feeling'.

If the ethnotheory embodied in the English language sees a human being as, above all, a 'res cogitans' ('a thing which thinks'), the ethnotheory embodied in the Russian lexicon sees a human being, above all, as a 'res sentiens, moralis et personalis', that is, a 'thing' which feels, which chooses between good and bad, and which needs intimacy with other similar 'things'. It may be useful to recall in this connection the sentence from *War and peace* which was quoted earlier and which was translated into English as "He is such a lofty, heavenly soul!" I have pointed out that in English the word *soul* would never be used like this. But in fact, the words *lofty* and *heavenly* would normally not be used like this either. The whole utterance reflects a mode of behaviour which is alien to Anglo-Saxon culture, with its double stress on the rational and pragmatic attitudes and with its avoidance of overly emotional behaviour and of absolute moral judgements.

To put it yet another way, the orientation of the old English *soul* was, above all, metaphysical and ethical; the orientation of the modern English *mind* is, above all, epistemological; the orientation of the Russian *duša* is, above all, phenomenological and ethical.

One is tempted at this point to raise the question of possible differences in behaviour corresponding to these differences in outlook. The stereotype of Russian behaviour suggests that the Russians not only tend to see human beings as composed of a body and a 'duša' but also tend to, and feel free to, behave as if they were composed of two such parts, and the stereotype of Anglo-Saxon behaviour suggests not only that the Anglo-Saxons tend to see human beings as composed of a body and a mind but that their cultural norms encourage them also to behave as if they were composed of two such parts and inhibit overt displays of their emotions and inner life. For example, Hedrick Smith's description of Russian behaviour would certainly fit in with such an idea. Smith is describing Russian viewers' reactions to the Western film version of Pasternak's novel *Doctor Zhivago:*

What stuck in my mind was the moment when everyone, foreigners and Russians alike, broke out laughing at the movie's portrayal of the meek, milquetoast welcome given by young Zhivago and his step-parents to his step-sister returning to Moscow by train from Paris. It was abrupt and cool, a quick, flat, unemotional Western peck on the cheek and a handshake, obviously directed and acted by people unaware of the effusive, emotional outpouring that occurs when Russians greet or part at a railroad station. They immerse each other in endless hugs, embraces, warm kisses on both cheeks, three times, not just kissing in the air for show, but strong, firm kisses, often on the lips, and not only between men and women, or between women, but man-to-man as well. Westerners used to discount this as an idiosyncrasy of Nikita Khrushchev with his famous bearhugs of Fidel Castro in fatigues and beard. But it is the Russian way. Russians relish the joy of reunion with gusto and they linger over the anguish of parting as if there were no onlookers and it were a private occasion. So tame and out of character was the movie version that night that the Russians were still chortling about it after the movie ended. (Smith 1976:134)

Studies of the Russian national character point in the same direction. For example, Gorer writes:

Great Russians, with the exception of the Soviet elite, do take much pleasure in expressing aloud the emotions which are momentarily possessing them. There is a considerable Russian vocabulary for the expressing of the emotions, 'pouring out one's soul' being one of the most common. For many Russians this is the most valued aspect of living. Indeed, feeling and expressing the emotions you feel is the sign that you are alive; if you don't feel, you are to all intents and purposes dead. (1949:160)

A further example comes from the following passage in Herling's book *A world apart,* to which Kevin Windle has drawn my attention:

Musical instruments were the most precious and most sought-after objects in the camp. The Russians love music quite differently from Europeans; for them it is not a mere distraction, or even an artistic experience, but a reality more real than life itself. I often saw prisoners playing their instruments, plucking the strings of a guitar, delicately pressing the keys of an accordion, drinking in music from a mouth-organ hidden in the grasp of both hands—full of great sadness, as if they were exploring the most painful places of their souls. Never has the word soul [i.e., *duša*] seemed so understandable and so natural to me as when I heard their awkward, hastily improvised compositions, and saw other prisoners lying on the bunks, staring vacantly into space and listening with religious concentration. The surrounding silence seemed to emphasise the power of that music and the emptiness in which it resounded like the sharp, sorrowful tones of a shepherd's pipe on a deserted mountainside. The player became one with his instrument, he pressed it hard to his chest, stroked it with his hands and, hanging his head reflectively, gazed with misty despair at the inanimate object which, at one dexterous touch, spoke and expressed for him all that he could never put into words. Sometimes these musicians were asked to stop: 'It tears one's soul.' (1951:115)

Dicks (1952:169) stresses "the overwhelming vitality and spontaneity" of the Russians, their need for "direct, spontaneous, heart-to-heart contact and communication", and their readiness to "lay bare their souls" (1952:159). A study at the Harvard Russian Research Center led to similar conclusions:

> In our clinical sample the modal subjects showed a great need for intensive face-to-face relationships, skill in creating such relationships, and deep satisfaction from them. They 'welcomed others into their lives'. . . . These Russians are expressive and emotionally alive. American stress upon autonomy, social approval, and personal achievement does not often appear in the Russian protocols. Russians demand and expect moral responses (loyalty, respect, sincerity). (Bauer, Inkeles, and Kluckhohn 1956:135)

The Russian need for intimate, 'emotional', 'soul-to-soul' communication with other people is reflected in the following passage from one of Tolstoy's letters:

> Milyj, dorogoj drug, Nikolaj Nikolaevič staršij. Uže tri dnja každyj den' sobirajus' pisat' vam, dumaju že o vas besprestanno i žaleju, čto ne čuju vas dušoj. (1984, v.19:140)

> 'My very dear friend, Nikolaj Nikolajevič senior. For three days I've been meaning to write to you; I think of you continually, and I am sorry that I can't feel you with my soul.'

Furthermore, the results emerging from the semantic analysis of the words *duša, soul,* and *mind* are quite remarkably consistent with the ideas put forward on an entirely different basis in Russian thought, especially in the theories of the so-called Slavophiles, who contrasted Russian culture with Western culture. Walicki summarises their views as follows:

> In their philosophy of man and their epistemology, the Slavophiles . . . were largely concerned with analysing the destructive influences of rationalism. Rationalism, they argued, is the main factor in social disintegration, and also destroys the inner wholeness of the human personality. . . . Natural reason, or the capacity for abstract thought, is only one of the mental powers and by no means the highest: its one-sided development impoverishes man's perceptive faculties by weakening his capacities for immediate intuitive understanding of the truth. The cult of reason is responsible for breaking up the psyche into a number of separate and unconnected faculties, each of which lays claim to autonomy. . . . Only faith, they claimed, could ensure the wholeness of the psyche. . . . Thanks to orthodoxy, Russians were still capable of attaining this kind of integration. . . . The inhabitants of Western Europe, on the other hand, had long since lost their inner wholeness, their capacity for inner concentration, and their grasp on the profound currents of spiritual life. Western thought was everywhere infected by the incurable disease of rationalism. (1980:100–103)

The Slavophiles not only described the differences between Russia and Western Europe (as they saw them), they also evaluated them. But whether or not one agrees with their evaluation, one must admit, I think, that the linguistic evidence tends to support their perception of the differences in question.

11. Concluding Remarks

"Inye vešči na inom jazyke ne mysljatsja", 'there are things which cannot be thought in another language', wrote Tsvetaeva (1972:151). Thoughts related to *duša* cannot be thought in English, and since in Russian a very high proportion of thoughts seem to be linked with the concept of *duša,* to a Russian the universe of Anglo-Saxon culture often seems to be characterised by *bezdušie,* lack of *duša.* Thus, in a characteristic passage, Tsvetaeva (1972:464) expresses her dislike for a fellow Russian émigré by accusing him of having become anglicised, and thus become affected with 'the English soullessness', "englizirovannoe bezdušie". This is no doubt a subjective and one-sided view, and one can well imagine English people similarly accusing the Russian national character of 'mindlessness'. In both cases, the contrast between the two cultures can be seen as epitomised in lexical differences ('they don't even have a word for *duša*', or 'they don't even have a word for *mind*').

But although lexical differences of this kind can be misinterpreted and exaggerated, nonetheless they do mean something, and if carefully and cautiously interpreted they can indeed be regarded as clues to the different cultural universes associated with different languages. In the case of Russian, the word *duša* seems to be one of the particularly valuable and revealing clues, and in the case of English, the decline and fall of the word *soul,* and the ascendancy of the word *mind,* seem to provide particularly significant evidence for cultural history and for prevailing modern ethnophilosophy.

2

Fate and Destiny

1. Fate, Karma, Kismet: Universals of Human Experience?

People can't always do what they want to, and they know it. Their lives are shaped, in some measure at least, by forces outside their control, and this seems as obvious and as universal as the fact that they have to die. It might seem reasonable to expect, therefore, that the concept of fate, or something very much like it, will be found in all cultures and will be reflected in all languages, as one might expect that the concept of dying, or something very much like it, would be present in all cultures and in all languages.

Heelas (1981:51) writes confidently: "I certainly think that there are adequate grounds for assuming that idealist indigenous psychology must acknowledge the experience of being under control, the impact on the self of external powers and the feeling that one is being made to do things in an involuntary fashion. Hence the universality of notions of the kind: fate, destiny, predestination, karma and the involuntary."

Is this true? Do all languages have words roughly similar to the English words *fate* and *destiny?*

Very many languages from different cultural spheres do indeed have such words. For example, the entry on *fate* in Hastings' *Encyclopaedia of religion and ethics* (1908–26) cites the ancient Greek concept of *moira,* the Roman concept of *fatum,* the Moslem concept of *kismet,* the Babylonian concept of *šimtu,* the Buddhist concept of *karma,* the Chinese concept of *ming,* the Egyptian concept of *šau,* and so on. (Cf. also Fortes 1959 and Cowan 1910 on similar concepts in West Africa and in New Zealand, respectively.)

At the same time, however, the entry in question notes that ancient Hebrew didn't have a word corresponding to *fate.* "Based on the Old Testament, which on the whole acknowledges freedom of choice, Judaism does not, and consistently cannot, hold the pagan doctrine of Fate. The subject never entered Jewish consciousness, and therefore there is not even a Hebrew word in the Old Testament corresponding to *moira* or *fatum*" (Suffrin 1912:793).

Concepts such as *fate* or *destiny* seem also to be alien to Australian Aboriginal languages. For example, R. M. W. Dixon (p.c.) states authoritatively that the Dyirbal language of North Queensland has no words of this kind. According to Dixon, the Dyirbal people believe in 'clever people' (witch doctors) and in ancestors (which is another side of the same coin) manipulating events, but not in some abstract fate/destiny, the idea of fate/destiny being alien to their world view. The same appears to be true of other Aboriginal languages.

It would appear, therefore, that Heelas went too far when he assumed the universality of notions of this kind. Dorner's (1910:777) conclusion to his introductory outline to the entry on *fate* seems more valid: "From the above outline we see the wide diffusion of the belief in Fate among mankind, and the manifold forms it assumes." The cautious phrase "wide diffusion" is clearly more appropriate than "universality".

But if "the belief in Fate assumes manifold forms among mankind", what is it exactly that has "wide diffusion"? Is it the belief in the English notion of fate? But, for example, the Turkish *kismet* is so different from *fate* that it can scarcely be seen as a form of it; nor should it be viewed through the prism of the English concept. For example, *kismet* is good, whereas *fate* tends to be bad. If one says in Turkish:

I'll see you on Saturday, if it is kismet.

this implies that I want to see you on Saturday, and that I hope I will (Aysun Adams, p.c.). The sense is much closer to the rather old-fashioned English expression "God willing" than to any expression involving *fate*.

But this means that *fate* is not a culture-independent notion which could be used as a descriptive tool in cross-cultural surveys. It is a folk concept, no more culture-independent than *kismet, karma,* or *ming*.

Furthermore, even within Anglo-Saxon culture *fate* is not the only folk concept relevant to the topic under discussion. There are also *destiny, providence, predestination, fortune,* and *luck*. In older English, there was also the concept of *weird*. Furthermore, *fate* itself appears to have changed its meaning in the course of the history of English, and so has *destiny* (see the following discussion). Similarly, in Turkish, *kismet* is not the only relevant term. Equally or more common is the term *kader,* which refers to what is believed or imagined to be written on a person's forehead (the future events which *must* happen in that person's life, Aysun Adams, p.c.). If we want to be able to compare such concepts in different languages, and in different strata of the same language, we need analytical tools which are more language- and culture-independent than any of the complex concepts under discussion. I suggest that here as elsewhere, elementary concepts such as 'want', 'don't want', 'happen', or 'know' provide the necessary tools.

2. The Russian *Sud'ba*

Sud'ba is a key concept in Russian culture. It has no equivalent in English—neither a linguistic equivalent nor a cultural one. Dictionaries usually offer *fate* as the closest English word, but actually the meaning of *fate* differs considerably from that of *sud'ba*. In fact, *fate* has perhaps a closer counterpart in the Russian word *rok* (and the adjective *fateful* can be said to have a counterpart in the Russian adjective *rokovoj*). In addition to the semantic difference, however, there is a huge cultural difference: In English, *fate* is not a particularly salient concept and it is not often mentioned in English discourse; for example, one can easily read a long English novel, or a volume of letters or memoirs, without encountering *fate* once; similarly, it is possible to read a comparable Russian book without encountering *rok* once, but it is impossible to read a Russian novel, or a volume of memoirs or letters, without coming across many references to *sud'ba*—often several references on the same page, as in the following passage from Grossman's novel *Žizn' i sud'ba*, 'Life and fate', where *sud'ba* is repeated again and again:

> V èti minuty rešalas' sud'ba osnovannogo Leninym gosudarstva . . . Rešalas' sud'ba nemcev voenno-plennyx, kotorye pojdut v Sibir'. Rešalas' sud'ba sovetskix voennoplennyx v gitlerovskix lagerjax, kotorym volja Stalina opredelila razdelit' posle osvoboždenija sibirskuju sud'bu nemeckix plennyx. . . . Rešalas' sud'ba Pol'ši, Vengrii, Čexoslovakii i Rumynii. Rešalas' sud'ba russkix krest'jan i rabočix, svoboda russkoj mysli, russkoj literatury i nauki. (Grossman 1980:450)

> What was being decided now, what was at stake, was the fate of the State Lenin had founded. . . . What was at stake was the fate of the German prisoners-of-war who were to be sent to Siberia; what was at stake was the fate of the Soviet prisoners-of-war in Hitler's camps who were also to be sent to Siberia. . . . What was at stake was the fate of Poland, Hungary, Czechoslovakia and Rumania. What was at stake was the fate of the Russian peasants and workers, the freedom of Russian thought, literature and science. (1985:646)

The subjective impression that the word *sud'ba* is used much more frequently in Russian than the word *fate* is used in English is confirmed by computational analysis of large corpora. In a corpus of one million English words, Kučera and Francis (1967) have recorded 33 occurrences of the word *fate* (and 22 occurrences of the related word *destiny*); by contrast, in a corpus of one million Russian words, Zasorina (1977) has recorded 181 occurrences of the word *sud'ba*. In Šteinfeldt's (1974) *Russian word count* the corresponding figure for *sud'ba* is 148 (based on a corpus of 400,000 words). The corresponding figures for *rok* (2 in Zasorina 1977 and none in Šteinfeldt 1974) show the relative insignificance of this concept in Russian in comparison with *sud'ba*.

I have quoted earlier Heelas' (1981:51) claim that "idealist indigenous psychology must acknowledge the experience of being under control". If one were to judge by lexical and lexicostatistical evidence, one would have to conclude that in the Russian "indigenous psychology" the experience of "being under control" is particularly salient.

The cardinal importance of the concept of *sud'ba* in the Russian discourse, and Russian thought, is summed up in Okudžava's song "Zaezžij muzykant" (quoted for a different purpose in Mel'čuk et al. 1984:35):

> Tebja ne soblaznit' ni plat'jami, ni sned'ju . . .
> Zaezžij muzykant igraet na trube.
> Čto mir ves' rjadom s nim, s ego gorjačej med'ju?
> . . . sud'ba, sud'by, sud'be, sud'boju, o sud'be.

> 'One cannot seduce you with fancy dresses or food . . .
> The visiting musician is playing his trumpet.
> What's the whole world next to him, to his hot copper?
> . . . Destiny, of destiny, to destiny, by destiny, about destiny.'

Sud'ba is usually rendered in English as either *fate* or *destiny*, but neither of these glosses is fully appropriate. For example, the title of Bondarchuk's film "Sud'ba čeloveka" (based on a short story by Sholokhov) has been rendered in English as 'The destiny of a man', but in fact it could probably be better rendered as 'A human life', or 'The story of a human life'. (It is worth noting that Mel'čuk and Žolkovskij (1984) give the word *žizn'* 'life' as a synonym of *sud'ba*.) But if *sud'ba* is translated simply as *life*, something important is lost, too: a certain way of looking at human life, which is written into *sud'ba* and which is not written into any English word or expression. To understand fully the flavour of this title, one should add: a human life seen from the vantage point of Russian folk philosophy.

Similarly, consider the lines from Pasternak's poem "Rassvet"

> Ty značil vse v moej *sud'be*
> Potom prišla vojna, razruxa.
> (1965:443)

which have been translated by Max Hayward and Manya Harari as follows:

> 'You meant everything in my destiny.
> Then came the war, the disaster.'
> (1958:496)

could perhaps be better rendered with *life* rather than *destiny:*

> 'You meant everything in my life.'

But again, what is meant is not simply 'life', but life seen through the prism of a prevailing Russian folk philosophy.

It is important to stress in this connection that the use of *sud'ba* with reference to human life is by no means restricted to poetry or to a poetical mood. It is used very widely, in very different registers, from everyday speech to scholarly discourse. For example, a collection of Tsvetaeva's poetry which was published in Moscow in 1965 is preceded by a scholarly introduction with the following heading: "Marina Tsvetaeva (Sud'ba. Xarakter. Poezija.)", 'Marina Tsvetaeva (Life. Personality. Poetry.)' The word *sud'ba* could be translated here as *life* or *biography*, but hardly as *fate* or *destiny*, but the use of the word *sud'ba* suggests here a characteristically Russian way of looking at a person's life.

An interesting parallel to this use of *sud'ba* as a quasi-synonym of 'life' is provided by Chinese. According to Walshe (1912:783), "the Chinese equivalent of 'fate', viz. *ming*, . . . is often used as synonymous with 'life'—regarded as the span of existence, whose limits are irrevocably fixed, so that a long *ming* is but another name for long life." But the Russian *sud'ba* emphasises not so much "the *span* of existence whose *limits* are irrevocably fixed" as the *course* of life, or what Russians call 'life's journey' (*žiznennyj put'*), and in Russian, it is this entire *course*, rather than the extreme points, which is viewed as 'fated' (not in every detail, but in its general character). This difference is important, as it seems to be correlated with a different kind of fatalism—a point to which we will return later.

Trying to understand the peculiar folk philosophy reflected in the word *sud'ba* it is useful to consider more closely the use of this word with reference to an imaginary force. Consider, for example, the following stanza from Pasternak's poem "Razluka" ('Parting'):

V goda mytarstv, vo vremena
Nemyslimogo byta
Ona volnoj *sud'by* so dna
Byla k nemu pribita.
(1965:441)

Hayward and Harari have rendered this into English as follows:

'In the years of trial,
When life was inconceivable,
From the bottom of the sea the tide of destiny
Washed her up to him.'
(PASTERNAK 1958:489)

But *destiny* is misleading as a translation of *sud'ba*, because of its optimistic and purposeful overtones: it suggests vaguely that at the end 'all was well', and an important goal was achieved.

Sud'ba implies neither a 'good' or meaningful outcome, like *destiny,* nor a 'bad' or meaningless outcome, like *fate;* nor is it totally neutral between good and bad (like the Polish *los,* which I will discuss later); it hints that one can expect more bad things than good things to happen to one, but it presents human life as incomprehensible (as well as uncontrollable) rather than as meaningless and necessarily tragic. This aspect of *sud'ba* is reflected rather well in Mel'čuk and Žolkovskij's (1984) definition, which includes the component "obyčno—vopreki namerenijam ili oži-danijam Y-a", 'usually against a person's intentions or expectations' (cf. also Radzievskaja 1991).

Another interesting feature of *sud'ba* as an imaginary force has to do with, so to speak, its ontological status, rather than with the good-bad dimension. Unlike *rok, fate,* or *destiny, sud'ba* doesn't necessarily imply the existence of other-worldly forces, controlling human life. It presents life as not subject to the individual's control, while evoking the idea of an external controller, but it leaves the possibility open that the external control may come from other people—for example, from social tyranny or political oppression—rather than from other-worldly sources. Hence one can say, for example,

Jurka Šarok—verši'tel' *sudeb,* prokuror. (Rybakov 1987, pt.2:86)

'Jurka Šarok—the arbiter of fates, the prosecutor.'

Oni s Šarokom veršat *sud'by* i žizni. (Rybakov 1987, pt.2:13)

'Šarok and his likes decide people's lives and fates (destinies).'

Na odnoj čaše vesov vy—ssyl'nyj kontrrevolucioner, na drugoj—predsedatel' kol-xoza, on sila, vlast', xozjain ix *sud'by.* (Rybakov 1987, pt.3:32)

'On one side of the scales you—the exiled counter-revolutionary, on the other, a kolkhoz chairman, power, authority, the master of their fates.'

The word *rok* cannot be used in this way, and *fate* and *destiny* are normally not used like this either.

One might say that *sud'ba* has a much more empirical, much more experiential, and much more down-to-earth character than either *destiny* or *fate*. Consider, for example, the following passage:

> Pečal'noj okazalas' *sud'ba* kota. . . . [o]dna iz sosedok to li slučajno, to li s dosady, ošparila ego kipjatkom, i on umer. (Grossman 1980:72)

> 'The cat came to a sad end. [Lit., 'The fate/*sud'ba* of the cat was sad'.] He died after being scalded with boiling water by one of the women, perhaps accidentally, perhaps not.' (Grossman 1985:120)

The word *destiny* would be ludicrous in a context such as this ('the cat's destiny'), and even *fate* would sound somewhat inappropriate except for humorous effect ('the cat's fate'), and Chandler used neither of these words in his sentence. But *sud'ba* does not sound similarly humorous in the Russian sentence, because *sud'ba* focusses above all on good and bad things which can happen to one (especially bad things), without necessarily evoking supernatural powers of any kind and without implying the inevitability that *fate* suggests.

In fact, *sud'ba* can even be used with respect to inanimate objects, as in the following example:

> Včera byla u Čirikovyx, oni očen' ozaboč eny *sud'boj* posylki. (Tsvetaeva 1972:108)

> 'Yesterday I went to see the Čirikovs. They are very concerned about the *sud'ba* (fate) of the parcel.'

Sud'ba refers here, roughly speaking, to the sequence of decisive events which happen to something, which are not determined by the will of the person involved (in this case, the sender of the parcel) and which are likely to be 'bad'. It is a moot point whether this use of *sud'ba* illustrates a different (though closely related) meaning or whether it is a metaphorical application of the basic, people-oriented meaning. In either case, it highlights the empirical (rather than mythological) emphasis of the basic meaning of *sud'ba*.

Nevertheless, the etymological link of *sud'ba* with *sudit'* 'judge' and *sud* 'court of law, trial' seems synchronically valid, and the past participle *suždeno* is often used as a quasi-synonym for *sud'ba*. This highlights the reference to 'someone', to an imaginary judge, in the concept of *sud'ba*. This 'someone' used to be interpreted as God, and the link between *sud'ba* and God's judgement is clearly visible in older Russian texts such as the old translation of Psalm 35, quoted in SAR (1971/1970): "*sud'by* Bož'i neispovedimy", 'God's judgements are inscrutable'. In present-day Russian the imaginary judge doesn't have to be interpreted as God, and *sud'ba* is compatible with both a religious outlook and an irreligious, or agnostic, one. It does, however, seem to imply an attitude of acceptance and resignation; one should accept whatever happens to one as if it were assigned to us by God's judgement.

This attitude of acceptance and resignation is reflected in a particularly striking way in the use of the loving diminutive *sud'binuška,* 'dear little fate', characteristic of folk literature, and in collocations such as *zlaja sud'binuška,* 'malign/malevolent dear-little-*sud'ba'.* (For a detailed discussion of the emotional value of the suffix *-uška,* see chapter 7.) For example:

Sokol . . . sokol moj ljubimyj! Ždala ja tebja dni i noči, nadejalas' vskorosti svidet'sja. No zlaja sud'binuška razlučila nas navsegda. (Priboj, Lišnij, quoted in AN SSSR 1963:1165)

'My angel . . . my beloved angel [lit., 'falcon']! I waited for you days and nights, I hoped to see you soon. But malign/dear-little-fate separated us forever.'

Mne žrebij nevoli sud'binuškoj dan. (Lermontov, Ataman, quoted in AN SSSR 1963:1165)

'On me, dear-little-fate has bestowed captivity.'

Oj, sud'ba ty moja, sud'binuška, goremyka kovarnaja! (Skitalec, Za tjuremnoj stenoj, quoted in AN SSSR 1963:1165)

'O my fate, my dear little fate, that sly wretch!'

This loving attitude to *sud'ba,* however bitter or cruel it may be, is reminiscent of the Stoic idea of *amor fati,* 'the love of one's fate'. (Marcus Aurelius (1964:115) said, "Love nothing but that which comes to you and is woven in the pattern of your destiny".) But in the Stoic version, this 'love of fate' implied a non-emotional attitude, with anything like pity (for others or for oneself) being disapproved. In the Russian version, 'the love of *sud'ba'* is accompanied by an intense pity and compassion, and, one might say, by a love of suffering.

The positive acceptance of one's *sud'ba* even when its blows are crushing and, humanly speaking, undeserved is illustrated very well in Dmitrij Karamazov's attitude to the sentence which he receives for a crime which he had not committed:

Ponimaju teper', čto na takix, kak ja, nužen udar, udar sud'by, čtob zaxvatit' ego kak v arkan i skrutit' vnešneju siloj. Nikogda, nikogda ne podnjalsja by ja sam soboj! No grom grjanul. Prinimaju muku obvinenija i vsenarodnogo pozora moego, postradat' xoču i stradaniem očiščus'! (Dostoevsky 1958:63)

'I understand now that such men as I need a blow, a blow of destiny to catch them as with a noose, and bind them by a force from without. Never, never should I have risen of myself! But the thunderbolt has fallen. I accept the torture of accusation, and my public shame, I want to suffer and by suffering I shall be purified.' (Dostoevsky 1974:539)

Before proposing a semantic explication of the concept *sud'ba,* I will quote one formulated almost a hundred years ago by the great Russian nineteenth-century thinker Vladimir Solov'ev, in his essay "Sud'ba Puškina" ('Pushkin's *sud'ba'*):

'There is something called *sud'ba,* something that is not material but that is none-theless fully real. By *sud'ba,* I understand that fact that the course and the outcome of our life depends on something other than ourselves, on some overwhelming necessity to which we must submit. As a fact this is beyond question.' (Solov'ev 1966–70, 9:34; my translation)

Concluding his outline of Pushkin's life (which ended tragically in a duel, at the age of thirty-eight), Solov'ev comments:

> 'Such was Pushkin's *sud'ba*. In conscience, we have to recognise that firstly, it was good, because it led a human being [i.e., Pushkin] to the best goal—to a spiritual rebirth, that is, to a supreme good, the only one worthy of him; and secondly, we should recognise that it was rational, because it attained that goal in the simplest and easiest way, under the circumstances, that is, in the best possible way.' (Solov'ev 1966–70, 9:59; my translation)

Solov'ev's purpose was not semantic, but ethical; but the fact that he finds his ethical conception of human life compatible with the concept of *sud'ba* provides valuable evidence as to the meaning of this concept. One could hardly say in English that 'the existence of Fate is an indubitable fact' or that the fate of a great poet who was killed in a duel at the height of his creative powers was 'good and rational'. Of course ideas such as Solov'ev's could be expressed in English, but wanting to express them one wouldn't use the word *fate* (or *Fate*).

I will now attempt to spell out the folk philosophy encapsulated in the word *sud'ba* in a semantic explication. I will not explicate separately the use of *sud'ba* as a personified imaginary force and its use in the sense of a person's life story, because I believe that both these senses assume the same folk philosophy, and it is this folk philosophy which I would like to articulate.

sud'ba
(a) different things happen to people
(b) not because they want it
(c) one can think this: more bad things will happen to me than good things
(d) one cannot think: these things will not happen to me if I say: 'I don't want it'
(e) it would be bad to say: 'I don't want it'
(f) I imagine I know that things happen to people because someone says: 'I want it'
(g) I imagine this someone can say things about people that other people can't say
(h) I think: all good and bad things that happen to a person are parts of one thing

Turning now briefly to the Russian concept of *rok,* I will first note that in English it can be approximated not only by *fate* but also by *doom,* since its connotations are even more final, ominous, and calamitous than those of *fate.* I will also stress that, judging from its frequency of use, the concept of *rok* is not nearly as central to Russian culture as is *sud'ba.* As an illustration of the use of *rok,* consider the following passage:

> Nad ètimi det'mi byl *rok* rannej smerti. Ne ulybajtes', on est'. I Ilovajskij, kak v mife, možet byt' byl tol'ko orudiem. (Xronos dolžen požirat' svoix detej.) Vina est', kogda est' ee osoznanie. Kogda ee osoznanija net, ona ne vina, xotja možet byt' i

smertonosna. Ilovajskij že žil—v Ilovajskom žilo nepopravimoe soznanie pravoty. Kak sudit' nepogrešimost'?

I možet-byt' to, čto vsem kazalos' volej žit', byla nevolja nad nim roka, rok obratnyj detskomu, byl rok nad nim dolgoj žizni, kak nad temi—rannej smerti: dolgoletija, stavšego prokljatiem? (Sivilla, ne moguščaja umeret'). (Tsvetaeva 1972:554)

'These children were foreordained (doomed) to an early death. Don't smile, doom (*rok*) does exist, Ilovajskij was perhaps only an instrument, as in the legend. (Time must devour its own children.) Guilt comes only with awareness. Where awareness is lacking, guilt is not guilt even when it spreads death. Ilovajskij lived—in him there lived an invincible sense of rightousness. How can one condemn infallibility?

Perhaps that which everyone took to be a will to live was a subordination to fate (*rok*), a fate (*rok*) opposed to that of the children, a fate (*rok*) that imposed a long life on him just as it imposed an early death on them: a longevity that became a curse (a Sybil unable to die).'

I would propose the following explication of the concept *rok:*

rok

(a) bad things happen to people
(b) I imagine I know that some bad things happen to some people because someone wants it
(c) it is not someone like a human being
(d) one can say that it is something, not someone
(e) one cannot know what it is
(f) it is not part of this world
(g) it is something bad
(h) if this someone or something wants something it will happen
(i) one cannot think: 'if I say: I don't want it, it will not happen'
(j) it cannot not happen

In present-day Russian, the noun *rok* sounds archaic, but the adjective *rokovoj,* which can be regarded as metaphorical, is still current, and it carries tragic and mythological overtones which are not inherent in *sud'ba*. The following passage from a recent newspaper story contains both the noun *sud'ba* and the adjective *rokovoj,* and it highlights the semantic relation between these concepts:

Ona k tomuže avtomatičeski utratila pravo na kojku v fabričnom obščežitii. Poslednij fakt okazalsja osobenno rokovym v sud'be Ljudmily. . . . Vyxod najden: otpravit' pod kryšu psixuški, zatem v invalidnyi dom požiznenno. (Ginzburg 1988:2)

'In addition, she automatically lost her right to a bed in the factory hostel. This last fact proved to be *rokovoj* (fateful) in Ljudmila's *sud'ba* (life). . . . A solution was found: to despatch her to a mental hospital, and then, for the rest of her life, to a home for invalids.'

In this passage, the word *sud'ba* clearly refers to an entire course of a person's life, whereas the adjective *rokovoj* ('fateful') refers to a single fact. *Sud'ba* doesn't imply that the whole of life is tragic, although it does imply an expectation that 'bad', 'sad', and difficult events will happen, and that the pattern of one's existence as a whole is independent of one's will. *Rokovoj,* however (and the noun *rok*), does imply something tragic. Both *sud'ba* and *rok* imply that what happens is independent of human will, but *rok* implies also an absolute, inexorable inevitability; this is stronger than the 'irresistibility' implied by *sud'ba.*

In a person's *sud'ba* even chance can play a certain role, although it is seen as subordinated to an overall design. One can say, for example:

> Sud'ba včera svela slučajno nas. (Lermontov)
>
> 'Yesterday fate accidentally brought us together.'

In the English gloss, the combination of the words *fate* and *accidentally* sounds odd, and a combination of the words *rok* and *slučajno* ('accidentally') is simply unthinkable, but a combination of *sud'ba* and *slučajno* does not sound odd.

Rok is seen also as arbitrary and meaningless, as if it were due to some incomprehensible, irrational power. There is no point in rebelling against *rok* because it is absolute and inexorable, nor is there room for accepting it. But *sud'ba* can be accepted in a positive way, as something that possibly does have sense, although this sense may transcend our comprehension. For this reason, if both these concepts, *sud'ba* and *rok,* may be said to be 'fatalistic', they represent different kinds of fatalism. The 'fatalism' of *sud'ba,* unlike that of *rok,* is compatible with the teachings and traditions of Orthodox Christianity which have shaped Russian spirituality, and in fact it finds its echo in one of the highest moral ideals of Orthodoxy: the ideal of *smirenie,* 'holy resignation' (see chapter 5).

An old proverb, quoted by Dal' (1955, v.4:623), highlights this difference between the two concepts: "Ne *rok* slepoj, premudrye *sud'by*", 'not blind *rok* (fate), but profoundly wise *sud'by* (i.e., divine decrees).' Although in present-day Russian *sud'ba,* as mentioned earlier, is no longer felt to be necessarily a religious concept referring to God's judgement, it is still compatible with such an interpretation (and some of my informants find the expression *slepaja sud'ba,* 'blind *sud'ba*', unacceptable).

Furthermore, even when *sud'ba* is seen as 'blind' and irrational, it is still compatible with the image of a judge delivering a sentence, as the following sentence from Dostoevsky's *Crime and punishment* indicates:

> On stydilsja imenno togo, čto on, Raskol'nikov, pogib tak slepo, beznadežno, gluxo i glupo, po kakomu-to prigovoru slepoj sud'by, i dolžen smirit'sja i pokorit'sja. (Dostoevsky 1957:417)
>
> 'What he was ashamed of was that he, Raskol'nikov, should have perished so utterly, so hopelessly, and so stupidly because of some blind decision [lit., 'sentence'] of fate, and that he should have to humble himself and submit to the absurdity of that sort of decision.' (Dostoevsky 1951:551)

It might be mentioned that Russian also has some other concepts belonging to the field under discussion, in particular *žrebij* ('lot/destiny') and *učast'* ('lot', 'portion assigned by fate'), but these, like *rok,* are rather marginal in Russian. *Žrebij* is archaic and poetic (AN SSSR 1955, 4:183, qualifies it as "ustareloe" 'obsolete'), whereas *učast'* is somewhat poetic; their importance in Russian thinking cannot be even compared with that of *sud'ba.* Unquestionably, it is *sud'ba,* rather than *rok, žrebij,* or *učast',* which is the key Russian concept, endlessly echoing in Russian literature and in Russian everyday speech as in Okudžava's song ("sud'ba, sud'by, sud'be, sud'boju, o sud'be . . .").

3. The Polish *Los*

Like the Russian *sud'ba,* the Polish *los* can refer either to an imaginary force or to the course of a person's life viewed in the light of a certain folk philosophy. But whereas *sud'ba* represents either an imaginary judge or an imaginary 'sentence', *los* has no such courtroom connotations. Rather, it evokes the image of a great lottery, where different people draw different tickets. The Polish word for a lottery ticket is also *los,* and although we have to treat '*los*-fate' and '*los*-lottery ticket' as two distinct meanings of the word *los,* these two meanings are clearly related, not only in the etymological but also in the semantic sense. The synchronic reality of a link between los_1 and los_2 is supported by songs such as the following, where *los* can be interpreted as ambiguous between los_1 and los_2:

> Bo taki los wypadł nam
> Że dzisiaj tu a jutro tam.
>
> 'That's the ticket we've drawn from the lottery of life
> That today we are here and tomorrow we are gone.'

The common expression *wygrać los (na loterii),* 'to win a lottery', can be used to refer to any unusual 'stroke of luck'.

The link between los_1 and los_2 highlights the image of human life as a kind of lottery, where different things happen to different people and 'luck' is distributed unevenly and unpredictably. There is no reference to 'someone' who knows the outcome and can control the outcome (although personification is of course possible). The stress is on unpredictability rather than on uncontrollability. The concept *sud'ba* implies a world controlled by someone who can decide the course of people's lives; the concept of *los* implies a world where 'anything can happen'.

It should be added that los_2 refers not only to the institution of the lottery but also to any situation where lots are drawn. The action of drawing lots is called in Polish *losowanie* (infinitive *losować*), and this word, too, is felt to be semantically related to *los* in the sense closer to *fate,* as the following sentence from one of Mickiewicz's letters indicates:

> Losowali na ten urząd i los z woli wyższej Jeżewskiego naznaczył. (Adam Mickiewicz, quoted in SJP 1958–69:199)
>
> 'They drew lots for the position, and *los,* by divine will, chose Jeżewski.'

In some ways, therefore, the Polish *los* is closer to the Roman *fortuna* than to the Roman *fatum*. Stock (1912:786) writes: "Fate is the counterpart of Fortune. They are two ways of looking at life; both are essentially connected with man. From the point of view of Fortune all is indeterminate; from the point of view of Fate all is determined."

What both these ways of looking at human life have in common is the assumption that it depends on factors other than human will. It would seem, however, that the Russian concept of *sud'ba* leans more toward a Fatum-like interpretation of these factors, whereas the Polish concept of *los* favours a Fortuna-like interpretation. Expressions such as *zmienne koleje losu* 'changing fortunes' or *na los szczęścia* 'counting on luck and hoping for the best' point in the same direction. Even formal expressions such as *wypadek losowy* or *wiza losowa* emphasise the accidental, rather than predetermined, character of events due to *los:* the former is a social security term and it refers to sudden, unpredictable social needs generated by accident, illness, death, and the like; the latter is a special category of visa, granted without the usual delays and restrictions in the case of a sudden misfortune in the family such as illness or death.

Since the Polish *los* evokes the image of a lottery rather than of a courtroom, it is not slanted toward suffering and misfortune in the way *sud'ba* is. A 'sentence' delivered by an imaginary judge can be seen as 'good' if it is less bad than one might have expected, but generally speaking, one expects from a 'sentence' bad things rather than good things. But the image of a lottery of life is not similarly pessimistic. One can lose one's money in a lottery, but one can also win. People's *losy* (plural) are seen as changeable and unpredictable, but there is no evidence that the concept *los* includes the 'adversative' component 'one can think: more bad things will happen to me than good things', which has been assigned to *sud'ba*.

Nor is there any evidence which would suggest that the Polish concept of *los* includes the somewhat fatalistic component 'one cannot think that if I say: "I don't want it", these things will not happen to me'. The Polish concept of *los* does, of course, present human life as not being controlled, or not fully controlled, by human will, and it includes a component such as 'different things happen to different people not because someone wants it'. But this lack of controllability, or full controllability, is something different from the idea of being subject to an irresistible higher power.

To account for all these aspects of *los*, I would propose the following explication:

> *los*
> (a) different things happen to different people
> (b) sometimes good things, sometimes bad things
> (c) more good things happen to some people than to others
> (d) more bad things happen to some people than to others
> (e) not because someone wants it
> (f) a person cannot think: I know what things will happen to me
> (g) one cannot know this

Component (a) in this explication is almost identical with component (a) of *sud'ba*. Components (b), (c), and (d), which show that good and bad things are distributed among people unevenly, have no counterpart in *sud'ba*. Component (e) has its counterpart in component (b) of *sud'ba*, but it is phrased differently: *sud'ba* stresses that people don't control their own lives, whereas *los* stresses that people don't control human life in general. (This leaves more room for optimism and an active attitude in one's own case.) Components (f) and (g) stress the unpredictability of people's fortunes. Component (e) of *sud'ba*, which encourages resignation, has no counterpart in *los*. Nor have components (f) and (g), which conjure up an imaginary judge, or component (h), which presents the vicissitudes of a person's life as a coherent whole (cf. Radzievskaja 1991).

A further difference between *sud'ba* and *los*, closely related to those which have been discussed so far, is related to the unity and cohesiveness of the former, but not necessarily of the latter. Since a person's *sud'ba* is likened to a 'sentence', it is viewed as a whole, perhaps as a coherent whole, but a *los* is more easily seen as determined by a series of 'accidents'. This difference in conceptualisation is reflected in a difference in grammar, *los* being much more readily used in the plural than *sud'ba* is. Just as in English one can speak much more readily of a person's *fortunes* (in the plural) than of his or her *fates*, in Polish one can speak of a person's *losy* (in the plural), in particular, *dalsze losy* (subsequent 'fates', that is, all the things that happened to a person 'later', all the subsequent turns in the course of his or her life).

Sud'ba can also be used in the plural, but normally not with respect to a single person. For example, as Mel'čuk and Žolkovskij (1984) note, one can speak of the *sud'by* (plural) of a large category of people, of a historical process, or of a social, cultural, or historical phenomenon, such as the Russian intelligentsia, the British fleet, Mediterranean civilisation, or the folk ballad. I have attempted to account for the inner unity of *sud'ba* by positing for it the component 'I think of good and bad things that happen to a person as parts of one thing', and I have not posited a similar component for *los*.

The conceptual differences between *sud'ba* and *los* are also reflected in the phraseology of the two words, and in the range of proverbs and other traditional sayings in which they are involved. In Polish, the most common proverb involving *los* is "każdy jest kowalem własnego *losu*", 'every one forges his own fate' (the only proverb involving *los* cited in SJP 1958–69). For *sud'ba*, Dal' (1955) cites a number of proverbs, nearly all of which have a fatalistic ring and have no Polish counterparts, for example: "Čto *sud'ba* skažet, xot' pravosud, xot' krivosud, a tak i byt'." 'Whatever *sud'ba* decrees, be it just or unjust, will come to pass.' "*Sud'ba* ruki svjažet." '*Sud'ba* will tie your hands.' "Vsjakaja *sud'ba* sbudetsja." 'Every *sud'ba* will come true.' (As pointed out by Dal', this last proverb involves a symbolic consonantal play on the noun sUD'Ba and the verb sBUDetsja 'will come true'.)

Another interesting Russian proverb cited by Dal', which has no counterpart in Polish, is "vsjakomu svoja *sud'ba*", 'to each his own *sud'ba*'. This idea that one's fate is unique and that it ought to be cherished for this reason is also characteristically Russian, and it would seem to be incompatible with the image of a lottery of life, where people compare their luck with that of others. This idea of precious uniqueness of one's fate is aptly expressed in a line from one of Pasternak's poems, in which he humbly asks God to teach him "sebja i svoj žrebij podarkom bescennym tvoim soznavat'"', 'to be conscious of oneself and one's fate as your priceless gift'. *Žrebij* means literally 'lot', and *metat' žrebij* means 'to cast lots', but under the pressure of Russian folk philosophy (best expressed in the word *sud'ba*), even this word for 'lot' (now archaic in the sense of 'fate') acquired connotations of something sacred, uniquely personal, and meaningful.

The phraseological differences between *sud'ba* and *los* can be illustrated with the Russian phrase *pokorjat'sja sud'be*, 'to submit (humbly) to one's *sud'ba*', which has no equivalent in Polish, the closest Polish counterpart being *pogodzić się z losem*, 'to come to terms with one's *los*, to make peace with one's *los*'.

Similarly, whereas both *sud'ba* and *los* can be seen as 'implacable' (*neumolimaja sud'ba, nieubłagany los*), *sud'ba*, in contrast to *los*, is also seen as *neotvratimaja*, 'irreversible' (cf. Mel'čuk and Žolkovskij 1984:857). Furthermore, *sud'ba*, in contrast to *los*, invites anthropomorphic imagery, such as *v rukax sud'by* 'in the hands of sud'ba', or *ruka/perst sud'by* 'the hand/finger of *sud'ba*' (cf. Mel'čuk and Žolkovskij 1984:858). In Polish, people speak of *palec Boży* 'the finger of God' (pointing to what God wants to happen), but not of any 'finger of *los*'. It is true that Polish can attribute to *los* irony or humour (as Russian can to *sud'ba*), but it doesn't favour the imagery of purposeful, rational behaviour, more compatible with the idea of an imaginary judge than of a master of ceremonies at the lottery of life.

The common Russian expressions *voleju sudeb, voleju sud'by*, and *po vole sud'by* 'by the will of *sud'ba*' point in the same direction. The Polish *los* can 'want' something, as it can have whims (for example, *los chciał inaczej* '*los* wanted otherwise'; *kapryśny los* 'capricious *los*'), but it cannot have a 'will'. Only God (or Heaven) can have a 'will' in Polish. The expressions *wola Boża* or *wola Boska* 'God's will' are extremely common in everyday Polish, but *wola losu*, 'the will of *los*' would sound strange in Polish, since it would attribute to *los* a rational purpose, and a kind of authority, which is incompatible with the 'capricious', fortuitous, and 'contingent' connotations of this concept.

Since the Polish *los* does not imply any 'higher' necessity to which one must submit and before which one must humble oneself, it is more conducive to the idea that one can influence, actively shape, one's life, either by resisting one's *los* (cf. the common expression *wyzywać los* 'to defy *los*') or by actively cooperating with it. The latter idea is reflected in the expression *zrobić los* or *zrobić świetny los* (*wielki los*), literally, 'to make a *los*' or 'to make an excellent/great *los*', that is, 'to make an excellent life for oneself' (for example, in terms of career or marriage).

Generally speaking, the phraseology of *los* seems to reflect an ethos which leaves more room for an active attitude, more in the spirit of the Latin proverb "audaces fortuna iuvat", 'fortune helps those who dare', whereas the phraseology of *sud'ba* seems to stress more the need for submission and resignation. As we will see in section 8 (and in chapter 12), this is entirely in line with what great Russian thinkers and writers (such as Dostoevsky, Tolstoy, Chekhov, or Solov'ev) have said about the Russian 'national character', and the difference between the 'Oriental ethos' (such as the Russian one) and the 'Western ethos' (one version of which they saw in the Polish ethos).

4. The German *Schicksal*

Brockhaus Wahrig Deutsches Wörterbuch (1983:545) attributes to the German word *Schicksal* two different meanings: (1) everything which happens to a human being, that determines his existence, without being influenced by human will and without being able to be changed by the person in question; (2) a power which governs and determines human life and which is independent of human will.

This double use of *Schicksal* parallels that of *sud'ba* and *los*. But what kind of folk philosophy is reflected in this word? One way of approaching this problem is to start with the Roman contrast between 'Fatum' and 'Fortuna', determinism and indeterminism, mentioned earlier, and to look at this contrast in terms of two poles toward which related concepts in other languages can be seen as gravitating. Clearly, the Russian *sud'ba* gravitates toward 'Fatum' rather than toward 'Fortuna', whereas equally clearly, the Polish *los* gravitates more toward 'Fortuna' than 'Fatum'. And *Schicksal?*

Unlike *los, Schicksal* does not evoke the image of a lottery or of people drawing lots of any kind. This doesn't mean that this image is totally alien to German folk philosophy, but it is associated with a different word: *Los* (in fact, the etymological source of the Polish *los*). But whereas in Polish *los* is a core concept in the area under discussion, in German *Los* is quite marginal. *Schicksal* is clearly the dominant concept in this area (and in fact the only one which is commonly used), and this vital, basic concept has no association with any drawing of lots.

But neither is it associated with the image of a supreme judge, whether divine or any other. As German dictionaries usually put it, *Schicksal* suggests "eine jenseitige Macht" (WDG 1975), 'an other-worldly power', or "eine höhere Macht" (Duden 1980), 'a higher power', which determines and governs human life in an absolute (*bedingungslos*) manner. The inevitability of *Schicksal* is reminiscent of the meaningless and 'blind' inevitability of the Russian *rok* rather than of the potentially meaningful irresistibility of *sud'ba* (which one might want to accept as God's personal 'gift' with a sense of dignity due to voluntary submission).

The inevitability encoded in *Schicksal* manifests itself in its adjectival use and, in particular, in the adjective *schicksalsbedingt*. For example, WDG (1975) cites the following sentence from the journal *Gesundheit* 'Health' (1966): "dass das Krebsleiden nicht *schicksalsbedingt* . . . ist", 'that cancer is not a *Schicksal*-determined malady'. Similarly, "nur relativ wenig Säuglingstodesfälle sind *schicksals*-bedingt, d.h. durch schwere Missbildungen und Erbkrankheiten verursacht" (from the journal *Urania*, 1962, quoted in WDG 1975); 'only relatively few cases of infant death are determined by *Schicksal*, that is, by severe anatomical abnormalities and hereditary diseases'. Clearly, illnesses described as *schicksalsbedingt* ('determined by *Schicksal*') are those which cannot be prevented, no matter what one does.

It is interesting to note that whereas hereditary diseases can be described as *schicksalsbedingt,* inherited talents (for example, a musical talent) cannot. This fact highlights the 'pessimistic' orientation of *Schicksal,* which is also manifested in the fact that although a person's *Schicksal* can be described as *schreckliches* 'terrible', *trauriges* 'sad', *tragisches* 'tragic', or *schweres* 'hard', it can hardly be described as *glückliches* 'happy' or *leichtes* 'easy'.

> Sie hatte ein schreckliches/schweres *Schicksal.*
>
> 'She had a terrible/difficult *Schicksal.*'
>
> *Sie hatte ein glückliches/leichtes *Schicksal.*
>
> 'She had a happy/easy *Schicksal.*'

Schicksal as an abstract force can be said to have been kind, or good, to somebody, but a person's *Schicksal* cannot be described as good or happy. This is all the more interesting since in Russian one *can* speak of a happy or enviable *sud'ba* (*ščastlivaja sud'ba, zavidnaja sud'ba; talan-sud'ba,* cf. Mel'čuk and Žolkovskij 1984:862). This suggests that if *sud'ba* implies that more bad things can be expected in life than good things, *Schicksal* has the stronger implication that bad things can be expected in life.

The analysis of *Schicksal* proposed here may seem to be incompatible with Bruno Bettelheim's observations on the relationship between *Schicksal* and the English *fate:*

> In translating the title of Freud's important paper 'Triebe und Triebschicksale' (1915), the translators have made two grievous mistakes. Not only have they rendered *Triebe* as 'instincts' but they have replaced *Schicksale* ('fates', 'destinies') with 'vicissitudes.' . . . It is true that both 'fate' and 'destiny' carry the implication of inevitability, which neither the German *Schicksal* nor the English 'vicissitudes' does. And Freud certainly did not mean that there is any inevitability inherent in the changes our inner drives are subject to. But if the translators rejected 'fate' because of its implication of immutability, they could have used 'change' or 'mutability' instead. They could, for example, have translated the title as 'Drives and their Mutability'. (1983:105)

The main point to be made here is that it is *Schicksale* (plural) rather than *Schicksal* which is free of the implication of inevitability (and probable misfortune). The Russian word *sud'ba,* too, loses many of its implications when it is used in the plural, as when one speaks of the *sud'by* of the Russian intelligentsia, the British fleet, or French literature. AN SSSR (1963:1163) glosses this use of *sud'ba,* in the plural, as "istorija suščestvovanija, razvitija čego-libo", 'the history of the existence, [and/or] development of something', and a similar rough definition could be assigned to *Schicksale,* although Bettelheim is quite right in stressing the idea of 'changes' inherent in this use. But this plural, *Schicksale,* should be regarded as an extension from, and a reduction of, the meaning of the singular form *Schicksal,* which, I would argue, does imply something like inevitability—in the sense that if the imaginary force 'wants something to happen it will happen'.

A related point concerns the relationship between *Schicksal* and chance. We have seen that *sud'ba* is fully compatible with chance because it can be seen as using chance for 'higher purposes'. But *Schicksal* does not seem to be similarly compatible with chance, and according to my informants sentence (b) sounds odd, though perhaps less odd than sentence (c):

    a. Sud'ba včera svela slučajno nas. (Lermontov)

    b. ?Gestern hat uns Schicksal zufällig zusammen geführt.

    c. ??Yesterday, fate accidentally brought us together.

Sud'ba seems to know what it is doing (even when it is making use of chance) and it can be respected and humbly cherished. *Schicksal* doesn't seem to know what it is doing: even when it is good to us its favours seem capricious and incomprehensible, and probably devoid of meaning. Expressions such as *Gunst des Schicksals* 'arbitrary benevolence of *Schicksal*', *Ungunst des Schicksals* 'arbitrary malevolence of *Schicksal*', *eine Laune des Schicksals* 'a whim of *Schicksal*', or *ein Wink des Schicksals* 'a nod from *Schicksal*' suggest that *Schicksal* is seen as arbitrary and capricious—more like the Polish *los* in this respect than like the Russian *sud'ba*. Admittedly, some expressions of this kind are also possible in the case of *sud'ba*, but, in addition, there are many others which present *sud'ba* in a different light and which have no equivalents in German. It would appear, then, that *Schicksal* is conceived of as an incomprehensible power, which determines the course of human life and which is expected to cause 'bad' things to happen to people in what appears to be an arbitrary fashion.

I asked at the outset whether *Schicksal* is closer to Fatum or to Fortuna. The short answer to this question seems to be that it is closer to Fatum. In some respects, however, it is closer to the Polish *los* than to the Russian *sud'ba*, since it suggests no 'amor fati' and stresses 'blindness' rather than 'judgement'. Judges may be just or unjust (recall the proverb about *sud'ba* quoted earlier: 'what *sud'ba* decrees, be it just or unjust, will come to pass'), but *Schicksal* is not seen as a 'judge' at all; rather, it is seen—as German dictionaries rightly express it—as a *jenseitige Macht*, a mysterious supernatural force, fearsome, all-powerful, arbitrary, and incomprehensible (like God's impenetrable secret decree in Luther's theology; cf. Weber 1968:102).

It is interesting to note, in this connection, that in the following context, where both *fate* and *sud'ba* are judged to be fully acceptable, *Schicksal* is not:

Dem Gefangenen war es niemals vergönnt den Richter zu sehen, der über sein Los (?Schicksal) Recht sprach.

'The prisoner (was tried in absentia and) never even saw the judge who was to determine his fate.'

A judge may determine a person's *fate*, or *sud'ba*, but not his or her *Schicksal*, because, I suggest, *Schicksal* is felt to be too supernatural and mysterious for that.

I propose the following explication:

Schicksal
(a) different things happen to people
(b) not because they want it
(c) more bad things happen to some people than to others
(d) one can think: bad things will happen to me
(e) I imagine I know that good and bad things happen to people because someone wants it
(f) it is not someone like a human being
(g) one can say that it is something, not someone
(h) it is not part of this world
(i) if this something wants something, it cannot not happen

Components (a), (b) and (d) link *Schicksal* with *sud'ba* (although the pessimistic expectation contained in component (d) of *Schicksal* is stronger than that contained in component (c) of *sud'ba*). Components (e), (f), (g), (h), and (i) link *Schicksal* with *rok*. But *rok* is seen definitely as something 'bad' ('it is something bad'), whereas this does not apply to either *Schicksal* or *sud'ba*. Furthermore, the inevitability of *Schicksal* does not mean specifically the inevitability of *bad* things, as in the case of *rok*. It is not accompanied by the resignation of *sud'ba*, suggested in component (e) of *sud'ba*, or by the image of a judge (component (g) of *sud'ba*), or by the idea of a coherent existential whole (component (h) of *sud'ba*). Component (c) of *Schicksal* hints at its 'capriciousness' and links it with the Polish *los*. But components (e) and (d) of the Polish *los*, which stress its unpredictability, are absent from the explication of *Schicksal* which stresses inevitability rather than unpredictability.

Finally, it should be pointed out that *Schicksal* does not have the existential and empirical ring of *sud'ba*, which almost identifies a person's life with his or her *sud'ba*. For example, a dry introduction in a German poetry volume would be unlikely to be entitled 'Rainer Maria Rilke. (*Schicksal*. Personality. Poetry.)', like a Russian scholarly introduction (Orlov 1965) entitled 'Marina Tsvetaeva. (*Sud'ba*. Personality. Poetry.)'. *Schicksal* implies something special, whereas *sud'ba* is the very stuff of human existence, and it is taken for granted in Russian as the only conceivable way of viewing human life. (Recall that according to Solov'ev, it is an indisputable "fact".) Linguistic evidence suggests that *Schicksal* is not similarly central to the German view of life. *Schicksal* is a common word in German, but its frequency appears to be nowhere near that of *sud'ba*. Both *sud'ba* and *Schicksal* present human life as something that a person cannot fully control and that is controlled by 'higher powers', but *sud'ba* implies that this is the 'normal' way of viewing human life, whereas *Schicksal* implies that this is a 'special', mythological way of viewing it. Components (f), (g), and (h) of its explication attempt to reflect that.

In support of the analysis of *Schicksal* sketched here I will adduce three passages from Erikson's essay entitled "The legend of Hitler's childhood" (chapter 9 in Erikson 1963). Erikson points to the extraordinary role that *Schicksal* (which he translates as Fate, with a capital *F*), plays in Hitler's account of his own life in *Mein Kampf* (cf. also Guardini 1961:186):

> His Reichs-German fairy tale does not simply say that Hitler was born in Braunau because his parents lived there; no, it was "Fate which designated my birthplace." This happened when it happened not because of the natural way of things; no, it was an "unmerited mean trick of Fate" that he was "born in a period between two wars, at a time of quiet and order." When he was poor, "Poverty clasped me in her arms"; when sad, "Dame Sorrow was my foster mother." But all this "cruelty of Fate" he later learned to praise as the "wisdom of Providence," for it hardened him for the service of Nature, "the cruel Queen of all wisdom."
>
> When the World War broke out, "Fate graciously permitted" him to become a German foot soldier, the same "inexorable Goddess of Fate who uses wars to weigh nations and men." When after the defeat he stood before a court defending his first revolutionary acts, he felt certain "that the Goddess of History's eternal judgment will smilingly tear up" the jury's verdict.
>
> Fate, now treacherously frustrating the hero, now graciously catering to his heroism and tearing up the judgment of the bad old men: this is the infantile imagery which pervades much of German idealism. (1963:339)

According to Erikson, *Schicksal* (which this time he renders in English as *destiny*) has a magic meaning in German thinking in general. He writes:

> At the end of the first World War Max Weber wrote that destiny had decreed (even a realistic German says "destiny," not "geography" or "history") that Germany alone should have as its immediate neighbors three great land powers and the greatest sea power and that it should stand in their way. No other country on earth, he said, was in this situation.
>
> As Weber saw it, the necessity to create national greatness and security in a thoroughly encircled and vulnerable position left no alternatives. . . . (1963:345)

Erikson here renders *Schicksal* as *destiny,* which is misleading, because what Weber had in mind was clearly something 'bad' and 'inevitable,' "an encircled and vulnerable position", which is very different from what *destiny* implies in English (discussed later). Yet, according to Erikson, in the German national mythology, the idea of *Schicksal* was felt to be perfectly compatible with the idea of being a 'chosen nation'. For example, after the defeat of 1918 it was felt that

> *Fate* had sent defeat to Germany in order to single her out from among the nations. *Fate* had elected her to be the first great country to accept defeat voluntarily. . . . Even in this very depth of masochistic self-abasement—impressively decried by Max Weber—world history was still a secret arrangement between the Teutonic spirit and the Goddess of Fate. (1963:350)

These passages should not be taken to imply that the idea of *Schicksal* is linked with nations rather than with people. It is linked above all with people. But the way it is applied to nations illuminates certain elusive aspects of this concept and, in particular, certain important differences between, on the one hand, a belief in

Schicksal (inevitable, superhuman, and awesome) and, on the other, that which Solov'ev and others saw as 'fatalism Russian style', encouraging humble resignation, non-resistance, and passivity rather than determined (and possibly even fanatical) action. The notion of *sud'ba* seems to reflect that "grudging idealisation of a strong and arbitrary authority" (Dicks 1952:169) which students of Russia see as one of its most characteristic features. By contrast, *Schicksal* seems to suggest a mysterious and inexorable other-worldly power rather than a "grudgingly idealised authority".

5. The Italian *Destino* and *Sorte*

In Italian, the most common word for something like the German *Schicksal* or the Russian *sud'ba* appears to be *destino*. Devoto and Oli (1977) offer the following definition of this concept: "the imponderable complex of causes that are thought to have determined (or to be going to determine) events which are decisive and immutable".

This sounds rather similar to most dictionary definitions of *Schicksal*. There are good reasons, however, to think that in fact *destino* encapsulates a different concept.

To begin with, Italian also has two other words whose dictionary definitions are similar to those of *Schicksal: fato* and *sorte* (not to mention *fortuna*, which is closer to *luck*), and since these four Italian words, *destino, fato, fortuna*, and *sorte*, are not always mutually substitutable, they can't all be exact equivalents of *Schicksal*. Devoto and Oli (1977) define *fato* as "*destino* especially [seen] as a supreme and ineluctable necessity or as a mysterious and irresistible power". This special stress on the inevitability of *fato* suggests that in some respects this concept may be closer to *Schicksal* than *destino* is.

In another respect, however, *destino* seems to be closer to *Schicksal* than *fato* is, because *fato* seems to be applicable mainly to an abstract force, not to an individual human life, whereas *destino*—like *Schicksal* or *sud'ba*—is often used precisely for that, and in fact it seems to stress the individual character of a person's existence.

As for *sorte*, Devoto and Oli (1977) define it as "an impersonal force which is supposed to regulate, in an unforseeable fashion, the events of a human life", and as "any condition which is thought of as due to contingencies independent of human will, or even to a course of events which is fatal and inscrutable". Despite the use of the adjective *fatale*, 'fatal', the emphasis seems to be in this case on the unpredictable, unforseeable character of the events of human life, rather than on their inevitability.

But the picture suggested by the dictionaries is confused, and the definitions provided do not make the relations among *destino, fato*, and *sorte* at all clear (although they do provide many helpful hints).

When we compare the abstract force of *fato* with the abstract use of *sorte* and *destino*, we notice not only the greater stress on inevitability but also the inherent orientation toward 'bad things'—perhaps not quite as strong as in the Russian *rok*, but probably stronger than in the German *Schicksal*.

Both the inevitability and the grimness of *fato* are highlighted in a short poem by Leopardi:

> Al gener nostro il fato
> Non donò che il morire. Ormai disprezza
> Te, la natura, il brutto
> Poter, che, nascosto, a comun danno impera,
> E l'infinita vanità del tutto.
>
> (quoted in Guardini 1961:170)

> 'To humankind fate has decreed nothing but death.
> Scorn now thyself, and Nature, and that brutal power
> That, hidden, governs to the universal hurt,
> And the infinite vanity of all things.'

It must be remembered, however, that the grim concept of *fato* is marginal in modern Italian culture and that in modern Italian the word *fato* is not a common word at all. By contrast, *destino* and *sorte* are both common, and they present two alternative ways of viewing human existence which are both characteristic of that culture. Of the two, *destino* is definitely more common (a point whose significance will be discussed later).

Nonetheless, as Zingarelli (1970) notes, one can "credere/non credere al *destino*", that is, 'believe or not believe in *destino*', and this suggests that unlike the Russian *sud'ba* or the Polish *los,* the idea of *destino* is not taken for granted as the 'normal' way of viewing human existence (one cannot *believe* or *not believe* in *sud'ba* or *los,* as one cannot *believe* or *not believe* in *life*). On the other hand, *sorte* does seem to be taken for granted, since one cannot "credere/non credere alla *sorte*", 'believe, or not believe, in *sorte*' (just as one cannot *believe,* or *not believe,* in *sud'ba* or *los*).

To see the difference between *sorte* and *destino* which may be responsible for the fact that one can *believe* in *destino,* but not in *sorte* it may be helpful to consider the following examples

> His destiny (*fate) was to become a great leader. [*destino, *sorte*]
> His fate was life imprisonment. [*sorte,* ?*destino*]

As the indicated differences in acceptability suggest, *sorte* is an empirical concept, which refers to what has actually happened, and it cannot be used to refer to something which is 'meant to happen'. *Destino* can also refer to what has actually happened (as in the second sentence), but only if the event is seen as somehow predetermined or preconceived, and, unlike *sorte,* it can also refer to something which has not (yet) happened, and which is, as it were, 'meant to happen'.

Sorte cannot be seen as predetermined or preconceived, because *sorte,* in contrast to *destino,* is seen largely as a domain of chance. Like the Polish *los, sorte* implies something like a lottery of life (and *tirare a sorte* means 'to draw lots'). But *destino* seems incompatible with this image and with the idea of chance in general. Hence the following contrast:

> We didn't meet by chance: it was fate/destiny that brought us
> together. [*destino*, **sorte*]

Zingarelli (1970) describes *destino* as "indipendente dalla volontà umana", 'independent of human will', and Devoto and Oli (1977) describe *sorte* in terms of "contingenze indipendenti dalla volontà", 'contingencies independent of human will'. But these descriptions are misleading, as the following sentences show:

  a. Bush and Gorbachev have the power to determine the fate of millions of people.
     [*destino*, **sorte*]
  b. The prisoner was tried in absentia and never saw the judge who was to determine his fate. [*sorte*, *?destino*]
  c. She thinks that we are masters of our own fate/destiny, but I don't agree.
     [*destino*, *?sorte*]

Sentences (a) and (b) show that both *destino* and *sorte* can be seen as determined, in some sense, by human will, whereas sentence (c) shows that *destino*, but not *sorte*, can also be seen as determined by one's own will.

The differences in the behaviour of *destino* and *sorte* in sentences (a) and (b) seem at first very mysterious. If a judge can determine the *sorte* of a prisoner, why cannot Gorbachev and Bush determine the *sorte* of 'millions of people', given that they *can* determine their *destino?* But the two cases are not really parallel. One difference can be summarised in terms of the contrast between the words *determine* and *predetermine*. A judge may determine the fate of the prisoner but cannot predetermine it (that is, determine it in advance of all the relevant events). By contrast, Bush and Gorbachev can be seen as predetermining (well in advance) the future of 'millions of people'. Another difference is related to the specificity of what is being determined. A judge assigns to the prisoner a very specific sentence, which can be seen as something very concrete that happens to the prisoner. Bush and Gorbachev, however, cannot determine the future of millions of people in a similarly specific and concrete way.

The same two (interrelated) differences between *sorte* and *destino* are inherent in the imagery of drawing lots and of moving toward a certain 'destination'. The 'destination' is in the future, and the path leading toward it does not have to be determined in every detail, but the drawing of lots happens at a particular time, and the lot that a person draws has a very specific value.

The idea of 'direction' inherent in *destino* is also supported by the expression *seguire il proprio destino*, 'to follow one's own *destino*', cited by both Zingarelli (1970) and Devoto and Oli (1977). One cannot similarly **seguire la propria sorte*, 'follow one's *sorte*', because *sorte* doesn't have any constant direction. In fact, *sorte* can refer to individual events rather than to any course of events (for example, *per mala sorte* 'unluckily'), whereas *destino* refers either to a course of events (to an imaginary 'line' of a person's life) or to one 'fateful' event which can decide that 'line'. *Sorte* can be seen as changeable ("nella buona e cattiva *sorte*" 'in good and bad stretches of life, independent of one's will' (part of the marriage formula)), but *destino* is not seen as similarly changeable: it evokes the image of a line rather than of a zigzag.

The association of *sorte*—but not *destino*—with the contrast between 'good' and 'bad' ("buona e cattiva *sorte*") points in the same direction. *Sorte* presents human life in terms of a sequence of good and bad events, distributed unevenly and unpredictably (although in present-day usage *sorte* tends to be expected to be bad). But *destino* presents life rather like a journey along a road, in the spirit of the opening line of Dante's (1980) *Divine comedy:* "Nel mezzo del cammin di nostra vita . . . " 'In the middle of the journey of our life . . . '; and in a journey of this kind lots of things happen to the traveller which cannot be neatly categorised as 'good' or 'bad'. The metaphor of a journey is useful here also because it doesn't present life as entirely independent of one's own will. *Sorte* implies that good and bad things happen to us that are totally independent of our will (especially bad things); *destino* implies that our life is going in a certain direction and that *we* are going in a certain direction, and it leaves room for the idea that the course of the 'journey' may depend to some extent on ourselves.

Destino does not have the melancholic ring of either *sud'ba* or *Schicksal,* and it doesn't suggest resignation. For example, the Italian magazine called *Kiss* published in 1985 a so-called *foto-romanzo* (photo-novel) of the soap opera genre, entitled "Destini" (plural), which presented human lives in terms of who fell in love with whom, who had an affair with whom, who married (or divorced) whom, who inherited a fortune, who had interesting adventures in a Brazilian jungle, and so on. If a Russian novel was entitled "Sud'by", it could not be concerned with matters such as these. *Sud'by* would not be all 'bad', but they would have to feature, prominently, misfortunes and things that happen to people against their wishes, and they would imply life patterns independent of human will. *Schicksal,* too, would have to suggest an emphasis on misfortunes and vicissitudes of life, and it would also suggest something unusual, dramatic, and unpredictable (as in the phrase "die Schicksale der Flüchtlinge", 'the fate of the refugees', cited in Collins 1980).

It might be added that although *sorte* (like *sud'ba*) does seem to stress bad things rather than good things, it has its positive counterpart in the concept of *fortuna,* which seems to have a wider scope than the English *luck* or the Russian *sčast'e* (in the sense of 'luck', not in the sense of 'happiness'). For example, in Italian one can wish people *Buona fortuna!* in general terms (cf. *All the best!* in English), whereas Russian *sčast'e,* or English *luck,* is not used like that. For example:

> Addio, caro amico. . . . Buona fortuna a lei e a suoi cari. (Bassani 1980:106)
>
> 'Goodbye, dear friend. . . . All the best (??good luck) to you and to those dear to you.'

It might also be added that in the history of the Italian language the role of *destino* seems to be growing, and that of *sorte* declining (so much so that some informants regard the marriage formula "nella buona e cattiva *sorte*", 'in good and bad *sorte*', as somewhat archaic). Reportedly (Antonella Salpietro, p.c.), *sorte* is used much more in Southern Italy (poor and rural) than in the (prosperous indus-trial) North. This suggests that the more active and dynamic *destino* is a more modern idea than *sorte* and that its increasing role may reflect more modern condi-tions of life, with greater mobility and a greater sense of personal opportunity.

Gipper (1976) points out that the concept of time in peasant societies tends to be different from the modern Western idea of time. The modern Western time is linear, and it moves forward; the time in traditional peasant societies is 'cyclic' and, one might add, more static. What applies to the perception of time in general applies also to the perception of human life. If one sees human life in terms of *destino*, one sees it as essentially linear and moving forward. By contrast, concepts such as *sorte* (or the English *lot,* or the German *Los,* or the folk Polish *dola*) are all static: they present a person's life as given, as being of a certain kind, and not as moving onward and being full of possibilities. The fact that static concepts such as *sorte, lot, Los,* or *dola* are generally declining in Europe seems to reflect social change and changes in cultural expectations. The apparent difference between Northern Italy and Southern Italy in this respect highlights these correlations.

I propose the following explications of *destino* and *sorte:*

destino
- (a) different things can happen to different people
- (b) not because they want it
- (c) I imagine I know that someone wants it
- (d) I imagine I know that someone can say of a person: 'these things will happen to this person, one after another'
- (e) this someone is not a part of this world

sorte
- (a) different things happen to people
- (b) not because someone wants it
- (c) one can think: more bad things will happen to me than good things
- (d) one cannot think: I know what will happen to me
- (e) one cannot know this

The distinction between things that 'happen' (*sorte*) and things that 'can happen' (*destino*) attempts to capture the sense of openness and possibilities inherent in *destino* but not in *sorte*. The phrase 'one after another' attempts to capture the linear conception of life. The phrase 'I imagine I know that someone wants it' endows *destino* with an imaginary intentionality and with potential meaning.

6. The French *Destin* and *Sort*

In French, the two main words in the area under discussion are *destin* and *sort,* which are both common words and which are close in meaning to the Italian words *destino* and *sorte*. It is noteworthy, however, that although these two core concepts are similar to their Italian counterparts, the more marginal concepts are different. Modern French has no equivalent of *fato,* but additionally it has the word *destinée,* which (in its modern sense) has no equivalent in Italian. These fairly clear differences between the marginal concepts *fato* and *destinée* may help us to detect some possible differences between the core concepts (*destin* and *destino, sort* and *sorte*), though these are undoubtedly quite close, as the following parallelisms in acceptability show:

a. The prisoner was tried in absentia and never even saw the judge who was to determine his fate [*sort, ?destin;* cf. *sorte, ?destino*].
b. The city of Pompeii suffered a terrible fate [*sort, ?destin;* cf. *sorte, ?destino*].
c. The wicked ogre deserved his fate [*sort, ?destin; sorte, ?destino*].
d. The fate of our children is at stake. We must stop pollution [*destin, ?sort;* cf. *destino, ?sorte*].
e. We didn't meet by chance; it was fate/destiny that brought us together [*destin, ?sort;* cf. *destino, ?sorte*].

A detailed investigation would be needed to establish whether *destin* and *sort* differ from *destino* and *sorte* at all. It seems possible, however, that although the semantic evolution of these concepts in Italian and French went in the same direction, French has gone further in that direction than Italian. For example, if *sorte* seems to suggest bad things rather than good, *sort* seems to have an even stronger negative bias. If in Italian it is still possible to speak of *buona sorte* and *cattiva sorte* (if only in formulaic language), in French informants find the expression *le bon sort* 'good *sort*' distinctly odd, whereas *le mauvais sort* 'bad *sort*' is very common.

Furthermore, if the Italian *destino* has begun to be used in a more active and a more positive way than it used to, the same applies even more to the French *destin*. This suggestion is supported by the fact that of the three meanings of *destin* singled out in *Le grand Robert* (1986), the third one, which can be interpreted as active and positive, is illustrated only with twentieth-century citations, whereas the first two, which cannot be interpreted as positive, are illustrated amply with seventeenth-, eighteenth-, and nineteenth-century citations.

This does not mean, however, that *destin* and *sort* have become symmetrical in French, in the way the adjectives *lucky* and *unlucky* are symmetrical in English. The considerable similarity in use between the French *sort* and the Italian *sorte* suggests that *sort*, too, is a more empirical concept, which has to do with things that 'simply happen' to people and with their chance distribution, whereas *destin* has more to do with an imaginary 'design' or with an imaginary 'destination'. But if Italians can still view contingent events in terms of a lottery of life, where either bad or good things can happen to people (as did, apparently, the seventeenth- and eighteenth-century French), modern French appears to view chance events with greater suspicion and to link 'good things' with what can be planned, chosen, or otherwise influenced by will rather than with any vagaries of chance.

The third, apparently most recent, meaning of *destin* singled out in *Le grand Robert* is formulated as follows: "Le cours de l'existence considéré comme pouvant être modifié par celui qui la vit", 'the course of existence considered as capable of being modified by the person who lives it'. If one compares this with the first meaning: "Puissance qui, selon certaines croyances, fixerait de façon irrévocable le cours des événements", 'a power which is believed to fix in an irrevocable manner the course of events', one must conclude that the shift from the original meaning to the current one is most remarkable and that it is pregnant with cultural implications (see section 8).

The changes in the meaning of *sort* and *destin* noted appear to be interrelated: the changing expectations associated with *sort* (from 'unpredictable, good or bad', to 'unpredictable and not wanted') went hand in hand with the changing expectations associated with *destin* (from 'irrevocable and independent of human will' to 'partly dependent on human will and therefore potentially a realm of freedom and responsibility'). This modern way of viewing *le destin* is reflected in the following sentences from a work by Daniel-Rops (cited in *Le grand Robert*):

> Ce dont chacun de nous est responsable, ce n'est pas d'un destin anonyme, c'est de son propre destin, reflet temporale de son éternité. Lorsque les hommes renoncent à considérer leur destin personnel comme quelque chose dont ils sont responsables, les destins du siècle fléchissent et mènent le monde aux faillites.

> 'What everyone among us is responsible for is not some anonymous *destin*, but one's own *destin*, a temporal reflection of one's eternity. When men cease to regard their personal *destin* as something for which they are responsible, the *destins* (plural) of the epoch wilt and lead the world to catastrophe.'

Compare the following twentieth-century example:

> L'humanité . . . allait pouvoir de nouveau travailler à se faire un destin meilleur. (Martin du Gard, quoted in Ramage 1904)

> 'Mankind was going to be able once more to fashion itself a better *destin*.'

It is interesting to note here that the title of Mauriac's (1983[1928]) novel *Destins* (in the plural) has been rendered into English as *Lines of life* (Mauriac 1957). Clearly, *fates* was felt to be unacceptable as an English rendering of *destins*, because what is meant is 'lines of life' seen as dependent not only on circumstances independent of human will but also on human choices.

The third French word in the domain under discussion, *destinée*, appears to have had an evolution similar to that of *destin,* with the result, however, even more 'positive'. The older citations often present *destinée* as a power totally independent of human will, for example:

> C'est notre destinée d'être soumis aux préjugés et aux passions. (Voltaire, 1769)

> 'It is our *destinée* to be subject to prejudice and passion.'

> Nous sommes . . . les jouets de la destinée. (Voltaire, 1769)

> 'We are the playthings of *destinée*.'

> L'essentiel, pour être le moins mal possible, est de se soumettre à sa destinée. (D'Alembert)

> 'To be the least bad possible (as a person), the essential thing is to submit to one's *destinée*.'

But in nineteenth-century citations, a different tone makes itself heard; for example:

La providence s'écrit souvent en toutes lettres dans la destinée des grands hommes. (Victor Hugo)

'Often, Providence inscribes itself clearly in the *destinée* of great people.'

Vous êtes promis à de plus hautes destinées. (Stendhal, quoted in Ramage 1904)

'You are ordained for the highest *destinée*.'

Mon père se faisait de l'âme humaine et de sa destinée une idée sublime: il la croyait faite pour les cieux; cette foi le rendait optimiste. (Anatole France)

'My father had a very elevated idea of the human soul and its *destinée:* he believed it made for the heavens and this faith made him an optimist.'

Twentieth-century citations present *destinée* as largely dependent on human will, for example:

. . . pour ce qui ne dépend pas de nous, notre manière d'y réagir est l'expression de notre caractère même; et là encore, nous modelons la destinée. (François Mauriac)

'As for the things that do not depend on us, our way of reacting to them is the expression of our character; and even here, we are shaping our *destinée*.'

What is, then, the difference between *destinée* and *destin?* It appears that, in a sense, *destinée* is a more 'glorious' or 'sublime' version of *destin*. It seems significant that in the Victor Hugo quote adduced *destinée* is linked with the lives of 'great people'. In contemporary French, this link seems even more pronounced: although everybody has a *destin,* it would appear that not everybody has a *destinée*—just as in English although everybody has a *life,* not everybody has a *destiny*. *Destinée,* rather like *destiny,* although not to the same degree, points to 'higher things'. If *destin* is still close to the Italian *destino* (existential, but not deterministic, and potentially meaningful), *destinée* is even more clearly meaningful, free, and goal-oriented (rather than determined by blind causes).

In the present context, I will limit myself to proposing explications for the more common concepts *destin* and *sort:*

destin
  (a) different things can happen to different people
  (b) I imagine I know that someone can say of a person: 'these things will happen to this person, one after another'
  (c) I imagine I know that this someone wants it
  (d) this someone is not part of this world

sort
  (a) different things happen to people
  (b) not because someone wants it
  (c) one can think: bad things will happen to me
  (d) one cannot think: I know what will happen to me
  (e) one cannot know this

These definitions are very close to those of *destino* and *sorte,* but there are some differences: *destin* does not include the component 'not because they want it', which has been assigned to *destino,* and so it suggests a greater degree of potential mastery over one's life, and *sort* includes a negative component which is worded more strongly than the corresponding component of *sorte* ('one can think: bad things will happen to me' versus 'one can think: more bad things will happen to me than good things').

7. The English *Fate* and *Destiny*

The picture presented by modern English is most remarkably different from what we find in the other European languages considered. The two relevant English words are *fate* and *destiny*. Neither of them is a common everyday word, like *sud'ba, los, Schicksal, destino, sorte, destin* and *sort,* and the fact that English doesn't have such a common colloquial word is in itself rather extraordinary. The specific semantic load of both *fate* and *destiny* is also quite remarkable. A good starting point for the discussion of this topic is provided by the following passage from Norman Davies' history of Poland:

> In the long run, the fate of the Polish People's Republic is of little significance; it is rotten to the core. But the fate of the Poles themselves must be of the greatest concern to everyone. Poland's destiny, in the cockpit of European conflict, is one of the few indicators of the destiny which lies in store for the rest of the continent. (1984:462)

English dictionaries are usually totally at a loss to explain how *destiny* differs from *fate.* For example, SOED (1964) suggests rather miserably that *destiny* is "that which is destined to happen; FATE" [*sic*], whereas LDOTEL (1984) informs us that *fate* is "destiny or fortune apparently determined by fate" [*sic*]. On the other hand, the old dictionary of synonyms by Charles Smith (1903) is full of insight (and it is a great pity that it wasn't consulted by the more recent lexicographers). I quote:

> The idea of destiny involves elements of greatness and immutability. It is not applicable to common things or persons or details of life, but to its apparent purpose and consummation. . . . Anyone might speak of his fate or his lot; only those who run important careers could speak of their destiny. . . . Fate . . . is seldom used in a favourable sense, as, 'In travelling it is almost always my fate to meet with delays'. So far as a man's condition has resulted from unconscious causes, as the laws of the material world, we speak of his fate. So far as we attribute it to the ordainment of more powerful beings, we speak of his destiny. Fate is blind; destiny has foresight. (1903:319)

Fate is a deterministic concept. It refers to things which 'happen' and it presents them as inevitable, irreversible, uncontrollable, and determined by earlier causes. Yet this emphasis on inevitability and uncontrollability is very different from that embodied in the German *Schicksal. Fate,* as it is used in modern English, doesn't suggest any impenetrable mystery behind the events, and if it has residual other-worldly connotations they are relatively slight. It breathes the atmosphere of English empiricism, and scepticism, the atmosphere of Hobbes, Hume, and Locke, and it feels thoroughly at home in scientific discourse. Thus a list of book titles in a library catalogue offers among others, the following items: *The fate of drugs in the organism, Fate of pesticides in the environment, The fate of fossil fuel CO_2 in the ocean,* and *Fate of pollutants in air and water environments.* It is inconceivable that *sud'ba, los, Schicksal, destino, sorte, destin,* or *sort* could be used like that. The titles starting with *Schicksal* in the same catalogue have an entirely different orientation—*Schicksal und Wunder 'Schicksal* and wonder', *Schicksal und Wille in den Märchen der Brüder Grimm, 'Schicksal* and Will in the brothers Grimm's fables', *Schicksale und Abenteuer, 'Schicksals* and adventures' and so on—and the judgements of my informants point in the same direction.

In fact, even the title of Jonathan Schell's (1982) book, *The fate of the Earth,* perplexed all the non-English informants whom I have asked for a translation, and after much mind searching, they all offered the equivalent of the English *future* rather than any putative equivalent of *fate* (*Zukunft, l'avenir, l'avvenire,* and so on). Similar perplexity was caused by the English sentence

The fate (*destiny) of our children is at stake. (We must stop pollution, etc.)

and here, too, all the informants finally settled on the equivalent of the English *future* rather than on any putative equivalents of *fate.* The reason is, I think, that if the lives of our children are presented as determined by material, well-understood causes such as pollution, this perspective is felt to be incompatible with the somewhat mysterious, metaphysical implications of concepts such as *Schicksal, destino,* or *destin.* But there is nothing metaphysical about the modern English concept of *fate.*

There seems to be another reason, however, why native speakers of European languages other than English feel so uncomfortable when confronted with a phrase such as "The fate of the Earth". The point is that *Schicksal, destino, destin, los,* and *sud'ba* all have a strongly existential and anthropocentric perspective, which modern English *fate* doesn't have. Apparently, a similarly existential and anthropocentric perspective was embodied in the old English concept of 'weird', illustrated in the following quotes from OED (1933):

Had neuer womman sa blisful wird . . . as maria maiden . . .(1300, Cursor M)

those whose weird is still to creep, alas! Unnoticed among the humble grass. (1774, Fergusson, "On seeing butterflies")

It was one more of those hammer-blows of Fate exactly coincident with the sequence of the Queen's weird. (1909, Belloc, "Marie Antoinette")

But in modern English, this numinous and anthropocentric concept of 'weird' has been replaced by the sober, this-worldly, 'objective', and positivistic concept of 'fate'. The mythological Fate, usually with a capital *F,* has also remained in literary

English, but it clearly has the character of a rhetorical figure and a mythological allusion. The mysterious, anthropocentric *weird* acquired negative connotations (as something 'weird', in the modern sense of the word) and has ceased to be used at all as a noun (presumably, as alien to the modern Anglo-Saxon folk philosophy).

I am not suggesting that concepts such as *Schicksal* or *destin* can be used only with respect to people. In fact, it is quite common to apply such concepts to countries or to cities. A country, or a city, can be treated as an individual among other comparable individuals and as endowed with a human-like personality (it can 'want', it can 'decide', it can 'suffer', and so on). But a title like *The fate of the Earth* suggests an entirely different, non-anthropomorphic perspective, and this is partly why it cannot be felicitously translated with a word such as *Schicksal* or *destin*.

This means that although the modern English lexicon recognises, and even emphasises, the operation of irreversible causes which fully determine observable events, it does not encourage the view that it is the general human condition (Malraux's "La condition humaine") to be subject to impenetrable forces, which influence, if not shape, the course of every human life. This is a remarkable new development in social psychology, which testifies to a new cultural orientation of the modern English-speaking Western societies.

The changes in the concept of *destiny,* concomitant to those in the concept of *fate,* are equally pregnant with cultural implications. In older English, *destiny* was seen as irrevocable, uncontrollable, and likely to be 'bad', as the following citations from OED (1933) indicate:

> The common people lamented their miserable destiny. (1548)
> The force of ruthless destiny. (1781)

In the nineteenth century, however, examples such as the following started to predominate more and more:

> Our manifest destiny is to overspread the continent allotted by Providence for the free development of our yearly multiplying millions. (John L. O'Sullivan, *United States Magazine and Democratic Review* 1845, in an editorial article denouncing the opposition to the annexation of Texas, quoted in Stevenson 1946:64)

The new concept of *destiny,* which spread in nineteenth-century America, was noted at the time as a new phenomenon (especially in the phrase "manifest destiny"). Emerson called this use "profane", contrasting it implicitly with the older, numinous sense:

> That word, "manifest destiny," which is profanely used, signifies the sense all men have of the prodigious energy and opportunity lying idle here. (Emerson, Journals, 1865, quoted in Stevenson 1946:64)

It is interesting to note a contrasting definition of *fate* by the same author:

> Whatsoever limits us, we call Fate. . . . The limitations refine as the soul purifies, but the ring of necessity is always perched at the top. (Quoted in Stevenson 1946:642)

The American writer William Woodward offers the following helpful comment:

> In the autumn of 1844 the question of annexation [of Texas] was one of the chief issues of the presidential campaign. The Democrats made "Manifest Destiny" the cornerstone of their political philosophy of the moment. (Woodward, quoted in Stevenson 1946:64)

The polarisation between *destiny* (good) and *fate* (bad) was accompanied by a restriction of destiny to 'somebody's destiny', whereas *fate* continues to be used to refer to 'fate in general', as well as to 'somebody's fate', but it is also increasingly used as 'something's fate' (for example, the *fate* of pollutants or pesticides in the environment).

In modern English, as Smith says, "Fate is blind, destiny has foresight". But *fate* is not blind in the way *Schicksal* is 'blind' (it doesn't act in an unpredictable, mysterious, or capricious way), and although *destiny* has foresight, it is not because we attribute it "to the ordainment of more powerful beings".

I propose the following explications:

> *destiny*
> (a) different things can happen to different people
> (b) different people can do different things
> (c) some people can do things that other people can't do
> (d) I imagine I know that someone wants it
> (e) this someone is not part of this world

> *fate*
> (a) different things happen in the world that are bad for people
> (b) these things happen because some other things happen
> (c) if those other things happen, these things cannot not happen

If these explications are basically correct, *destiny* would be the only concept among those considered here which focuses on what people can *do* (not all people but *some* people), and in fact on what *some* people appear to be *meant* to do. All the non-English concepts considered refer to things that *happen* to people, and not to some people, but to *all* people. The only possible exception to this may be the French *destinée*, which is, however, much more marginal in French than either *destin* or *sort*.

8. Sociocultural Correlates

Why is the Russian concept of *sud'ba* so different from the Polish concept of *los?* Why is the German *Schicksal* so different from the Italian *destino* or from the French *destin?* And why are the English *fate* and *destiny* so very different from all of those?

Presumably, the answers to these questions lie largely in the history of the peoples in whose cultures these concepts have evolved and in their national characters, shaped by their history. I have neither the space nor the expertise to engage here in an extensive discussion of the vast issues involved; I would like, however, to note some key points which emerge from the existing literature.

8.1 Why *Sud'ba?*

It is a truism to say that the history of Russia is a history of despotism and subordination. Marx and Engels called Russian society "semi-Asiatic", and the Tsarist regime "Oriental despotism", and so did Lenin (cf. Wittfogel 1963:379). If we look back into the Russian past,

> we discover a differentiation between Western and Eastern Europe which goes back to the direct and indirect effects of Mongol rule (1240–1452). . . . As Mongol rule declined . . . , the Grand Dukes of Moscow achieved ascendancy over their rivals, eventually attaining a supremacy which equaled or exceeded that of the Mongols. During two centuries prior to the industrialization and democratization of Western Europe, the Russian Tsars succeeded in subordinating all ranks of society to their autocratic commands. . . . The symbol of this social structure was the liability to corporal punishment of *all* sections of the population on one hand, and the legendary sanctification of many Tsars as a retrospective legitimation toward the end of their reigns on the other. . . . These attributes of the Russian social structure indicate a subordination of society to the autocratic ruler, which, albeit in significantly altered form, has lasted to the present day. (Bendix 1977:178)

Bendix (1977:178) points out that "The sanctification of Tsarist rule is symbolic of the absence in Russian civilization of that conflict between church and secular authority which in Western Europe provided one basis for the development of representative institutions". The Orthodox church has traditionally emphasised "how sacred is the duty of submitting to the authorities" (statement of the Metropolitan Filaret of Moscow, quoted in Curtis 1940:30). As Bendix points out,

> The distinctive feature of such appeals is the emphasis upon submission to the government as the principal rule of conduct. Subordination to his own lord or employer is, therefore, only a token of the . . . submission to the highest authority, an idea expressed with classic simplicity in the following address of an aristocratic landowner to his peasants: "I am your master, and my master is the Emperor. The Emperor can issue his commands to me, and I must obey him; but he issues no commands to you. I am the Emperor upon my estate; I am your God in this world, and I have to answer for you to the God above." (1977:184)

But it is not necessarily blind submission based on fear which is seen by students of Russia as a distinct feature of the Russian national tradition (although Russian writers and thinkers have often complained about the "izvečnaja rossijskaja pokornost'", the 'eternal Russian humility/submissiveness'; cf. Solzhenitsyn 1986:436). It is also a humble, uncomplaining acceptance of hardship and suffering, epitomised in the Russian Orthodox ideal of *smirenie,* which has become a distinctive mark of Russian spirituality (see chapter 5). A nineteenth-century Russian *starets* (an "elder, a discerning man of God to whom many came for advice, and to whom some entrusted their entire lives", Ellis 1986:124) expressed this ideal as follows:

> We must not try to find out why this happened in this way, and not in that, but with childlike obedience we must surrender ourselves to the holy will of our heavenly

Father and say from the depth of our soul: "Our Father, thy will be done!" (Igumen Antonij, quoted in Bolshakoff 1977:176)

It seems clear that the Russian concept of *sud'ba* bears the imprint of these traditions.

8.2 Why *Schicksal?*

In trying to understand the German idea of *Schicksal,* the most obvious place to look for a possible explanation is in the formative influence of the Lutheran Reformation. "The deep imprint left on German minds by the Lutheran Reformation" (Dumont 1986:593) seems to be generally acknowledged by students of German culture. It is also generally accepted that Luther exercised a profound influence on the German language and the conceptualisations reflected in that language. (Cf., for example, Weber 1968:206.) The crucial point here is the view of the role of human will and human freedom in people's lives. As Kane points out,

> Among the controversies of the reformation, the doctrine of free will was a crucial point of difference between Protestant and Catholic theologians. Martin Luther and John Calvin strongly denied freedom of the will. . . . Luther concluded that man is predestined to such an extent that he can never truly be said to have power over his own fate. (1967:90)

Luther saw human beings as, essentially, evil and powerless. "The depravity of man's nature and its complete lack of freedom to choose the right is one of the fundamental concepts of Luther's whole thinking" (Fromm 1980:63). He taught "that man was a powerless tool in God's hands and fundamentally evil, that his only task was to resign to the will of God, that God could save him as the result of an incomprehensible act of justice" (Fromm 1980:65). He did not deny completely that a human being had a free will, but he maintained that it applied "not in respect of those who are above him, but in respect only of those who are below him. . . . Godward man has no 'free will', but is a captive, slave, and servant either to the will of God or to the will of Satan" ("The bondage of the will", quoted by Fromm 1980:64). Fromm goes on to comment that "This dichotomy—submission to powers above and domination over those below—is . . . characteristic of the attitude of the authoritarian character".

In Luther's picture of the world, "Man is free from all ties binding him to spiritual authorities, but this very freedom leaves him alone and anxious, overwhelms him with a feeling of his own individual insignificance and powerlessness. This free, isolated individual is crushed by the experience of his individual insignificance. Luther's theology gives expression to this feeling of helplessness and doubt" (Fromm 1980:68).

Comments of this kind go, it seems to me, a long way toward explaining the German concept of *Schicksal,* and in particular, the similarities and the differences between *Schicksal* and the Russian concept of *sud'ba.*

As for the relationship between *Schicksal* and the English *destiny,* a particularly helpful clue is contained in Max Weber's (1968:160) discussion of the Protestant concept of 'calling'. According to both Lutherans and Puritans, every human being has his or her own 'calling', assigned by God. The idea of 'calling' first appeared in Luther's translation of the Bible. "After that it speedily took on its present meaning in the everyday speech of all Protestant peoples. . . . The idea is new, a product of the Reformation" (Weber 1968:79). But the Puritan interpretation of this idea was, according to Weber, different from that given it by the Lutherans.

> For everyone without exception God's Providence has prepared a calling, which he should profess and in which he should labour. And this calling is not, as it was for the Lutheran, a fate to which he must submit and which he must make the best of, but God's commandment to the individual to work for the divine glory. This seemingly subtle difference had far-reaching psychological consequences, and became connected with a further development of the providential interpretation of the economic order. . . . (1968:160)

Weber's discussion of this point offers insight into the differences not only between the Lutheran-inspired concept of *Schicksal* and the Puritan-inspired concept of *destiny* but also between *Schicksal* and concepts such as *sorte, sort,* or *los* (or the Spanish *suerte*), which we find in the languages of Catholic Italy, Catholic France, Catholic Poland, or Catholic Spain, that is to say, as Weber calls Catholic nations, among "the peoples of the *liberum arbitrium*":

> The phenomenon of the division of labour and occupations in society had, among others, been interpreted by Thomas Aquinas, to whom we may most conveniently refer, as a direct consequence of the divine scheme of things. But the places assigned to each man in this cosmos follow ex causis naturalibus and are fortuitous (contingent in the Scholastic terminology). The differentiation of men into classes and occupations established through historical development became for Luther, . . . a direct result of the divine will. The perseverance of the individual in the place and within the limits which God has assigned to him was a religious duty . . . the world had to be accepted as it was, and this alone could be made a religious duty. But in the Puritan view, the providential character of the play of private economic interests takes on a somewhat different emphasis. True to the Puritan tendency to pragmatic interpretations, the providential purpose of the division of labour is to be known by its fruits. (1968:160–61)

The new concept of *destiny* which spread in nineteenth-century America is astonishingly congruent with Weber's analysis. (Recall the sentence quoted earlier: "Our manifest *destiny* is to overspread the continent allotted by Providence for the free development of our yearly multiplying millions.")

Destiny will be discussed in more detail later, and so will *sorte, sort* and *los.* The key points to be noted now are these: the Lutheran view presents a person's life as due to an impenetrable decree of God and therefore as something to which one must submit and which one must make the best of; the Puritan view presents human life as a task assigned by Providence; the Catholic view presents human life as a direct consequence of the divine scheme of things but nonetheless as woven out of events which are fortuitous and contingent.

8.3 Why *Sorte* and *Sort?* Why *Destino* and *Destin?*

The Italian concept of *sorte* and the French concept of *sort* both focus on the contingent, fortuitous aspect of human life. Both words are used also with reference to drawing lots, and both suggest that human life is largely unpredictable and that chance plays a considerable role in it. The concomitant concepts of *destino* and *destin* play a complementary role. Since chance plays a considerable role in human life, one can view life from the point of view of what is contingent, fortuitous in it, and this is one valid way of looking at it, but this is not the only valid perspective: one can also view life as a "journey in a certain direction", that is, a *destino* or *destin*.

Catholic theology has always insisted that human beings are free in their choices and in their decisions—that they are free, so to speak, to go the way they want. As Nolan (1967:91) says, "The term free will is customarily regarded as an accurate translation of the Latin expression *liberum arbitrium;* yet the more exact translation is free choice or free decision". Regan (1967:93) points out that "In the context of the strong statements of the Reformers, . . . the [Catholic] Church defined as a dogma that even sinful man has a truly free will".

Once again, theology and semantics seem to meet on this point. Unlike your *Schicksal,* your *destino* or your *destin* is something that you can control yourself, to some extent. There are of course limits to one's freedom of movement (dictated, one might say, by one's *sorte* or *sort*), but within these limits one might consider oneself as free. According to Weber, this idea of human life, inspired by Catholicism, was not as conducive to the development of capitalism as the Protestant idea, whether in the Lutheran or in the Calvinist version. The idea that one can do what one wants to can be easily interpreted in the sense that one can do as one pleases. This can breed attitudes such as unscrupulousness, unconsciousness, and plain laziness ("il dolce far niente", "la dolce vita"), which are incompatible with the spirit of capitalism. As Weber put it,

> The universal reign of absolute unscrupulousness in the pursuit of selfish interests by the making of money has been a specific characteristic of precisely those countries whose bourgeois-capitalistic development, measured according to Occidental standards, has remained backward. As every employer knows, the lack of *coscienziosità* of the labourers of such countries, for instance Italy as compared with Germany, has been, and to a certain extent still is, one of the principal obstacles to their capitalistic development. Capitalism cannot make use of the labour of those who practice the doctrine of undisciplined *liberum arbitrium,* any more than it can make use of the businessman who seems absolutely unscrupulous in his dealings with others. (Weber 1968:57)

Weber's theses were much discussed, in the subsequent literature, and various aspects of his interpretation met with considerable opposition, but these controversies are not relevant from the present point of view. The basic idea that "peoples of the *liberum arbitrium*" may differ in their attitudes to life, in their assumptions, and in their values from peoples of other religious backgrounds, seems uncontroversial and very fruitful. In seeking to understand the differences in folk philosophy which semantic analysis of words such as *Schicksal, destiny,* or *destin* brings to light, the religious history of the nations involved appears to contain particularly helpful clues.

When we compare the modern French and Italian concepts of *destin* and *destino* with the German concept of *Schicksal,* we discover that they make much more room for both chance and freedom than *Schicksal* does. It seems to me that this difference echoes in a remarkable way the differences between the Catholic and the Lutheran religious traditions. We have already seen that where Catholic theology allowed for contingencies Luther saw inescapable necessities, and where Catholic theology allowed for free choice (*"liberum arbitrium"*), Luther denied free choice and opposed to it his doctrine of *"servum arbitrium"*. Luther's American biographer John Todd summarises the debate between Luther and Catholic theologians (represented here by Erasmus of Rotterdam) as follows:

> The controversy with Erasmus becomes the practical statement of what man's situation really is, a pilgrimage during which he is tested and must make responsible choices, against a statement of the domination of the spiritual so extreme that man seems to be predestined either to heaven or to hell. (1964:225)

I submit that Luther's view of human life finds its echo in the German concept of *Schicksal,* whereas the Catholic view finds its echo in concepts such as *destino* or *destin,* which have evolved in 'the countries of *liberum arbitrium*'.

Of course native speakers of German are not all Lutherans, and they are not culturally homogeneous (cf. Lowie 1954). It is possible that their considerable cultural heterogeneity is reflected in some semantic and lexical variation in the area of *Schicksal*-like concepts. The problem requires further investigation. Nonetheless there is of course a shared core of German cultural traditions, and there can be little doubt that this core bears some imprint of Luther's teachings.

8.4 Why *Los?*

I have postponed the discussion of the Polish *los* till this point because it is important to compare it not only with the Russian *sud'ba* but also with the Italian concepts *destino* and *sorte,* with the French *destin* and *sort,* and with the German *Schicksal.*

Poles are Slavs, like Russians, so one might expect that *los* will be similar to *sud'ba.* But it isn't. Poles are Catholics, like the Italians or the French, so one might expect that *los* will be similar to its Italian and French counterparts. But it isn't—or rather, it is and it isn't. The Polish word *los* is a borrowing from German, so one might expect that the concept is similar to its counterpart in German. But it isn't. Why then, is the Polish *los* the way it is?

There are three factors which help to explain the apparent enigma of the Polish *los:* history, religion, and cultural affiliation.

Starting from the last of these three points, Poland has always had a very strong bond with Western Europe. As the British historian of Poland Norman Davies (1984:343) has put it, "Geographically, Poland belongs and always has belonged to the East. In every other sense, its strongest links have been with the West". In fact, he goes so far as to say that "The Poles are more Western in their outlook than the inhabitants of most Western countries" (1984:345). Thus although both the Poles and the Russians are Slavs, their cultural orientations are, one might say, diametrically opposed. To quote Davies (1984:345) again, "Russia is East, and Poland is West; and never, it seems, the twain shall meet".

The nineteenth-century Russian philosopher Vladimir Solov'ev stresses this profound cultural divergence in even stronger terms. According to Solov'ev (1966–70, v.4:3), "a great debate between East and West runs like a thread throughout human history"; and the dividing line between the two is that between Russia and Poland.

> Poland represents in Eastern Europe this spiritual principle which lies at the foundation of the history of the West. In its spiritual essence, the Polish nation . . . belongs to the Western world. Spirit is stronger than blood. . . . A Western European, even a Protestant, is spiritually closer to the Catholic Pole than an Orthodox Russian. . . . The main debate goes not between Christianity and Islam, not between the Slavs and the Turks, but between the European West (mainly Catholic) and the Orthodox Russia. (Solov'ev 1966–70, v.4:15)

Davies similarly links the Western orientation of Poland with its Catholicism.

> Poland's Catholicism determined that . . . all her cultural ties lay with the Latin world; . . . and, in the age of faith, that most of her sympathies lay with the Catholic peoples of the West rather than with the pagans, schismatics or infidels of the East. (1984:343)

If, as Solov'ev presents it, "East" stand for a tendency to fatalism, resignation, and submission, and "West" for an active attitude to life and for a glorification of freedom, then the Polish national ethos is indeed definitely Western. In fact, the British historian Timothy Garton Ash (1983:3) summarises his description of Poland and her history in what he calls the three basic points: "the Poles are an old European people with an unquenchable thirst for freedom; freedom in Polish means, in the first place, national independence; the Polish national identity is historically defined in opposition to Russia."

The ten centuries of Polish history have been characterised succinctly on the jacket of Davies' (1981) book *God's playground: a history of Poland:*

> Early Poland became a major power in the East, and was deeply involved in the Renaissance, the Reformation, the Counterreformation, and the Enlightenment. Before the notorious Partitions of 1773–95 [i.e., between Russia, Prussia, and Austria] the United Republic of Poland-Lithuania was at once one of the largest states, and the home of one of the most extraordinary cultures, of the continent. In the period since the Partitions, the Poles have been engaged in an endless struggle for survival against the empires, ideologies, and tyrannies of Eastern Europe, sustaining a national crusade of wonderful tenacity.

Given all these ingredients—a Western orientation, Catholicism, and a history of 'power and glory' followed by a loss of independence and a series of uprisings, defeats, and renewed uprisings—how did the Polish concept of *los* come to be formed?

When we compare it with the Russian *sud'ba*, we notice above all the absence of any trace of respect for 'holy resignation'. This is well illustrated by the motto which Timothy Garton Ash (1983) chose for his book about "Solidarity": "The Poles rebel against a mild oppressor, because they can; against a harsh one, because they must" (according to Garton Ash, a Polish saying of the 1860s, the time of one of the most desperate Polish risings). If there is in the Russian *sud'ba*, putting it crudely, a touch of fatalism, quietism, and humble acceptance of life, there is nothing of the kind in the Polish *los*. On the contrary, *los* emphasises the elements of hazard, changing fortunes, and unpredictability, life being seen as a kind of a game of chance, a gamble.

The image of a lottery of life is of course not unique to Polish; for example, it is also implied by the Italian *sorte*, the French *sort*, or the Spanish *suerte*. But all these languages have in addition lexicalised another image: that of life's 'taking its course' and 'moving forward', like a journey (*destino, destin, destino*). But the Polish cultural lexicon has only one image, which seems to present life in terms of ups and downs rather than any smooth movement toward a destination.

The element of a chance game where one is likely to lose but where one can always hope to win, and where one may act freely, putting all one's money on one card, seems to play an important role in the Polish military folklore, which, as has often been pointed out, has played a crucial role in the formation of the Polish national ethos. What matters most for our present concerns is that the concept of *los* plays an important role in this folklore. As one characteristic example I will adduce here, following Davies (1984:24), the words of the "March of Piłsudski's Legions" (1914–17):

> Legiony to—żołnierska buta;
> Legiony to—ofiarny stos;
> Legiony to—żebracka nuta;
> Legiony to—straceńców los;
> My, Pierwsza Brygada,
> Strzelecka Gromada,
> Na Stos, rzuciliśmy,
> Swój życia los
> Na stos, na stos.

> 'The Legions stand for a soldier's pride;
> The Legions stand for a martyr's fate;
> The Legions stand for a beggar's song;
> The Legions stand for a desperado's death:
> We are the First Brigade,
> A regiment of rapid fire.
> We've put our lives at stake,
> We've willed our fate,
> We've cast ourselves on the pyre.'

Piłsudski was the main figure in Poland's liberation in 1918 and the first leader of independent Poland. Davies (1984:241) observes: "As Piłsudski himself freely admitted, when he founded the Legions, there were only two things in prospect: 'either death or great glory'. He fully expected the former". He also quotes Piłsudski's motto: "Defeat . . . is not to have fought. Victory is to have fought, and not to have submitted" (1984:243).

Polish history and traditions being what they are, attitudes of this kind have always been greatly admired in Poland (at the expense, it has often been pointed out, of civic virtues and, in particular, of those virtues which Max Weber saw as the core virtues of the Protestant ethic).

It might be added that the Polish national ethos is, as Davies puts it, a "noble ethos", that is, the ethos of the Polish nobility (more properly gentry or *Szlachta*). "Individualism lay at the heart of the noble ethos. Once the legal and social barriers had been dismantled in the nineteenth century—and particularly after the Emancipation of the serfs, it could spread into the wider strata of Polish society as a whole" (1984:331).

The idea of *los* bears an imprint of this 'noble ethos', and it is interesting to note that before this ethos spread to the population at large, Polish folk culture viewed human life not in terms of *los* but in terms of a different concept, *dola*, much closer to the English *lot* than to the Polish *los*. This is in marked contrast with Russian culture, where the concept of *sud'ba* was a key concept in all social strata (as the loving folk form *sud'binuška* indicates). In Poland, the spread of the idea of *los* to the entire population can be regarded as a symbolic expression of the spread of the 'noble ethos' and of its identification with the national ethos. (For further linguistic evidence of this ethos see chapters 6 and 8.)

It is important to stress that the Polish ideal of a desperado and a daredevil should not be confused with that of a Japanese kamikaze or of a Shiite Muslim seeking martyrdom in a 'holy war' (*jihad*). The Polish ideal extols the courage of people who willingly take very high risks, fully accepting the possibility of death but hoping for the best. The Polish concept of *los*, which is more closely related to 'luck' and to 'chance' than *sud'ba*, *Schicksal*, *destino*, *destin*, or *fate* are, seems to bear an imprint of these traditions.

8.5 Why *Destiny*? And Why *Fate*?

Returning now to the English scene, we must note, above all, the polarisation between *fate* ('bad') and *destiny* ('good'), which has taken place in modern English, and the divisive nature of this polarisation (with some people apparently having a 'destiny' and others having a 'fate').

> Our destiny (*fate) is to rule the world.
> His destiny (*fate) was to become a great leader.
> His fate (*destiny) was life imprisonment.
> The prisoner was tried in absentia and never even saw the judge who was to determine his fate (*destiny).

When one thinks of the modern Anglo-Saxon culture as of something that was shaped, to some extent, by its Puritan past, it is hard not to be impressed by the analogy between this semantic polarisation of words and the religious polarisation of people in Calvinist theology. As Weber (1968:98) points out, at the time when "the great political and cultural struggles of the sixteenth and seventeenth centuries were fought, . . . and in general even today, the doctrine of predestination was considered its most characteristic dogma". Luther, too, accepted this dogma, but "not only did the idea not assume a central position for him, but it receded more and more into the background. . . . With Calvin, the process was just the opposite; the significance of the doctrine for him increased perceptibly in the course of his polemical controversies with the logical opponents".

It will be useful to recall at this point Smith's observation that "only people with important careers could speak of their destiny". Everybody has a *sud'ba,* a *los,* a *Schicksal,* a *destino,* or a *destin,* but not everybody has a *destiny.* I am suggesting, however (in this case, against Smith), that not everybody has a *fate* either. Normally, people speak of a person's *fate* only if some 'terrible fate' befalls him or her (an incurable and frightening illness, a rape, an unexpected death in unusual circumstances, etc.) One might say that only 'chosen people' have a *destiny* and only 'particularly unfortunate' people have a *fate.* Neither of these words suggests a common human lot, a universal human condition (*lot* itself being no longer a common word in English, comparable with commonly used words such as *Schicksal* or *destino*).

I suggest, then, that *fate* and *destiny* reflect, to some extent, the Calvinist element in the Anglo-Saxon past. But of course in modern English both these concepts have become, as Emerson put it with respect to *destiny,* profane, and they have developed further, each in its own way. How and why could these changes have happened?

As for *destiny,* the literature on Puritanism and the 'spirit of capitalism' provides plenty of suggestions. As pointed out by Weber (1968:232), "Fatalism is, of course, the only logical consequence of predestination. But on account of the idea of proof the psychological result was precisely the opposite". Calvinism placed a tremendous emphasis on action, on effort, and on secular success, because it was considered that only through such action, bearing tangible fruits, can one fulfil one's 'calling', give glory to God, and be able to convince oneself that one is among the chosen. "The will of God, God's own glory, which is at the same time the chief end of man, combined with the soul's necessity of gaining an assurance of election, produces a tremendous drive towards action", "the terrific Puritan drive toward intense activity" (Fullerton 1959:14,17).

But once started, a process may have a logic of its own. As Weber and others have pointed out, there is a built-in secularisation in the Puritan ethics, "which John Wesley noted when he says that piety produces riches, and riches a decline of religion" (Bendix 1977:193). Piety (of the Puritan kind) leads to intense activity, intense activity leads to secular success, and secular success achieved through one's own effort undermines the view of human life as dependent on impenetrable supernatural powers.

Speaking of the "spirit of capitalism", Weber quotes Benjamin Franklin's "Advice to a Young Tradesman":

> Remember that time is money. . . . Remember that money can beget money. . . .
> He who wastes five shillings murders . . . all that might have been produced by it,
> whole columns of pounds sterling. (quoted after Fullerton 1959:7)

Speaking of the "specifically bourgeois ethic represented in Franklin's maxims", Fullerton comments:

> No longer was money-making a means, by which the assurance of salvation could
> be secured or God be glorified. It had become an end in itself. . . . Puritanism had
> led to the rationalization of life as calling. Then a tragic thing happened. Capitalism
> saw the business significance of calling, removed the transcendental, otherworldly
> motive, and transformed "calling" into a job. (1959:20)

I suggest that this change of perspective, from transcendental and other-worldly to secular, and this change of orientation, from glorification of God to glorification of self (as someone who is successful in worldly endeavours), is epitomised by the change in the meaning of the word *destiny.* ("Our manifest destiny to overspread the continent allotted us by Providence for the free development of our yearly multiplying millions . . . ")

As for *fate,* clearly, it, too, lost its other-worldly orientation. It also lost much of its power, becoming a matter of concern for some unfortunate people, not a matter of universal human concern. Clearly, the idea of Fate with a capital *F* is inimical to the 'spirit of capitalism'. Drive toward action, free enterprise, initiative, striving for individual success in life, competition—all these things are hard to reconcile with the idea that one's life does not depend on one's own efforts.

The semantic evolution of *fate* seems also to have been affected by an additional set of factors, which had their source not in religion but in philosophy. The changing interpretation of *fate* can almost be pinpointed in the writings of the most influential British philosophers such as Hobbes, Hume, or Locke. What these thinkers were primarily interested in, and attracted to, was not predestination but determinism, and the relation between freedom and necessity. (I do not mean that these writings influenced the meaning of English words such as *fate* directly but that they contributed to an intellectual atmosphere, and to a specifically Anglo-Saxon style of thinking, which found their expression in English ways of speaking and, ultimately, in the English language.)

"Hobbes held that the notion of free subject was as self-contradictory as that of a round quadrangle" (Nolan 1967:90). "Hume held that from one standpoint man's acts are free, whereas from another standpoint they are not. . . . Acts of choice are strictly determined by preceding feelings or motives, as well as by character." And Locke (1959:327) maintained that although people are free to act as they will, they are determined as to what they do will: "a man is not at liberty to will, or not to will, anything in his power that he once considers of: liberty consisting in a power to act or to forbear acting, and in that only." (Cf. also Aaron 1955:268.)

As far as the concept of *fate* goes, perhaps what influenced it most was Hobbes' identification of inevitability with causal explicability.

> Hobbes . . . implied that if a causal explanation can be given of an action, then it could not have happened otherwise than it did. 'Determined', in other words, has often meant, by those who have shared his scientific optimism, inevitable as well as causally explicable. 'This concourse of causes, whereof everyone is determined to be such as it is by a like concourse of former causes, may well be called (in respect they were all set and ordered by the external cause of all things, God Almighty) the decree of God'. (Peters 1956:184)

In passages like this quote from Hobbes we can almost see the meaning of *fate* changing before our eyes, from 'inevitable and transcendental' to 'causally explicable'. When one compares, for example, the use of *fate* by Shakespeare ("O God! that one might read the book of fate!", *II Henry IV*) with its use in modern titles such as "Fate of pesticides in the environment", one can appreciate both the extent and the direction of the change. What was written in the book of Fate was inevitable; what happens to pesticides in the environment can be causally explained; the path from the former to the latter position leads via the Hobbesian assumption 'causal explicability equals inevitability'.

A different, but related, switch in the interpretation of *fate* is connected with the links between inevitability and irreversibility. When it is said in present-day English that a terrible *fate* befell a person, this is not meant to imply inevitability: perhaps the 'terrible fate' may well have been prevented if the victim had not voluntarily exposed himself or herself to danger. But what has happened is irreversible. What is inevitable is also irreversible. In the modern Anglo-Saxon atmosphere of rational empiricism events tend to be viewed as irreversible and explicable rather than 'inevitable'. Or rather, they are viewed as inevitable in a given causal context. The sense of mystery, which still permeates concepts such as *Schicksal, destino,* or *sud'ba,* has evaporated from the English *fate.*

8.6 How Universal Is 'Fate'?

Is *fate* a universal human concept? Clearly not: the evidence discussed here suggests that, on the contrary, it is highly culture-specific. But are concepts "such as *fate, karma, kismet,* or *Schicksal*" universal? This depends on what is meant in this case by "such as". If the hypothetical universal is that all languages embody a concept of 'being controlled by an impenetrable, supernatural power', then modern English provides a sufficient counter-example. This is not to say that there is no universal, or near-universal, in this area of thought, but before a hypothesis along those lines can be verified it has to be first formulated in a clear way, and in terms of concepts which are not highly culture-specific themselves.

One temptation in cross-cultural research is to postulate vague and unverifiable universals described in terms of English folk concepts (such as *mind, soul,* or *fate*). Another common temptation is to posit sweeping cross-cultural generalisations formulated in terms of dichotomies opposing the 'West' to 'non-Western society'. This last practice was forcefully challenged, from a psychiatric perspective, by the psychiatrist Atwood Gaines:

> My research in Western Europe and a reading of the now-growing anthropological literature on Western Society suggest that the West is not constituted by one major cultural tradition. Rather, it may be suggested that there are two distinct major cultural traditions in the West. . . . What are these two Great Traditions in the West? Basically, we can distinguish the Northern European Culture Area from the Mediterranean Culture Area. (1984:178)

Following Max Weber, Gaines links the basic differences in question with differences in religion and with their impact on social life.

> Northern Europe is home to the world view which Weber (1964) referred to as 'disenchanted' and is heir to the Magisterial Protestant Reform which symbolised a practical, empiricist, non-magical approach to the social and natural world. Goals of this world are to be achieved by action in this world, not by the intercession of preternatural forces and beings into this life. Action in this world is caused by physical factors, not by fate, immaterial saints, genies (as in Islamic lands), devils or miracles (which are the touch of divinity itself). . . . Latin Europe, a species of Mediterranean tradition, is that of the enchanted world view. (1984:179)

This is certainly an improvement on the stereotyped dichotomy: 'West versus non-West'. Yet this, too, represents an oversimplification of the real picture. Gaines' picture of the "Northern European tradition" presents correctly the predominant Anglo-Saxon tradition but may be less adequate for the German tradition. Gaines refers to Max Weber, but Weber saw great differences between the Calvinist tradition and the Lutheran tradition in Northern and Central Europe. The linguistic evidence discussed in this chapter supports Weber's views, rather than Gaines' simplified version of those views. The German concept of *Schicksal* is not consistent with the picture of "a practical, empiricist, non-magical approach to the social and natural world". (Recall Erikson's (1963) remark that even a "realistic German" says *Schicksal* instead of history and geography.) The old English concept of *weird* was not consistent with such an empiricist approach either, and it has disappeared from the English cultural lexicon. But *Schicksal* has not disappeared from the German cultural lexicon.

But although religion is no doubt a crucial factor determining cultural differences, it is not the only one. If modern English is, as it seems to be, the only European language which doesn't have some 'mysterious', non-empirical concept such as *destino, Schicksal,* or *weird* in its lexicon, this must be due partly to the empirical, pragmatic tradition of Anglo-Saxon culture, which expressed itself most fully in empiricist philosophy. It is worth noting in this connection that even Dutch culture, despite the Calvinist element in its past, does have a non-empirical concept of *noodlot* (the word being cognate to the English words *need* and *lot;* Bert Peeters, p.c.). Judging by lexical evidence of this kind, neither German nor Dutch suggests the thoroughly 'dis-enchanted' world view embodied in the English language. The huge differences between the still flourishing if diminished German *Seele* and the withered English *soul* point of course in the same direction. (See chapter 1.)

But the idea that "Latin Europe, a species of Mediterranean tradition, is that of the enchanted world view (Erickson 1976)" (Gaines 1982:179) seems to me to be supported by lexical evidence of the kind discussed here. Concepts such as *destino* and *destin, sorte* and *sort* (and also the Spanish *destino, suerte,* and *fortuna*), are all highly compatible with "a belief in a magical, enchanted world, wherein threads of this world and those of the world beyond are woven into a single fabric of perception and experience as in the medieval (e.g., Latin) world view (Erickson 1976)" (Gaines 1984:180). The rather grim German *Schicksal* doesn't suggest an "enchanted" world of this kind, but neither does it suggest the world view labelled by Gaines as "Northern European" and "Protestant". "In Protestant Europe's world view, the physicalist, empiricist tendencies find expression as the world of wonders is obliterated. Explanations are sought in the tangible, empirical world" (Gaines 1984:181).

The latter world view is not "Northern European" or "Protestant" but Anglo-Saxon, and nothing illustrates this better than the fate of the concept of *weird*, which modern Anglo-Saxon culture has come to see as "weird" and dispensable.

9. Grammatical Correlates of Key Lexical Concepts: Reflections of *Sud'ba* in Russian Grammar

Concepts and attitudes which are fundamental in a given culture usually find their expression not only in the lexicon but also in the grammar of the language of that culture. For example, to appreciate the role of kinship in Australian Aboriginal culture one must understand not only the lexicon of kinship but also the grammar of kinship in Australian languages (cf., for example, Hale 1966; Dixon 1989; Dench 1987).

Differences in values and in attitudes reflected in lexicalised key concepts such as *sud'ba, Schicksal,* or *fate* find their expression also in the grammar of the languages in question, as well as in their phraseology, proverbs, folk literature, and so on. Limitations of space preclude any discussion here of the grammatical correlates of more than one 'fate-type' concept. I have chosen for this purpose the Russian *sud'ba,* whose importance in Russian culture seems quite unique, in comparison with other European languages and cultures. (Recall the relative frequency data, which are of course not conclusive but which are nonetheless highly suggestive: *fate:* 33:1,000,000; *sud'ba:* 181:1,000,000.)

Seen from a Western perspective, Russian grammar is quite unusually rich in constructions referring to things that happen to people against their will or irrespective of their will. Some of these constructions reflect, more specifically, a folk philosophy at the heart of which appear to lie a kind of 'fatalism' and a kind of resignation.

Russian folk literature abounds in negative sentences referring to desirable states of affairs which—alas—will never eventuate because 'they were not fated to do so'.

For example (several of the examples in this section are cited after Galkina-Fedoruk 1958),

> Ne vidat' tebe ètix podarkov.
>
> 'You'll never see these presents.'

> Ne guljat' emu na vole.
>
> 'He'll never walk in freedom again.'

> Ne stat' tebe so mnoj boj deržat'.
>
> 'You are not fated to do battle with me.'

Frequently, utterances of this kind occur in the folk genre called "plač", that is, lamentation (lit., a 'weep'). For example:

> Ne raskryt' tebe svoi očen'ki jasnye
> Ne vzmaxnut' tebe da ručen'ki belye,
> Ox, da ne toptat' tebe dorožki torenye . . .

> 'You'll never open those bright little eyes
> Those little white hands will never wave
> Oh, and you will never set foot on boarded paths again.'

According to Galkina-Fedoruk (1958:214) and many other observers, "this is the most often used, the most beloved form of expression in Russian folk speech; these negative impersonal-infinitival sentences occur very frequently in *byliny* (folk epic), in folksong, in proverbs and sayings".

The canonical form of this construction can be represented as follows:

> Neg. + Infinitive + Dative (human) [indefinite time]

Some variation in this basic formal structure is possible, but departures from it are marked and require some sort of justification. For example, in the following sentence the dative is placed before the infinitive, but this 'inversion' is justified by the preposing of the adverb:

> Ne dolgo našej Mašen'ke vo devuškax sidet'.
>
> 'Our dear Maša wasn't fated to remain unmarried for long.'

The usual initial position of the infinitive in this construction contrasts with the unmarked initial position of the dative in other Russian constructions based on the infinitive, which do not have anything to do with 'fate', for example,

> Im ètogo kurgana nikak ne minovat'. (A. Kalinin)
>
> 'They cannot possibly pass that barrow.'

As for the semantic category of the noun in the dative, it *can* be inanimate rather than human, but this usually implies either a personification or a parallel between nature and events in human life, and the over-all perspective behind such parallelisms is always anthropocentric. For example, the sentence

> Ne rasti trave zimoj po snegu. . . .
> 'Grass cannot grow in winter on snow. . . .'

clearly implies a comment on human life, not a biological observation. The parallel is explicit in the following example:

> Ne dolgo cvetiku v sadiku cvesti,
> Ne dolgo venočku na stenočke viset',
> Ne dolgo nasej Mašen'ke vo devuškax sidet'.
>
> 'A flower is fated not to blossom in a garden for a long time,
> A wreath is fated not to hang on the wall for a long time,
> Our dear Maša is fated not to remain an unmarried girl for a long time. . . .'

The indefinite time is another characteristic feature of this construction. The iterative verbs *byvat'* 'to be', *vidat'* 'to see', and *slyxat'* 'to hear' are particularly characteristic of this construction and seem to mark it quite unambiguously for the 'fated' interpretation. For example:

> Ne byvat' Egorju na svjatoj Rusi,
> Ne vidat' Egorju sveta belogo,
> Ne obozret' Egorju solnca krasnogo,
> Ne vidat' Egorju otca-materi,
> Ne slyxat' Egorju zvona kolokol'nogo,
> Ne slyxat' Egorju pen'ja cerkovnogo.
>
> 'Egor wasn't fated to be (ever again) in holy Russia,
> Egor wasn't fated to see (ever again) the light of the day
> Egor wasn't fated to see the red (or: beautiful) sun,
> Egor wasn't fated to see (ever again) his father or mother,
> Egor wasn't fated to hear (ever again) the bell from the belfry,
> Egor wasn't fated to hear (ever again) church singing.'

A vague reference to something like *fate* can also be detected in positive infinitival sentences such as the following, which are, however, incomparably rarer in Russian:

> Byt' byčku na verovočke.
> 'The little bull will be tied; it's fated to happen.'

Often negative and positive sentences of this kind occur together in parallel sentences; for example:

> Ne byt' mne za knjazem,
> Ni za knjazem, ni za bojarinom,
> A byt' mne za vorom,
> Za razbojnikom.

> 'I am not fated to be married to a prince,
> Not to a prince, not to a nobleman,
> I am fated to be married to a thief,
> To a robber.'

As justly noted by Galkina-Fedoruk (1958:215), sentences of this kind suggest that the events in question are "inevitable and predetermined by *sud'ba*". Note, in this connection, the following recent example, where the 'fated construction' under consideration is linked explicitly with the concept of *sud'ba*:

> No, uvy, mne nikogda ne byt' za granicej, tak kak brat'ja (èto ty i Faskitdin) otsidevšie. . . . Ty tol'ko radi Boga, ne podumaj, čto èto ja tebja rugaju, ili obiža-jus', ili tam ešče čego-to. Èto ja prosto dumaju o tebe, o *sud'ba*x našix, o tom, kak u kogo skladyvaetsja žizn'. (Pis'mo 1988:7)

> 'But, alas, I am not fated to go abroad, as my brothers (you and Faskitdin) have served terms in prison [or labour camps]. But, for God's sake, don't think that I am reproaching you, or complaining, or something: I am simply thinking about you, about our *sud'ba*s, about the different patterns of our lives.'

The semantic core of the negative constructions in question can be represented as follows:

> (a) X will not happen to Y
>   (not because someone doesn't want it)
>   one can't think: 'if I want it, it will happen'
>   it cannot happen

The semantic core of the positive construction can be represented as follows:

> (a′) X will happen to Y
>   (not because someone wants it)
>   one can't think: 'if I don't want it, it will not happen'
>   it cannot not happen

It appears, however, that in addition to that core (either positive or negative) the constructions in question also carry some additional components, which link them even more closely with the concept of *sud'ba*. The additional components form two groups, which I will call (b) and (c):

> (b) some things that people want will not happen
>   some things that people don't want will happen
>   one couldn't say why

(c) I imagine I know this:
some things happen to people and other things don't happen to people
because someone says: I want this

It can of course be claimed that the components (b) and (c) are suggested by the interaction between the construction under discussion and the context rather than by the construction itself, and I agree that the matter requires further investigation. But there are enough formal clues to posit components (a) and (a') as part of Russian grammar.

From a syntactic point of view, a dative 'victim' can be interpreted either as a non-agentive subject or as a complement of an 'understood' predicate *suždeno* ('was fated/was sentenced'), and this double-entendre is often intentionally highlighted, as in the following passage:

> Začem sud'boj ne suždeno
> Moej nepostojannoj lire
> Gerojstvo vospevat' odno?
>
> 'Why wasn't my changeable lyre
> fated by *sud'ba*
> to sing only in honour of heroism?'

Formally, the dative *lire* is here an indirect object of *suždeno,* but if the phrase *sud'boj ne suždeno* were omitted, the sense of the sentence would remain essentially the same, and the dative *lire* would be the subject.

Similarly, in the following lines by Zinaida Gippius the dative *mne* is both the indirect object of *suždeno* 'fated' and the experiencer of the 'fate' referred to by the infinitive:

> O, počemu Tebja ljubit'
> Mne suždeno neodolimo? (1972(1910):12)
>
> 'Oh, why was I fated overpoweringly to love you?'

Consider also the juxtaposition of *sud'ba* and the 'fated' dative in the following passage:

> Stoim my slepo pred Sud'boju.
> Nam ne sorvat' s nee pokrov. (Tjutčev 1976:201)
>
> 'We stand blind before Fate.
> We (Dat.) [can]not tear off (Inf.) its cover.'

It is interesting to note how the most dramatic exchange of love letters in Russian literature, that between Tat'jana and Onegin in Pushkin's *Eugene Onegin,* hinges crucially on the fatalistic infinitive phrase *tak i byt'* echoed by the inevitable key words *sud'ba* and *suždeno:*

Byt' možet, èto vse pustoe,
Obman neopytnoj duši!
I suždeno sovsem drugoe!
No tak i byt'! sud'bu moju
Otnyne ja tebe vručaju. . . .
(1981:95)

'Perhaps, 'tis nonsense all,
an inexperienced soul's delusion, and there's destined
something quite different. . . .
But so be it! My fate
henceforth I place into your hands. . . .'
(1964:171)

No tak i byt': ja sam sebe
Protivit'sja ne v silax bole;
Vse rešeno: ja v vašej vole
I predajus' moej sud'be.
(1981:220)

'But let it be: against myself
I've not the force to struggle any more;
all is decided: I am in your power,
and I surrender to my fate.'
(1964:309)

In general, *sud'ba* and *suždeno* co-occur very frequently in Russian poetry and prose, and often *sud'ba* is presented as the agent of *suždeno*. For example:

I načinaet ponemnogu
Moja Tat'jana ponimat'
Teper' jasnee—slava Bogu—
Togo po kom ona vzdyxat'
Osuždena sud'boju vlastnoj.
(1981:186)

'And my Tatiana by degrees
begins to understand
more clearly now—thank God—
him for whom by imperious fate
she is sentenced to sigh.'
(1964:273)

Compare also:

Uželi žrebij vam takov
naznačen strogoju sud'boj?
(1981:108)

'Can it be true that such a portion
is by stern fate assigned to you?'
(1964:188)

Tak, vidno, nebom suždeno. . . . (1981:108)

'By heaven thus 'tis evidently destined. . . .'

(1964:189)

It should be added that a 'fatalistic' dative construction can also be used to refer to inevitability of a different kind. In particular, if the state of affairs desired by one person depends entirely on the arbitrary decision of another, that arbitrary decision may appear to be as inexorable as a verdict of *sud'ba;* in fact, such an arbitrary decision by someone else can be seen as *being* part of our *sud'ba*. This is illustrated in the following examples:

Esli nynče nočju Bèla ne budet zdes', to ne vidat' tebe konja. . . . (Lermontov 1959:379)

'If tonight Bèla is not here you'll never see that horse. . . .'

Vižu, Azamat, čto tebe bol'no ponravilas' èta lošad'; a ne vidat' tebe ee, kak svoego zatylka. (Lermontov 1959:378)

'I see, Azamat, that you have fallen in love with that horse; but you will never see it, as you will never see the back of your head.'

And here is a contemporary quote:

Staroe foto. . . . Svetlolikaja devuška—xarkovčanka Lena Danilovič. . . . Ona daže ne trockistka, a—strašno skazat'—'decistka'. I ženix u nee 'decist', v drugoj kakoj-to ssylke. My uže znaem, čto im ne svidet'sja—usatyj koldun zakoldoval ix namertvo. (*Glasnost'* 1988, 12:43)

'An old photo. . . . A bright-faced girl from Kharkov, Lena Danilovič. . . . She wasn't even a Trotskyite, but—dare one say it—a "Decist". And her fiancé was a "Decist" also, in exile somewhere else. And we can sense that they'll never see [i.e., they are fated not to see] each other again. The mustachioed sorcerer [i.e., Stalin] had cast a fatal spell on them.'

Sentences of this kind seem to carry the same components which constitute the core of the negative 'fated' construction:

X will not happen to person Y
one can't think: 'if I want it, it will happen'
it cannot happen
[because someone says: I want this: it will not happen]

Generally speaking, Russian is extraordinarily rich in constructions referring to events and states of affairs which go against human will or cannot be influenced by human will. One formal reflection of this is the major, and ever growing, role which dative subject constructions play in Russian grammar. Nominative-subject constructions referring to people indicate volition or at least some degree of responsibility; the all-pervasive dative-subject constructions reflect a perspective in which human beings are seen as not being in control. A number of such constructions will be surveyed in chapter 12. In the present context, I will mention only one other construction of this kind, which seems to echo in a remarkable way the content of the word *sud'ba*. First an illustration:

> No znaju, miru net proščenija,
> Pečali serdca net zabvenia,
> I net molčaniju razrešenija,
> I vse na vek bez izmenenija,
> I na zemle, i v nebesax.
>
> (Gippius 1972, v.1:24)

'I know, there is no forgiveness for the world,
There is no oblivion for the heart's sadness,
There is no resolution for the silence,
And everything will remain forever without change,
On earth and in heaven.'

The syntactic pattern used in the first three lines is this:

> Noun:Dat. + Negation ('there isn't') + Noun:Gen.

The noun in the dative indicates an experiencer, or an aspect of the experiencer, and the noun in the genitive indicates some unattainable 'good'. The meaning of the pattern is, roughly, this:

> X would want this: Y will happen
> Y cannot happen
> one couldn't say why
> (I imagine I know this: some things that people want will not happen
> they cannot happen
> because someone says this: I want this: it will not happen.)

Those readers who are familiar with Russian literature will perhaps also recall Pushkin's frequent references to his youth, for which "vozvrata net", 'there is no return', and "vozroždenija net", 'there is no rebirth'.

It should be added that in folk speech, the 'fated' construction seems nearly always to refer to 'bad', undesirable events, and it might seem justified to include this 'badness' in the semantic formula. I have refrained from doing so, however, because there are exceptions. For example, in 1932, when the poet Marina Tsvetaeva, then living in Paris, reflected in "Stixi k synu", 'A poem for my son', on her son's future using the 'fated' construction, she didn't seem to see it as 'bad':

> Ne byt' tebe buržuem. . . .
> Ne byt' tebe Francuzom. . . .
>
> (1965:296)

'You are not fated to be a bourgeois,
You are not fated to be a Frenchman. . . .'

Tsvetaeva's prophecies had an appalling though totally misguided prescience: her son did not become a bourgeois, and he did not become a Frenchman. The family returned from emigration to the Soviet Union, where his father was promptly arrested and shot, his sister was sent to a labour camp, his mother hanged herself, and he himself was killed by the Germans, at the age of nineteen, as a Russian soldier. As a Russian might say, "vpolne russkaja sud'ba", 'a typically Russian *sud'ba*'.

II

EMOTIONS ACROSS CULTURES

3

Are Emotions Universal
or Culture-Specific?

As pointed out in a recent article by Ben Blount (1984:130), "The past decade has witnessed, in contrast to earlier periods, an efflorescence of interest in emotions". Some scholars proclaim the birth of a new science, a science of emotions (cf., for example, Izard's statements quoted in Trotter 1983). One of the most interesting and provocative ideas that have been put forward in the relevant literature is that it is possible to identify a set of fundamental human emotions, universal, discrete, and presumably innate; and that in fact a set of this kind has already been identified. According to Izard and Buechler (1980:168), the fundamental emotions are (1) interest, (2) joy, (3) surprise, (4) sadness, (5) anger, (6) disgust, (7) contempt, (8) fear, (9) shame/shyness, and (10) guilt. (Cf. also, for example, Ekman 1980 and 1989; Johnson-Laird and Oatley 1989.)

I view claims of this kind with scepticism. If lists such as the preceding are supposed to enumerate universal human emotions, how is it that these emotions are all so neatly identified by means of English words? For example, Polish does not have a word corresponding exactly to the English word *disgust*. What if the psychologists working on the 'fundamental human emotions' happened to be native speakers of Polish rather than English? Would it still have occurred to them to include 'disgust' on their list? An Australian Aboriginal language, Gidjingali, does not lexically distinguish 'fear' from 'shame', subsuming feelings kindred to those identified by the English words *fear* and *shame* under one lexical item (Hiatt 1978a:185). If the researchers happened to be native speakers of Gidjingali rather than English, would it still have occurred to them to claim that fear and shame are both fundamental human emotions, discrete and clearly separated from each other?

English terms of emotion constitute a folk taxonomy, not an objective, culture-free analytical framework, so obviously we cannot assume that English words such as *disgust, fear,* or *shame* are clues to universal human concepts or to basic psychological realities. Yet words such as these are usually treated as if they were objective, culture-free 'natural kinds'.

The fallacy in question has been exposed very well by Catherine Lutz:

> American psychology has taken English emotion words (such as 'fear', 'love', and 'disgust'), has reified what are essentially American ethnopsychological concepts, and has accepted them, often unquestioned, as the conceptual apparatus of scien-

tific inquiry. Given the limited cultural base, it would be surprising if the emotions, exactly as distinguished, conceptualized, and experienced in American society, emerge as universals. Exactly this has been assumed, however, and then 'proven' by Western researchers (Ekman 1974, Sorenson 1976). While it has been considered of great importance to ascertain whether some non-Western peoples 'feel guilt', the question does not arise as to whether Americans experience the New Guinea Highlanders' emotion of *popokl* 'outrage over the failure of others to recognize one's claims' (Strathern 1968) or whether they are deficient in the ability to experience the Ifaluk emotion of *fago* 'compassion/love/sadness'. (1985b:38)

It is not my purpose to argue against the "assumption of the innateness and universality of the fundamental emotions" (Izard 1969:260) or against the thesis that "the emotions [presumably, the "fundamental" ones] have innately stored neural programs, universally understood expressions, and common experiential qualities" (Izard 1977:18). The search for fundamental emotions, innate and universal, is akin to the search for fundamental concepts ('semantic primitives'), similarly innate and universal, in which I have been engaged for more than two decades (see, in particular, Wierzbicka 1972a, 1980, 1985d, 1989a and b, 1991a and c, and In press e). I want to stress, therefore, that although many scholars may question this undertaking from a position of relativism or narrow empiricism, my own strictures have a totally different basis. I am in sympathy with the attempts to capture what is fundamental, universal, and presumably innate. I am also in sympathy with attempts to discover discrete categories behind the apparent 'fuzziness' of human cognition.

I would like, however, to point to some aspects of the task at hand that so far have not received due attention and that seem to me important. My suggestions can be outlined as follows: (1) If we want to posit universal human emotions we must identify them in terms of a language-independent semantic metalanguage, not in terms of English folk words for emotions (or in terms of English scientific expressions such as "a loss of situational self-esteem" for shame-like emotions). (2) Lexical discriminations in the area of emotions (as in other semantic fields) provide important clues to the speakers' conceptualisations. (3) The study of the interplay between the universal and the culture-specific aspects of emotions must be seen as an interdisciplinary undertaking, requiring collaboration of psychology, anthropology, and linguistics. (4) A considerable amount of lexical data collection, and of serious semantic analysis, is needed before any tenable universals in the area of emotion concepts can be plausibly proposed.

1. The Need for Reductive Analysis

In addition to the reification of English folk categories (such as *anger, shame,* or *disgust*), which have been treated as culture-independent realities (cf. Kleinman 1977; Lutz 1985b), the conventional analysis of emotion terms has been plagued, as much as any other semantic domain, by direct or indirect circularity. For example, Izard (1977:288) writes: "Even so common a feeling as that of distress is not altogether easy to describe. To feel distressed is to feel sad, downhearted, discouraged." If one attempts to define one emotion word via others one will never be able to elucidate the meaning of any of them. If one defines *distressed* via *sad* or *downhearted,* the chances are that one is going to define *sad* and *downhearted* via *distressed,* and so on, ad infinitum. No real analysis is performed, only a semblance of analysis. But if emotion terms are decomposed into simpler concepts, such as 'want', 'feel', 'think', 'say', 'good', or 'bad', then there is no threat of overt or covert circularity, and both the similarities and the differences between different emotion concepts are made explicit.

At the same time, a basis is reached for illuminating cross-linguistic comparison of emotions, because although concepts such as 'distress' or 'sadness' are highly language-specific, concepts such as 'want', 'think', 'good', or 'bad' can be presumed to be universal, or at least very widespread across languages and cultures.

2. Cross-Cultural Comparison of Emotions

Consider the Polish words *tęsknota* (noun) and *tęsknić* (verb). Although they have no simple, monolexemic English equivalents, it is possible to explain in English what the relevant feeling is, if one decomposes the complex Polish concept into parts whose names do have simple English equivalents. I think this can be done as follows:[1]

> X *tęskni* do Y   →
>
> X thinks something like this:
>   I am far away from Y
>   when I was with Y I felt something good
>   I want to be with Y now
>   if I were with Y now I would feel something good
>   I cannot be with Y now
> because of this, X feels something bad

Several English words may come to mind as potential translation equivalents of the Polish word (*homesick, long, miss, pine, nostalgia*), but they all differ from one another and from the Polish term as well. For example, if a teenage daughter leaves the family home and goes to study in a distant city, her Polish parents would usually *tęsknić,* but one could not say that they were *homesick* for the daughter, that they felt *nostalgia* for her, and one would hardly say that they were *pining* after her. One could say that they *missed* her, but *miss* implies much less than *tęsknić.* One could say to a friend, 'We missed you at the meeting', without wishing to imply that anything remotely similar to pain or suffering was involved, and yet *tęsknić* does imply something like pain or suffering (in fact, the best gloss I have come across is 'the pain of distance'). The word *miss* implies neither pain nor distance. For example, one can *miss* someone who has died ('My grandmother died recently. You have no idea how much I miss her'). But one would not use *tęsknić* is a case like this, because *tęsknić* implies a real separation in space.

In this respect, *tęsknić* is related to *homesick*. But of course *homesick* implies that the experiencer himself or herself has gone far away from the target of the emotion. The exact similarities and differences between *tęsknić* and *homesick* can be seen if one compares the explication of the former concept, given earlier, with the explication of the latter, given here:

X is *homesick* →

X thinks something like this:
  I am far away from my home
  when I was there, I felt something good
  I want to be there now
  if I were there now, I would feel something good
  I cannot be there now
because of this, X feels something bad

Pining differs from *tęsknić*, above all, in its single-mindedness and its, so to speak, debilitating effect ('because of this, X can't think of other things'). Furthermore, *pining* does not refer to separation in space; for example, a dog can *pine* for his dead master; by contrast, *tęsknić* can only be used with respect to dead people metaphorically.

X is *pining* after(/for) Y →

X thinks something like this:
  I am not with Y
  when I was with Y, I felt something good
  I want to be with Y now
  I cannot be with Y now
because of this, X feels something bad
because of this, X can't think of other things

Longing doesn't refer to separation in space either. More importantly, however, it is future-oriented and includes no reference to the past or to the present. For example, one can *long* to have a baby, but *tęsknić* cannot be used like that: *tęsknota* can have as its target one's real children who are far away but not children who haven't been born yet. (In this respect, *homesick* and *pine* are like *tęsknić*, not like *long*.)

Furthermore, *longing* is not person- (or place-) oriented, as the other words discussed are: one *longs* for something to happen, not for a person or a place.

X is *longing* for Y →

X thinks something like this:
  I want Y to happen
  because of this, if I could I would do something
  I can't do anything
because of this, X feels something bad
when X imagines 'Y is happening', X feels something good

In addition to this basic difference between *long* and *tęsknić,* there seem to be two further ones: *long* is more helpless ('I can't do anything'), and yet it is sweeter, less painful than *tęsknić*—presumably, because it involves an act of imagination (if the feeling of 'not having what one desires' is painful, the 'imagining' that one does have it is sweet).

Miss, as a form of emotion, can be explicated as follows:

> X *misses*₁ person Y   →
> X thinks something like this:
> I was with Y before now
> when I was with Y, I felt something good
> I cannot be with Y now
> because of this, X feels something bad

> X *misses*₂ doing Y   →
> X thinks something like this:
> I did Y before now
> when I did Y, I felt something good
> I cannot do Y now
> because of this, X feels something bad

The fact that one can *miss* certain events, or states of affairs, as well as people, highlights the relatively mild nature of the emotion involved. If someone says, "I miss our walks in the forest" or "I miss bowling", he does not want to imply any particular love for the things mentioned. Rather, he wants to imply that he thinks of the things in question as pleasurable, that is, as things that have caused him to feel something good in the past and presumably would cause him to feel something good now.

The absence of acute suffering is shown by the absence of a volitive component ('I want to be with X'). In the case of *tęsknić, pine, long,* and *homesick,* X wants something that X knows is impossible (e.g., to be at home 'now'), hence the suffering. In the case of *missing,* there is no similar elan toward an inaccessible target.

3. No Word—No Feeling?

English has no word for the feeling encoded in the Polish word *tęsknić.* Does this mean that native speakers of English do not know (never experience) the feeling in question? Not necessarily. Individual speakers of English have no doubt experienced this feeling. But the Anglo-Saxon culture as a whole has not found this feeling worthy of a special name.

Nor does the fact that a language has not encoded a particular emotion in a separate word mean that the speakers of this language cannot perceive that emotion as a distinct, recognisable feeling or that they cannot talk about it. Both everyday speech and psychologically sensitive literature are full of attempts, often highly successful, to convey feelings for which there is no simple word. The following

examples are from Tolstoy's *Anna Karenina* (for more examples and discussion see
Wierzbicka 1972a): (1) Kitty Ščerbatskaja is awaiting the decisive visit of Levin and
Vronskij: "From after dinner till early evening, Kitty felt as a young man does
before a battle" (1953:52) (2) Hitherto, his wife's soul had been open to Karenin:
"He felt now rather as a man might do on returning home and finding his own house
locked up" (1953:159).

There are countless human emotions that can be perceived as distinct and
recognisable. Possibly, all these emotions can be, better or worse, expressed and
described in words—in any human language. But each language has its own set of
ready-made emotion words, designating those emotions that the members of a given
culture recognise as particularly salient. Presumably, these language-specific sets
overlap and, presumably, the closer two cultures are, the greater the overlap between their respective sets of emotion words.

But although the absence of a word does not preclude the ability of experiencing
an emotion, or of perceiving it as distinct and identifiable, there are good reasons to
think that differences in "emotion talk" (Heelas 1984:27) are linked with differences
in the emotions themselves. The emotional lexicons of different languages vary
considerably, and this points to profound differences between ideas and beliefs
about emotions and between cultural models of emotions. But, as Mischel (1977:21)
points out, "if people raised in different cultures or sub-cultures come to internalise
different ways of describing their experience, this may make what they experience
different".

Some scholars have stressed these differences in how people feel in different
cultures in very strong terms, for example, Rosaldo:

> [I]t seems easier to insist that people elsewhere think differently about their agricul-
> ture or gods than to insist . . . that there is nothing universal about such things as
> happiness and anger. But that the Balinese no more feel 'guilt' than we feel *lek*, the
> Balinese emotion closest to our 'shame'—and that these differences relate to how
> we think about the world—is, to me, equally clear. (1984:142)

I think that Rosaldo is making an important point here: that *guilt* is no more a
culture-independent psychological construct than *lek* is. But she may be going too
far in asserting confidently that the Balinese don't feel guilt. Perhaps they do, and
perhaps Americans do feel *lek* sometimes, as they may feel *tęsknota* sometimes,
without having a lexicalised concept of either *lek* or *tęsknota*. What is really important, I think, is that the feelings of *lek* and of *tęsknota* are not sufficiently salient in
American culture to have merited lexicalisation. And if it is true that "our descriptions of our experience are, in part, constitutive of what we experience" (Mischel
1977:21), then lexical differences between *lek* and *guilt*, or between *tęsknić* and
miss, may not only reflect but also encourage different, culture-specific, modes of
thinking and feeling.

Are there any emotion concepts which have been lexically recognised as distinct
and identifiable in all languages of the world?

The evidence available suggests that there are no such emotions. (Cf.
Wierzbicka, In press a and b.) Emotions which may appear to be particularly strong

candidates for this status, such as *anger, fear,* or *shame,* on closer inspection turn out not to have been universally lexicalised. But this is an issue which will be discussed in more detail in the following chapter.

4. Emotion Terms as Clues to Different Cultures

I believe that the emotion terms available in a given lexicon provide an important clue to the speakers' culture. Arguably, the Polish concept 'tęsknota' discussed previously is a good case in point.

In older Polish, this word designated a kind of vague sadness, as the related Russian word *toska* does even now. Apparently, it was only after the partitions of Poland at the end of the eighteenth century, and especially after the defeat of the Polish uprising of 1830 and the resulting 'Great Emigration', that this word developed its present meaning of, roughly, 'sadness caused by separation'. When one considers that after that time the best and most influential Polish literature started to develop abroad, among the political exiles, and that it became dominated by the theme of nostalgia, it is hard not to think of the emergence of the new meaning of the word *tęsknota* as a reflection of Poland's history and the predominant national preoccupations.

An even clearer illustration is provided by a whole series of words referring to emotions (and to bodily results of emotions) akin to both sadness and love in the Australian Aboriginal language Pintupi, which demonstrates a degree of love and concern for one's kin and one's land unparalleled in Western culture (cf. Myers 1976; Morice 1977a:105). This is entirely in line with what is otherwise known about Aboriginal culture and Aboriginal society. I will discuss the Pintupi words in question, as well as several other culturally salient emotion concepts from many other languages, in the following chapter.

5. Disgust—Universal or Language-Specific?

Izard (1969) and others hypothesise that feelings such as fear, shame, and disgust are perceived universally as distinct emotions, recognisable by the way they are expressed. It seems to me that this claim would be much more credible if the feelings in question were lexically encoded in all natural languages.

As mentioned earlier, however, I do not wish to rule out the possibility that psychologists may find some universal human emotions, distinct and clearly identifiable, among emotions that have not been widely lexicalised in different languages. I am merely suggesting that emotions proposed as universal, in the sense under discussion, must be identified in terms of a maximally language-independent semantic metalanguage, not in terms of English folk taxonomy. For example, if someone wants to claim that something such as 'disgust' is indeed a universal human emotion, then he or she should identify this emotion in terms of lexical universals or near-universals such as *say, want, feel,* or *bad* rather than in terms of the English-specific lexical item *disgust.* The fact that the same scholar can sometimes say *disgust* and sometimes *disgust/revulsion* (cf. Izard 1969) wishing to identify the same "fundamental" emotion, shows the inadequacy of English-specific emotion terms as analytical tools. After all, the words *disgust* and *revulsion* do not mean the same thing; the feelings they identify are different from each other (though not widely different). Which feeling, than, is really claimed to be universal, that designated by the word *disgust* or that designated by the word *revulsion?*

Izard (1969:337) writes: "Theorists since Darwin have suggested that the emotion of disgust may have its origin in biological phenomena associated with the hunger drive and the eating process. The expression of disgust can be simulated by a person posing as though he is refusing or rejecting from the mouth something which tastes bad."

I think that the image of a person "rejecting from the mouth something which tastes bad" may indeed provide a useful reference point for the feeling identified in English by means of the word *disgust*. But *revulsion* evokes a different image: that of a person who wants to withdraw his or her body from contact with something unwanted, or more than that, something with which the person cannot bear to be in contact. *Repugnance* is associated with a different image again: that of a person who is near (rather than in contact with) something that he or she does not want to be near to and who experiences an impulse to move away from it. (It is similar in this respect to *repulsion.*) *Distaste* evokes the image of a person who has had something in his or her mouth that tasted bad, but it lacks the idea of rejecting anything from the mouth. Accordingly, it suggests a 'milder' dislike and a 'milder' disapproval than *disgust*. Thus, the feelings identified in English by means of the words *disgust, distaste, revulsion,* and *repulsion* are different feelings and they cannot all correspond to the same "discrete fundamental human emotion".

Trying to explicate the concepts in question we cannot always rely on the prototypical image evoked by them. For example, the meaning of the word *fear* cannot be explicated simply in terms of an impulse to run away. Similarly, the synchronic meaning of *disgust* cannot be explicated simply in terms of spitting out and bad taste. At a dinner table, one would be more likely to experience *disgust* watching other people's behaviour than concentrating on one's food, no matter how unsatisfactory. One might also experience disgust when thinking of the cook's incompetence or of his or her dirty habits rather than when focussing on the food as such.

For the same reason, I think, worms or insects are more likely to be called *repulsive* or even *revolting,* than *disgusting:* if one called them *disgusting,* this would sound jocular and anthropomorphic.

The noun *revulsion* does not involve a judgement concerning human action and in fact does not seem to imply a negative judgement of any kind. For example, one can feel revulsion toward mice or frogs without thinking anything bad about them, let alone attributing to them any "bad actions". *Revulsion* may differ in this respect from the adjective *revolting: revolting* food must be thought of as bad food, whereas, for example, slugs don't have to be thought of as "bad creatures" to cause someone's revulsion.

The adjective *revolting* may also differ from the noun *revulsion* in another respect: in its apparent link with something like vomiting, which could perhaps be represented as follows: 'when I think about it, I couldn't have something in my mouth; if I did I would feel something bad.'

Interestingly, the adjective *revolting* can apply to both things and animals or people (or their behaviour), whereas the adjective *repulsive* appears to apply almost exclusively to living beings: a lecherous old man can be called both *repulsive* and *revolting,* but excrement or food would only be called *revolting,* not *repulsive.*

I think the reason is that bad food may cause one to want to avoid any contact with it (especially, contact through the mouth), but it can hardly cause people to want to avoid being anywhere near it (the presence of bad food behind our back can hardly matter to us). But living creatures, such as rats or people, can have a different effect on people: if they are particularly unpleasant, then even being in close proximity to them can be hard to bear. Being able to move, to look, to breathe, to spit, and so on, they create around themselves a sphere of potential influence, which people may feel like avoiding. To account for both the similarities and the differences in the use of the terms under discussion, the following rough explications can be proposed.[2]

disgust

X thinks something like this:
    I now know: this person did something bad
    people shouldn't do things like this
    when one thinks about it, one can't not feel something bad
because of this, X feels something bad
X feels like someone who thinks something like this:
    I have something bad in my mouth
    I don't want this

distaste

X thinks something like this:
    Y did something bad
    when I think about it, I feel something bad
because of this, X feels something bad
X feels like someone who thinks something like this:
    I now had something bad in my mouth

revulsion

X thinks something like this:
    Y is in this place
    a part of my body could be in the same place
    if this happened, I would feel something bad
    when I think about it, I can't not feel something bad
because of this, X feels something bad
(of the kind people feel when they think something like this)

(Y is) *repulsive*

X thinks something like this:
    Y is near me
    I don't want this
    when I am near Y, I can't not think that Y is bad
because of this, X feels something bad
(of the kind people feel when they think something like this)

A few explanations are in order.

First, the phrase "I now know" is meant to indicate perception: one feels *disgust,* or *distaste,* when one first realises (sees, hears, etc.) that someone did something "bad", not later.

Second, the references to the mouth in the explication of *disgust* and *distaste* are supported by facial expressions characteristic of these emotions (although *disgust* appears to be also associated with a wrinkled nose; cf. Ekman and Friesen 1975).

Third, *distaste* is, intuitively speaking, a milder emotion than *disgust.* This is accounted for by the difference in tense in the components 'I have something bad in my mouth' (*disgust*) and 'I now *had* something bad in my mouth' (*distaste*), and also by the absence of a volitive component 'I don't want this' in *distaste* and its presence in *disgust* (the *disgusted* person rejects, so to speak, an unacceptable current experience, but *distaste* is more like a kind of unpleasant after-taste).

Fourth, *disgust* implies that something is objectively bad and that other people, too, would feel something unpleasant if they were confronted with it or even if they contemplated it ('when one thinks about it, one can't not feel something bad'); by contrast, *distaste* seems to be more subjective ('when I think about it, I feel something bad').

Fifth, both *revulsion* and *repulsive* are represented here as referring to undesirable objects (or creatures). This may seem too restrictive, as it can also refer to human behaviour and to abstract entities (such as, "revolting rhymes"). It is possible, however, that the uses which are not accounted for by the formulae posited here should be regarded as metaphorical or otherwise extended. Furthermore, the phrase "revolting behaviour" brings to mind above all physical behaviour (for example, by a drunk), and the formula proposed applies in this case, too (one could well shrink from physical contact with a drunk behaving in a revolting manner).

Sixth, the phrasing 'one/I can't not feel something bad' in the explications of *disgust* and *revulsion* (and a parallel component in the explication of *repulsive*) is an attempt to reflect the instinctive character of the negative reactions in question.

Seventh, the explications of *revulsion* and *repulsion* (*repulsive*) may seem circular ('X thinks such and such and feels the way people usually do when they think this'). I don't think there is anything wrong with this kind of apparent circularity, but I regard it as quite likely that further research into emotion concepts may suggest a better phrasing. (Cf. Wierzbicka In press a and c.)

All the points mentioned require further investigation, and the explications sketched should be regarded as no more than first approximations.

What I want to stress here is that the exact boundaries drawn between the related feelings of *disgust, distaste, revulsion,* and *repulsion* (not to mention *aversion*) are language-specific. For example, Polish has several words that can be used as translation equivalents of the words in question: *niesmak* (roughly, 'distaste'), *wstręt* (roughly, 'revulsion'), *obrzydzenie* (roughly, 'disgust'), *odraza* (roughly, 'repulsion'), *brzydzić się* (roughly, 'feel revulsion for'), but the émigré Polish writer Jan Lechoń, writing his diaries in America, repeatedly uses in his diaries the word *dyzgust,* a loan from English, despite his otherwise puristic attitude to his own Polish (Lechoń 1973). Clearly, Lechoń feels that the Anglo-Saxon concept of 'disgust' has no equivalent in Polish (and I agree). Having developed, under the influence of Anglo-Saxon culture, a need to use the Anglo-Saxon concept 'disgust', he also feels compelled to borrow the word to convey this concept in Polish.

It is particularly worth noting that the English word *disgust* does not mean the same as the related French word *dégoût*. Izard (1969) reports that French and American children show very similar patterns of growth of recognition of individual emotions with age. He notes, however, that with respect to disgust there is an unexpected difference: the French slightly exceed the Americans at most age levels. Izard tries to explain this puzzling fact in terms of greater emphasis placed on the culinary art in French culture:

> It is a well-known fact that the French are very proud of their culinary art. . . . The French art of cooking is matched by an equally refined art of eating. . . . The existence of the French traditions in cooking and eating are undoubtedly partly dependent on the parallel processes of teaching and learning fine discriminations in the appearance, smell, taste and texture of differently prepared foods. In these processes, the French child might well be expected to have greater opportunity to witness and to experience the emotion of disgust. (1969:338)

All this is very well, but one crucial point is clearly being missed: that the French word *dégoût* and the English word *disgust* do not mean the same thing. When the French children learn to use the word *dégoût*, they are not learning to recognise and to label the same feeling which American children associate with the word *disgust*. The feeling designated by the word *dégoût* is associated much more closely and much more directly with eating than is that designated by the word *disgust*. Thus, one can say in French *avoir du dégoût pour le lait* (the first example for the use of *dégoût* offered in Harrap's (1961) *Standard French and English dictionary*). This does not mean that *dégoût* cannot be used in situations in which *disgust* can, but there are situations where *dégoût* can be used and *disgust* cannot. As I have suggested earlier, the English word *disgust* encodes a feeling caused by 'bad and ugly' human actions (or their results), not by food as such. This is not to deny that the English concept 'disgust' contains a reference to 'something *like* bad taste and an impulse to get something out of one's mouth', but in 'disgust' this reference serves merely as a simile. By contrast, in the concept of 'dégoût' the reference to the same sensation ('oral avertive reflex') constitutes the core of the meaning:

> *dégoût*
> X thinks something like this: this is bad
> because of this, X feels something bad
> X feels like someone who thinks this:
>   'I have something bad in my mouth'
>   'I don't want this'

This more physical emphasis of *dégoût* is, of course, related to the absence from this concept of the "judgemental" and moral components of *disgust*: 'this person did something bad', 'people shouldn't do things like this'.

My question is, Is it likely that the language-specific concept encoded in the

English word *disgust* corresponds to a discrete, fundamental human emotion? Why the concept encoded in *disgust* rather than that encoded in the Polish word *obrzydenie* or *odraza* or in the French word *dégoût?* And if what is meant is not 'disgust' but a kind of feeling that corresponds equally well to *odraza, obrzydzenie,* or *dégoût* as it does to *disgust,* then what exactly is being postulated here as a discrete universal human emotion?

I am not saying that this cannot be spelt out. I am saying that this has to be spelt out if the claim that 'disgust' (or "something like disgust") is a fundamental human emotion is to have a precise meaning.

6. Shame, Embarrassment, and Fear

The inadequacy of the analytical framework which relies on English folk terms to identify supposedly universal feelings is particularly clear in that part of the spectrum of emotions which includes the feeling that English calls *shame.* English distinguishes shame from both fear and embarrassment, but many other languages draw different conceptual distinctions in this area.

As was noted already by Darwin, the concept of shame (obviously, in the English sense of the word) is associated with a desire not to be seen. Izard (1969:275) writes: "When subjects are asked how they feel or what they do when they experience shame, they very frequently indicate that they want to disappear; they want very badly not to be seen. In a recent film of hypnotically induced fundamental emotions (Izard and Bartlett 1968), the disappearance theme was quite evident. The subject experiencing hypnotically induced shame lowered her head and pulled her legs and arms up very close to her body. On inquiry the subject reported that she was making herself as small as possible in order not to be seen."

But the closest equivalent of the English word *shame* in the Australian language Gidjingali doesn't seem to associate the feeling it designates with a desire not to be seen. Rather (as Hiatt 1978a plausibly suggests) it seems to associate this feeling with a desire to retreat, to run away. Consequently, the word in question can be used not only in situations in which the English word *shame* would be appropriate but also in a situation in which the English word *fear* rather than *shame* would be used. From an English speaker's point of view, shame and fear are two different emotions. But from the point of view of the speakers of Gidjingali, apparently they are not, because both are seen in terms of the same impulse to retreat.

It should also be noted that in the passage on shame quoted (from Izard 1969:275) two prototypical impulses are mentioned side by side: the desire not to be seen and the desire to disappear. I believe that the English concept of shame relies crucially on the former standard rather than the latter. It is striking how the author imposes an interpretation in terms of 'disappearance' on a report of an experience couched in terms of a desire not to be seen, not in terms of a desire to disappear. But disappearance may be simply one way of ceasing to be seen, and therefore a desire to disappear may be simply one particular manifestation of a more general desire not to be seen. The desire to disappear is perhaps associated with embarrassment rather than with shame as such.

Many languages of the world (for example, Korean, Ewe in West Africa, and Kuman in Papua) don't lexically distinguish shame and embarrassment. In fact, the same word also seems to be applied to situations in which English would use the word *shy* rather than either *embarrassed* or *ashamed*.

Furthermore, in many non-Western cultures a concept related to 'shame', but by no means identical with it, plays an important social role. In particular, this point has often been made with respect to Aboriginal Australia. For example, Myers (1976:151) writes this about the Pintupi: "The concept of 'shame' [*kunta*] is a cultural form, something which is learned in growing up. . . . The concept . . . is a major construct in the Pintupi view of what it means to be a person and how a person should comport himself in social relations."

According to Myers (1976:171), "the Pintupi concept of *kunta* includes within its range the English concepts of 'shame', 'embarrassment', 'shyness' and 're-spect'". The feeling of 'kunta' is crucially linked with rules of avoidance, which play an important role in regulating conduct in Aboriginal society. Myers writes (1976:148–49): "A number of social relationships are characterised by 'shame' (*kunta*). One should avoid one's 'wife's mother' because of 'shame', and also one should be very restrained with one's 'wife's father' because of 'shame'. . . . The relationship between brothers-in-law is supposed to show 'shame' or 'respect' (*kunta*). This entails a special avoidance language between these peoples. . . . The restrained behaviour of the Pintupi in the public domain is largely a concomitant of the concept of 'shame/respect'. The reluctance to openly disagree with others is based on avoidance of 'embarrassment'."

Myers doesn't really define the concept of 'kunta', but his discussion of this concept makes it quite clear that although related to 'shame' it is far from identical with it.

The difference between the Australian Aboriginal concepts encoded in words such as *kunta* and the concept encoded in the English word *shame* comes across very clearly in the following account, referring to another Aboriginal language, Ngiyambaa:

> The general attitude towards anything to do with white people, whether initially mysterious or not, was avoidance wherever possible. After cars had become com-monplace: 'If we was walking along the road and heard a motorcar, we still scooped into the scrub'.
> This attitude was partly dictated by fear: 'If we saw anybody with a camera we'd reckon, "They going to shoot us" and run off away and hide. That was a gun, we thought.' But it was also partly the result of *kuyan,* an expression of respectful behaviour usually talked of in English as 'shame' or 'shyness'. Its full force is liable to be missed by non-Aboriginal speakers of English for whom the words shame and shyness rarely have positive connotations. According to the Ngiyambaa scheme of things, *kuyan* is not an uncomfortable feeling to be overcome, but an appropriate and expected reaction in many social situations:
> > 'We were brought up to know right from wrong in our own way. We wasn't cheeky to anyone. We had to respect them for what they were to us in the blacks' law. We carried that out. Our people told us how to treat others that weren't in our tribe, how to treat strangers.'

> In the system of etiquette which provided the ground rules for everyday life, various sorts of avoidance were prescribed as the chief means of showing respect—both physical avoidance and restrictions on conversations. . . . So Eliza and her sisters grew up feeling 'ashamed' or 'shy', as a matter of normal propriety, in the presence of many people, including strangers both black and white. (Kennedy and Donaldson 1982:7)

This account makes it clear that the Aboriginal concept is more closely related to avoidance, and therefore to fear, than the English concept of shame. In a prototypical situation of 'shame' something 'wrong' has already taken place. The Aboriginal concepts such as 'kunta' or 'kuyan' seem to evoke a situation when nothing 'wrong' has taken place, yet might happen and is to be avoided.

The future orientation of these concepts makes them closer to 'fear' than the English concept of 'shame', which is focussed on something real, not on something potential. The fact that in a prototypical situation of 'kunta' or 'kuyan' nothing wrong has happened (yet) makes this feeling closer to 'embarrassment' or 'shyness' than is English 'shame'. The fact that in a prototypical situation of 'kunta' or 'kuyan' the experiencer desires to avoid doing anything 'wrong' makes this feeling closer to 'respect' than is English 'shame'. It is understandable why a feeling such as 'kunta' or 'kuyan' can be used in regulating social conduct in Aboriginal society, in a positive way, in contrast to the negative way in which 'shame' or 'guilt' is used in Western societies.

It is worth noting, however, that in older English the word *shame* had (as the German word *Scham* still does) a meaning rather different from the one it has now and apparently closer to the concepts encoded in present-day Aboriginal languages. Consider, for example, the following line from Shakespeare, cited in SOED (1964):

> Have you no modesty, no maiden shame, no touch of bashfulness?

Clearly, in this passage the word *shame* doesn't imply anything *shameful* in the modern sense of the word, i.e., anything 'bad'. A maiden's 'shame' is a feeling which should protect a maiden from something bad, rather than a feeling resulting from something bad.

The Ngiyambaa concept of 'kuyan' could perhaps be explicated along the following lines:

> *kuyan*
> X thinks something like this:
>   I am near person Y
>   this is bad
>   something bad could happen because of this
>   people could think something bad about me because of this
>   I don't want this
> because of this, X feels something
> because of this, X wants to do something
> X wants not to be near this person

(For an illuminating discussion of the related concept of *getting shame* in Aboriginal English, see Harkins 1988 and 1990.)

A particularly interesting case of a language-specific conceptualisation of 'shame-like' emotions is provided by the Australian language Kayardild (Nicholas Evans, p.c.) In this language there are at least two words that the speakers themselves translate into English as *shame* (although they use also the word *shy,* as an alternative translation of both words). One of these words, *ngankiyaaja,* is based on the word *nganki* 'side of head', and it designates a kind of emotion that men are expected to feel in the presence of their mothers-in-law, or their sisters, whom they are supposed to avoid. The significance of the morphological clue is obvious, in the light of the strong taboo against facing one's mother-in-law or one's sister and against interacting with her directly. Evans reports that he has also heard the same word applied to small children's reaction to strangers (turning the head away in shyness). The other word, *bulwija,* is derived from the word for eyelashes, and it designates a kind of emotion that men and women are expected to exhibit in the presence of potential sexual partners. There, too (as Evans suggests), the meaning of the morphological clue is rather transparent: the lowering of the eyelashes can be expected to prevent the eyes of the two parties from meeting and from sending provocative gazes.

The present-day English concepts of 'shame', 'embarrassment', and 'fear' can, I think, be explicated as follows (for slightly different explications along similar lines, see Dineen 1990; Harkins 1990; Osmond 1990; see also Wierzbicka 1990b and In press c):

(X is) *ashamed*
X thinks something like this:
    people can know something bad about me
    because of this, people can think something bad about me
    I don't want this
    because of this, I would want to do something
    I don't know what I can do
because of this, X feels something bad

(X is) *embarrassed*
X thinks something like this:
    something happened to me now
    because of this, people here are thinking about me
    I don't want this
    because of this, I would want to do something
    I don't know what I can do
    I don't want to be here now
because of this, X feels something bad

(X is) *afraid*
X thinks something like this:
    something bad can happen
    I don't want this
    I want to do something because of this
    I don't know what I can do
because of this, X feels something bad

The concepts explicated here are perfectly discrete, because they can be represented by means of discrete semantic components (for a defence of discreteness in semantic analysis, see Wierzbicka 1985d). But are the feelings corresponding to concepts such as 'shame', 'fear', and 'embarrassment' discrete? Are they universally perceived and conceptualised as discrete, even in those cultures where they are not lexically distinguished from one another? And if not, then in what sense are they "discrete, fundamental emotions common to all mankind" (Izard 1969:265)?

7. Conclusion

In recent psychological literature, the thesis that emotions are "innate, universal" (Izard 1977:17) goes hand in hand with the claim (Izard 1969:265) that "each of these emotions has a characteristic expression or pattern which conveys particular meaning or information for the expresser and the perceiver". (Cf. also Ekman 1980, 1989; Ekman and Oster 1979.)

Nonetheless, the "analyses of Emotion Recognition tasks" based on these two assumptions "showed some differences between cultures and emotions". For example, some tests showed that pre-literate subjects in New Guinea failed to distinguish between fear and surprise. Trying to explain this discrepancy between prediction and empirical results, Izard (1969:264) does acknowledge that "it is quite possible that concepts like shame and contempt, and a fine distinction such as that between surprise and fear, will be extremely hard to translate into the spoken languages of preliterate cultures". But he does not see the linguistic problem as one of fundamental importance: "When we manage to surmount the language and communication barriers, it is entirely conceivable that the other emotions which I have termed fundamental can be validated in the pre-literate cultures."

But to say this is to underestimate the real conceptual differences between cultures. If a language does not discriminate lexically between, say, shame and fear, then an investigator may be unable to make its speakers perceive fear and shame as two different feelings by somehow simply "surmounting the language and communication barriers".

Different systems of emotion terms reflect different ways of conceptualising emotions, and conversely, any cross-cultural similarities in the conceptualisation of emotions will be reflected in the ways different societies converge in the labelling of emotions. But the extent of similarities and differences in the labelling and conceptualisation of emotions cannot be assessed without rigorous semantic analysis, and without a language-independent semantic metalanguage.

4

Describing the Indescribable

The idea that "not only ideas, but emotions, too, are cultural artefacts" (Geertz 1973:81), at one time described by a distinguished anthropologist as "complete rubbish" (Leach 1981), is becoming increasingly well documented. (Cf., in particular, Briggs 1970; Geertz 1974; Gerber 1985; Levy 1983; Rosaldo 1980; Scruton 1985; or Lutz 1983, 1985a and b, 1987.)

Solomon (1984:253) writes: "[V]ariation in emotional life is a very real part of cross-cultural differences, and not only in the more obvious variations in circumstances and expression". To develop this insight as a constructive thesis, he urges, "it would be necessary to turn to a piece by piece investigation of the concepts that make up our various emotions and their complex permutations, side by side with more holistic investigations of a number of other societies, such as those offered us by Levy (1973) and Briggs (1970). The flat-footed question 'Do these people get angry or not, and if so under what circumstances?' would be replaced by a broader inquiry into the over-all evaluative-conceptual schemes of appraisal and self-identification that give structure to emotional life. . . ."

It is the purpose of this chapter to undertake such a piece by piece investigation of the concepts that make up a number of different emotions in a number of societies, placing the semantic analysis of the concepts in question in the context of a broader inquiry into the culture. In many cases, it has been claimed that the emotion in question epitomises the culture as a whole. In all cases, it has been claimed that the emotion term in question is 'untranslatable', because the concept is unique.

I maintain, however, that no matter how 'unique' and 'untranslatable' an emotion term is, it can be translated on the level of semantic explication in a natural semantic metalanguage and that explications of this kind make possible that "translation of emotional worlds" (Lutz 1985a) which seems otherwise impossible to achieve.

The format used in the explications which will be proposed requires some discussion. Since, however, this discussion is not essential for my present purpose, I will postpone it until after the present survey. If some readers have doubts or reservations as to the general format used here, they are asked to suspend their judgement on this point until the final section of this chapter.

1. Survey of Some 'Untranslatable' Emotion Concepts

1.1 *Amae:* A Concept Representing "the True Essence of Japanese Psychology"

According to Doi (1981:169) *amae* is "a peculiarly Japanese emotion", although it has "universal relevance". It is "a thread that runs through all the various activities of Japanese society" (1981:26). It represents "the true essence of Japanese psychology" and is "a key concept for understanding Japanese personality structure" (1981:21). It is also a concept which provides "an important key to understanding the psychological differences between Japan and Western countries" (1974:310).

But what exactly is *amae?* Doi (1974:307–8) is convinced that there is no single word in English (or in other European languages) equivalent to it, a fact that "the Japanese find . . . hard to believe". Nonetheless, in his writings, Doi has offered innumerable clues which enable us to construct an English version of the concept of *amae*, not in a single word, of course, but in an explication. Doi has himself devoted an entire book (1981) to the elucidation of this concept and its ramifications.

As Doi (1974:307) explains, "*amae* is the noun form of *amaeru*, an intransitive verb which means 'to depend and presume upon another's benevolence'". It indicates "helplessness and the desire to be loved" (1981:22). The adjective *amai* means 'sweet', both with reference to taste and with reference to human relations: "If A is said to be *amai* to B, it means that he allows B to *amaeru*, i.e. to behave self-indulgently, presuming on some special relationship that exists between the two" (1981:29).

Amaeru can also be defined "by a combination of words such as 'wish to be loved' and 'dependency needs'" (1974:309). The Japanese dictionary *Daigenkai* defines *amae* as "to lean on a person's good will" (Doi 1981:72) or "to depend on another's affection" (1981:167).

But the most useful clue to the concept of *amae* is provided by the reference to the prototype on which this concept is based—a prototype which is not difficult to guess. "It is obvious that the psychological prototype of *amae* lies in the psychology of the infant in its relationship to its mother"; not a new-born infant but an infant who has already realised "that its mother exists independently of itself"; "[A]s its mind develops it gradually realises that itself and its mother are independent existences, and comes to feel the mother as something indispensable to itself; it is the craving for close contact thus developed that constitutes, one might say, *amae*" (1981:74).

On the basis of these and other similar clues we can explicate the concept of *amae* as follows:

> *amae*
> X thinks something like this:
> > Y feels something good toward me
> > Y wants to do good things for me
> > when I am with Y nothing bad can happen to me
> > I don't have to do anything
> > I want to be with Y
> because of this, X feels something

Doi stresses that *amae* presupposes conscious awareness. The subcomponent 'X thinks . . .' reflects this. The presumption of a "special relationship" is reflected in the component 'Y feels something good toward me'. The implication of self-indulgence is rooted in the emotional security of someone who knows that he is loved: "it is an emotion that takes the other person's love for granted" (1981:168); it is accounted for by the combination of components: 'Y feels something good toward me' and 'when I am with Y nothing bad can happen to me'. The component 'I don't have to do anything because of this' reflects the 'passive' attitude of an *amae* junior, who doesn't have to earn the mother figure's good will and protection by any special actions. The craving for close contact is accounted for in the component 'I want to be with Y'.

What are the reasons for "the prominence of *amae* in Japanese society" (Doi 1981:173)? According to Doi himself (1981:16), and to a number of other observers of Japanese society, this is linked with an "affirmative attitude toward the spirit of dependence on the part of the Japanese". Murase (1984:319) points out that "Unlike Westerners, Japanese children are not encouraged from an early age to emphasise individual independence or autonomy. They are brought up in a more or less 'interdependent' or *amae* culture. . .". He contrasts the Western culture, which he calls "ego culture", with the Japanese culture, which he calls "*sunao* culture", where *sunao*—like *amae*—symbolises "trustful relationships" fostering "openness and dependence" (1982:325). He also cites some other key words (besides *amae*) which "have been proposed as representing the essential nature of Japanese culture" and notes that they all point in the same direction: "empathy culture" (Minamoto 1969), "maternal principle" (Kawai 1976), "egg without eggshell" (Mori 1977), and so on.

According to Murase (1982:321–27), the Western "ego culture" is individual-centred, and the personality type which it promotes is "autonomous", "self-expanding", "harsh and solid", "strong", "competitive", "active, assertive, and aggressive"; by contrast, the Japanese "*sunao* culture" is "relationship-oriented", and the personality type which it promotes is "dependent", "humble, self-limiting", "mild and tender", "flexible and adaptable", "harmonious", "passive, obedient, and non-aggressive". The relationships fostered by the "ego culture" are "contractual", whereas the relationships fostered by the "*sunao* culture" are "unconditional". Murase links this with the prevalence of the "maternal principle" in Japan as against the prevalence of the "paternal principle" in the West. He also stresses such specifically Japanese values as "adaptation through accommodation", "conformity, or the merging of self and other", "a naive, trusting and empathic relationship with others", "obedience and docility" ("without the negative connotation in English"), and, again and again, "dependence".

It seems to me that these features of Japanese culture are indeed highly consistent with the prominence of the feelings of loving dependence elucidated by Doi (1974 and 1981). I hope that the explication of this crucial concept proposed here can help to make it a little more intelligible to the cultural outsider. (For further discussion of *amae* and a number of related concepts see Wierzbicka, 1991b.)

1.2 Respect and Etiquette: The Javanese Concept of *Sungkan*

According to Hildred Geertz (1974:257–58), *sungkan* "is something peculiarly Javanese". It is one of "three Javanese words, *wedi, isin,* and *sungkan,* which denote three kinds of feeling states felt to be appropriate to situations demanding respectful behavior".

The fundamental role of "respectful behavior" in Javanese culture is well known from the writings of Clifford Geertz, Hildred Geertz, and other scholars. It is reflected in a number of Javanese words and other linguistic devices which have no exact equivalents in European languages. To begin with, "the central concept of 'respect' (*urmat, adji*) is a notion so peculiarly Javanese that it cannot be easily translated" (Geertz 1974:257).

But what is 'untranslatable' on the level of words is nonetheless translatable on the level of universal semantic primitives and near-primitives. Since the limitations of space prevent any detailed discussion of all the Javanese emotion concepts mentioned by Geertz, I will confine myself here to an attempt to 'translate' into a universal semantic metalanguage that one which Geertz presents as the most peculiarly Javanese: the concept of *sungkan*.

Hildred Geertz (1974:259) writes: "Roughly speaking, *sungkan* refers to a feeling of respectful politeness before a superior or an unfamiliar equal, an attitude of constraint, a repression of one's own impulses and desires, so as not to disturb the emotional equanimity of one who may be spiritually higher. . . ." "If a delegation of official visitors comes to my house and they sit at my table, I sit off in a chair in the corner; that's *sungkan*." "If a guest comes to my house and I give him dinner, I say, 'sampun sungkan-sungkan' [don't be *sungkan*] and I mean, 'Don't stand on ceremony, eat a lot as if you were in your home.'"

In the socialisation, that is, "javanisation", of a Javanese child, *sungkan* comes at the end, after *wedi* (roughly, 'fear') and *isin* (roughly, 'shame/guilt'). It is the "last, culminating, ultra-Javanese kind of respect" (Geertz 1974:260), and it is a sign of refinement. In fact, "some village people in Java do not . . . make the distinction between *isin* and *sungkan,* considering the latter simply a more refined synonym. They associate the word with the world of aristocratic townsmen and its ranks and values, where the ritual of politeness is practiced with subtlety and sensitivity. To know *isin* is simply to know the basic social properties of self-control and avoidance of disapproval, whereas to know *sungkan* is to be able to perform the social minuet with grace" (1974:259).

But from Geertz's discussion it is quite clear that *sungkan* is not merely a refined synonym of *isin*. It is a word which designates a special emotional attitude cultivated by Javanese townspeople, an attitude which—unlike *isin*—doesn't seem to have semantic equivalents in any other parts of the world. This attitude can be portrayed as follows:

> *sungkan*
> X thinks something like this:
>   I cannot do what I want
>   another person is here

this person is not someone like me
this person could feel something bad if I did what I want
this person could think something bad of me
I don't want this
I want this person to think something good of me
because of this, X feels something
because of this, X doesn't do some things
because of this, X does some things

An emotional attitude of this kind is so elaborate, and implies such a complex conceptual structure, that it is not surprising that it takes years to acquire and that it has to be taught, for years, at home and at school. "How does the child learn this last, culminating, ultra-Javanese kind of respect? He has already learned an acute awareness of other people's moods and opinions, an attitude of tuning in on the desires of the other person, through his education in *isin*. And towards the end of the second phase he has begun to learn self-renunciation and impulse-control, for now he is likely to have a younger sibling to care for, one who, like himself as an infant, may not be permitted to be frustrated or upset. And now his father, formerly warm and affectionate, like an 'insider', begins to act like an 'outsider' toward him, and to expect him to behave in his presence according to the social forms appropriate to outsiders. The child finds himself now feeling *isin* in front of his father, and being told, moreover, to be *sungkan* in his presence" (Geertz 1974:260).

Geertz's comments on the importance of the "emotional lexicon" as an instrument of socialisation and acculturation seem to me penetrating and insightful. In particular, she points out (1974:262) that "the cultural system . . . provides recipes for the child's reactions" to the "various transitions through which he must pass". "The culture presents not only a set of suggested answers on *how to behave* in these situations, but also clues to *how to feel* about his actions."

The crucial point is that these clues are encoded in the emotion terms provided by a given culture. If we manage to decode such terms and to translate them into a universal semantic metalanguage, we can make the cultural recipes provided by different cultures comparable and intelligible to outsiders.

1.3 *Liget:* The Driving Force of the Headhunting Ilongots

As shown by Rosaldo (1980), the concept of *liget* is of fundamental importance in the culture of the Ilongot tribe of the Philippines. Glossed as 'energy, anger, passion', *liget* is clearly the driving force in the lives of the Ilongots. It expresses itself equally in the passion to kill as in the passion to work. It implies vitality and fierceness, a will to compete, and a will to triumph. "Without liget to move our hearts," the Ilongots say, "there would be no human life" (1980:47). In fact, even babies "are the product of male *liget*, 'concentrated' in the form of sperm".

By a revealing metaphorical extension, *liget* is also ascribed to certain inanimate objects and to the forces of nature, such as chili pepper, liquor, storm, wind, rain, or fire. *Liget* suggests here "potency, energy, intensity, the irritating heat of chili peppers, the rush of rapids, or the force of wind" (Rosaldo 1980:45–46). *Liget* implies not only "energy and irritation, but also a sense of violent action and of intentional shows of force". Typically, *liget* is born not so much of inherent qualities of things as of their interaction. For example, "tobacco gives desired *liget* to the yeast that people use in making wine. Winds grow fiercer when they bump into a fence or an obstruction; an irritating whiff of ginger revitalises 'passion' in a killer; chili can give *liget* to a stew".

In human life, however—which is the basic domain of *liget*—*liget* is typically born of 'envy', of a desire to compete and to triumph over one's equals.

Manifestations of *liget* in human life can be manifold, focussed or chaotic, productive or destructive. *Liget* can express itself in "fierce work", when one's heart "goes beyond its limits" (Rosaldo 1980:46) and when one sweats and pants in quest of admiration and envy. It can also express itself in fierce killing and in celebration of killing.

"Concentrated *liget* is what makes babies, stirs one on to work, determines killers, gives people strength and courage, narrows vision on a victim or on a task" (Rosaldo 1980:48–49). Good *liget* "is realised in activity and purpose, in a willingness to stay awake all night and travel far when hunting, in a readiness to climb tall trees or harvest in hot sunlight, in an aura of competence and vitality". But bad *liget* is frightening, "paralysing and confusing"; it can lead to "sporadic bursts of basket-slashing, knife-waving violence".

Liget plays a key role in the conceptualisation of experience: "Ilongots use the vagaries of *liget* as a frame for understanding their experience at the same time that they experience it as difficult to control" (Rosaldo 1980:51). "The energy that is *liget* can generate both chaos and concentration, distress and industry, a loss of sense and reason, and an experience of clarification and release. These various possibilities are imaged in terms that link the emotional dilemmas of individual human actors to certain general conditions of human existence. . . ; these constitute a system that embodies not only the core of Ilongot emotion, but also the stuff of life and human effort as Ilongots in their reflections know them" (1980:47).

Rosaldo makes it clear that the concept of *liget* plays an absolutely essential role in the Ilongot culture. But what exactly is *liget*? Rosaldo herself is at pains to show that *liget* is a unique Ilongot concept with no equivalent in English, and that it reflects attitudes different from those codified in Western culture. Nonetheless some other anthropologists were able to conclude from Rosaldo's data that *liget* is essentially the same as the English *anger*. For example, Spiro writes:

> I would suggest that it is not the case, insofar as anger is concerned at least, that 'in important ways [Ilongot] feelings and the ways their feelings work must differ from our own' (Rosaldo [1984]). To be sure, their anger seems to be much more intense than ours, and its expression is much more violent, but, these quantitative dimensions aside, their anger and ours seem to work in similar ways. They, like we, get angry when frustrated, and they, like we, usually repress their anger in culturally appropriate contexts only to express it symbolically in culturally appropriate ones. This indicates, I would suggest, that human feelings and the ways in which they work are determined not so much by the characteristics of particularistic culture

patterns but by the transcultural characteristics of a generic human mind. (1984:334)

In my view, there is no reason why someone's faith in the existence of certain "transcultural characteristics of a generic human mind" should be undermined by data such as those concerning the Ilongot conceptualisation of emotions, but the confident identification of the Ilongot concept of *liget* with the English concept of *anger* seems to me to involve a serious error.

Careful examination of the evidence shows that the differences between *liget* and *anger* are not quantitative but qualitative, and that in fact the two words embody two entirely different (though overlapping) concepts. The following explications make these qualitative differences explicit:

> *liget*
> X thinks something like this:
>   other people can do something
>   they could think that I can't do it
>   I don't want this
>   because of this, I want to do something
>   I can do it
> because of this, X feels something
> because of this, X wants to do something
> when someone feels like this, they can do things
>   that they can't do at other times

> *angry*
> X thinks something like this:
>   this person (Y) did something bad
>   I don't want this
>   I would want to do something bad to this person
> because of this, X feels something bad toward Y
> because of this, X wants to do something

(For a slightly different analysis of 'anger', see Wierzbicka, In press a and Forthcoming. See also Goddard 1991.) As these explications show, *liget* has a competitive character and is related to envy and ambition, but there is nothing like that in the concept of *anger*. *Anger* has its basis in the thought that 'someone did something bad', but there is nothing like that in the concept of *liget*.

Consequently, *anger* implies a negative feeling toward the target person ('because of this, X feels something bad toward Y'), but *liget* doesn't. In fact, *liget* doesn't imply that there is any specific target person at all. Moreover, the feeling associated with *liget* doesn't have to be a 'bad feeling'. It *can* be a 'bad feeling', but it can also be an intoxicatingly 'good feeling' (depending on one's perception of one's chances of success).

It is true that both *anger* and *liget* are likely to hurt somebody, that is, to cause someone to 'feel something bad'. But in the case of *liget,* one doesn't necessarily have an urge to hurt somebody, as one does in the case of *anger* (whether or not one acts on that urge is another matter). The fierce headhunter kills not because he wants to hurt, to punish, to inflict pain, but because he wants to prove to himself and to others that he is as good as anybody else (and perhaps better). There is nothing like that in the concept of *anger*.

Furthermore, the person who is likely to get hurt through *liget* may well be the experiencer of *liget* himself. When one is sweating and panting in "fierce" work, one is disregarding one's own 'bad feelings' (tiredness, aches, pain, and so on). One is determined not to let such 'bad feelings' (whether in oneself or in another person) interfere with one's action. This is ruthless determination, which "narrows vision on a task", not an urge to hurt.

Finally, *liget* spurs people to action, gives them strength and courage, enables them to go beyond their limits, and leads them to achievements and to triumphs. This is reflected in the component 'when someone feels like this, they can do things that they can't do at other times'. Since, however, *liget* can also lead to destructive and unplanned actions, for example, "basket-slashing, knife-waving violence", the things that one can do because of *liget* are not described in the explication as 'good things', or as 'things that one wants to do'.

It seems to me that the explication of *liget* sketched here accounts correctly for the entire range of this concept's use, as reported by Rosaldo, and explains adequately "the ambivalence surrounding *liget*" and deriving "from the fact that it can lead in a variety of directions" (Rosaldo 1980:47). Anger is not similarly ambivalent, and if it is not repressed or sublimated, it can lead only in one direction, that of intentionally 'doing something bad to someone'.

I conclude that the Ilongot concept of *liget* is indeed unique and cannot be identified with the English concept of *anger*. If there are any "transcultural characteristics of a generic human mind", conceptualisation of emotions in terms of either *anger* or *liget* is certainly not among their number. It is an illusion to think that "in the human being the expression of anger and the experiential phenomenon of *anger* are innate, pan-cultural, universal phenomena" (Izard 1977:64). There is no reason to think that *anger* is any more 'innate', 'pan-cultural', or 'universal' than *liget*.

1.4 Emotions on a Pacific Atoll: Ifaluk Feeling States

Lutz (1985a:83) paints a vivid and rather moving picture of human existence on the tiny Ifaluk atoll in the Western Pacific. "Seen from a steamship offshore, the atoll of Ifaluk seems a tightly bounded and somewhat precarious community, sitting as it does at most fifteen feet above sea level in an area of frequent typhoons and few neighboring islands. Four hundred thirty people share one-half square mile of land, and survive through fishing, the gathering of fruits and coconut and taro cultivation. The cooperative and non-aggressive patterns they have successfully developed, in part in response to these material conditions, have made for dense networks of connections between individuals."

What do people living on the Ifaluk atoll feel? How do they talk about their emotions? How do they conceptualise their feelings? Lutz has tried to explore these questions in a number of careful studies (1982, 1985a and b, 1987). The following analysis is based entirely on her data and on her observations. (For an earlier version of this analysis, see Wierzbicka 1988a.)

1.4.1 Fago

Lutz (1987) glosses the Ifaluk word *fago* by means of three English words: *compassion, love,* and *sadness*. In an earlier article on the same subject (Lutz 1982), *fago* is glossed as *love*. It is obvious that this word has in fact no exact equivalent in English and that it expresses some concept which is more salient in the Ifaluk culture than in Western culture. But what concept?

Lutz mentions the following situations as likely triggers of the feeling of *fago*: illness, a departure from the island, lack of food. In her view, this feeling has a hidden "goal" which can be formulated as follows: "change the situation, by filling the need of the unfortunate party" (1987:301). Actions which naturally follow from the feeling of *fago* include the following: to give the target person food, to cry, to speak to him or her kindly (1985a:295).

As a first approximation, I propose the following explication of the core sense of *fago:*

> *fago*
> X thinks of person Y
> X feels something good toward Y
> X thinks something like this:
>> something bad can happen to a person
>> when something bad happens to someone, some people should do
>>> something good for this person
>> I don't want bad things to happen to Y
> when X thinks that something bad can happen to Y, X feels something bad
> because of this, X wants to do something good for Y

This explication does not fit all the situations when *fago* can be used (as described, in particular, in Lutz 1988). The range of these situations, however, is so broad that I don't think any unitary formula could be proposed for them, beyond the following three components:

> X is thinking of person Y
> X feels something good toward Y
> X wants to do something good for Y

But a broad formula such as this would fail to account for the links between *fago* and *compassion* and *sadness,* repeatedly emphasised by Lutz. I suspect, therefore, that *fago* may be polysemous and that two different sense of this word should in fact be distinguished: the core sense explicated here and the more peripheral sense, which is closer to something like admiration than to something like compassion or sadness. Lutz (1988:137) describes this second type of *fago* as follows:

While most of the contexts in which the word *fago* is used represent major or minor disasters for those involved, the emotion is also importantly linked to encounters with people whom the Ifaluk define as exemplary in crucial kinds of ways. As one person told me, "You *fago* someone because they do not misbehave. You *fago* them because they are calm and socially intelligent."

The formula proposed in the present chapter is not meant to cover this second use of *fago,* for which a separate formula would probably be needed.

Nonetheless, the formula proposed here is still very comprehensive, and it covers a wide range of types of situations. In particular, it applies not only to people to whom something bad has already happened but also to those to whom something bad might happen. For example, it could apply to the feelings of a woman who heard "her younger brother singing as he fished from his canoe in the lagoon" and who said, as she heard him, "I had a bit of *fago* for him" (Lutz 1988:121). Apparently, nothing bad has happened to the young man yet, but his sister appears to think of him as vulnerable (as well as dear), and this thought activates her desire to protect him and to do good things for him.

The explication proposed here would also account for the fact that *fago* is seen "as an emotion that can prevent violence. . . . If one feels *fago* for a potential victim, the desire to hurt is short-circuited. In socializing children, a parent's appeal to *fago* is often made as a way of promoting gentle (as well as generous) behavior" (Lutz 1988:136).

Can the explication proposed here account for the association between *fago* and death? The fact that "the dying person is the prototypical object of *fago*" is easily accounted for in terms of this explication (one doesn't want something bad to happen to the dying person, one wants to do good things for him or her, and one is very much aware that bad things can happen to a person and that one should try to do good things for those to whom they happen). It is less obvious that the same explication applies also to *fago* which occurs *after* somebody's death, as in the following case: "The last time I [experienced] *fago* was when our 'mother' died two days ago. We really felt bad inside. It was like our insides were being torn. We beat our chests and scratched our faces because our *fago* was so strong, because there is no other time that we will see her" (Lutz 1988:125). But, in fact, I believe that the proposed formula applies here, too: the grieving woman who beats her chest and scratches her face does not (yet) accept the fact that "something bad" has happened to her mother, and she still wants to do good things for her (although there is perhaps nothing, or little, that can be done).

In other cases, it is the awareness that something bad has happened to a person (often, a stranger) that gives rise to a desire to do something good for him or her. (For example, "'we *fago* the new students [the freshmen] because they aren't used to Ulithian custom, and they don't know all of the taboos that exist there'. Implied here is that the boys must be anxious or afraid (. . .) in the new and unfamiliar setting" (Lutz 1988:135).)

It seems to me that the formula proposed is sufficiently vague and comprehensive to cover all these different cases of *fago* (though not those similar to admiration).

If this analysis of *fago* is even approximately correct, then *fago* does not have very much in common with *sadness* (cf. Wierzbicka, In press a and c). Nonetheless, here, as in *sadness,* there is an incompatibility between the real ('something bad can happen to a person') and the desired ('I don't want bad things to happen to Y'). In the case of *sadness,* however, this incompatibility takes a different form ('something bad happened'—'I would want: it didn't happen').

The closest English counterpart of the concept *fago* seems to be *compassion.* But the fact that bilingual informants gloss *fago* as *love* rather than *compassion,* and that Lutz, too, finds it necessary to add *love* and *sadness* to *compassion* in her gloss, suggests that *fago* is both 'warmer' and 'stronger' than *compassion.* Trying to capture both the similarities and the differences between *fago* and *compassion* I propose the following explication for the latter:

> *compassion*
>
> (a) X thinks something like this:
> (b)   something bad happened to Y
> (c)   because of this, Y feels something bad
> (d)   if it happened to me, I would feel something bad
> (e) when X thinks this, X feels something good toward Y

What *compassion* and *fago* share is the component 'X feels something good toward Y', linked with the idea of 'bad things happening to Y'. But *compassion* is much more specific in this respect than *fago: compassion* presupposes that something bad has already happened to Y, whereas *fago* allows for the possibility that nothing bad has happened yet but that the experiencer sees the target person as vulnerable and in need of protection.

Furthermore, *compassion* does not imply an active attitude ('X wants to do something good for Y') or the more general assumption that 'if something bad happens to someone, some people should do something good for this person'. *Fago,* Lutz (1985a:85) points out, is "a sadness that activates", but in the case of *compassion* neither the 'twinge in the heart' nor the 'warm feeling' towards the unfortunate person has to be sufficiently strong to lead to an urge to do something for that person. The concept of *compassion* differs in this respect from the concept of *love* (as in "X loves person Y", which always carries such an implication ('X wants to do something good for Y'); cf. Wierzbicka 1986c). But of course the Western concept of *love* is not limited to situations when something bad is happening to the target person. It implies a kind of universality (in the sense that it can be addressed to anybody and under any circumstances); but it is also individual and personal (in the sense that it implies a personal bond with the target person). It can be explicated as follows:

> *love* (X *loves* person Y)
>
> (a) X knows Y
> (b) X feels something good toward Y
> (c) X wants to be with Y
> (d) X wants to do good things for Y

The concept of *fago* doesn't include component (a) (it can be extended to strangers) or component (c) (which suggests a kind of personal attraction to another person). It does contain, however, components (b) and (d).

Clearly, the explication of *love* given here doesn't fit sentences like 'I love cottage cheese' or 'I love opera'. If one 'loves' cottage cheese or opera, one doesn't want to cause good things to happen to these things. This, however, is a different meaning of *love*. In support of this claim, I would adduce the following evidence: In sentences with inanimate objects, *love* is used hyperbolically, as an emphatic and deliberately exaggerated substitute for the unmarked and expected word *like*. The speaker wants to convey something along the following lines: 'I like it so much that I don't want to use the word which one would normally expect (*like*); I want to use a different word, which says more than that'. Consequently, when used with inanimate objects, *love* is usually endowed with special prosodic clues, which signal an expressive emphasis and an emotional attitude to the subject matter. In addition to prosodic clues, the emphatic exaggeration can also be signalled by particles, especially by *just*. A sentence such as 'I love cottage cheese' conveys something similar to what is conveyed by the sentence 'I just *love* cottage cheese'. But the sentences 'Robin loves Hilary' and 'Robin just *loves* Hilary' are not similarly close. It is normal for a mother to love her baby, but it would be odd to hear that somebody 'just *loves*' her baby. There are reasons, therefore, to distinguish the use of *love* as a hyperbolic emphasiser from its use as an ordinary verb.

A situation where a language doesn't have a word for *love* in general but does have a word combining 'good feelings' toward other people with elements of compassion, pity, or protectiveness (toward the unfortunate, weak, or helpless) is known from many other languages of the world (cf., for example, Levine's (1981) data for Tibetan; Briggs' (1970) data for Utku Eskimo; or Gerber's (1985) data for Samoan, some of which are mentioned in this chapter). This is a point which may be familiar to anthropologists but appears to have gone unnoticed in the majority of psychological literature on emotions. For example, Eibl-Eibesfeldt (1971), author of a book entitled *Love and hate: on the natural history of basic behaviour patterns*, apologises for extending, on occasion, the terms *love* and *hate* to animals, but he has not the slightest doubt that they can be extended, unreservedly, to all humans, and that they provide 'natural', 'basic' clues to human psychology. He writes (1971:6): "In this book I make quite frequent use of the term 'love'. By this I mean not only sexual love but more generally the emotional, personal bond between one man and another or the bond arising from identification with a particular group. The counterpart of *love* is hate. . . . Strictly speaking we can only use the terms 'love' and 'hate' in this sense in the case of man."

What most psychologists do not seem to realise is that *love* is no more a "basic human behaviour pattern" than *fago* is. The concept of *love* is not a universal human concept; it is not clear why one should regard *love* as more 'human' or more 'basic' than *fago*.

Of course different people can attach different importance to different concepts. It could be argued that the modern European concept of *love* (*amour, Liebe, amore*, and so on) is particularly important and that the emergence of this concept in Western folk philosophy constitutes a significant stage in the development of human ideas and human values. But whatever one thinks about the significance of *love,* it is an illusion to think that it is a universal, 'natural', or 'basic' human concept. It is no more such a concept than *fago* is.

1.4.2 Song

Lutz glosses the Ifaluk word *song* as 'justifiable anger'. Her discussion shows clearly, however, that this word doesn't mean the same as the English word *anger,* and not only because *song* is supposed to be 'justifiable'. Evidently, *song* is a less aggressive feeling than *anger,* a feeling which is less likely to lead to physical violence. Typically, *song* manifests itself in reprimands, refusal to eat, or pouting. What is more, in some cases *song* can lead to suicide, or in any case to an attempted suicide. The hidden "goal" of *song* is, according to Lutz (1987:301), "to change the situation by altering the behaviour of the offending person", but the actions caused by *song* are often directed toward oneself rather than toward the guilty person (for example, an attempted suicide rather than an attempted murder). From an earlier article on the same subject (Lutz 1982:121) we learn that *song* is regarded as "good for people (and especially parents) to feel and express when a wrongdoing has occurred. It is only through the observation of their parents' *song* in particular situations that children are said to learn the difference between right and wrong." Accordingly, people in a higher position, who are responsible for other people's behaviour, can be expected to feel and show *song* particularly frequently. "An elder is more often *song* (justifiably angry) at a younger person, than at a peer or at a higher-ranked individual. The chiefs are often said to be *song* at those who have broken rules or taboos" (1982:122).

All of these observations indicate that the concept of *song* differs from the concept of *anger* and suggest the following conceptual structure:

> *song*
> (a) X thinks something like this:
> (b)   this person (Y) did something bad
> (c)   people should not do things like this
> (d)   this person should know this
> (e) because of this, X feels something bad
> (f) because of this, X wants to do something

This is certainly close to the conceptual structure of *anger,* but it is by no means identical to it, as shown by the following explication, repeated from the previous section for the reader's convenience:

> *anger*
> (a) X thinks something like this:
> (b)   this person (Y) did something bad
> (c)   I don't want this
> (d)   I would want to do something bad to this person
> (e) because of this, X feels something bad toward Y
> (f) because of this, X wants to do something

Component (b) is identical in both cases: 'person Y did something bad'. Component (c), however, is in each case different. In the case of *song,* component (c) suggests that there is something 'objectively' wrong about Y's action ('Y shouldn't do things like this'); in the case of *anger* component (c) suggests that what is involved is the personal will of the experiencer, rather than an objective evaluation ('I don't want this').

This difference in component (c) is logically linked to a difference in component (e): in both cases, X feels 'something bad', but in the case of *anger* this feeling is directed toward the culprit ('X feels something bad toward Y because of this'), whereas in the case of *song* the feeling is not oriented specifically toward anyone ('X feels something bad').

This difference in component (e) is linked, in turn, with a difference in component (d): in the case of *anger,* the negative feeling is directed toward the guilty person and it leads to an urge to do something bad to that person ('I would want to do something bad to Y because of this'); in the case of *song,* the urge to do something is not oriented toward anyone, and it can express itself in a refusal to eat as much as in a reprimand ('X wants to do something because of this'). This doesn't mean, of course, that *song* can express itself in any action whatsoever. All the actions mentioned by Lutz (a reprimand, a refusal to eat, a pout, an attempted suicide) have a common denominator: X wants Y to know that Y has done something bad and reprehensible and to draw consequences from this. Hence the need for component (d): 'Y should know this'.

Lutz observes that the Ifaluk culture enjoins people to avoid aggression and that in its hierarchy of values it ranks this injunction much higher than Western culture, and in particular, than American culture: "[A]lthough both the Ifaluk and Americans may have the goal of avoiding violence, rules of physical aggression in the two societies and beliefs about those rules are in dramatic contrast, in part due to cultural differences in the importance attached to that goal" (1987:299–300).

The fact that the Ifaluk language has no word corresponding to the English word *anger* and that the closest Ifaluk counterpart of this concept is much 'softer' and closer to *reproach* seems to constitute a lexical confirmation of this difference between the two cultures. In the explications proposed earlier the conceptual relations in question are portrayed clearly and explicitly.

1.4.3 Ker

Lutz (1987) glosses the Ifaluk word *ker* as 'happiness/excitement', thus making clear that it cannot be matched exactly with any one English word. But the meaning of *ker* can be established on the basis of the information about the behaviour typically associated with the feeling in question. Typically, people who feel *ker* laugh, talk a lot, "misbehave", "walk around", neglect their work, show off, and so on. According to Lutz, the hidden "goal" of the feeling of *ker* consists in "making use of the resources of the situation" and in "maintaining the situation".

Ker is an emotion "people see as pleasant but amoral. It is often, in fact, *immoral* because someone who is happy/excited is more likely to be unafraid of other people. While this lack of fear may lead them to laugh and talk with people, it may also make them misbehave or walk around showing off or 'acting like a big shot'" (Lutz 1988:167).

All these clues together suggest the following conceptual structure:

ker
(a) X thinks something like this:
(b)   something good is happening to me
(c)   I want this
(d) because of this, X feels something good
(e) because of this, X doesn't think of what other people would think of X
(f) because of this, X could do things that X shouldn't do

The first three components of this explication taken together correspond roughly to the concept of *joy*, although it appears that *joy* is less egocentric than *ker* and at the same time a little more 'reflective' (thoughtful), that is, that it is based on the thought 'something good is happening' rather than 'something good is happening to me'. (*Happiness*, like *ker*, is egocentric, and it is based on the thought 'something good happened to me' (cf. Wierzbicka, In press a and c).)

In contrast to *joy* and *happiness*, however, *ker* implies a lack of concern for other people's reactions (component (e)) and, as a consequence, a danger of moral transgressions (component (f)).

If *joy* implies a thought of something good that is happening, *excitement* implies a thought of something that is to happen in the near future. Roughly (ignoring here the difference between *feeling excited* and *feeling excitement;* cf. Wierzbicka 1980:104):

excitement
(a) X thinks something like this: something good will happen to me now
(b) because of this, X feels something good
(c) because of this, X can't think of other things

Excitement, in contrast to *ker*, doesn't suggest that the person in question is likely to 'misbehave'. Moreover, *excitement* differs from *ker* in its temporal perspective: *ker* is rooted in the present, and this is why it can constitute a loose translation equivalent for both *happiness/joy* and *excitement*. If *happiness* involves something that has already happened, and *joy*, something that is happening *now*, *excitement* involves something that will happen in the near future. *Ker* doesn't presuppose a similar distinction, embracing in its temporal perspective a broadly understood 'present time', which can include both recent events that have already happened and forthcoming events (that are going to happen soon); as long as these events are so vivid in the experiencer's mind that they temporarily obscure everything else, including the sense of duty and the sense of propriety.

1.4.4 Nguch

According to Lutz (1982:119), *nguch* "is a much-used emotion word that labels feelings in situations where one must accept that one's individual goals are thwarted". It is used "in daily life to describe the frustration engendered by the obedience required to those of higher rank". But it can also be engendered by monotonous work, or by "a noxious but unavoidable situation" such as repeated requests for tobacco from a mentally retarded youth. "If a woman has been grating coconut in the midday heat for three hours, she will often declare herself *nguch*. If someone makes repeated requests for cigarettes or some other object, that request cannot be legitimately denied, but the severe drain on one's tobacco supply is nonetheless seen as a loss. To call oneself *nguch* in that situation is to call for some relief from a frustration while at the same time recognizing that the drains on one's time and resources are legitimate" (Lutz 1985a:87).

All of these comments, and illustrations, suggest the following conceptual structure:

> *nguch*
> (a) X thinks something like this:
> (b)   this (Z) has been happening to me for a long time
> (c)   because someone else (Y) wants it
> (d)   I don't want it (Z) to happen any more
> (e)   because of this, I would want to do something bad to Y
> (f)   I shouldn't do it
> (g)   I can't do anything
> (h) because of this, X feels something bad

The English expression *sick and tired* implies a component similar to (b), but not necessarily a reference to another person: because, unlike *nguch*, the feeling in question doesn't have to be caused by "noxious social obligations" (Lutz 1987:307). Components (d) and (h) of *nguch* are no doubt present here as well ('I don't want this to happen any more', 'because of this X feels something bad'). But unlike *nguch*, *sick and tired* doesn't convey a feeling of helplessness (component (g)) or of an obligation to put up with the situation (component (f)). It is often used to express 'rebellion', whereas *nguch* suggests a readiness to submit to a frustrating situation, rather than potential defiance.

> *sick and tired*
> (a) X thinks something like this:
>   this (Z) has been happening for a long time
> (b)   I don't want it (Z) to happen any more
> (c) because of this, X feels something bad

As this explication (similar to that proposed in Osmond 1990) suggests, the expression *sick and tired* doesn't necessarily have to refer to interpersonal relations, in the way *nguch* does: *nguch* is a reaction to other people's behaviour, but *sick and tired* doesn't have to be (although it is likely to be).

As for *boredom*, it has even less to do with social relations, being predominantly psychological in nature. Nonetheless, it does have components in common with *nguch*, apart from the obvious 'X feels something bad'. Like *nguch*, it implies that something has been going on for a long time, that one feels something bad because of that, that one doesn't want it to continue, and that one would want to do something because of that. There is also a vague implication that one cannot do what one wants to do, though in this case one doesn't necessarily know what one would want to do. Unlike in the case of *nguch,* the main problem is that one's thoughts are not occupied with anything interesting (either because one is doing nothing or because one is doing something uninteresting).

As a first approximation, the following formula could be proposed for *boredom:*

> *boredom*
> (a) X thinks something like this:
> (b)   for some time, I haven't been doing anything that I would want
>   to think about
> (c)   I don't want this
> (d)   I would want to do something that I would want to think about
> (e)   I can't do anything like this now
> (f) because of this, X feels something bad

1.4.5 Waires

Lutz (1982, 1987) glosses *waires* as 'worry/conflict'. As an example of a characteristic situation associated with the feeling of *waires,* she mentions the case of a young woman who learned about the illness of her 'mother', living on a different island. The young woman wants to visit her mother, but she also wants to stay with her sister, who is in her ninth month of pregnancy. Hence a conflict of motivations and a feeling of *waires.*

According to Lutz (1987:303), "by asserting her *waires* she declared herself to simultaneously hold those two, now conflicting goals". The "program of action" associated with the feeling of *waires* can be formulated as follows: "Seek further information. Seek assistance in decision making".

These clues suggest the following conceptual structure:

> *waires*
> X thinks something like this:
>   I want to do two things
>   I know that if I do one, I cannot do the other
>   if I don't do one, it will be bad
>   if I don't do the other, it will be bad
>   I don't know what I should do
> because of this, X feels something bad

As this explication suggests, the concept of *waires* is close to the concept encapsulated in the English expression *to be in two minds.* The latter expression, however, is not the name of a feeling; moreover, it does not imply an unpleasant state of mind, as *waires* does. It appears that the English expression doesn't refer to any 'bad' consequences; it can be applied to a situation when the choice involves two 'good' possibilities:

X is *in two minds*
X thinks something like this:
    I want to do two things
    I know that if I do one, I cannot do the other
    I don't know what I should do

Returning to *waires,* it is interesting to note that like most of the other Ifaluk concepts discussed here, it links the concept of 'feel' with the concepts of 'should', 'do', and 'bad' or 'good'. This is consistent with Lutz's (1985a:91) claim that in many non-Western cultures "emotions may be grouped with moral values" and that this may reflect a cultural orientation different from that reflected in "the middle-class Euro-American stance toward the value of a 'rich' (i.e. introspective) inner emotional life".

According to Lutz (1987:292) there are between ten and fifteen Ifaluk emotion terms "which can be heard in daily conversation" (and there are almost one hundred words in at least occasional use that represent these concepts). The five emotion terms analysed here belong to the former category, and thus they constitute between one third and one half of the basic emotional vocabulary used by the Ifaluks. They are indeed culture-specific, but they are not impenetrable to outsiders. When they are translated into the universal semantic metalanguage, the similarities and the differences between these concepts and their closest counterparts elsewhere in the world become apparent and their cultural significance can more easily be appreciated.

1.5 "Hawaii—the World of *Aloha*"

To anyone passing through Hawaii the concept of 'aloha' imposes itself as an intriguing riddle. One encounters the word everywhere, especially in the tourist industry. Ubiquitous signs welcome one "to the *Aloha* state". There are "*Aloha* buses" (sightseeing buses), "*Aloha* restaurants", shopping centres "Where *Aloha* comes alive", "*Aloha* Towers", "*Aloha* Stadiums", "*Aloha* Funway Rentals", "*A-loha* Airlines"; there is an "*Aloha* Flea Market"; and so on, ad infinitum. In fact, even before one goes to Hawaii, advertisements in travel agencies lure one with that key word: "Discover a different world . . . a world of private coves, native hearts filled with *aloha,* a world where the sun sets each evening just for you" (*Guide to Oahu,* February 5–11, 1988, which also lists the businesses mentioned).

What exactly is *aloha,* the bewildered tourist asks? "It seems to mean every damned thing", I have heard one tourist exclaim.

The anthropologist Francis Newton (1984:88) replies characteristically: "*Aloha* is a complex and profound sentiment. Such emotions defy definition. . . ." Some writers on the subject (for example, Ito 1985:308) gloss *aloha* as 'love', but others insist that *aloha* cannot be identified with love and suggest that it is a much more elusive and mysterious feeling. For example, Andrews (1974:51) describes *aloha* as "A word expressing different feelings; as love; affection; gratitude; kindness; pity; compassion; grief; the modern common salutation at meeting, at parting". In a similar vein, Pukui and Elbert (1986:21) gloss *aloha* as "love, affection, compassion, mercy, sympathy, pity, kindness, sentiment, grace, charity; greeting; salutation, regards . . ." , and so on and so on. (Cf. also Akoka 1966.)

What descriptions of this kind make clear is, first, that the concept of 'aloha' is related to the concept of 'love'; second, that *aloha* is not identical with *love;* and third, that *aloha* encapsulates a concept for which no word is available in English. I suggest that this concept can be spelt out as follows:

> *aloha*
> X feels something good toward Y
> X wants Y to feel something good

Unlike *love* ("X loves Y"), *aloha* doesn't imply personal acquaintance (although it is of course compatible with it), and it is readily extended to strangers. Consequently, the component 'X knows Y', which I have postulated for *love* (see Wierzbicka 1986c and the preceding section of this chapter), is not included in the explication of *aloha*.

Since *aloha*, unlike *love*, doesn't imply any 'special relationship' between the experiencer and the target person, it implies no feeling of personal happiness caused by contact with the target person and no desire for such a contact. Unlike *love*, therefore, it doesn't include the components 'X wants to be with Y' or 'when X is with Y, X feels something good'.

Finally, *aloha* doesn't imply any desire to do something good for the target person (although it is of course compatible with such a desire). It doesn't warrant, therefore, the inclusion of the component 'X wants to do something good for Y', which has been postulated for *love*.

Generally speaking, therefore, *aloha* implies 'good feelings' toward other people and 'good wishes' for other people, without any implication of personal bond, commitment, or active concern. Its component 'X wants Y to feel something good' makes it very appropriate for use in greetings and leave-takings, but it differs from English good wishes by its emotional component ('X feels something good toward Y'). If it is related to love, it is a very diluted kind of love; it is warmer, however, than mere good wishes, or mere friendliness.

The Hawaiians are quite right, therefore, when they insist that their *aloha* is something unique, something with no equivalent in English. It is certainly not *love*, but it is a word which implies a general attitude of 'good feelings' toward other people, combined with a kind of light-hearted good wishes ('I want you to feel something good'). These good wishes focus not so much on good things that the speaker wants to happen to the other people as on good feelings that he or she would want other people to have. When advertising brochures alternate their titles between "Welcome to Paradise", "Welcome to the World of Polynesia", and "Welcome to the Aloha State", they exploit, I think, the implication that the target person will 'feel something good' and that the Hawaiians want other people to 'feel something good'. The invitation "discover a world of native hearts filled with *aloha*, a world where the sun sets each evening just for you!" promises no less than that—but probably no more.

Anticipating the following discussion of concepts related to *aloha* in other Polynesian languages (Tahitian, for example, Levy 1973; Samoan, cf. Gerber 1985; for a discussion of a similar concept in Marquesan, see Kirkpatrick 1973), I will note here that *aloha* differs from them considerably, in lacking their seriousness and their link with 'sadness' or 'compassion'. It is tempting to speculate that this difference may be the result of a change in the meaning of *aloha*, which in turn may be an effect of the americanisation of Hawaii over the last century. In support of this suggestion I would adduce the fact that the use of *aloha* in conventional formulae such as 'good morning', 'good-bye', or 'hello' (Pukui and Elbert 1986) is a recent phenomenon. Thus, Andrews (1974:51) writes of *aloha: "Aloha,* as a word of salutation, is modern; the ancient forms were *anoai, welina,* etc." He ends the list of English emotion terms which can be used as translation equivalents of *aloha* (love, affection, gratitude, pity, compassion, grief) with the most recent usage: "The modern common salutation at meeting and parting." This new use of *aloha* in greetings suggests a certain devaluation of the concept. It is more consistent with fairly superficial good wishes and with a kind of obligation-free optimistic friendliness (cf. "Have a nice day!") than with a meaning closer to love, empathy, or loving compassion.

Whether or not the meaning of *aloha* has been affected by the americanisation of Hawaii, it would appear that in modern use this term doesn't refer to misfortune in any way (unlike the Tahitian *arofa,* the Samoan *alofa,* the Ifaluk *fago,* the Utku Eskimo *naklik,* or the Russian *žalost').* Compare, for example, the following comment (Gallimore and Howard 1968a:11): "When one's friends and kinsmen arrive, it is time to relax, to talk, to bring out for everyone's enjoyment what there is to share, and to promote as much as possible the feeling of *aloha.*"

Accounts of this kind cannot always be trusted, because they sometimes focus on the anthropologist's idea of what "true" *aloha* (or any other emotion) is, instead of focussing on the empirical evidence as to how the term in question is used. For example, Newton (1984:88) says: "I witnessed true *aloha* most commonly within kin groups—especially within nuclear families—during moments of good fortune or crisis involving loved ones. With regard to the community as a whole I observed expressions of true *aloha* during major village crises." From Newton's observations, it seems clear that the Hawaiians themselves do not link *aloha* specifically with crises, but he chooses to dismiss this fact because it doesn't fit his notion of what "true *aloha*" is:

> On a more ordinary, day-to-day basis there is a substantial amount of cooperation and good fellowship among the villagers—although such positive interactions did tend to be largely confined to circles of close kin and friends. . . . Such behavior is another form of *aloha* and it is commonly referred to by the villagers as '*aloha*'. However, this type of *aloha* in my opinion was not altruistic because such cooperation carried with it expectations of reciprocity. (1984:488)

This is in keeping with Newton's criticism of the dictionary definition of *aloha* quoted earlier, which describes it as "love, affection, compassion, mercy, pity, kindness and charity". Newton comments (1984:88): "what this definition lacks,

from my personal observations, is a sense of altruism in true expressions of *aloha*."
But this distinction between *aloha* and "true *aloha*" only obscures the real meaning
of the concept. The way Hawaiian villagers use the word *aloha* (as reported, for
example, by Gallimore and Howard 1968a or Newton 1984) is not compatible with
the claim that *aloha* (in its present use) implies something like compassion or pity.
Whatever "true *aloha*" was one hundred years ago, the meaning of this concept
appears to have changed. In fact, this change in the meaning of *aloha* seems to
epitomise the broader cultural change which has affected Hawaii since its annexa-
tion by the United States.

1.6 The Tahitian Concept of *Arofa*

"*Arofa*, we do not really know what is its nature", says Manu, one of Levy's
(1973:321) Tahitian informants. Levy himself (1973:342) glosses *arofa* as "empa-
thy/pity/compassion". He writes: "*Arofa* in its broadest sense implies 'empathy',
although it usually is used for 'empathic suffering because of the sufferings of
others'. It implies caring about someone." Thus, Levy posits for *arofa* two components: something like suffering of the target person and something like empathy of
the experiencer. He is very emphatic on both points: "One feels *arofa* for cripples,
for hungry people, for people who have undergone calamities. It indicates 'pity'.
But it also means that one feels the suffering of these people as they feel it; thus it
indicates 'empathy' " (1973:342). "It implies caring for someone else" (1973:321).

The general 'tone' of *arofa*, therefore, is quite different from that of the
Hawaiian *aloha*. When one is welcomed to the "*aloha* state", that is, to the "Polyne-
sian paradise", one is not being welcomed to a state of pity or compassion. The
'good feelings' toward the target people are of course present in both cases, but the
Tahitian *arofa* refers also to 'bad things' that happen to people. On the basis of
Levy's discussion and examples, it can be explicated as follows:

> *arofa*
> (a) X thinks something like this:
>   something bad happened/will happen to Y
> (b)   if this happened to me, I would feel something bad
> (c)   Y feels/will feel something bad
> (d)   I don't want this
> (e) because of this, X feels something bad
> (f) because of this, X feels something good toward Y

The disjunctive components in this explication ('happened/will happen',
'feels/will feel') could be avoided if we assumed that future events ('will happen',
'will feel') are really involved in an anticipation of *arofa* rather than in the *arofa*
itself; I suspect this is really the case, but this is a point which is not entirely clear in
Levy's description.

Levy (1973:321) suggests that "*arofa* is a significant aspect of moral controls"
and that (1974:294) "*arofa* also has an aspect of avoidance of mistake. By empathet-

ically knowing which aspects of action will hurt someone else, by accepting the clues of compassion and pity, one can then avoid behavior which would produce harm, punishment, and inchoate guilt feelings."

If we took this aspect of *arofa* as part of its semantic invariant, we should probably add to the proposed explication the following component: 'I don't want to do something bad' or 'I don't want to do something that would cause someone to feel something bad'. Some of Levy's examples would clearly support some such component. For example, Levy quotes the following comments by an informant:

> If [I decided to] go and get money, I would go and get money . . . but I don't want to do such things because it is forbidden to me, I am prevented from doing them because of *arofa* . . . (*Arofa* for whom?) *Arofa* for the person to whom I have done a bad thing, and *arofa* toward myself. I am jumping into a hole. (Levy 1974:294; cf. also 1973:321)

Nonetheless, I have not included in the explication the hypothetical component in question ('I don't want to do something bad'), because it seems to me that it doesn't always apply to instances of *arofa*. One may be trying to "avoid making a mistake" when one refrains from stealing or from "trying to initiate a sexual relationship with the *vahine* [woman] of another villager" (Levy 1973:321), but when one feels *arofa* for people who are impaired, is one also trying to "avoid making a mistake"? Presumably not.

On the other hand, if we posit for *arofa* the component 'I don't want Y to feel something bad', this will account, it seems to me, for both kinds of situations (compassion for someone who is suffering and avoidance of an action which would lead to someone's suffering).

1.7 The Samoan Concept of *Alofa*

According to Gerber (1985:151), *alofa* is "the most culturally salient emotion" in Samoa. Gerber, reluctantly, glosses this term as 'love'. In fact, however, her discussion, and examples, make it quite clear that *alofa* means something different from *love*. Evidently, Gerber herself feels uncomfortable with her equation of *alofa* with *love*, and she comments that "the study of such functional equivalencies would be put on a firmer basis if it rested on a systematic framework of comparison" (1985:147).

I submit that a systematic framework is provided by the natural semantic metalanguage, based on universal semantic primitives. Within this framework, both the similarities and the differences between *alofa* and *love*, and also among *alofa*, *arofa*, and *aloha*, can be accurately portrayed. Although Gerber herself glosses *alofa* as 'love' (though with reservations), she reports that "bilingual Samoans . . . frequently say that three English words—*love, charity,* and *sympathy*—are needed to translate the word *alofa*" (1975:190). This is a very revealing statement. It suggests that the Samoan *alofa* is closer in meaning to the Tahitian *arofa* than to the English *love*. The following comment on *alofa*, attributed to a native informant, confirms this: "If someone gets hurt, and he needs your help, he's lying on the ground, calling for help. Then you start to feel *alofa,* then you start to give him help" (Gerber 1975:190). Gerber (1975:190) comments: "When *alofa* is used to indicate giving any sort of aid to the unfortunate, the Samoan contention that they 'love all people' is quite literally true." But this is an illusion. In fact Samoans do not claim that they *love* all people; they only claim that they have *alofa* for all people, and the two concepts are clearly very different. If Samoans *alofa* all people, this means that *alofa* doesn't imply a 'special relationship', as *love* does.

Given this general nature of *alofa,* which implies no special personal bond, it is not at all surprising that it doesn't tend to express itself in kissing, hugging, and smiling, as *love* does.

> Based on several informal interviews with Americans, one important connotation of the term 'love' is the physical demonstration of affection, embraces and smiles being particularly salient. . . . These associations never appear in Samoan descriptions of the term *alofa.* Smiling (a minor Samoan category) appears only in association with *fiafia,* 'happiness'. Embraces, even between husbands and wives, are not mentioned as expressing *alofa:* sexual love is glossed by other terms, such as *mana'o* 'want' and *tu'inanau* 'desire' or 'eagerness'. (Gerber 1985:146)

The discussion so far suggests that the Samoan concept of *alofa* is very close to the Tahitian concepts of *arofa.* But Gerber insists that the two are not identical:

> I have never had the impression that [*alofa*] was a particularly powerful feeling. This contrasts strongly with Levy's (1973:340–346) description of how the feeling *arofa* can overwhelm Tahitians. The connection with giving and helping is much more important, and appears to be universal in all descriptions of *alofa.* This is true in intimate relationships as well as more casual ones. The *alofa* between parents and children, between siblings, and even husbands and wives, is described in terms of giving and helping. The emphasis, even in these close relations, is on mutual obligation rather than intimacy. (1985:145)

This suggests that the element of empathy, present in *arofa,* is absent from *alofa* and that *alofa* implies a more active attitude ('I should do something good for this person; I want to do something good for this person'). The need for a reference to 'should' in the definition of *alofa* is supported by the gloss in Gerber's (1985:162) "glossary": "*alofa*—love, stresses social bonding and obligation".

Before I propose an explication for *alofa,* we should first clarify the relationship between *alofa* and misfortune or suffering. According to Gerber (1975:191), "when the term is used in connection with closer people, the general association of giving aid remains important, but the feeling is not necessarily connected with another person's misfortune". She also says about the Ifaluk concept of *fago* that "it is clearly a similar concept, but it is more definitely sad in tone than is *alofa*" (1985:145). "For a few informants, however, the connotation of *alofa* as a reaction to the misfortune of another remains strong even in the context of close relationships. For example, one informant said . . . : I think I feel *alofa* especially when people are sick or in trouble" (1975:191).

I think this ambivalence concerning the link between *alofa* and misfortune doesn't reflect any sociolectal or idiolectal variation but a somewhat different, less specific conceptual structure. Perhaps *arofa* is "sadder in tone" than *alofa* because it assumes a misfortune ('X thinks: something bad happened to Y'), whereas in the case of *alofa* the link with misfortune may be more hypothetical ('X thinks: bad things can happen to a person'). This applies both to a situation when a misfortune has actually occurred and to a situation when it is merely envisaged as a possibility. As for *fago,* its "sad" tone is perhaps accounted for by the component 'when X thinks that something bad can happen to Y, X feels something bad' (*alofa* doesn't seem to imply that the experiencer feels "something bad").

Gathering all these different clues together, I would propose the following explication:

> *alofa*
> X thinks of person Y
> X thinks something like this:
>> bad things can happen to a person
>> if something bad happens to a person, I should do something good
>>> for this person
> X feels something good toward Y
> X wants to do something good for Y

This is neither particularly 'sad' (as *fago* is) nor particularly 'intense' (as *arofa* is); yet it reflects that emphasis on 'giving and helping', with which, as Gerber (1985:151) assures us, informants primarily associate it.

1.8 Warm Feelings in an Igloo: Some Emotion Concepts of the Utku Eskimos

Emotion concepts of the Utku Eskimos have been studied, with remarkable care and discernment, by Jean Briggs (1970) in her book *Never in anger: portrait of an Eskimo family.* The analysis proposed here is based entirely on her data and observations.

Some of Briggs' emotion concepts seem familiar from other cultures, and these will not be analysed here. Others seem to have no parallels elsewhere in the world, as far as one can judge from studies available to date. The most persistent and striking image of the Utku Eskimos emerging from Briggs' study is that of people huddling together for warmth and affection, as if trying to find in that emotional closeness a protection against the cold outside, especially protection for their children.

1.8.1 Iva

One characteristic Utku term worth mentioning here is *iva,* which Briggs (1970:314) glosses as follows: 'to lie next to someone in bed ("under the same covers", p.319), with connotations of affectionate cuddling'. Strictly speaking, this is not an emotion term, as it focusses on a certain type of behaviour rather than a certain mental state, but it clearly has an important emotional dimension. The importance of this behaviour among the Utkus is illustrated in the following quote: "Small children are *iva*d (cuddled) by their parents and usually by most other close relatives as well, being carried from iglu to iglu or from tent to tent in the mornings, to be tucked into bed with aunts, uncles, grandparents, and cousins. Sometimes when a child is displaced from its mother's side by a younger brother or sister the father may continue to *iva* the child. . . . Often, however, some other older family member of the household: an older sibling, an uncle, or an aunt, may take over the role of cuddler. In some cases, it is said that the person who *iva*s a child as a substitute parent 'adopts' him, that is, the *iva* relationship itself constitutes a sort of 'adoption', developing into an especially close bond. . ." (Briggs 1970:319).

But although the concept of *iva* clearly takes an adult-child relationship as its prototype, this relationship cannot be represented as a necessary condition, because "when husbands and wives lie together under one cover, as they usually do, this is also called *iva*ing" (Briggs 1970:320). As a first approximation, I propose the following explication:

> *iva* ('X *iva*s Y')
> if a person feels something good toward a small child, this person wants to lie
>   in bed with this child covered by the same thing
> so that their bodies can touch
> and so that they can be warm and feel something good
> X feels like this toward Y
> because of this, X does this with Y

1.8.2 Niviuq

A related concept is that of *niviuq,* which informants gloss as 'to want to kiss' but which according to Briggs "also seems to include the wish to touch or to be physically near someone". The importance of the element of touch for this concept is highlighted by its humorous use in a situation when mosquitoes light on someone's arms and the person laughs: "They feel *niviuq* toward me" (Briggs 1970:322).

The concept of *niviuq* contains, evidently, at least two concepts: 'X wants to touch Y' and 'X feels something good toward Y'. Briggs' data on the use of this word suggest, however, that this is not the whole story. First, there is a question of 'littleness' or 'babyishness' as a basis of *niviuq* feelings. Briggs writes:

> Littleness seems to be a central characteristic of objects that are considered *niviuq-naqtuk*. In addition to babies, a great variety of small things, both live and inanimate, may produce *niviuq* feelings; newborn puppies (especially when there are no small children in the household), baby birds, a doll's dress, even the inch-long slips of paper on which I recorded vocabulary—people used the term *niviuq* in connection with all these things. (1970:316)

But despite the reference to the small slips of paper I believe it is not 'littleness' which is the crucial factor here but the association with babies. Clearly, *niviuq* is not restricted to babies, but it seems equally clear that babies provide the prototype for the feeling in question.

Second, there is also a question of 'attractiveness', 'cuteness', as a necessary dimension of *niviuq*. A doll's dress, or a new-born puppy, can remind one of babies not only because it is seen as 'small' but also because it is seen as 'cute', 'nice to look at'. Briggs describes "*niviuq* qualities" of things and creatures as their "kissable qualities" (1970:319). Other English adjectives which come to mind here are *lovable* and *adorable*. To account for all these aspects of *niviuq*, I would propose, tentatively, an explication along the following lines:

> *niviuq* ('X *niviuq*s Y')
> X thinks something like this:
>> looking at Y one feels something good of the kind that one feels
>> looking at a baby
> because of this, X wants to touch Y
> because of this, X feels something good toward Y

1.8.3 Aqaq

A third Utku concept focussed on babies or small children is *aqaq*. Briggs (1970:314) glosses this word as 'to communicate tenderly with another by speech or by gesture (other than touch)', but she makes it clear that what is involved is above all "cooing" addressed at small children, which she describes as a highly patterned activity. Some forms of *aqaq*ing are generally available, others are strictly dyadic, being restricted to individual adult-child relationships. For example, "Mannik. . . , when *aqaq*ing Saarak, repeats one endearing phrase again and again: '*Niviuqnaqtuguuuuli* (you are kissable)'; the vowel is drawn out tenderly." To account for both the content and form of "*aqaq*ing" utterances, I would propose the following explication:

> *aqaq* (X *aqaq*s Y)
> X says things to Y
> like one says things to babies
> when one feels something good toward them
> and when one wants them to know it

1.8.4 Unga

Briggs (1970:315) glosses *unga* as 'the desire to be with a loved person'. "Being with" can be interpreted here as being very close indeed. For example, a little girl, Raigili, who "after her baby sister's birth, refused to sleep by herself—next to her father, as before, but under separate quilts", was said to feel *unga*. But the 'togetherness' in question doesn't have to be interpreted quite as strictly. For example, when the boy Ukpik "decided to stay at home instead of returning to school", he, too, was said to feel *unga*.

The concept of *unga* seems to imply three distinct elements: a desire to be with another person, a 'good' (love-like) feeling toward that person, and something like pleasure experienced in contact with that person. This last element is particularly clear in the following example: "Inuttiaq's children were said to *unga* him, to want to be with him, because he was never annoyed (*urulu*) with them."

The following explication can be proposed for the concept of *unga:*

> *unga* ('X *unga*s Y')
> X thinks something like this:
>   I want to be with Y
>   when I am with Y, I feel something good
> X feels something good toward Y

1.8.5 Naklik

From a Western perspective, it might be said that *unga* and *naklik* represent two faces of love: its self-oriented and its other-oriented aspect. *Unga* implies that one feels good in another person's presence and that one wants to be with that person. By contrast, *naklik* implies that one wants to do good things for the other person. In the Utku view, "small children are thought to feel *unga,* to want to be with people they love, but they only gradually begin to love in a nurturant (*naklik*) way" (Briggs 1970:323). Briggs (1970:320) reports that when she asked people what *naklik* meant, she was always told "that it referred to the desire to feed someone who was hungry, warm someone who was cold, and protect someone who was in danger of physical injury".

Her examples of *naklik* include both actual misfortunes and situations when no misfortunes have happened and apparently none is looming on the horizon. For example, Briggs (1970:321) reports that Pala said of his daughter, Akla, "She makes one feel *naklik;* she *unga*s me very much", and she comments: "Here the *naklik* response seems to be a reaction to emotional rather than physical need."

The active nature of *naklik* and also the fact that it can be translated as *pity* (1970:321) make this concept similar to the Tahitian *arofa* and to the Ifaluk *fago*. But *naklik* doesn't seem to have the 'sad tone' of *arofa* or *fago*, and Briggs presents it as 'protective' rather than 'compassionate'. In her examples, she mentions *naklik* for people who are hungry or for people who are cold, but not for people who are impaired physically. "*Naklik* feelings are given as reasons for taking care of the ill, for adopting orphans, and for marrying widows, all categories of people who are in need of physical assistance" (1970:321). Perhaps all these situations can be thought of as being 'improvable', as not being 'beyond remedy'?

The wide range of situations where *naklik* is applicable means that we can posit for this concept none of the following components:

> (a) X thinks this: something bad happened to Y
> (b) X thinks this: something bad will happen to Y
> (c) X thinks this: something bad may happen to Y

We cannot posit (a) as part of the invariant because the misfortune may not yet have happened, and we cannot posit (b) or (c) as part of the invariant because the misfortune may have already happened. It appears, however, that what we *can* posit is the following component: 'X thinks; I don't want bad things to happen to Y'. This leads to the following explication:

> *naklik* ('X *nakliks* Y')
> X thinks something like this: I don't want bad things to happen to Y
> X feels something good toward Y
> X wants to do something good for Y

1.9 "Poor Fellow My Country": Emotions in an Australian Desert

The phrase "poor fellow my country" is the title of a massive novel by an Australian writer, Xavier Herbert, who had a long and close involvement with Aboriginal people. The novel was published in 1975 and was dedicated "to my poor destructed country". The emotion expressed in the phrase "poor fellow" (which appears to be widely used by Aboriginal speakers of English in the Northern Territory, and which is found in the Kriol language as *bobala* (Jean Harkins p.c.)), is designated by different words in different Australian Aboriginal languages (possibly, with different shades of meaning). In the Western Desert language Pintupi the word in question is *kuunyi*. Myers (1976:131) glosses this word as 'compassion', 'concern' or 'feeling sorry for another', and he notes that it is usually rendered as 'poor bugger' in Pintupi English. Myers (1979:132) writes: "Another context of occurrence [of the word *kuunyi*] is related to mention of or thought of one's home country: 'poor fellow, my country' (*kuunyi, ngurra ngayuku*). The emphasis is on the sentiments of a feeling of relatedness towards the country."

Kuunyi is just one of a number of Pintupi emotion terms which have no exact equivalents in English and which are, or can be, used to express warm feelings to people and places in ways which have no parallels in English. Unlike *kuunyi* itself, some of these words appear to refer inherently to one's homeland or to one's kinsfolk.

The psychiatrist Rodney Morice (1978:87), who worked among the Pintupi in Central Australia, found that "in a transcultural setting, psychiatric diagnosis is often impeded by language and cultural barriers. . . . When language and cultural barriers intervene, the expression and interpretation of symptoms can become exceedingly difficult, and mental state examination even more so". The main difficulty, according to Morice, consists in understanding what the patients feel: that is, in translating the patients' words describing their symptoms into terms intelligible to him:

> The most stable set of cognitions available to a person is contained in his language and its lexical categories. By examining these in a particular Aboriginal speech community it has been possible to predict the most likely responses of its members to the effects of anxiety and depression. For example, many Pintupi words for sadness and depression imply that the sufferer is 'worrying' for his land or his

relatives, concepts understandable in the light of Aborigines' strong attachment to their country of birth, and of the complex kinship system. Most Pintupi when experiencing a depressed affect can therefore be expected to interpret this as resulting from separation from their land or relatives, and a behavioral response to this may be the sudden embarkation on a journey or 'walkabout'. (1978:94)

Other writers on the subject, too, emphasise the extraordinary importance of the Aboriginal "spiritual kinship with the land" (Myers 1979:350; cf. also Berndt and Berndt 1968), "the special identification of persons with 'place' in Aboriginal thought" (Myers 1979:350), and "a sense of belonging together, or shared identity", with one's kin (Myers 1979:350). Myers (1979:350) refers in this connection to Munn (1970:158), who "has tried to show that among Central Australian Aborigines, important external objects—parts of the material world like the 'country'— come to provide the individual with images or 'fragments' of himself".

The fact that the Pintupi language has "many words for sadness and depression" which imply "that the sufferer is 'worrying' for his land or his relatives" does support, indeed, the general conviction of all observers that the Pintupi are strongly attached to their country and to their kin, that they somehow identify with them, and that this attachment constitutes an important part of their culture. But this fact suggests also that the words in question are not really words "for sadness, depression or worry". They are really words for something else—all of them being somehow different in meaning from each other, as well as from the English words *sadness, depression,* and *worry.*

What, then, *is* the meaning of these words? Morice (1977a:105) offers the following glosses (quoted verbatim):

watjilpa: preoccupation with thoughts of country and relatives. To become sick through worrying about them. Other people may try to assuage worry, or traditional doctor may treat.

wurrkulinu: excessive concern for, and worry about, land or relatives, as for *watjilpa.*

yiluruyiluru: dejection caused by worrying too much for absent relatives, for example if they are in hospital.

yirraru: as for *watjilpa.*

yulatjarra: sympathy or sorrow for sick or deceased relatives. If a death has occurred this state is accompanied by self-inflicted wounds—'sorry cuts'. Not treated by traditional doctor.

In a later article, Morice (1977b:24) adds one more Pintupi emotion concept focussed on attachment to relatives, *nantungu,* which he defines as follows:

nantungu: to become stiff or paralysed from too much worry, from thinking too much about relatives who have been dead for a long time.

But glosses of this kind, useful as they are, cannot be taken as adequate definitions. To begin with, *yirraru* hasn't received any definition at all, except for the unconvincing comment that it is like *watjilpa,* and *yiluruyiluru* hasn't really been differentiated from *watjilpa* either. Clearly the other glosses are also not intended to be taken literally. For example, *yulatjarra* can hardly mean "sympathy for deceased relatives" (if they are dead, they are no longer a suitable target for *sympathy*). In the other glosses, too, words such as *preoccupation, worry, concern, sympathy, sorrow,* or *dejection* appear to be used almost at random, indiscriminately. This negligent attitude to the choice of English emotion words tallies well with the author's (admitted, and well-justified) lack of faith in such matching procedures.

In any case, what such half-hearted matching achieves is an ethnocentric look at the Pintupi emotion concepts through the prism of the English emotion concepts, not an understanding of the Pintupi conceptualisation in its own right. As a result, the relations among the different Pintupi emotion words discussed remain obscure, as do the relations between the Pintupi and the English emotion terms.

The data provided by Morice are not sufficient for well-justified explications of the relevant Pintupi concepts to be posited confidently (and there appear to be some inconsistencies between Morice's data and Myers' (1976 and 1979) data). Consequently, the explications to be proposed have to be regarded as no more than first approximations.

I will start with the concept of *watjilpa,* which Myers (1979:361) glosses as 'homesick', 'pining', 'lonely', 'worry', or 'melancholy', and which he describes as follows: "The core of the concept refers to *separation* [Myers' emphasis] from objects or persons of security and familiarity—family and home—places and people among which and whom one grew up and where one feels safe and comfortable. . . . Time and again in the life histories collected, Pintupi talked of their travels and the 'homesickness' (*watjilpa*) that made them come back to their home country. One friend (who had not seen his country for a long time) explained to me, 'I close my eyes and I can see that place. It's very green. There's a rockhole and a hill where I used to play. My brother pushed me down—it makes me "homesick".'"

watjilpa
X thinks something like this (of a place):
   I am like a part of this place
   I am not in this place now
   I want to be in this place
   I can't be in this place now
      because of this, something bad can happen to me
   because of this, X cannot think of other things

wurrkulinu
X thinks of place Y
X feels something good toward the people in this place
X thinks something like this:
   something bad could happen to people in this place
   these people are like a part of me
   because of this, X feels something bad

yulatjarra

X thinks of person Y
X feels something good toward Y
X thinks something like this:
   something bad happened to Y
   Y is like a part of me
because of this, X feels something bad
X doesn't want not to feel this

yiluruyiluru

X thinks of person Y
X feels something good toward Y
X thinks something like this:
   I am not with Y
   something bad is happening to Y
   Y is like a part of me
because of this, X feels something bad

nantungu

X thinks of people Y
X feels something good toward Y
X thinks something like this:
   people Y are dead now
   this is bad
   these people are like a part of me
because of this, X feels something bad
because of this, X cannot think of other things
because of this, X cannot feel anything good
because of this, something bad happens to X's body

    I conclude that Morice's lexical data do support his claim that Aboriginal people have very close ties with their land and with their relatives; they do not, however, give any support to his ethnocentric conclusions (1977a:92) that "as with anxiety, depression is an affect inherent to the human condition and psyche"; that "to assume its absence from groups of preliterate people would therefore seem, on theoretical grounds, to be untenable" or that "in practice, it has been observed to occur, and the degree of differentiation in the Pintupi lexicon of grief and depression would seem to suggest that it is a not uncommon experience".

    What seems to have been observed among the Pintupi is not the occurrence of *anxiety, depression,* or *grief* but the occurrence of *watjilpa, yulatjarra,* or *yiluruyiluru,* and the existence of lexical categories such as these does not support the view that *anxiety* or *depression* is a universal human concept "inherent to the human condition and psyche", just as the existence of lexical categories such as *anxiety* and *depression* in English doesn't support the view that *watjilpa* or *yulatjarra* are universal human concepts, inherent in the human condition and psyche. (Cf. Lutz 1985a; Kleinman and Good 1985.)

1.10 The Czech Concept of *Litost* and the Russian Concept of *Žalost'*

The Czech writer Milan Kundera devoted to the concept of *litost* a brilliant mini-study entitled "What is *litost?*", the core of which I am going to quote in extenso:

> *Litost* is a Czech word with no exact translation into any other language. It designates a feeling as infinite as an open accordion, a feeling that is the synthesis of many others: grief, sympathy, remorse, and an indefinable longing. The first syllable, which is long and stressed, sounds like the wail of an abandoned dog.
>
> Under certain circumstances, however, it can have a very narrow meaning, a meaning as definite, precise, and sharp as a well-honed cutting edge. I have never found an equivalent in other languages for this sense of the word either, though I do not see how anyone can understand the human soul without it.
>
> Let me give an example. One day the student went swimming with his girl-friend. She was a top-notch athlete; he could barely keep afloat. He had trouble holding his breath underwater, and was forced to thrash his way forward, jerking his head back and forth above the surface. The girl was crazy about him and tactfully kept to his speed. But as their swim was coming to an end, she felt the need to give her sporting instincts free rein, and sprinted to the other shore. The student tried to pick up his tempo too, but swallowed many mouthfuls of water. He felt humiliated, exposed for the weakling he was; he felt the resentment, the special sorrow which can only be called *litost*. He recalled his sickly childhood—no physical exercise, no friends, nothing but Mama's ever-watching eye—and sank into utter, all-encompassing despair. On their way back to the city they took a shortcut through the fields. He did not say a word. He was wounded, crestfallen; he felt an irresistible desire to beat her. 'What's wrong with you?' she asked him, and he went into a tirade about how the undertow on the other side of the river was very dangerous and he had told her not to swim over there and she could have drowned—then he slapped her face. The girl burst out crying, and when he saw the tears running down her face, he took pity on her and put his arms around her, and his *litost* melted into thin air.
>
> Or take an instance from the student's childhood: the violin lessons that were forced on him. He was not particularly gifted, and his teacher would stop him and point out his mistakes in a cold, unbearable voice. It humiliated him, he felt like crying. But instead of trying to play in tune and make fewer mistakes, he would make mistakes on purpose. As the teacher's voice became more and more unbearable, enraged, he would sink deeper and deeper into his bitterness, his *litost*.
>
> Well then, what is *litost?*
>
> *Litost* is a state of torment caused by a sudden insight into one's own miserable self. (1980:121)

From further comments (Kundera 1980:122), however, it would appear that *litost* is in fact a little more than that feeling of torment "caused by a sudden insight into one's own miserable self", because "*Litost* works like a two-stroke motor. First comes a feeling of torment, then the desire for revenge. The goal of revenge is to make one's partner as miserable as oneself". I suggest that (if Kundera is correct) the whole conceptual 'script' for *litost* can be spelt out as follows:

> *litost*
> X thinks something like this:
>   something bad is happening to me
>   I can't do something
>   this other person (Y) can do it
>   because of this, Y can think something bad about me
> because of this, X feels something bad
> because of this, X wants Y to feel something bad

It is fascinating to consider the differences, and the similarities, between this concept and the related Polish concept encapsulated in the word *litość* (obviously a cognate of *litost*). *Litość* can be roughly glossed as 'pity', and the relationship between *litość* and *litost* can be likened to that between pity and self-pity.

> *litość* (*pity*)
> X thinks something like this:
>   something bad is happening to person Y
>   something like this is not happening to other people
> because of this, X feels something bad

Unlike *compassion, litość* (or *pity*) does not imply that the target person feels anything bad (for example, one could pity a child whose parents have been killed even if the child doesn't know this yet).

Another Polish word cognate to *litost* and semantically related to it is *politowanie*, a kind of patronising and smug pity, which can be portrayed as follows:

> *politowanie*
> X thinks something like this:
>   this other person (Y) cannot do things well
>   this is bad for Y
>   I am not like this
> because of this, X feels something

But *litost* is not simply self-pity: it is a kind of self-pity born of humiliation, and Kundera is, of course, quite right in stressing its uniqueness and 'untranslatability'. It can be 'translated', however, at the level of semantic explications.

It is tempting to link the emergence of the unique concept of *litost* with the sad history of the Czech nation—defeated, humiliated, and for three hundred years deprived of its independence and its national dignity. To substantiate this suggestion, however, we would need to know more about the semantic history of the word *litost*. I will not pursue this question here.

It is interesting to note that if the closely related language, Polish, doesn't have a word for *litost,* Russian doesn't have a word for either *litost* or *litość* (*pity*). Dictionaries usually equate both the Polish *litość* and the English *pity* with the Russian word *žalost'*, but this is inaccurate and misleading. When the Russian religious philosopher Vladimir Solov'ev (1966, v.7:57) calls *žalost'* "the root of an ethical

attitude towards . . . other human beings and towards living creatures in general",
he doesn't mean *pity*. He means something that constitutes, roughly speaking, a
kind of cross between *pity* and *love*. It can be spelt out as follows (for another
analysis of *žalošt'*, along rather similar lines, see Zaliznjak 1988):

> *žalost'*
> X thinks something like this:
>   something bad is happening to Y
>   because of this, Y feels something bad
>   I would want it didn't happen [i.e., I wish it hadn't happened]
>   because of this, X feels something good toward Y
>   if X could, X would want to do something good for Y

Žalost' differs from *pity*, and from the Polish *litość*, in the presence of 'loving'
feelings toward the unfortunate target person ('X feels something good toward Y')
and in its absence of potentially invidious comparisons with other people: the target
person is not thought of as being any 'worse off' than other people. Unlike *pity*,
žalost' is, potentially, a feeling that can embrace all living creatures, just as *love* can.
Solov'ev (1966, v.5:421) points out that Russian peasant women simply merge
žalost' and *ljubov'* 'love' (using the verb *žalet'* instead of *ljubit'*), and he himself
often brings the two concepts together, as if they were almost identical (for example, 1966, v.5:422). He also claims (1966, v.8:960) that "*žalost'* est dobro; čelovek
projavljajuščij èto čuvstvo nazyvaetsja dobrym" ('*žalost'* is goodness; a man who
shows *žalost'* is called a good man'). All this sets *žalost'* apart from *pity*, and from
litość.

   Žalost' is morphologically related to *žal'* (roughly, 'regret'), and both are closely
linked with the verb *žalet'*, whose transitive use corresponds to *žalost'*, and its
intransitive use, to *žal'*. This semantic link between *žalost'* and *žal'* is accounted for
in the component 'I would want it didn't happen'. The difference between *žalost'*
and the closest Russian counterpart of *compassion* (*sočuvstvie*, lit., 'co-feeling') is
highlighted in the following passage from Solzhenitsyn's novel *Cancer Ward:*

> Kostoglotov smotrel na nego ne s *žalost'ju*, net, a—s soldatskim *sočuvstviem:* èta
> pulja tvoja okazalas', a sledujuščaja, možet, moja. (1968a:231)

> Kostoglotov regarded him not with pity, but with a soldier's sympathy: 'This bullet
> was yours; the next may be mine.' (1968b:243)

But the word *sympathy*, used in the English translation quoted, is not a good
rendering of the Russian *sočuvstvie*, and it doesn't really help to elucidate Solzhenitsyn's distinction between *sočuvstvie* and *žalost'*. In fact, *sočuvstvie* is closer to
the English *compassion*, discussed earlier; like *compassion*, it implies that the
experiencer puts himself mentally in the place of the suffering person and imagines
his own feelings ('if this happened to me, I would feel something bad'), and it
doesn't imply an impulse to do something. *Žalost'* is more altruistic, so to speak,
and more likely to "activate"—rather like the Ifaluk *fago*, though its close link with
žal' 'regret' highlights the experiencer's feeling of helplessness and impotence ('X

would want to do something good for Y' in *žalost'* versus 'X wants to do something good for Y' in *fago*).

The importance of the concept *žalost'* in Russian culture was well perceived in Geoffrey Gorer's studies of the "Russian psychology" and of the Russian "national character". For example, Gorer (1949a:165), observes that of all "the tender emotions which Russians express . . . the most dramatic is love, but far and away more widespread is that which the Russians call *žalost'*, and which is inadequately translated as 'pity'. There is no single English word to carry all the connotations: it means a sympathetic understanding of and feeling for the moral and spiritual anguish which other people are undergoing. In contrast to pity, it is perhaps even more desirable to receive *žalost'* from another than to offer it. It can be, and often is, felt for all undergoing moral and spiritual anguish, whether personally known or not."

Gorer rightly points out (1949b:183) that the Russian concept of *žalost'* is epitomised in Aleksandr Blok's poem which begins as follows:

> Devuška pela v čerkovnom xore
> O vsex ustalyx v čužom kraju,
> O vsex korabljax, ušedšix v more,
> O vsex, zabyvšix radost' svoju.

> 'A girl was singing in the church choir
> Of all the tired in foreign lands,
> Of all the ships that went to sea,
> Of all who lost their joy. . . .'

The great significance of the concept of *žalost'* in Russian culture is also confirmed by statistical data. Thus, in Zasorina's (1977) megacorpus of one million running words, the noun *žalost'*, the verb *žalet'*, and the adverbial *žalko* have a joined frequency of 218, whereas in Kučera and Francis' (1967) data for American English *pity* has a frequency of merely 14. It is true that in Russian *žalet'* and *žalko* can also stand for *regret*, but the Russian noun for *regret*—*žal'*—has also a high frequency of 74, whereas the English word *regret* (whether noun or verb) has a frequency of only 23. This means that in Russian the combined frequencies of *žalet'*, *žalost'*, *žalko*, and *žal'* are 294, whereas in English the combined frequencies of *pity* and *regret* are only 39. These are, I think, spectacular differences.[1] (For further discussion of *žalost'*, see chapter 7, section 2.2.5.)

1.11 The 'Broad Russian Nature' and the Russian Concept of *Toska*

Toska is one of the key words in Russian culture. More than that, it is a word that can be seen as a key to the 'Russian soul'. In fact the two words *toska* and *duša* ('soul') often come together in Russian speech, as if one concept evoked the other, and as if they had something in common. For example, Tsvetaeva (1969:131) wrote this about her ten-year-old son, Mur:

> Menee vsego razvit—duševno: ne znaet *toski*, sovsem ne ponimaet. Lob—serdce—
> i potom uže—duša: 'normal'naja' duša desjatiletnego rebenka, t.e.—začatok. (K

serdcu—otnošu ljubov' k roditel'jam, žalost' k životnym, vse elementarnoe—k
duše—vse bespričinnoe bolevoe.) (1969:131)

He is least advanced emotionally [lit. soul-wise]: he doesn't know what *longing*
[*toska*] is, doesn't understand it in the least. The forehead—the heart—and only
then—the soul: the 'normal' soul of a ten-year-old child, i.e. its embryo. (To the
heart I relate love for parents, pity for animals, all that is elementary.—To the soul I
relate all that is painful without seeming cause.) (Translation from Proffer 1980:99)

Before we explore these somewhat mysterious links among 'longing', 'soul',
and 'inexplicable pain', it should be pointed out that unlike words such as *longing*
and *soul* in English, *toska* is a common everyday word in Russian. In fact, Russians
seem to refer to their *toska* more often than speakers of English refer to any emotion
whatsoever. This impression is confirmed by the data from the available 'megacorpora' of English and Russian speech. Thus, in Kučera and Francis' (1967) corpus of
one million words of running text, the closest equivalents of *toska* show the following frequencies:

melancholy	9
yearning	14
longing	12
boredom	11

The corresponding frequency for *toska* (Zasorina 1977) is 53, and if we also include
the verb *toskovat'*, then it is 69. It might be objected that since *melancholy, longing,*
and *yearning* are not common everyday words in English, one should rather compare *toska* with common English words such as *sadness* and *sad*. The frequency of
sadness (including *sad* and *sadly*) is indeed much higher (55), but *sadness* does have
its close counterpart in Russian, in fact two such counterparts, *grust'* and *pečal'*,
whose frequency is also very high, in fact much higher than that of *sadness:* for
grust' (including the adjective *grustnyj,* the adverb *grustno,* and the verb *grustit'*)
the figure is 99, and for *pečal'* (including the adjective *pečal'nyj,* the adverb
pečal'no, and the verb *pečalit'sja*) the frequency is 102.

It cannot be said, therefore, that *toska* is the Russian cultural equivalent of the
English *sadness*. *Sadness* has its closest equivalents in *grust'* and *pečal'*, and *toska* is
something special, something peculiarly Russian. So what exactly is it?

Consider the following passage from a poem (Tsvetaeva's "Sereže", 'To Se-
reža'):

Po tebe vnizu *toskuet* mama,
V nej duša grustnej pustogo xrama,
Grusten mir. K sebe ee zovi. (1980, v.1:6)

'Your mother longs for you below
Her soul sadder than an empty shrine
Her whole world sad. Call her to yourself.'

I believe these three lines (of an invocation to a dead boy) offer a good introduction
to the concept of *toska,* as they highlight several important aspects at the same time:

the link of *toska* with *grust'* 'sadness', the implication of emptiness caused by the absence of someone or something of great value (the empty temple image); the intensity and pervasiveness of the feeling, which seems to throw a shadow on the whole world ("the world is sad"); the implication of yearning, of wanting to be elsewhere; the idea of a call coming to us from 'beyond', from another world, the contrast between the world of here and now, which has lost its appeal to us, and another, inaccessible world, which contains a lost treasure. All these elements are relevant to the concept of *toska* and have to be accounted for in its explication.

Can they all be accounted for in one explication? In dealing with complex and difficult concepts such as *toska,* there is a natural temptation to treat them as polysemous and to link different aspects of their meaning with different senses of the word. Not surprisingly, bilingual dictionaries of Russian usually succumb to this temptation in the case of *toska.* For example, Smirnickij (1961) assigns to *toska* two different meanings—(1) melancholy, depression, yearning, anguish, agony; (2) ennui, weariness, tedium—whereas Wheeler (1972) attributes to it three different meanings: (1) melancholy, anguish, pangs; (2) depression, ennui, boredom; (3) longing, yearning; nostalgia; *po rodine* ('after homeland')—homesickness.

But in fact there is little justification for assigning two, three, or more different meanings to *toska.* The nature of *toska* is such that elements of something similar to melancholy, something similar to boredom, and something similar to yearning are blended together and are all present at the same time, even though different contexts may highlight different components of this complex but unitary concept.

One could of course try to separate different senses of *toska* on the basis of their syntactic properties: distinguishing *toska* without any complements from *toska* used with one prepositional phrase (*toska po* N) and again from *toska* with another prepositional phrase (*toska o* N). But although there is no doubt some merit in considering these three syntactic contexts separately, the fact of the matter is that in each case we discover the same blend of something like melancholy or sadness, of something like boredom, and of something like yearning or nostalgia. The prepositional phrases '*po* N' and '*o* N' add something to the bare *toska,* but despite the appearances, a common core remains. In particular, it is not the case that *toska* with a prepositional phrase implies an identifiable cause or target and a bare *toska,* an inexplicable feeling with no specific target. A bare *toska* is quite compatible with a specific target, as in the following sentence about an orphan boy's anguish:

'Mamočka,'—v dušerazdirajuščej toske zval on ee s neba, kak novopričtennuju ugodnicu. . . (Pasternak 1959:19)

'Mama!'—in his heartrending anguish he called her down from heaven like a newly canonised saint. . . (Pasternak 1958:21)

The orphan boy's *toska* (*without* a prepositional phrase) is not different in kind from the *toska* of the mother of a dead boy mentioned earlier (*with* a prepositional phrase). The point is that whether or not a specific target of *toska* is mentioned, something inexplicable and indefinite is always implied in this word. *Toska* implies the absence and the inaccessibility of something good; a thought of a loved person who has died may provide a crystallising point for this feeling, but the feeling goes far beyond any such point.

Similarly, in the following sentence:

S toskoj i blagodarnost'ju vspominala naši gimnazii so 'svoimi slovami' ('Rasskaži svoimi slovami'). (Tsvetaeva 1969:44)

'I recalled with nostalgia and gratitude our high schools, with their "in your own words" ("Tell it in your own words").'

the *toska* is focussed on the old schools, with their traditional teaching methods, but it goes far beyond that, hinting at old values and a bygone world, and perhaps at the loss of childhood.

Toska is always indefinite, even if it does have a specific crystallising point, because it always hints at an unappeasable heartache, at an insatiate longing which seems to reach out beyond the boundaries of 'this world', of the accessible reality. This is why, I think, *toska* can so easily develop both positive connotations (poetic and metaphysical) and negative ones (connotations of despair and hopelessness), as in the following two contrasting quotes:

U mamy—muzyka, stixi, toska, u papy—nauka. (Tsvetaeva 1972:29)

'Mother had her music, her poetry, her *toska;* father had his scholarship.'

Takoj toski Saša ne ispytyval ni v Butyrke, ni na peresylke, ni na ètape. V Butyrke byla nadežda—razberutsja, vypustjat, na ètape byla cel'—dojti do mesta, obosnovat'sja. . . . Zdes' net ni nadeždy ni celi. (Rybakov 1987, pt.3:54)

'Saša had never experienced such anguish (*toska*) before, not at any of the camps or staging posts along the way into exile. In Butyrka there was still the hope that they would discover their mistake and release him. Along the way there was the goal of reaching the next point, getting settled. . . . Here there was no hope, no goal.'

Trying to account for all these different and seemingly contradictory aspects of *toska,* I propose the following explication of this protean concept:

> *toska*
> X thinks something like this:
>   I want something good to happen
>   I don't know what
>   I know: it cannot happen
> because of this, X feels something

The fact that the person who experiences *toska* wants something good, vague, and inaccessible accounts for the link between *toska* and *yearning.* The fact that the experiencer knows that the desired state of affairs cannot come true accounts for the links between *toska* and concepts such as *melancholy* and *sadness.* The fact that people in the grip of *toska* can see no attainable goals, that there is nothing else that they think they want to do and can do, accounts for the links between *toska* and concepts such as *boredom* and *ennui.* Finally, the implicit contrasts between the things of here and now, that could happen, and good things to which one aspires and which could not happen (as if they belonged to another, better, world) accounts for the intuitively felt link between *toska* and *duša* ('soul'); see chapter 1.

As Andrzej Bogusławski (p.c.) has pointed out to me, Sukalenko (1976:144) quotes the following definition of *toska* by the Gorky scholar Pocepnja: "čuvstvo mučitel'noj, nevynosimoj neudovletvorennosti, tomjaščego dušu protesta", 'a feeling of tormenting, unbearable "unsatisfiedness", of a protest nagging at the soul'. Pocepnja noted that this meaning is not stated in the general dictionaries of the Russian language; Sukalenko retorts that such an interpretation of *toska* is idiosyncratic and should *not* be noted in general Russian dictionaries. In fact, however, Pocepnja's definition captures remarkably well the invariant core of *toska,* missed in the conventional definitions, which treat the word as polysemous.

One might say that the essence of *toska* is expressed in the following poem by Zinaida Gippius (translated by Jarintzov 1916:190):

> Ja umiraju,
> Stremljus' k tomu, čego ja ne znaju,
> Ne znaju . . .
> I èto želanie ne znaju otkuda
> Prišlo otkuda,
> No serdce xočet i prosit čuda,
> Čuda!
> O, pust' budet to, čego ne byvaet,
> Nikogda ne byvaet,
> Mne blednoe nebo čudes obeščaet,
> Ono obeščaet,
> No plaču bez slez o nevernom obete,
> O nevernom obete . . .
> Mne nužno to, čego net na svete,
> Čego net na svete.

> 'Alas, I'm dying with sadness that's gnawing me,
> Gnawing me,
> Longing for things unknown to me,
> Unknown to me.
> Where has it come from? I cannot grasp it . . .
> Cannot grasp it.
> I am drawn by things which have not passed yet,
> Not passed yet.
> My heart is praying for miracles,
> Miracles,
> High above earthly pinnacles,
> Pinnacles! . . .'

The last two lines mean, literally, 'I feel I need that which doesn't exist in the world'.

One final question imposes itself at this point: why are the Russians so prone to *toska?* And why does this concept play such a significant role in Russian culture?

We could of course say that once a key concept such as *toska* has been explicated, the linguist's job is done and that the rest should be left to cultural historians, social psychologists, anthropologists, and other scholars. I do not wish to indulge in speculations, and I do prefer to keep close to the area of my professional competence. But perhaps I could be allowed to point to some views of experts in Russian history, in Russian thought, and in the Russian 'soul', which seem to be particularly relevant in the present context. Thus, the Russian philosopher Berdyaev has this to say about "the Russian national type":

> There is that in the Russian soul which corresponds to the immensity, the vagueness, the infinitude of the Russian land, spiritual geography corresponds with physical. In the Russian soul there is a sort of immensity, a vagueness, a predilection for the infinite, such as is suggested by the great plains of Russia. (1947:2)

The Russian poet Esenin in his poetical portrait of Russia explicitly linked the concept of *toska* with this feature of Russian geography:

> I toska beskonečnyx ravnin . . . (Esenin 1933:284)
>
> 'And the *toska* of the endless plains . . .'

Thinking along similar lines, another expert in Russian culture, Fedotov (1981:92), sees the key to the Russian soul in "that aspect of Russian nature which is called its 'broadness'—its unrestrainedness, . . . its organic dislike for any finiteness of form"; he describes the vague Russian yearnings as characterised by two contrasting features—"mračnost' and detskost'", 'childlikeness and gloom'. The Russian gaiety, he says, "is transient, unrestrained joy cannot satisfy a Russian for a long time. It always ends seriously, tragically". Fedotov mentions in this connection, as probably relevant, "the Tartar blood and the Moscovite oppression". Furthermore, Fedotov (like many other commentators) describes the "Russian national type" as that of "an eternal seeker" (1981:86), and he characterises the Russian religious orientation as "an eschatological type of Christianity, having no earthly 'home' but yearning for a heavenly one".

Berdyaev echoes this, describing as "an extraordinary property of the Russian people" "a capacity for the endurance of suffering and a mind directed ardently towards the other world" (1947:14), and saying (1947:253): "The Russian Idea is eschatological, it is oriented to the end; it is this which accounts for Russian maximalism".

It seems to me that comments of this kind fit in very well with the emergence of the unique concept of *toska* in Russian language and with the salience of this concept in Russian culture.

2. Conclusion

Can a feeling such as, for example, anger be a universal human emotion? Solomon (1984:242) observes, "Anger is an emotion that would seem to be universal and unlearned if any emotion is, however different its manifestations in various cultures". Most scholars involved in the controversy about the universality of emotions would probably agree with this judgement (whether they accept or reject the universality thesis). It is therefore convenient to use anger as a focal example. Solomon himself stresses the "if", and he doesn't forget this "if" in the subsequent discussion. He doesn't deny the possibility "that some emotions may be specific to *all* cultures", but he insists that "this should remain an open question for cross-cultural inquiry, not an a priori supposition" (1987:249–50). Personally, he is sceptical: "one might find anger (or some similar emotion) in every society, but the evidence seems to suggest that this is not the case". Many other scholars, however, have asserted (or assumed) the universality of anger without the slightest hesitation; for example, Izard (1977:64) declared flatly, "in the human being the expression of anger and the experiential phenomenon of anger are innate, pan-cultural, universal phenomena".

Some other writers on the subject have been attracted to a compromise solution suggested by the prototype theory of semantics. Rosch herself (1975:196) seemed quite happy to accept Ekman's (1974) "six basic emotions"—happiness, sadness, anger, fear, surprise, and disgust—as universal prototypes. Rosch wrote: "In domains in which prototypes are biologically 'given', categories can be expected to form around the salient prototypes and, thus, to have elements of content as well as principles of formation which are universal."

Gerber (1985:143) is inclined to accept this idea: "It seems possible . . . that basic affects serve as prototypes for the development of a series of more culturally specific categories." In her "conclusion", she is even more definite (1985:159): "In this analysis, I have assumed the existence of inborn patterns of affective arousal. . . . Basic affects pattern the conceptual system of emotion, and serve as centers around which clusters of meaning develop. This is similar to the 'natural prototype' structures suggested by Rosch (1975). . . . Because these basic affects are panhuman, they will provide a basis for comparison and translation between systems of emotion in different societies." (Here Gerber speaks as if the pan-human character of the "basic affects" in question had already been established.)

Levy (1984) is similarly inclined to apply the prototype theory to emotions, although his phrasing is much more cautious than Gerber's. Referring to Berlin and Kay's (1969) work on colour categories, Levy (1984:229) writes: "Tahitian and Newar data suggest that in some similar fashion the central tendencies named by various emotional terms are probably universal but that the borders of the categories may differ. . . . That is, whatever the cultural peculiarities in the relations and associated meanings of Tahitian emotional terms, I had little trouble in recognizing, say, *ri'ari'a* as 'fear', *riri* as 'anger', *hina'aro* as 'desire', *'oa'oa* as 'happiness', *ha'ama* as 'shame'. That is, if an emotion was recognized and named at all, its 'central tendency' seemed to be universally human."

The data discussed in this book, however, do not support Levy's or Gerber's position. Even if the Tahitian word *riri* or or the Samoan word *ita* can be recognised as meaning, "essentially", the same as *anger*, Rosaldo's and Lutz' data show that the Ilongot word *liget* and the Ifaluk word *song* do not mean "essentially" the same as *anger*. It is not just the boundaries that are different: the prototype itself is different. The explications phrased in the natural semantic metalanguage show these differences in an explicit and precise form.

There is no reason to think that the English word *anger* represents a "pan-human prototype" any better than the Ilongot word *liget* or the Ifaluk word *song* does, and once the differences between these concepts have been clearly represented, the untenability of the view which regards *anger* as a pan-human prototype (let alone a pan-human invariant) becomes, it seems to me, self-evident.

Does it mean that there are definitely no universal human emotions? Or that there are no recognisable "pan-human prototypes" in the area of emotion?

I would repeat, like Solomon, that "this should remain an open question for cross-cultural inquiry". One thing, however, seems to be certain: if there are some universal human emotions, or at least some pan-human emotional prototypes, they cannot be identified by means of English folk categories such as *anger, shame,* or *disgust;* they can only be identified in a culture-independent semantic meta-language.

3. Retrospect: The Format of the Explications

As mentioned earlier, the format of the explications sketched in the present chapter (and in the preceding one) requires some discussion. The two most important issues involved concern the role of thoughts in emotion concepts and the role of feelings. I will start with the role of thoughts in the conceptualisation of emotions.

That thoughts do play a major role in emotion concepts is in my view beyond question, and I hope that the present analysis helps to make this point clear. What is not clear, however, is in what *form* thoughts enter the structure of emotion concepts.

Many different views can of course be taken on this point, and many have been expressed in the philosophical and psychological literature on emotions. It seems to me, however, that these different views can be reduced, essentially, to two possibilities: the thoughts characteristic of a given emotion can be seen either as its cause or as its situational prototype.

The causal view goes back to Aristotle, who (as pointed out in Gordon 1978:125) defined *fear* (or rather, a Greek word meaning something similar to *fear*) as "a kind of pain or perturbation arising from the idea of impending evil".

The prototype view was put forward in a pioneering study by Iordanskaja (1970, 1974); it also underlies the analysis of a number of emotion terms developed in my own earlier work on emotions (cf. Wierzbicka 1972, 1973, 1980, and 1986a). It assumes that if we say, for example, "John is sad" we mean that 'John is in a state like that which is normally triggered by certain thoughts' (without prejudging whether in this particular case the 'state of sadness' was triggered by 'sad thoughts' or not).

The causal view of emotion concepts is sometimes stated in terms of the 'about-ness of emotions'. For example, Gordon (1974) argues that if one is angry one is angry *about* something, which is taken to indicate that one is *thinking* about something, and that any experiential, physiological, or behavioural components of anger are triggered by those underlying thoughts.

This seems very reasonable. On the other hand, one may doubt whether the same argument would apply to all emotion terms. For example, if one is sad or depressed, does one have to be sad or depressed 'about something'? In ordinary language (as distinct from the terminology of psychologists or psychiatrists), sentence (a) sounds odd but sentence (b) does not seem similarly odd (cf. Johnson-Laird and Oatley 1989):

> (a) ?John was angry (surprised, indignant) without knowing why.
> (b) John was sad (depressed) without knowing why.

One possible conclusion is that different emotion concepts have different structures and that some of them specify certain thoughts as the causes of the emotional state, whereas others do not. From a semantic point of view, there would be nothing odd in such a situation. In fact, the long impasse in the semantic study of many other semantic domains may have been partly due to the assumption that all words in a given domain must necessarily have the same kind of semantic structure, for example, that the meaning of *mother* must be symmetrical to the meaning of *father* (cf. on this point the interesting discussion in Mufwene 1983).

It is possible, therefore, that some emotion concepts do have the feature of 'aboutness', whereas others don't. In fact, we will see in chapter 12 that in Russian emotion verbs do seem to have that feature and can combine with an 'about' complement, whereas emotion adjectives and adverbs do not.

In this chapter, I do not wish to take a definite stand on the "*because* versus *like*" (i.e., causal versus prototypical) issue, because my purpose here is different. I am interested here in developing a framework for a cross-cultural comparison of emotion concepts, and I think this can be done without prejudging the outcome of the *because* versus *like* debate. For example, whether *anger* and *liget* are ultimately analysed in the causal mode or in the prototypical mode will not affect the aspects of these concepts which have been discussed here. (For further discussion of the semantics of emotions, see Wierzbicka, In press a and c.)

Turning now to the role of the concept 'feel' in emotion concepts, we should note that in many non-Western societies, less emphasis seems to be placed on 'feeling' than is done in European culture, presumably because of European individualism, tendency to introspection, and so on (cf., for example, Lutz 1985a and 1988; Howell 1981; Johnson 1985; Solomon 1984; Shweder and LeVine 1984; Heelas 1984). In many cultures emotions appear to be linked very closely with moral and social concerns and to be seen largely in terms of social behaviour and moral appraisal rather than in terms of 'private', subjective feelings. But if so, is it justified to posit a 'feel' component in the explications of all emotion terms?

An objection along these lines appears to be strengthened by the reports that not all languages have a word for 'feeling' distinct from the words for thinking and wanting (cf. Lutz 1985a; Howell 1981; Levy 1973).

I do not think, however, that reports of this kind should be accepted at face value. In particular, I am not quite convinced that Ifaluk doesn't have a word for *feel*. Notably, Ifaluk has the word *niferash,* which Lutz (1988:92) glosses as 'our insides' and which she calls "the most general term used to describe internal functioning". As she points out herself (Ibid.), "To say 'My insides are bad (*Ye ngaw niferai)*' may mean one is either feeling physically bad or experiencing bad thoughts and emotions, or both, the exact meaning, as with the English phrase 'I feel bad,' being determined by context".

It is possible, then, that despite Lutz' protestations (and despite very real and important differences in their use), Ifaluk does distinguish lexically among the three crucial concepts of thinking (*nunuwan*), wanting (*tip-*), and feeling (*niferash*), and, on further investigation, the same may prove true of all the languages of the world.

The status of 'feeling' as a possible conceptual universal is important because it is now quite clear that the concept of 'emotion' is not universal and cannot be used as a common measure in investigating and comparing different languages and cultures.

In the scholarly literature on 'emotions', 'emotions' are usually contrasted with 'sensations', but natural languages rarely draw a similar distinction, the two being usually subsumed under one category of 'feelings'. In fact, even in English the verb *feel* applies to both bodily and mental phenomena. Scholars committed to the emotion/sensation distinction may deplore this "vagueness" of the verb *feel*, or may even regard this verb as polysemous, but linguistic evidence does not support this view. In other languages, which do not distinguish lexically between "body" and "mind" or between "sensations" and "emotions", there is even less reason to suspect that the equivalent of the word *feel* is polysemous (and that is has two distinct meanings, 'emotion' and 'sensation').

The concept of 'emotion' (born out of the distinction between "emotions" and "sensations") seems to be one of those concepts which originate in the English language and in the ethnopsychology embodied in it and which have become taken over by the language of scholarship as one of its basic concepts.

There is of course nothing wrong with such an elevation in status of an ordinary English concept; but it should be remembered that from a universal, language-independent point of view it is probably the undifferentiated 'feel' which is a truly fundamental human concept, not the more elaborated, more culture-dependent and theory-laden 'emotion'.

The concept of 'emotion' involves a combination of 'feeling', 'thinking', and an unspecified internal process. In the language of universal semantic primitives this can be represented as follows:

> *emotion*
> person X thought something
> because of this, X felt something
> because of this, something happened to X

One could say that the English concept of 'emotions' picks out one type of feeling (cognitively based feelings) as an important category, distinct from other types of feelings; and that, moreover, it links it with a vague reference to something that 'happens' to or in a person as a result of the feeling in question.

I am suggesting, then, that while the concept of 'feeling' is universal (or near-universal) and can be safely used in the investigation of human experience and human nature, the concept of 'emotion' is culture-bound, and cannot be similarly relied on.

As for the observation that in many non-Western societies "emotions may be grouped with moral values . . . , and . . . may be seen as characteristics of situations or relationships rather than as the property of individuals" (Lutz 1985a:81), it seems to me important, but perfectly compatible with the framework proposed here. After all, if we want to compare 'emotions across cultures', we must have in mind some stable and culture-independent concept to guide us; otherwise, we will not be able to compare anything at all. The format used here allows for considerable differences among 'emotion concepts' belonging to different cultural spheres, and in fact it highlights differences in cultural preoccupations, emphasised by Lutz, Geertz, Scruton, Russell, and others. Above all, it makes it possible to compare 'emotion concepts' across cultures in a rigorous and, I hope, illuminating way.

III

MORAL CONCEPTS
ACROSS CULTURES

5

Apatheia, Smirenie, Humility

The philosophical literature on ethical concepts is so old and so extensive that its size has to be counted not in pages but in yardage of bookshelves, and in age, not in decades or in centuries but in millennia. For a linguist, this literature constitutes an inexhaustible source of delight, enlightenment, inspiration—and frustration.

The frustration is due to the profound ethnocentrism of much of this literature. In particular, what most Anglo-Saxon ethical works tend to do is to discuss ethical concepts embodied in certain English words as if they were language-independent moral ideas, culture-free and fully transferrable from one language to another. For example, concepts such as 'justice', 'honesty', 'hypocrisy', or 'greed' are discussed as if they stood for some universally valid categories, rooted in human nature and human reason rather than in the English language and in the broad cultural tradition which has given the English lexicon its present shape.

Before the reader categorises this chapter as an attempt to promote shallow cultural—and perhaps moral—relativism, I hasten to say that nothing could be further from my intentions. I simply want to point out that ethical concepts embodied in the words of this or that natural language are language-specific and culture-specific. If we wish to compare ethical concepts embodied in different natural languages or to discuss ethical concepts from some universal, philosophical perspective, we must somehow 'liberate' these concepts from the chains which tie them to a particular natural language. I am not saying that this 'conceptual liberation' cannot be achieved. On the contrary, it is my purpose to propose an analytical framework within which it can be. But it will never be achieved at all if we don't first become fully aware of the bondage and of the need to overcome this bondage.

English ethical vocabulary constitutes a folk taxonomy (cf., for example, Frake 1969; Conklin 1967; Hunn 1976; or Bright and Bright 1969), not an 'objective', culture-free analytical framework. To treat English words such as *justice, courage,* or *self-indulgence* as language-independent realities or norms means to fall into the same trap into which some philosophers of language (for example, Searle 1979:ix) fall when they treat concepts such as *promise, warn,* or *request* as universal, objective realities of human communication or human thought. (Cf. Wierzbicka 1985a; see also Verschueren 1985.)

As Humboldt never tired of pointing out, meaning is all in the mind and reflects ways of thinking characteristic of a given speech community. The meanings of ethical terms such as *honesty, kindness,* or *hypocrisy* are not determined by some pre-existing, objectively delimited, discrete phenomena but represent an interpretation imposed on the reality by the semantic system of a given natural language. If we want to be able to compare ethical concepts across language boundaries, we have to translate them, first, into simple concepts—as close as possible to the level of universal semantic primitives.

The use of relatively simple terms in the explications, which makes possible a rigorous comparison of concepts both cross-linguistically and within one language, also ensures the elimination of the vicious circles which have plagued traditional definitions of ethical concepts as much as of any other kind of concept. Traditionally, a word such as *humility* has usually been defined with reference to *pride*, and vice versa. And even modern analysts have often defined *good* via *commend*, *approve*, or *praise* without giving any consideration to the question whether the notions encapsulated in these verbs would not have to be explicated, in turn, via the concept *good*. (Cf., for example, Hare 1961.)

In my analysis, no ethical concept can be defined via another ethical concept; the only words pertaining to the ethical field which can occur in the explications are *good* and *bad*, which are regarded as basic to this field. Whether or not these two concepts have the status of universal semantic primitives, for the present purposes they can be treated as indefinables.

As the title of this chapter suggests, the following discussion will focus on three concepts which embody three different though related moral ideals: 'apatheia', 'smirenie', and 'humility'.

Because of the obvious etymological links, 'apatheia' will also be briefly compared with the modern concept of 'apathy', and since opposites and quasi-opposites are as instructive in semantic analysis as synonyms and quasi-synonyms, I will complement my discussion of 'smirenie' and 'humility' with a brief analysis of 'pride', 'orgueil', and 'fierté'. Before turning, however, to these three focal concepts, I will illustrate the proposed method of analysis with a simpler example: I will discuss the Roman concept encoded in the Latin word *pietas*, comparing it with the concept encoded in the English words *piety* and *pious*, and *gratitude*.

1. *Pietas* and *Piety*

The Roman ideal of 'pietas' is very easy to misconstrue as identical with 'piety', because of the obvious etymological link between the two words. Authors discussing the concept of 'pietas' (for example, Ferguson 1958:164–72) have tried very hard to show that 'pietas' and 'piety' are very different from one another, but without two definitions which could be compared with one another, such discussions are bound to suffer, to a greater or lesser degree, from vagueness and inconclusiveness.

Ferguson (1958:164) writes: "*Pietas* is not 'piety'; indeed Cicero at one point insists that proper behaviour in relation to the gods is not *pietas* but *religio* . . . ; *pietas* is proper behaviour towards parents". He adds, however, that there were three main fields within which *pietas* could be exercised: one's family, one's country, and one's gods. *Pietas* involves loyalty, duty, but also real affection. "It does genuinely represent an inward disposition and not merely an outward observance . . . ; it is realised in personal relationships" (1958:171). It is neither abstract nor cold; in fact, he says, "the human quality of *pietas* has more kindling power than the volcano" (1958:171).

I think that many different aspects of *pietas* discussed in the literature (loyalty, affection, indebtedness, 'kindling power', personal bond, and so on) can be summarised in the following definition:

> *pietas*
> (a) X thinks something like this:
> (b)　Y did something good for me
> (c)　I couldn't do something like this for Y
> (d)　if Y wants me to do something, I should do it
> (e) because of this, X feels something good toward Y
> (f) X wants to do good things for Y
> (g) [I think this is good][1]

Components (b) and (e) show how *pietas* is related to *gratitude*, since both these attitudes imply a recognition of some 'debt' and a resulting 'good feeling' directed toward the other person:

> *gratitude*
> (a) X thinks something like this: Y did something good for me
> (b) because of this, X feels something good toward Y

But *pietas* also has a component, called here (c), which shows that *pietas*, unlike *gratitude*, is inherently asymmetrical and implies a kind of dependence: *gratitude* could be mutual, but *pietas* could not. Component (f) spells out the 'kindling power' of *pietas:* the debt which one can't fully repay makes one nonetheless want to try to repay it, at least potentially. Component (d) spells out the obligation of loyalty and obedience. Component (g) shows that *pietas* was seen as a virtue.

All this differs considerably from the concept encoded in the modern English words *pious* and *piety,* which are normally restricted to the religious domain, which refer above all to external behaviour, and which lend themselves very easily to ironic usage. For example, the *Pocket Oxford* (1969) entry for *pious* reads: 1) devout in religion, 2) ostentatiously virtuous. I don't think, however, that there is any need to postulate polysemy here. We can account for all the different aspects of the word's use by means of a unitary formula:

> *piety*
> X does many things
> because of these things, people could think something like this:
> 　X thinks much about God
> 　X feels something good toward God
> 　X wants to do good things for God

The existence of the phrase *filial piety* may seem to contradict this formula. In fact, however, the semantic structure of this phrase is not taxonomic but analogical:

a *mock orange* is not 'a kind of orange', but something that without being an orange (tree) looks *like* an orange (tree); an *artificial leg* is not a kind of leg, but something that without being a leg is *like* a leg; similarly, *filial piety* stands for an attitude which is not piety (because it is directed toward one's parents rather than toward God) but which is *like* piety. An alternative interpretation of *filial piety,* suggested to me by Thomas Mautner (p.c.), would treat this use as a separate meaning of *piety,* which may be an attempt to represent in English the meaning of Latin *pietas.*

This formula does not present the words *piety* and *pious* as unambiguously pejorative (as the words *sanctimonious* or *hypocritical* are), but in stressing observable behaviour and observable displays of religious feeling it does invite suspicions as to the sincerity, depth, and 'kindling power' of the attitude in question. At the same time, it does not exclude the possibility that the person may be sincere. Explicit evaluative components ('I think this is good' or 'I think this is bad') are simply absent from this explication.

2. *Apatheia* and *Apathy*

Hearing for the first time about the ancient Greek concept of 'apatheia', one is naturally inclined to link it with the modern concept encoded in the English word *apathy.* (In fact, that is how *apatheia* is sometimes translated; cf., for example, Tsanoff 1947:26 or McIntyre 1966:106.) One is quickly disabused, however, when one learns that *apatheia* was seen as a virtue, not as a pathological state. For example, Ferguson (1958:96) says that "the Stoics sought *apatheia*", and he defines it as "freedom from emotional disturbance". Von Arnim (1964:50) quotes the following passage from Cicero's *Tusculanae:* "est igitur Zenonis haec definitio ut perturbatio sit, quod *pathos* ille dicit, aversa a recta ratione contra naturam animi commotio" ('According to Zeno's definition, an (inner) disturbance (*perturbatio*), or what he calls *pathos,* is a movement of the spirit, contrary to nature and inimical to reason'). Pohlenz (1948:276) mentions the fact that Cicero rendered the Greek word *pathos* as *perturbatio* and *apatheia* as *tranquilitas (animi),* and although Pohlenz thinks these renderings didn't exactly match the Greek concepts, they are nonetheless highly revealing. Pohlenz himself emphasises "Verstandes-klarheit" 'clarity of reason' and "Seelensfrieden" 'peace of mind/soul' as the main content of the Stoic concept.

Edel and Edel (1968:201) characterise the Stoic ethic as follows: "It has a distinctive set of austere virtues and a general end of peace of mind construed as a kind of *apathy* or dominating independence of spirit through resignation, in which will is detached from ordinary aims and human relations." McIntyre (1966:106) writes: "Desire, hope, fear, pleasure and pain are against reason and nature; one should cultivate a passionless absence of desire and disregard of pleasure and pain. This is what the Stoics called *apathy*". And Tsanoff offers the following account:

> The man in the grip of passion is consumed with desire for some thing or condition
> which is not in his power, but on which he hangs his happiness or well-being. Be
> the end desired sensual pleasure or wealth or any other external mastery, the

infatuate pursuit of it enslaves the passionate man and finally exposes his entire life as futile. For nothing is gained where self-knowledge or self-mastery is not realised. In his pursuit of the good life the Stoic concentrated on the rational will as the distinctively human faculty, but unlike Aristotle and Plato, who advocated the moderation or control of the passions, the Stoics demanded their utter repression, *apathy*, the life of reason sovereign and uncontested. (1947:26)

Tsanoff adds (1947:30): "The spirit of lofty disinterestedness is characteristically Stoic. . . . This serene spirit of cosmic acquiescence is the high closing note of Roman Stoicism. But it has the overtones of resignation".

Accounts of this kind show that the concept of 'apatheia' was in fact much closer to the Christian concept of 'detachment' than to morally neutral concepts such as 'apathy' or 'indifference'. It is also related to the Orthodox Christian concept of 'smirenie', to be discussed later. Yet neither lengthy discussions nor vague analogies from other languages and other cultures can show us clearly and precisely the unique nature of a concept such as 'apatheia'. This can be done only by means of an explicit semantic formula. As a first approximation, I propose the following:

apatheia
  (a) X thinks something like this:
      different things happen to people, good things and bad things
      one cannot think: if I say: 'I don't want this', it will not happen
  (b) because of this, X doesn't think of anything that happens:
      'I don't want this'
  (c) because of this, when something bad happens to X, X doesn't think: 'I don't want this'
  (d) because of this, when things happen that X doesn't want,
      X doesn't feel anything bad
  (e) because of this, X can at all times think about what one should do and doesn't do anything that X thinks one shouldn't do
  (f) [I think this is good]

Component (a) reflects the Stoic recognition of the sovereign power of 'fate' in human life. Component (b) reflects a 'philosophical' attitude to 'fate' and the importance attached to 'reason' and wisdom in the conduct of one's life. Component (c) accounts for the Stoic freedom from desire for things which are not in one's power, for the 'resignation' mentioned by Tsanoff, and for the ideal of willingness reflected in Seneca's formula, "ducunt volentem fata, nolentem trahunt" (McIntyre 1966:106), 'him who is willing the fates lead, but the unwilling they drive' (Tsanoff 1947:25). Component (d) accounts for the Stoic serenity and absence of bad feelings such as frustration, indignation, and despair. Component (e) accounts for the Stoic tranquillity and control of the passions (neither pain nor pleasure can cause the 'wise man' to lose his tranquillity—either to cry or to laugh excessively or to display any other uncontrolled and 'unwise' reaction of any kind). Component (f) shows that 'apatheia' was seen as a virtue.

The modern concept of 'apathy' (encapsulated in the English word *apathy*) is related to the Greek 'apatheia' in implying a certain unconcern (lack of wanting) and a lack of feeling. Here, too, one could speak loosely of 'indifference'. Frankl (1964:21) glosses *apathy* as "the blunting of emotions and the feeling that one could not care any more". But the unconcern and the absence of emotion exhibited by an apathetic person are involuntary and are viewed by the speaker as pathological phenomena. Another gloss for *apathy* offered by Frankl (1964:18) is "emotional death". By contrast, the Stoics' absence of emotions was voluntary, and it followed from a voluntary acceptance of one's fate. Tentatively, I propose the following explication:

> *apathy*
> X thinks something like this:
>   one cannot think:
>   if I say: 'I want this', it will happen
>   if I say: 'I don't want this', it will not happen
>   I don't want anything
> because of this, X doesn't want to do things
>   X cannot feel much
>   X doesn't do much
> [I think this is bad]

Frankl (1964) and others have suggested that in certain abnormal circumstances (such as life in a concentration camp) 'apathy' could have a positive and indeed a salutary function. I have nonetheless postulated for *apathy* the component 'I think this is bad' because I think that the word implies that the state in question is pathological, abnormal, and there is no contradiction in saying that under abnormal conditions, 'bad', pathological states may have a positive function.

3. *Smirenie*

A particularly clear example of cultural significance of the lexicalisation of ethical concepts is provided by the Russian word *smirenie,* which has no exact equivalent in English and which identifies a religious attitude to life quite crucial to the traditional (Orthodox) Russian outlook. The significance of *smirenie* in this tradition is clearly reflected in the following quotes from Dostoevsky's *The Brothers Karamazov:*

> No spaset bog ljudej svoix, ibo velika Rossija smireniem svoim. (1976:286)
>
> 'But God will save His people, for Russia is great in her humility.' (1974:328)
>
> A Rossiju spaset gospod', kak spasal uže mnogo raz. Iz naroda spasenie vyjdet, iz very i smirenija ego. (1976:286)
>
> 'But God will save Russia as He has saved her many times. Salvation will come from the people, from their faith and their meekness.' (1974:328)
>
> Smirenie ljubovnoe—strašnaja sila, izo vsex sil'nejšaja, podobnoj kotoroj i net ničego. (1976:289)

'Loving humility is marvellously strong, the strongest of all things and there is nothing else like it.' (1974:332)

Dictionaries usually equate the verb *smirit'sja* with English verbs such as *submit* or *resign (oneself);* the noun *smirenie* with English nouns such as *humbleness, humility,* or *meekness;* and the adjective *smirennyj* with English adjectives such as *humble, meek,* and *submissive.* (Cf., for example, Smirnickij 1961.)

In fact, however, translations of this kind give very little insight into the concept of 'smirenie', so crucial to the traditional Russian culture. Tendentious, hostile glosses such as "*smirenie*—outsutstvie gordosti, gotovnost' podčinjat'sja čužoj vole" ('absence of dignity, readiness to submit to somebody else's will'; Ožegov 1972:676) are even more misleading, although their very tendentiousness is also revealing. Glosses of this kind imply that *smirenie* has negative connotations. In fact, the opposite is true. To use this word in a negative sense, one would have to use it sarcastically, as a quote from a language which one does not speak oneself. Speaking seriously, one can only use it in a positive sense—as it has been used, for example, in the sentences quoted.

From this it is evident that some Soviet lexicographers felt that ideologically undesirable attitudes such as 'smirenie' cannot be neutrally reflected in a dictionary, without some sign of disapproval. In fact, the word *smirenie* denotes a religious attitude of serene acceptance of one's fate, achieved through moral effort, through suffering, and through realisation of one's total dependence on God, an acceptance resulting not only in an attitude of non-resistance to evil but also in profound peace and a loving attitude toward one's fellow human beings.

In natural language, one can always violate certain semantic components of a word by using it in what is called a 'powerful context' ("moščnyj kontekst", cf. Paduçeva 1985:56). For example, one can say in Russian:

Ivan ne vyzdorovel—on voobšče ne bolel.

'Ivan hasn't recovered (from illness)—he hasn't been ill at all.'

but this doesn't show that the word *vyzdorovet'* 'recover' lacks any presupposition of an earlier illness. Typically, violations of this kind occur when a word is used as a reaction to someone else's utterance and when it constitutes a crypto-quotation. A 'quotative' use of the word *smirenie* can, I think, be illustrated with the following sentence from Berdyaev:

Rab'e učenie o smirenii isključaet vozmožnost' bunta i vosstanija, ono trebuet poslušanija i pokornosti daže zlu. (1949:68)

'The slavish doctrine of "smirenie" excludes any possibility of rebellion and of protest; it demands obedience and submission even with respect to evil.'

In this passage Berdyaev is distancing himself from a certain interpretation of *smirenie;* the word itself is for him neither negative nor even neutral. It is positive, as one can seen when one considers his use of the collocation *nastojaščee smirenie* 'genuine *smirenie*', as in the following passage:

Kogda v kakom-nibud' sobranii menja sčitali očen' počtennym i izvestnym, to ja
xotel provalit'sja skvoz' zemlju. Èto ne est' nastojaščee smirenie. Tut sliškom
mnogo ot gordosti, ravnodušija, izolirovannosti, čuždosti vsem. . . . (1949:39)

'When in some gathering I was treated as a celebrity, I wanted to sink into the
ground. This is not genuine *smirenie*. There is too much in this of pride, indifference, intentional isolation and alienation from everyone. . . .'

In some ways, the Orthodox concept of 'smirenie' is related to the Stoic concept
of 'apatheia'. Loosely speaking, both *smirenie* and *apatheia* could be glossed as
'acceptance of fate' or as 'attainment of emotional peace'. But formulae of this kind
would gloss over some crucial differences between the two concepts—as one can
see comparing the following explication of *smirenie* with the explication of *apatheia*
given earlier:

smirenie
(a) X thinks something like this:
         things happen to people because someone (God) wants it
(b)   this someone knows why they happen
(c)   I cannot know it
(d) because of this, when something bad happens to X, X doesn't think: 'I don't
       want this'
(e) because of this, X doesn't feel anything bad toward anyone
(f)   and feels something good toward everyone
(g) [I think this is good]

For one thing, 'smirenie' is a religious concept: it refers not to fate but to God.
(For example, one could hardly speak of a *smirennyj kommunist,* a '*smirennyj*
communist'.) This difference between *apatheia* and *smirenie* is reflected in the
component (a) of the two explications.

Second, *smirenie* implies a submission not only of one's will but also of one's
reason to God: a person who has achieved *smirenie* does not merely accept what he
or she recognises as inevitable but also recognises the inherent limitations of his or
her judgement in assessing things that happen. By contrast, *apatheia* suggests
confidence in human reason: one can't change one's 'fate', but recognising this, one
can conduct one's life rationally, mastering one's emotions and doing only what one
thinks a person guided by reason should do. (See component (e) of *apatheia* and (b)
and (c) of *smirenie*.)

Third, 'smirenie' is a positive concept in the sense that it implies warm feelings
toward the world, achieved through an unconditional surrender to God's will. By
contrast, 'apatheia' seems to be conceived of more negatively, as 'freedom from
emotional disturbance'. It appears that *apatheia* aimed at creating an emotional
distance between a person and the world; *smirenie,* on the other hand, aims at
making a person emotionally close to everyone and everything. I have reflected this
difference by assigning to *smirenie,* but not to *apatheia,* the component 'because of
this, X doesn't feel anything bad toward anyone and feels something good toward
everyone' (components (e), (f) of *smirenie*).

Fourth, *apatheia* was meant to create a wall around those who possessed it: a wall which would protect them from all 'bad feelings' (anger, despair, frustration, pain, and so on). By contrast, *smirenie* is meant to deliver those who possess it from any bad feelings *toward other people*, without necessarily protecting them from inherent 'bad feelings' such as sadness, sorrow, or suffering. The holy figures of Mater Dolorosa and the Man of Sorrows are quite compatible with the ideal of 'smirenie', but not with the Stoic ideal of 'apatheia'. (Compare the phrasing of component (e) of *smirenie*, 'X . . . feels something good toward everyone', with the phrasing of component (d) of *apatheia*, 'X doesn't feel anything bad. . .' .)[2]

Fifth, *apatheia* implies self-control, tranquillity, ability to maintain at all times the same cool and 'philosophical' attitude to the world (component (e)); no such component, however, is contained in the concept of 'smirenie'.

Finally, *smirenie* easily lends itself to an interpretation in the spirit of non-resistance, submission, and passivity, whereas *apatheia* doesn't invite such an interpretation.

The following passage by a nineteenth-century *starec* (charismatic spiritual director) reflects the flavour of *smirenie* very well:

> Peace of soul is acquired by a perfect surrender to the divine will, without which nothing happens. . . . He in whose heart humility and meekness are reborn, will find true rest for his soul. He will be satisfied with everything, grateful for everything, peaceful and full of love for everybody. He will judge none and will feel no anger. His heart will be filled with divine sweetness, that is, he will feel in himself the Kingdom of God because God grants his grace only to the humble. (Bolshakoff 1977:176)

4. *Humility*

The Christian ideal of 'humility' is more difficult to articulate than one might initially expect. Metaphors come readily to mind: X is humble: X wants to be 'small'; "X wants to be a 'servant' of all; X is 'lowly of mind'" (Turner 1980:718); X wants to be 'lowly'. But when one tries to explicate 'humility' in non-metaphorical terms, the task proves unexpectedly hard—despite the extensive Christian literature devoted to the problem.

According to St John of the Cross (1979:300–301), souls "who are advancing in perfection . . . receive great benefit from their humility, by which they not only place little importance on their deeds, but also take very little self-satisfaction from them. They think everyone else is far better than themselves. . . . They think they themselves are insignificant, and want others to think that too and to belittle and slight their deeds. . . . They are more eager to speak of their faults and sins, and reveal them to others, than their virtues."

Comments of this kind offer valuable clues to the concept of 'humility', and yet they do not provide a sufficient basis for a definition, since they don't predict correctly the entire range of the concept's application. In particular, they do not account for the possibility that the word *humility* can be used with respect to Jesus

Christ. Positive words such as *mercy, justice,* or *goodness* can be applied to both
God (God the Father) and Christ. The word *humility* cannot be applied to God, but
(unlike *self-abasement*) it can still be applied to Jesus. (Cf. Matt. 11:29: "discite a
me quia mitis sum et humilis corde", "learn from me, for I am gentle and humble-
hearted" (NEB 1970). I presume that the Latin adjective *humilis,* unlike the English
adjective *humble,* corresponds in meaning to the noun *humilitas* 'humility'.) This
shows that an adequate explication of 'humility' cannot contain components such as
'X thinks bad things about himself', 'X thinks that everyone is better than X', or 'X
wants people to think bad things about X', as might be suggested by St John's
discussion quoted earlier.

To solve the problem of the applicability of the concept in question to Jesus, I
propose, tentatively, the following phrasing of the relevant components (for a full
explication, see below):

> X doesn't think things like this:
>   I am someone good
>   people can know good things about me
>   I know much

It seems to me that, phrased in this way, these components are not incompatible
with the assumptions of Jesus' sinlessness and of His awareness of His special status
as Son of God.

In discussing the concept of 'humility' with respect to Jesus, I do not wish to
imply that Jesus is the prototypical model of 'humility'. I simply think that if one
considers Jesus' personality, it becomes easier to separate 'humility' from concepts
such as 'self-abasement' or 'inferiority complex'.

Furthermore, in calling 'humility' a Christian concept I am not suggesting that it
can be used only within the context of a Christian outlook, although the origin is no
doubt Christian. (As shown by Turner 1980, in secular Greek the word *tapeinos*
meant 'low', 'flat', and when it was used as a moral concept it was clearly pejorative, meaning something like 'mean' or 'base'. It was only in Biblical Greek that the
new, distinctly Christian sense of *tapeinos* 'humilis' as something good was born.)
Extended use of the concept, going beyond a Christian outlook, seems possible. For
example, one can speak of atheist scientists who felt 'humility' when they thought
of the mysteries of the Universe. One can say that the contemplation of the sky on a
starry night can teach people (and especially scientists) humility, without any religious overtones. It is also possible for politicians who have just been elected to
say, in their first public statement after the event, that they feel great humility
thinking of the great task before them and of the trust that people have placed in
them.

The components proposed so far seem to be applicable, by and large, to both the
hypothetical scientist and the hypothetical politician. But even if we decide (as I
think we should) to treat scientists' or politicians' 'humility' as an extended use of
the term, extensions of this kind are still instructive. In particular, they point to
some incommensurability between the experiencers and the target of their thoughts:
politicians don't feel humility when thinking of their fellow politicians but when

thinking of the needs of the nation, and scientists don't feel humility when thinking of fellow scientists but when thinking of the vastness of the Universe or the vastness of our ignorance. This highlights the fact that Christians whose hearts are full of humility don't really compare themselves with other people: they feel humility because their thoughts are focussed on someone incommensurably greater than either they or their fellow human beings. They may feel humility thinking of God and of the 'distance' which separates human beings from God. By extension, perhaps, it can be said that scientists feel 'humility' thinking of the distance which separates what they know from what remains to be discovered (and from what will never be discovered).

To account for the different aspects of the concept 'humility' I would propose the following semantic formula:

> *humility*
> X often thinks something like this:
> > Y is someone good
> > no one can be like Y
> because of this, X feels something good toward Y
> because of this, X doesn't think things like this:
> > I am someone good
> > people can know good things about me
> > I know much
> X doesn't want other people to think these things about X
> [I think this is good]

Defined like this, 'humility' looks like a predominantly negative concept: it consists largely in 'not thinking' certain things rather than in thinking something. Since, however, those things that a person of humility doesn't think are among the most natural and wide-spread human inclinations, humility would often be a result of profound inner work, aimed at eradicating attitudes which appear in the human heart quite naturally. Nonetheless, the concept of 'humility' as such doesn't entail the idea of an inner struggle and of an inner transformation. Rather, it suggests the image of a person whose inner sight is focussed on something other than and greater than himself or herself. It is the contemplation of something other than oneself that cleanses the heart of a person of humility from the natural human tendencies toward self-aggrandisement and self-glorification. Thomas à Kempis wrote:

> The saints highest before God are lowest in their own sight. And the more their glory, the deeper their humility. Full of heaven's truth and glory, they are not eager for empty praise. . . . And they who ascribe to God whatever good they have received will not look for another's praise, but long for the glory that is God's above, and desire that God may be praised beyond everything in themselves and in all the saints. (1952:66)

If we compare the concept of 'humility' with the concept of 'smirenie', we see that the differences between them are really quite considerable. The main difference is, I think, this: *Smirenie* implies above all a serene acceptance of everything that happens, because everything that happens is seen as due to God's will, to which one has submitted one's own will; this may well include acceptance of one's own lowly status, as well as acceptance of suffering, violence, persecution, and so on, but the main stress is not on the 'lowliness' but on acceptance. To the extent to which 'a lowliness of mind and heart' is implied by *smirenie*, it follows from the submission of one's will to God's will.

By contrast, in *humility* the stress is not on acceptance and submission of will but on a preference for the last place, on a desire not to be treated as someone who is better than other people, on a deep dislike of *vana gloria* 'empty glory'. The great symbolic scene in which Jesus washes the feet of His disciples is symbolic of 'humility', not of 'smirenie': there is no question there of His submitting His will to theirs, but only of His wish not to derive any glory from any comparisons between Him and His fellow human beings. If one wanted to point to a scene in the Gospels which could serve as a prototype of 'smirenie', one would have to point to a different scene: the scene in the Garden of Gethsemane, when Jesus submits His will to His Father's will.

A person who has achieved *smirenie* doesn't rebel against anything. A person who has achieved *humility* would never rebel against his lowly status, lowly opinion of other people, and so on, but could well rebel against other things—things that he or she sees as 'bad'. Hence, the ideal of *smirenie* leads more easily to the ideal of non-resistance to evil than the ideal of *humility* does. Furthermore, the ideal of *humility* is more easily reconciled with Western ideals of individualism, personal independence (in outward affairs, not only in inner life), struggle for freedom, and so on.

The explications of *humility* and *smirenie* proposed here are perhaps surprisingly different from one another (given the traditional assumptions that *smirenie* is simply the Russian term for *humility*). Of course the extent of the difference may be partly due to some inadequacies of the formulae. But I think that even allowing for this one must admit that detailed semantic analysis shows these concepts to be much further apart than has been traditionally assumed. When one considers that in the translations of the Bible and other crucial documents of Christianity, the same words which are translated into English as *humility* are translated into Russian as *smirenie*, one must conclude that these different translations suggest to their readers rather different moral ideals. The difference between *humility* and *smirenie* is highlighted by sentences such as the following:

> No uže togda u Solov'eva bylo protivojadie protiv soblaznov sverxčelovečeskoj gordyni v čuvstve smirenija. (Solov'ev 1977:151)
>
> 'But by that time there was in Solov'ev an antidote against superhuman pride in the feeling of *smirenie.*'

It would be odd and self-contradictory to speak of a person's *humility* as an antidote against his or her *pride* (or *hubris*), because the two are direct opposites of one another, but *smirenie* is not a real opposite of *pride* or *gordost'* (the Russian equivalent of *pride*).

I am not suggesting that closer attention to semantic details can overcome the problem of non-equivalence between the moral ideals promoted by different transla-tions, because this non-equivalence is an inherent feature of the languages in ques-tion. I would suggest, however, that it is important to be aware of such differences—and to be aware of the new shades of ethical teaching which originate in the process of translation and which are absent from the semantic content of the original. Subtle differences of this kind, which can be revealed in painstaking semantic analysis, are easily overlooked, not only by the general reader but also by scholars whose attention is focussed on the theological, historical, philological, or exegetic aspects of their area of study, but who may be unaware of its semantic dimension.

Linguistic difficulties which arise when one tries to translate ethical terms from one language into another have of course often been noted. For example, Edel and Edel write:

> To pursue such analyses in other cultures is not a simple matter. Considering the difficulty in getting at the precise meaning of terms in ethical discourse in our own usage, despite the centuries of practice from Socrates to the modern analysts, it is not surprising that one may sometimes find it hard to ferret out with exactness the meaning of an ethical term in some other language and cultural situation. But it is also clear that such comparative inquiry may yield some very interesting clues. (1968:114)

Yet even such perceptive and linguistically aware authors as May Edel and Abraham Edel seem to underestimate seriously the real difficulty of the task they discuss. For example, they see no problem in analysing the Navajo term *bahazid* (which they say Ladd (1957) regards as the critical term of the Navajo ethical system) via the English terms *reverence* and *fear*. But as long as ethical terms in one language are explained via ethical terms of another language (which constitute a different folk taxonomy of ethical concepts), ethnocentrism cannot be prevented. It can only be avoided if the introduction of a language-independent metalanguage puts an end to the use of language-specific ethical terms as supposedly culture-free analytical tools.

Of course the idea that in translation concepts, including moral concepts, are often more or less inevitably altered is hardly new. What I think *is* new about the present approach is that it offers an analytical framework within which such subtle alterations can be made explicit, so that their character can be brought to the level of awareness and be made a subject of study.

5. *Humility* Versus *Pride*

Having defined *humility,* it is good methodology to verify the adequacy of the proposed definition by comparing it with the definition of the closely related con-cept of 'pride', or rather, with that encoded in the clearly pejorative words such as the Latin *superbia,* the French *orgueil,* or the Polish *pycha.*

It is quite remarkable that, unlike many other European languages, English

doesn't encode lexically the notion of 'bad pride', of 'superbia'. English dictionaries often include the word *hubris* and allege that this is the English equivalent of
orgueil, but of course *hubris* is not a colloquial English word, and the need to use it
(or the specialised phrase *overweening pride*) occasionally in English highlights the
lexical gap in question. In fact, even in scholarly books which are written in a non-
pretentious style, *superbia* is rendered as *pride* rather than *hubris,* as, for example,
in the following sentence: "Do not let nineteenth-century anticlericals persuade you
that in the Judaeo-Christian tradition the mere vices of the flesh are ranked as
deadlier sins than the great evils of pride, bad faith, cruelty" (Brinton 1959:116).

The fact that English has no special word for 'bad pride' (*orgueil*) may well be
related to the fact that it has no adjective corresponding precisely to the noun
humility. Both of these lexical gaps may reflect a relative unconcern of the Anglo-
Saxon cultural tradition with 'superbia' and 'humility'. The adjective *humble* (as
pointed out to me by Jean Harkins) differs in meaning from the noun *humility,* in
being oriented more toward external behaviour than toward the dispositions of the
heart and in implying certain comparisons (between the 'humble' person and other
people). It seems that the ideal of incommensurability between the subject and the
target of his or her thoughts, which lies at the heart of *humility,* has been replaced in
the concept of *humble(ness)* with something more superficial and external.

I will now proceed to explicate three concepts, all related to 'humility' and to
each other: the negative concept encoded in words such as *orgueil* ('bad pride'), the
positive concept encoded in words such as *fierté* ('good pride'), and the neutral or
ambivalent concept encoded in the English word *pride.*

> *orgueil*
> X doesn't think things like this of anyone:
>> Y is someone very good
>> no one can be like Y
> X often thinks something like this:
>> I am someone very good
>> I am not someone like other people
>> I want this
> because of this, X feels something good
> X wants other people to think the same
> [I think this is bad]

> *fierté*
> X often thinks something like this:
>> people can know something very good about my Y
>> because of this, they cannot *not* think something good about me
>> I can think something good about me
> because of this, X feels something good
> [I think it is good if someone can think something like this]

> *pride* (X is *proud* of Y)
> X often thinks something like this:
>> people can know something very good about my Y
>> because of this, they cannot *not* think something good about me
>> I can think something good about me
> because of this, X feels something good

I will comment on these definitions as briefly as possible.

The definition of *orgueil* is not exactly like a mirror image of the definition of *humility* but comes pretty close to it. Persons guilty of this vice are self-centred, have an exceedingly high opinion of themselves, and are incapable of an adoring contemplation and glorification of anything other than themselves. They seek gratification by comparing themselves (favourably) with other people and want other people to see them in the same light. They are hardly capable of acknowledging anybody else's superiority, or even the possibility of such superiority.

Of course the sin of *orgueil* is not incompatible with a belief in God. It seems, however, that even in relationship to God, an *orgueilleux* is incapable of sincerely acknowledging and accepting an incommensurability between himself and God.

The concept encoded in the French word *fierté* (or the Polish word *duma*) is much simpler, but it doesn't represent simply an extract from the concept encoded in the word *orgueil*. For one thing, this concept reduces the self-centredness of *orgueil* by shifting the attention from ego to something related to ego (ego's children, ego's creation, ego's work, and so on). This does not represent a real shift from 'self' to 'other', but it can be seen as a move in that direction. For that reason, no doubt, the attitude in question is no longer seen as ugly or sinful, and the words which designate it acquire almost positive connotations. I have refrained, however, from assigning to *fierté* the positive evaluative component 'I think this is good' because *fierté* is not seen as a virtue. Rather it is seen as a recognition of something positive in one's life. To account for the positive connotations of *fierté*, I have posited a different component: 'I think it is good if someone can think something like this'.

As for *pride*, I have represented it as differing from *fierté* in just one component (the last one). The fact that *pride* shares with *fierté* an orientation toward something related to ego (rather than to ego as such) accounts for the fact that *pride* can be used in a positive sense and can be conjoined with a positive word such as *dignity*. The fact that the explication of *pride* contains no evaluative component of any kind accounts for the possibility of using this word in purely negative contexts and of conjoining it with such unambiguously pejorative words as *cruelty* or *greed* (cf. Brinton 1959:116, quoted earlier).

I must add that in Russian literature, the concepts of 'gordost'' ('pride') and 'gordynja' ('orgueil') are often contrasted with 'smirenie', as, for example, in the following sentence:

Taina Golgofy, prinjatie kotoroj trebuet smirenija, ne vozmeščaetsja v ego gorduju dušu. (Solov'ev 1954:15)

'In his proud soul there is no room for the mystery of Golgotha, the acceptance of which requires *smirenie*.'

This may suggest that not only *humility* but also *smirenie* should be represented as a semantic opposite of *orgueil* and that the definitions of *humility* and *smirenie* proposed here are in fact too far apart.

Admitting this as a real possibility, I would, however, point out that the apparent incompatibility between *smirenie* and *orgueil* may not necessarily reflect a symmetrical semantic structure of the two concepts. There are many different kinds of conceptual incompatibility (cf., for example, Lyons 1977; cf. also Russell 1962;

Apresjan 1974). *White* is incompatible with *black,* but they are not opposites in the same sense in which *big* and *small* or *long* and *short* are. *Smirenie,* like *humility,* is perceived as an opposite of *orgueil,* but unlike *humility* it is also perceived as an opposite of *rebellion.* This suggests that *smirenie* is not as direct an opposite of *orgueil* as *humility* is. It should also be pointed out in this connection that although in Russian literature *smirenie* is often contrasted with *gordynja* or *gordost',* it is sometimes presented as *difficult* rather than *impossible* to reconcile with these latter attitudes. (Cf., for example, Berdyaev 1949:38.) By contrast, *humility* seems to be directly opposed to *orgueil* and to be not *difficult* but *impossible* to reconcile with it.

The quote from Vladimir Solov'ev adduced earlier is illuminating in the way it brings together the concept of 'smirenie' with the concept of 'mystery'. *Smirenie* does seem to imply a recognition that one's capacity for understanding is limited and an acceptance of these limitations. I have tried to account for this aspect of *smirenie* in the components of its explication: 'this someone (God) knows why they happen; I cannot know why they happen'. There is no exact parallel to this in the proposed explications of either *humility* or *orgueil.*

6. Language and Culture

In medieval Europe, including England, the sin called "superbia" (that is, 'bad pride') was regarded as "king of all vices" (Bloomfield 1952:183), as "the eldest daughter of hell" (1967:172), and as "leader of Sins" (1967:145). Yet in modern English there is not even a word to refer to this concept. Is this an accident of language or a meaningful expression of culture and society?

I believe it is the latter. The idea that it is good to view oneself as 'small' and that it is bad to view oneself as 'great' lay at the heart of the medieval European world view and was expressed in the contrast between the virtue of 'humilitas' and the vice of 'superbia'.

The spread of the ideology of humanism was of course hard to reconcile with that idea, and from the time of the Renaissance both 'humility' and 'superbia' lost their central place in the European moral outlook. It appears, however, that in the Anglo-Saxon culture this process of decline of both 'humilitas' and 'superbia' went further than in other European countries. Presumably, one relevant factor was religion, and it appears that in Catholic countries the concepts in question maintained their position better than they did in Protestant countries. Weber's speculations about the link between the Protestant ethic and the development of capitalism may apply to the concepts of 'humility' and 'bad pride' as much as they do to the concepts of 'weird', 'fate', and 'destiny' (see chapter 2). If an ethical ideology places a great emphasis on individual success and on competition, then it is hard for it to continue to regard 'pride' as the "king of all vices". The thought 'I am better than other people' can no longer be regarded as the root of all evil; on the contrary, it must come to be seen as linked with 'cardinal virtues' rather than with cardinal sins.

The downfall of the concept of 'humility', and, in particular, the shift in the meaning of the English adjective *humble,* points in the same direction. In modern Anglo-Saxon consciousness, the idea of a 'humble person' is associated more with a

Uriah Heep personality than with any positive hero of modern times.

As for the contrast between the Western European concept of 'humility' and the Russian concept of 'smirenie', the emphasis in the former seems to be on what one *thinks* of oneself, whereas in the latter it seems to be on what one *wants*. It is *smirenie*, then, but not *humility*, which involves 'giving up one's will' to some extent. This is entirely compatible with what cultural historians have said about the role of 'Eastern passivity' in the Russian cultural tradition and in the Russian national outlook and about the role of 'activism' in the Western European cultural tradition. The Russian philosopher Vladimir Solov'ev presented this contrast in the following terms (for further discussion of this area, see chapter 12):

> Western culture was forged in the ancient world by the Greek republics and by Rome. Greek cities were founded by teams of homeless settlers and Rome was founded by a gang of robbers. Hence the virtues of the Western man: independence and energy; and vices: personal pride, a tendency to wilfulness and internecine conflicts.

> Eastern culture has its basis in complete subordination of man to a superhuman force; Western culture—in autonomous human activity. . . . On the basis of the subordination to superhuman forces, Eastern thought developed its specific moral ideal, whose main features are resignation and complete submission to 'higher powers'. (1966, v.4:21)

The moral ideal in question, 'smirenie', has never had an equivalent in the Western cultural lexicon. But the Western Christian ideal of 'humilitas' ('humility') has declined, too, whereas virtues such as 'independence', 'self-reliance', 'self-confidence', or 'ambition' have been consistently gaining ground (see, for example, Arensberg and Niehoff 1975 and Hsu 1975).

It is interesting to note in this connection that in Russian, the closest equivalent of *ambition*, *čestoljubie*, is a somewhat marginal and rather pejorative word. For example, Ušakov's (1940) dictionary of Russian glosses this word, and its derivatives, as *knižnoe, neodobritel'noe* 'bookish, somewhat negative'. Literally, *čestoljubie* means something like 'fondness for honours', and it doesn't have the goal-oriented character of *ambition*. Consequently, *čestoljubie*, in contrast to *ambition*, cannot be used with reference to an important goal, and Gal'perin's (1977) English-Russian dictionary translates the English sentence "It is his *ambition* to become a writer" as "Ego mečta—stat' pisatelem", lit., 'It is his dream to become a writer'. This equation of the English *ambition* with the Russian *mečta* 'dream' corresponds in a striking way to what has been claimed by Solov'ev and others about the different cultural orientations characterising 'the East' and 'the West'.

The impression that *čestoljubie* is a marginal concept in Russian whereas *ambition* is a very important and salient one in English is confirmed in a spectacular way by data on their frequency provided by corpora such as Zasorina's (1977) and Kučera and Francis' (1967). In Zasorina's megacorpus of one million words *čestoljubie* occurs just once, and the clearly pejorative noun *čestoljubec* ('an over-ambitious person') also once, whereas in Kučera and Francis' corpus *ambition* and *ambitious* have (jointly) a frequency of 50. It would be hard to find more telling evidence for a cultural difference.

7. Conclusion

Countless studies have been devoted to subjects such as 'the idea of justice in Plato's philosophy', 'the idea of courage in Aristotle's writings', 'the concept of law (sacrifice, faith, etc.) in Jewish thought', and 'the concept of obligation in the Japanese ethics'. The abundance of the literature on such topics is only natural, given their inherent interest and importance. But this very abundance creates a danger, lending the scholarly tradition in question an air of naturalness and undisputed legitimacy and thereby masking its precarious and vulnerable character.

A fresh look at the tradition in question quickly exposes its inherent vulnerability. The point is familiar but all the more easily forgotten: ideas are only accessible to us through language, and not through 'language' in the abstract but through concrete lexical items of a particular natural language. It is legitimate to talk about the Roman ideal of 'pietas', but not about the Roman ideal of 'courage'; about the Stoic ideal of 'apatheia', but not about the Stoic ideal of 'apathy', 'indifference', or 'detachment'; about the Orthodox Russian ideal of 'smirenie', but not about the Orthodox Russian ideal of 'humility'.

The use of authentic lexical labels enables us to identify ideas, and ideals, with precision and without ethnocentrism. At the same time, however, exclusive use of such labels prevents cross-cultural comparison of ideas and ideals, and although preventing ethnocentric distortions, it may also prevent insight and understanding.

I believe that contrary to appearances, the dilemma in question is not insoluble. Cross-cultural translation in the area of ethical ideals is possible, as it is possible (also contrary to appearances) in the area of kinship terminologies, terms for emotions, or terms for speech acts and speech genres. What is needed is simply a culture-independent semantic metalanguage, based on an 'alphabet of human thought': that is to say, on a non-arbitrary system of universal semantic primitives.

6

Courage, Bravery,
Recklessness

What is *courage?* What does it mean to be *brave* or to be a *coward?* Questions such as these have been pursued in European thought at least since the time of Socrates, and it is astonishing to see how little progress has been made in defining concepts of this kind. Despite all the efforts of philosophers and of lexicographers, dictionaries still content themselves to say, in essence, that *courageous* means *brave* and that *brave* means *courageous.* For example, *Webster* (1965) takes the reader on the following tour:

courageous	=	brave, bold
brave	=	bold, courageous, intrepid
bold	=	courageous, venturesome
intrepid	=	bold, fearless
fearless	=	intrepid

If a rare dictionary does manage to define one of these words without a vicious circle, it will pay for it by not even attempting to capture the invariant. For example, LDOTEL (1984) defines *courage* as follows:

courage = mental or moral strength to confront and withstand danger, fear, or difficulty

It doesn't even try to say what "danger", "fear", and "difficulty" may have in common, thus violating the fundamental principle of sound defining laid down by Socrates on the very occasion of searching (with Laches) for a definition of *courage* (or rather, of the Greek concept *andreia,* usually rendered in English as *courage*).

I meant to ask you not only about the courage of the heavily-armed soldiers, but about the courage of cavalry and every other style of soldier; and not only who are courageous in war but who are courageous in perils by sea, and who in disease, or in poverty, or again in politics, are courageous; and not only who are courageous against pain or fear, but mighty to contend against desires and pleasures, either fixed in their rank or turning upon the enemy. There is this sort of courage—is there not, Laches?

LACH.: Certainly, Socrates. . . .

SOC. What is that common quality, which is the same in all these cases, and which is called courage? (Plato 1970:116–17)

Philosophers who have written about *courage* and related concepts appear to be more aware of the need to search for a semantic invariant. For example, Wallace (1978:78–79) offers the following definition of *courage* (in the form of a set of four conditions):

(a) A believes that it is dangerous for him to do Y
(b) A believes that his doing Y is worth the risks it involves
(c) A believes that it is possible for him not to do Y
(d) The danger A sees in doing Y must be sufficiently formidable that most people would find it difficult in the circumstances to do Y

But philosophical definitions of this kind usually fail to pay attention to the actual usage and aim at some language-independent fictions rather than at the concepts authentically encoded in real words such as the English *courage,* the Latin *fortitudo,* or the Greek *andreia.* It is often recognised at the beginning of a discussion that words of this kind do not match up across language boundaries, but on the second or third page this crucial fact is already forgotten, and the writer proceeds to offer a definition of some hypothetical concept not encoded in any real word of any known language.

In Wallace's case, it is easy to see that his definition of *courage* doesn't fit, for example, the case of someone who shows the quality in bearing a painful and incurable illness. In a case like this, no dangers, and no risks, are involved in behaving in a dignified, patient, and serene fashion, and yet in English such behaviour *can* be called *courageous.*

What applies to much of the philosophical literature on character traits applies also to a good deal of the psychological literature, including cross-cultural personality studies.

As Wagatsuma (1977:142–43) points out, cross-cultural research in the area of personality studies often proceeds as follows: "a questionnaire or psychological list developed in one language is translated into another language and responses to the 'same' questionnaire or test in 'different' languages are used for a cross-cultural comparison". To Wagatsuma, who has compared a number of Japanese character terms with their closest counterparts in European languages, it is perfectly clear that "words that describe behavioral characteristics or social phenomena may connote one thing in one language and another in another language". In view of this, "the stimulus value of the original questionnaire or test certainly becomes lost when translated into another language and used in another culture. And yet, many cross-cultural studies have been carried out precisely in this manner".

Even anthropologists who are aware of the language problem sometimes underestimate the dangers involved in similar procedures. For example, White (1980:776) postulates some "universal conceptual schemata in the personality lexicon", "using English translations of the Melanesian and Indian word-sets". He admits that "there are real dangers in matching English glosses which mask the range of culture-specific meanings" (1980:760), but he dismisses this difficulty, on the grounds that "models of conceptual organization derived independently from these distinct languages show remarkable similarities in over-all structure" (p. 760)—"independently", but always by using English glosses. For example, White's (1980:762) figure 1 "represents a two-dimensional model of conceptual structure in 37 personality descriptors of the A'ara language of Santa Isabel, Solomon Islands". These 37 "A'ara descriptors" include items such as *possessive, individualistic, irresponsible, haughty, bold, aggressive, selfish.*

But if the A'ara descriptors are studied through their English glosses, can we fully trust the conclusion that they "show remarkable similarities in over-all structure" to the English terms?

The crucial fact that many researchers seem still to be unaware of is that character terms encapsulate specific cultural models (D'Andrade 1985), associated with specific languages, and that if we want to elucidate these models, and to be able to compare them, we need a culture-independent semantic metalanguage. We cannot achieve these ends relying on English folk concepts such as *brave, coward, bold,* or *reckless,* and we cannot achieve them using relatively complex and language-specific terms such as *formidable, danger, risk,* or *fear.* We can, however, reach them—or at least make considerable progress toward reaching them—by using simpler, less culture- and language-dependent concepts as our analytical tools. I believe that *bad* and *good, do* and *happen* should be among our main tools when approaching the task in question.

1. English

1.1 *Coward*

Coward is a noun, and as such it indicates not only a simple property (as the adjectives *brave* or *courageous* do) but a categorisation: 'the kind of person who . . . ' (cf. Wierzbicka 1988c:469). It refers to a certain type of behaviour, but it describes this behaviour in terms of hypothetical thoughts and motivations. The thoughts in question can be represented as follows:

> I think I should do Y
> I don't want to do it
> if I do it, something bad could happen to me

Thus, a *coward* knows what he should do, or at least he thinks he knows what he should do, but he doesn't want to do it because he knows, or thinks, that if he does it, something bad could happen to him. As a result, he doesn't do it. The speaker who is describing someone as a *coward* is definitely expressing a negative opinion about this behaviour ('I think this is bad'). This opinion applies to the entire construct of the 'coward' concept, as a kind of 'editorial' comment on it.

In addition to a negative opinion, the word *coward* seems also to convey the speaker's negative feeling toward the person spoken of, as *nomina personae* (i.e., nouns) describing character traits generally tend to do. For example, the verb *to lie* or the adjective *foolish* is negative, without, however, implying a 'bad feeling', whereas the nouns *liar* and *fool* seem to imply both a bad opinion and a bad feeling. (The special status of these two components is indicated by square brackets in the following.) This leads us to the following explication:

> X is a *coward*.   →
> X is the kind of person who thinks something like this:
>   I should do Y
>   I don't want to do it
>   if I do it, something bad could happen to me
> and because of this, feels something bad
> and because of this, doesn't do Y
> [I think this is bad]
> [because of this, I feel something bad toward X]

One aspect of this explication[1] which should perhaps be explained is the absence of any explicit reference to fear. In fact, something very much like fear is implied in the combination of components 'X thinks something like this: if I do it something bad could happen to me', and 'because of this, X feels something bad'. The concept 'fear' is complex and language-specific; it is undesirable, therefore, to employ it in the semantic metalanguage—and it is unnecessary, if we have at our disposal simpler concepts: *bad, feel, happen,* and so on.

1.2 *Courageous*

Courageous is an adjective, not a noun, and it doesn't categorise a person in the way *coward* does ('X is the kind of person who . . .'; cf. Wierzbicka 1988c). Rather, it ascribes to a person (or an action) a single property ('X is someone who . . . '). *Courageous* people, like *cowards,* know, or think they know, what they should do, but unlike *cowards,* they want to do it, and they do it because of that. Do they think, as *cowards* do, 'if I do it, something bad could happen to me', and do it in spite of that, or is any thought of possible bad consequences absent from their minds?

People do say sometimes that *courageous* people "have no fear", or, on the contrary, that they feel fear but have to overcome it. For example, in a recent article, Johnson-Laird and Oatley (1989:111) define *courage* as "control, or lack, of fear in relation to danger". But according to this definition a madman, or a baby, both of whom may 'lack fear in relation to danger', could be called *courageous*. In fact, it seems that neither the presence nor the absence of fear is necessary. What is necessary is that there is something objectively bad or threatening about the situation that would be recognised by other people and that would be likely to stop them from doing what they think they should do—them, but not our hero (the *courageous* person).

The proviso 'bad or threatening' is necessary, because *courage*—unlike *cowardice*—can be shown in a situation which is already bad, not only in a situation which threatens to be bad. For example, an incurable and painful illness can be borne with *courage*, but if it is not borne with courage, and if the sick person complains and moans all the time, this would not be called *cowardice*. *Cowardice* really has to involve the possibility that something bad will happen, whereas *courage* may refer to bad things happening now, as well as to those which may happen in the future.

For this reason, we cannot postulate for *courage* or *courageous* the component which we have postulated for *coward:* 'if I do it, something bad could happen to me'. What we can postulate instead is a vaguer component covering both the future and the present, the possible and the real: 'I don't want bad things to happen to me'. The thing that the *courageous* person does, and that other people might not do (Y), consists either in a specific action or simply in a certain way of behaving (being quiet, serene, uncomplaining, and so on). Inner qualities such as serenity, calm, and dignity, 'shining through' the *courageous* behaviour, seem so important to this concept as to warrant an explicit denial of any 'bad thoughts'. This can be done by means of the following component:

> X doesn't think: 'I don't want bad things to happen to me'

The speaker's attitude to the *courageous* person is clearly positive ('I think this is good'); it is less clear, however, that a positive feeling toward the person (such as admiration) is also necessarily implied, in the way a negative feeling is implied by the noun *coward*.

There is one further semantic difference between the words *courageous* and *coward*, suggested by their very form: *courageous* is derived from the abstract noun *courage*, whereas the abstract noun *cowardice* is itself derived from *coward*. This morphological contrast is parallelled by a contrast in frequency: *courage* appears to have a much higher frequency than *courageous* (a ratio of 32:4 in Kučera and Francis' (1967) data, and >50:8 in Thorndike and Lorge (1963)), whereas *cowardice* appears to have a much lower frequency than *coward* (2:8, 5:52). What these differences suggest is that *coward* is focussed primarily on the behaviour of a person (interpreted in terms of hypothetical motivations), and the abstract noun *cowardice* constitutes a more abstract description of that kind of behaviour, whereas the abstract noun *courage* refers to a virtue, to a moral quality, which one can 'have in one's heart' and which can be manifested in certain behaviour. But *cowardice* is not something that one has in one's heart.

To account for such differences as these in semantic representations, I would propose that features of behaviour, such as *cowardice*, be portrayed in terms of what one does, or doesn't do, whereas features of character, such as *courage*, be represented in terms of what one *can* do or not do. Since this ability to do something (that other people can't do) is caused by a conscious, or semi-conscious, act of will, I would also include in the explication of *courage* the component 'I want to think: I will do it'.

This leads us to the following explication (to facilitate comparison with other character terms such as *coward* or *brave*, I will explicate the adjective *courageous* rather than the noun *courage*):

X is *courageous*. →

X is someone who thinks something like this:
   I should do Y
   because of this, I want to do it
   I want to think: I will do it
and because of this, can do Y and does Y,
and doesn't think something like this:
   I don't want bad things to happen to me
when other people would think this
and because of this, wouldn't do Y
[I think this is good]

1.3 *Brave*

We have seen that the concept *courageous* is not as symmetrical with respect to the concept *coward* as one might expect. Is it possible that *brave* is more closely related to *coward* than *courageous* is?

In one respect at least this is undoubtedly the case. *Brave*, like *coward*, is focussed primarily on behaviour, even though this behaviour has its basis 'in the heart'. (For example, a small child running onto a busy road to retrieve a ball would not be called *brave*. *Brave* acts have to be seen as having 'brave' motivations.) The morphological relationship between *brave* and the abstract noun *bravery* is similar to that between *coward* and the abstract noun *cowardice: bravery* is derived from *brave*, not vice versa. The frequency relations are also similar: *bravery* is much less common than *brave* (a ratio of 4:24, 18:>50), just as *cowardice* is much less common than *coward* (2:8, 5:22), whereas *courage* is, as we have seen, much more common than *courageous* (32:4, >50:8). One doesn't have *bravery* 'in one's heart', whereas one does have *courage* 'in one's heart'. Similarly, one can *take courage* but not **take bravery*.

For example, in Shakespeare's line "but screw your courage to the sticking place, and we'll not fail" (*Macbeth*, I, 7), *bravery* could not be substituted for *courage*. This suggests that *brave* should be represented in terms of things one *does* rather than in terms of things one *can* do. In fact, among all the English words to be considered in this section, *courageous* is the only one which refers primarily to an inner propensity rather than to external behaviour.

In another respect, however, *brave* seems to be less closely related to *coward* than *courageous* is. Consider, for example, the case of two children ice skating for the first time in their lives. One child (A) keeps holding on to the rail and is afraid to let go and to expose himself to the possibility of falling, whereas the other child (B) does let go, falls, gets up, falls again, and finally skates across the ring. B's behaviour could no doubt be described as *brave* ('Jimmy was very brave'), and it wouldn't be described as *courageous*.

Child A could be jocularly described as a *scaredy-cat*, a *chicken*, a *wimp*, or (in Australia) a *sook*, but he wouldn't be seriously described as a *coward*. The reason seems to be that both *courageous* and *coward* imply a moral dimension, which is inappropriate in the situation described. *Brave* doesn't imply that, although it is of course fully compatible with such a dimension. To account for this difference between *brave* on the one hand and *courageous* and *coward* on the other, we can phrase one component in terms of 'what I should do' (as we have already done for *coward* and *courageous*) and the other in terms of 'what would be a good thing to do'. In sport or adventure, people often overcome their fear to do something that seems to be 'a good thing to do', under the circumstances, without feeling any moral obligation to do so.

Furthermore, *brave* is more 'unthinking' than *courageous,* less a matter of conscious thought and conscious will. Accordingly, I have not posited for it the component 'I want to think: I will do it'. Nonetheless, the *brave* person is aware that something bad can or will happen to him or her but brushes this thought aside. To account for this, I have postulated the component 'I don't want to think: I don't want something bad to happen to me'.

A final difference between being *brave* and being *courageous* has to do with the serenity and dignity mentioned earlier in connection with *courage.* A *brave* person would not complain and would not let any 'bad thoughts' stop him or her from behaving in the right way, but the presence of such thoughts does not seem to be excluded in this case, as it is in the case of someone who is *courageous.* (One can perhaps be *brave*—though not *courageous*—in a somewhat grim way.) For this reason, I will not postulate for *brave* the component 'X doesn't think: I don't want bad things to happen to me', which has been included in the explication of *courageous.*

The speaker's evaluation is positive, as it is in the case of *courageous* ('I think this is good').

> X is *brave.* →
> X is someone who thinks something like this:
>> it would be good if I did Y
>> because of this, I want to do it
>> I don't want to think: 'I don't want something bad to happen to me'
> and because of this, does Y
> when other people would think something like this:
>> I don't want something bad to happen to me
> and because of this, wouldn't do Y
> [I think this is good]

The component 'if I do it', which is present in *coward,* is absent from *brave,* as it is absent from *courageous.* Children who scream during injections and thus are not "being *brave*" do not think: 'if I do it (i.e., if I behave stoically), something bad will happen to me'. Similarly, people who fail to show *courage* in the face of an incurable illness do not think: 'if I behave serenely something bad will happen to me'. On the other hand, the word *coward* does seem to attribute to the person so described a thought of the 'if . . . then' kind ('if I do this, something bad could happen to me').

1.4 *Fearless*

A fearless person is not someone who doesn't feel any fear but someone who shows
no fear in a situation when other people would and who does things that other
people would be afraid to do, as if he or she didn't feel any fear.

For example, if bombs are being dropped onto a certain district and everybody is
screaming and shaking with fear, but one person is sleeping undisturbed, one
wouldn't describe that person as 'sleeping fearlessly'. Clearly, to be *fearless* one has
to do something, rather than fail to do anything, and the action has to involve a
certain risk.

Fearless differs in this respect from *brave* and *courageous*. One can face a
painful injection *bravely*, but not *fearlessly*, and one can bear a severe illness
courageously, or *bravely*, but not *fearlessly*. This suggests that *fearless* is restricted
to situations of real danger. But a lunatic jumping off the roof of a house would not
be described as *fearless*. A child playing unknowingly on a mine-field would not be
described as *fearless*. On the other hand, a soldier making his way swiftly across a
mine-field to get to a wounded comrade could well be described as *fearless*. This
suggests that the *fearless* person must be seen as someone who is capable of
appreciating the danger involved but who doesn't pay any attention to it.

> X is *fearless*.   →
> X is someone who thinks something like this:
>   it will be good if I do Y
>   because of this, I want to do it
> and because of this, does Y
> and doesn't think something like this:
>   if I do it, something bad will happen to me
> when other people would think this,
> and couldn't do Y because of this
> [I think this is good]

The component 'other people . . . couldn't do it' suggests that there is a situation of real danger, where other people would be simply paralysed by fear. This
accounts for the 'exceptional' character of *fearlessness*.

The element of personal risk ('if I do Y . . . ') separates *fearless* from both
courageous and *brave* and links it with *bold*, which, however, doesn't imply any
real danger.

1.5 *Bold*

According to LDOTEL (1984), the basic meaning of *bold* is "fearless in the face of
danger; intrepid; showing or requiring a fearless adventurous spirit". Since *fearless*
already implies 'in the face of danger', what this definition amounts to is an
identification of *bold* with *fearless* (which, incidentally, is not defined at all, simply
listed as an "adjective" under *fear*).

But of course *bold* doesn't mean the same as *fearless*. Nor does it necessarily imply that something is done 'in the face of danger'. For example, if a child *boldly* asks an adult a question, this doesn't imply that this adult constitutes a danger for the child.

One crucial feature of *boldness* that no other words considered here seem to have is its focus on other people's reaction to the act in question. One can behave *bravely, courageously,* or even *fearlessly* when there are no other people around, but it would be very difficult to act *boldly* on a desert island (unless even there one imagined that other people were looking at one). If a robber can *boldly* barge into an empty house, the implication is that somebody might see him or her do it or at least that people may find out about it later.

Christian martyrs could face wild animals *bravely,* and they could speak *boldly* to their Roman persecutors, but it would be odd to say that they faced the animals *boldly.* This suggests that what a *bold* person is unafraid of is a very specific kind of 'danger': other people's bad thoughts about him or her. This is confirmed by frequent collocations such as *bold plans* or *bold ideas,* which don't imply any physical danger, but rather a danger of making a fool of oneself, of being laughed at, of failing spectacularly and very noticeably. The derived sense of *bold* as in *bold print* points in the same direction: *bold print* is more noticeable than ordinary print; it refers, therefore, to other people's attention. The primary sense of *bold* appears to do the same. (Cf. Locke's (1959 [1690], v.1:387) definition of *boldness:* "*boldness* is the power to speak or do what we intend, before others, without fear or disorder".)

Bold people seem not only to disregard but even to defy other people's opinion. They are aware that people may think something bad about them because of their action, and they choose to ignore that.

Another obvious difference between *bold* and the other words which we have considered so far is that being *bold* is not concerned with what one *should* do, and not even with what would be a *good thing* to do; rather, it is concerned with what one *wants* to do.

Furthermore, *bold* doesn't imply the speaker's positive evaluation. It is neither negative like *coward* nor positive like *brave, courageous,* or *fearless,* and it is compatible with either evaluation.

> X is *bold.* →
> X is someone who thinks something like this:
>   I want to do Y
>   I know that if I do it, something bad could happen
>   I know that other people could think something bad about me
>   I don't want not to do it because of this
> and because of this, does Y

1.6 *Daring*

According to Merriam-Webster (1972:9), the word *daring* "heightens the implication of fearlessness and may suggest boldness in action or thought". But in fact, *daring* doesn't imply all the components of fearlessness, since *fearless* implies a positive evaluation ('I think this is good') and also a situation of real danger, probably physical danger, when other people would be paralysed by fear. For example, ideas and plans can be *daring* but not *fearless*. (Cf. also "a daring outfit" and "*a fearless outfit".)

Nonetheless, *daring* does imply that something bad is likely to happen to the person in question, and in this respect it has more to do with danger than *bold* does. *Bold* doesn't necessarily imply any bad consequences other than other people's negative reactions; but *daring* may refer to real physical danger (as in the case of "the daring young man on the flying trapeze" of the popular song, who "flies through the air with the greatest of ease").

Intuitively, *daring* is more extreme than *bold*, and in this respect it is closer to *fearless* than *bold* is. It implies a considerable risk, which would deter other people from doing the thing in question (and which might even cause their disapproval). The performer of the *daring* act is aware of this—and is likely to derive from this an additional frisson (as one may from a spectacular sporting feat, or from a spectacular escape). There is an element of 'showing off' about *daring*, and although *daring* acts cause admiration, the term does not necessarily imply a positive opinion about the act. To account for this aspect of *daring*, it seems justified to posit for it the component 'I feel something good toward X because of this' without positing the component 'I think this is good'.

Normally, *daring* is used to describe exceptional acts rather than exceptional people; since, however, it *can* be used to describe people (like the "daring young man on the flying trapeze"), I will explicate the latter use, to facilitate comparison with other character terms:

X is *daring*.   →
X is someone who thinks this:
   I want to do Y
   I know that if I do it, something bad can happen to me
   I know that other people wouldn't do it
   I know that they would say that I shouldn't do it
   I don't want not to do it because of this
and because of this, does Y
[because of this, I feel something good toward X]

X did something *daring*.   →
X did something (Y) that other people wouldn't do
I imagine that X thought something like this:
   I want to do it
   I know that if I do it, something bad can happen to me
   I know that other people wouldn't do it
   I know that they would say that I shouldn't do it
   I don't want not to do it because of this
and because of this, did Y
[because of this, I feel something good toward X]

1.7 *Reckless*

Reckless is similar to *bold* in so far as the agent does what he or she wants and disregards what other people might think about it. It is different from it, however, in involving a danger for other people and in the speaker's negative evaluation.

Normally, a person wouldn't be described as simply *reckless*, but as *reckless* in some particular activity, that is, as *a reckless V-er*.

> X is a *reckless* V-er. →
> X does V like someone who thinks something like this:
>   I want to do Y
>   I know that if I do it, something bad can happen to someone
>   I don't want to think about this
>   I don't want not to do Y because of this
> and because of this, does Y
> [I think this is bad]

Another negative word related to the field under discussion is *foolhardy*, with its combination of foolishness and something like bravery or courage. Since, however, its emphasis is on stupidity rather than courage, I will not try to explicate this concept here.

2. Polish

It is widely assumed that virtues such as *courage* and valued behavioural propensities such as *bravery* are features of 'human nature', independent of individual languages and of their semantic options. In fact, however, even European languages differ considerably in their conceptualisations in this area.

For example, in Polish only the word *coward* appears to have an exact semantic equivalent: *tchórz*. All the other concepts in the semantic domain under discussion are different from those encoded in the English lexicon.

2.1 *Odważny*

The adjective *odważny* is regarded as the Polish equivalent of the English adjective *courageous*. Like *courageous*, it is derived from an abstract noun, *odwaga*, and refers primarily to a 'virtue' rather than to a feature of behaviour. This is supported by the common expression *dodać komuś odwagi*, lit., 'to give someone more courage', which refers exclusively to a psychological effect, not to a way of influencing someone's behaviour. (Similarly, in English only *courage*—not, for example, *bravery* or *fearlessness*—can be "given" or "taken".)

Unlike *courageous*, however, *odważny* cannot be applied to situations such as an incurable illness, when the 'bad thing' is present and actual, rather than future and potential. It involves an element of personal risk (like *fearless*), and it is more directly opposed to *tchórz* than *courageous* is to *coward*. The Polish lexicon seems to offer a straightforward alternative: you can either be a *tchórz* ("coward") or you can be *odważny*. English doesn't present a similar alternative, as it has no positive concept directly opposed to *coward*.

> X is *odważny*. →
> X is someone who thinks something like this:
>> I should do Y
>> because of this, I want to do it
> and because of this, does Y
> when other people would think something like this:
>> if I do Y, something bad could happen to me
>> I don't want this
> and because of this, wouldn't do Y
> [I think this is good]

2.2 *Śmiały*

> Żył lotnik, który był tak śmiały
> jakby się jego ciała kule nie imały.
> (Słonimski, quoted in SJP 1958–69)
>
> 'There once was a pilot who was so *śmiały*
> as if he thought no bullets could touch him.'

The quality of *śmiałość* (noun), that is, of being *śmiały* (adjective), occupies a particularly important place in the pantheon of Polish national values. For example, one of the most admired Polish kings was given the nickname *śmiały*, whereas no king was given the nickname *odważny*. Loosely speaking, *śmiałość* constitutes a combination of *bravery, daring,* and *boldness*.

Morphologically, *śmiały* is related to the verb *śmieć* 'dare', and this link highlights the element of personal risk and of a certain bravado implied by this adjective. One can speak in Polish of *śmiałe plany* ('*śmiałe* plans', PL) or *śmiałe idee* ('*śmiałe* ideas', PL), as one speaks in English of *bold plans* and *bold ideas*.

Śmiały has its opposite—morphologically, if no longer semantically—in *nieśmiały*, which means something like *timid* or *shy*. This relationship, too, highlights the similarity between *śmiały* and *bold*. But, as pointed out earlier, *bold* is not inherently positive, whereas *śmiały* is. There is something admirable about being *śmiały*, though not about being *bold*, and *śmiały* has more to do with danger than *bold* does. *Śmiały* is also used frequently to translate *brave*. It suggests the same kind of unreflective and spectacular simplicity in action that *brave* does. For example, a *brave* physical act, such as jumping off a cliff, would be described in Polish as *śmiały*. But a child expecting a painful injection would be encouraged in Polish to be *dzielny* (see next section), not *śmiały*, because *śmiały* requires an element of personal risk.

In English, a willingness to take a personal risk seems to be implied only by the somewhat extreme adjectives *daring* and *fearless*. But *daring* is not inherently positive, and it has a 'showing-off' quality which makes it unsuitable as a moral or social ideal. *Fearless* is inherently positive, but it implies a situation of extreme danger (where other people *couldn't* do what the *fearless* person does). In Polish the closest counterpart of fearless is *nieustraszony,* lit., 'unfrightened' or 'unfrighten-able'. The word *śmiały* hails the willingness to take a personal risk in all situations, both ordinary and extraordinary. It hails the attitude of eagerness to take risks in all circumstances, in daily life as much as in extraordinary situations which call for *fearlessness* or *nieustraszoność* (abstract noun).

> X is *śmiały*. →
> X is someone who thinks something like this:
>> I think it would be good to do Y
>> because of this, I want to do it
> and because of this, does Y
> when other people would think something like this:
>> if I do Y, something bad could happen to me
>> I don't want this
> and because of this, wouldn't do Y
> [I think this is good]

The main difference between this explication and that of *odważny* is in line two: *odważny* implies a kind of moral obligation ('should'), whereas *śmiały* doesn't. For this reason, a 'brave' but morally neutral jump from the top of a cliff would be called in Polish *śmiały* rather than *odważny*. A second difference is related to a more 'unthinking' character of *śmiały,* which links it with the English concepts *brave* and *fearless*.

2.3 *Dzielny*

As mentioned earlier, to encourage a child to be *brave* when faced with a painful injection, one would use the word *dzielny,* not *śmiały*. This doesn't mean, however, that *dzielny* has the same meaning as *brave*. For example, a person who has to walk for hours in hot weather carrying a heavy load and doesn't complain would be called *dzielny* but wouldn't be called *brave*. I presume the reason is that nothing bad is going to happen to such a person (the situation is difficult and/or unpleasant, but not necessarily 'bad'). Nor would such a person be called *courageous*—presumably because nothing bad is happening to him or her in the present either (unlike the case of a person who is *courageously* bearing an incurable illness). But if so, why can such a person be called *dzielny,* if *dzielny* is related to *brave?*

I think the reason is that *dzielny* refers to 'feeling something bad' rather than undergoing or facing something bad. A person carrying a heavy burden for a long time feels something bad (for example, tiredness), but nothing bad is actually happening, or is going to happen, to such a person. A painful injection can also be seen in that light. Whenever a 'bad feeling' interpretation is possible, the word *dzielny* can be used. For *brave*, this is not enough: it is possible only when a 'bad event' interpretation is possible. A painful injection is open to either interpretation, but mere tiredness is not. Consider, however, the following, very characteristic, use of *dzielny:*

> To bardzo dzielna dziewczyna. Wiesz, całą rodzinę utrzymuje. (Andrzejewski, quoted in sjp 1958–69)
>
> 'She is a very *dzielna* girl. You know, she supports the whole family.'

In this case, *dzielność* (abstract noun) consists not in bearing an unpleasant feeling but, I suppose, in not allowing 'bad feelings' (fear, discouragement, depression, worry) to find their way into one's heart (and to prevent one from doing what one should do).

It might be added that *dzielny* is etymologically related to the verb *działać* 'to act'. This supports the idea that a *dzielny* person is seen as someone who 'can do' things when other people can't (that is, when feeling something bad).

This leads us to the following explication:

> X is *dzielny.* →
> X is someone who thinks something like this:
>   I should do Y
>   because of this, I want to do it
> and because of this, does Y
> when other people would think this:
>   I feel something bad
>   because of this, I can't do Y
> and because of this, wouldn't do Y
> [I think this is good]

There may appear to be one problem with this explication: how would it apply to the case of a child bravely facing the prospect of a painful injection? The painful feeling is not there yet, so why is the word *dzielny* suitable? I think the answer is that although the pain is not there yet, fear or apprehension is, and it is this fear, not pain, which is the bad feeling that has to be overcome and which could stop other people from behaving the way they should. Since this interpretation is possible, the invariant posited in the explication can be maintained.

2.4 *Mężny*

Mężny, etymologically 'virile' or 'manly', is also used to translate *brave*. In particular, military *bravery* would normally be described in Polish as *męstwo* (noun). But a child would be encouraged to be *dzielny,* not *mężny,* and a 'brave' jump from the top of a cliff would never be described as *mężny.*

This doesn't mean, however, that only military bravery is called *męstwo.* One can also bear a disaster or a misfortune *mężnie* (adverb), although one cannot bear tiredness *mężnie*. The crucial factor seems to be that something bad is actually happening to us (for example, the enemy is trying to kill us, or we have found out that we have cancer) and that despite this, we do what we should be doing.

Since actual misfortunes are also compatible with the English word *courage*, *męstwo* can sometimes be translated into English as *courage*, and *mężny* as *courageous*. But *courage* is also applicable in the case of danger, that is to say, in the case of potential rather than actual 'bad events'. *Mężny* requires that bad things are already happening and that one 'soldiers on' (that is, does what one should do) in spite of them.

Prototypically, *męstwo* (the quality of being *mężny*) is undoubtedly linked to the situation of war and, in particular, to 'fear-less' defence: 'bad things are happening to us' because of the actions of a powerful enemy, but despite those 'bad things' we continue doing what we believe we should do. By extension, *męstwo* can also be applied to metaphorical struggles (a 'struggle' against temptation, illness, etc.), but the image of an 'onslaught' which should be withstood and overcome has to be present.

> X is *mężny.* →
> X is someone who thinks something like this:
>   something bad is happening to me
>   I don't want to think: 'I don't want this'
>   I should do Y
>   because of this, I want to do it
> and because of this, does Y
> when other people would think something like this:
>   something bad is happening to me
>   I don't want this
> and because of this, wouldn't do Y
> [I think this is good]

2.5 *Waleczny*

Waleczny is a word which is used specifically for military valour; for example, the phrase *zginąć śmiercią walecznych*, 'to die the death of the *waleczny* ones', means 'to be killed in battle'. It is derived from the noun *walka* 'struggle', and it is normally used in the plural, of soldiers. *Krzyż Walecznych*, 'the cross of the *waleczny* ones', is a decoration for military valor.

Perhaps the closest English adjectives are *valiant* and *valorous*, but these are marginal in modern English, whereas *waleczny* is not an uncommon word in Polish. Furthermore, *valiant* is not restricted to military valour, and one can speak, for example, of a *valiant effort* with regard to some other cause. As for *valorous* and *valour*, the *Concise Oxford* (1964) describes them as "now chiefly poetic, rhetorical, or jocular". By contrast, *waleczny* is a perfectly normal Polish word, despite its military character and its heroic connotations.

In this explication of *waleczny* I will not try to explicate the idea of 'fighting in battle' (which could, of course, be decomposed), but I will include it in that form, to highlight the specifically military character of this concept, linked no doubt with the important role that memories of struggles for freedom and independence play in Polish culture and in the Polish collective consciousness.

> Xs are *waleczny* (PL).   →
>
> Xs are people who think something like this:
> we should "fight in battle"
> because of this, we want to do it
> we want to do it well
> and because of this, do it
> when other people would think something like this:
> if we do it, something bad could happen to us
> we don't want this
> and because of this, wouldn't do it
> [I think this is good]

3. 'Courage' and Culture

We have seen that concepts such as 'brave', 'courageous', or 'bold' are language-specific and that the distinctions drawn in Polish are different from those drawn in English. Can these differences between English and Polish be somehow made sense of and explained in terms of culture and history?

I think that, to some extent at least, they can. To begin with, Polish clearly pays more attention than English to military valour, having a special adjective (*waleczny*) just for that and another, *mężny,* which is used primarily for that. This can hardly come as a surprise to anybody who knows anything about the history of Poland— "God's playground", in Norman Davies' (1981) well-chosen metaphor. ("For Poland is the point where the rival cultures and philosophies of our continent confront each other in the most acute form, where the tensions of the European drama are played out on the flesh and nerves of a large nation" (Davies 1984:463).)

Furthermore, English provides lexically for a wider range of attitudes toward those who are in some sense 'above fear' than does Polish. Next to adjectives full of admiration or approval such as *courageous* or *brave,* English has also some negative adjectives such as *reckless* and *foolhardy;* by contrast, Polish doesn't seem to have any conterparts of such terms of negative evaluation. For example, the following sentence about the Polish campaign of September 1939, quoted in Merriam-Webster (1972:9), can hardly be translated into Polish, as there is in Polish nothing similar to *foolhardy:*

"Brave and valiant and foolhardy though they were, the Poles were simply overwhelmed by the German onslaught." (W. L. Shirer)

One Polish adjective which might be proposed as a quasi-equivalent of *foolhardy, szalony* ('foolish/mad/wild') is not inherently negative and in fact is often used as a word of high praise, especially in Polish military folklore (see the next section, on the Polish concept of 'honor'). Another Polish adjective which glorifies 'mad courage' is *straceńczy* (roughly, 'desperado'), frequently used in the phrase *straceńcza odwaga* (roughly, 'the courage of a desperado'). But in English, *desperado* implies distance rather than deep admiration and respect, which are inherent in the Polish word. In fact, Polish doesn't even seem to have neutral terms such as *bold* or *daring,* the only reasonably close counterpart of these words, *śmiały,* being a word of high praise.

The Polish counterpart of *courage, odwaga,* praises an ability to take risks (in a good cause) and doesn't allow for 'noble endurance', as *courage* does; the Polish term refers specifically to 'noble action'. In fact, both the basic English words of positive evaluation in the domain under discussion, *courageous* and *brave,* equate risky actions with endurance: one can be *courageous* in action and one can be *courageous* in an illness; one can be *brave* in battle and one can be *brave* when faced with an injection. In Polish, the two most basic words of positive evaluation, *odważny* and *śmiały,* both focus on a 'risky' action and cannot be stretched to endurance.

All these lexical differences between Polish and English, minor and insignificant as they might seem at first sight, are so remarkably consistent with the stereotypes of the Polish national character and national ethos that it would require a great deal of determination (or foolhardiness) to dismiss them as accidental.

The conclusions emerging from the semantic analysis presented here are remarkably consistent with those emerging from studies of the Polish national character, such as Benet (1953), where military valour and "high standards of death" are presented as lying at the core of the national values and ideals.

> [T]he measure of success is not so much the achieved goal and the results of the battles as it is the conduct during action, and the demonstration of the indomitable qualities which in Poland spell honor. . . . Poles identify honor with bravado, regardless of the price they pay for it, and regardless of the total situation. . . . During the 'blitz' in London, Polish air units were sent aloft to fight the Germans. The Poles were reckless both of their own lives and of the planes. Although the English appreciated their bravery, they could not afford to lose the planes and were forced constantly to curb the enthusiasm of the Poles. There have been other misunderstandings between the Poles and their allies. Poles fighting in foreign lands consider that they have a mission to fulfil. . . . Their allies regard them as lunatics, maniacs, and adventurers. The Poles think of their allies as too sober, too commercial, too much given to compromise. (1953:417–18)

The last comment has also a clear confirmation in the Polish lexicon, where the words *bezkompromisowy* 'uncompromising' and *nieugięty* 'inflexible' (lit., 'unbendable') are just as unquestionably positive as *szlachetny* 'noble', *bohaterski* 'heroic', or *niezłomny* 'unbreakable' ('a person whose spirit cannot be broken by anyone'). In English, *inflexible* is a negative word, not a positive one, and *unbreakable* (as a character term) doesn't exist at all. The Polish word *kompromis* also lends itself more easily to negative interpretations than the English word *compromise*.

English expressions such as "to reach a compromise" or "the art of compromise", which imply a positive evaluation, have no equivalents in Polish, and the closest corresponding Polish expression, *pójść na kompromis,* implies not appreciation but contempt. (For some further discussion, see Wierzbicka 1984b.)

Benet points out that although "[t]he everyday life of a nation, one could say, is not occupied just with wars . . . , these values receive attention not in extraordinary circumstances only. On the contrary, since they are so integrated into home life and school education, they leave their imprint in every sphere of the people's activities."

The data discussed in this chapter show, I think, that they also leave their imprint in the lexicon.[2]

4. The Concept of 'Honor'

The high priority of virtues similar to bravery and daring in the Polish national ethos, and its link with the vicissitudes of Polish history, is reflected in a particularly illuminating way in the modern Polish concept of 'honor'. At first sight, 'honor' may seem to be a common European concept, lexicalised not only in the Polish word *honor* but also in the English word *honour,* the French *honneur,* the German *Ehre,* the Russian *čest',* and so on. On closer inspection, however, this uniformity turns out to be more apparent than real.

The first point which must be noted is that Polish has not one but two words in this general area, *honor* and *cześć,* and that these two words are not synonymous. A second important point is that the Polish concept of *honor* has changed in the course of the last two centuries, and from a concept similar to the English *honour* or to the French *honneur* it has evolved in a rather unique way, coming to be linked not so much with human 'glory and respect' as with sacrifice and death.

I cannot undertake here a detailed analysis of the English concept of *honour,* or of the French concept of *honneur,* and I will limit myself to pointing out, informally, that they appear to have two different aspects: a positive quality that can be seen as something that every human being of a certain category of people would have (as in "word of honour") and a special claim to other people's regard and deference (as in the phrase "it's a great honour", or in a "guard of honour", or in the name of the French decoration *Légion d'Honneur,* which is a mark of very high distinction).[3]

As the citations in the extensive *Dictionary of the Polish language* (sjp 1958–69) show, until, roughly speaking, the period of the partitions of Poland (among Russia, Prussia, and Austria), the Polish word *honor* had a range similar to that of the English *honour,* or to the French *honneur,* as had its quasi-synonym *cześć.* From that time onward, however, a curious polarisation began to develop between these two concepts: *cześć* retained its association with human regard and 'glory', while *honor* began to develop a link with bravery, sacrifice, and voluntarily chosen death.

This modern sense of the word *honor* is echoed in the title of a recent book about the Warsaw Uprising of 1944, described by a British historian (Bruce 1972:9) as "a drama of unexempled heroism, ending in appalling tragedy". The book is entitled *Nothing but honor* (Zawodny 1978; cf. also Michnik 1985).

Generally speaking, the word *honor,* in its new sense, plays an essential role in Polish national lore. For reasons of space, I'll quote here only three characteristic citations. One concerns the famous last words of the Polish military leader General Józef Poniatowski, who sought to liberate Poland by linking her fate with that of Napoleon's campaign against Russia in 1812. As the British historian Norman Davies (1984:162) points out, "Napoleon called the war of 1812 his 'Polish War', and in crossing the frontier of the Russian Empire the *Grande Armée* was in fact restoring the historic border of Poland and Lithuania, annulled in 1795. Inexorably, the Russian victory spelt disaster no less for the Polish cause than for that of Napoleon". As Davies describes it elsewhere (1984:186), "Mortally wounded by three bullets, Poniatowski scorned all suggestions of surrender or retirement. Spurring his horse into the water, in a flurry of sniper fire, he sank from view". His legendary last words were "Bóg mi powierzył honor Polaków, Bogu go tylko oddam." 'God entrusted Polish honour to me, and I will yield it only to him.' Davies (1984:186) observes that "Poniatowski's death is often quoted as yet another example of suicidal Polish courage. . . . Like the rest of his generation he hoped; he fought; he served, and only found rest in honourable defeat".

Another characteristic quote involving *honor* comes from a popular mariners' song:

> Morze, nasze morze!
> Wiernie ciebie będziem strzec!
> Mamy rozkaz cię utrzymać,
> Albo na dnie na dnie twoim lec,
> Albo na dnie—z honorem—lec!

> 'Our sea, our sea!
> We will faithfully guard thee!
> We are commanded to preserve thee,
> Or to sink forever in thy depths,
> To sink—with honour—in thy depths!'

As a final example, particularly salient in Polish national memory, I will quote two lines from an extremely popular Polish song, celebrating the battle of Monte Cassino in 1944, an event described by an historian as follows:

> When allied armies from various lands failed to take the stronghold which the Germans had established next to the Monastery of Monte Cassino thus blocking the way to Rome, the Polish corps under the command of General Władysław Anders started another attack on 11 May and after eight days of desperate fighting, suffering the heaviest losses, finally broke the German resistance, and in a well-deserved triumph planted the Polish flag on the ruins of the monastery. (Halecki 1983:322)

Referring to the endless rows of Polish soldiers' graves on Monte Cassino, the song asks:

> Czy widzisz ten rząd białych krzyży?
> To Polak z honorem brał ślub. . . .

> 'Do you see that row of white crosses over there?
> They are Poles who have wedded death with honour. . . .'
> (lit., 'They are Poles who wedded honour'.)

As a result of very frequent use in contexts of this kind, the Polish concept of *honor* shifted away from human regard in the direction of readiness for sacrifice and death. Consequently, it can no longer be used (in the singular) in contexts like this:

> Honor to dla mnie, że gość tak dostojny
> raczył nawiedzić mój zamek.
> (Słowacki, Balladyna, quoted in sjp 1958–69)
>
> 'It's a great honour for me that such a distinguished guest should be
> pleased to visit my castle.'

Similarly, one can no longer speak in Polish of a 'great honour' (*wielki honor*). *Honor* is no longer seen as something which could have different degrees: one couldn't have 'more of it' than one has, but one can always lose it, if one doesn't act (in crucial situations) in the way one should, no matter what the cost.

Before I attempt an explication of the Polish concept of *honor,* I will point out that the special character of this concept, and its special place in the Polish national ethos, was noted, and was often referred to, by many Russians, and in particular by Dostoevsky. Dostoevsky (of distant Polish extraction himself) was virulently anti-Polish, and he liked to include in his novels satirical episodes about Poles and their exaggerated, as he saw it, sense of "*gonor*", that is, as he put it, *pol'skaja čest'*, "the Polish *čest'*" (*čest'* being the closest Russian word for something like *honour,* in the English sense of the word, and of course a cognate of the Polish word *cześć* (cf., for example, Dostoevsky 1958:531)). For example:

> Pan zapyxtel ot gonora. (Dostoevsky 1958:535)
>
> 'The Polish gentleman spluttered from [outraged] honour.'

Typically, the word *gonor* is used in Russian to refer to the Polish value of 'honor', and (as pointed out to me by Andrzej Bogusławski, p.c.) it is by no means identical with the latter in meaning: rather, it represents a stereotyped Russian view of Polish 'honor'. According to the authoritative Russian dictionary of Dal' (1914), *gonor* is a loan from Polish, which means "a jealous protection of one's dignity in other people's eyes", and it is used ironically, in the sense of "an exaggerated notion of one's dignity". The Academy dictionary of Russian (AN SSSR 1950–65), too, assigns to *gonor* pejorative overtones, defining it as "an exaggerated notion of one's dignity; excessive pride, conceitedness". But, needless to say, no such pejorative overtones are present in the Polish concept of *honor,* which embodies one of the highest national values.

As a first approximation, I would propose the following explication of the modern Polish concept of *honor:*

> *honor*
> it is like a part of a person
> if something bad happens to a person
>   nothing bad can happen to this thing
> if one doesn't do something that one should do
>   something bad can happen to this thing

if something bad happens to this part
    one cannot think good things about oneself any more
        and one cannot want people to think good things about one any more
    it is better if bad things happen to a person
        than if something bad happens to this thing

5. A Parallel from Africa?

The contrast between Polish and English, investigated in the present chapter, may bring to mind contrasting attitudes to fear in two African societies, the Maasai and the Sukuma, described by Hatfield (1986).

According to Hatfield, the Maasai institution called *e murano* "introduces a situation in which expression of fear is deliberately suppressed in young men. . . . The Maasai appear to have founded the entire ethos of warriorhood on means of achieving and maintaining that state." A Maasai warrior is characterised by the term *api* 'sharp', which carries with it a cluster of similar meanings: courageous and self-reliant (Jacobs 1979), brave, bold, strong (Mol n.d.). "*Api* is a term also used to describe important accoutrements of a warrior, his spear and stabbing sword. Just as he hones his weapons to be *api*, so must he also hone himself. The opposite of this ideal is *ol kuret*, the coward, derived from the verb *a-re*, to fear" (Hatfield 1986:92).

The equivalent age group among the Sukuma, called *basumba batale*, has a rather different ethos (Hatfield 1986:96–98). "Rather than be characterized by independence and fearlessness, they are considered self-reliant and reliable." . . . "The Sukuma organization is not formed for the pursuit of danger and cultivation of fearlessness. . . . Sukuma youth are not required to pay so much attention to promoting notions of their bravery as they are to developing and demonstrating their skills at organization, cooperation, and negotiations." . . . "Confrontation with and courting of physical danger does not form an essential part of the *basumba batale*."

Should we conclude from this that the ethos of the Maasai warriors, reflected in concepts such as *api*, is similar to the traditional Polish ethos, reflected in concepts such as *odważny, śmiały,* or *waleczny?*

Some similarities in outlook seem to be undeniable—as well as some similarities in history and geography which might partially explain them. Hatfield (1986:113) observes that the Sukuma "have far less to fear from external forces than the Maasai. The simple fact of scale, that the Sukuma number perhaps twenty times more than the Maasai, has a great deal to do with their relaxed defenses. . . . The Maasai realise that their case is different and the threats to the integrity of their existence are very real ones indeed."

Nonetheless, there are also certain striking differences between the Maasai ethos as described by Hatfield and the relevant aspect of the Polish ethos reported here. The main difference involves the drastic separation, physical and psychological, of the Maasai warriors from the rest of the society. Among the Maasai, "fearlessness" is institutionalised, according to Hatfield (1986:101), in a special "force" of warriors, who are "conditioned to act as if fear did not exist". "They emphasize visible signs of difference: elaborate skin skirts, dazzling arrays of necklaces, earrings and other decorations, complex hair styles, gravure, spears and swords for warriors, all of which call attention to their aloofness from and lack of concern for other ways of life" (1986:112).

Being a warrior means entering an exclusive age set, which is clearly distinct from "ordinary people". At the end of the relevant period, the warrior "removes the gravure of warriorhood, its taboos, and discards the persona of fearless paragon of Maasai virtue in order to get on with the business of living as a real person in a whole community" (Hatfield 1986:96).

These observations suggest that the ideal of a Maasai warrior embodied in the term *api* may encapsulate the following concept:

> X is *api*. →
> X is someone who thinks something like this:
>   we are not like other people
>   we can do things that other people can't do
> because of this, X doesn't think something like this:
>   something bad can happen to me
>   I don't want this
> because of this, X can do things that other people can't
> [I think this is good]

This explication is based entirely on Hatfield's discussion, and since the information on the use of the word *api* provided by Hatfield is very sketchy, this formula cannot be more than a very rough approximation. I hope, however, that it identifies correctly at least some of the differences, and the similarities, between the Maasai ideal of *api*-ness and the ideals encoded in the Polish words discussed in this chapter. Above all, *api*-ness implies *apart*-ness, being apart, being special, belonging to a special clan of people—and being 'fearless' (or something rather like fearless) because of that. Since the word *api*, however, can be applied to spears and swords as well as to warriors, presumably the emphasis is on abilities rather than on thoughts and intentions. An *api* warrior 'can do things that other people cannot do' (as an *api* 'sharp' sword can 'do' things that other swords cannot 'do'), because he doesn't think, as other people do, 'something bad can happen to me; I don't want this'. This applies not only to acts of bravery but also to 'wild' behaviour, expected of and excused in warriors.

One can gather from Hatfield's discussion that, as one would expect, the Sukuma language, too, has certain words embodying the characteristic Sukuma ideals in the field under discussion. Not enough information is provided, however, for even tentative explications to be sketched on that basis. Rigorous contrastive analysis of ethical and social ideals embodied in the lexicons of different languages is, in a sense, a new field of study, where nearly everything remains to be done.

IV

NAMES AND TITLES

7

Personal Names
and Expressive Derivation

In many languages, for example, in many Slavic and Romance languages, expressive derivation plays a role that can hardly be overstated. In particular, the functional load of many so-called diminutive suffixes is simply colossal. Yet the meaning of such suffixes (and other related morphological devices) has never been studied in depth, and a suitable methodology for a rigorous study of this kind has never been developed. Labels such as 'diminutive' or 'augmentative', which may be useful as pointers to certain areas of meaning, prove hopelessly inadequate when treated as serious analytical devices (for semantic purposes). Even within individual languages, each such label covers a wide range of different functions, whose nature and interrelations remain a (usually unacknowledged) mystery. When it comes to cross-linguistic comparisons, the inadequacy of such labels as analytical tools becomes even more acute.

In this chapter, I will try to develop a methodology suitable for the study of expressive derivation. As my illustrative material, I will use mainly Russian and Polish. But to enable the reader unfamiliar with these languages to understand the approach advanced here I will start with some data from English. In a sense, the need for such a methodology is perhaps less clear in the case of English than it is in languages such as Russian. The limited range of English expressive derivation may make a few conventional labels such as 'formal' and 'informal', 'affectionate' and 'neutral', seem sufficient. In what follows, I will try to show that even with respect to English such labels are far from adequate. At the same time, the relatively limited role of English expressive derivation combined with the general accessibility of the English data makes the area of English personal names a suitable preliminary testing field.

1. English Personal Names

Van Buren (1977:112) divides (American) first names into male and female, and, within each of these macro-classes, three further categories—first full names (FFN e.g., *Thomas, Pamela*), nicknames (Nn, e.g., *Tom, Pam*), and affectionate nicknames (AfNn, e.g., *Tommy, Pammy*)—and he tries to assign to these three categories certain constant pragmatic meanings (such as formality, informality, masculine connotation, feminine connotation, or childish connotation). He sets himself the goal of showing that "the inventory and usage of American names" forms a system and that as it is a system, it can be taught to and learned by non-native speakers of English (1977:128). I agree that despite all the individual, sociolectal, and regional variation, there is an underlying system, and I regard Van Buren's analysis as valuable and pedagogically useful, to some extent. In my view, however, this analysis is far too simplistic and far too mechanical to explain adequately how the system of American names really works.

Before I try to show why it is too simplistic and too mechanical, let me point to a few simple facts which might otherwise confuse the reader and cloud the systematic nature of the phenomena under discussion.

First, in this area as in any other, different regional varieties of English may differ from one another. For example, *Dave* is a standard short form of *David* in American English, but not in Australian English. This variation is worth a separate study, and it will not be discussed here.

Second, individual names have individual histories, individual frequencies, and individual associations. For example, although the forms *Pammie* and *Katie* both sound rather childish, *Pammie* is widely regarded as being more childish than *Katie*. Individual differences of this kind are no doubt real and worth studying, but they are a matter of degree, and they should be distinguished from discrete, categorical differences such as that between *Pam* and *Kate* on the one hand and *Pammie* and *Katie* on the other. (Cf. section 3.5.2.)

Third, the semantics of proper names is a large field which cannot be discussed exhaustively here. What will appear to the reader to be counter-examples to the generalisations proposed may in fact be examples of sub-regularities which couldn't be discussed here for reasons of space. For example, if forms such as *Jimmy* or *Gracie* are characterised as, roughly speaking, 'childish', this might seem to be contradicted by habitual designations of some well-known personalities such as Jimmy Carter or Gracie Allen. But in fact the names of politicians and other celebrities constitute a category of their own, which has its own rules (cf. Poynton 1982:265).

Another objection which I anticipate is this: "different forms of names are used in different social milieus; just as the choice between *Mum, Mother* and *Mummy* depends largely on the social milieu, so does that between *Patricia, Pat, Trish,* and *Patty;* it has nothing to do with semantics". But in fact there is no conflict between semantic and social explanations. On the contrary, semantic distinctions may be explainable in terms of social ones. For example, the attitudes encapsulated in the form *Mum* (or those encapsulated in the form *Pat*) may be more relevant in a given social milieu than those encoded in the forms *Mother* or *Patricia* (cf. section 1.1).

And so on. It is impossible to discuss everything here, and even more impossible to discuss everything at once. I have to ask the readers, therefore, to be patient and not to close their eyes to the systematic aspects of the use of proper names just because some other aspects of their use are, or appear to be, variable, unsystematic, and a matter of degree.

With all these provisos in mind, why should we regard Van Buren's three categories, FFN, Nn, and AfNn, as too mechanical and too simplistic?

To begin with, full first names such as *Thomas* and *William* don't have the same pragmatic value as, for example, *Andrew, Martin,* or *Matthew,* and female names such as *Pamela* or *Katherine* don't have the same pragmatic value as, for example, *Helen, Ruth, Janet,* or *Clare.* In most cases, full first names are marked if they have unmarked standard abbreviations (e.g., *Tom* for *Thomas, Bill* for *William, Pam* for *Pamela,* and *Kate* for *Katherine*), and unmarked, if they don't (e.g., *Martin* or *Clare*). If one addresses someone as *Thomas* or *Pamela,* these full names are felt to be chosen in preference to the expected standard abbreviations (*Tom, Pam*), but this is not the case with *Martin* or *Clare.* (In some cases, however, full first names can be unmarked even though they do have unmarked standard abbreviations, e.g., *Michael* > *Mike, Matthew* > *Matt, Stephen* > *Steve,* or *David* > *Dave.*)

Consider, for example, the opening paragraph of the following (authentic) letter which the author received from a firm of accountants:

> Dear Client,
> We are pleased to advise that Chris Fearon and Stephen Brennan together with Bill
> Bowd will be commencing practice at Deakin from 1st June 1988.

The names *Christopher* and *William* are both marked and have been shortened here to *Chris* and *Bill,* but the name *Stephen* is unmarked and has not been shortened to *Steve.* Yet *Steve,* too, is an unmarked abbreviation, and in fact the same letter is signed (by hand) as follows: *Steve Brennan, Chris Fearon.*

Similarly, 'nicknames' such as *Tom, Bill,* or *Bob* don't have the same value as, for example, *Ger* or *Ter* (which Van Buren puts in the same category), and female 'nicknames' such as *Pam, Kate,* or *Sue* don't have the same values as, for example, *Deb, Pen,* or *Beck* (which Van Buren also puts in the same category). The reason is that *Tom, Bill,* and *Bob* are unmarked, standard short forms for *Thomas, William,* and *Robert,* and *Pam, Kate,* and *Sue* are standard forms for *Pamela, Katherine,* and *Susan.* But *Ger* and *Ter* are not similarly standard and unmarked, and neither are *Deb, Pen,* and *Beck.* For *Deborah* or *Penelope,* the forms in *-ie/-y* (*Debbie* or *Penny*) are in fact the unmarked standard abbreviations rather than 'affectionate' or 'childish' derivatives of *Deb* or *Pen.* Similarly, for *Terrence* or *Gerald, Terry* and *Gerry* are the standard abbreviations, and not 'affectionate' or 'childish' derivates of *Ter* and *Ger.*

Thus, despite all the individual, sociolectal, and regional variation, one *can* say, that, in a sense, *Bobby* = *Jimmy* or *Pammy* = *Ruthie,* but one *cannot* say that *Bobby* = *Terry* or that *Debbie* = *Pammy.* We need, therefore, not three categories (FFN, Nn, and AfNn) but at least six: unmarked full name (e.g., *Martin, Clare*) and marked full name (e.g., *William, Deborah*); unmarked short form (e.g., *Tom, Pam*) and marked short form (e.g., *Ter, Ger, Deb, Pen*); unmarked *-ie/-y* forms (e.g., *Penny, Debbie, Terry, Jerry*) and marked *-ie/-y* forms (e.g., *Jimmy, Bobby, Pammy, Ruthie*).

I say "at least" because a good case can be made for assigning, in some cases, different values to male and female names. Thus, Van Buren (1977:122–23) has claimed that short names such as *Bob, Bill,* or *Tom* have masculine connotations, and it seems to me that this may well be right. It is as if the shortness of such forms and their typical phonological shape (CVC) serve to heighten the masculine identification of the names themselves. Since for many feminine names the standard phonological shape of an unmarked short form is different (two syllables, with a final *-ie/-y* suffix, e.g., *Debbie* or *Cindy*), the one-syllable short form can naturally be seen as implying a heightened masculinity.

Logically, I can understand why Van Buren has also attributed masculine connotations to short forms of feminine names such as *Pam, Jill, Kate,* or *Sue,* which are also one syllable long and contrast formally with clearly feminine names such as *Debbie* or *Cindy.* But this attribution seems to be unsupported by any evidence other than theoretical speculation based on somewhat mechanical comparison of formal patterns. In fact, native speakers' intuitions seem to point in a different direction. All the native speakers whom I have consulted agree that forms such as *Pam, Jill, Kate,* or *Sue* sound non-sentimental, non-childish, and not particularly feminine (as compared with *Debbie* or *Cindy*), but they don't agree that they sound masculine.

Judging by the native speakers' reactions, it would appear that although a symmetry between formal and functional patterns is indeed involved, it is a symmetry of a less mechanical kind than Van Buren assumed. Rather than asking about the value of a one-syllable short form, we should ask about the effect of a morphological process. It appears that the shortening of a name which is inherently masculine (e.g., *Robert, William,* or *James*) heightens, so to speak, the masculinity of that name, whereas the shortening of a name which is inherently feminine (e.g., *Pamela, Katherine,* or *Susan*) lowers, so to speak, the femininity of that name. Both effects are iconic and based on sound symbolism, but not in the way Van Buren suggested:

William (masculine name) > *Bill*	(heightened masculinity; prototype: man or boy)
Pamela (feminine name) > *Pam*	(lowered femininity; prototype: person)
Deborah (feminine name) > *DebbIE*	(heightened femininity; prototype: woman or girl, or child)

Accordingly, I have framed the explication of masculine short forms such as *Bob, Bill,* or *Tom* in terms of 'boys and men'; the explication of feminine short forms such as *Debbie* or *Cindy* in terms of 'women and girls' (but also 'children'); and the explication of feminine short forms such as *Pam* or *Kate* in terms of 'people'. Of course forms such as *Pam* or *Kate* can only refer to females, but this is determined by the female reference of the underlying full names. The short forms themselves do not emphasise this female reference. (I will return to this problem later in this section.)

Furthermore, I think that a good case can be made for assigning different values to female *-ie/-y* forms (such as *Debbie* or *Penny*) and to male *-y* forms (such as *Terry* or *Jerry*). The fact that these standard male forms are always spelt with *-y,* never with *-ie,* provides some evidence for this suggestion. 'Childish' male forms such as *Billie, Eddie,* or *Frankie* can be spelt with either *-ie* or *-y,* but these are felt to be derived from standard short forms such as *Bill, Ed,* and *Frank,* whereas standard *-y* forms such as *Terry* or *Jerry* are not felt to be similarly derived from *Ter* or *Jer*

(Ger). In fact, it appears that, mutatis mutandis, the short masculine *-y* forms such as *Terry* or *Jerry* have the same pragmatic value as feminine short forms ending in a consonant, such as *Pam* or *Kate*. Masculine short forms of a 'non-masculine' phonological shape seem to de-emphasise the inherent masculinity of the full name, just as the feminine short forms of a 'non-feminine' phonological shape seem to de-emphasise the inherent femininity of the feminine full name:

> *Gerald* (masculine name) > *Gerry*   (de-emphasised masculinity; prototype: person)
>
> *Pamela* (feminine name) > *Pam*   (de-emphasised femininity; prototype: person)

The fact that masculine short forms such as *Gerry* (*Jerry*) or *Terry* can also be used for women seems to support this interpretation.

Before I propose a set of explications to show how pragmatic meanings encoded in different forms of personal names can be modelled in the natural semantic metalanguage, I must make some general comments, without which these explications could prove incomprehensible. First, the value of a given form, spelt out in the explications, depends on with what other forms this form competes, or rather, is felt to compete. For example, the form *James* (as a form of address or a form of reference) is felt to compete with *Jim* and with *Mr Herriot* (*Mr X*), not with *Jimmy;* in choosing *James* as a form of address, the speaker indicates that *Mr Herriot* is too formal and *Jim* too informal or too boyish. The form *Jimmy* is felt to be chosen in preference to *Jim*, not to *James* or *Mr Herriot*, and *Jim* is normally not felt to be chosen in preference to *Jimmy*.

Of course in a given personal relationship there may be personal conventions running counter to those inherent in the system itself. For example, if a mother normally calls her young son *Jimmy*, and only occasionally switches from *Jimmy* to *Jim*, then in her speech *Jim* will feel marked in relation to *Jimmy*. Nonetheless the habitual choice of *Jimmy* in preference to *Jim* means something (roughly speaking, that she treats him like a child, not like a man or a 'big boy'), and it means something because there are certain constant values attached to forms such as *Jimmy* and to forms such as *Jim*, values determined by the system itself and independent of personal conventions. In the system, *Jim* is unmarked with respect to *Jimmy* and to *James; Pam* is unmarked with respect to *Pamela* and with respect to *Pammie; Cindy* is unmarked with respect to *Cynthia; Debbie* is unmarked with respect to *Deborah* and also with respect to *Deb; Andrew* is unmarked with respect to *Andy;* and so on. Personal conventions can be superimposed on the social ones, but they don't cancel them out.

The second general comment concerns the different expressive possibilities of different names. Looking at different names superficially, one might assume that one full first name, for example, *Andrew,* is equivalent to another, for example, *Timothy,* and one 'diminutive' in *-ie/-y,* for example, *Debbie,* is equivalent to another, for example, *Pammie*. But in fact this is not true. *Timothy* is a marked full name, and if it is used as a form of address, it has an expressive value which simply cannot be achieved with a name such as *Andrew,* which is an unmarked full name.

Similarly, *Debbie* is an unmarked short form of *Deborah* (even though it conveys a certain warmth and a certain appeal to the addressee's femininity); it has therefore an expressive value which simply cannot be achieved with a name such as *Pamela*, whose unmarked short form is *Pam*, not *Pammie*. *Pammie* sounds childish as well as warm, whereas *Debbie* can sound warm without sounding childish. Differences in the expressive range of different names can of course be taken into account by parents bestowing names on their babies, but they cannot be changed at will.

Third, to claim that different forms of names constitute a system in which certain constant meanings can be assigned to certain categories of forms is not to deny that individual names, or groups of names, may have their individual features. For example, an unusual name such as *Prudence* or *Gertrude* may be perceived as more 'marked' than a relatively common one such as *Deborah* or *Thomas*. Similarly, to some people, Old Testament names such as *Joshua* or *Jonathan* may have an 'entirely different value' from New Testament names such as *Peter* or *Paul*, and Christian names such as *Mary* and *Clare* may have an 'entirely different value' from 'invented names', such as *Raylene* or *Kelly;* names of French origin such as *Michelle* or *Nicole* may be perceived as having a different value from, say, borrowings from Russian such as *Natasha* or *Tanya;* and so on. I am not denying the reality of such differences, but I believe that they are independent of the systematic, discrete, categorical differences such as those between marked full names (e.g., *Pamela* or *James*) and unmarked full names (e.g., *Mary* or *John*).

Finally, it should be mentioned that names—like any other words in natural language—can be polysemous. For example, *Sally* may be either an unmarked full name or a short form of *Sarah; Suzie* may be used either as an unmarked short form similar in value to *Debbie* or *Cindy* or as a marked, 'childish' form similar in value to *Pammie* or *Ruthie; Vic* can be either a standard short form of *Victor* or a back-formation of *Vicki* (from *Victoria*). Naturally, a polysemous form of this kind has two different values, not one. But this doesn't mean that a form such as *Sally* or *Vic* is somehow 'vague and indescribable'.

With these general considerations in mind, I propose the following set of explications:

STANDARD MALE SHORT FORMS (e.g., *Tom, Jim, Bill*)

I want to speak to you the way people speak
   to men and boys whom they know well

STANDARD FEMALE SHORT FORMS (e.g., *Pam, Kate, Sue*)

I want to speak to you the way people speak
   to people whom they know well

CHILD-ORIENTED *-ie/-y* FORMS (e.g., *Jimmy, Tommy, Pammie, Ruthie*)

I want to speak to you the way people speak
   to children whom they know well and toward whom they feel something good

STANDARD FEMALE *-ie/-y* FORMS (e.g., *Debbie, Penny*)

I want to speak to you the way people speak
   to girls and women whom they know well or to children

UNISEX STYLE -*y* FORMS (e.g., *Terry, Jerry*)
I want to speak to you the way people speak
  to people whom they know well

NON-STANDARD SHORT FORMS, BACK-FORMATIONS FROM -*ie*/-*y* FORMS (e.g., *Deb*
  from *Debbie*, *Pen* from *Penny*, *Sal* from *Sally*)
I want to speak to you the way people speak
  to people whom they know well
I don't want to speak to you the way people speak
  to women or girls whom they know well and to children
I feel something good toward you
  not of the kind that people feel toward children

UNMARKED MALE AND FEMALE FULL FORMS (e.g., *Ruth, Clare, Andrew, Martin*)
I don't want to speak to you the way people speak
  to people whom they don't know well

MARKED MALE AND FEMALE FULL FORMS (e.g., *James, Deborah*)
I don't want to speak to you the way people speak
  to people whom they don't know well
I don't want to speak to you the way people speak
  to boys and girls
I want to speak to you the way people do not speak to children

Some comments and explanations are in order. To begin with, it should be pointed out that these formulae have been phrased in such a way as to account for the use of names as forms of address. To account for the use of a name in reference all we would have to do is to replace the expression 'to you' with the expression 'of (person) X', for example:

I want to speak to you the way people speak to boys . . . →
I want to speak of X the way people speak of boys . . .

In saying this, I do not wish to imply that a given form, for example, *Janey* or *Deb,* will have exactly the same expressive value whether it is used in reference or in address. It is more usual to express in speech feelings directed at the addressee than feelings directed at a third person, and an affectionate form used as a form of reference may be felt as more unusual, and more emotionally loaded, than the same form used as a form of address. In fact, some highly expressive forms of names (such as *Svetik* or *Ljusik* in Russian or *Basiulka* or *Ewulka* in Polish) are normally used only as forms of address. This doesn't mean, however, that the attitude encoded in a form used as a form of address should be represented (in the semantic formula) as different from that encoded in the same form used as a form of reference.

Furthermore, even though first names can be said to form a system, in a sense, in fact they belong to a larger system of forms of address and forms of reference, which includes combinations of first names with surnames, surnames with titles, titles alone, and so on. For example, forms of address such as *James* or *Pamela* contrast not only with unmarked short forms such as *Jim* or *Pam* but also with combinations such as *James Herriot* or *Mr Herriot*. If this were not taken into account, it might seem odd that marked full names such as *James* or *Pamela* have been assigned, among others, the 'quasi-familiar' component 'I don't want to speak to you the way people speak to people whom they don't know well'. This is not to deny, of course, that full names such as *James* or *Pamela* may sound 'distant', 'formal', 'lacking in familiarity', and so on. But first, I have not assigned to them the component of true familiarity, which I have assigned to short forms such as *Bob* or *Sue:* 'I want to speak to you the way people speak to people whom they know well'. Instead, I have only assigned to them the component of quasi-familiarity: 'I don't want to speak to you the way people speak to people whom they don't know well'. And second, the serious and formal effect of such names can be largely accounted for by the component 'I want to speak to you the way people do not speak to children'.

Van Buren (1977:114) stresses the fact that in speaking to children, full names often sound angry or disapproving and that "the fiercer the scolding the more fully the names owned are used" (for example, "Jessie, no", "Jessica, don't do that!"). But apart from the fact that this effect applies only to marked full names which do have unmarked short forms (that is, to *James* or *Jessica* but not to *Martin* or *Clare*), this 'disapproving' connotation is by no means a part of the invariant interactional meaning of such forms. A proud father may say to his little boy, "Well done, James!" just as well as an angry one may say, "Stop it at once, James!" What both of these uses have in common can be captured in terms of components such as 'I want to speak to you the way people (normally) don't speak to children'.

Interactional meanings of this kind can account, to some extent, for stable personal conventions as well as for variable usage of names. For example, if in a certain relationship a boy is called *Jim, James,* or *Jimmy,* depending on the speaker's mood, the choices can clearly be accounted for in terms of the semantic formulae proposed here, but if in a particular relationship (for example, between Helen and James Herriot in James Herriot's (1986) *Dog stories* and the television series based on them) one person always calls the other *James* (rather than *Jim* or *Jimmy*), this usage, too, can be accounted for in terms of the proposed formulae. For example, the component 'I want to speak to you the way people do not speak to children' fits in quite well with the general tenor of that particular relationship. (As one would expect, when Helen and James Herriot have a son, whose name is also *James,* they normally call him *Jimmy,* not *James.*)

However, interactional meanings are not always a matter of free choice. For example, if a woman has been introduced to us as *Katie,* and if she calls herself *Katie* and expects us to call her that, we may well feel obliged to use that form in speaking both to her and about her, even if we felt that a different interactional meaning (for example, that encoded in the full name) would suit this particular relationship better. Similarly, if a cute little girl insists on being called *Cynthia* rather than *Cindy,* we may feel that we have to call her *Cynthia*. We may feel that we have no choice in the matter. This doesn't mean, however, that in this particular case the form *Katie* or *Cynthia* has no special interactional meaning or that it has a meaning different from that of the same form chosen freely. The use of a word or expression with a certain meaning may be forced on us by circumstances or by a social convention (for example, "Nice to see you" or "Nice to have met you"). But this doesn't mean that this meaning is no longer there.

By contrast to marked full names such as *James*, unmarked full names such as *Matthew* or *Ruth* don't have that serious and adult effect, because it is quite common to apply them to children. Accordingly, I have not postulated for them the component 'I want to speak to you the way people do not speak to children' (see section 1.1). But they have been assigned the component of quasi-familiarity 'I don't want to speak to you the way people speak to people whom they don't know well'. (I have not assigned to them the component of 'true familiarity'—'I want to speak to you the way people speak to people whom they know well'—in order to distinguish them, in this respect, from shortened forms such as *Bob* or *Kate*.)

It should also be pointed out that the formulae proposed here have been phrased, for the most part, in terms of prototypes rather than necessary conditions. For example, I do not claim that by calling or addressing somebody as *Jimmy* or *Bobby* the speaker is conveying the message 'I think of you as a child' or 'I feel something good toward you'. Rather, the speaker is conveying a more oblique message: 'I want to speak to you the way people speak to children whom they know well or toward whom they feel something good'. If the addressee is a small child (and the speaker an adult), the use of forms such as *Jimmy* or *Bobby* can of course be interpreted as conveying a certain warmth, as well as a grown-up-to-child attitude. If both the speaker and addressee are small children, forms such as *Jimmy* or *Bobby* may be unmarked in their use, convey no warmth, and in fact be compatible with personal 'bad feelings'. Still, the general meaning 'I want to speak to you the way people speak to children whom they know well' is compatible with this use, too. If the person spoken of, or spoken to, is an adult, forms such as *Jimmy* or *Bobby* may have a patronising, condescending, or disparaging effect (as, for example, does the form *Pammy* used in reference and address to a female clerk in Alexander Buzo's (1974) play *The front room boys*), but here, too, this effect is compatible with, and explainable in terms of, the postulated meaning 'I want to speak to you the way people speak to children'.

On the other hand, back-formations of feminine names such as *Beck* from *Becky*, *Pen* from *Penny*, *Vic* from *Vicki*, or *Deb* from *Debbie* do seem to express personal good feelings, as well as a claim to a 'special relationship'. Casual acquaintances, or people newly introduced at a party, may well start calling a woman *Penny, Vicki*, or *Debbie* but not *Pen, Vic* or *Deb*. Back-formations of this kind carry an element of playful distortion, as if the speaker were saying, 'I don't want to use that boring conventional -*ie*/-*y* form that anybody can use to a female acquaintance or to a child; I want to use something special because our relationship is special'. For example, in any Anglo-Saxon high school girls may well call their close friends *Pen, Deb*, or *Vic*, but the teachers would normally call them *Penny, Debbie*, or *Vicki*, rather than *Pen, Deb*, or *Vic*, since it would be inappropriate for a teacher to claim a 'special relationship' with a student.

Personal good feelings of a 'special kind' are also encoded in Australian personal names such as *Johnno, Sallo, Thommo*, or *Bronno* (from *Bronwyn*), and in -*z* or -*za* forms such as *Baz, Bazza* (from *Barry*), or *Kez, Kezza* (from *Kerry*), which I discuss in more detail in chapter 11. (See also Poynton 1982 and 1989.)

As mentioned earlier, Van Buren (1977:122) has claimed that in English "the Nn has a masculine connotation and the AfNn has a feminine connotation, especially for adults", and in support of this claim he points out that when John F. Kennedy was president of the United States, "the general public and all the news media could and often did call the President *Jack* (never *Jackie*) and the President's wife *Jackie* (never *Jac*, the Nn for *Jacqueline*)".

The observation is interesting, but the generalisation does not seem to be correct. When President Nixon was sometimes called "Tricky Dicky", this was certainly disparaging, but there is no evidence of any feminine connotations of the form *Dicky*. Childish connotations of all forms such as *Bobby*, *Jimmy*, or *Johnny* are sufficient to explain the sometimes disparaging effect of the form *Dicky*, especially of course if it is combined with the adjective *tricky*.

Similarly, as pointed out earlier, it seems incorrect to claim that all 'nicknames'—that is, short forms such as *Kate*, *Sue*, *Bob*, or *Liz*—have masculine connotations in English. If forms such as *Kate*, *Sue*, or *Liz* may seem to have masculine connotations at all, it is only because they don't have the feminine connotations of *-ie/-y* forms of feminine names such as *Debbie*, *Vicki*, or *Penny*. To account for this, however, we should include a reference to 'girls and women' in the explications of the latter forms (and only those), not a reference to 'men' in the explication of the former. There is a difference between the presence of masculine connotations and the absence of feminine connotations. By choosing a form without feminine connotations in preference to one which does have such connotations, one may sometimes create an effect of an 'anti-feminine' style. But semantically, names such as *Kate*, *Sue*, *Liz*, or *Pam* don't have inherent masculine connotations.

The same applies to back-formations such as *Deb*, *Vick*, *Pen*, or *Beck:* they do not have inherent masculine connotations, although they contrast with *Debbie*, *Vicki*, *Penny*, or *Beckie* in their absence of the feminine connotations carried by the *-ie/-y* forms of feminine names.

As for the reasons why the media didn't call Jacqueline Kennedy *Jac*, I suggest these may have been related not to the alleged masculinity of English 'nicknames' but to the affectionate special relationship implied by all back-formations such as *Deb*, *Pen*, *Beck*, or *Jac* (*Jack*), particularly common in Australian English (cf. chapter 11). In the Australian high school that one of my daughters attended, a girl called *Jackie* was often called *Jac/Jack* by her close friends, though never by the teachers, just as *Lydia* and *Alison* were often called *Lyd* and *Al* by their close friends though never by the teachers. The use of such back-formations seems to be much more common in Australia than it is in the United States, but in both cases, whatever restrictions there are, they are due to the 'special relation' claim inherent in such names and not to their alleged masculine connotations.

1.1 Family Relation Terms

The semantic system to which personal names belong also includes, as an important sub-system, the kin terms used in family life. At the core of this sub-system lie two crucial terms normally acquired early in life, on which the rest is normally built. These two terms are *Mummy* and *Daddy*. The pragmatic meaning of these words used as terms of address (which can also be assigned to *Auntie* and to *Granny*) can, I think, be spelt out along the following lines:

> I want to speak to you the way children speak
> to people toward whom they feel something good
> and who feel something good toward them

Of course a very young child may be unaware of the inherent social meaning of the forms *Mummy* and *Daddy*. Presumably, it is only when the alternative forms— *Mum* and *Dad, mother* and *father*—are acquired that the implicit meaning of *Mummy* and *Daddy* becomes a part of the child's semantic system. What matters in the present context is what this meaning is, not when or how it is acquired.

It is culturally significant, of course, that although the meaning assigned here to *Mummy* and *Daddy* can also be assigned to *Auntie* and *Granny* (and the now-outdated *nanny*), there are no similar masculine forms for uncle and grandfather in general use (and of course *Granny* cannot stand for grandfather). It is also significant (though less culture-specific; cf. Greenberg 1980) that there are no parallel forms for 'horizontal' or descending relationships: brother, sister, daughter, grandson, granddaughter, nephew, or niece. (The form *sonny* does exist in English, but it is rarely used for one's own sons, and its pragmatic meaning is different, cf. Zwicky 1974:790.) In this respect, the forms *Mummy, Daddy, Auntie,* and *Granny* are different from child-oriented personal names such as *Bobby, Johnny,* or *Ruthie,* which are used both horizontally (between children) and vertically, but if vertically then (prototypically) in a descending rather than ascending manner (see the accompanying figure).

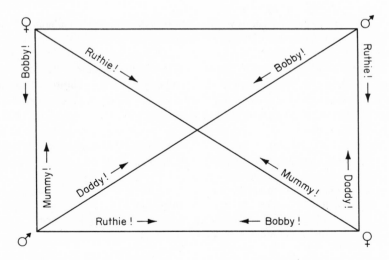

Thus, both *-ie/-y* kin terms such as *Mummy* and *Daddy* (and also *Auntie* and *Granny*) and *-ie/-y* names such as *Bobby* and *Suzie* are child-centered, but the first category is essentially from a child to a (close and caring) adult, whereas the second

category is essentially from anyone (close) to a child. These differences are reflected in the explications:

> CHILD-TARGET NAMES (e.g., *Bobby, Ruthie*)
>
> I want to speak to you the way people speak
>   to children whom they know well
>   and toward whom they feel something good
>
> CHILD-SOURCE FAMILY TERMS (*Mummy, Daddy, Auntie, Granny*)
>
> I want to speak to you the way children speak
>   to people who are not children, who do good things for them,
>   and toward whom they feel something good

The terms *Mum* and *Dad* should, I think, be seen against the background of earlier
terms of address used by children: they represent, essentially, a rejection of the
"childish" forms *Mummy* and *Daddy,* combined, however, with a recognition of a
continuing asymmetry in the relationship and with a preservation of something of the
close child-parent relationship. When used by adults, these forms sound warm
(especially when compared to *mother* and *father,* to be discussed later), and even in
the speech of teenagers the rejection of the "childish" style of relationship does not
seem to include a rejection of the warm component 'toward whom they feel something good'. This double message of the forms *Mum* and *Dad* (used as forms of
address) can be represented as follows:

> NON-CHILDISH BUT INTIMATE (*Mum* and *Dad*)
>
> I don't want to speak to you the way children speak
>   to people who are not children
>   (and who do good things for them)
> I don't want to speak to you the way people who are not children
>   speak to people who are not children

The words *Mother* and *Father* used as forms of address represent a very different
style of the child-parent relationship: they embody a positive claim of a symmetrical, adult-to-adult style of relationship, and an overt rejection of any show of 'good
feelings'. This can be represented as follows:

> NON-CHILDISH, NON-INTIMATE, FAMILY TERMS (*Mother* and *Father*)
>
> I don't want to speak to you the way children speak
>   to people who are not children
>   (who do good things for them
>   and toward whom they feel something good)
> I want to speak to you the way people who are not children speak
>   to people who are not children
> I don't want to show good feelings toward you

As this formula indicates, the terms *Mother* and *Father* are in some ways
parallel to the use of marked full first names such as *James* or *Deborah*. But the

component of 'rejection' is in each case somewhat different: the terms *Mother* and *Father* reject the style of adolescent dependence (being chosen in preference to *Mum* and *Dad*), whereas forms such as *James* or *Pamela* reject the style proper for addressing adolescents (being chosen in preference to *Jim* and *Pam,* as well as to *Mr Herriot* or *Mrs Brown*).

The structural similarity between the two patterns, that of family relation terms and that of proper names, is indeed quite striking and it is tempting to posit semantic proportions along the following lines:

Mother	:	Mum	:	Mummy	=
Pamela	:	Pam	:	Pammie	=
Father	:	Dad	:	Daddy	=
James	:	Jim	:	Jimmy	

Van Buren (1977:123) in fact succumbs to this temptation when he writes: "[E]ven the terms . . . used within the family share the paradigm of FFN, Nn, AfNn and exhibit the same usage patterns and connotations as do regular proper names."

But this is misleading and inaccurate. *Mum* and *Dad* are felt to be replacements of earlier forms *Mummy* and *Daddy* and are perceived as an expression of growing up. But 'nicknames' such as *Jim* or *Pam* are not felt to be replacements for *Jimmy* and *Pammy* (we usually don't first get to know people as *Jimmies* or *Pammies* and then move on to more 'mature' forms such as *Jim* or *Pam*). In a sense, *Mum* and *Dad* are anti-diminutives, based on rejection of the previously expected suffix *-ie/-y*. In this respect, they are analogous to affectionate back-formations such as *Deb, Vick, Beck,* or *Pen* rather than to unmarked short forms such as *Jim* or *Pam*. On the other hand, however, *Mum* and *Dad* are not necessarily affectionate. Consequently, they are neither exactly parallel to affectionate back-formations such as *Deb* or *Beck* nor exactly parallel to unmarked short forms such as *Jim* or *Pam*. There are similarities, but there are also differences. It is not true, therefore, that family terms "exhibit the same usage patterns and connotations as do regular proper names". Categories such as "FFN", "Nn", and "AfNn" are far too simplistic to be adequate analytical devices for describing or comparing the usage of family terms and of "regular" proper names in English. When it comes to cross-linguistic comparisons the total inadequacy of such categories becomes even more immediately apparent.

2. Russian Personal Names

In languages with rich expressive derivation such as Russian any tripartite division of names similar to that into full first names, nicknames, and affectionate nicknames is unthinkable in view of the exceedingly wide variety of alternative forms of address (and reference), unimaginable to native speakers of a 'sober' language such as English. For example, a study of colloquial speech in the Russian town of Penza and the surrounding area (Bondaletov and Danilina 1970) has revealed the use of as many as eighty different expressive suffixes, each with its own pragmatic meaning.

In literary Russian, expressive forms commonly used in names are probably closer to twenty. What is particularly important in this connection is that the same name, for example *Ivan,* may have a large number of possible derivational forms for speakers to choose from and that speakers' choices may depend on their momentary mood and on the specific attitude that they wish to convey at that particular moment, rather than on any stable and rigid personal and interpersonal conventions (as is usually the case in English).

Some scholars have tried to cope with this wealth of expressive possibilities by postulating a larger number of analytical categories. For example, Witkowski (1964) has proposed for German and Slavic names more than ten categories, including *Koseform* (caressing), *Schmeichelform* (flattering/cajoling), *Scherzname* (jocular), *Spottname* (mocking), *Stichelname* (taunting), *Stochelname* (derisive), and *Scheltname* (scolding). (Cf. Bondaletov and Danilina 1970:195.) For Russian, Superanskaja (1969, quoted in Comrie and Stone 1977:183) offers a different grid:

1. The short forename (without 'emotionally loaded' suffixes), e.g., *Júra*
2. Forms with suffixes of 'subjective assessment':
   (a) Caressing (*laskatel'nyj*), e.g., *Júročka*
   (b) Diminutive (*umen'šitel'nyj*), e.g., *Júrik*
   (c) Familiar/vulgar (*familiarnyj/vul'garnyj*), e.g., *Júrka*
   (d) Teasing (*podraznivajuščij*), e.g., *Juríšče*
   (e) Scornful (*prenebrežitel'nyj*), e.g., *Juráška*
   (f) Pejorative (*uničižitel'nyj*), e.g., *Juríška*
   (g) Contemptuous (*prezritel'nyj*), e.g., *Jurčíšče*

(According to my informants, some of these forms do not in fact exist.) But the task of translating dozens of expressive categories into descriptive adjectives such as 'caressing' or 'teasing' is a hopeless and futile one. There is simply no one-to-one match between expressive suffixes and descriptive adjectives, so translations of the kind attempted by Witkowski or by Superanskaja are clearly arbitrary. If a form such as *Júročka* can be said to be 'caressing', so can *Káten'ka* or *Il'júšečka,* and yet the expressive value of each of these forms is different. Similarly, if *Júrik* can be said to be diminutive (cf. *sad* 'garden', *sádik* 'little garden'), so can *Júročka* (cf. *zvezdá* 'star', *zvëzdočka* 'little star').

As a framework for cross-linguistic comparisons, grids such as those proposed by Witkowski or Superanskaja are even more futile. There is no way of knowing, for example, how Witkowski's *Spottname* or *Stochelname* is related to Superanskaja's *podraznivajuščij* or *prenebrežitel'nyj*. Conventional linguistic labels such as 'diminutive' or 'pejorative' prove singularly unhelpful when it comes to describing a language which has dozens of different 'diminutive' or 'pejorative' forms, like Russian.

In addition to the formidable wealth of expressive forms, which have no exact equivalents of any kinds in typologically different languages like English, a different but no less formidable difficulty lies in the protean nature of many of these forms, some of which seem to have an extremely broad range of possible interpretations. (This applies in particular to the Russian suffix -*ka,* which is treated in detail in section 2.3.)

Apart from dialectal variation, a changeable value of a given expressive form can be accounted for, to some extent, in terms of irony, sarcasm, jocularity, and other similar devices. For example, although the unmarked value of forms in *-en'ka* (e.g., *Natášen'ka, Káten'ka*) is, roughly speaking, affectionate and caressing, the character in Tolstoy's (1953) novel *Anna Karenina* who is normally referred to as *Vasen'ka Veslovskij* is rather unpleasant, and the effect of the form *Vásen'ka* is in his case disparaging, almost contemptuous, rather than affectionate. This reversal, however, is easily explained in terms of irony, and it presupposes rather than casts doubt on the basically positive value of names in *-en'ka*.

Similarly, forms which are basically somewhat pejorative, such as *Katjúxa* or *Andrjúxa*, can be used lovingly, to express jocularly rough affection. It would be entirely inadmissible to say, however, that the same suffix can be either positive or negative in value, depending on the idiolect, or depending on the context or the situation, and that no stable pragmatic meanings can be assigned to any expressive forms as such. Bondaletov and Danilina are perhaps not sufficiently clear on this point when they say:

> Svoim budet delenie na položitel'nye i otricate'lnye formy i na urovne individu-al'nogo jazyka—idiolekta. Zdes' obščeprinjatye laskatel'nye formy (tipa *Nikólen'ka, Petrús', Lénočka* i dr.) neredko vystupajut v kačestve imenovanij, a v kačestve laskatel'nyx imen upotrebljajutsja formy s pejorativnymi suffixami (*Kát'ka, Katjúxa* i dr.) (1970:198)
>
> 'The division of forms into positive and negative can also vary according to individual usage, that is at the level of individual language—the idiolect. At this level, forms which in common usage are affectionate/caressing (e.g. *Nikólen'ka, Petrús', Lénočka*, etc.) are often used as habitual designations, and forms with pejorative suffixes (e.g. *Kát'ka, Katjúxa*, etc.) are used with an affectionate value.'

It is important to stress that reversals of this kind—whether habitual or spontaneous—don't cancel the basic social value of a form but exploit it for a further expressive purpose. Just as in Australian friendly insults (e.g., "You old bastard!"), the friendly effect depends on the insulting literal meaning and draws from it its specific quality of 'matey' rough affection, so the specific quality of affection conveyed by forms such as *Katjúxa* or *Andrjúxa* depends on and exploits, rather than cancels, the somewhat negative literal value of the form as such.

Expressive devices such as jocularity or irony must be distinguished from genuine vagueness (compatible with a more or less wide range of interpretations), and vagueness must be distinguished from polysemy. For example, in Australian English the word *bastard* (apart from its sense of 'illegitimate child') is neither vague nor polysemous in its evaluation (it is not 'either good or bad'). It is always bad (pejorative), although this very badness can be exploited in jocular insults.

I would suggest that Russian forms such as *Katjúxa* or *Andrjúxa* operate in the same way as *bastard*, whereas forms such as *Kát'ka*, which Bondaletov and Danilina mention in one breath with *Katjúxa*, do not work in the same way. But this is a point which I will discuss in more detail later (see section 2.3.1).

Polysemy of expressive forms can be illustrated for Russian with the suffix *-ik*.

For some masculine names, e.g., *Stanisláv, Vladisláv,* or *Aleksándr,* it is used as an unmarked short form: *Stásik, Vládik, Álik* (cf. Suslova and Superanskaja 1978:109). For other masculine names, however, e.g., for *Mark,* it is used as an affectionate form: *Márik.* (For *Aleksándr,* there is another *-ik* form, *Šúrik,* which can also be used as affectionate.) For feminine names, *-ik* is always affectionate, and in fact more so than it can ever be for masculine names, e.g., *Svétik (Svetlána), Ljúsik (Ljudmíla).* Thus, three different pragmatic meanings need to be postulated for the *-ik* suffix, two for its use in masculine names and one in feminine ones.

Before I attempt a detailed semantic analysis of a number of expressive types, I must warn the reader that the meanings in question may prove extremely rich and complex and that one should not expect that they can be represented by means of simple global labels such as 'affectionate', 'caressing', 'contemptuous', or 'scornful'. In many cases, as many as six different components will be posited for one expressive category, each of these components being spelt out in one or two lines (although more convenient abbreviations will also be provided). The length of the proposed explications will no doubt strike some readers as shocking and off-putting. I believe, however, that it reflects the richness of the concepts themselves—a richness that conventional global labels such as diminutive, augmentative, or pejorative are utterly unable to capture, or even to approximate.

The discussion will be divided into three parts: 2.1, full forms and short forms of names; 2.2, the meaning of expressive suffixes (which are added to either short or long forms of names); and 2.3, the semantics of the versatile suffix *-ka* in names. It should be stressed that the survey of expressive types is by no means intended to be an exhaustive one.

2.1 Full Forms and Short Forms

2.1.1 Full Forms

For a native speaker of English, full forms of first names present the easiest part of the Russian use of personal names, because they are closest to the English usage of full first names. In Russian, as in English, there are two types of full first names: marked ones and unmarked ones. Addressing someone in Russian as *Konstantín, Nikoláj, Natál'ja* or *Evgénija* has an effect somewhat similar to addressing someone in English as *James, Nicholas, Deborah,* or *Pamela* (which doesn't mean that they are used under the same conditions, or that their value is exactly the same). In different contexts, a full form of this kind may imply anger, disapproval, coldness, distance, solemnity, pride, respect, and so on. The invariant of Russian full first names, however, can be spelt out as follows:

> a. I don't want to speak to you the way people speak
>   to people whom they don't know well
> b. I want to speak to you the way people don't speak
>   to children or to people whom they know well
>   and toward whom they feel something good

Component (a), which is identical with the first component of marked full first names in English, accounts for the contrast between the use of full first names as such and that of full first names with patronymics, which is the unmarked usage in situations of social distance (*Konstantín* vs. *Konstantín Petróvič, Evgénija* vs. *Evgénija Ivánovna*). Component (b) accounts for the contrast between marked full first names and unmarked short forms (*Konstantín* vs. *Kóstja, Nikoláj* vs. *Kólja, Natál'ja* vs. *Natáša, Evgénija* vs. *Žénja*). But in Russian, it seems even less common and even more marked than in English to call one's friends or relatives by their marked full name, except for ad hoc expressive purposes (for example, to show anger, pride, or a solemn feeling). For example, in Dostoevsky's (1976) novel *The brothers Karamazov*, the two brothers to whom the author (or narrator) feels close, *Alëša* and *Mítja*, are never called by their full names (*Alekséj* and *Dimítrij*), but the distant, aloof, and somewhat mysterious third brother is always called by his full first name: *Iván*. I have tried to account for the highly marked character of such forms in the way I have phrased their second component: 'I want to speak to you the way people don't speak to children or to people whom they know well and toward whom they feel something good'.

The unmarked type of full first names, e.g., *Andréj, Ígor', Véra, Nína*, parallels (to some extent) unmarked full first names in English, such as *Andrew, John, Mary*, or *Clare*. They imply something like familiarity because they contrast with combinations of such names with patronymics (*Andréj Petróvič, Véra Ivánovna*), but they are not too familiar, as they do not carry any expressive suffixes, which in Russian would be perfectly natural in familiar adult-to-adult speech.

When names of this kind are applied to adults, they don't seem to imply more than that, and so their value might seem to be the same as that of *Ruth, Clare*, or *John* in English. However, when names of this kind are applied to children, their value is clearly different. The point is that in an English or American kindergarten there is nothing unusual about calling small children *Ruth, Clare*, or *John*. But in a Russian kindergarden it is not unmarked to call three- or four-year-olds *Véra* or *Nína*. With small children, names of this kind sound very grown up and more marked than the corresponding diminutives *Véročka* or *Nínočka*. In adult-to-adult speech, forms such as *Véra* or *Nína* can be perceived as 'neutral', but in adult-to-child speech they are perceived against the background of the more usual *Véročka* or *Nínočka*. To account for both of these possibilities, names of this kind should, I think, be analysed as follows:

> *Véra, Nína*
>
> a. I don't want to speak to you the way people speak
>   to people whom they don't know well
> b. I don't want to speak to you the way people speak
>   to children

The first of these two is the quasi-familiarity component, which I would also assign to unmarked full first names in English (as well as to marked full first names in both English and Russian). Since, however, in Russian such forms are less appropriate for children than forms such as *Ruth* or *Matthew* are in English, and since they are chosen in preference to readily available diminutives (e.g., *Véročka, Nínočka*), I have also assigned them the quasi-serious component 'I don't want to speak to you the way people speak to children'. But this quasi-serious component is still not as serious as that assigned to marked full first names: 'I want to speak to you the way people don't speak to children'.

The double negative contained in component (a) may seem unnecessarily complex: why not say simply 'I want to speak to you the way people speak to people whom they know well'? But in fact, this double negative allows us to distinguish quasi-familiar full names such as *Nína, Véra,* or *Andréj* from familiar derived forms such as *Lída* (from *Lídija*) or *Ljúba* (from *Ljubóv'*), which will be discussed in the following section.

2.1.2 Short Forms with Soft and Hard Stems

Turning now to short forms, at least three different types must be distinguished here: names with a soft (palatalised) stem-final consonant, e.g., *Kóst'ja* (for *Konstantín*), *Ván'ja* (for *Iván*), or *Kát'ja* (for *Katerína*); those with a hard (non-palatalised) stem-final consonant, e.g., *Lëva* (for *Lev*), *Díma* (for *Dmítrij*), *Júra* (for *Júrij*), *Lída* (for *Lídija*), *Ljúba* (for *Ljubóv'*), or *Lára* (for *Laríssa*); and those with a stem expanded by the suffix -*š*, e.g., *Gríša* (for *Grigórij*), *Máša* (for *Márija*), or *Natáša* (for *Natál'ja*).[1]

In the literature on Russian names these different types are usually not distinguished from a semantic point of view, although they are subdivided into categories from a morphological standpoint (cf., for example, Benson 1967 or Stankiewicz 1968). The reason for this undoubtedly lies in the fact that from a functional point of view the proportions such as the following ones are in a sense valid:

Katerína:Kát'ja = Lídija:Lída = Natál'ja:Natáša

The point is that *Kát'ja* *is* the unmarked short form for *Katerína, Lída* for *Lídija,* and *Natáša* for *Natál'ja,* so structurally as well as functionally these short forms occupy the same slot in the relevant pattern. This doesn't mean, however, that the semantic value of these different short forms is exactly the same. To put it crudely, the soft consonant suggests a shade of semantic 'softness' which the hard consonant doesn't suggest, and the stem final -*š* occupies, in a sense, an intermediate position between the other two, both structurally and semantically.

As a parallel to 'soft' short forms such as *Vánja* or *Kátja* consider 'soft' family terms such as *tëtja* 'auntie', *djádja* 'uncle', and *njánja* 'nanny', which come close in 'warmth' to English terms such as *Auntie, Granny, Mummy,* and *Daddy.* The symbolic effect of soft consonants in expressive derivation is also visible in the formation of diminutive adjectives and adverbs, as the expressive diminutive suffixes such as -*en'kij/-on'kij* and -*en'ko/-on'ko* indicate (e.g., *bélyj* 'white' > *bélen'kij; molodój* 'young' > *molóden'kij; légkij* 'light' > *légon'kij*).

'Hard' short forms such as *Lída, Ljúda, Lára, Ljúba, Lëva,* or *Júra* don't have such associations and they are felt to be closer to unmarked full names (e.g., *Véra, Nína*). When applied to small children, they appear to be marked, 'grown-up'. There is nothing unusual about addressing small children as *Mítja* or *Sónja* (although more affectionate *Míten'ka* and *Sónečka* are also quite standard in this situation), but it is more unusual, and marked, to address them as *Lída, Lára,* or

Lëva. It appears, therefore, that names of this kind should be assigned the same 'anti-childish' semantic component which has been assigned to unmarked full first names such as *Véra* or *Nína:* 'I don't want to speak to you the way people speak to children'. Structurally, the position of short hard names such as *Lída* and *Ljúba* is different from that of unmarked full names such as *Véra* and *Nína,* because *Lída* and *Ljúba* occupy an intermediate position between full names *Lidija* and *Ljubóv'* and the 'diminutives' *Lídočka* and *Ljúbočka,* but semantically, their value seems to be the same as that of unmarked full names. Field theorists notwithstanding, the semantic value is not always determined by an item's position in the field of related items.

To put it crudely, only what seems big may need to be 'diminished'. Full names (e.g., *Véra, Nína*) have an adult ring to them and may need to be 'diminished' when applied to children (*Véročka, Nínočka*), and the same applies (though to a lesser extent) to hard short forms (*Lída > Lídočka, Ljúba > Ljúbočka*). But soft short forms (e.g., *Kátja, Mítja*) don't have an adult ring to them and don't need to be 'diminished' when applied to children. On the other hand, they, too, may need to be replaced with something more tender or affectionate; this need is fulfilled by the suffix *-en'ka* (*Káten'ka, Míten'ka*).

In support of the semantic distinction between soft and hard short forms drawn here I will adduce the fact—whose significance will become more clear later—that usually the hard short forms take the diminutive hypocoristic (affectionate) suffix *-očka,* whereas the soft short forms take the non-diminutive hypocoristic suffix *-en'ka.*

Lída	>	Lídočka
Lëva	>	Lëvočka
Kátja	>	Káten'ka
Mítja	>	Míten'ka

(There are exceptions to these generalisations, but I will not discuss them here.) Hard short forms parallel in this respect unmarked full names:

Véra	>	Véročka
Nína	>	Nínočka

I will also mention here the fact—whose full significance will also become more clear later—that usually only soft stem short forms can take the 'serious and intimate' suffix *-úša:*

Katjúša	cf. ?Lidúša
Vanjúša	cf. ?Levúša
Nadjúša	cf. ?Larúša

My explanation for this fact is that hard stem short forms such as *Lída, Lëva,* or *Lára* are sufficiently 'serious' themselves as not to need such a derivational form or as to need it less than soft stem short forms such as *Kátja, Vánja,* or *Nádja.* (Forms in -*ša*, such as *Natáša* or *Gríša*, cannot take the suffix -*uša* for obvious phonetic reasons.)

2.1.3 Short Stems with Suffix -ša

For many names, for example, *Grigórij*, *Natál'ja*, or *Maríja*, forms in -*ša* present the most basic, unmarked short forms: *Gríša*, *Natáša*, *Máša*. Functionally, they are therefore parallel to 'soft' short forms such as *Kátja* or *Sónja*, or to hard forms such as *Lída* or *Svéta*, which are also the most basic, unmarked short forms of the corresponding names *Katerína* and *Sófija* or *Lídija* and *Svetlána*. For example, in Tolstoy's (1949) *War and peace* the two young girls Nataša and Sonja are treated in the same way, and their names (*Natáša* and *Sónja*) are also felt to be on the same level of intimacy (as against the name of the eldest Rostov sister, *Véra*, a more distant and less personable character, habitually called by an unmarked full first name). Similarly, in *Anna Karenina* (Tolstoy 1953) the two elder children of the Oblonsky family, *Tanja* and *Griša*, are also treated as being on a par, and so are their names (a soft short form and a short form in -*ša*).

Nonetheless, I would like to argue that from a semantic point of view short forms in -*ša* such as *Natáša* or *Gríša* are not exactly equivalent to forms such as *Sónja* or *Tánja*. Phonetically, *š* is a hard consonant in Russian, and apart from lovable characters such as *Nataša* in *War and peace* names in -*š* such as *Míša* or *Sáša* don't sound quite as 'soft' and warm as soft short forms such as *Sónja* or *Mítja*.

To appreciate the exact semantic value of forms in -*ša*, it is helpful to consider the structural position of the consonant *š* in the Russian sound system. Phonetically, *š* is hard, and in this respect names in -*ša* such as *Gríša* or *Sáša* evoke hard short forms such as *Lída* or *Lëva* rather than soft ones such as *Mítja* or *Kátja*, but morphologically, *š* is treated in the same way as soft consonants, and, for example, the names in -*ša* can be further combined with the affectionate suffix -*en'ka*, like soft short forms, not with the affectionate suffix -*očka*, like hard short forms:

Kátja	>	Káten'ka
Mítja	>	Míten'ka
Lída	>	Lídočka
Lëva	>	Lëvočka
Gríša	>	Gríšen'ka
Máša	>	Mášen'ka

From the point of view of form, therefore, names in -*ša* are, so to speak, half way between soft short forms and hard short forms. I would suggest that semantically, too, they are half way between the soft and the hard short forms, being just a shade less 'soft' than the soft ones, and just a shade less serious than the hard ones. To capture this intermediate shade of the -*ša* forms, I would propose for them an explication which does refer to children but does not refer to 'good feelings':

   Sáša, Máša, Natáša
   I want to speak to you the way people speak
    to people whom they know well and to children

  The reference to children distinguishes this formula from that of hard short forms:

   Lída, Lëva, Ljúba
   I want to speak to you the way people speak
    to people whom they know well
   I don't want to speak to you the way people speak to children

  The absence of a reference to good feelings distinguishes the formula assigned to -*ša* forms from that assigned to soft short forms:

   Kátja, Sónja, Mítja
   I want to speak to you the way people speak
    to people whom they know well
    and toward whom they feel something good, and to children

2.1.4 Summary of Full and Short Forms of Russian Names

SHORT FORMS WITH A HARD CONSONANT AND -*a* (e.g., *Lída, Lëva*)
I want to speak to you the way people speak
 to people whom they know well
I don't want to speak to you the way people speak to children

SHORT FORMS WITH A SOFT CONSONANT AND -*a* (e.g., *Kátja, Vánja*)
I want to speak to you the way people speak
 to people whom they know well
and toward whom they feel something good, and to children

SHORT FORMS WITH SUFFIX -*š* AND -*a* (e.g., *Gríša, Máša*)
I want to speak to you the way people speak
 to people whom they know well and to children

MARKED FULL NAMES (e.g., *Konstantín, Evgénija, Ól'ga*)
I don't want to speak to you the way people speak
 to people whom they don't know well
I want to speak to you the way people don't speak
 to children and to people whom they know well and toward whom they feel
 something good

UNMARKED FULL NAMES WITH A HARD STEM (e.g., *Véra, Nína*)
I don't want to speak to you the way people speak
 to people whom they don't know well
I don't want to speak to you the way people speak to children

2.2 Russian Expressive Derivation

2.2.1 The Suffix -očka

For many names, especially for those whose unmarked short form has a hard stem, the forms in *-očka* constitute the basic, unmarked affectionate choice. For example:

$$
\begin{array}{lcl}
\text{Lídija} & > & \text{Lída} & > & \text{Lídočka} \\
\text{Ljubóv'} & > & \text{Ljúba} & > & \text{Ljúbočka} \\
\text{Júrij} & > & \text{Júra} & > & \text{Júročka}
\end{array}
$$

Nonetheless, I would argue that the form in *-očka* conveys something more specific than simply 'good feelings'. Bratus (1969:36) says of these forms that "the predominant meaning is diminutive-hypocoristic, sometimes only hypocoristic, especially when talking to children". This is partly right, I think, in so far as *-očka* does suggest 'smallness' as well as good feelings, but I can't agree that the 'smallness' is not relevant, or less relevant, when speaking to children. On the contrary, forms in *-očka* evoke a combination of smallness, good feelings, and child orientation.

Morphologically, *-očka* constitutes a double diminutive, and from a semantic point of view this is relevant, as what it suggests are a particularly small size (relative to a given kind) and good feelings associated not simply with children but with small children:

$$
\begin{array}{lcl}
\text{krovát' 'bed'} & > & \text{krovátka} & > & \text{krovátočka} \\
\text{lóšad' 'horse'} & > & \text{lošádka} & > & \text{lošádočka}
\end{array}
$$

Names in *-očka* are particularly common in speech directed at children, whose world is naturally viewed as full of miniature versions of things encountered in the adult world. From the point of view of emotions, too, the 'good feelings' implied by forms in *-očka* seem to be of a kind associated with small children. Forms such as *krovátočka* or *lošádočka* evoke the world of small children and the emotional aura associated with interaction with small children. The adult entering this world and attempting to interact with its inhabitants feels a mixture of something like tenderness, endearment, playfulness, non-seriousness, and so on.

This aura is transferred to names in *-očka* when they are not used speaking to, or of, small children. For example, the word *páročka* (lexicalised as a word for a couple of lovers or sweethearts) clearly expresses a light-hearted, slightly playful, and slightly indulgent tone (as if serious adults were speaking of people who are a bit like children—endearing but not serious). The word *mórdočka* (from *mórda*, 'snout') would be commonly used with reference to 'cute' small animals such as squirrels or puppies (or in jocular reference to children's faces).

I suggest that this basic flavour of *-očka* is also transferred to personal names in *-očka*, whether they are applied to children or to adults. To capture this particular flavour, I propose the following explication:

Lídočka, Ljúbočka, Lëvočka
I feel something good toward you
  of the kind that people feel speaking to small children

This formula doesn't mean, needless to say, that forms of this kind are used only, or even mainly, when speaking to (or of) children. Rather, it tries to spell out the particular expressive flavour they have when they are used—whether they are used to (or of) children or adults. For example, when in Solzhenitsyn's (1968a) novel *Rakovyj korpus* the old doctor Oreščenkov calls the middle-aged doctor Ljudmila Doncova (his former student) "Ljudočka", this is perfectly normal, and in fact this is the most natural form that he can use (given the nature of their relationship), despite—and perhaps because of—the light-hearted and slightly playful, as well as affectionate, character of this form.

2.2.2 The Suffix -en'ka

For many names, the suffix *-en'ka* occupies the same slot in the structural-functional pattern as *-očka* does for others: marked full name (e.g., *Katerína, Lídija, Ljubóv'*), unmarked short form (*Kátja, Lída, Ljúba*), basic affectionate form (*Káten'ka, Lídočka, Ljúbočka*). It is not surprising, therefore, that names in *-očka* and *-en'ka* are often treated as being on the same pragmatic level. For example, in Tolstoy's (1978) *Childhood, boyhood and youth* the two little girls, who are treated in exactly the same way, are habitually called *Káten'ka* and *Ljúbočka*.

Generally speaking, names with soft short forms such as *Kátja* or *Mítja* normally take the suffix *-en'ka* (*Káten'ka, Míten'ka*), whereas names with hard short forms such as *Ljúba* or *Júra* usually take *-očka* (*Ljúbočka, Júročka*). In the case of soft short forms ending in *-n'*, however, the combination *-nen'ka* is usually avoided, and *-ečka* (a variant of *-očka*) takes the place of the expected *-en'ka:*

Ánja	>	Ánečka
Vánja	>	Vánečka
Sónja	>	Sónečka

This apparent substitution of *-ečka* (*-očka*) for *-en'ka* strengthens the impression that the two suffixes are exactly equivalent semantically.

Nonetheless, I would like to argue that this impression is mistaken and that just as short forms such as *Kátja* and *Ljúba* may be on a par without being semantically equivalent, so forms such as *Káten'ka* and *Ljúbočka* are not exactly equivalent either. They are often equivalent pragmatically, but they are not exactly equivalent in terms of their semantic value; consequently, they have a slightly different flavour.

In the case of short forms in *-ša*, too, both *-ečka* and *-en'ka* are available, e.g., *Natášen'ka, Natášečka*. In this case, however, *-en'ka* is more common, and more unmarked than *-ečka*. As a result, a form such as *Natášečka* may seem more affectionate and more personal than *Natášen'ka*. But here, too, *Natášečka* sounds a bit more playful.

It might seem that the difference between the two forms can best be seen in the case of those names which can take either *-očka* (or its variant *-ečka*) or *-en'ka* (or its variant *-on'ka*). For example, in the case of unmarked full names with a stem ending in *-j* such as *Zója* and *Rája* we get either *Zóen'ka, Ráen'ka,* or *Zóečka, Ráečka;* in the case of hard short forms such as *Lída* and *Ríta* we get either *Lídočka, Rítočka* or *Lídon'ka* or *Ríton'ka;* and in the case of short forms in *-ša* such as *Natáša* we get either *Natášen'ka* or *Natášečka.* In fact, however, minimal pairs of this kind don't help much because in each case one of the two affectionate forms is more common and represents an unmarked choice. The less usual form is naturally interpreted as a more 'special' one, with a greater expressive loading. For example, *Ríton'ka* is less usual, and has a greater expressive load, than *Rítočka;* and *Natášečka* is less usual, and may seem to have a greater expressive load, than *Natášen'ka.* Furthermore, if a form in *-ša* such as *Natáša* is already applicable to children, even small children, without the magnifying effect that hard stem names such as *Ljúda* or *Ríta* have, the 'diminishing' effect of *-očka/-ečka* is in any case more noticeable. As a result, *Natášečka* sounds more endearing than *Rítočka* even though *Ríton'ka* may sound more endearing than *Rítočka.* For this reason, minimal pairs such as *Rítočka* and *Ríton'ka* or *Natášen'ka* and *Natášečka* are not as helpful as one might expect them to be.

There are other minimal pairs of Russian diminutives, such as *mámočka* vs. *mámen'ka* 'mummy' or *pápočka* vs. *pápen'ka* 'daddy' or *dúšen'ka* vs. *dúšečka* 'dear soul', but these, too, are not as helpful as one might expect, because their members usually turn out to differ in more than one respect. Some further evidence comes from lexicalised contrasts such as *dévka* 'maid' or 'whore' vs. *dévočka* 'little girl', and from the fact that the names of 'serious' and 'big' phenomena can occasionally take *-en'ka* (*-on'ka*) but never *-očka* (*-ečka*), e.g., *bóžen'ka* nursery word for 'God', vs. **bóžečka; zóren'ka* poetic/folk-style word for 'dawn' vs. **zórečka.*

The main evidence, however, for the 'endearing' character of *-en'ka* (*-on'ka*) and 'diminutive-endearing' character of *-očka* (*-ečka*) arises from the fact that outside the area of proper names *-očka* is used to indicate small size (as well as good feelings), whereas *-en'ka* is never so used. In fact, the Academy grammar of Russian (AN SSSR 1960:267,269) describes the meaning of *-očka* as 'diminutive-endearing' and that of *-en'ka* as 'endearing'. I think this distinction is essentially correct and applies also—in a sense—to the use of these suffixes in proper names. This doesn't mean, of course, that a *Ljúbočka* is smaller than a *Káten'ka,* but it means that the expressive flavour conveyed by names such as *Ljúbočka* has more to do with the world of adult-child interaction than does that conveyed by names such as *Káten'ka.*

A further clue to the flavour of the suffix *-en'ka* comes from the area of adjectives which take what is arguably the same suffix (*-en'k*), such as *bélen'kij* (from *bélyj* 'white') or *žëlten'kij* (from *žëltyj* 'yellow'). The value of such adjectives depends on the character of the base (and on some other factors), in ways which are complex and which cannot be discussed here, but if the base is neutral (neither 'good' nor 'bad'), as in the case of colour terms, the suffix *-en'k* definitely implies good feelings, as well as a kind of delight due to the perception of a certain object or at the thought of that object. If the speaker describes an object as *žëlten'kij* ('yellow' + Dim.), this implies that thinking of that object and visualising its yellow colour he finds it endearing, is well disposed toward it, and also feels a small rush of something like pleasure. To capture this basic flavour of adjectives in *-en'k,* I propose tentatively the following explication:

> *žëlten'kij, pérven'kij, práven'kij*
> I think of X as Adj.
> I feel something good toward it
> I feel something good thinking of it

I believe that a similar attitude is expressed in the case of family terms in *-en'ka,* such as *dóčen'ka* (from *doč'* 'daughter'), *tëten'ka* (from *tëtja* 'auntie'), or *djáden'ka* (from *djádja* 'uncle'), but in the case of the adjective, the expressive attitude is linked with a specific feature, whereas in the case of nouns it is linked with the interaction itself. This can be represented as follows:

> *dóčen'ka, tëten'ka*
> I feel something good toward you
> because you are my X
> I feel something good speaking to you

I suggest that essentially the same attitude is conveyed in names in *-en'ka* such as *Káten'ka* or *Míten'ka:*

> *Káten'ka, Míten'ka*
> I feel something good toward you
> I feel something good speaking to you

If speaking to you causes me to feel something good, this means that I like you, perhaps love you; a happy feeling stirs within me when I am in contact with you. The combination of components

> a. I feel something good toward you
> b. I feel something good speaking to you

may seem redundant, but I don't think it really is so. Component (a) seeks to capture, roughly speaking, the speaker's affection for the addressee, and component (b), the speaker's pleasure experienced in speaking to that particular addressee. We need both components to account for the intuitively felt difference between forms in *-en'ka* (e.g., *Zóen'ka*) and forms in *-ečka* (e.g., *Zóečka*) and for the difference in their respective ranges of use.

I am not suggesting that all names in *-en'ka,* e.g., *Zóen'ka, Káten'ka,* and *Natášen'ka,* have exactly the same value; they don't, because in each case the suffix *-en'ka* is added to a different kind of base (a full form in the case of *Zója,* a soft short form in the case of *Kátja,* and a short form in *-ša* in the case of *Natáša*). But the value of *-en'ka* is in each case the same. It is affectionate, but not in the same way as *-očka* is affectionate. The difference is qualitative, not quantitative, but in a sense

-en'ka can be said to be more 'caressing' and more intimate than *-očka*. Since *-en'ka* is never used for designating small things used by children (such as *krovátočka* 'bed-Dim.' or *rubášečka* 'shirt-Dim.'), *-en'ka* doesn't evoke the world of small children, which may be seen as 'cute' and endearing but not fully serious. At the same time, *-en'ka* suggests a personal response to the interaction with the other person.

For what it is worth I might mention here that according to all the Russian parents whom I have consulted, if they had to choose between *Zóen'ka* and *Zóečka*, *Natášen'ka* and *Natášečka,* and *Ríton'ka* and *Rítočka*, using one form to a very sick child, and the other to a happily playing child, they would rather use the *-en'ka* (*-on'ka*) forms in the former case and the *-očka* (*-ečka*) in the latter. I think this is because of the playful connotations of the forms in *-očka* (*-ečka*) and the more personal and intimate connotations of the forms in *-en'ka* (*-on'ka*).

2.2.3 The Suffixes -ik and -ók

With some names, the suffix *-ik* can form unmarked short forms of some masculine names (especially polysyllabic names of Polish origin, e.g., *Vladisláv* > *Vládik, Stanisláv* > *Stásik*); more commonly, however, it is used as an affectionate form, derived either from a full form or a short form, especially if the stem ends in *-r,* e.g., *Mark* > *Márik, Lavréntij* > *Lávrik, Júra* > *Júrik,* or *Šúra* > *Súrik*.

Like affectionate names in *-očka*, those in *-ik*, too, have a counterpart in diminutives designating 'small things', e.g., *most* 'bridge' > *móstik; xolm* 'hill' > *xólmik; kovër* 'carpet' > *kóvrik; xvost* 'tail' > *xvóstik*.

Bratus (1969:18) suggests that forms in *-ik* don't always imply smallness, because, for example, "the form *bilétik* (<*bilét*) in *kupite bilétik!* 'Do buy a ticket!' does not mean a small ticket (the ticket may be of the usual dimensions) but adds an emotional nuance, suggesting, 'Be so kind as to buy . . . '". In fact, however, *bilétik* does refer to something small, although the nature of this reference is interpreted in the light of the entire speech act. Roughly:

kupite bilet!	=	I want you to do something (to buy a ticket)
kupite biletik!	=	I want you to do something small (to buy a ticket)

But unlike the common names in *-očka*, those in *-ik* are never double diminutives suggesting not small but very small forms of certain objects:

krovát' 'bed'	>	*krovátka*	>	*krovátočka*
lóšad' 'horse'	>	*lošádka*	>	*lošádočka*
most 'bridge'	>	*móstik*		
xolm 'hill'	>	*xólmik*		

Consequently, forms in *-ik* such as *móstik* or *xólmik* don't evoke the world of small children in the way forms in *-očka* such as *krovátočka* or *lošádočka* do.

As a result, of two affectionate forms such as *Júročka* and *Júrik*, both diminutive, *Júrik* has more boyish associations and *Júročka* more childish ones. This impression is strengthened by the fact that *-ik* is essentially a male form, whereas *-očka* is equally applicable to males and females. It is true that forms in *-ik* are also derived from feminine names, e.g., *Svéta* > *Svétik*, *Ljúsja* > *Ljúsik*, but forms of this kind are felt to be playful, affectionate 'distortions', which exploit for expressive purposes the essentially boyish character of the suffix *-ik*. No such effect, however, is created when the suffix *-očka* is applied to boys or men, and in fact, male forms such as *Júročka* or *Lëvočka* have exactly the same expressive value as feminine names such as *Lídočka* or *Ljúbočka*.

But the expressive value of feminine forms such as *Svétik* or *Ljúsik* is different from that of masculine forms such as *Júrik* or *Márik*. It establishes a 'special relationship', private and playful, whereas affectionate masculine names in *-ik* do not.

To account for these facts, I propose the following explications:

Júrik, Márik (masculine names, forms in *-ik*)
I feel something good toward you
   of the kind that people feel toward small boys

Svétik, Ljúsik (feminine names, forms in *-ik*)
I feel something good toward you
I feel something good speaking to you
I don't want to speak to you the way other people speak to you
I want to speak to you as if you were a small boy, not a girl

It might be added that a similar device of using inherently masculine forms to express special affection for girls can also be observed in feminine names in *-ók*, such as *Ninók* (from *Nína*) or *Irók* (from *Íra*). These are formed on the model of affectionate masculine names such as *Igorëk* (from *Ígor'*) or *Dimók* (from *Díma*).

Forms such as *Ninók*, too, are affectionate and playful, and they too imply a 'special relationship'. They sound, however, a little rougher, a little more tomboyish and more jolly than feminine forms in *-ik* such as *Svétik* or *Ljúsik*. I conjecture that this rougher character of the forms in *ók* is due to the intermediate position of the suffix *-ók* between a base form and a form in *-óček*:

véter 'wind'	>	*veterók*	>	*veteróček*
gólos 'voice'	>	*golosók*	>	*golosóček*
den 'day'	>	*denëk*	>	*denëček*
čas 'hour'	>	*časók*	>	*časóček*

With respect to the base form, the form in *-ók* is a diminutive. For example, if *čas* means an hour, *časók* means something like 'just an hour', that is, an hour thought of as something small (and seen in a pleasant light). But the form in *-óček* designates something thought of as still smaller (and still more pleasant). Forms in *-óček* are similar in this respect to forms in *-očka*:

> *krovát'* 'bed'   >   *krovátka*   >   *krovátočka*
> *čas* 'hour'   >   *časók*   >   *časóček*

Seen in this perspective, *-ók* is a diminutive, but a 'big' diminutive, whereas *-óček* is a 'small' diminutive. But the suffix *-ik* doesn't occupy a similarly intermediate position:

> *most* 'bridge'   >   *móstik*
> *bilét* 'ticket'   >   *bilétik*

Forms in *-ik* cannot be perceived, therefore, as 'big' diminutives.

What applies to common nouns applies also, mutatis mutandis, to personal names in *-ók,* such as *Ninók* or *Lizók:* they are perceived not only as affectionate and playful diminutives based on the model of masculine names but as 'big' diminutives. Hence the rougher and more jolly effect than that of feminine names in *-ik,* such as *Svétik* or *Ljúsik.* Arguably, all we need to capture this effect in an explication is to replace 'small boy' in the fourth component of forms such as *Svétik* or *Ljúsik* with 'boy', but it might also be justified to remove the second component.

> *Ninók, Lizók* (feminine names, forms in *-ók*)
> I feel something good toward you
> (I feel something good speaking to you)
> I don't want to speak to you the way other people speak to you
> I want to speak to you as if you were a boy

Presumably, the masculine model of such names differs from the masculine model of names in *-ik* along the same lines:

> *Júrik, Márik* (masculine names, forms in *-ik*)
> I feel something good toward you
>   of the kind that people feel toward small boys

> *Igorëk, Dimók* (masculine names, forms in *-ók*)
> I feel something good toward you
>   of the kind that people feel toward boys

2.2.4 *The Suffixes* -ënok *and* -ënyš

A jocular and loving 'distortion' is also involved in forms in *-ënok* such as *Katënok* or *Nikitënok,* and in forms in *-ënyš,* which affectionately liken the target person to a baby animal:

> *svinjá* 'swine'   >   *svin'ënok* 'piglet'
> *myš* 'mouse'   >   *myšónok* 'baby mouse'
> *Kátja* 'Kate'   >   *Katënok* 'baby Kate'
> *Nikíta* 'Nikita'   >   *Nikitënok* 'baby Nikita'

According to Stankiewicz (1968:167), the suffix *-ënok* in personal names "expresses an affectionate and protective attitude". I wonder, however, whether the "protective attitude" doesn't constitute an inference rather than a semantic component: if a child is likened, affectionately, to a baby animal, this can be interpreted as implying a protective attitude, but it can also be interpreted (and intended) as implying a loving and jocular attitude, rather than a protective one.

The suffix *-ënyš*, which like *-ënok* is used for deriving words for baby (or non-adult) animals, can be used in a similar way, as in the following sentence from Solzhenitsyn's novel *The first circle:*

> Rešila vybor Dinera—ona očen' nastaivala v pis'max i zaezžala prostit'sja pered frontom—čtoby Klarënyš postupala na literaturnyj. (1968c:210)

> 'It was Danera [*sic*] who made the choice for her; in her letters and on her farewell visit before leaving for the front she insisted that Clara should study literature at the university.' (1976:273)

In this passage, an older sister lovingly accepts responsibility for a younger sister's future, and her attitude is summed up in, and highlighted by, the use of the form *Klarënyš* ('kid-sister-Clara', 'fledgling-Clara'). This effect is of course lost in the English translation, where *Klarënyš* is rendered in the same way as *Klára* and *Kláročka*, becoming simply *Clara*. (When citing published translations, I quote them verbatim; although ways might be found to improve them, this is not attempted here.)

The flavour of *-ënyš* is not exactly the same as that of *-ënok*. It conveys less overt tenderness and more jocularity of a slightly patronising, or teasing, character. In pairs such as *svinënok–svinënyš* (from *svinjá* 'swine'), the forms in *-ënok* suggest some nice babyish qualities, but the forms in *-ënyš* don't have to be taken that way. For example, a *zmeënyš* (from *zmejá* 'snake') could be an adolescent snake, rather than a baby snake, and would not be necessarily attractive.

These differences between forms such as *zmeënok* and forms such as *zmeënyš* are exploited in the expressive use of personal names. A form such as *Klarënyš* has to be affectionate (just like *Nikitënok*), but it sounds as if the speaker is trying to hide affection behind a mask of teasing and patronising jocularity.

To account for these differences in flavour between forms in *-ënok* and forms in *-ënyš*, I propose for them the following explications:

Katënok, Nikitënok

I feel something good toward you
I feel something good speaking to you
I don't want to speak to you the way other people speak to you
I want to speak to you as if you were a baby animal, not a child

Katënyš, Klarënyš

I feel something good toward you
I don't want to speak to you the way other people speak to you
I want to speak to you as if you were a young, not full-grown, animal

I have assigned to forms in *-ënok* but not to those in *-ënyš* the loving component 'I feel something good speaking to you' and a positive reference to baby animals.

2.2.5 The Suffix *-uška*

The suffix *-uška* (with the stress on the last vowel of the stem) encodes a particularly interesting type of expressivity, which is clearly positive without being in any way child-oriented.

To see this, it is useful to compare common family terms in *-uška* with those in *-en'ka:*

mátuška 'mother'	*mámen'ka* 'mother'
	mámočka
bátjuška 'father'	*pápen'ka* 'father'
	pápočka
bábuška 'grandmother'	**bában'ka* 'grandmother'
déduška 'grandfather'	**déden'ka* 'grandfather'
tëtuška 'aunt'	*tëten'ka* 'aunt'
	djáden'ka 'uncle'
njánjuška 'nanny'	
	dóčen'ka 'daughter'

First, the family forms in *-uška* are reserved for adults and old people, whereas the family forms in *-en'ka* are not restricted to adults and are unsuitable for old people (grandparents).

Second, the family forms in *-uška* tend to be derived from 'adult' words such as *mat'* 'mother' and *ded'* 'grandfather', whereas the forms in *-en'ka* tend to be derived from children's words such as *máma* 'mummy' and *pápa* 'daddy'.

In the case of proper names, too, forms in *-uška* usually (or at least very frequently) take the full name as their basis, that is, a form which small children might not even know, whereas forms in *-en'ka* or *-očka* are normally based on short forms, which are more commonly used at home, e.g., *Avdót'ja* > *Avdót'juška* (cf. *Dúnja* > *Dúnečka*), *Ánna* > *Ánnuška* (cf. *Ánja* > *Ánečka*), *Nikíta* > *Nikítuška*, *Egór* > *Egóruška*, *Maksím* > *Maksímuška*, and so on.

Significantly, forms in *-uška* (and even more in *-uško; cf. Bratus 1969:32) are particularly characteristic of peasant speech and of folk literature, whereas forms (of names) in *-en'ka* have a more literary flavour and apparently were seldom used in peasant speech (Suslova and Superanskaja 1978:116).

Furthermore, names in *-uška* are as (or more) likely to be used when addressing (or speaking about) adults as they are when addressing or speaking about children.

As I have argued earlier, forms in *-en'ka* such as *Káten'ka* or *Míten'ka* are not quite as child-oriented as are forms in *-očka* (*-ečka*). However, their soft bases themselves contain a reference to interaction with children, and this carries over to their derivates. Forms in *-ik* such as *Márik* or *Svétik* and forms in *-ók* such as *Igorëk* or *Ninók* do not refer directly to children but to 'small boys'. But forms in *-uška* such as *Avdótjuška* contain no reference to children (or boys) whatsoever.

What they typically seem to convey is not so much endearment as a kind of pity, of feeling sorry for people. For example, the form *Nikítuška* is repeatedly used by a peasant woman in Dostoevsky's (1976) novel *The brothers Karamazov,* in reference to her unhappy husband, whom she loves and above all pities. The form *Avdótjuška* is used in a stylised recent story (Gorenštejn 1982) about a poor old woman struggling with the vicissitudes of life. In Tolstoy's (1949) *War and peace* the form *Nikóluška* is used for a child, not an adult, but the child in question is an orphan; this contrasts significantly with the choice of the form *Nikólen'ka* for another hero, Rostov, successful and adored by his family. And so on—examples can be multiplied.

Furthermore, forms in *-uška* (or *-uško*) can be combined (in folkloric style) with words encoding abstract existential concepts, such as *góre* 'grief' > *górjuško; vólja* 'freedom' > *vóljuška; rabóta* 'work' > *rabótuška; smert'* 'death' > *smértuška; dúma* 'thought' > *dúmuška; zabóta* 'care' > *zabótuška; síla* 'strength' > *síluška;* or *dólja* 'fate' > *dóljuška* (cf. Bratus 1969:68). But suffixes such as *-en'ka* or *-očka* can never be used like that.

All these facts suggest that the expressivity encoded in the suffix *-uška* has no relation to children's speech or speech to children but has its axis of orientation elsewhere. It seems to reflect an important feature of Russian folk philosophy, which views the human condition as pitiful and which encourages both resignation and compassion. Words such as *zímuška* (winter—a Russian winter), *vóljuška* (freedom—desired but often unattainable), *smértuška* (death—inevitable and therefore to be lovingly accepted), *nevéstuška* (bride, seen as someone to be pitied—a flower to be cut tomorrow), *golóvuška* (head, especially in lamentations such as *bédnaja mojá golóvuška* 'oh my poor little head'), *górjuško* (grief—to be accepted), *xlébuško* (bread—often lacking), *soséduška* (female neighbour—'life is hard', 'let's help one another'), *mórjuško* (sea—mysterious expanse which can take people away) have a strong existential flavour and evoke strongly traditional Russian attitudes, expressed in Russian folk literature.

With these considerations in mind, I tentatively propose the following explication of names with the suffix *-uška:*

> *Nikítuška, Avdótjuška, Ánnuška*
> I feel something good toward you
>   of the kind that people feel toward people
>   when they think of bad things that can happen to people

There are many cultures in the world in which something like pity or compassion seems to be more salient than something like love, affection, or fondness. For example, the Ifaluk language of Micronesia has a word for something like compassion but not for something like love (Lutz 1987; cf. chapter 4). Similarly, Tibetan has a word for something like pity and desire to protect but not for something like love (Levine 1981). In Russian culture, warm pity encoded in the verb *žalét'* seems also to be particularly salient (as noted by a number of observers). For example, Fedotov comments as follows on the Russian 'national character':

My privykli dumat', čto russkij čelovek dobr. Vo vsjakom slučae, čto on umeet žalet'. V russkoj mučitelnoj, kenotičeskoj žalosti my videli osnovnoe različie našego xristianskogo tipa ot zapadnoj moral'noj ustanovki. (1952:61)

'We are used to thinking that the Russian people are good. In any case, that they know how to pity. In the Russian painful, kenotic pity we see the main difference between our Christian type and the Western moral orientation.'

Particularly revealing, however, is the observation of the great Russian thinker Vladimir Solov'ev that Russian peasant women ("*russkie baby*") use the word *žalét'* 'to pity/to have compassion' in lieu of *ljubít'* 'to love'. Solov'ev himself makes a characteristically Russian remark when he says:

Nikakaja svjatost' ne možet byt' tol'ko ličnoj, . . . ona nepremenno est' ljubov' *k drugim*, a v uslovijax zemskoj dejstvitel'nosti èta ljubov' [k drugim] est', glavnym obrazom, *sostradanie*. (1966–70, v.5:421)

'No holiness can be purely personal; it is necessarily love *for others*, and in the conditions of earthly reality this love is, above all, *compassion*.'

Not surprisingly, perhaps, in Solov'ev's own ethical philosophy *žalost'* 'pity' occupies a central place. (See in particular his book *Opravdanie dobra*, 'The justification of the good', 1966–70, v.8:57–59.)

I suggest that that the preponderance of the suffix *-uška* (*-uško*) in Russian folk literature points in the same direction as the use of *žalét'* for *ljubít'*, noted by Solov'ev.

If the analysis proposed here seems far-fetched, it could perhaps be made more acceptable by removing the word *bad* from the semantic formula. This would maintain the idea that forms in *-uška* have an existential ring to them and that they convey a warmth caused not so much by any endearing features of the person spoken to as by the speaker's experience of life. I feel, however, that the following comment by Bratus (1969:32) supports my original analysis: the suffix *-uška* (and *-uško*) "convey endearment, a kindly attitude, sometimes jocularity". The key word here is "kindly". Suffixes such as *-en'ka*, *-očka*, or *-ik* have nothing "kindly" about them. But *-uška* often does sound "kindly". It suggests a warm attitude to people shaped by the speaker's experience of life and an awareness of bad things that can happen to people. The folk philosophy reflected in forms in *-uška* suggests that life is such that people ought to be pitied and treated kindly. (This does not necessarily exclude the speaker. For example, a child's cry *njánjuška!* 'nanny!' may express the speaker's anguish or anxiety, as in Mussorgskij's nursery songs, rather than pity. But this, too, is compatible with the proposed formula.)

2.2.6 The Suffix -úša

Names in *-úša* such as *Katjúša, Tanjúša,* or *Andrjúša* have a somewhat ambivalent character, sometimes being felt to be affectionate and sometimes apparently lacking in any warmth. According to Stankiewicz (1968:159) *-úša* "carries a familiar and affectionate meaning". Since other affectionate suffixes, such as *-en'ka* or *-očka*, are called simply "affectionate", by saying in this particular case "familiar and affectionate" Stankiewicz is hinting, I think, at a sometimes less than affectionate nature of names in -*úša*. He seems to be suggesting that sometimes they sound affectionate but sometimes sound merely "familiar".

Bratus (1969:33) says of the same suffix that it "forms a few diminutives from proper names:

Il'já	Elias	Il'júša
Kátja	Kate	Katjúša
Pável	Paul	Pavlúša

and a few diminutives of endearment from nouns and adjectives, which have, however, a dialect flavour". This seems to imply that proper names in -*úša* do not convey endearment.

In Tolstoy's (1928) novel *Resurrection* the peasant girl who lives with an aristocratic family as something between an adoptive daughter and a maid is called "*Katjuša*". Tolstoy explains that this form was felt to be appropriate given the girl's intermediate status: *Káten'ka* would sound too soft for her and *Kát'ka*, too harsh. "[B]etween these two influences, the girl grew up half servant, half young lady. They called her Katusha, a sort of compromise between Kat'ka and Katen'ka" (1928:5).

But a Russian acquaintance named *Sónja* has informed me that her casual friends and acquaintances commonly call her *Sónečka*, whereas the form *Sonjúša* is only used by her close friends and is perceived by her as more intimate and carrying a greater emotional weight. Several other native speakers have made similar comments.

When confronted with such apparently contradictory data, both native speakers and linguists tend to conclude that everything depends on the context, on people's individual usage, or perhaps on their private conventions; in other words, that names in -*úša* have no semantic invariant whatsoever.

I do not believe that this is true. Certainly, the exact pragmatic interpretation of names in -*úša* does depend on the context, on individual preferences, and on private conventions, but there is also a semantic invariant. This invariant is compatible with a wide, but by no means unlimited, number of interpretations, and although it is certainly difficult to capture, difficult does not mean impossible.

If we look first at unmarked full names such as *Véra* or *Andréj*, which don't have unmarked short forms, it will be fairly clear that their derivates in -*úša* (*Verúša*, *Andrjúša*) sound more intimate and more affectionate. When we turn, however, to names which do have unmarked short forms, if these short forms have a soft stem, as in *Kátja*, the affectionate value of the form in -*úša* may well seem less clear, because in the pair *Katjúša* and *Káten'ka*, *Káten'ka* will be felt to be more endearing (recall Tolstoy's (1928:5) remark on the relationships among *Kát'ka*, *Káten'ka*, and *Katjúša*).

But to say that *Káten'ka* is more endearing doesn't mean that *Katjúša* will normally be felt to be less affectionate. There is a qualitative difference between the light, caressing endearment conveyed by *Káten'ka* and the 'heavier', more serious, more adult affection conveyed by *Katjúša*. In the popular World War II song the girl waiting in anxiety for her sweetheart who has gone to war, whose love is protecting him, is called *Katjúša*, not *Káten'ka:*

> [V]yxodila na bereg Katjuša,
> na vysokij na bereg krutoj
>
> 'Katjuša walked to the edge of the river,
> to its high steep bank'

In this case, *Káten'ka* would sound rather less appropriate than *Katjúša*, presumably because what is called for is an atmosphere of seriousness and anxiety rather than one of caressing endearment.

What applies to the pair *Katjúša* and *Káten'ka* applies even more to the pair *Sonjúša* and *Sónečka*. Informants might say that *Sónečka* is more endearing, but they might also say that *Sonjúša* has a greater emotional load; these two statements are not necessarily incompatible. In Russian culture, endearments tend to be showered on people easily and lightly, whereas 'more serious' forms such as *Sonjúša* or *Vanjúša* may in fact carry a greater weight and may be felt to mean more than a casual endearment. (As a remote and imperfect analogy I might mention the fact that in Australia, the terms "dear" and "love" are routinely addressed by shop assistants and bar attendants to all and sundry, whereas less overtly affectionate forms such as *Deb* for *Debbie* or *Pen* for *Penny* are kept for intimate friends.)

Bratus (1969:33) calls forms such as *Katjúša* or *Il'júša* "diminutive", but in fact they could in a sense be regarded as affectionate 'augmentatives' rather than diminutives. For example, if a little girl commonly called *Sónečka* or *Tánečka* is occasionally called *Sonjúša* or *Tanjúša*, this has a 'magnifying' effect rather than the reverse. It sounds as if she is being treated as a 'big person', seriously and affectionately at the same time. It will probably mean more to her than being called *Sónečka* or *Tánečka*, endearments routinely given to little girls called *Sónja* or *Tánja*. The existence of a diminutive suffix *-úška* (e.g., *Petrúška*, *Vanjúška*) is partly responsible, perhaps, for this magnifying effect, just as the existence of *-óček* makes *-ók* seem less than a diminutive. But, unlike *-ók*, *-úša* never functions as a diminutive of common nouns at all. Apart from a few de-verbal or de-adjectival *nomina personae* such as *klikúša* 'epileptic woman', *-úša* is used exclusively with proper names.

The suffix *-úška* (with the stress on *ú*, as in *Petrúška*) is not widely used in literary Russian, but it is not unknown, and in a pair such as *Petrúška* and *Petrúša*, *Petrúša* must seem an anti-diminutive rather than a diminutive, given that *-úška* is used as a diminutive of common names (e.g., *derévnja* 'village' > *derevúška* 'little villate'; *kómnata* 'room' > *komnatúška* 'little room'; *cérkov'* 'church' > *cerkvúška* 'little church'), whereas *-úša* is not used with common nouns at all.

Of course in the case of unmarked full names such as *Véra*, forms in *-úša* (e.g., *Verúša*) don't have a similarly strong magnifying effect, because they are seen against the background of *Véra* as well as *Véročka* (as well as *Vérúška* or other affectionate forms). With respect to *Véročka*, *Verúša* is magnifying, but with respect to *Véra* it isn't. In the case of unmarked full names such as *Andréj*, which have neither an unmarked short form nor an unmarked affectionate form of any kind, the form in *-úša* (*Andrjúša*) is even less 'magnifying': *Andrjúša* is seen against the background of the unmarked full form *Andréj*, so there is no reason why it should seem to be 'magnifying'. For example, when Tolstoy (1985) in his diaries refers to his son Andréj (of whom he didn't think much) as *Andrjúša*, this sounds patronising and certainly not particularly dignified. Being a kind of 'familiar' form, *Andrjúša* sounds less 'adult' than *Andréj*; at the same time, *Sonjúša* sounds more dignified and adult than *Sónečka*, and *Katjúša*, more than *Káten'ka*.

In a sense, forms such as *Andrjúša* occupy vis-à-vis their full form a position similar to those that short forms in *-ša* (such as *Gríša* or *Natáša*) occupy with respect to their full names. They are more affectionate, however, although this affection is not of an 'endearing' kind as in *-en'ka* or *-očka* (*Káten'ka* or *Sónečka*) forms.

Before I attempt to gather all these various clues together and to propose a semantic formula consistent with them all, let me draw the reader's attention to one especially vibrant and emotionally rich example of use of a name with the suffix *-úša*. I have in mind Dostoevsky's (1976) little hero Iljúšečka in *The brothers Karamazov*.

The suffix *-ečka* (as in *Sónečka*) gives this name a childlike ring and expresses, as usual, light endearment. But the combination of *-ečka* with *-úš(a)* endows this name with an emotional significance which goes far beyond that of any *Sónečka* or *Vánečka*. The first suffix, *-úš(a)*, conveys here (as usual), an intimacy of a kind normally not associated with small children. The second suffix, *-ečka*, conveys a tenderness of a kind which *is* associated with small children. As a result, Iljúšečka's name conveys both tenderness and intimacy; it caresses and dignifies the little hero at the same time and fits this charming character to perfection.

A momentary shift from an unmarked form to a form in *-úša* implies in Russian a change of attitude, normally in the direction of warmth, seriousness, and intimacy. For example, when in Solzhenitsyn's novel *The first circle* a roommate switches from the usual form *Nádja* to *Nadjúša*, this is taken as an expression of sympathy:

> 'Čto s toboj, Nadjuša? Ty utrom ušla veselaja.' Slova byli sočuvstvennye, no smysl ix byl—razdraženie. (1968c:247)
>
> ' "What's wrong with you, Nadya? You were cheerful enough when you left this morning." The words were sympathetic in themselves, but they conveyed her irritation.' (1979:337)

But in the English translation of this passage, the words are not particularly sympathetic. What makes the original sentence sound sympathetic is the use of *Nadjúša*. The good feelings and the seriousness encoded in that form, combined with the question "What's wrong?", do convey something like sympathy. In English, this is bound to be lost, and as a result, the whole passage loses its logic.

To account for all these different aspects of forms in *-úša*, the following formula can be proposed:

> *Katjúša, Sonjúša, Andrjúša*
> I feel something good toward you
> not of the kind that people feel toward children

2.2.7 Summary of Russian Expressive Derivation

FORMS IN *-očka (-ečka)* (e.g., *Lídočka, Gáločka, Lëvočka, Sónečka*)
I feel something good toward you
   of the kind that people feel speaking to small children

FORMS IN *-en'ka (-on'ka)* (e.g., *Káten'ka, Míten'ka*)
I feel something good toward you
I feel something good speaking to you

MASCULINE NAMES, FORMS IN *-ik* (e.g., *Márik, Júrik*)
I feel something good toward you
   of the kind that people feel toward small boys

FEMININE NAMES, FORMS IN *-ik* (e.g., *Svétik, Ljúsik*)
I feel something good toward you
I feel something good speaking to you
I don't want to speak to you the way other people speak to you
I want to speak to you as if you were a small boy, not a girl

MASCULINE NAMES, FORMS IN *-ók* (e.g., *Sašók, Dimók*)
I feel something good toward you
   of the kind that people feel toward boys

FEMININE NAMES, FORMS IN *-ók* (e.g., *Ninók, Lizók*)
I feel something good toward you
(I feel something good speaking to you)
I don't want to speak to you the way other people speak to you
I want to speak to you as if you were a boy, not a girl

FORMS IN *-ënyš* (e.g., *Katënyš, Klarënyš*)
I feel something good toward you
I don't want to speak to you the way other people speak to you
I want to speak to you as if you were a young, not full-grown, animal

FORMS IN *-ënok* (e.g., *Katënok, Nikitënok*) (cf. Benson 1967:167)
I feel something good toward you
I feel something good speaking to you
I don't want to speak to you the way other people speak to you
I want to speak to you as if you were a baby animal, not a child

FORMS IN *-uška* (e.g., *Nikítuška, Avdótjuška*)
I feel something good toward you
   of the kind that people feel toward people
   when they think of bad things that can happen to people

FORMS IN *-úša* (e.g., *Katjúša, Sonjúša, Andrjúša*)
I feel something good toward you
   not of the kind that people feel toward children

2.3 The Semantics of Russian Names in -*ka*

2.3.1 The Protean Nature of the Suffix

The suffix -*ka* is the most versatile and the most elusive of all the Russian expressive suffixes. In linguistic literature, names in -*ka* are generally regarded as pejorative (except in dialectal use; cf., for example, Bondaletov and Danilina 1970:198). Some books for the general reader go as far as condemning it as ideologically unsound. For example, Suslova and Superanskaja (1978:116) write (my translation): "The -*ka* has kept until the present day its traditional aspect conveying a contemptuous attitude to a person, and diminishing the addressee's dignity in his or her relationship with the speaker." The authors note that Pushkin, who liked to make use of Russian peasants' speech, was not above using that form and called his dearly loved children *Máška, Sáška, Gríška,* and *Natáška.* In that sense, names with the suffix -*ka* are also used in present-day colloquial speech. Nonetheless, Suslova and Superanskaja go on to condemn this usage: "But in our times social interaction should use new forms. In courteous, respectful speech, treating other people as equals, there is no room for forms such as *Vas'ka* or *Máška,* which are incompatible with cultured social interaction" (Ibid.).

This is a very curious passage. In Pushkin's use forms in -*ka* were all right, because he liked simple folk's speech. But in our times, they are not all right—even though in everyday colloquial speech they are used in the same sense in which they were used by Pushkin!

A similar ambivalence (though without the normative and ideological overtones) can be seen in Stankiewicz's (1968:156) account of this troublesome suffix: "The meaning of this suffix is pejorative, especially among children or when used by adults in address to children. In pre-Revolutionary Russia it was used for people of lower class and the peasantry. Among adolescents and young adults, the pejorative meaning is now attenuated, and the derivative conveys, among friends, the meaning of familiarity or intimacy."

But what does it mean for a pejorative meaning to be "attenuated"? *Is* this meaning pejorative or *isn't* it?

Similarly, Benson (1967:152) says that "the suffix -*ka* is familiar, often derogatory: *Egór–Egórka*". He doesn't make it clear, however—and perhaps he hasn't made it quite clear to himself—what exactly he is claiming: are some *categories* of names in -*ka* derogatory (so that 'derogatoriness' is part of their semantic invariant) or are some *instances* of such names intended in a derogatory way, without there being any derogatoriness in the semantic invariant of any names in -*ka?*

Furthermore, it is not true that among children forms in -*ka* are generally speaking pejorative. For example, in Arkadij Gajdar's (1957) children's novel *Škola* 'The school', schoolboys generally call and address one another by means of -*ka* forms (*Vál'ka, Gríška, Féd'ka, Mít'ka,* and so on), without any pejorative connotations whatsoever; it would appear that for schoolboys (though not for schoolgirls) they are in fact standard and unmarked.

Nor is it true that in the relationship between an adult and a child a form in -*ka* would normally sound pejorative. To begin with, as pointed out by Suslova and

Superanskaja (1978:113), forms of this kind are often used by adults when talking to other adults about their own children (e.g., *moj Pét'ka,* 'my boy Pete', *moja Kát'ka* 'my small daughter Kate'), with no pejorative connotations at all. The poet Aleksandr Blok referred even to his baby son (who only lived a week or so) as *Mit'ka,* wondering, lovingly, prematurely:

> Kak ego teper, Mit'ku . . . vospityvat? (Gippius 1971:40)
>
> 'How should we bring him up, our Mit'ka?'

Consider also the following two examples from Gajdar's novel *Timur and his team,* where the form in *-ka* conveys a father's affectionate attitude to his young daughter:

> Papa, priezžaj skoree! Papa! Mne, tvoej Žen'ke, očen' trudno! (1957:471).
>
> 'Daddy, come back quickly! Daddy! Things are hard for me, your Žen'ka!'

> Čerez polčasa ja uedu. . . . žal, čto tak i ne prišlos' povidat' Žen'ku. (1957:503)
>
> 'I'll be leaving in half an hour. What a pity that I didn't manage to see Žen'ka!'

Among male friends (not necessarily young), forms in *-ka* such as *Kól'ka* or *Bór'ka* are also very common, and they don't have to sound pejorative at all. They are compatible not only with affection, but even with respect, as Okudžava's song about "Lën'ka Korolëv" illustrates:

> Rebjata uvažali očen' Lën'ku Korolëva.
>
> 'The lads (his mates) had great respect for Lën'ka Korolëv.'

Given this capacity of the suffix *-ka* (even when used after a soft consonant) to be used either affectionately or in a friendly spirit, and not only in jocular reversals, we cannot regard it as inherently negative in its semantic structure. What we should try to do instead is to assign to it a kind of semantic structure which would explain its tendency to be interpreted as negative but which would also be compatible with a positive interpretation.

2.3.2 Two Types of Forms in -ka: *Positive and Neutral*

I believe that one reason (though not necessarily the main one) why names in *-ka* seem so confusing and so difficult to give a consistent account of is that the suffix *-ka* is in fact polysemous—or rather, that it is linked with a number of different morphological constructions (which can be described in terms of different morphological processes) and that in each case the meaning of the construction including *-ka* is different.

First of all, three-syllable forms based on the full (hard) stem of (full) three-syllable feminine names (such as *Marínka, Irínka, Tat'jánka*) are not only not pejorative but unquestionably positive. Like names in *-en'ka* and *-očka,* they convey (among others) the component 'I feel something good toward you'. If we want to describe this category in processual terms, we can say that in this case the suffix *-ka* is added to a full, hard, three-syllable stem (of a feminine name).

No other category of names in *-ka* has that inherent positive value. From this point of view, then, names such as *Marínka* or *Irínka* have more in common with affectionate names in *-očka* or *-en'ka* (*Iročka, Káten'ka*) than with the other types of names in *-ka*.

In contrast to these three-syllable *-ka* forms based on feminine full names, other *-ka* forms (for example, *Vérka, Lídka, Natáška, Kát'ka,* or *Sáška*) are neither positive nor negative. They are casual, off-hand, informal, familiar, and unceremonious. Given these qualities, it is not surprising that in some situations they can be interpreted as lacking in (due) respect and therefore as pejorative, but in other situations, they can be interpreted as friendly and intimate.

The general message 'with you I don't have to stand on ceremony' is compatible with disrespect, but it is also compatible with friendly closeness. In the semantic formulae assigned to Russian names in *-ka* I have formulated this component as follows: 'I don't want to show that I feel something good toward you of the kind that people show they feel toward people whom they don't know well and who are not children'. For mnemonic reasons, I have labelled this component 'anti-respect', but this should not be confused with disrespect.

I believe that the use of *-ka* forms in pre-Revolutionary Russia can be explained along similar lines. When peasants were called by their landlords *Kát'ka* or *Féd'ka,* these forms sounded disrespectful, because they implied a lack of distance without signalling any affection and because no intimacy or affection was implied by the social situation itself. But among peasants themselves, the same forms were interpreted differently, as pointed out by Suslova and Superanskaja (1978:116): "they showed a simplicity in interpersonal relations, and endowed these relations with closeness and even warmth". I believe that both these contrasting interpretations are compatible with the same semantic structure. If a form explicitly signals 'no distance' and doesn't overtly signal affection, it is still compatible with a 'close and warm' interpretation if intimacy and affection are implied by the social situation (as in the case of the villagers' speaking among themselves).

In addition to 'anti-respect', neutral forms in *-ka* (that is to say, all of them except those in the *Irínka* category) also convey an unspecified expressive component, which I would represent as 'I feel something toward you', but they don't specify the nature of the speaker's attitude, and this is why they lend themselves to a very wide spectrum of interpretations, from loving to offensive and contemptuous.

In one respect, however, this expressive character of names in *-ka* is specified: it has to be of, roughly speaking, an anti-sentimental nature. I have represented this aspect of their value in the form of the following component: 'I don't want to show that I feel something good toward you of the kind that people feel toward children'.

Everything that has just been said about the unceremonious, expressive, and anti-sentimental character of names in *-ka* (other than those of the *Irínka* category) applies equally to hard stem forms, such as *Lídka* or *Dëmka;* to soft stem forms, such as *Kát'ka* or *Ván'ka;* and to forms with the *-š* suffix, such as *Gríška* or *Sáška*. In the formulae, these common features have been labelled, for the reader's convenience, *expressivity, anti-respect,* and *anti-sentimentality.* A fourth feature, called here *familiarity,* is simply carried over from the base and belongs in fact to all expressive forms of Russian names.

In addition to these common features, however, neutral names in *-ka* (that is, all names other than those in the *Irínka* category) also display certain differences, which are linked with the character of the stem and with the nature of the morphological process involved. Three subtypes should be distinguished here, depending on the nature of the stem-final consonant.

2.3.3 Three Subtypes of Neutral Forms in -ka

If we disregard different social connotations of individual names, we can say that names in *-ka* based on short forms with a hard stem (e.g., *Lída > Lídka, Zína > Zínka*) seem to have the same expressive value as those based on unmarked full forms (e.g., *Véra > Vérka, Nína > Nínka*). I will treat them together, therefore, as the subtype with a hard stem. Forms in *-ka* based on a short form with a soft stem (e.g., *Kátja > Kát'ka, Vánja > Ván'ka*) have a somewhat different value, and the *-ka* forms with the suffix *-š* behave somewhat differently from the other two. We are left, therefore, with three different subtypes, which can be called hard stem forms, soft stem forms, and *-š* forms. Since the *-š* form occupies an intermediate position between the other two, we will start by comparing hard stem forms with soft stem forms in *-ka*.

It is my hypothesis that, generally speaking, soft forms in *-ka* tend to sound more rough, disrespectful, unceremonious, rude, and even vulgar than their counterparts with a hard stem. For example, if a family had two small daughters, named *Svetlána* and *Katerína,* they would be more likely to call them *Kátja* and *Svétka* than *Svéta* and *Kát'ka* or *Svétka* and *Kát'ka,* and if they did call them *Svéta* and *Kát'ka,* or *Svétka* and *Kát'ka,* this would suggest a rougher attitude to the girl called *Kát'ka.* This roughness could of course be jocular and affectionate rather than unloving, but this doesn't affect the point that *Kát'ka* and *Svétka* don't have exactly the same expressive value. In fact I suspect that when linguists and others write about the supposedly pejorative nature of the suffix *-ka,* which "conveys a contemptuous attitude and diminishes the addressee's dignity vis-à-vis the speaker" (Suslova and Superanskaja 1978:116), they are thinking of names with soft stems, such as *Kát'ka* or *Ván'ka,* not of hard-stemmed ones such as *Lídka, Svétka,* or *Rómka.*

In Russian literature, switches from a habitual soft stem short form to its counterpart with *-ka* usually signal an onset of 'bad feelings'. For example, in Gajdar's (1957) novel *Timur and his team,* the older sister, Ol'ga, usually calls her younger sister *Žénja,* but when she is displeased with her she switches to *Žén'ka.* Similarly, in Dostoevsky's (1957:174) novel *Crime and punishment,* the hero's (Raskolnikov's) best friend, Razumixin, usually calls him *Ródja,* but when on a particular occasion he gets very angry with Raskolnikov and starts yelling at him, he calls him *Ród'ka.* But it is difficult to find any similar switches involving hard stem short forms.

Contrasts in habitual designations, such as *Mítja* vs. *Mít'ka* or *Kátja* vs. *Kát'ka,* are also used as indicators of different attitudes. For example, in Dostoevsky's

(1976) novel *The brothers Karamazov*, people who love Dmitrij Karamazov (Aleša and Grušen'ka) usually call him *Mítja*, whereas his father, who hates him, usually calls him *Mít'ka*. But hard stem forms such as *Dëmka* or *Svétka* are seldom, if ever, used in such contrasts. In fact, they are frequently used as habitual designations of characters presented in a positive light. For example, in Solzhenitsyn's (1968a) novel *The cancer ward*, the generally liked lad named *Dëma* (presumably from *Demján*) is normally called *Dëmka* and this sounds friendly rather than pejorative.

One is also reminded in this connection of a reference to the young Roman Jakobson in one of Mayakovsky's poems:

> Glaz
> > kosja
> > > v pečati surguča
> > naprolét
> > > boltal o Romke Jakobsone
> > i smešno potel,
> > > stixi uča.
> > > > (1958:163)

> 'One eye cocked
> > towards your red-sealed cargo,
> nights on end,
> > while others snored away,
> about old Romka Jakobson
> > you'd argue,
> memorising poems
> > in your funny way.'
> > > (1972:69)

Clearly, in Mayakovsky's mouth, the phrase "Romka Jakobson" sounds friendly rather than pejorative.

Finally, I will recall here a song by Vladimir Vysockij, in which a form in *-ka* (*Nínka*) has clearly positive connotations:

> Segodnja žizn' moja rešaetsja,
> Segodnja Ninka soglašaetsja.

> 'Today my life is being decided,
> Today Ninka is saying "yes".'

In other contexts, *Nínka* may sound vulgar and pejorative, but here it is clearly anything but pejorative.

I must reiterate, however, that I am not saying that hard stem *-ka* forms (such as *Rómka*) are inherently positive whereas soft stem *-ka* forms such as *Kát'ka* are inherently negative. I am only saying that soft forms in *-ka* are more likely to be interpreted as negative. Since the stems themselves have different value, they react differently to the adding of *-ka*. Looking at the proposed explications of hard stem names such as *Lída* and soft stem names such as *Kátja*, we see that they differ in two respects: first, names like *Lída* exclude children as part of their prototype, whereas names like *Kátja* include children as part of their prototype; second, names like *Kátja* include a friendly attitude as part of their prototype, whereas names like *Lída* don't. I believe that both these features interact with the 'operator' *-ka*.

First, it should be recalled that in the area of common nouns, too, the suffix *-ka* is somewhat ambivalent: if *-očka* suggests 'much smaller than [the base]', *-ka* suggests 'not much smaller than [the base]'. In a series such as *gorst'* 'handful' > *górstka* > *górstočka* the form in *-ka* acts as a diminutive with respect to the base but as an anti-diminutive, so to speak, with respect to the form in *-očka*.

Furthermore, for many nouns a form in *-ka* represents in fact the norm, whereas the corresponding form in *-očka* (*-ečka*) represents a diminutive. As pointed out by Bratus (1969:37), "In these instances, the word from which the diminutive in *-očka/-ečka* is formed, is 'augmented', as it were, i.e. acquires the meaning of a relative augmentative".

At the same time, it should be mentioned that outside the area of proper names the suffix *-ka* is normally combined with hard stems, not with soft stems:

krovat' 'bed'	>	*krovatka*	**krovat'ka*
ploščad' 'city square'	>	*ploščadka*	**ploščad'ka*

This means that hard stem names in *-ka* such as *Lídka* or *Nínka* can be perceived as mildly 'diminutive', presenting a person as rather 'small' (in size, status, dignity, age, etc.) Consequently, they can be perceived as disrespectful, but they can also be perceived as affectionately familiar. By contrast, soft stem names in *-ka* such as *Kát'ka* or *Ván'ka* can never be perceived as 'diminutive' because there are hardly any 'diminutive' models for such forms in the area of inanimate nouns.

What I am trying to suggest is that if the suffix *-ka* is inherently somewhat ambivalent, different types of names may tend to invite different interpretations; in particular, hard stem names may tend to invite a diminutive interpretation, whereas soft stem names may tend to invite an 'augmentative' interpretation.

Since hard stem names take adults as their prototype, they may seem to be 'big' names, more suitable for big people than for children. If a little girl is called *Ljúdka* or *Svétka*, this is likely to be interpreted as a diminutive (in the sense of small size). But soft stem short forms such as *Kátja* or *Vánja* are not perceived as 'big names'; they are felt to be equally suitable for children as for (likeable) adults. Consequently, forms such as *Kát'ka* or *Ván'ka* are less likely to be interpreted as diminutives. Consequently, a *Svétka* can be felt to be a 'smaller version' of *Svéta*, but *Kát'ka* will not be felt to be a 'smaller' version of *Kátja*.

This ambivalence of the suffix *-ka* can also be seen in the area of family terms. For example, the form *dóčka* is said to be a diminutive of *doč'* 'daughter' (cf., for example, AN SSSR 1960:265), but the form *tëtka* is felt to be an 'augmentative' rather than a diminutive of the form *tëtja* 'auntie'. In the case of *djádja* 'uncle' the form in *-ka* not only is a kind of anti-diminutive but is in fact often used not in the sense of 'uncle' but in the sense of 'a rather unpleasant-looking man, a stranger'.

The 'augmentative' function of a form such as *tëtka* (vs. *tëtja*) can, I think, be represented as follows:

I don't want to speak to you (of her) the way children speak

The 'augmentative' character of a soft stem name such as *Kát'ka* or *Žén'ka* can be represented in a similar (though not identical) way:

I don't want to speak to you the way people speak to children

The 'diminutive' character of a hard stem form such as *Svétka* or *Ljúdka* can be represented in the following way:

I don't want to speak to you the way people speak
to people who are not children

Turning now to the second difference between hard stem forms such as *Lídka* and soft stem forms such as *Kát'ka*, it will be recalled that their bases differ also in what I have called 'personal distance': 'I want to speak to you the way people speak to people whom they know well' (hard stem) versus 'I want to speak to you the way people speak to people whom they know well and toward whom they feel something good'. In the case of the bases themselves, a soft stem form such as *Kátja* can be said to imply less personal distance than *Lída*. I believe that this difference is carried over to forms in *-ka* (*Kát'ka*, *Lídka*), but that in the context of the semantics of *-ka* it appears here in a different light. Since *-ka* carries with it an 'anti-respect' component and an 'anti-sentimental' component, the lack of distance implied by the base acquires here a rather *razvjaznyj* 'laid back' character. Forms in *-en'ka* such as *Káten'ka* don't imply personal distance either, but they signal affection, and therefore they cannot sound offensive. But forms such as *Kát'ka* don't signal affection and do signal a lack of distance. This combination is likely to be interpreted as disrespectful and offensive.

To portray this difference between *Kát'ka* and *Lídka*, I have postulated for the former a component which for convenience could be called 'roughness': 'I don't want to show that I feel something good toward you'. The soft stem itself, for example, *Kát'-*, signals, 'I want to speak to you the way people speak to people whom they know well and toward whom they feel something good'. By adding *-ka* to this, the speaker makes sure that this lack of personal distance is not interpreted here as a show of personal affection ('I don't want to show that I feel something good toward you').

As for forms in *-ška* such as *Sáška* or *Gríška*, they seem to occupy an intermediate position between hard stem forms such as *Svétka* and soft stem forms such as *Kát'ka*. This makes sense, in view of the intermediate position that the base forms in *-ša* such as *Sáša* occupy with respect to soft stem bases such as *Kátja* and hard stem bases such as *Lída* or *Svéta*.

Since forms in *-ška* have neither the diminutive effect of hard stem forms in *-ka* nor the augmentative effect of soft forms in *-ka*, I have included in their explication neither the component of 'diminution' nor that of 'augmentation'. But since forms in *-ška* are no less applicable to children than those in *-ša*, I have kept the reference to children, giving it in this case the conventional label 'patronising'. In the case of names of -*ša,* the reference to children doesn't have a patronising effect, but in the context of the semantics of -*ka,* it does acquire some such flavour. A component of 'roughness' is not called for in this case, because the base itself doesn't signal any lack of personal distance.

I am now going to propose semantic formulae for the different types of names in -*ka* which have been discussed here: first, three formulae for the three subtypes of the semantically neutral names in -*ka,* and then a formula for positive named in -*ka,* such as *Marínka.* In each case, the formula will include a considerable number (from three to seven) of fairly complex components. To make the formulae easier to read, therefore, I have provided each component with a convenient short label, which gives a rough summary of this component's meaning. It should be remembered, however, that it is the full formula rather than the set of short labels which is being proposed as the statement of meaning.

2.3.4 Summary of Russian Forms in -ka

A. NEUTRAL NAMES IN -*ka*

I. -*ka* AFTER A HARD CONSONANT (e.g., *Lídka, Rómka, Vérka, Nínka*)

[FAMILIARITY]
> I want to speak to you the way people speak
> to people whom they know well

[DIMINUTION]
> I don't want to speak to you the way people speak
> to people who are not children

[EXPRESSIVITY]
> I feel something toward you

[ANTI-SENTIMENTALITY]
> I don't want to show that I feel something toward you
> of the kind that people feel toward children

[ANTI-RESPECT]
> I don't want to show that I feel something good toward you
> of the kind that people show they feel toward people
> whom they don't know well

II. -*ka* AFTER A SOFT CONSONANT (e.g., *Kát'ka, Mít'ka, Ván'ka*)

[FAMILIARITY]
> I want to speak to you the way people speak
> to people whom they know well

[NO DISTANCE]
> and toward whom they feel something good

[AUGMENTATION]
> I don't want to speak to you the way people speak to children

[EXPRESSIVITY]
> I feel something toward you

[ROUGHNESS]
> I don't want to show that I feel something good toward you

[ANTI-SENTIMENTALITY]
> I don't want to show that I feel something toward you
>> of the kind that people show they feel toward children

[ANTI-RESPECT]
> I don't want to show that I feel something good toward you
>> of the kind that people show they feel toward people
>> whom they don't know well

III. *-ka* AFTER THE SUFFIX *-š* (e.g., *Gríška, Sáška*)

[FAMILIARITY]
> I want to speak to you the way people speak to people
>> whom they know well

[PATRONISING]
> and to children

[EXPRESSIVITY]
> I feel something toward you

[ANTI-SENTIMENTALITY]
> I don't want to show that I feel something toward you
>> of the kind that people show they feel toward children

[ANTI-RESPECT]
> I don't want to show that I feel something good toward you
>> of the kind that people show they feel toward people
>> whom they don't know well

B. POSITIVE FORMS IN *-ka* (e.g., *Irínka, Marínka, Tatjánka*)
(*-ka* after a hard consonant, three syllables, based on full feminine name)

[FAMILIARITY]
> I want to speak to you the way people speak
>> to people whom they know well

[DIMINUTION]
> I don't want to speak to you the way people speak
>> to people who are not children

[POSITIVE EXPRESSIVITY]
> I feel something good toward you

3. Polish Personal Names

The system of Polish personal names and their expressive derivates is in many ways similar to the Russian system. Given the close genetic relationship between the two languages and the over-all similarity of their expressive systems, it is all the more fascinating to discover, through detailed semantic analysis, the subtle differences between the two systems and to ponder their cultural significance.

One general difference, however, lies on the surface: Polish names, in contrast to Russian names, are sex-differentiated, right throughout the expressive system. In Russian, the repertoire of full masculine names differs from that of feminine ones, but the system of expressive derivation is by and large the same for both sexes.

Among full names, feminine names tend to end in *-a* and masculine names in a
consonant, but even here there are many exceptions; for example, there are masculine names such as *Gavríla, Il'já, Kuz'má, Nikíta*. But in the area of short forms
and of expressive derivates, forms in *-a, -ša, -en'ka, -očka, -úša, -uška*, or *-ka* can
all equally well be masculine or feminine. Amazingly to an outsider, the bulk of
these 'unisex' expressive forms are in fact morphologically feminine (that is to say,
they use suffixes which in the area of inanimate nouns are feminine), a fact which
would seem to be rich in cultural implications. In Polish this is not the case, the
inflectional patterns of masculine and feminine names being different. Apart from
cases of affectionate distortion, a name ending in *-a* (*-eńka, -eczka, -ulka, -usia,
-unia, -ka*, and so on) will always be feminine, and a name ending in a consonant
(or in *-o*) will always be masculine. (The only exception to this that I am aware of is
the name *Kuba*, from *Jakub*.) As we will see, this formal differentiation of names
into masculine and feminine is accompanied in Polish by a high degree of semantic
differentiation. Seen against this background, the Russian system of expressive
derivation strikes one as semantically uniform, with males and females being treated in largely the same way.

Another general difference between the Polish and Russian system is related to
the role of formality and courtesy and the interaction between formality and affection. In fact, these two differences between the Russian and the Polish system are
related, since courtesy, Polish style, is of the chivalrous and asymmetrical kind and
so depends on gender: for example, if in Poland courtesy requires that men should
kiss a woman's hand in greeting and leave-taking, this tradition manifests both
ritualised courtesy and different treatment of women and men (cf. Wierzbicka
1985c). As in the case of the Russian names, the survey of Polish expressive types is
by no means intended to be exhaustive.

3.1 Full First Names

Like Russian (and like English), Polish has two types of full first names: marked
ones, such as *Jan, Maria* or *Zofia*, and unmarked ones, such as *Adam, Ewa,
Michał*, and *Marta*. The fact that in recent fashion many full names which used to
be treated as marked (e.g., *Tomasz* or *Małgorzata*) are beginning to be treated as
unmarked and to be used instead of short forms doesn't affect this basic distinction.
Generally speaking, the use of these forms in Polish is similar to the use of the
corresponding forms in Russian.

In a Polish kindergarten, children named *Adam, Ewa, Michał*, and *Marta* would
be less likely to be called by these (unmarked) full names than in an Anglo-Saxon
kindergarten children named *Matthew, Andrew, Clare*, or *Ruth* would be likely to be
called by their (unmarked) full names. Marked full names such as *Kazimierz* (as in
Pułaski), *Tadeusz* (as in Kościuszko), or *Maria* (as in Skłodowska Curie) are very
unlikely to be used in normal everyday relations with one's spouse, relatives, and
friends; and if they are so used, they are highly marked.

It appears, however, that there is one difference between the Polish and the
Russian usage: in Polish, full names are not used as commonly as they are in

Russian to express disapproval to children. For example, the switching from *Žénja* to *Evgénija* in the speech of an older sister addressed at a younger (thirteen-year-old) sister in Gajdar's (1957) novel *Timur and his team* sounds natural in Russian, but in Polish it would be less natural to keep switching in this way from *Genia* to *Eugenia*, or from *Zosia* to *Zofia*. To account for this apparent difference between Russian and Polish, I have included in the Russian formula for marked full names a component which denies overt affection, and I have not included such a component in the corresponding Polish formula.

> MARKED FULL NAMES (e.g., *Kazimierz, Tadeusz, Maria*)
> I don't want to speak to you the way people speak
>   to people whom they don't know well
> I don't want to speak to you the way people speak
>   to people whom they know well and to children

> UNMARKED FULL NAMES (e.g., *Adam, Ewa*)
> I don't want to speak to you the way people speak to children
> I want to speak to you the way people speak
>   to people whom they know well

Nonetheless, Polish differs from Russian with respect to the elaboration of formality and respectful politeness, and this affects the use of full names. Professional titles aside, in Russian formality is conveyed by combining a full first name with a patronymic, for example, *Lev Nikolaevič* (Tolstoy), *Anna Andréevna* (Akhmatova). Expressive variants of people's names cannot be combined with a patronymic (**Ánja Andréevna, *Ánečka Andréevna*, and so on). In Polish, formality is expressed by means of the words *pan* (roughly, 'Mr'), *pani* (roughly, 'Mrs'), and *panna* (roughly, 'Miss'), but in contrast to Russian, these titles *can* be combined with short forms and with expressive derivates (at least with those which are semantically compatible with the respect encoded in the title itself). As a result, in Polish one doesn't have to choose between expressing an emotional attitude and maintaining some distance, and one can combine the two in various proportions and in different combinations. For example, speaking of a girl called *Zofia*, one can maintain formality and still choose among forms such as *panna Zofia, panna Zosia,* and *panna Zosieńka,* and for a man called *Tadeusz* one can maintain formality and still choose among forms such as *pan Tadeusz, pan Tadzio,* and *pan Tadek.* The range of possibilities is particularly wide in the vocative, which Polish has maintained as a separate case (e.g., *panie Tadeuszu, panie Tadziu, panie Tadku*).

The rich system of expressive derivation links Polish with Russian (and with other Slavic languages) and reflects the 'emotional' character of human interaction in Slavic culture. But the combination of emotionality and formality, of affection and somewhat ritualised courtesy, is a specifically Polish feature, which is expressed also in non-verbal behaviour. The need to maintain a certain formality even in relationships in which one also feels the need to express affection or other feelings is an important feature of traditional Polish culture, which is reflected in the Polish language. (It is also a feature which has sometimes been mocked and satirically portrayed in Russian literature, especially in Dostoevsky's novels.)

3.2 Short Forms

3.2.1 Soft Stem Forms, and Hard Stem Forms in -ek

Speaking of Russian short forms, we have distinguished three classes: soft stem forms (e.g., *Kátja*, *Vánja*), hard stem forms (e.g., *Lída*, *Díma*), and forms in *-ša* (e.g., *Natáša*, *Gríša*). In Polish, however, short forms present a rather different picture, because in contrast to Russian, feminine and masculine names are not treated in the same way.

For feminine names, short forms are based on a soft stem or include a suffix with a soft consonant such as, above all, *-sia* (e.g., *Zosia*). These soft-stemmed feminine forms correspond in value to Russian soft stemmed short forms such as *Kátja* or *Ánja*. But for masculine names, no forms of the same expressive value are available in Polish. From a morphological point of view, many names do present a perfect symmetry, and in fact many feminine short forms are formed by adding a feminine suffix *-a* to a masculine short form or by replacing a word-final masculine *-o* with the feminine *-a:*

MASCULINE		FEMININE	
Jaś	(from *Jan*)	*Jasia*	(from *Janina*)
Staś	(from *Stanisław*)	*Stasia*	(from *Stanisława*)
Kazio	(from *Kazimierz*)	*Kazia*	(from *Kazimiera*)
Henio	(from *Henryk*)	*Henia*	(from *Henryka*)

Yet from a pragmatic and, I would claim, semantic point of view the value of the masculine and feminine forms is not exactly the same: the masculine soft stem forms are perceived as 'softer' and more childish than the corresponding feminine forms.

It is true that in small children's stories masculine and feminine soft forms often seem to be on a par, as in the Polish version of Grimm's fairy tale about Hansel and Gretel: *Jaś i Małgosia*. But in the generally used *Elementarz* (a book teaching children to read and write; Falski 1976), the stereotypical boy and girl are called *Ala* (feminine, soft stem) and *Janek* (masculine, hard stem), not *Ala* and *Jaś*. The other girls' and boys' names similarly paired in the *Elementarz* include the following:

Ola	—	*Olek*
Tola	—	*Tolek*
Cela	—	*Lucek*

This suggests that the basic short form of marked feminine names, such as *Zofia*, *Anna*, or *Maria*, is a soft stemmed one, *Ala*, *Zosia*, *Ania*, *Marysia*, but for marked masculine names such as *Jan*, the basic, unmarked short form is a hard-stemmed one with the suffix *-ek: Janek*, not the soft-stemmed *Jaś*.

In support of this claim, I would adduce the fact that marked masculine names normally do have a short form in *-ek*, whereas forms in *-ś* (not to be confused with *-uś*) exist only for a handful of such names (in addition to what is felt as a more neutral form in *-ek*). For example:

MARKED FULL NAME	FORM IN -*ek*	FORM IN -*ś*
Jerzy	*Jurek*	∅
Jan	*Janek*	*Jaś*
Władysław	*Władek*	∅ (archaic babyish: *Władyś*)
Bolesław	*Bolek*	∅ (*Boleś*)
Aleksander	*Olek*	*Oleś*
Józef	*Józek*	∅
Antoni	*Antek*	*Antoś*

For the majority of marked full masculine names, the form in -*ś* is either non-existent or highly marked as child-oriented and affectionate. For unmarked full names, all derivates, whether in -*ek* or in -*ś*, sound child-oriented (to some extent) and affectionate, because it is the full form which plays the unmarked role:

UNMARKED FULL NAME	FORM IN -*ek*	FORM IN -*ś*
Michał	*Michałek* (affectionate)	*Michaś* (affectionate)
Adam	∅	*Adaś* (affectionate)
Rafał	*Rafałek* (affectionate)	∅
Marcin	*Marcinek* (affectionate)	∅
Andrzej	*Andrzejek* (affectionate)	∅

(Polysyllabic names in -*ek* such as *Michałek* are all affectionate and will be discussed in section 3.5.)

Thus, in Polish, the basic unmarked short form of a marked masculine name is the form in -*ek*, not the form in -*ś* (or its equivalents with a soft stem). The value of this form in -*ek* is a little 'tougher' than that of the basic unmarked short form of a marked feminine name. At the same time, the value of the form in -*ś* is a little 'softer' and more child-oriented than that of the soft stem short forms of feminine names. The semantic relations between these three forms can be portrayed as follows:

FEMININE NAMES, SOFT STEM SHORT FORMS (e.g., *Zosia*)
I want to speak to you the way people speak
   to girls and women whom they know well and toward whom they feel
   something good, and to children

MASCULINE NAMES, STANDARD FORMS IN -*ek* (hard stem, two syllables, e.g., *Janek, Antek*)[2]
I want to speak to you the way people speak
   to boys and men whom they know well
I don't want to speak to you the way people don't speak to children

MASCULINE NAMES, SOFT STEM SHORT FORMS (e.g., *Jaś, Adaś; Józio*)
I want to speak to you the way people speak
   to boys toward whom they feel something good, and to children

What this means is that in Polish, masculine and feminine names are treated differently. Within the masculine names, a polarisation has developed between boy- and man-oriented names, which encode familiarity without encoding warmth or 'softness' (e.g., *Janek*), and between boy- and child-oriented names, which do combine familiarity with warmth and 'softness' (e.g., *Jaś*). Within the feminine names, however, familiarity is generally combined with softness and warmth, so that no distinction is drawn in this respect between women and girls on the one hand and girls and children on the other.

Despite this polarisation, however, it should be noted that Polish two-syllable forms in *-ek*, which are the basic short form of masculine names, are nonetheless less 'tough' and 'manly' than English short forms of masculine names such as *Bob, Bill*, or *Jim*. In Polish inanimate nouns, the suffix *-ek* after a hard stem implies 'smaller size', for example:

> *dom* 'house'   >   *domek* 'little house'
> *nos* 'nose'   >   *nosek* 'little nose'

In names such as *Janek* or *Tomek*, this diminutive value of the suffix *-ek* is not equally strong, but it still plays a certain role. The suffix *-ek* doesn't make names of this kind 'child-oriented', but it ensures that they have a mildly 'diminutive' component: 'I don't want to speak to you the way people don't speak to children'. English names such as *Bob, Bill*, or *Jim* do not have this component, and this is why they sound 'tougher' than Polish names such as *Janek* or *Tomek*. The formulae assigned to these types make this relationship clear:

> *Janek, Tomek*
> I want to speak to you the way people speak
>   to boys and men whom they know well
> I don't want to speak to you the way people don't speak to children

> *Bob, Bill, Jim*
> I want to speak to you the way people speak
>   to boys and men whom they know well

3.2.2 *Feminine Forms in* -ka *(Two Syllables, Hard Stem; e.g.,* Janka*)*

Formally, many feminine names in *-ka* seem to be perfect counterparts of masculine names in *-ek*, for example:

Janek	(from *Jan*)	—	*Janka*	(from *Janina*)
Bronek	(from *Bronisław*)	—	*Bronka*	(from *Bronisława*)
Mirek	(from *Mirosław*)	—	*Mirka*	(from *Mirosława*)
Mietek	(from *Mieczysław*)	—	*Mietka*	(from *Mieczysława*)

In fact, however, forms of this kind do not have exactly the same value. (Forms in *-ek* and *-ka* after a soft stem, such as *Wiesiek* and *Wieśka,* or polysyllabic forms, such as *Michałek* and *Dorotka,* will be discussed in sections 3.5.1 and 3.5.2.)

The subtle difference in value between feminine names such as *Janka* and masculine names such as *Janek* is easier to see when one considers some other names in *-ka* (after a hard stem), derived from names which have no masculine counterparts, for example:

Hanna	—	*Hanka*	—	*Hania*
Danuta	—	*Danka*	—	*Danusia*

Names such as *Hanka* sound completely non-sentimental and non-childish, being seen against the background of friendly, feminine forms such as *Hania.* But although *Hanka* is felt to be chosen in preference to *Hania, Janek* is not felt to be chosen in preference to *Jaś,* because *Jaś* is more marked than *Janek.* As a result, *Janek* and *Hanka* are not felt to be exactly on the same level. A boy and a girl treated by their family in the same way would normally be called *Janek* and *Hania,* rather than *Janek* and *Hanka* (not to mention *Jaś* and *Hanka*).

Not all feminine names in *-ka* (after a hard stem) have their counterparts with a soft stem (such as *Hania* vs. *Hanka*), but this doesn't seem to affect their value. There is no **Jania* next to *Janka,* and yet *Janka* sounds just as non-sentimental as *Hanka.* In fact, the value of such names appears to be rather similar to that of English short names such as *Kate, Sue,* or *Pam.* It must be remembered, however, that in Polish *-ka* is, basically, a diminutive suffix:

krowa 'cow'	>	*krówka* 'little cow'
głowa 'head'	>	*główka* 'little head'

Since in Polish non-sentimental names such as *Hanka* are chosen in preference to 'warm and feminine' names such as *Hania,* and since in form they are diminutive rather than augmentative, one is led to conclude that this non-sentimentality of names such as *Hanka* derives from their avoidance of 'warm femininity' rather than from any explicit avoidance of child orientation. These considerations lead us to the following formula for feminine names in *-ka* such as *Hanka* or *Janka* (two syllables, hard stem):

    a. I want to speak to you the way people speak
       to women and girls whom they know well
    b. I don't want to show that I feel something good toward you
       of the kind that people show they feel toward women and girls

For comparison, I will repeat here the formula which was assigned in section 1 to English names such as *Kate* or *Pam:*

ENGLISH FEMININE SHORT FORMS (e.g., *Kate, Pam*)
I want to speak to you the way people speak
    to people whom they know well

The contrast between these formulae reflects the fact that forms such as *Kate* or *Pam* are not felt to be chosen in preference to forms such as *Katie* or *Pammie* (as the latter are more marked than the former), whereas Polish forms such as *Hanka* or *Bronka* would be perceived against the background of 'softer' forms such as *Hania* or *Bronia*.

3.2.3 Summary of Full and Short Forms of Polish Names

MARKED FULL NAMES (e.g., *Kazimierz, Tadeusz, Maria*)

I don't want to speak to you the way people speak
  to people whom they don't know well
I don't want to speak to you the way people speak
  to people whom they know well and to children

UNMARKED FULL NAMES (e.g., *Adam, Ewa*)

I don't want to speak to you the way people speak to children
I want to speak to you the way people speak
  to people whom they know well

FEMININE NAMES, SOFT STEM SHORT FORMS (e.g., *Zosia*)

I want to speak to you the way people speak
  to girls and women whom they know well
  and toward whom they feel something good, and to children

MASCULINE NAMES, STANDARD FORMS IN -*ek* (hard stem, two syllables, e.g., *Janek, Antek*)

I want to speak to you the way people speak
  to boys and men whom they know well
I don't want to speak to you the way people don't speak to children

MASCULINE NAMES, SOFT STEM SHORT FORMS (e.g., *Jaś, Adaś, Józio*)

I want to speak to you the way people speak
  to boys toward whom they feel something good, and to children

FEMININE NAMES, FORMS IN -*ka* (hard stem, two syllables, e.g., *Hanka, Janka*)

I want to speak to you the way people speak
  to women and girls whom they know well
I don't want to show that I feel something good toward you
  of the kind that people show they feel toward women and girls

3.3 Forms with Expressive Suffixes

Expressive derivation of names in Polish is similar in richness and scope to the corresponding phenomena in Russian. Some expressive suffixes are in fact 'the same' (etymologically and in the perception of bilingual speakers). Nonetheless there are also considerable differences, and these are very revealing. In what follows, I will first discuss a dozen or so commonly used morphological constructions one by one and then summarise the uses of the vital suffix -*ka* in Polish, comparing them with the uses of 'the same' suffix in Russian. (For some earlier discussion of the value of Polish hypocoristic suffixes, see, e.g., Dłuska 1930; Gawroński 1928; Obrębska 1929; Urbańczyk 1968; Wędkiewicz 1929; and Zarębina 1954.)

3.3.1 Forms with the Suffix -eńk(a)

Polish names in -eńka such as *Zosieńka* or *Marysieńka* seem to correspond closely to Russian names with the related suffix -en'ka, such as *Káten'ka* and *Míten'ka*. Nonetheless here, too, there are some interesting differences. Most importantly, in Russian the suffix -en'ka applies equally to masculine and feminine names; by contrast, in Polish, the suffix -eńk(a) is by and large restricted to feminine names. Masculine names such as *Jasieńko* or *Jasieniek* are known from folk poetry and folksongs, but they are not used in literary language except for the vocative case, e.g., *Jasieńku, Stasieńku, Michasieńku.*

The restrictions on masculine names in -eńk can be explained not only in general cultural terms (although it is undoubtedly true that Polish culture tends to reserve overt expression of extreme tenderness for women and children and to use it more sparingly for men) but also in linguistic terms. As I have argued earlier, soft bases of masculine names, such as *Jaś* or *Staś*, are already 'softer' (semantically) than soft bases of feminine names, such as *Zosia*. As a result, a masculine vocative such as *Michasieńku* or *Jasieńku* sounds even 'softer' than a feminine vocative such as *Zosieńko*, and a masculine nominative **Michasieniek* doesn't exist at all. But it goes without saying that this 'purely linguistic' difference is, ultimately, culturally determined as well.

It might be added that in the area of family terms, too, affectionate forms with the suffix -eńk are by and large restricted to feminine terms: *mateńka* (for mother), *córeńka* (daughter), *cioteńka* (aunt), *syneńku* (son, vocative only).

In the area of expressive adjectives, too, -eńk is more restricted in Polish than -en'k is in Russian, because it occurs only in combination with other expressive suffixes: -ut-eńk, -usi-eńk (e.g., *bieluteńki, bielusieńki* 'white').

These restrictions support the impression that the Polish -eńk, although very similar in flavour to the Russian -en'ka, is even more tender and loving. It would seem reasonable to propose for it the same two components (a and b) which have been proposed for the Russian suffix -en'ka, but it might be justified to add to them an additional component (a'), which would account for this apparent greater 'tenderness' of the Polish suffix and for its more restricted use:

> FORMS IN -eńk(a) (e.g., *Zosieńka*)
> a. I feel something good toward you
> a'. of the kind that people feel toward girls, women, and children
> b. I feel something good speaking to you

3.3.2 Forms with the Suffix -eczka

Polish names in -eczka seem to correspond exactly to the Russian names with the related suffix -očka (-ečka). I would assign to them, therefore, the same semantic representation:

FORMS IN -eczka (e.g., Haneczka)

I feel something good toward you
of the kind that people feel toward children

I have argued that in Russian, names in -očka (-ečka) are not quite as tender as those in -en'ka. The same applies to the respective value of Polish names in -eczka and in -eńka. For example, in Wyspiański's (1901) drama Wesele 'The wedding', two young girls are treated as similar characters: Zosia and Haneczka. Of the two names, Haneczka sounds a little more affectionate than Zosia, but they can still be treated as being on a par, because if the girls were called Zosieńka and Haneczka, Zosieńka would sound a shade more affectionate than Haneczka. On the other hand, had the author called his heroines Hania and Zosieńka, this would imply a different attitude toward them, because Zosieńka is far more affectionate than Hania. In other words, a soft short form such as Zosia can be perceived as being somewhere between the tender Zosieńka and the cheerful, affectionate Haneczka.

This analysis is supported by the fact that feminine names in -eczka, unlike those in -eńka, do have some masculine counterparts: e.g., Jureczek, Tomeczek, Jareczek.

Although these masculine names, too, are used mostly in the vocative, nonetheless they are not as strictly restricted to the vocative as the names with the suffix -eńk. Furthermore, vocative forms such as Michasieńku or Stasieńku sound far more tender than Jureczku or Tomeczku. (If I may be permitted a personal note at this stage, I have a nephew called Michał and a young cousin called Tomek, and I often address them as Tomeczku and Michałeczku, but I never use the form Michasieńku, which sounds far too tender to use for anyone other than a small son, a husband, or a lover.)

3.3.3 Forms with the Suffix -cia

Names with the suffix -cia, such as Ewcia, Klarcia, Julcia, or Helcia, are a specifically Polish category, with no parallel in Russian. They are used very widely, and they have a very specific flavour, which can be described roughly as affectionate and patronising. Typically, they are used in speaking to children and young girls, but when they are used for young girls, they tend to be used by mothers and aunts rather than by boyfriends: they don't lend themselves to romantic use at all. For example, in Bolesław Prus' (1890) novel Lalka 'The doll', the beautiful heroine, Izabela, is often called Belcia by her aunts, but it is inconceivable that her ardent admirer, Wokulski, might call her so. Speaking to my twelve-year-old daughter, named Klara, I might use the form Klarcia to issue cheerful instructions but never to comfort her when she is sick or feels unhappy. I also use for her the playful nickname Żabcia (from żaba 'frog'), but again only when in a playful and cheerful mood. It is true that the basic Polish word for grandmother, babcia, also includes the suffix -cia and that in that word -cia doesn't have the value which I am ascribing to it. But babcia is a separate lexical entity. On the other hand, the form wujcio (from wuj 'uncle') does have the value which I am ascribing here to -cia, and so does the form córcia (from córka 'daughter').

To account for the characteristic flavour of names in -*cia*, I would propose for them the following formula:

FORMS IN -*cia* (e.g., *Ewcia*)

[AFFECTION]

  a. I feel something good toward you

[CHILD ORIENTATION]

  a'. of the kind that people feel toward children

[ANTI-RESPECT]

  b. I don't want to show that I feel something good toward you
     of the kind that people show they feel
     toward people whom they don't know well

The 'anti-respect' component which appears in these names is the same as the one we have encountered in the Russian names in -*ka*, such as *Kat'ka;* this time, however, it appears in combination with clearly expressed affection ('I feel something good toward you'). The character of that affection ('of the kind that people feel toward children') links names in -*cia* with those in -*eczka*. The whole combination of affection, child orientation, and 'anti-respect' produces a characteristic non-serious flavour, which can easily be interpreted as patronising, although it can also be perceived as cheerful or playful.

Informants of the older generation (i.e., those who are now in their seventies or eighties) tend to see several names in -*cia* (e.g., *Karolcia, Julcia,* or *Mańcia*) as typical of the social position of *służąca* 'housemaid' in pre-war Poland. This is understandable, in view of the combination of affection and lack of respect encoded in such names. Other names in -*cia*, however (e.g., *Ewcia* or *Belcia*), although also patronising, don't sound as 'housemaid-like', because the base names *Ewa* and *Izabela* have quite different social connotations.[3]

I would add that -*cia* does have a masculine counterpart -*cio*, e.g., *Romcio, Tomcio*. These masculine forms are not nearly as common as the feminine forms in -*cia*, but they do exist, and they have the same flavour. For example, in the Polish version of the fairy tale about Tom Thumb the little hero is called *Tomcio Paluch* 'Tomcio Thumb'; in a children's poem by Julian Tuwim (1955–64, v.2:315), a lap-dog is called *Dżoncio* (from the Polish rendering of the English name John, plus the suffix -*cio*); and so on.

3.3.4 Forms with the Suffixes -usia *and* -uś

For many masculine names, the most common form used in reference or address to children is a form with the suffix -*uś*, e.g., *Maciej* > *Maciuś*, *Piotr* > *Piotruś*, *Jakub* > *Kubuś, Jacek* > *Jacuś*. Functionally, these forms in -*uś* often seem more or less equivalent to those in -*ś*, such as *Jaś* (from *Jan*), *Michaś* (from *Michał*), or *Antoś* (from *Antoni*), in the sense that if a couple have two small sons, named *Jan* and *Wojciech*, they will probably call them in everyday usage *Jaś* and *Wojtuś*, and if the small boys' names are *Antoni* and *Maciej*, they will probably call them in everyday usage *Antoś* and *Maciuś*. However, as the boys get older, the chances are that *Maciuś* and *Wojtuś* will become *Maciek* and *Wojtek* some time before *Jaś* and *Antoś* become *Janek* and *Antek*. The point is that if masculine names in *-ś* such as *Jaś* or *Antoś* are child- and boy-oriented, the names in *-uś* such as *Maciuś*, *Wojtuś*, *Kubuś*, or *Jędruś* are simply child-oriented: they have a nice kindergarten flavour about them.

The same atmosphere also surrounds feminine names in *-usia*, such as *Hanusia*, *Magdusia*, *Martusia*, *Klarusia*, or *Ewusia* (not *Danusia*, from *Danuta*, which has the suffix *-sia*, not *-usia*).

Being both affectionate and child-oriented, names in *-uś* and *-usia* may well seem to be similar in value to names in *-eczka* and in *-eczek*. And yet there is a difference in flavour, which is highlighted by the existence of some forms in *-uś* or *-usia* outside the area of personal names. Words such as *dzidziuś* 'baby', *kiciuś* 'kitten', *kaczusia* 'baby duck', *Żabusia-Skaczusia* (a character from a fairy tale, from *żaba* 'frog' and *skacze* 'jump'), or *trusie* 'rabbits' all point in the same direction: they all designate nice, cute, adorable creatures. In Gabriela Zapolska's (1950) short story entitled (ironically) *Żabusia* (from *żaba* 'frog') the heroine is a brainless pretty young woman, nicknamed by her adoring and trusting husband *Żabusia;* the name expresses the loving husband's view of his wife as small, cute, and adorable. In a well-known nursery song the suffix *-usia* is added to the adjective *mała* 'small' (*malusia*) and to the adverb *dokoła* 'around' (*dokolusia*) to evoke a similar impression:

> Ta Dorotka ta malusia ta malusia
> tańcowała dokolusia dokolusia. . . .

> 'That Dotty, that tiny one, tiny one,
> danced away all around all around. . . .'

In the final stanza of this nursery song, the words for 'pillow', *poduszka*, and 'cradle', *kolebka*, also receive a form in *-usia:*

> A teraz śpi w kolebusi, w kolebusi
> Na różowej, na podusi, na podusi.

> 'And now she sleeps in her little cradle, little cradle,
> on her pink little pillow, little pillow.'

Normally, inanimate nouns don't take the suffix *-usia,* but in a lullaby *podusia* ('pillow' + *-usia*) and *kolebusia* ('cradle' + *-usia*) sound just right. As far as I know, the only two other inanimate nouns which are used with *-usia* are *kawa* 'coffee' and *chleb* 'bread': the forms *kawusia* and *chlebuś* suggest appetising, fragrant, 'lovable' coffee and bread.

Family terms such as *córusia* 'daughter' and *synuś* 'son' have a similar ring. Even *dziadziuś* (from *dziadek* 'grandfather') suggests a lovable little old man, and *matusia* (from *matka* 'mother') suggests a poor sweet little woman, as in the popular Christmas carol:

> Jezus malusieńki
> Leży śród stajenki
> Płacze z zimna, nie dała mu
> Matusia sukienki. . . .

> 'The tiny Jesus
> Is lying in a little stable,
> He's crying from cold,
> For his *matusia* (mother) had no clothes for him'

(The two other family terms with *-uś, mamusia* and *tatuś,* 'mummy' and 'daddy', don't have the flavour which I am attributing here to names with the suffix *-uś/-usia* and should, I think, be treated as separate lexical items.)

All these facts point clearly in the same direction: *-uś* and *-usia* evoke lovable delightful small creatures. Significantly, the only two adjectives which can take this suffix seem to be *mały* 'small' (*malusi*) and *miły* 'nice' (*milusi*). The derived forms *malusi* (feminine *malusia*) and *milusi* (feminine *milusia*) can be glossed as 'tiny' and 'cute'. Other adjectives (and adverbs) can take the suffix *-uś* only in combination with the suffix *-eńk* (e.g., *cichusieńki* from *cichy* 'quiet'; *bielusieńki* from *biały* 'white'; *leciusieńki,* from *lekki* 'light in weight'; *jaśniusieńki* from *jasny* 'light in colour'). The range of these adjectives, however, is also restricted to qualities perceived as nice and as 'small'. For example, one cannot coin forms such as **głośniusieńki* (from *głośny* 'loud'), **ciemniusieńki* (from *ciemny* 'dark'), or even **czerwoniusieńki* (from *czerwony* 'red'). All these facts suggest that an explication along the following lines may be suitable for names in *-usia* or *-uś:*

> FORMS IN *-usia* OR *-uś* (e.g., *Martusia, Wojtuś*)
> I feel something good toward you
>   of the kind that people feel toward children
> I imagine that looking at you, people feel something good

3.3.5 *Forms with the Suffix* -unia *(-*unio*)*

The difference between names in *-usia* such as *Martusia* and *Klarusia* and those in *-unia* such as *Martunia* and *Klarunia* may seem to be purely stylistic and sociolectal, as the choice seems to depend largely on the speaker's generation. It appears that in pre-war literary Polish *-uś* was used in masculine names (*Jędruś, Maciuś, Piotruś*), whereas feminine names normally took *-unia* rather than *-usia* (*Ewunia, Martunia, Klarunia*). Feminine names in *-usia* such as *Jagusia* and *Hanusia* had a dialectal, peasant-style flavour. Significantly, the main heroine of Władysław Reymont's (1949) highly popular novel *Chłopi* 'The peasants', an attractive peasant girl, was called *Jagusia*. But after the war, feminine forms in *-usia* became fashionable in literary Polish; they replaced to a large extent forms in *-unia* and started to be used as widely as masculine forms in *-uś*.

In my view, however, this apparent competition between *-unia* and *-usia* (and the increasing popularity of *-usia*) doesn't mean at all that the two suffixes were, and are, semantically equivalent. On the contrary, the growing success of *-usia* and the decline of *-unia* were due, I think, to the subtle semantic differences between the two suffixes. What became fashionable after the war was not just a certain combination of sounds but a certain style of parent-child interaction, and this new style of interaction was better served by *-usia* than by *-unia*.

An important clue to the specific semantic flavour of the suffix *-unia* is offered by the affectionate family terms, such as *babunia* and *dziadunio* (from *babka* 'grandmother' and *dziadek* 'grandfather'). In the case of grandmother, a form in *-usia* doesn't exist at all; in the case of grandfather, a form in *-uś* does exist (*dziadziuś*) but has an entirely different flavour than *dziadunio*. Another minimal pair is *córunia* and *córusia* (from *córka* 'daughter'); again, both these forms are affectionate but have different flavour.

In my view, *babunia* and *dziadunio* evoke the image of frail old people. Strong, healthy, active grandmothers or grandfathers in their fifties or early sixties can be called *babcia* or *dziadek,* but it is inconceivable that they should be called *babunia* and *dziadunio* (except jocularly). *Ciotunia* (from *ciotka* 'aunt'), too, suggests a frail elderly aunt rather than a vigorous young auntie. *Córunia* 'daughter' can of course refer to someone very young, but it doesn't have the cheerful and exhilarating ring of *córusia*.

What I am trying to suggest is that forms in *-unia* link affection with the perception of a loved person as someone rather frail. If a prototypical *Jagusia* is a strong, healthy, attractive peasant girl, eager to laugh and dance, a prototypical *Martunia* or *Helunia* is a delicate girl from a non-peasant family, young and loved by the speaker but rather frail and in this respect not unlike an old *babunia* or *dziadunio*. (It seems inconceivable that in a fairy tale a merry jumping frog could be called "*Żabunia Skaczunia*" rather than *Żabusia Skaczusia*.)

The value of forms in *-unia* (in contrast to other affectionate diminutives) is epitomised in the following little poem by Kazimiera Iłłakowiczówna:

Babunia

Babunia jest taka chudziutka.
Babunia siedzi w ogródku.
Czepek ma czarny, a chustkę białą.
Zimno jej w ręce, nogi ma skostniałe.
Marcia i Janek, Janka i Jadwisia
są przy Babuni łagodni i cisi.
Tato głos zniża, donośny i gruby,
stąpa na palcach ogromny wuj Kuba.
Krzykliwa ciocia Ewcia tylko Babci słucha. . . .
Bo wszyscy sie boją. . . .
Bo Babunia taka krucha.

(1980:107)

'Granny

Granny is so tiny.
Granny sits in the garden.
She has a black hat and a white scarf.
Her hands are cold, her legs are numb.

Marty and Johnny, Janie and Winnie
Are quiet and gentle with Granny.
Daddy lowers his rough loud voice,
Uncle Jake steals about on tiptoe.
Raucous Auntie Evie listens only to Grandma. . . .
Because they're all afraid. . . .
Because Granny's so frail.'

Trying to capture this peculiar flavour of names in *-unia*, I propose for them the following semantic formula:

FORMS IN *-unia* (e.g., *Ewunia*)
I feel something good toward you
   of the kind that people feel toward small children
   and toward old people (to whom bad things could happen)

3.3.6 Forms with the Suffixes -ulka or -ulek

Names in *-ulka* (*-ulek*) such as *Basiulka, Asiulka, Marysiulka,* or *Stefulek* are clearly child-oriented, but in contrast to other child-oriented names they are also slightly jocular. I would suggest that this slightly jocular character is based on an attempted 'reification' of the addressee, who is perceived not only as a child but also as a 'small thing'. For this reason, forms in *-ulka* seem incompatible with an overt show of respect. Hence the following contrasts in the acceptability of forms of address (vocative case):

Panno Zosiu!	Panie Jasiu!
Panno Zosieńko!	*Panie Jasieńku!
Panno Haneczko!	(?)Panie Jureczku!
Panno Ewuniu!	?Panie Stefuniu!
Panno Jagusiu!	(?)Panie Piotrusiu!
?Panno Basiulko!	??Panie Stefulku!

Generally speaking, the title *panna* 'Miss' is fairly easy to combine with child-oriented names, certainly easier than *pan* 'Mr' or *pani* 'Mrs', but not even *panna* can combine with forms in *-ulka*.

Family terms such as *córulka* ('daughter') or *babulka* ('grandmother') have the same flavour as names with these suffixes. There are also a handful of other words in *-ulka*, in particular *biedulka* 'poor little thing' (from *biedna* 'poor', feminine) and *czarnulka* 'pretty little dark-haired thing' (from *czarna* 'black', feminine). The two masculine words in *-ulek* which come to mind are *mężulek* (from *mąż* 'husband') and *księżulek* (from *ksiądz* 'priest'). Both these words are jocular or ironic, and they seem to suggest that the speaker perceives the person in question as a non-serious 'small thing'.

FORMS IN *-ulka* OR *-ulek* (e.g., *Basiulka, Stefulek*)
I feel something good toward you
    of the kind that people feel toward small children
I feel something good speaking to you
I want to speak to you as if you were a small thing

3.3.7 Affectionate 'Distortion': Names in -ik, -usik, and -ątko

Feminine names in *-ik* appear to be used in Polish in exactly the same way as
feminine names in *-ik* are used in Russian: they have the same air of jocular and
loving distortion, and they are similarly restricted to close, intimate, asymmetrical
relations such as those between parents and their daughters. In Polish, too, the
expressive 'distortion' goes so far that the name in *-ik* becomes masculine not only
in its inflectional type but also in its agreement pattern. For example:

> Kazik się przestraszył.
>
> 'Kazik (boy's name) got frightened (Masc.).'
>
> Marysia się przestraszyła.
>
> 'Mary (girl's name) got frightened (Fem.).'
>
> Marysik się przestraszył.
>
> 'Mary + *-ik* got frightened (Masc.).'

The remarkable thing is that in Polish, unlike Russian, masculine names in *-ik* are
not at all common and some of them, e.g., *Tadzik,* are small-boy-oriented. It seems
possible that it is the common noun *chłopczyk* 'small boy' which acts here as a
model, rather than, or in addition to, boyish names in *-ik.*
   The formula for feminine names in *-ik* is the same as that assigned to Russian
feminine names in *-ik.*

FEMININE NAMES, FORMS IN *-ik* (e.g., *Marysik*)
I feel something good toward you
I feel something good speaking to you
I don't want to speak to you the way other people speak to you
I want to speak to you as if you were a small boy, not a girl

   The suffix *-usik* represents a combination of *-usia* (e.g., *Martusia*) and *-ik* (e.g.,
Marysik). It is loving, jocular, playful, and very tender, more tender and caressing
than *-ik* alone. The *-ik* element contributes the loving playfulness ('I want to speak
to you as if you were a small boy, not a girl', 'I feel something good speaking to
you'), and the *-usia* implies that the target person is viewed as a delightful child.
Since not all names have forms in *-usia,* and *-usik* is based on *-usia,* not all names
can have forms in *-usik,* but in those cases where a form in *-usik* exists, its value
seems to combine that of *-usia* and that of *-ik:*

FEMININE NAMES IN -*usik* (e.g., *Martusik*)
I feel something good toward you of the kind that people feel toward children
I imagine that looking at you/speaking to you people feel something good
I feel something good speaking to you
I don't want to speak to you the way other people speak to you
I want to speak to you as if you were a small boy, not a girl

Names in -*ątko* such as *Jasiątko* or *Marysiątko* are used in Polish in a way similar to Russian names in -*ënok*. Outside the area of personal names the suffix -*ątko* is used to denote baby animals:

kot 'cat'	>	*kociątko* 'kitten'
cielę 'calf'	>	*cielątko* 'baby calf'
osioł 'donkey'	>	*oślątko* 'baby donkey'

Nouns in -*ątko* are neuter in gender, and the transposition of a feminine or masculine noun into a neuter derivate in -*ątko* highlights the jocular and affectionate effect due to the semantics of the suffix. Names of this kind are clearly aimed at small children, and they are highly expressive. In my experience, they are usually used in address, not in reference, being even more restricted in this respect than feminine names in -*ik*.

NAMES IN -*ątko* (e.g., *Jasiątko, Marysiątko*)
I feel something good toward you
  of the kind that people feel toward baby animals
I feel something good speaking to you
I want to speak to you as if you were a baby animal, not a child

3.3.8 Summary of Polish Expressive Suffixes

FORMS IN -*eńk(a)* (e.g., *Zosieńka*)
I feel something good toward you
  of the kind that people feel toward girls, women, and children
I feel something good speaking to you

FORMS IN -*eczka* (e.g., *Haneczka*)
I feel something good toward you
  of the kind that people feel toward children

FORMS IN -*cia* (e.g., *Ewcia*)
I feel something good toward you
  of the kind that people feel toward children
I don't want to show that I feel something good toward you
  of the kind that people show they feel toward people whom they don't know

FORMS IN -*usia* OR -*uś* (e.g., *Martusia, Wojtuś*)

I feel something good toward you
   of the kind that people feel toward children
I imagine that looking at you people feel something good

FORMS IN -*unia* (e.g., *Ewunia*)

I feel something good toward you
   of the kind that people feel toward small children and toward old people
   (to whom bad things could happen)

FORMS IN -*ulka* OR -*ulek* (e.g., *Basiulka, Stefulek*)

I feel something good toward you
   of the kind that people feel toward small children
I feel something good speaking to you
I want to speak to you as if you were a small thing

FEMININE NAMES, FORMS IN -*ik* (e.g., *Marysik*)

I feel something good toward you
I feel something good speaking to you
I don't want to speak to you the way other people speak to you
I want to speak to you as if you were a small boy, not a girl

FEMININE NAMES, FORMS IN -*usik* (e.g., *Martusik*)

I feel something good toward you
   of the kind that people feel toward children
I imagine that looking at you/speaking to you people feel something good
I feel something good speaking to you
I don't want to speak to you the way other people speak to you
I want to speak to you as if you were a small boy, not a girl

FORMS IN -*ątko* (e.g., *Jasiątko, Marysiątko*)

I feel something good toward you
   of the kind that people feel toward baby animals
I feel something good speaking to you
I want to speak to you as if you were a baby animal, not a child

3.4 'Augmentative' Forms

In Polish, augmentative forms of names are usually formed with the help of the suffix -*ch* (a voiceless velar fricative). Among those forms which employ this suffix for purposes which can be roughly called 'augmentative', at least three different types should, I think, be distinguished. I will discuss these in three separate subsections of the present section (3.4.1, 3.4.2, and 3.4.3). In combination with other suffixes, -*ch* can also have, or appear to have, other functions. These other uses will be discussed in sections 3.4.4 and 3.4.5.

3.4.1 Forms in -ch

Most of the expressive categories discussed so far were child-centred, some were centred on women and girls, and a few others were oriented toward small boys, baby animals, and frail human creatures, either very young or very old. But Polish also has expressive categories of a different kind, categories which link affection with strength, robustness, and masculinity. The most important category of this kind is illustrated by masculine names such as *Stach, Krzych,* or *Zdzich,* formed by truncation from marked full names such as *Stanisław, Krzysztof,* and *Zdzisław.*

Outside the area of personal names, the 'augmentative' suffix *-ch* (derived from the underlying consonant *s* or *š* (in the orthography *sz*)) can take the place of the suffix, or pseudo-suffix, *-k,* as in the following examples. (The element *-k* suggests something like smallness, even in those cases where there is no corresponding word without *-k.*)

kluski	=	noodles
*klusy		
kluchy	=	big noodles (pejorative or jocular word)
misa	=	a big bowl
miska	=	bowl
micha	=	a huge bowl (especially with reference to the contents, as in *micha klusek,* or *micha kluch,* a huge bowl of noodles)

In the case of masculine names, too, a form in *-ch* can be formed only if the base contains, after the first syllable, *s* or *š* (and even then, not always):

Leszek	>	*Lech*
Zbyszek	>	*Zbych*
Krzysztof	>	*Krzych*
Zdzisław	>	*Zdzich*
Stanisław	>	*Stach*
Jan	>	**Jach*
Adam	>	**Adach*

Inanimate nouns in *-ch* often have coarse, almost vulgar connotations, e.g., *flacha* (from *flaszka* 'bottle'), *mięcho* (from *mięso* 'meat'), or *kichy* (from *kiszki* 'guts'). But in the area of personal names, forms constructed by adding *-ch* to the first syllable of a full masculine name are not coarse at all. The most refined and lady-like woman can call a man *Stach* or *Krzych* to convey her admiration for his manly qualities. For example, in Henryk Sienkiewicz's (1949) novel *The Połaniecki family,* the dainty little heroine, a sickly, delicate young girl, usually calls the protective adult hero, the strong and manly Stanisław Połaniecki, *"Pan Stach"*, 'Mr. Stach'.

To portray this kind of attitude, I propose the following semantic formula:

FORMS IN -*ch* (e.g., *Stach*)
I feel something good toward you
  of the kind that people feel toward men and don't feel toward children

In the life of many Polish boys, the moment when they change from being a *Staś*, a *Zdziś*, or a *Krzyś* to being a *Stach*, or *Zdzich*, or *Krzych* plays the role of an important 'rite of passage'. Naturally, many boys remain a *Staś*, a *Krzyś*, or a *Zdziś* in their mother's or grandmother's speech long after they have become a *Stach*, a *Krzych*, or a *Zdzich* in the speech of others, particularly that of their peers.

The serious, 'augmentative', and yet affectionate flavour of names in -*ch* makes them similar, to some extent, to Russian names in -*uša*, such as *Katjuša, Tanjuša*, or *Il'juša*. The two categories differ, however, in one important respect: the Russian names in -*úša* are not sex-differentiated, whereas the Polish names in -*ch* are masculine. This is yet another manifestation of the general difference between the two systems of names, which we have noted earlier: the Polish system is much more sex-differentiated than the Russian one; that is, in the Polish system, attitudes toward women and girls tend to be different from those toward boys and men. In particular, the combination of affection with a 'strong, big, grown-up' flavour occurs in Polish only in the context of masculinity.

In support of the analysis of Polish names in -*ch* proposed here I will mention the fact that the use of the suffix -*ch* has spilled over to one family term: *brachu*. *Brachu* (in current use largely replaced by *stary* 'old') is a vocative of an unattested *brach*, an expressive substitute for *brat* 'brother'. SJP (1958–69) glosses the form *brachu* as "poufała rubaszna", 'familiar and coarse/jovial'. Since in the word *brat* there is no *s* or *š*, the form *brachu* must be due to the pressure of names such as *Stach* or *Lech*, in the vocative *Stachu* and *Lechu*. The form *brachu* implies affection, robustness, and masculinity, adding to them, however, coarseness, which is not present in the personal names themselves.

3.4.2 Forms in -cho *or* -chu

Although names in -*ch* convey a certain admiration for robust masculinity, they do not seem to be any more likely to be used by males than by females. In fact, the opposite seems to be true. Two slightly 'tougher' (but still positive) alternatives to names in -*ch* are provided by forms with a word-final -*o* or -*u*, e.g., *Krzycho* or *Krzychu*. The Solidarity leader Lech Wałęsa was normally referred to by the workers in Gdańsk as *Lechu*, and the value of this form *Lechu* seems to correspond to that of *Krzychu* or *Stachu*, even though in Wałęsa's case *Lech* is not an expressive derivate but a full first name.

Forms in -*u*, however, are characteristic of workers' speech rather than of literary Polish. On the other hand, forms in -*o* such as *Krzycho*, though highly colloquial, can also be heard in the speech of the intelligentsia. What they add to the expressive value of forms such as *Krzych* or *Stach* is a component which I have called 'anti-respect':

MASCULINE NAMES IN -*cho* (e.g., *Krzycho, Zdzicho*)

I feel something good toward you
  of the kind that people feel toward men and don't feel toward children
I don't want to show that I feel something good toward you
  of the kind that people show they feel toward people whom they don't know
  well

As far as I can see, forms in -*chu* such as *Lechu* or *Stachu* convey the same, or a very similar, attitude. It should be mentioned, however, that the same sociolect which has forms such as *Lechu* or *Stachu* also has other forms in -*u*, such as *Jasiu*, *Stasiu*, or *Heniu*. In literary Polish, such forms occur only in the vocative case, whereas the nominative uses a zero ending or a word-final -*o: Jaś, Staś, Henio*. The spread of the vocative form into the nominative position seems to fit in very well with the greater intimacy and expressivity of forms in -*u*. But the precise semantics of such forms, and also of the forms in -*chu*, requires further investigation.

3.4.3 Forms in -cha

Feminine names in -*cha*, such as *Marycha, Małgocha,* or *Krycha,* are superficially similar to masculine names in -*ch,* such as *Krzych* or *Stach.* Functionally, however, the two categories are different. Feminine names in -*cha* don't have the positive character of the masculine forms in -*ch* and unlike the masculine forms tend to sound coarse, although they are not incompatible with friendliness and affection. They appear to be used most widely among teenagers, eager to establish a rough and anti-sentimental style of relations in a peer group.

The difference in semantic value between the two categories may be due to the fact that despite the superficial similarity, two different morphological processes are in fact involved.

In masculine names, the 'augmentative' suffix -*ch* replaces a meaningless sound (*s* or *š*) and in some cases an emotionally neutral suffix (or pseudo-suffix) -*ek*. But in feminine names, the augmentative suffix -*cha* replaces a warm and feminine suffix -*sia* (regardless of whether or not there is a *s* or *š* in the base); as a result, feminine forms in -*cha* are felt to be ostentatiously non-warm and non-feminine (because they represent a rejection of warmth and femininity).

Zofia	>	*Zosia*	>	*Zocha*
Małgorzata	>	*Małgosia*	>	*Małgocha*
Katarzyna	>	*Kasia*	>	*Kacha*
Kazimiera	>	*Kazia*	>	**Kacha*
Anna	>	*Ania*	>	**Acha*

It is important to stress that masculine forms in -*ch* do not depend on the existence of corresponding forms in -*š* and therefore that the masculine -*ch* cannot be seen as a replacement of the affectionate suffix -*š*. Consider, for example, the following contrasts:

Stanisław	—	Staś	—	Stach
Zdzisław	—	Zdziś	—	Zdzich
Kryzsztof	—	Krzyś	—	Krzych
Leszek	—	*Leś	—	Lech
Zbyszek	—	?Zbyś	—	Zbych (full name Zbigniew)
Jan	—	Jaś	—	*Jach
Adam	—	Adaś	—	*Adach

As these examples show, what is needed for a form in -*ch* is not the existence of a form in -*ś* but the presence of a *s* or *š* (*sz*) in the base. But the feminine names in -*cha*, such as *Marycha*, do depend on the existence of a corresponding form in -*sia*, and therefore -*cha* can be felt to be a replacement of the warm and feminine -*sia*.

Needless to say, these 'anti-warm', 'anti-feminine' names are in fact perfectly compatible with rough, 'tough', teenager-style affection. They do not imply, 'I feel something bad toward you' or 'I don't feel anything good toward you'. Rather, they imply, 'I don't want to show that I feel something good toward you', and more specifically:

a. I don't want to show that I feel something good toward you
   of the kind that people show they feel toward women and girls
b. I don't want to show that I feel something good toward you
   of the kind that people show they feel toward people whom they don't know
   well

The second of these components has been labelled 'anti-respect', and the first one can be labelled 'anti-femininity'. Consequently, the relationship between feminine names in -*sia* (section 3.2) and feminine names in -*cha* can be presented in terms of a denial:

Małgosia, Basia

I want to speak to you the way people speak
   to girls and women whom they know well
   and toward whom they feel something good, and to children

Małgocha, Bacha

I want to speak to you the way people speak
   to people whom they know well
I feel something toward you
I don't want to show that I feel something good toward you
   of the kind that people show they feel toward girls and women
I don't want to show that I feel something good toward you
   of the kind that people show they feel toward people whom they don't know
   well

The combination of an emotional component ('I feel something toward you') with a clear refusal to express either polite respect or any good feelings of the kind traditionally shown to women and girls gives these forms a rough and coarse character. One possible inference is that the speaker actually feels something bad toward the addressee, but an equally plausible inference is that the speaker feels something good, though not of the gentle kind traditionally associated with female addressees and certainly not of the respectful kind associated with formal relationships.

In support of the distinction which I have drawn here between feminine names in -*cha* such as *Bacha* or *Małgocha* and masculine forms in -*ch* such as *Stach* or *Zdzich* I will point out the following contrast in acceptability:

Panie Stachu!	*Panie Zdzichu!*	(Vocative)
*Pani Bacho!	**Pani Małgocho!*	(Vocative)

The feminine forms in -*cha* cannot be combined with the polite respectful title *pani* because they imply anti-respect, but masculine forms in -*ch* don't imply anti-respect, and so they can be combined with the polite respectful title *pan*.

Admittedly, individual names may differ somewhat from one another in this respect, presumably depending on their past history and social spread. For example, the form *Zocha* (from *Zofia*) is much more common than *Bacha* (from *Barbara*) and doesn't seem so 'rough'. Consequently, the combination *pani Zocha* seems much more acceptable than *pani Bacha*. Similarly, *Stach* is more common than *Zdzich*, and *pan Stach* is more common than *pan Zdzich*. But individual differences of this kind—which are usually a matter of degree—do not cancel the reality of the categorial differences in question.

It is interesting to compare feminine names in -*cha*, such as *Marycha*, with feminine names in -*ka*, such as *Janka* or *Hanka*, which were discussed in section 3.2 and which were also called non-sentimental. The crucial difference is that forms in -*ka* such as *Janka* or *Hanka* have no emotional component at all, whereas forms in -*cha* are highly emotional. *Janka* and *Hanka* convey familiarity and a wish not to sound sentimental. By contrast, *Marycha* and *Małgocha* convey an emotion, and they ostentatiously qualify this emotion as being of an anti-sentimental, anti-feminine, and anti-respectful kind. As a result, *Marycha* and *Małgocha* are expressive and rough (if not coarse), whereas *Janka* and *Hanka* are merely cool and composed.

It should be added that Polish also has two or three feminine names in -*cha* whose value is not rough and coarse but 'augmentative' in the way *Stach* and *Zdzich* are augmentative. These are feminine names derived from the corresponding masculine names:

Stanisław (Masc.)	—	*Stanisława* (Fem.)
Zdzisław (Masc.)	—	*Zdzisława* (Fem.)
Stach	—	*Stacha*
Zdzich	—	*Zdzicha*

The forms *Stacha* and *Zdzicha* convey the same robust and 'masculine' affection which is associated with masculine names such as *Stach* and *Zdzich* but which is felt to be even more 'robust and masculine' when addressed to a girl or a woman:

I feel something good toward you
of the kind that people feel toward men and don't feel toward children

3.4.4 Forms in -ucha, -uch

Forms in *-ucha* or *-uch* are highly expressive, and they are similar, both formally and semantically, to forms in *-cha,* such as *Małgocha* or *Bacha*. They are rough and anti-sentimental, anti-respectful, and intimate. But unlike the names in *-cha,* they clearly imply, or pretend to imply, something bad.

Outside the area of personal names, the suffix *-ucha* is pejorative in Polish. It has a clearly pejorative character in three crucial human nouns: *dziewucha* 'girl', *starucha* 'old woman', and *staruch* 'old man':

dziewczyna	—	girl (neutral, unmarked)
dziewuszka	—	nice young girl (positive and 'diminutive')
dziewucha	—	girl (probably peasant, coarse and augmentative)
staruszka	—	old woman (unmarked, but with positive and diminutive connotations)
starucha	—	old woman (seen as someone big and rather repulsive, coarse and augmentative)
staruszek	—	old man (unmarked, but with positive and diminutive connotations)
starzec	—	old man (marked: someone looking noble, grand, impressive)
staruch	—	old man (seen as someone big and rather repulsive, coarse and augmentative)

In personal names, too, the suffix *-uch* (*-ucha*) sounds coarse and pejorative. It implies that the person spoken to, or spoken of, is seen in a negative light and that the speaker's feelings toward that person are negative, too. For example, in Henryk Sienkiewicz's novel *Pan Wołodyjowski,* a tyrannical old father, who treats his daughter, Ewa, with hostility and contempt, frequently calls her *Ewucha,* a form which sums up his attitude to her:

Gdy syn uciekł, ów wyręczał mnie w gospodarstwie, póki mu się amorów z Ewuchą nie zachciało, co ja spostrzegłszy kazałem go wychłostać. (1950, v.2:98)

'When my son ran away, this one helped me in management until he wished to make love to Eva [lit., to Ewucha, to that good-for-nothing Eva]; seeing this, I had him flogged.' (1897:239)

The following formula can be proposed for personal names in *-ucha:*

FORMS IN *-ucha* (e.g., *Ewucha*)
I want to speak to you the way people speak
    to people whom they know well
I feel something bad toward you
I think something bad about you

I don't want to show that I feel something good toward you
  of the kind that people show they feel toward women and girls
I don't want to show that I feel something good toward you
  of the kind that people show they feel toward people whom they don't know
  well

The combination of overtly expressed bad feelings and bad thoughts with an 'anti-feminine' component and a component of 'anti-respect' makes such forms sound unambiguously contemptuous and coarse. They can, nonetheless, also be used in a loving and tender way on the basis of an expressive reversal. If the speaker clearly conveys 'good feelings' toward the addressee, then the component of 'bad feelings' encoded in the form in *-ucha* acts as a signal that a reverse meaning is intended. This is neither polysemy nor vagueness but a conscious expressive device, which is not linked in any special way to names in *-ucha*.

3.4.5 *Forms in* -chna *and* -uchna

Forms in *-chna*, such as *Marychna, Zochna, Kachna*, or *Joachna*, are very affectionate in Polish. Unlike forms in *-ucha*, they do not pretend to be coarse and pejorative. Rather, they sound cheerful and feminine.

But if so, why do they have the augmentative suffix or pseudo-suffix *-ch?* Is it arbitrary and unmotivated, from a synchronic point of view?

I do not think it is, because forms such as *Zochna* and *Kachna* convey affection and even delight, while denying that these feelings are in any way child-oriented. A two-year-old girl named *Zofia* would commonly be called by her family *Zosieńka* or *Zosiunia*, but probably not *Zochna*. The form *Zochna* or *Marychna* suggests a young woman rather than a child. A speaker who calls someone *Zochna* or *Marychna* is definitely conveying 'good feelings' toward her, but not of the kind associated with children. Rather, they are good feelings of a kind that people feel toward a girl who is no longer a child, especially if she is nice and attractive.

These observations lead us to the following semantic formula:

FORMS IN *-chna*

I feel something good toward you
  of the kind that people feel toward girls and women
  not of the kind that people feel toward children
I feel something good speaking to you
I imagine that looking at you/speaking to you
  people feel something good

I think it is this combination of a feminine prototype with the explicit denial of a child prototype which gives forms in *-chna* their cheerful character. If the speaker merely denied a child orientation, this could imply roughness. If both women and children were included in the prototype, this might suggest a soft, lyrical flavour (as in forms in *-eńka*). But if the prototype includes women and especially girls, while excluding children, this precludes both a soft and sentimental flavour and a rough, masculine flavour. The effect is feminine but rather cheerful and spirited at the same time. In folk poetry and folksongs, a girl called *Kasieńka* would often pine after an absent lover or mourn a dead one, but a girl called *Kachna* is more likely to be getting ready to dance.

The feminine orientation of names in *-chna* also manifests itself in the fact that they have no masculine equivalents: there are no masculine names parallel to *Zochna, Kachna,* or *Marychna.*

By and large, the same holds for names in *-uchna*, such as *Anuchna, Martuchna,* or *Ewuchna,* although these have a twist of their own, which is due to their formal relationship with forms in *-usia* and also with forms in *-ucha.* I will not discuss this special twist here. I will mention, however, that if some boys or men can sometimes be called, very tenderly, *Piotruchna* or *Januchna,* this is clearly done by an expressive reversal, playing on the feminine form of the suffix.

The idea that names in *-chna* may suggest someone attractive, someone nice to look at and to talk to (as well as someone for whom the speaker personally feels something good), derives some support from adjectival forms in *-uchny* (fem. *-uchna*). For example, when Mickiewicz (1955, v.1:120–25) in his ballad "Rybka", 'The mermaid', describes a mermaid as having a *szyjka cieniuchna,* a 'thin little neck', with a diminutive suffix *-ka* on the word for 'neck' and with an adjective in *-uchna,* he clearly intends to evoke a pretty picture, not a pitiful one. Similarly, when he says in "Pan Tadeusz" (1955, v.4) that the heroine, *Zosia,* is a *młodziuchną, prześliczną dziewczyną* 'lovely young girl', he clearly intends to add charm to the picture by adding the suffix *-uchna* to the word for 'young'.

It is instructive to compare, from this point of view, two adjectives, *mały* ('small', used of children) and *młody* ('young', used only of young people who are no longer children):

> *mała* — *malusia* (as in "ta Dorotka, ta malusia")
> *młoda* — *młodziuchna* — **młodziusia*

Both *-usia* and *-uchna* suggest that the target is delightful. But as I have argued earlier, speaking of names in *-usia, -usia* evokes a delightful child, whereas by contrast, *-uchna* suggests a charm of a different kind—perhaps the charm of a young girl rather than that of a child.

For example, of the two affectionate words for 'auntie', *ciotuchna* and *ciotunia,* *ciotuchna* sounds younger and more charming than *ciotunia.* If one had two dear aunts, one young and charming and the other old and frail, one would be more likely to call the younger *ciotuchna* and the older *ciotunia* than the other way around. (The third highly affectionate word for 'auntie', *cioteczka,* also sounds young, and somewhat flirtatious, which is understandable given the child orientation of the suffix *-eczka.*)

3.4.6 Summary of Polish 'Augmentative' Names

FORMS IN *-ch* (e.g., *Stach*)
I feel something good toward you
  of the kind that people feel toward men
  and don't feel toward children

FORMS IN *-cho* (e.g., *Krzycho, Zdzicho*)

I feel something good toward you
  of the kind that people feel toward men
  and don't feel toward children
I don't want to show that I feel something good toward you
  of the kind that people show they feel
  toward people whom they don't know well

FORMS IN *-cha* (e.g., *Małgocha, Bacha*)

I want to speak to you the way people speak
  to people whom they know well
I feel something toward you
I don't want to show that I feel something good toward you
  of the kind that people show they feel toward girls and women
I don't want to show that I feel something good toward you
  of the kind that people show they feel
  toward people whom they don't know well

MASCULINE-DERIVED FEMININE NAMES, FORMS IN *-cha* (e.g., *Stacha, Zdzicha*)

I feel something good toward you
  of the kind that people feel toward men
  and don't feel toward children

FORMS IN *-ucha* (e.g., *Ewucha*)

I want to speak to you the way people speak
  to people whom they know well
I feel something bad toward you
I think something bad about you
I don't want to show that I feel something good toward you
  of the kind that people show they feel toward women and girls
I don't want to show that I feel something good toward you
  of the kind that people show they feel
  toward people whom they don't know well

FORMS IN *-chna* (e.g., *Zochna*)

I feel something good toward you
  of the kind that people feel toward girls and women
  not of the kind that people feel toward children
I feel something good speaking to you
I imagine that looking at you/speaking to you people feel something good

3.5 Expressive forms in *-ka* and *-ek*

Polish names in *-ka* fall into three semantic categories:

1. Non-expressive names such as *Hanka* or *Janka* (which convey no emotion);
2. Expressive names conveying a positive emotion (e.g., *Dorotka* or *Karolinka*);
3. Expressive names conveying an unspecified emotion (e.g., *Zośka, Baśka*).

Generally speaking, these three semantic categories correspond to distinct morphological types: non-expressive names have a hard stem and are two syllables long, positive expressive names have a hard stem and are more than two syllables long, and unspecified expressive names have a soft stem and any number of syllables. There are a few feminine names in *-ka* which do not seem to fit into this general schema (e.g., *Ewka*), but by and large the three semantic categories do correspond to the three formal ones.

The masculine names in *-ek* fall into similar formal and semantic types:

1. Non-expressive names such as *Janek, Jurek,* or *Antek* (hard stem, two syllables);
2. Expressive names conveying a positive emotion such as *Michałek* or *Andrzejek* (hard stem, more than two syllables);
3. Expressive names conveying an unspecified emotion, such as *Krzysiek, Heniek,* or *Wiesiek* (soft stem, two syllables; in most cases, the final segment is *-siek*).

The non-expressive names in *-ka* and *-ek* have already been discussed (in section 3.2). I will now discuss the expressive forms in *-ka* and *-ek,* first those conveying a positive emotion and then those conveying an unspecified emotion.

3.5.1 Positive Forms in -ka *and* -ek

In Polish, as in Russian, positive names in *-ka* are based on a non-truncated form of a full first name (usually a name ending in *-ota, -ata,* or *-ina*), which doesn't have a soft short form. They are usually three syllables long, but sometimes they can be four syllables long, for example:

Renata	>	*Renatka*
Agata	>	*Agatka*
Dorota	>	*Dorotka*
Beata	>	*Beatka*
Małgorzata	>	*Małgorzatka*
Grażyna	>	*Grażynka*
Sabina	>	*Sabinka*
Karolina	>	*Karolinka*
Teresa	>	*Tereska*

Names of this kind appear to have a similar value to polysyllablic masculine names in *-ek,* which were mentioned earlier (in section 3.2.1). These masculine names are usually derived from unmarked full names, which don't have an unmarked short form, for example:

Michał	>	*Michałek*
Łukasz	>	*Łukaszek*
Rafał	>	*Rafałek*
Andrzej	>	*Andrzejek*

If they are derived from full names which either are marked or do have an unmarked short form, they are felt to be archaic or old-fashioned, for example:

Tomasz > Tomaszek

Tadeusz > Tadeuszek

Polysyllabic names in *-ka* and *-ek* convey affection ('I feel something good toward you'), and they have a 'diminutive' flavour. They are not, however, as child-oriented as the names in *-eczka* or *-eczek* such as *Haneczka* or *Jureczek*, to which I have attributed the component 'I feel something good toward you, of the kind that people feel toward children'. I believe that the slightly 'diminutive' flavour of polysyllabic names in *-ka* and *-ek* can be captured differently, without referring to the precise quality of the 'good feelings':

POLYSYLLABIC FORMS IN *-ka* AND *-ek* (e.g., *Dorotka, Michałek*)
I want to speak to you the way people speak
　to children and to people whom they know well
　and toward whom they feel something good
I feel something good toward you

In speaking to adults, masculine polysyllabic forms in *-ek* are probably less used than feminine polysyllabic names in *-ka,* and forms such as *Rafałek* or *Łukaszek* seem more childish than *Dorotka* or *Agatka,* although much seems to depend on the name itself. For example, *Halinka* seems much less 'childish' than *Karolinka,* presumably because it has been around (as a common name) for much longer. Names which have become popular fairly recently were at first fashionable names for babies, toddlers, and kindergarten children, and presumably they tend to retain this aura for some time, at least for many speakers. I believe, however, that differences of this kind are pragmatic rather than semantic. The only invariant value which can be attributed to polysyllablic forms in *-ka* and *-ek* is that which has been spelt out in the preceding formula.

3.5.2 *Forms in* -ka *Conveying an Unspecified Emotion*

Polish soft-stemmed names in *-ka* such as *Maryśka* or *Zośka* are in many ways similar to Russian names of unspecified emotion such as *Kat'ka* or *Van'ka.* One major formal difference is that the Polish names are sex-differentiated, *-ka* being in Polish only a feminine suffix, but semantically, soft-stemmed feminine names in *-ka* seem to correspond quite closely to masculine soft-stemmed names in *-ek,* such as *Wiesiek* or *Krzysiek.*

As in Russian, names of this kind are often felt to be somewhat rough and even pejorative. But clearly, these pejorative leanings must be of a pragmatic rather than a semantic character, because in an appropriate context, names of this kind can also be interpreted as affectionate. For example, in Sienkiewicz's (1950) novel *Pan Wołodyjowski,* the hero's beloved wife, *Basia* (from *Barbara*), is called *Baśka* by those who love her most: her adoring husband, Wołodyjowski, and her equally adoring 'adoptive father', Zagłoba.

The romantic poet Słowacki dedicated a nostalgic lyrical poem to a girl whom he called *Zośka* ("niechaj mnie Zośka o wiersze nie prosi", 'let Zośka not ask me for poems'), and in this context the form *Zośka* sounds lyrical, not rough, let alone pejorative.

Among teenage girls, forms in *-śka* are often used for the speaker's closest friends, without any pejorative overtones whatsoever, and with a value rather similar to that of names in *-cha,* such as *Zocha* or *Marycha.*

Nonetheless, although an adoring husband, or a romantic poet, can call a woman *Baśka* or *Zośka,* they would be most unlikely to call her *Bacha* or *Zocha.* This suggests that forms in *-ka* such as *Baśka* and *Zośka* are in fact much less rough than forms in *-cha.* The formal differences between the two categories point in the same direction. Both *Zocha* and *Zośka* are felt to be derived from *Zosia,* but whereas in the case of *Zocha,* the semantically 'soft' feminine suffix *-sia* is rejected and replaced with an 'augmentative' suffix *-cha,* in the case of *Zośka,* this 'soft' feminine suffix is retained.

Moreover, the suffix added by forms such as *Zośka* may be anti-sentimental, but it is not augmentative. With a semantically neutral base, it in fact forms a diminutive, and with a semantic base marked for affection and/or for child orientation, it acts as a kind of anti-diminutive:

głowa 'head'	>	*główka* 'little head'
kobieta 'woman'	>	*kobietka* 'little woman'
ciocia 'auntie'	>	*ciotka* 'aunt' (anti-sentimental)
babcia 'grandma'	>	*babka* 'grandmother' (anti-sentimental)
niania 'nanny'	>	*niańka* 'nanny' (anti-sentimental)

As these facts suggest, names in *-ka* such as *Zośka* are anti-sentimental but they are not inherently anti-feminine or inherently 'augmentative', whereas forms in *-cha* are.

Consequently, although the semantic formula of forms in *-ka* such as *Zośka* should include something like 'anti-sentimentality' and 'anti-respect', it should not contain anything like 'anti-femininity'.

I propose the following formula:

FORMS WITH *-ka* ADDED TO A SOFT STEM (e.g., *Zośka*)

[FAMILIARITY]
I want to speak to you the way people speak
  to girls and women whom they know well

[AUGMENTATION]
I don't want to speak to you the way people speak to children

[EXPRESSIVITY]
I feel something toward you

[ANTI-SENTIMENTALITY]
I don't want to show that I feel something good toward you
  of the kind that people show they feel toward children

[ANTI-RESPECT]
I don't want to show that I feel something good toward you
  of the kind that people show they feel toward people whom they don't know well

This formula is almost identical to that which has been posited for Russian names such as *Kát'ka* and *Ván'ka*, but it has one component less: the one which I have labelled as 'roughness' ('I don't want to show that I feel something good toward you'). I may be wrong on this point, but there are indications that the Russian forms are a little 'rougher' than the Polish ones. My Russian informants find it easier to imagine (or to recall) that a man would use masculine names such as *Mit'ka* or *Kol'ka* for his close male friends than to imagine a female name such as *Kat'ka* or *Tan'ka* to be put to a romantic use. The label usually given to such names in Russian linguistic literature ("uničižitel'naja forma", a 'disparaging form') points in the same direction.

Again, different individual forms tend to have different connotations, depending on their past history and on their links with different social strata. For example, *Mańka* (from *Mania*, *Maria*) and *Jadźka* (from *Jadzia*, from *Jadwiga*) tend to be seen as coarse and vulgar, whereas *Zośka* (from *Zosia*, from *Zofia*) and *Baśka* (from *Basia*, from *Barbara*) do not sound coarse at all, and *Maryśka* (from *Marysia*) and *Kaśka* (from *Kasia*, from *Katarzyna*) seem to be occupying an intermediate position between the vulgar *Mańka* and the totally non-vulgar *Zośka*. I believe that individual differences of this kind are also interesting and worth studying but that they don't invalidate the reality of the categorial differences between different classes of names.

3.5.3 Forms in -ek Conveying an Unspecified Emotion

Soft-stemmed masculine names in *-ek* (in most cases, names ending in *-siek*) are similar in value to feminine names in *-ka,* in being expressive and anti-sentimental at the same time. Their derivation is also similar:

Krystyna	>	*Krysia*	>	*Kryśka*
Barbara	>	*Basia*	>	*Baśka*
Jan	>	*Jaś*	>	*Jasiek*
Stanisław	>	*Staś*	>	*Stasiek*

But if it is true that, as I have suggested, there is a subtle difference in value between feminine forms such as *Krysia* or *Basia* and masculine forms such as *Jaś* or *Staś,* one would expect that this difference would carry over to feminine forms such as *Kryśka* and *Zośka* on the one hand and masculine forms such as *Jasiek* and *Stasiek* on the other. According to my observations, this appears to be true. For example, I personally know men who are usually referred to in their wider circle of friends as *Wiesiek, Krzysiek,* and *Stasiek,* but in my experience, if women are referred to as *Baśka, Zośka,* or *Kryśka,* this indicates a considerable degree of intimacy or emotion. This seems to suggest that feminine names of this kind are a little more expressive than their masculine counterparts in *-ek.*

On the other hand, this apparent difference in use may well be due to purely pragmatic reasons: the 'anti-sentimental' character of names in *-ka* and *-ek* may make them appear more marked if used for women simply because 'anti-sentimentality' is less expected in reference and address to women.

Be that as it may, as a first approximation I would propose for soft-stemmed forms in *-ek* a formula which differs from that assigned to soft-stemmed feminine forms in *-ka* in one respect, and in that one respect only—that which distinguishes their respective bases (*Zosia, Basia* vs. *Jaś, Staś*):

MASCULINE FORMS IN *-ek* ADDED TO A SOFT STEM (e.g., *Krzysiek*)

[FAMILIARITY]
I want to speak to you the way people speak to boys whom they know well

[AUGMENTATION]
I don't want to speak to you the way people speak to children

[EXPRESSIVITY]
I feel something toward you

[ANTI-SENTIMENTALITY]
I don't want to show that I feel something toward you
  of the kind that people feel toward children

[ANTI-RESPECT]
I don't want to show that I feel something good toward you
  of the kind that people show they feel toward people
  whom they don't know well

3.6 Forms with the Suffix *-uśka*

Forms in *-uśka* are perhaps more affectionate than any others available in Polish. Like forms in *-eńka*, they have no masculine counterparts except in the vocative:

Zosia	>	*Zosieńka*
Jaś	>	**Jasieniek* (dialectal *Jasieńko*)
		Jasieńku (Voc.)
Martusia	>	*Martuśka*
Piotruś	>	**Piotrusiek*
		Piotruśku (Voc.)

But forms such as *Martuśka* seem to have even more expressive power, and emotional weight, than those in *-eńka*. One is of course tempted to try to account for this particularly loving effect of forms in *-uśka* by deducing it somehow from the combined force of *-usia* and *-ka*, and perhaps this is not impossible. It should nonetheless be stressed that, deducible or not, *-uśka* has a special loving force, which neither *-usia* nor *-ka* has by itself.

It will be recalled that forms in *-usia* have been described as, roughly speaking, affectionate and child-oriented and as implying that the person so called is seen as somehow delightful:

I feel something good toward you
  of the kind that people feel toward children
I imagine that looking at you people feel something good

We have seen that when the suffix *-ka* is used as an operator acting on a 'soft' base, it carries a, so to speak, anti-diminutive and anti-sentimental-force. When *-ka* and *-uś* (*-usia*) are used together, they seem almost to contradict one another:

> I feel something good toward you
> of the kind that people feel toward children
> I don't want to show that I feel something good toward you
> of the kind that people show they feel toward children

But in fact there is no contradiction. A tender feeling is conveyed anyway, and the speaker's avowed effort not to sound sentimental and not to display sentiments usually shown to children rather than adults only reinforces that feeling and makes it sound more serious and more irrepressible.

The 'anti-diminutive' component of *-ka,* too, seems to contribute to that serious and irrepressible lyrical effect. The 'anti-sentimental' *-ka* suggests, 'I don't want to speak to you the way people speak to children', but the 'soft' suffix *-uś* suggests, 'I feel something good toward you, of the kind that people feel toward children'. The combination suggests an intense tenderness, breaking through the barrier of the speaker's wish to avoid 'childish' forms.

As for the 'anti-respect' component of soft-stemmed forms in *-ka,* it can be interpreted either as implying disrespect or as implying closeness and intimacy ('no need to show respect'). But in the context of the semantics of *-uś,* the former (negative) interpretation is out of the question, and consequently, this component can only be taken as implying closeness and intimacy. As a result, this component, too, intensifies the overall positive effect of forms in *-uśka.*

A suitable semantic formula for forms in *-uśka* should, I think, combine the components of forms in *-usia* and of those in *-ka.* I propose the following:

> NAMES IN *-uśka* (e.g., *Martuśka*)
> I feel something good toward you
> of the kind that people feel toward children
> I imagine that looking at you people feel something good
> I don't want to speak to you the way people speak to children
> I don't want to show that I feel something good toward you
> of the kind that people show they feel toward children
> I don't want to show that I feel something good toward you
> of the kind that people show they feel toward people
> whom they don't know well and who are not children

3.6.1 *Summary of Polish Forms in* -ek, -ka, *and* -uška

MASCULINE NAMES, STANDARD FORMS IN *-ek* (hard stem, two syllables; e.g., *Janek, Antek*)

> I want to speak to you the way people speak
> to boys and men whom they know well
> I don't want to speak to you the way people don't speak to children

FEMININE NAMES, FORMS IN -*ka* (hard stem, two syllables; e.g., *Hanka, Janka*)

I want to speak to you the way people speak
  to women and girls whom they know well
I don't want to show that I feel something good toward you
  of the kind that people show they feel toward women and girls

POLYSYLLABIC FORMS IN -*ka* AND -*ek* (e.g., *Dorotka, Michałek*)

I want to speak to you the way people speak
  to children and to people whom they know well
  and toward whom they feel something good
I feel something good toward you

FORMS WITH -*ka* ADDED TO A SOFT STEM (e.g., *Zośka*)

I want to speak to you the way people speak
  to girls and women whom they know well
I don't want to speak to you the way people speak to children
I feel something toward you
I don't want to show that I feel something good toward you
  of the kind that people show they feel toward children
I don't want to show that I feel something good toward you
  of the kind that people show they feel
  toward people whom they don't know well

FORMS WITH -*ek* ADDED TO A SOFT STEM (e.g., *Krzysiek*)

I want to speak to you the way people speak
  to boys whom they know well
I don't want to speak to you the way people speak to children
I feel something toward you
I don't want to show that I feel something toward you
  of the kind that people feel toward children
I don't want to show that I feel something good toward you
  of the kind that people show they feel toward people
  whom they don't know well

FORMS IN -*uśka* (e.g., *Martuśka*)

I feel something good toward you
  of the kind that people feel toward children
I imagine that looking at you people feel something good
I don't want to speak to you the way people speak to children
I don't want to show that I feel something good toward you
  of the kind that people show they feel toward children
I don't want to show that I feel something good toward you
  of the kind that people show they feel toward people
  whom they don't know well and who are not children

4. Concluding Remarks

Names mean something—not just in an etymological sense but in a synchronic
sense. They carry important pragmatic meanings, which colour, and even shape, the

character of human interaction. In the past, a number of obstacles have conspired to make the recognition of this fact difficult.

First, the fact that (within certain limits) parents can choose their children's names arbitrarily has the consequence that the same form, e.g., *Debbie* or *Cindy*, can be either treated as a short form derived from a full name or as a full name in its own right, with a different pragmatic value. This measure of freedom creates an impression that names are arbitrary and that they have no stable pragmatic meanings at all.

Second, traditional attempts to assign stable meanings to different categories of names were usually based on the assumption that these meanings should be stated in the form of quite specific expressive values: 'affectionate', 'contemptuous', 'disparaging', and the like. But descriptions of this kind were always contradicted by evidence. For example, any Russian speaker knows from experience that the "uničižitel'naja forma", the 'disparaging form', can be used in a friendly and even affectionate spirit. Consequently, traditional descriptions of names in terms of specific attitudinal values have always met with a sound and well-justified scepticism. This reinforced the conviction that names had no stable meanings at all.

Third, even in the case of those expressive forms which do have quite specific emotional values, for example, the Russian names in *-uška*, the attempts to portray that value were vitiated by the assumption that what was needed was some simple label, such as 'affectionate' or 'caressing'. The idea that a simple suffix may carry with it a very complex semantic structure, which cannot be matched with any one global emotion term, or even with a few such terms, and which in fact may need several lines to be spelt out fully, was far beyond the limits of what was expected and imagined in the traditional descriptions of meaning.

Fourth, the idea was missing that the attitudinal meanings of names may be structured in terms of prototypes rather than in terms of explicit emotional and attitudinal features. Yet it is precisely that idea which provides a clue to the semantics of names.

The analysis of English, Russian, and Polish names presented here suggests that in these three languages the main prototypes—that is, the main orientation posts in the universe of interpersonal relations—involve fundamental human categories based on age and sex—children, women, men—and, to a lesser extent, boys, girls, small children, small boys, small girls, and old people.

Traditional descriptive categories such as 'diminutives' and 'augmentatives' conceal the fact that what is really important in the semantics of human relations is not the notions of 'small things' and 'big things' but notions such as children, women, and men.

In the area of inanimate objects, the notions of 'small things' and 'big things' may indeed play an important role. In some languages, for example, Polish, size is an obligatory morphological category: for example, one cannot speak in Polish, as one can in English, of a 'bottle', whether it is a tiny bottle of perfume or a huge bottle of champagne. Instead, one has to choose between *butelka* ('normal size', e.g., a wine bottle), *buteleczka* ('small size', e.g., a bottle of perfume), and *butla* ('big size', e.g., a bottle (magnum) of champagne).

But in the area of human relations, what matters is not size but existential status determined by age and by gender.

One would expect that categories based on age and on gender will turn out to play an important role in the semantics of names in many, perhaps most, languages of the world. At the same time, the specific existential prototypes, and the exact role assigned to age and sex distinctions, will no doubt vary considerably from language to language. It is instructive to discover that even two closely related languages such as Russian and Polish may differ in this respect to a quite considerable extent. A rigorous analysis of the semantics of names reveals to what extent different attitudes are linked in a given culture to different genders and to different age statuses, for example, to what extent overt displays of affection and similar feelings depend on the addressee's being seen as a woman, a child, or a girl.

Furthermore, the semantics of names reveals the extent to which emotions are expected to be shown in human relations in general, and the kind of emotions. It is of course well known that different cultures differ greatly in this respect, and differences of this kind have often been described on an impressionistic basis. But a rigorous analysis of names allows us to go beyond impressionistic comments in this area and to develop an objectively valid comparative framework.

The survey offered in the present study substantiates the impression that the culture reflected in the English language discourages a display of emotions in interpersonal relations, whereas the culture reflected in either Russian or Polish, on the contrary, promotes such open displays, on an extraordinary scale.

In Russian, affection and other 'warm feelings' are expressed so freely that they can be poured out to men and women almost in equal measure (although there are special categories of forms focussed on little boys, such as the names in *-ik* or *-ok* (*-ëk*), e.g., *Jurik* or *Igorëk,* and special expressive devices focussed on little girls, such as the combination of feminine names with the masculine suffix *-ik,* for example, *Svetik*).

In Polish, this is not quite the case, feminine forms being privileged over the masculine ones in their capacity to encode 'good feelings'. Even more importantly, however, feminine and masculine forms differ from one another in the quality of emotions and attitudes encoded in them. For example, forms in *-ch* single out men as the focus of a special men-oriented positive emotion, and they assert adult masculinity as a value (seen as such by both sexes), and forms in *-chna* single out women and girls as the focus of a special, positive emotion and assert femininity as a value (also seen as such by both sexes).

English forms such as *Bob* or *Bill,* too, assert adult masculinity as an orientation post in human relations, but they don't link it with affection ('good feelings') as the Polish forms in *-ch* do. This is of course in keeping with the over-all nature of the English system, where the place of affection is very limited in general and where it is strongly biased toward children and, to a lesser extent, women. Forms such as *Bobby, Jimmy, Pammie,* or *Katie* sound childish as well as warm in English, whereas forms such as *Debbie, Cindy, Nicki,* or *Jenny* sound feminine as well as potentially warm, but there are, generally speaking, no forms which sound manly and warm, or potentially warm, at the same time. A somewhat exceptional category in this respect is provided by Australian forms such as *Bazza,* which combine 'manliness' with a 'tough' and anti-sentimental kind of warmth (see chapter 11).

The emotions conveyed by different categories of names can sometimes be very specific. But they are not linked directly with words designating emotions, or attitudes, such as affectionate, tender, admiring, disparaging, friendly, and teasing. The precise emotional tone and flavour of a category of names are suggested rather than spelt out in its semantic structure. Often, it is spelt out in negative as well as positive terms, as when, for example, Polish forms in -*ch* signal the following meaning:

> I feel something good toward you
> of the kind that people feel toward men
> and don't feel toward children

Very frequently, the means used to encode a particular attitudinal meaning are partly iconic or based on sound symbolism (cf. Volek 1987:221). For example, the rejection of the affectionate suffix -*si(a)* in Polish names such as *Krycha* and *Marycha*, derived from *Krysia* and *Marysia,* has an iconic effect (the speaker is rejecting overt affection), and the replacement of this -*si(a)* with -*ch(a)* (a sound which in inanimate nouns implies a big size and a coarse attitude) involves a good deal of sound symbolism. Frequently, it is such processes of formal rejection and replacement which contribute the negative components in the semantic structure ('I feel something toward you not of the kind that people feel toward . . . ')

A rigorous analysis of the semantics of names gives us an adequate framework not only for cross-linguistic and cross-cultural comparisons but also for a cultural analysis of change and variation within one language. For example, if we know the exact expressive value of Polish forms in -*unia* and in -*usia*, we can better understand, and better document, changes in social attitudes, reflected in the wider spread of -*usia* over -*unia.*

Since different types of names have different derivational possibilities, and consequently a different expressive range, a better understanding of the semantics of names can lead to a better understanding of the cultural significance of fashions in names. For example, Poland appears to have witnessed in recent decades a fashion (among the intelligentsia) for polysyllabic feminine names which form polysyllabic derivates in -*ka,* e.g., *Dorota* > *Dorotka, Agata* > *Agatka, Renata* > *Renatka, Beata* > *Beatka, Karolina* > *Karolinka,* or *Grażyna* > *Grażynka.* Since names of this kind don't have commonly accepted forms in -*sia,* -*eńka,* -*eczka,* or -*chna,* one can hypothesise that the semantics of polysyllabic feminine names in -*ka* well meets the expressive needs of the generation of parents who tend to choose such names in preference to the names lending themselves most naturally to other types of expressive derivation. Facts of this kind provide clues to social and cultural history, but to understand and to be able to utilise such clues, we must be able to decode the different expressive meanings in question.

Social and cultural change is undoubtedly mirrored in the changing trends in the expressive derivation of names, and the links between the two domains offer a fascinating field of study. On the informal level, native speakers are often aware of such links. With respect to Polish, Gabriela Zapolska's (1907) comedy 'Mrs Dulska's morality' offers a good illustration of this point (as Nina Zagórska, p.c., has pointed out to me). In this comedy, the teenage daughter of the bourgeois Dulski family comments that if her brother marries the housemaid *Hanka* (as he is threatening to do), this *Hanka* will have to start to be called *Andzia* (both forms being derived from *Anna*). Presumably, soft stem forms such as *Andzia* were perceived in that milieu as 'genteel', whereas the hard stem form *Hanka* sounded too 'rough' to be suitable for a lady. (Soft-stemmed forms in *-cia,* however, such as *Karolcia,* were seen as quite suitable for a housemaid, because of their patronising character.)

It would appear that in post-war Poland the contrast between soft forms and hard forms is no longer seen (by anybody) in terms of 'gentility' and 'non-gentility'. As independence, strength, and self-reliance in girls came to be cherished in all social milieus more than 'softness' and 'genteel femininity', hard stem forms such as *Hanka* came to be perceived in a more positive light. The growing fashion (among the intelligentsia) for unmarked full names such as *Dorota, Agata,* or *Beata,* which don't have soft short forms, may have a similar social explanation. The same may apply to the growing tendency to use full names (e.g., *Dorota, Małgorzata, Ewa*) instead of any expressive forms, and also to the fact that many soft short forms which used to be common among the nobility and among the intelligentsia are now perceived as old-fashioned and seen to be going out of use (e.g., *Terenia, Marynia, Jadwinia, Jadwisia, Elżunia*). The popular name *Magdalena* provides a characteristic example in this respect, with its shift from the once 'normal' soft short form *Madzia* (as in Bolesław Prus' (1894) novel *Emancypantki* 'Feminists') to the now 'normal' hard short form *Magda.*

Furthermore, the use of truncated soft forms whose base forms are not recoverable (e.g., *Dziunia, Dusia, Niusia, Nusia, Misia,* and also *Lala, Lola, Lula, Lela,* etc.) seems to have declined greatly and to be perceived today as excessively sugary.[4]

At this stage, however, observations of this kind are necessarily speculative, and they need to be supported by empirical research.

Brown and Ford (1964:238) have pointed out that in American English, "A speaker may use more than one form of the proper name for the same addressee, sometimes saying TLN, sometimes FN (first name) or LN (last name) or a nickname, sometimes creating phonetic variants of either FN or the nickname." They suggest that there may be a universal correlation between intimacy and address variation.

> The tendency to proliferate proper names in intimacy is interesting because it accords with a familiar semantic-psychological principle. For language communities the degree of lexical differentiation of a referent field increases with the importance of that field to the community. To cite a fresh example of this kind of thing, Conklin (1957) reports that the Hanunóo of the Philippine Islands have names for 92 varieties of rice which is their principal food. In naming ferns and orchids, with which they are little concerned, the Hanunóo combine numerous botanical species under one term whereas the rice they differentiate so finely is for the botanist a single species. The proper name constitutes the individual as a unique organism. Beyond the single proper name, however, where interest is still greater the individual is fragmented into a variety of names. Perhaps this differentiation beyond individuality expresses various manifestations or ways of regarding someone who is close. (1964:238)

But what does one say of a culture where most individuals are normally "fragmented into a variety of names" (one is tempted to say, into an orgy of different names) and where the linguistic system itself provides the resources for such an orgy? Wouldn't it follow from Brown and Ford's hypothesis that in such a culture the general level of closeness and intimacy is higher than it is in cultures which are more restrained in this respect? And doesn't the ever-present freedom of choice among numerous expressive possibilities contribute considerably to the general atmosphere of spontaneity and emotional richness, characteristic of Slavic interaction and Slavic discourse?

It seems to me that questions of this kind are legitimate and worthy of further investigation. If they are answered affirmatively, then systems of productive expressive derivation of names could offer some kind of index to important cultural differences which are easy to see with the naked eye but which are not easy to document objectively.

Finally, a systematic investigation of the semantics of names could, I think, have important consequences for psychology and psychotherapy, since it can provide an objective and reliable guide to subconscious attitudes.

Imagine, for example, a Polish family with two daughters, named *Klara* and *Ewa,* one of whom tends to be called by the parents *Klarcia,* and the other, *Ewuśka.* Or perhaps the father usually calls the girls *Klarcia* and *Ewuśka,* and the mother, *Klareczka* and *Ewunia.* Some difficulties develop in the family relations and the parents seek professional guidance and therapy. The counsellor or the psychotherapist wants to understand the dynamics of inter-familial relations. The forms of names used by the parents offer invaluable clues—but these clues cannot be utilised unless the precise attitudinal meanings encoded in these forms are reliably revealed.

Examples can be multiplied. I think, however, that enough has been said to show that the semantics of names is potentially an important field of inquiry—not only from a linguistic point of view but also with respect to psychology, anthropology, sociology, and cultural history. It is particularly important, however, from the point of view of cross-cultural studies, both in a theoretical and in an applied perspective.

Names mean something. The meanings encoded in them can be revealed and described; they can be learned and they can be taught.

8

Titles and Other Forms of Address

1. The Semantics of Titles

1.1 English Titles

What is the difference in meaning among the following four utterances?

1. Good-bye, Mr Brown.
2. Good-bye, Andrew.
3. Good-bye, Sir.
4. Good-bye, Father.

Questions of this kind have hardly ever been raised in semantic literature, presumably because it is usually taken for granted that differences of this kind are 'sociolinguistic' or 'pragmatic' rather than 'semantic', and 'sociolinguistic' or 'pragmatic' differences can be *talked about* but cannot be *defined*. (For excellent discussions from a sociolinguistic point of view, see, in particular, Brown and Gilman 1960; Brown and Ford 1964; and Ervin-Tripp 1974.)

I don't accept the position that differences of this kind cannot be defined, and I believe that the question of the differences in meaning is valid, important, and answerable.

For example, a combination of the title *Mr* with a surname (e.g., *Mr Brown*), used as a form of address, can be said to carry with it the following semantic components: (a) 'I want to speak to you the way people speak to men whom they don't know well' (if I thought of you as someone whom I know well, I would probably use the first name); (b) 'and the way people don't speak to men whom they don't know' (if I didn't know you, I wouldn't know your surname), (c) 'or whom they know well' (as in (a)), 'or to children' (if I thought of you as a child, I wouldn't call you *Mister*). Furthermore, the same phrase *Mr Brown* carries with it something like respect, of the kind usually shown to all adult acquaintances (but not to strangers or to friends); 'I want to show that I feel something good toward you, of the kind that people show they feel toward people whom they don't know well'.

As a first approximation, then, I propose the following set of explications:

> *Mr Brown*
> [DISTANCE]
> (a) I want to speak to you the way people speak
>   to men whom they don't know well

and the way people don't speak to men whom they don't know
or whom they know well, or to children

[RESPECT]
(b) I want to show that I feel something good toward you
of the kind that people show they feel
toward people whom they don't know well

Andrew

[LACK OF DISTANCE]
(a) I don't want to speak to you the way people speak
to people whom they don't know well

Sir

[DISTANCE]
(a) I want to speak to you the way people speak
to men whom they don't know or whom they don't know well
and the way they don't speak to men whom they know well

[RESPECT]
(b) I want to show that I feel something good toward you
of the kind that people show they feel
toward people whom they don't know well

[DEFERENCE]
(c) I want to show that I think of you as someone
to whom I couldn't say:
'I don't want to do what you want me to do'

Father

[DISTANCE]
(a) I want to speak to you the way people speak
to men whom they don't know well

[RELIGIOUS STATUS]
(a') and who are thought of as God's people

[RESPECT]
(b) I want to show that I feel something good toward you
of the kind that people show they feel
toward people whom they don't know well

[DEFERENCE]
(c) I want to show that I think of you as someone
to whom I couldn't say:
'I don't want to do what you want me to do'

[FILIAL ATTITUDE]
(d) I want to show that I feel something good toward you
of the kind that one feels toward one's father

The explications proposed will no doubt strike many readers as unconventionally
long and 'long-winded'. Wouldn't it be better to propose instead short, crisp abstract features similar to the widely used 'power', 'solidarity', 'intimacy', 'familiarity', 'distance', 'deference', and the like?

I agree that for mnemonic purposes, features of this kind are superior to long explications, and I have nothing against supplementing explications with convenient abbreviatory labels. As indicated in the square brackets, for the forms under consideration, this could be done as follows:

1. Mr X — (a) distance, (b) respect
2. First name — (a) lack of distance (or: familiarity)
3. Sir — (a) distance, (b) respect, (c) deference
4. Father — (a) distance, (a') religious status,
   (b) respect, (c) deference, (d) filial attitude

I do not accept the idea, however, that convenient mnemonic labels of this kind can be used *instead* of verbal explications.

One reason is that labels of this kind are arbitrary. For example, first names can be assigned either the feature 'lack of distance', or the feature 'familiarity', or some other similar feature. If these features are to have some real explanatory value, they have to be defined; consequently, they cannot replace verbal explications.

A related point is that although features of this kind appear to be self-explanatory, in fact they are not, and their meaning shifts more or less imperceptibly when they are applied to different forms. For example, both *Sir* and *Mr* imply a certain distance, but this 'distance' is in each case different, since *Sir* can be applied to strangers whose name one doesn't know, whereas *Mr* requires a degree of familiarity linked with the knowledge of the target person's surname. Similarly, *Father* can be applied to people whom one knows sufficiently well to use their first name (in addition to the title)—*Father John*—but *Mr* or *Sir* cannot be used like that.

When a first name (e.g., *Andrew*) is compared with a combination of *Mr* with the surname (*Mr Brown*), it can be said to imply 'familiarity', but when it is compared to a derived form (e.g., *Andy*), it is the derived form, not the full first name, which can be said to imply familiarity. So what exactly is the supposed constant meaning behind labels such as 'distance' or 'familiarity'?

Verbal explications can accurately portray these different kinds and different degrees of what might be called 'distance' and 'familiarity' (I am ignoring at the moment the dimension of 'respect'):

Andrew

I don't want to speak to you the way people speak
  to people whom they don't know well

Mr Brown

I want to speak to you the way people speak
  to men whom they don't know well
  and the way people don't speak to men whom they don't know
  or whom they know well, or to children

Sir

I want to speak to you the way people speak
  to men whom they don't know or whom they don't know well
  and the way people don't speak to men whom they know well
  and the way people don't speak of anyone

Andy
I want to speak to you the way people speak
   to boys whom they know well
   and toward whom they feel something good

Furthermore, consider the kind of respect encapsulated in the titles *Mr, Mrs, Miss, Ms,* and *Professor.* I think one can argue that *Mr, Mrs, Miss,* and *Ms* all convey a kind of respect accorded to all people on the basis of their social status as adults and as individuals, their individuality being symbolised by their surname. (They differ of course in terms of their status on the basis of gender and marriage, but this can be regarded as a separate dimension, and I will discuss it separately.) But the kind of respect embodied in the form *Professor* is different, being based not on adulthood and individuality but on professional status. The difference in question can be portrayed as follows:

Mr Brown
I want to speak to you the way people speak
   to men whom they don't know well
   and the way people don't speak to men whom they don't know
   or whom they know well, or to children
I want to show that I feel something good toward you
   of the kind that people show they feel
   toward people whom they don't know well

Professor Brown
I want to speak to you the way people speak
   to people whom they don't know well
   and who can be called 'Professor'
   and the way people don't speak to people whom they don't know
   or whom they know well
I want to show that I feel something good toward you
   of the kind that people show they feel
   toward people whom they don't know well
   and who can be called 'Professor'

Like the formulae in chapter 7, these formulae have been phrased in such a way as to account for the use of names as forms of address. To account for the use of a name in reference, all we would have to do is to replace the expression 'to you' with the expression 'of (person) X', for example:

I want to speak to you the way people speak to men . . . $\rightarrow$
I want to speak of X the way people speak of men. . . .

However, a given form may not have exactly the same expressive value when it is used in reference as it has in address, and some forms, like *Sir* and *Professor,* are not normally used in reference at all.

Turning now to a comparison of the forms *Mr, Mrs, Miss,* and *Ms,* it should be noted that although they could be easily described in terms of abstract features such as 'male', 'female', 'married', 'unmarried', and '±married', a description of this kind would not be fully adequate and would imply false symmetries. In fact, the unspecified status of *Mr* is quite different from the unspecified status of *Ms*, because *Mr* doesn't refer to marriage at all, whereas *Ms* does, albeit in a consciously negative way. As a result, *Ms* is pragmatically much more marked than *Mr* in present-day usage, though its advocates would of course hope that it will eventually become the unmarked title for women. The differences in question can be captured accurately in verbal explications:

> *Mr Brown*
>
> I want to speak to you the way people speak
>> to men whom they don't know well
>> and the way people don't speak to men whom they don't know
>> or whom they know well, or to children
>
> I want to show that I feel something good toward you
>> of the kind that people show they feel
>> toward people whom they don't know well

> *Mrs Brown*
>
> I want to speak to you the way people speak
>> to women whom they don't know well
>> and whom they think of as married women
>> and the way people don't speak to women whom they don't know
>> or whom they know well
>
> I want to show that I feel something good toward you
>> of the kind that people show they feel
>> toward people whom they don't know well

> *Miss Brown*
>
> I want to speak to you the way people speak
>> to women whom they think of as unmarried and to girls whom they
>> don't know well
>> and the way people don't speak to women whom they don't know
>
> I want to show that I feel something good toward you
>> of the kind that people show they feel
>> toward people whom they don't know well

Under certain circumstances, *Miss* can also be used to (or of) married women (as, for example, in speaking of well-known actresses). The definition has been phrased in such a way as not to exclude this possibility. *Miss* further differs from *Mr, Mrs,* and *Ms* in one additional respect: it can be used on its own (in older English, also in combination with a first name); I will return to this point in a later section. (In American English it is possible, under certain circumstances, to use *Mister*—but not *Mrs*—without a surname. I will not discuss this usage here.)

> *Ms Brown*
>
> I want to speak to you the way people speak
>> to women whom they don't know well

and whom they don't want to think of as married women
or unmarried women
and the way people don't speak to women whom they know well
or to children
I want to show that I feel something good toward you
of the kind that people show they feel
toward people whom they don't know well

1.2 French Titles

But if it is an illusion to think that labels such as 'distance', 'familiarity', 'respect', or 'married status' have constant meaning within a given language, it is an even greater illusion, I believe, to think that they can be transferred, with a constant value, across language boundaries.

For example, at first sight one might be tempted to assign the same features to English titles such as *Mr, Mrs,* and *Miss* and to French titles such as *Monsieur, Madame,* and *Mademoiselle.* On closer inspection, however, one discovers that the value of these forms is not the same (cf. Ervin-Tripp 1974:237). In particular, in French one can address a man as *Monsieur,* without a surname, but in (standard) English one cannot address a man as *Mister* (although *Miss* is possible). In French, one can address a male stranger as *Monsieur,* but in English, to use the form *Mister,* one must know the target person's surname; that is, one cannot treat the person as a total stranger. In this respect, therefore, *Monsieur* is rather like the English word *Sir.* But of course *Sir* implies a kind of (real or imaginary) subordination, which *Monsieur* doesn't. In this respect, then, *Monsieur* is like *Mr,* not like *Sir.*

I am not saying that differences of this kind haven't been noticed and commented on in the sociolinguistic and pragmatic literature. They have. But I don't think they have been—or can be—adequately portrayed in descriptions operating with obscure and undefined features such as 'familiarity' or 'solidarity'. (Cf. Wierzbicka 1991a.)

For example, Ervin-Tripp (1974:231) asserts (on the basis of data from Geoghegan 1971) that in the Bisayan language spoken in the Philippines there are forms "uniting informality and deference", whereas in English informality and deference cannot be similarly combined; or that in the Korean system "intimacy is separable from solidarity", whereas in the European languages studied by Brown and Gilman (1960) solidarity and intimacy are normally linked together.

Observations of this kind are intriguing and they offer valuable hints for further investigation, but in the absence of any definitions of concepts such as 'informality', 'deference', 'solidarity', or 'intimacy' one cannot really be sure exactly what the writer is referring to, or that each time he or she uses a given term it refers to the same thing.

It is the old problem of translating meanings into a 'Markerese' of one kind of another (cf. Lewis 1970:18–19; Wierzbicka 1980:10–14). If the markers of the 'Markerese' are not interpreted in terms of concepts which either are self-explanatory themselves or have already been defined in terms of concepts which are self-explanatory, then the translation into 'Markerese' leaves us in the previous obscurity.

On the other hand, verbal explications which rely on what appear to be universal semantic primitives and on concepts which have already been defined in terms of such primitives lead us in the direction from the obscure to the clear, from the unknown to the known.

For example, the relation between the French title *Monsieur* and the English titles *Mr* and *Sir* can be portrayed in the following way. For the reader's convenience, I have used capital letters for the subcomponents which distinguish the components (a) and (a'):

Mr Brown

(a) I want to speak to you the way people speak
to men whom they don't know well
AND DON'T SPEAK TO MEN WHOM THEY DON'T KNOW
OR WHOM THEY KNOW WELL, OR TO CHILDREN
(b) I want to show that I feel something good toward you
of the kind that people show they feel
toward people whom they don't know well

Monsieur

(a') I want to speak to you the way people speak
to men whom they don't know well
OR WHOM THEY DON'T KNOW
(b) I want to show that I feel something good toward you
of the kind that people show they feel
toward people whom they don't know well

Sir

(a') I want to speak to you the way people speak
to men whom they don't know well
OR WHOM THEY DON'T KNOW
(b) I want to show that I feel something good toward you
of the kind that people show they feel
toward people whom they don't know well
(c) I want to show that I think of you as someone
to whom I couldn't say:
'I don't want to do what you want me to do'

The French form *Madame* might seem to be related to *Mrs* in the way *Monsieur* is related to *Mr,* but this proportion is not really valid either, because *Madame* does not imply married status quite as clearly and emphatically as *Mrs* does. In French, if one wants to ignore a woman's married status, one can still use the form *Madame;* it is also possible to combine *Madame* with professional titles (e.g., *Madame le professeur*), but it is of course impossible to call anyone **Mrs Professor*. These facts suggest that whereas a *Mrs* is thought of as a married woman, a *Madame* is simply a woman whom the speaker doesn't think of as an unmarried woman.

Mrs Brown

I want to speak to you the way people speak
  to women whom they don't know well
  and whom they think of as married women
  and the way people don't speak to women whom they don't know
  or whom they know well

Madame

I want to speak to you the way people speak
  to women whom they don't know, or whom they don't know well,
  and whom they don't think of as unmarried women
  and the way people don't speak to children

There is, however, one further respect in which the French forms *Monsieur* and *Madame* differ from the English forms *Mr* and *Mrs:* their combinability with first names:

Monsieur Jean	—	*Mr John
Madame Marie	—	*Mrs Mary
Mademoiselle Jeanne	—	Miss Jane (acceptable in older English)

This contrast means that in English one has to choose between formal politeness (*Mr, Mrs*) and a claim to close acquaintance (first name), whereas in French one can combine the two, extending formal courtesy even into the area of close acquaintance (or perhaps preventing close acquaintance from becoming too close by maintaining formal courtesy despite the implicit claims of close acquaintanceship). To account for this difference, I have included in the explications of *Mr, Mrs,* and *Ms*—but not in those of *Monsieur* and *Madame*—the component 'the way people don't speak to people whom they know well'.

1.3 Polish Titles

Consider in turn the analogous Polish forms *pan, pani,* and *panna,* which correspond more closely to the French forms *Monsieur, Madame,* and *Mademoiselle* than to the English forms *Mr, Mrs,* and *Miss.* (For further discussion of the Polish system, see Stone 1981 and Bogusławski 1985.) Like the French forms, the Polish ones can be used without surnames and can be combined with professional titles and first names:

1. a. Bonjour Monsieur/Madame.
   b. Dzieńdobry Panu/Pani (dative).
   c. *Good morning Mr/Mrs
2. a. Monsieur/Madame le Professeur
   b. Pan/Pani Profesor
   c. *Mr/Mrs Professor
3. a. Bonjour Monsieur Paul.
   b. Dzieńdobry Panie Pawle (vocative).
   c. *Good morning Mr Paul.

But the Polish words *pan* and *pani* correspond not only to the French words *Monsieur* and *Madame* but also to *Seigneur* and *Dame* (roughly, 'Lord' and 'Lady'), and *maître* and *maîtresse* (roughly, 'master' and 'mistress'); and this wider range of their use suggests that their meaning is not identical with that of *Monsieur* and *Madame*.

Of course one could say—and I think rightly so—that the Polish words in question are polysemous. For example, in the title of the Polish translation of Thomas Mann's short story *Pan i pies* 'Master and dog', *pan* doesn't have the same meaning as in the title of Henryk Sienkiewicz's novel *Pan Wołodyjowski* 'Mr Wołodyjowski'. But there is evidence suggesting that in Polish, the two meanings of *pan* are felt to be related, and that *pan*$_1$ (roughly *Monsieur, Mr*) is semantically closer to *pan*$_2$ (roughly, *maître, master*) than *Mr* is to *master* or *Monsieur* to *maître*. Furthermore, *pan*$_2$ seems to correspond not only to *master* or *maître* but also to *Lord* or *Seigneur,* and this fact, too, seems to have a bearing on the meaning of *pan*$_1$.

The very fact that the communist regime in Poland regarded the forms *pan* and *pani* as offensive and incompatible with the communist ideology and struggled (in vain) to eradicate them and to replace them with the form *wy* ('you-plural') points in that direction. One argument which was often used in the propaganda war against the forms *pan* and *pani* was that "*w Polsce nie ma już panów*", 'there are no more *pan*s in Poland'; that is, 'there are no more masters/lords/overlords in Poland'.

In the past, the titles *pan, pani,* and *panna* were used in Poland only in speaking to (and of) the nobility. In contemporary Poland, they have lost their previous social significance, and they have become generalised in urban speech, but they are still not in general use among villagers. The social overtones of these words have changed, but their earlier status has not disappeared without a trace.

The intuitive links between the two meanings of the word *pan* are well reflected in the following passage from Sienkiewicz's novel *Pan Wołodyjowski* (for reasons of space, I quote only the English translation):

> 'Pan Mellehovich is an officer of the hetman,' said Basia; 'we have nothing to do with him.'
> 'Permit me; I will ask him. Let the other side be heard', said the little knight.
> But Pan Novoveski was furious. '*Pan* Mellehovich! What sort of a *Pan* is he?— My serving-lad, who has hidden himself under a strange name. Tomorrow I'll make my dog keeper of that *Pan;* the day after tomorrow I'll give command to beat that *Pan* with clubs. And the hetman himself cannot hinder me; for I am a noble, and I know my rights.' (1897:240)

Although Pan Novoveski in this passage is a seventeenth-century noble, very conscious of his superior social status as a member of the nobility (i.e., as a *Pan*), his protest at the use of the phrase *Pan Mellehovich* could well belong to a contemporary novel: today, too, a combination of a surname with the word *pan* implies not only 'ordinary' politeness due to anyone outside our immediate circle of relatives and friends but also a recognition of the target person's status as his or her 'own master' and an acknowledgement of a person's dignity based on that status. Concepts such as *Monsieur* or *Mr* do not imply that.

Subtle differences between concepts such as *pan* and *Mr* or *Monsieur* are lost in an analysis which operates only with abstract features such as 'distance', 'familiarity', 'solidarity', 'intimacy', and 'respect'. They can be captured, however, in verbal explications.

> *Monsieur*
> I want to speak to you the way people speak
>   to men whom they don't know well or whom they don't know
> I want to show that I feel something good toward you
>   of the kind that people show they feel
>   toward people whom they don't know well

> *Pan*
> I want to speak to you the way people speak
>   to men whom they don't know well or whom they don't know
> I want to show that I feel something good toward you
>   of the kind that people show they feel
>   toward people whom they don't know well
>   and whom they think of as people who can do what they want

> *Pan₂* (e.g., *X jest tutaj panem* 'X is the master/lord here')
> X can do what X wants here
> (other people can't)

It seems to me that explications of this kind account well for the synchronic links between *pan* and *pani* used as polite titles and the same forms used in the sense close to 'master/lord' and 'mistress/lady', and that they also account well for their social overtones, which reflect both their historical past and something of the national ethos. In the traditional hierarchy of values of the Polish nobility the *złota wolność* 'golden liberty' occupied a place of paramount importance, and as the ethos of the broad masses of Polish *szlachta* ('nobility' and the numerous 'lower nobility') turned into the Polish national ethos, the respect for individuals seen as people who are their own masters crystallised as one of the highest values in the national culture (cf. Davies 1984:331–36). The lexical blend of the equivalents of *lord, master,* and *Mr* (or *lady, mistress,* and *Mrs*) reflects and epitomises this cultural fact. (I shall return to this point in section 3.2.)

2. The Semantics of Agreement

The semantics of agreement can be illustrated from Polish. The forms *pan* and *pani* discussed in the preceding section take in Polish third-person agreement, not second-person agreement, even when they are used in address rather than in reference. But in Polish, other forms of address, too, can take third-person agreement, especially kinship terms. For example:

> a. *Mamusiu, widzisz?*
>   Mummy (you) see:2SG
>   'Mummy, you see?'
> b. *Mamusia widzi?*
>   Mummy sees:3SG
>   'Mummy, you see?'

Usually, third-person agreement is applied only to ascending kin terms (*mamusia* 'mummy', *ciocia* 'auntie', *wujek* 'uncle', etc.); same-generation terms *siostra* 'sister' and *brat* 'brother' normally take third-person agreement only when applied to nuns and monks, or to nurses. Descending kin terms (e.g., *córka* 'daughter', *syn* 'son', *siostrzeniec* 'nephew') never take that form of agreement:

<blockquote>
a. *Ciocia widzi?*
auntie sees
'Do you see, auntie?'
b. *Siostra widzi?*
sister sees
'Do you see, Sister?'
c. **Córka widzi?*
daughter sees
</blockquote>

In principle, third-person agreement can also be used with personal names (for example, in addressing maids, nannies, and other social inferiors who are treated in a familiar and courteous manner):

<blockquote>
a. *Marysiu, widzisz?*
Mary, (you) see:2SG
'Mary, you see?'
b. *Marysia widzi?*
Mary sees:3SG
'Mary, you see?'
</blockquote>

The semantics of different forms of personal names was discussed earlier. What matters in the present context is that the third-person version adds to the utterance one part of the second component of the meaning assigned here to the forms *pan* and *pani* (which normally also take third-person agreement):

<blockquote>
I want to show you that I feel something good toward you
of the kind that people show they feel
toward people whom they don't know well
</blockquote>

The reference to 'people thought of as people who can do what they want' is clearly not applicable here, and neither is the first component attributed to *pan/pani*:

<blockquote>
I want to speak to you the way people speak
to men/women whom they don't know well or whom they don't know
</blockquote>

Instead, forms such as *ciocia* 'auntie' or *Marysia* 'Mary-Dim.' carry with them their own first component, indicating how the speaker wants to speak to the addressee.

3. The Semantics of 'Polite' Pronouns

As Ervin-Tripp (1974:232) says, "The brilliant work of Brown and Gilman (1960), which initiated the recent wave of studies of address systems, was based on a study of T and V, the second person verbs and pronouns in European languages".

Brown and Gilman analysed the T:V alternations in different languages in terms of two features: 'power' and 'solidarity'. They were well aware, of course, that these alternations take different shapes in different languages, but they assumed that the underlying 'features' were the same. This attitude to pronominal alternations was largely adopted in the wave of studies which followed Brown and Gilman's pioneering work. It was assumed that the same underlying features (such as 'power' and 'solidarity') were at work in different languages, and that the languages differed in the way T and V forms were used, not in what they meant.

I want to challenge the assumption that forms of address in general, and pronouns in particular, involve a number of universal features of this kind, with a stable language-independent meaning, and I want to suggest that the differences in the way T and V forms are used may be determined, to some extent, by the differences in the meaning of these pronouns. (Cf. Mühlhaüsler and Harré 1990.)

More precisely, I maintain that the T forms in different languages are semantically equivalent, being all indefinable within their respective systems, whereas the V forms are definable and do differ in meaning from one another. For example, I believe that the Russian V form *vy* differs in meaning from the French form *vous*—despite the fact that in Russian "the T/V contrast itself came in from above as a borrowing from French" (Ervin-Tripp 1974:234).

As one piece of evidence for this view I will adduce the fact that whereas in French prayers and meditations God is commonly addressed as *vous,* in Russian God is always addressed as *ty,* and any attempts to address God as *vy* would produce an effect similar to addressing God in English as *Mr God.* What is involved is clearly not an arbitrary convention, because when conventions are violated, the effects are unconventional but not ludicrous. For example, in French, it may be unconventional to address God as *tu,* but there is nothing comical and unacceptable about it (for example, Pascal uses both *tu* and *vous*); but in Russian, it would be comical and unacceptable to address God as *vy.*

As for the T form, it may seem justified to assign to it abstract features such as 'intimacy' or 'solidarity', but to be really meaningful, features of this kind would have to be defined, and defined without circularity, and I don't think this has ever been attempted in the relevant literature. If one shouts at a dog, for example, *va-t-en!* 'go away (SG)', in what sense does this utterance imply 'intimacy'? Or in what sense does it imply 'solidarity'? And if one addresses God in Russian with a solemn prayer *Gospodi pomiluj!* 'Lord have mercy (SG)', in what sense can one claim that the singular form conveys intimacy? or solidarity? On the other hand, if we assume that the T form is indefinable, we *can* define the V form without circularity, and we can define it differently for different languages, thus accounting, to some extent at least, for the differences in their use.

3.1 The Russian *Vy* Versus the French *Vous*

I would suggest that the reason why the Russian *vy* is inapplicable to God is essentially the same why the English *Mr* is inapplicable: the prototype inherent in the meaning of these forms is clearly and unambiguously human, and it invites an interpretation in terms of worldly politeness. As a first approximation, I propose the following formula:

> RUSSIAN *vy*
>
> I want to speak to you the way people speak
>   to people whom they don't know, or whom they don't know well,
>   and who are not children

To account for the fact that the French *vous* can be applied to God we must assign to it a different meaning. I propose the following:

> FRENCH *vous*
>
> I want to speak to you the way people don't speak
>   to people whom they know well and to children

If these explications are correct, the French *vous* has no positive prototype and conveys, essentially, the speaker's reluctance to speak in an intimate and unceremonious way associated with a prototype which is felt to be inappropriate in a given situation. By contrast, the Russian *vy* does have a positive prototype (people seen as adult strangers or adult non-intimates). This explains, I think, why the French *vous* can be applied to God whereas the Russian *vy* cannot. (God is not 'people'; the French *vous* doesn't imply that He is, but the Russian *vy* would.)

The explications proposed present, however, one difficulty: They imply that the Russian *vy* has, so to speak, the 'distance' component of the French title *Monsieur* or of the English title *Mr* and differs from those titles mainly in the absence of a concomitant 'respect' component (as well as in the absence of sex differentiation). This is not counter-intuitive, but it fails to explain the fact that *vy* can be used, to some extent, among family members, whereas for *Monsieur* or *Mr* in present-day usage this is absolutely impossible (except in jest, irony, or sarcasm). For example, the poet Marina Tsvetaeva, throughout her married life, addressed her husband Sergej Efron as *vy*, although she addressed her great (platonic) love, the poet Boris Pasternak, as *ty*.

It seems reasonable to suppose that what makes forms such as *Monsieur* or *Mr* inapplicable to family members is the prototype of 'strangers' or 'partial strangers': it would be odd to imply, again and again, that one wants to treat some members of one's own family as people whom one doesn't know or whom one doesn't know well.

But if so, how is it possible that *vy* can be used for family members?

It seems to me that a possible explanation for this fact is suggested by the very form of the polite *vy*, that is, by its plural number. What a form such as *vy* implies is not necessarily a lack of familiarity: it may be also lack of intimacy, and non-intimacy may well have its prototype in a situation when one is speaking to more than one person at a time. This reasoning leads to the following revised explication of *vy*:

> *vy*
> I want to speak to you the way people speak
>   to people whom they don't know, or whom they don't know well
>   and who are not children
>   or the way people speak to more that one person at a time

The formula for the French *vous* cannot be amended in exactly the same way, because this would make it, wrongly, inapplicable to God (it would be odd to imply that one wants to speak to God in the way people speak to more than one person at a time). Since, however, the plural form of *vous* suggests a reference to plurality, it would be good if its explication could somehow account for this fact. I would suggest that this could be achieved in the following way:

> *vous*
> I don't want to speak to you the way people speak
>   to people whom they know well and to children
>   if they don't speak to more than one person at a time

The formulae proposed suggest that the Russian *vy* has a triple prototype, strangers, partial strangers, and also groups, whereas the French *vous* has no positive prototype at all and is based on an avoidance of two prototypes: well-known people and children. Another consequence of this difference is that in human relations the French *vous* appears to have a wider range of application than the Russian *vy* (at least in some registers). For example, in Tolstoy's *War and peace* the bilingual aristocrats often use the Russian *ty* (SG) and the French *vous* in the same situation, addressing the same person. For example, Prince Andrej addresses his wife in Russian using a singular *ty:*

> Čego ty boiš'sja Liza? Ja ne mogu ponjat'. (1949:33)
> 'What are you (SG) afraid of, Liza? I cannot understand.'

But a few lines later he switches in mid-sentence to French and uses a plural *vous:*

> Vse-taki ja ne ponjal, de quoi vous avez peur. (1949:34)
> 'I still can't understand (Rus.) what you (PL) are afraid of (Fr.).'

Half a page later, when Prince Andrej's mood has changed from mild annoyance to strong displeasure, he switches from the Russian singular *ty* to the plural *vy,* and this switch clearly reflects a change of attitude (cf. Friedrich 1966). But switching from a Russian *ty* (SG) to a French *vous* (PL) doesn't seem to be similarly conditioned.

I do not regard this last argument as very strong, because one could well argue that in the speech of bilingual Russian aristocracy French constituted a 'higher register', and that it tended automatically to induce greater formality. But the argument from prayers is, in my view, very strong and cannot be similarly dismissed.

3.2 The Polish *Wy*

Turning now to the Polish form *wy*, which was mentioned earlier, it must be stressed again that it differs in semantic value from the Russian *vy*, despite the formal, structural, and even functional similarity. When the Communist regime in Poland tried to force the form *wy* on the population, it was no doubt partly because of the Russian model, which was felt to be an appropriate tool for forging a 'bourgeois' country into a Communist one. But it was also a conscious attempt to eradicate the traditional Polish forms *pan* and *pani,* which—not surprisingly, in view of their semantics, as discussed earlier—were perceived as contrary to the spirit of Soviet-style Communism.

Given the different linguistic and cultural context, the form *wy* had a different pragmatic value in Polish than it did in Russian; nonetheless, given the historical circumstances in which it was imposed, it was felt to be not simply non-Polish but positively Soviet.

I would add that the contrast between the courteous, Polish-style form *pan/pani* and the impersonal, Soviet-style form *wy* is something that Poles are acutely aware of and often remark on. To illustrate this general awareness of the semantic implications of the two forms, I will quote a characteristic passage from an essay which was published in the leading Polish émigré monthly, *Kultura:*

> When the Russians speak of us ironically as *te polskie pany* ('those Polish gentle-men'), the connotations are of culture rather than class. The gentry as a class has long since ceased to exist, but we are still 'gentry' because we didn't submit to Soviet attempts at *'Gleichschaltung'*, at 'comradising' us, and the form *wy* ('you PL') didn't take. In communist Poland the only contrast really felt is that between *panowie* ('gentry', but also 'misters') and those who are generally referred to as *oni* ('they') [i.e., the regime people, the new ruling class]. (Schrett 1984:7; cf. also Torańska 1985)

The form *wy* favoured by the Communist regime carried with it implications of impersonal equality, as well as distance. To the Polish ear, it sounded cold, imper-sonal, and discourteous. It de-emphasised personal ties (either intimate, signalled by *ty,* or based on personal respect, signalled by *pan/pani*) in favour of an equality derived from membership in a collectivity. *Pan/pani,* on the other hand, is non-intimate, but it is also courteous and personal. I presume that the 'personal' charac-ter of *pan/pani* is due partly to its singular form, and possibly also to its sex differentiation, whereas the 'impersonal' character of the form *wy* is due partly to its plural and genderless form. (Polish courtesy stresses respect for every individual as a free individual and is highly sex-conscious. The collectivist and genderless ring of the form *wy* was jarring in that tradition.) It is important to mention, in this connection, that the officially supported form *wy* co-occurred with 'collectivist' vocatives and appellatives such as *towarzyszu, towarzysz* 'comrade', and, to a lesser extent, *obywatelu, obywatel* 'citizen', and was no doubt interpreted in conjunction with, or against the background of, those collectivist Soviet-style forms.

To account for the collectivist, impersonal, non-intimate, and anti-*pan/pani* character of the form *wy*, I would propose for it the following explication:

> *wy* (official)
> I want to speak to you the way people speak
>   to more than one person at a time
> I want to speak to you the way I speak
>   to all people who are not children and whom I don't know well
> I don't want to show that I feel something good toward you
>   of the kind that people show they feel
>   toward people whom they don't know well
>   and whom they think of as people who can do what they want

Finally, it should be mentioned that Polish dialects have a homophonous form *wy* (used, for example, to one's in-laws), which belongs to a system of only two contrasting members—*ty* (SG) and *wy* (PL)—and which has an entirely different value than the official regime-sponsored *wy*. It conveys a lack of intimacy and a respectful attitude, not normally shown to children and to intimates.

> *wy* (dialectal)
> I want to speak to you the way people speak
>   to more than one person
> I want to show that I feel something good toward you
>   of the kind that people don't show they feel
>   toward people whom they know well and toward children

4. Conclusion

I have claimed that 'pragmatic' meanings which are related to the speaker's attitude to the addressee can be described with the same degree of precision as any other meanings and that they can be described in the same framework, using the same semantic metalanguage. Since in natural language 'subjective' and 'objective', or 'pragmatic' and 'referential', meanings are inextricably linked, the availability of a unified descriptive framework in which 'pragmatic' meanings—as well as any other meanings—can be adequately described is, I have argued, a necessary condition of success in semantics of natural language.

I have tried to demonstrate that the semantic metalanguage derived from natural language and based on a system of universal semantic primitives provides an adequate basis for such an integrated semantic description.

I have argued that attitudinal meanings encapsulated in different forms of address (such as titles, 'polite pronouns', and personal names, including their expressive derivates) can be accurately portrayed in semantic explications, and that such explications allow us to make the relations between different pragmatic categories transparent—both within a language and in a cross-linguistic perspective.

I have also argued that many pragmatic meanings have a 'prototypical' semantic structure, that is, that they present emotions and attitudes in terms of certain prototypical human relationships, rather than in terms of fully specified mental states or social relations. In particular, social and existential categories, such as children and adults, women and men, or people whom one knows, people whom one knows well, and people whom one doesn't know, appear to provide important signposts in the universe of human relations. But these signposts are used differently in different linguistic categories, and they cannot be correlated in a straightforward manner with specific attitudes such as tenderness, respect, or intimacy.

Furthermore, I have argued that pragmatic meanings cannot be satisfactorily described in terms of abstract features such as 'solidarity', 'familiarity', 'respect', 'deference', and 'distance', because features of this kind do not have any constant, language-independent value. In fact, even within one language, the 'distance' implied by a certain pronoun may mean something different from the 'distance' implied by a title, or by a type of personal name. (For further discussion and illustration, see Wierzbicka 1991a.)

To describe a great variety of pragmatic meanings encoded in different languages, we need some reliable constants, and if this description is to be illuminating, the constants on which our analysis relies must be self-explanatory. I believe that concepts such as 'want', 'say', 'person', 'think', or 'know' are better candidates for self-explanatory universal semantic primitives than concepts such as 'distance', 'solidarity', or 'intimacy', and I hope that this chapter demonstrates the usefulness of such hypothetical primitives, and of a limited number of other concepts based on them, in portraying pragmatic meanings encoded in different languages of the world.

V

KINSHIP SEMANTICS

9

Lexical Universals
and Psychological Reality

For a semanticist, there can hardly be a question more vital and more disturbing than the one raised in a memorable article by Robbins Burling (1969:427): "When an anthropologist undertakes a semantic analysis, is he discovering some 'psychological reality' which speakers are presumed to have or is he simply working out a system of rules which somehow take account of the observed phenomena?"

Burling followed this question with an ironic remark: "It certainly sounds more exciting to say we are 'discovering the cognitive system of the people' than to admit that we are just fiddling with a set of rules which allow us to use the terms the way others do." He concluded, "Nevertheless, I think the latter is a realistic goal, while the former is not."

In the two decades which followed the publication of Burling's article many scholars have tried to "balance his scepticism with positive things that can be done" (Hymes 1969:431). For my part, however, I feel that it is vital to attempt more than that: the challenge formulated by Burling has to be met head on. The crucial problem is that of non-uniqueness in semantic analysis. To quote Burling again:

> Students who claim that componential analysis or comparable methods of semantic analysis can provide a means for "discovering how people construe the world" must explain how to eliminate the great majority of logical possibilities and narrow the choice to the one or few that are "psychologically real." I will not be convinced that there are not dozens or hundreds of possible analyses of Subanese disease terms until Frake presents us with the entire system fully analysed and faces squarely the problem of how he chooses his particular analysis. (1969:426)

In what follows I will try to do just that: to show how we can choose one particular analysis over any potential competitors. As my test case, however, I will use not disease terms but the meaning of kinship terms, because there seems to be a general consensus that any theoretical advance in semantic anthropology must prove itself above all in that area (cf., for example, Needham 1974:39). For another large body of data, fully analysed into components, see Wierzbicka (1987c).

1. Principles of Definition

To begin with, let us consider two componential definitions of the terms for 'father' in two Australian languages: Burling's own 'definition' of the Njamal word *mama* and Scheffler's (1978:102) 'definition' of the corresponding Pitjantjatjara word, also *mama:*

mama	G^{+1} M^e S^m	(Njamal)
mama	K.L.G1.$+.\delta$	(Pitjantjatjara)

In Burling's formula, G^{+1} stands for the first ascending generation, M^e for ego's moiety, and S^m for male sex. In Scheffler's formula, K stands for kinsman, L for lineal, G1 for one degree of generation removal, + for senior, and δ for male. For the sake of the exposition let us assume that Scheffler's formula could be assigned to the Njamal word as well as to the Pitjantjatjara word, and vice versa. How could we decide then which analysis to choose?

I submit that the correct answer to this question is simpler than might be assumed: the question of a choice between the two analyses does not even arise, because neither of them could possibly have any psychological reality. The point is that both formulae are circular. The problem of psychological reality arises only for definitions which are inherently tenable, that is, which are not circular. For circular definitions, it does not arise at all.

If one seeks to define the two concepts 'first ascending generation' and 'lineality', one will soon see that they are both dependent, ultimately, on the concepts 'mother' and 'father'. Very roughly, 'the first ascending generation' means, if we draw a diagram in which every person's mother and father are represented as being one level above that person, then the 'first ascending generation' stands for all the people who are represented as being one level above a given person. But this means that the concept of 'ascending generation' is more complex than the concept of 'mother' and 'father': if we define 'ascending generation' in terms of 'mother' and 'father,' then we cannot define 'mother' and 'father' in terms of 'ascending generation'. Clearly, what applies to the English terms *mother* and *father* applies also to Australian Aboriginal terms for mother and father. Trying to explain to an Aborigine what the term 'ascending generation' means, one would have to draw a diagram and to show on this diagram the position of a person's genetrix and begetter. But of course in order to do this one would have to use words which stand for genetrix and begetter, i.e., for 'mother' and 'father' in the English sense of these terms (cf. Keen 1985:77).

What applies to 'ascending generation' applies also to 'ancestors', 'parent', 'lineal', and many other features in terms of which the words for mother and father are typically analysed in the anthropological literature. For example, the concept 'X's ancestors' stands, roughly, for a group of people who lived before X, who include X's mother and father, and who are mutually related in such a way that everyone in that group is the father or mother of someone else in the group.

It must be stressed that in saying this I am not criticising anthropological formulae such as G^{+1}M^{e}S^m or K.L.G1.$+.\delta$, which may have great value for certain purposes. I only want to show that formulae of this kind cannot be regarded as *semantic* formulae, that is to say, as formulae which explicate the meaning of native terms such as *father* or *mama*. Viewed as *semantic* formulae, they are in the class of Pascal's (1963[1667]:580) mock definition of 'light': "La lumière est un mouvement luminaire des corps lumineux" ('light is the luminary movement of luminous bodies').

A definition as a semantic formula must be above all reductive: it must reduce relatively complex concepts to relatively simple ones (cf. Bogusławski 1978 and 1982; Apresjan 1974; Wierzbicka 1972a, 1980, 1985a, and 1987b). This principle in itself destroys the spectre of hundreds of alternative analyses raised by Burling. By itself, it doesn't perhaps guarantee uniqueness, but in each case it reduces valid alternatives to no more than a mere handful. To achieve uniqueness, which I see as a fully realistic, as well as the highest, goal of semantic analysis, two further methodological principles must be adhered to: the principle of indigenisation and the principle of translatability.

The principle of indigenisation can be formulated as follows (cf. chapter 10). If the semantic formulae are to constitute plausible hypotheses about the native speakers' meanings encoded in language A (say Pitjantjatjara), then those formulae must be translatable into language A. For example, it is permissible to use in the semantic formulae English words such as *person, say, good, bad, mother,* or *father* if the language whose meanings the analysis is trying to represent has words for such concepts, and it is not permissible to use words such as *sex, generation, sibling, parallel, opposite, senior,* or *moiety* if the language in question doesn't have words for such concepts.

The principle of indigenisation saves the analyst from the "almost unavoidable ethnocentrism" (Wallace and Atkins 1969:364) of conventional analyses of kinship terminologies, which has justly been recognised as a major obstacle in the path of anyone trying to attain the golden ideal of 'psychological reality'. Wallace and Atkins describe this obstacle as follows:

> The first of the methodological difficulties alluded to above is an almost unavoidable ethnocentrism. If the analyst is writing a paper in ethnographers' English (or any language other than the idiom of his informants), he is to a degree constrained by the terminological resources of his own language in his efforts to state the meaning of a foreign expression. Even the simple kin-type denotata of which we have made such heavy use are not, to my knowledge, absolutely universal human concepts. . . . Just as the physicist cannot measure both the position and the momentum of a particle under the same conditions, so the semantic analyst cannot state simultaneously the meaning of an event in his own language and in that of another person, because the two languages impose different conditions of analysis. (1969:364)

The ethnocentrism described in this passage would indeed by unavoidable if the authors were right in assuming that there are no 'universal human concepts', i.e., no concepts (relevant to kinship) which have been lexicalised in all, or nearly all, languages. I contend that—fortunately—they are wrong on this crucial point. There are concepts fundamental to the semantics of kinship which, I conjecture, have been lexicalised in nearly all human languages. Ethnocentrism *can* be avoided in semantic analysis, because the principle of indigenisation is in fact compatible with the other crucial principle of semantic analysis: the principle of translatability.

The principle of translatability can be formulated as follows (cf. chapters 3 and 10). If the meanings encoded in language A (say, Pitjantjatjara) are to be made intelligible to people from a different cultural and linguistic background B (say, English), then those meanings have to be expressed in semantic formulae constructed in (simple and generally understandable) words from language B.

The proviso 'simple and generally understandable' is important, for I don't regard artificial terms such as *consanguineal, cross-sibling,* or *parent-in-law* as genuine English words. The problem of cross-cultural translatability would be trivial if analysts were free to invent technical labels wherever the ordinary vocabulary failed them. The claim which I am making is much stronger: I submit that kinship terminologies can be explicated across language and culture boundaries because there are certain universal human concepts, relevant to kinship, which have apparently been lexicalised in the ordinary vocabulary of almost all human languages. The concepts in question are 'mother' and 'father' (but not 'brother', 'sister', 'son', 'daughter', or 'child').

2. The Problem of Polysemy

At first sight, counter-examples seem easy to find. For example, in many Australian Aboriginal languages the word for 'father' is also used for father's brother, for father's father's brother's son, for father's mother's sister's son, and for many other types of relatives, and the word for mother is also used for mother's sister, and for many other types of relatives. Can we maintain that these languages have lexicalised the concept of mother (birth giver) and the concept of father (begetter)?

I think we can, because there are compelling reasons to recognise that the terms in question are polysemous—as are, in fact, the corresponding English terms (for example, when we call a nun *Mother Superior* we don't mean that she has given birth to anybody).

Similarly, few linguists would deny that French and German have words for 'wife', even though the words in question (*femme* and *Frau*) also have another meaning: 'woman' (cf. Scheffler 1978:18). The evidence for polysemy can be lexical, syntactic, phraseological, morphological, or purely semantic. For example, a definition of *femme* or *Frau* which tried to cover both senses of the word at the same time would be so narrow as to exclude a large proportion of the people to whom these terms would in fact be applied (all unmarried women). On the other hand, a 'unitary' definition of *femme* or *Frau* along the lines of 'adult female human being' would make nonsense of sentences such as "avant d'être devenue sa femme elle était sa maîtresse" ('before she became his wife she was his mistress').

To take one last example, a definition of *brother* as 'someone for whom one can be expected to have fraternal feelings' has a certain amount of psychological plausibility with respect to certain uses of this word. Pursuing this semantic fantasy further, one could propose that a person's biological brother is simply a special kind of 'brother' in the sense defined, namely that kind of a person to whom one could be expected to have fraternal feelings who has the same father and mother as one.

In this case, the semantic fantasy in question would of course be rejected on the grounds of circularity: 'fraternal feelings' are feelings of the kind one would expect between brothers (say, feelings of affection and solidarity), but if the concept of 'fraternal' is based on the concept 'brother', then the word *brother* cannot be defined via the word *fraternal*. In my view, exactly the same considerations apply to the words for 'mother' and 'father'. As argued forcefully by Scheffler (1972 and 1978), a term such as *pipi* (the Ompela term for father) is polysemous between 'father$_1$' (begetter) and 'father$_2$' (as Scheffler puts it, 'man of my father's clan and of approximately his age and generation'). As Scheffler (1978:34) shows, an expression such as *pipi toipi* ('own father', i.e., begetter) cannot be analysed as a special case of *pipi* 'in general' (i.e., of the classificatory father) because the very concept of '*pipi* in general' treats ego's biological father as the focal or "logically prior" denotatum of the term, i.e., as the man by reference to whom all other men may also be reckoned as *pipi*.

What applies to terms for 'father' also applies to terms for 'mother'. It follows that even if a language doesn't have separate words used uniquely for the biological mother and father, it can nonetheless have separate lexical terms for the concepts in question. For example, the Ompela word *pipi* is used for classificatory fathers as well as for biological fathers, but the lexical item *pipi$_1$* encodes only the concept of biological father.

The point is so crucial to the semantics of kinship that although I regard the argument from circularity as decisive and as sufficient to justify the positing of polysemy, I will nonetheless try to support this position with additional arguments.

In particular, I would like to show that the concepts of (biological) 'mother' and 'father' play an important role in the semantic system of a language even if the words for 'father' and 'mother' are also used in this language in a classificatory sense. This is manifested, among other things, in the existence of numerous words whose meaning is based on these concepts. I will illustrate this with some Australian Aboriginal concepts, but first an analogue from English.

The English word *mother* is used as a religious title (as in *Mother Superior*), as well as a term for birth giver, but words such as *step-mother, mother-in-law, orphan, maternity,* or *motherhood* are derived semantically, quite unambiguously, from the sense 'birth giver'. This in itself constitutes a proof (if proofs are needed) that the sense 'birth giver' is a separate (and of course primary) sense of the English word *mother*.

Exactly the same applies to Australian Aboriginal languages, despite the classificatory nature of their kinship terminologies. For example, the Dyirbal terms *jarraga,* used for classificatory mothers who are not biological mothers, and *galŋan,* used for classificatory fathers who are not biological fathers (Dixon 1989), can be explicated along the following lines:

> Y is X's *jarraga.* →
> X can think of Y like X thinks of X's MOTHER
> Y is not X's MOTHER

> Y is X's *galŋan*. →
> X can think of Y like X thinks of X's FATHER
> Y is not X's FATHER

An alternative phrasing, a little more complex but probably preferable (because it can be treated as a more general model of kinship terms), would read as follows:

> Y is X's *jarraga*. →
> if a woman is not my MOTHER
> and if I can think of her like I think of my MOTHER
> I can say of her: 'this is my *jarraga*'
> X can think of Y like I would think of this woman
>
> Y is X's *galŋan*. →
> if a man is not my FATHER
> and if I can think of him like I think of my FATHER
> I can say of him: 'this is my *galŋan*'
> X can think of Y like I would think of this man

I am using the terms MOTHER and FATHER, in capital letters, as words of the semantic metalanguage, standing for the birth giver and the begetter. For definitions of these concepts in terms of more elementary concepts, see Wierzbicka (1972a and 1990a; see also chapter 10).

The Walmatjari word *kumpurru*, which is used for foster-mothers (cf. Hudson MS b), can be explicated along the following lines:

> Y is X's *kumpurru*. →
> X can think of Y like one thinks of one's MOTHER
> because Y did good things for X
> of the kind that one's MOTHER does for one
>   before one becomes a man or a woman
> Y is not X's MOTHER

It is easy to see how this formula would be rephrased to conform to the egocentric model.

Dyirbal possesses special verbs which Dixon (1989) calls "the verbs of begetting" and which are based on the concepts 'mother' and 'father'. Dixon glosses the word *bulmbi* as 'be the male progenitor of, beget', and *gulŋga* as 'give birth', and he offers the following translations for Dyirbal sentences containing those verbs:

> X *bulmbi* Y   'X (if a male) or one of X's brothers (for both males
>   and females) begot Y'
> X *gulŋga* Y   'X (if a female) or one of X's sisters (for both males
>   and females) gave birth to Y'

But this phrasing seems to suggest that the verbs in question have a different meaning depending on the speaker's sex; or, on a different interpretation, that the concept of 'begetting' is applicable to women as well as to men and that the concept of 'giving birth' is applicable to men as well as to women. Both these difficulties can be prevented if the following semantic formulae are adopted instead:

> X *bulmbi* Y. →
>
> if someone has the same MOTHER and FATHER as my FATHER
> I can say of this person: this person *bulmbi* me
> Y can say this of X
>
> X *gulŋga* Y. →
>
> if someone has the same MOTHER and FATHER as my MOTHER
> I can say of this person: this person *gulŋga* me
> Y can say this of X

It will be noticed that in this case, the kinship words signal how X is actually related to Y, not how X is thought of as related to Y.

The concepts of MOTHER and FATHER also play an important role in the semantic structure of numerous words for affines. For example, Hudson (MS b) offers the following terms from Walmatjari: *parnmarn* (a man's actual mother-in-law), *karntiya* and *wurruru* (a woman's actual son-in-law), and *wurturtu* (a woman's actual 'grandson-in-law'). As Hudson points out, in addition to referring to the biological motherhood, the terms in question encode a good deal of specific social information. It should be noted that these terms are all 'triangular' (cf. Evans 1985; Heath 1982; O'Grady and Mooney 1973), involving the addressee, the referent, and the speaker. Drawing on Hudson's analysis, I would explicate these terms as follows:

> *parnmarn*
>
> a woman
> she is your MOTHER
> I cannot speak to her
> I cannot look at her
> I cannot speak of her to you like I speak of other people
> because she is my wife's MOTHER
>
> *karntiya*
>
> a man
> you are his wife
> I cannot speak to him
> I cannot look at him
> I cannot speak of him to you like I speak of other people
> because I am his wife's MOTHER
>
> *wurruru*
>
> a man
> he is your FATHER
> I cannot speak to him
> I cannot look at him
> I cannot speak of him to you like I speak of other people
> because I am his wife's MOTHER

wurturtu

a man
you are his wife
I cannot speak to him
I cannot look at him
I cannot speak of him to you like I speak of other people
because I am the MOTHER of his wife's MOTHER

My argument is this: if the concept of 'one's wife's MOTHER' is sufficiently salient in a given culture to merit lexicalisation, then it can hardly be the case that the concept of MOTHER (or, for that matter, the concept of 'wife') would not be lexicalised.

For reasons of space, this chapter is confined to discussion of kinship terms, to the exclusion of affines. It appears, however, that just as kinship semantics requires two 'primitives' ('mother' and 'father'), so does the semantics of terms for affines. In this case, the primitives are 'husband' and 'wife'. It might seem that just one primitive would suffice—'spouse' or 'marry'—but in fact not all languages have words for these concepts, whereas it appears that all languages have words for 'husband' and 'wife'. Of course in some cases the words for husband and wife will be polysemous (for example, in German *Mann* means not only 'husband' but also 'man', just as *Frau* means not only 'wife' but also 'woman'), but this is not a reason not to regard the concepts 'husband' and 'wife' as possible lexical universals. Furthermore, in some languages (for example, in several Australian languages) the same word stands for both husband and wife. It appears, however, that here, too, a good case can be made for polysemy. For example, although Pitjantjatjara[1] uses the same word, *kuri,* for both husband and wife, it has, nonetheless, a special word (*waputju*) for wife's FATHER, and another special word (*umari*) for wife's MOTHER.[2] It also has a special word (*mingkayi*) based on the concept of 'husband', 'X's *mingkayi*' being someone related to X in the way one's husband's MOTHER or FATHER is related to one.

I do not wish to claim, however, that it is necessarily the word *kuri,* and its counterparts in other Australian languages, which are polysemous. Rather, it may well be that it is the words for woman and man which are polysemous (as they are in German). In support of this suggestion I would adduce the fact (cf. Goddard 1985:77) that in Yankunytjatjara a genitive construction is used to refer to a wife or a husband:

wati-ku kungka (man-Gen. woman)   'the man's woman = wife'

kungka-ku wati (woman-Gen. man)   'the woman's man = husband'

Returning to kinship, it is also relevant to note that at least some Australian languages do have special terms for the biological mother and father. For example, Evans (1985) cites the following Kayardild words:

ngijinmimatharrb   'begetter of me, i.e., my FATHER'

ngijinmimayarrb   'begotten by me, i.e., those whose FATHER I am'

ngijinbadiyarrb   'carrier of me, i.e., my MOTHER'

ngijinbadiind   'carried by me, i.e., those whose MOTHER I am'

If it is true, however, that all languages have special lexical items (whether monosemous or polysemous) for biological mothers and fathers, then the concepts of biological mother and father can be used as universal semantic primitives of kinship terminologies, that is, as terms whose use permits a simultaneous application of the principles of indigenisation and translatability. For example, the Pitjantjatjara terms *tjamu* and *pakali,* which Scheffler defines (in their 'primary senses') as K.L.G2. .♂ and K.L.G2.-.♂, respectively, can in fact be defined as follows:

> X and Y are *tjamu.* →
> if a man is the FATHER of another man's FATHER or MOTHER
> each of these men can say of the other: 'this is my *tjamu*'
> X and Y can think of each other like these men would think of each other

> Y is X's *pakali.* →
> if I am the FATHER or MOTHER of a man's FATHER or MOTHER
> I can say of this man: 'this is my *pakali*'
> X can think of Y like I would think of this man

It should be noted that these definitions do not imply that the terms *tjamu* and *pakali* apply only to adults: they mention 'two men' or 'a man' as prototypes, not as parts of the invariant. For example, the component 'X can think of Y like I would think of this man' does not imply that Y is necessarily an (adult) man. In an earlier version of the present study (Wierzbicka 1987c), I used in my explications of kinship terms the expression 'related in the way. . . '. In the present version I have replaced this expression with a combination of simpler concepts such as 'can', 'think', and 'like'.

In calling 'mother' and 'father' semantic primitives of kinship terminologies I do not wish to suggest that these concepts cannot be further decomposed. But they are sufficiently simple to be treated as primes for the purposes of kinship semantics, and it appears that they function as the basic units of that area of language.

An apparent counter-example to the claim that the concepts of both MOTHER and FATHER are universal is the fact that Yuman languages in Southern California distinguish lexically between a woman's FATHER and a man's FATHER, though, interestingly, not between a woman's MOTHER and a man's MOTHER. But in fact, these languages also have a separate word for FATHER, applicable to both a woman's FATHER and a man's FATHER (Margaret Langdon, p.c.).

As the proposed definitions illustrate, the admission that the terms for mother and father are polysemous and that they can be regarded as lexical universals makes most of the conventional features of kinship semantics (co-lineal, collateral, first ascending generation, second degree of genealogical distance, and so on) simply superfluous, as hypothetical *semantic features.* The proviso is important, because features of this kind may well be necessary for practical reasons, as part of the anthropologist's technical metalanguage, and of course there can be no objection to the use of such features as a convenient technical shorthand. But they cannot be regarded as *semantic* features, that is, as genuine components of meaning. They are precisely what Burling said they were: artificial devices introduced for the purpose of "fiddling with a set of rules which allow us to use the terms the way others do". So when, for example, Turner (1980:33) lists formulae such as the following:

maeli/kandari—people in my own and linked patri-group on 2a and 2d generation
levels with Ms in my M's or linked patri-group

under the heading "the meaning of Kariera kin terms", he is, I believe, using the
term *meaning* in a confusing and confused way. This may be what Turner and his
colleagues mean by such terms, but it is hardly what Kariera people mean by them.

Needless to say, componential analyses don't have a monopoly on psychological
implausibility. For example, definitions such as "sister = the female person who is
the child of one's parents or (=) one's parents' daughter who is not oneself" (cf.
Keen 1985:66) also seem rather implausible. It is unlikely that we think of our
sisters, on any level, as 'people who are not ourselves'. The following phrasing
overcomes this problem:

> Y is X's *sister*. →
> if a woman or a girl has the same MOTHER and FATHER as I
> I can say of her: 'this is my *sister*'
> X can say this of Y

In addition, this phrasing restores the relational aspect of the concept: 'X's sister' is
somebody who is not only related to X's parents in a certain way but, above all,
somebody who is related to X in a certain way.

3. The Social Nature of Kin Terms

It will be noticed that the natural language definitions proposed here are couched as
much in social terms as in genealogical terms: for example, the genealogical relationships FF and MF are used here as prototypes of the social relationship called
tjamu, not as its determinants.

Scheffler has argued—to my mind, quite conclusively—that in the case of
terms for mother and father the biological relationship is primary and has to be
treated as a separate sense of the term, because otherwise circularity sets in. I
believe, however, that this argument applies specifically to the terms for father and
mother, not to the whole class of kinship terms. The definitions proposed in this
chapter demonstrate, I hope, that other kinship terms can be defined, without
circularity, in social terms and that polysemy doesn't have to be posited for them.

I think the reason why Scheffler's claim concerning the polysemy of the terms
for mother and father met so much resistance may have lain largely in the fact that
Scheffler was willing to extend this claim to all kinship terms and so to posit
polysemy on a truly massive scale. But clearly, polysemy should never be posited
without absolute necessity, because "entia non sunt multiplicanda praeter neces-
sitatem" (Occam's razor). To be sure, an expression such as *pipi toipi* ('own father')
cannot be analysed as 'that classificatory father who is also the genitor' because the
very idea of 'classificatory father' is based on that of 'genitor'. X's classificatory
father is a man whose relationship to X is thought of as similar to that between a
person's genitor and that person. For this reason, for terms such as *pipi* polysemy
must be recognised (roughly, (1) genitor, (2) social analogue to genitor). Since,

however, the other kinship terms *can* be analysed as monosemous (without circularity), it is inadmissible, for general methodological reasons, to analyse them as polysemous.

I think Scheffler is still right in believing that a certain blood relationship is focal to every kinship term, but this view is quite compatible with an analysis which doesn't posit polysemy for any terms other than those for mother and father and which results in definitions couched in social (and psychological) terms as much as in biological ones. A definition such as that assigned to the Pitjantjatjara term *tjamu* links this term with a social and psychological relationship *like* that which holds between certain blood relatives. This is different from saying that the classificatory sense of *tjamu* constitutes an extension of its primary (genealogical) sense. There is no need to posit two different senses, a primary and an extended one, here. An expression such as 'one's own *tjamu* (grand-kinsman)' may indeed be semantically derived from 'one's (classificatory) *tjamu*', even though an expression such as 'one's own *mama*' (FATHER) cannot be regarded as semantically derived from 'one's (classificatory) *mama*'.

Polysemy should of course be distinguished from metaphorical and other extensions of the lexical meaning of a word. The distinction is not easy to draw, but 'not easy' is not the same as 'not possible'. The very fact that in Australian languages the great majority of kin terms can be used with respect to many different kin types suggests that what is involved here is a phenomenon of a very general nature, which operates on a level different from that of individual lexical items (see section 6). By contrast, the polysemy of the French word *femme* involves this particular lexical item.

It is worth noting in this connection that kinship terms also tend to be used, on a larger or smaller scale, as terms of address, to express a momentary emotional attitude to the addressee rather than a permanent interpersonal relationship. For example, in nineteenth-century Russian it was common for adults in a socially inferior position to address the children of their social superiors as *batjuška* ('dear little father') and *matuška* ('dear little mother'), in a spirit of familiarity, respect, and affection. Clearly, an explicatory formula along the lines of, 'I can think of you like I think of my MOTHER', would be inappropriate in this case. Instead, a formula along the following lines would be appropriate:

> speaking to you
> I feel something good toward you
> like what I would feel speaking to my MOTHER

There are good reasons to think that in languages with a classificatory system of kinship terminology, kin terms can also be used in this way. In fact, the phenomenon in question may well be a universal of language use. But it is a phenomenon apart, not to be confused with the use of kin terms in a genealogical sense (such as FATHER and MOTHER) or in a social (classificatory) sense.

The analysis suggested here offers a kind of compromise solution to the controversy between the genealogical and the social approach to kinship semantics, including, it seems to me, the important insights of both schools of thought.

It seems to me that the widely felt impasse in the controversy between the genealogical and the social approaches to kinship semantics (cf., for example, Keesing 1975:119) may have hinged precisely on that point: the unwarranted assumption that whatever solution is right for the terms for father and mother (which are usually used to illustrate the issue) is right for kinship terminology as a whole. I suggest that this assumption should be urgently re-examined.

I have argued that the problem of non-uniqueness can be remedied by setting three methodological requirements which have to be met jointly: the requirements of (1) reductiveness, (2) indigenisation, and (3) translatability. After the foregoing discussion, two further requirements can be added to those three: (4) non-proliferation of meanings and (5) preservation of the prototype.

Requirement (4) is a safeguard against unjustified polysemy. For example, when Scheffler proposes the formula K.L.G2. . δ as a definition of only one of the senses of the term *tjamu* (assuming that there is another sense of the term, which would require a separate definition), he seems to be multiplying meanings beyond necessity. A unitary formula such as that assigned by Burling (1970a:25) to the Njamal term *maili*, $G^2M^eO^m$ (two degrees of generation distance, ego's moiety, oldest member of the pair male), prevents this failing. On the other hand, one can argue that Burling's formula is unsatisfactory in so far as it treats a person's father's father in exactly the same way as his or her FFB, or FMBWB. This is counter-intuitive, since the FF relationship is no doubt more central to the concept than, say, the FMBWB one. I submit that a solution which saves both insights, and avoids both failings, is provided by the following formula (cf. Wierzbicka 1980:50):

> X and Y are *maili*. →
> if a man is a person's FATHER'S FATHER
> this man and this person can say of each other: 'this is my *maili*'
> X and Y can think of each other like this man and this person would think of
>   each other

This is a unitary formula, which doesn't assume the existence of two separate senses of the term *maili* (a primary genealogical one and a secondary social one), and which nonetheless treats the genealogical relationship FF as a focal one and as the prototype of the social relationship.

I am not saying that in any given kinship terminology the only terms affected by polysemy will be those for father and mother. A detailed investigation of a particular terminology may show that some other terms are also polysemous. But sound methodology requires that every time polysemy is posited, a special case has to be made for it. Consider, for example, the following statement:

> The evidence is quite clear that the so-called terms of relationship designate ego-centric, genealogically defined categories, and are polysemous; each term has a structurally primary and specific sense and a derivative, expanded, or broader sense (or senses). (Scheffler 1978:66)

In the case of 'father' and 'mother' the evidence is indeed quite clear. It is not justified, however, to extend this claim automatically to all terms of relationship. For example, Goddard's discussion of Yankunytjatjara terms of 'senior brother' and 'senior sister' seems to suggest that, unlike the terms for mother and father, these two are not polysemous. Goddard (1985:304) states: "Yankunytjatjara people have repeatedly stressed to me that one's first and second cousins are 'really' [original emphasis] one's *kuta* and *kangkuru*". By contrast, expressions such as *ngunytju mula* 'true mother' and *mama mula* 'true father' refer specifically to one's biological parents (1985:303).

4. Pitjantjatjara and Ompela: Two Illustrations

In issuing his challenge to believers in psychological reality, Burling (1969:426) demanded that the analyst "presents us with the entire system fully analysed and faces squarely the problem of how he chooses his particular analysis". I think that in the foregoing discussion I have met these requirements with my five explicit principles. It remains to present the reader with some examples of an entire system fully analysed on the basis of these principles.

To meet this challenge, I will use two illustrations. First, I will reproduce the entire set of Pitjantjatjara kinship terms, with Scheffler's 'componential definitions' of their 'primary senses', and I will contrast these with a set of natural language definitions based exclusively on the two proposed universals of kinship semantics, the concepts of MOTHER and FATHER, and formulated in a standardised semantic metalanguage derived from ordinary language. Second, I will reproduce Thomson's list of the Ompela kinship terms, with his specification of kin types covered by each term, and I will follow this, again, with a set of natural language definitions based exclusively on the concepts MOTHER and FATHER.

4.1 Pitjantjatjara Kin Classification: Componential Definitions of Primary Senses (from Scheffler 1978:102)

TERM	FOCI	DEFINITION
1. *tjamu*	FF, MF, SS, DS	K.L.G2. .♂
2. *pakali*	SS, DS	K.L.G2.−.♂
3. *kami*	FM, MM, SD, DD	K.L.G2. .♀
4. *puliri*	SD, DD	K.L.G2.−.♀
5. *mama*	F	K.L.G1.+.♂
6. *kamuru*	MB	K.C^1.G1.+.♂.X
7. *ngunytju*	M	K.L.G1.+.♀
8. *kuntili*	FZ	K.C^1.G1.+.♀.X
9. *kuta*	B+	K.Col.G=.+.♂
10. *kangkuru*	Z+	K.Col.G=.+.♀
11. *malanypa*	Sb−	K.Col.G=.−.
12. *watjira*		K.C^4.G=.
13. *untalpa*	D	K.L.G1.−.♀
14. *katja*	S	K.L.G1.−.♂
15. *ukari*	mZC, wBC	K.C^1.G1.−.X

Scheffler's notational conventions are as follows:

1. Kinsman (K) versus nonkinsman ($-$K).
2. Lineal (L) versus collateral (C) relationship.
3. Degree of generational removal: same generation as ego (G=) versus one generation removed (G1) versus two generations removed (G2).
4. Seniority: senior to ego (+) versus junior to ego ($-$).
5. Sex of alter: male (δ) versus female ($\female$).
6. Relative sex: same (//) versus opposite (X).
7. Sex of ego: male (δ ego) versus female ($\female$ ego).

4.2 Pitjantjatjara: Natural Language Definitions

1. X and Y are *tjamu*. $\rightarrow$

   if a man is the FATHER of another man's MOTHER or FATHER
   each of these men can say of the other: 'this is my *tjamu*'
   X and Y can think of each other like these men would think of each other

2. Y is X's *pakali*. $\rightarrow$

   if I am the FATHER or MOTHER of a man's FATHER or MOTHER
   I can say of this man: 'this is my *pakali*'
   X can think of Y like I would think of this man

3. X and Y are *kami*. $\rightarrow$

   if a woman is the MOTHER of another woman's MOTHER or FATHER
   each of these women can say of the other: 'this is my *kami*'
   X and Y can think of each other like these women would think of each other

4. Y is X's *puliri*. $\rightarrow$

   if I am the FATHER or MOTHER of a woman's FATHER or MOTHER
   I can say of this woman: 'this is my *puliri*'
   X can think of Y like I would think of this woman

5. Y is X's *mama*$_1$ = Y is X's FATHER

   Y is X's *mama*$_2$. $\rightarrow$

   if I can think of a man like I think of my FATHER
   I can say of him: 'this is my *mama*'
   X can think of Y like I would think of this man

6. Y is X's *kamuru*. $\rightarrow$

   if a man has the same MOTHER and FATHER as my MOTHER
   I can say of him: 'this is my *kamuru*'
   X can think of Y like I would think of this man

7. Y is X's *ngunytju*$_1$ = Y is X's MOTHER

   Y is X's *ngunytju*$_2$ $\rightarrow$

   if I can think of a woman like I think of my MOTHER
   I can say of her: 'this is my *ngunytiju*'
   X can think of Y like I would think of this woman

8. Y is X's *kuntili*. →

   if a woman has the same FATHER and MOTHER as my FATHER
   I can say of her: 'this is my *kuntili*'
   X can think of Y like I would think of this woman

9. Y is X's *kuta*. →

   if a man has the same MOTHER and FATHER as I
   and if I was born after him
   I can say of him: 'this is my *kuta*'
   X can think of Y like I would think of this man

10. Y is X's *kangkuru*. →

    if a woman has the same MOTHER and FATHER as I
    and if I was born after her
    I can say of her: 'this is my *kangkuru*'
    X can think of Y like I would think of this woman

11. Y is X's *malanypa*. →

    if a person has the same MOTHER and FATHER as I
    and if this person was born after me
    I can say of this person: 'this is my *malanypa*'
    X can think of Y like I would think of this person

12. X and Y are *watjira*. →

    if two people don't have the same MOTHER and FATHER
    and if the MOTHER or FATHER of one of them has the same MOTHER and
       FATHER as the MOTHER or FATHER of the other
    each of these two people can say of the other: 'this is my *watjira*'
    X and Y can think of each other like these two people would think of each
       other

13. Y is X's *untalpa*. →

    if I am a woman's MOTHER or FATHER
    I can say of this woman: 'this is my *untalpa*'
    X can think of Y like I would think of this woman

14. Y is X's *katja*. →

    if I am a man's MOTHER or FATHER
    I can say of this man: 'this is my *katja*'
    X can think of Y like I would think of this man

15. Y is X's *ukari*

    if two people have the same MOTHER and FATHER
    and if one of them is a man and the other is a woman
    and if one of them is my MOTHER or FATHER
    the other one can say of me: 'this is my *ukari*'
    X can think of Y like this person would think of me

This last definition may seem unnecessarily complex. I would argue, however, that
the simplicity of formulae such as 'cross-nephew/-niece' is more apparent than real.
Features such as 'lineal' or 'collateral', too, may seem simple, but when one tries to

decode them, long explicative formulae prove unavoidable. The idea of a 'cross-(sibling, etc.)' crucially involves a reference to a relationship between a man and a woman who have the same MOTHER and FATHER. A natural language definition simply makes this relationship explicit. In this case, the natural language definitions have the added advantage of highlighting the focal role of the relationship between a SEXUALLY MATURE male and female for the concept of 'opposite sibling'. (The idea of a 'parallel sibling' seems to be based on that of 'cross-sibling'.)

4.3 Ompela Kin Classification (from Thomson 1972:5)

TERM	DENOTATA
1. *pola*	FF, FFB, MMB, WMF, HMF
2. *poladu*	♂SC, ♂BSC, ♂ZDC, ♂MB+SSW, ♂DDH, ♂DSW
3. *mimi*	MM, MMZ, FFZ, WFM, HFM
4. *kamidjo*	♀DC, ♀ZDC, ♀BSC, ♀SDH, ♀SSW
5. *pa'i*	FM, FMZ, MFZ, WMM, HMM
6. *pa'idjo*	♀SC, ♀ZSC, ♀BDC, ♀DDH, ♀DSW
7. *ŋatji, ŋatjimo*	MF, MFB, FMB, WFF, HFF
8. *ŋatjidjo*	♂DC, ♂BDC, ♂ZSC, ♂SDH, ♂SSW
9. *pipi*	F, FB−, MZ−H, ♂SSS, ♂DDS, ♀SDS, ♀DSS
10. *pima*	FZ−, MB−W, ♂SSD, ♂DDD, ♀SDD, ♀DSD
11. *piado*	♂C, B+C, WZ+C, HZ+C, FFF, MMF, MFM, FMM
12. *pinya*	FB+, FZ+, MZ+H, MB+W, (♂MFZ+S)*
13. *pinyadu*	B−C, WC−C, HZ−C, (♂MB−DS)
14. *papa*	M, MZ−, FB−W, ♂SDD, ♂DSD, ♀DDD, ♀SSD
15. *kala*	MB−, FZH−, (♂FFZS), (♂MMZS), ♂SDS, ♂DSS, ♀SSS, ♀DDS
16. *mampa*	♀C, Z+C, WB+C, HB+C, (♂MBSS), (♂MZDS), FFM, MMM, FMF, MFF
17. *mukka*	MZ+, MB+, FB+W, FZ+H, (FFZ−C), (♀FMB+S)
18. *mukkadu*	Z−C, HB−C, WB−C, (MB+SC), (♂FZ−SD)
19. *yapu*	B+, FB+S, MZ+S, (♂MFZSS)
20. *ya'a*	Z+, FB+D, MZ+D
21. *ya'adu*	B−, Z−, FB−C, MZ−C, (♂FMBDS)
22. *ŋami*	MB+C, FZ+C, (♂FMBSS)
23. *tata*	MB−C, FZ−C, (♂FFZSS)

(Thomson uses the symbols B− and Z− for younger brother and younger sister and the symbols B+ and Z+ for elder brother and elder sister.)

4.4 Ompela: Natural Language Definitions

1. Y is X's *pola*. →

   if a man is my FATHER's FATHER
   I can say of him: 'this is my *pola*'
   X can think of Y like I would think of this man

2. Y is X's *poladu*. →

   if a man is my FATHER's FATHER
   he can say of me: 'this is my *poladu*'
   X can think of Y like this man would think of me

3. Y is X's *mimi*. →

   if a woman is my MOTHER's MOTHER
   I can say of her: 'this is my *mimi*'
   X can think of Y like I would think of this woman

4. Y is X's *kamidjo*. →

   if a woman is my MOTHER's MOTHER
   she can say of me: 'this is my *kamidjo*'
   X can think of Y like this woman would think of me

5. Y is X's *pa'i*. →

   if a woman is my FATHER's MOTHER
   I can say of her: 'this is my *pa'i*'
   X can think of Y like I would think of this woman

6. Y is X's *pa'idjo*. →

   if a woman is my FATHER's MOTHER
   she can say of me: 'this is my *pa'idjo*'
   X can think of Y like this woman would think of me

7. Y is X's *ŋatji* (*ŋatjimo*) →

   if a man is my MOTHER's FATHER
   I can say of him: 'this is my *ŋatji*'
   X can think of Y like I would think of this man

8. Y is X's *ŋatjidjo*. →

   if a man is my MOTHER's FATHER
   he can say of me: 'this is my *ŋatjidjo*'
   X can think of Y like this man would think of me

9. Y is X's *pipi₁* = Y is X's FATHER

   Y is X's *pipi₂*. →

   if a man has the same MOTHER and FATHER as my FATHER
   and if he was born after my FATHER
   I can say of him: 'this is my *pipi*'
   X can think of Y like I would think of this man

10. Y is X's *pima*. →

    if a woman has the same MOTHER and FATHER as my FATHER
    and if she was born after my FATHER
    I can say of her: 'this is my *pima*'
    X can think of Y like I would think of this woman

11. Y is X's *piado*.[3] →

    if a man is my FATHER
    or if he has the same MOTHER and FATHER as my FATHER
       and was born after my FATHER
    he can say of me: 'this is my *piado*'
    X can think of Y like this man would think of me

12. Y is X's *pinya*. →

    if a person has the same MOTHER and FATHER as my FATHER
    and if my FATHER was born after this person
    I can say of this person: 'this is my *pinya*'
    X can think of Y like I would think of this person

13. Y is X's *pinyadu*. →

    if a person's FATHER has the same MOTHER and FATHER as I
    and if he (this person's FATHER) was born after me
    I can say of this person: 'this is my *pinyadu*'
    X can think of Y like I would think of this person

14. Y is X's *papa*$_1$ =   Y is X's MOTHER

    Y is X's *papa*$_2$. →

    if a woman has the same MOTHER and FATHER as my MOTHER
    and if she was born after my MOTHER
    I can say of her: 'this is my *papa*'
    X can think of Y like I would think of this woman

15. Y is X's *kala*. →

    if a man has the same MOTHER and FATHER as my MOTHER
    and if he was born after my MOTHER
    I can say of him: 'this is my *kala*'
    X can think of Y like I would think of this man

16. Y is X's *mampa*. →

    if a woman is my MOTHER
    or if she has the same MOTHER and FATHER as my MOTHER
       and was born after my MOTHER
    she can say of me: 'this is my *mampa*'
    X can think of Y like this woman would think of me

17. Y is X's *mukka*. →

    if a person has the same MOTHER and FATHER as my MOTHER
    and if my MOTHER was born after this person
    I can say of this person: 'this is my *mukka*'
    X can think of Y like I would think of this person

18. Y is X's *mukkadu*. →

    if a person has the same MOTHER and FATHER as my MOTHER
    and if my MOTHER was born after this person
    this person can say of me: 'this is my *mukkadu*'
    X can think of Y like this person would think of me

19. Y is X's *yapu*. →

    if a man has the same MOTHER and FATHER as I
    and if I was born after him
    I can say of him: 'this is my *yapu*'
    X can think of Y like I would think of this man

20. Y is X's *ya'a*. →

    if a woman has the same MOTHER and FATHER as I
    and if I was born after her
    I can say of her: 'this is my *ya'a*'
    X can think of Y like I would think of this woman

21. Y is X's *ya'adu*. →

    if a person has the same MOTHER and FATHER as I
    and was born after me
    I can say of this person: 'this is my *ya'adu*'
    X can think of Y like I would think of this person

22. Y is X's *ŋami*. →

    if two people have the same MOTHER and FATHER
    and if one of them is a man and the other is a woman
    and if one of them is my MOTHER or FATHER
      and was born before the other one
    this other person can say of me: 'this is my *ŋami*'
    X can think of Y like this person would think of me

23. Y is X's *tata*. →

    if two people have the same MOTHER and FATHER
    and if one of them is a man and the other is a woman
    and if one of them is my MOTHER or FATHER
      and was born after the other one
    this other person can say of me: 'this is my *tata*'
    X can think of Y like this person would think of me

In all of the explications proposed in this chapter, with the exception of 22, seniority has been represented in terms of 'after', not 'before', and in principle it would seem desirable to do so consistently in all the explications. Nonetheless, for the term *ŋami*, an explication phrased in terms of 'before' seems simpler and more intelligible. This may not be accidental. It is possible that 'seniority' is usually conceived of in egocentric terms rather than in terms of 'who was born after whom', for example: 'if I was born before this person', 'if I was born after this person', 'if my MOTHER was born before this person', 'if my MOTHER was born after this person'. The problem requires further investigation.

5. Some Comments on the Definitions

Several aspects of the definitions proposed here require some explanation. First, there is the question of reciprocal and non-reciprocal terms. Componential formulae such as (Burling 1970a:25):

$$maili \quad - \quad G^2M^eO^m$$
$$karna \quad - \quad G^{+1}M^oS^m$$

(where G^{+1} stands for the first ascending generation, G^2 for two degrees of genealogical distance, M^e for ego's moiety, M^o for the opposite moiety, O^m for 'oldest member of the pair male', and S^m for male sex of the referent) blur the difference between terms such as *maili,* which are reciprocal, and terms such as *karna,* which are not. Verbal explications make this difference explicit. Thus:

X and Y are *maili.* $\rightarrow$

X and Y can think of each other like they (the prototype kin) would. . . .

X is Y's *karna.* $\rightarrow$

X can think of Y like I would. . . .

Second, there is the question of asymmetry between the terms for senior and junior members of various pairs of relatives (cf., for example, Scheffler 1978; Thomson 1972; Greenberg 1966 and 1980). Conventional componential formulae such as

$$tjamu \quad - \quad K.L.G2. \; .\delta$$
$$pakali \quad - \quad K.L.G2.-.\delta$$

do not show that *pakali* is in fact a marked term, not on a level with *tjamu.* The semantic asymmetry between the senior and junior terms is reflected in a particularly striking way in the morphology of the Ompela terms: *pola* versus *poladu, pa'i* versus *pa'idjo, pinya* versus *pinyadu,* and so on. But componential analysis doesn't reflect this semantic asymmetry, whereas natural language definitions make it explicit. Compare:

X's *pola*   =   X can think of Y like I would think of this man
X's *poladu*   =   X can think of Y like this man would think of me

In fact, I believe that similar asymmetries may exist in English, though they are never reflected in the componential analysis of English kin terms. The following explications attempt to show how, for example, *uncle* may differ in its semantic structure from *nephew:*

Y is X's *uncle.* $\rightarrow$

if a man has the same MOTHER and FATHER as my MOTHER or FATHER
I can say of him: 'this is my *uncle*'
X can think of Y like I would think of this man

Y is X's *nephew.* →

if a person has the same MOTHER and FATHER as a man's MOTHER or FATHER
this person can say of this man: 'this is my *nephew*'
X can think of Y like this person would think of this man

These explications suggest that *uncle* has an egocentric perspective, whereas *nephew* takes the 'objective' perspective of an outside observer. The greater semantic complexity of the terms *nephew* and *niece* as compared with *uncle* and *aunt* is reflected, among other things, in the fact that the former two are acquired later, are used less frequently, are not used as terms of address, cannot be used with names and without articles (*Uncle Bill rang* vs. **Nephew Bill rang*), don't participate in morphological and semantic derivation (cf. *auntie* vs. **niecie, Unc* vs. **Neph*), and so on.

Third, the components 'born before' and 'born after' deserve a brief comment. I have chosen these components in preference to the usual 'older' and 'younger' (or 'senior' and 'junior'), because an early death of one person can make any comparisons of age between this person and other persons impossible, but the relationship 'born before/born after' is an absolute one. (In English, where a concept such as 'first-born child' is not equivalent to 'oldest child (in the family)', in inheritance laws and the like, the former concept has often been treated as more important than the latter.)

It is interesting to note in this connection that in some Australian languages expressions such as 'gone before' and 'gone after' are in fact used as kinship terms, standing, respectively, for 'actual older sibling' and 'actual younger sibling'. This is what Evans (1985) notes for Kayardild.

6. Interpretation Rules

Needless to say, a formula such as 'someone thought of as related to X like (or *in the way*) one's FATHER is related to one' has only a very limited predictive power, since it is not clear what kinds of relationship would count in a given society as analogous to fatherhood. I believe, however, that the principles for extending focal relationship should be stated in the form of general interpretation ('extension') rules rather than be included in the explications of individual lexical items, since these principles operate on a level much more general than that of lexical items (cf. Lounsbury 1964 or Scheffler 1978).

An analogy from English may be useful at this point. The English expression 'X's brother' can be applied not only to a man or a boy who has the same mother and father as X but also to someone who has the same mother *or* father as X. Technically, such a person would be classified as 'half-brother' rather than 'brother', but in ordinary language he would be called *brother*, without any qualms. It would not be justified, however, to make provisions for this in the definition of the English word *brother*, because the equivalence in question applies also to half-sisters, 'half-uncles', 'half-aunts', and so on, so evidently it operates on a level more general than that of individual lexical items.

In fact, I believe that such rules represent cultural knowledge rather than purely linguistic knowledge. Cultural knowledge of this kind is of course essential for successful linguistic communication, but this doesn't mean that it would be either feasible or desirable to put it all into a dictionary. It must be simply recognised that to achieve a full communicative competence in a society, we need a cultural encyclopaedia, as well as a dictionary and a grammar.

If, however, our postulated interpretation ('extension') rules aspire to psychological reality, then the problem of non-uniqueness arises for them too, and so they, too, have to be formulated according to the methodological principles which guarantee uniqueness. For example, I would reformulate Scheffler's (1978:101) "half-sibling merging rule"

> (PC → Sb), self-reciprocal. Let anyone's parent's child be regarded as structurally equivalent to that person's sibling (or parents' child).

along the following lines:

> if a person has the same MOTHER or FATHER as I
> I can think of this person like I would think of a person
> who has the same MOTHER and FATHER as I

(Note the contrast between *or* in the first line and *and* in the third.)

I believe, however, that interpretation rules of this kind should be regarded as culture-specific and should be formulated accordingly (even if some of them operated in fact in many different languages and societies). For example, for Pitjantjatjara and Ompela one might propose, among others, the following interpretation rules:

> *Pitjantjatjara*
>
> if a man has the same MOTHER and FATHER as my FATHER
> I can think of him like I think of my FATHER
>
> if a woman has the same MOTHER and FATHER as my MOTHER
> I can think of her like I think of my MOTHER
>
> *Ompela*
>
> if a man has the same MOTHER and FATHER as my FATHER
> and was born after my FATHER
> I can think of him like I think of my FATHER
>
> if a woman has the same MOTHER and FATHER as my MOTHER
> and was born after my MOTHER
> I can think of her like I think of my MOTHER

If extension rules of this kind prove valid, it might be possible to simplify the definitions of words for classificatory mothers and fathers along the following lines:

> Y is X's *papa*$_1$ = Y is X's MOTHER
> Y is X's *papa*$_2$ = Y can think of X like I think of my MOTHER

But the matter requires further investigation.

7. Social and Psychological Components of Meaning

As has sometimes been pointed out (cf., for example, Leach 1961; Heath 1982), componential analyses of kinship terminologies present them in a form of abstract 'algebras', of rigid grids of symmetrically structured kin categories. But in fact, kinship words often incorporate behavioural norms and emotional expectations which don't lend themselves to representation in the form of such algebraic systems. There is no problem, however, in incorporating information of this kind in natural language explications. Some examples of this type have already been adduced (cf. the Walmatjari terms for affines explicated in section 2). As a further example, I will adduce the Russian word for grandmother, which incorporates affection and which is closer in meaning to the English word *granny* than to the English word *grandmother,* although it is the basic, and in fact the only, Russian word for grandmother. The meaning in question can be represented as follows:

> Y is X's *babuška.*   →
> if a woman is the MOTHER of my MOTHER or FATHER
> I can say of her: 'this is my *babuška*'
> X can think of Y like I would think of this woman
> one would think that I would feel something good toward this woman
> and that this woman would feel something good toward me

It should be obvious that both the 'good feelings' and a child's (rather than an adult's) perspective embodied in this concept are totally lost in descriptions such as MM, FM, or 'lineal female relative of the second ascending generation'.

Given that social and psychological information can be easily incorporated in natural language explications, the question should be raised whether rights, obligations, expectations, and so on, should not be incorporated in the definitions of kin terms on a much greater scale than has been done in the present chapter. Let us consider as an example the Ompela term *ya'a* 'older sister'. Since a girl "often teaches her younger siblings how to behave, much as their FZ does" (Thomson 1972:13), shouldn't we incorporate a component of this kind in the definition of the word *ya'a?*

It would be very easy to do so, but I don't think it would be justified. The point is that, as Thomson (1972:13) observes, a girl teaches her younger siblings *when they are children,* "but a pattern of avoidance between brother and sister develops as they grow up. A woman avoids her brother on the path, and a man may not sit down near or at the same fireside as his sister (elder or younger)". Since the same term *ya'a* is used for an elder sister regardless of her age, it is clear that no behavioural norms are encoded in the words as such.

Similarly, the Ompela term *pola* 'grandfather' implies a relationship based on respect and deference in the case of a close relative but a joking relationship in the case of a distant relative. Since the same kin term is used in both cases, evidently no behavioural norms are encoded in the word as such. This is quite different from what holds for the Walmatjari terms for affines discussed earlier, where the idea of certain behavioural norms is inseparable from the words themselves.

Scheffler (1978:32) has asserted (with respect to Australian languages) that "any

one kinship term may designate more than one kin class and that the connotations (if
any) of a kinship term are connected with the kin class it designates rather than
directly with the term itself".

I believe that this assertion is largely correct, but not entirely so. In some cases,
social and/or psychological connotations do become attached to the kin term itself.
In English the kin terms *father* and *dad* stand for the same kin type, but the social
and psychological connotations are in each case different. There is little doubt that
Aboriginal languages, too, possess kin terms which are similarly charged. For
example, Evans (1985) cites the Kayardild word *wangkurda,* which he glosses as
'darling opposite sex sibling', and which I would explicate as follows:

> X is my *wangkurda.* →
> X and I can think of each other like a man and a woman who have the same
>   MOTHER and FATHER think of each other
> I feel something good toward X

I would argue that every kin word should be examined on its own terms and that
social and psychological components should be included, or not included, in the
explication, depending on whether or not they are invariably associated with the use
of the word in question.

On the whole, it seems safe to say that Australian languages have many more
words which combine in their meaning genealogical information with social and
psychological components than European languages. A good case in point is provided by bereavement terms, for example, the Ompela words for a bereaved child of
a man or a bereaved elder sibling (Thomson 1972:20).

Special terms for prospective wives and husbands also exist, it seems. For
example, Thomson notes that the Ompela terms *wullomo, piloba* and *moryu*

> are applied to daughters and sons of 'outside'—distant or classificatory, as distinct
> from actual—'mother's brother's' and 'father's sister's' children and these are
> potential wives and husbands. But to the sons and daughters of own close mother's
> brothers and father's sisters, the terms *ŋami* and *tata* are applied. (1972:27)

"People say", he notes, that "it would be tactless and imprudent to address a BW as
wullomo, for this might suggest a sexual interest and give rise to jealousy between
brothers" (1972:8). This suggests, it seems to me, that the word *wullomo* as such
encodes a reference to marriageability and that it should be explicated (at least in
part) as follows:

> Y is X's *wullomo.* →
> if a man can think of a woman: 'this could be my wife'
> he can say of her: 'this is my *wullomo*'
> X can think of Y like this man would think of this woman

Clearly, being a man's *wullomo* is not just a matter of being related to that man in a
certain way but also of being *thought of* as related to that man in a certain way.

Generally speaking, whether a given term should be defined in genealogical terms alone, in terms of prospective marriageability, or both, is something that should be decided on an individual basis, not on the basis of some general principles, applied sweepingly to the entire lexical field of kinship.

8. The Practical Value of Natural Language Definitions

In searching for the optimal definition of kinship terms, my main goal has been to grasp what native speakers mean by them. I believe that a formula such as K.Col.G=.+.♂ or G°M°A°S^m, whose components have been arbitrarily chosen and do not correspond to any indigenous lexical items, can hardly aspire to the status of the native speakers' meanings. By contrast, formulae couched in terms of components which do correspond to indigenous lexical items can well aspire to that status.

But although the goal of such explications is primarily scientific (to discover 'the truth', i.e., to reveal the cognitive world of the speakers of a given language), it seems to me that they are also potentially useful from the point of view of applied linguistics and that they may provide practical assistance to all those who want to bridge the abyss between different cognitive worlds associated with different languages: teachers, social workers, compilers of dictionaries, devisers of bilingual education programs, and so on.

I do not claim that explications of the kind proposed here are all utterly simple and easy to read. But they do seem to be easier to comprehend than componential formulae. In principle they can, I think, be comprehended even by school-children. At this stage, I can only express hope that pedagogical experiments along these lines will soon be undertaken.

9. Conclusion

The universality of the concepts MOTHER and FATHER couldn't have been recognised before the myth was cleared away that some tribal peoples, and in particular Australian Aborigines, don't understand the mechanics of human reproduction. Scheffler writes:

> Contrary to the fantasies of some Western observers, Australian concepts of kinship are rooted in concepts of bisexual reproduction. As understood in Australian cultures, fertile sexual intercourse is necessary and sufficient to produce an animate human being. The man and woman who produce such a being are known as his or her 'father' and 'mother'. . . . (1978:515)

This is a statement of fundamental importance. I would argue, however, that the last clause of this sentence, "and he or she is known as their 'child'", should not be included. Australian Aboriginal languages have *words* for mother and father, but in many cases, they don't have any word for one's 'child' (regardless of this child's sex and regardless of the parent's sex). Putting the concepts 'mother', 'father', and 'child' on the same level, Scheffler undermines the importance of lexical evidence, which otherwise could be seen as a powerful source of support for his claim concerning the concepts 'mother' and 'father'. It is lexical data, I believe, which provide decisive evidence that the concept of biological fatherhood is relevant to Australian Aboriginal culture: the existence in Aboriginal languages of words such as *ngijinmimatharrb* (Kayardild for 'begetter') or *galŋan* (Dyirbal for classificatory father who is *not* a begetter) seems to prove this quite conclusively. Lexical data provide clues to cognition. Without such data, the spectre of 'hocus-pocus' (cf. Burling 1969) raises its ugly head again.

If we really want to avoid imposing alien forms on social and cultural categories and to comprehend them on their own terms, we should try to describe them without categories deeply rooted in anthropological culture, such as 'lineal', 'collateral', or 'ascending generation', and without categories rooted in European languages such as 'child' (regardless of sex) or 'brother' (regardless of relative age). But the concepts 'mother' and 'father' can be legitimately used, because—as lexical evidence suggests—these two are truly fundamental to the way human beings conceptualise their world, and this applies to Australian Aborigines as much as the rest of humankind.

Talking about categories such as 'lineal', 'consanguineal', or 'second ascending generation', Greenberg notes that they

> constitute what in the 60s came to be called a universal etic framework by means of which individual systems could be described. The parallel is close, and in fact recognised, to the phonemic theory of American structuralism of this period, which operated with a universal phonemic theory and a universal set of procedures whose purpose was to analyse each phonemic system as a unique structure, with the hope for many, that the phonemic analysis would reveal the psychologically real categories which underlay the speakers' linguistic behavior. (1980:13)

Fully recognising the historical value and importance of the introduction of componential analysis of kinship referred to in this passage, I would like to submit that an alternative 'universal etic framework' is available, in the form of the categories MOTHER and FATHER (and perhaps HUSBAND and WIFE), supplemented by universal semantic primitives such as 'person', 'think of', 'want', 'say', and their semantic derivates. Since the categories proposed here free the analysis from inherent circularity, and since at the same time they are supported by verifiable lexical evidence, they have, I believe, a better claim to being semantically viable and psychologically real.

10

'Alternate Generations' in Australian Aboriginal Languages

Two decades ago Rodney Needham (1971a:xxviii) issued a challenge to linguists and mathematicians: "If a mathematician or a linguist thinks that he can see how to extend into the elucidation of social classification and corporate institutions certain methods which have proved revealing in his own subject, it is entirely to the good that he should try his hand at it and show the anthropologists what his method is. The decisive point, though, is whether the formal analyses really do provide students of society with advantageous methods of understanding what they are trying to understand". (Cf. also Leach 1971.)

In this chapter, I would like to take up Needham's challenge. The method I propose can be regarded as formal and, in a sense, componential. It is very different, however, from the kind of componential analyses which scholars such as Needham or Leach have repeatedly denounced. In essence, the method advanced here aims at capturing "the native's point of view" (cf. Geertz 1971) in terms of a postulated set of non-arbitrary universal semantic primitives.

Cognitive anthropology, like semantics, is, essentially, a search for meaning. Commonly, however, the results of cognitive anthropology are expressed in a meta-language which cannot possibly reflect the native speakers' perspective and which cannot be expected to show the kind of meaning that the native speakers wish to convey. Consider, for example, the way the meaning of the word for 'mother' in the Australian languages Njamal and Pitjantjatjara is stated in Burling (1970a:24; Njamal) and Scheffler (1978:102; Pitjantjatjara):

$$\textit{ngardi} \quad — \quad G^{+1}M^{o}S^{f}$$
$$\textit{ngunytju} \quad — \quad K.L.G1.+.♀$$

In Burling's formula, G^{+1} stands for the first ascending generation, M^o for opposite moiety, and S^f for female sex. In Scheffler's formula, K stands for kinsman, L for lineal, G1 for one degree of generation removal, + for senior to ego, and ♀ for female. It seems clear (as pointed out in chapter 9) that formulae of this kind reflect the anthropologist's perspective, the anthropologist's 'meaning', rather than the native speakers' meaning. (Cf. Burling 1969 and 1970b; see also Wierzbicka 1972a, 1975, and 1980.)

Naturally, cultural anthropologists need and are entitled to their own technical metalanguage, as are linguists and other social scientists. But surely, the interpretation of cultures requires more than translation of native categories into an arcane technical language of the scientist. It also requires a translation of native categories into a kind of language which would make it possible both to capture the native speakers' meaning and to make that meaning accessible, intelligible to people from other cultures.

Semantic formulae of the kind just quoted achieve neither of these goals (and, presumably, they are not meant to). But what could and should an anthropologist, or a linguist, do if a group of ordinary people in an English-speaking country (high school students, teachers, social workers, and so on) asked him or her what was the meaning of a word such as *ngunytju*—i.e., what the native speakers meant by it when they used it?

I believe that the correct, and illuminating, answer to this question would be that the term in question has two meanings. One meaning is the same, or roughly the same, as that of the English word *mother,* and the other can be stated, roughly, as follows: 'she is his *ngunytju$_2$* = she is thought of as related to him like one's mother (*ngunytju$_1$*) is related to one'.

Contrary to appearances, in positing for this particular term two meanings rather than one we would not be acting in an ethnocentric way, because there is overwhelming anthropological and linguistic evidence that the terms for 'mother' and 'father' in Australian languages are indeed polysemous. (See Scheffler 1972 and 1978; Mufwene 1980 and 1987; see also Wierzbicka 1980 and chapter 9.) But this is not the place to try to establish the correctness of the definition proposed. My present concern is to draw attention to a methodological problem and to the availability of a framework which would make it possible to try to capture the native speakers' meaning and to make it intelligible to people from other linguistic and cultural backgrounds.

I agree entirely with Leach (1961:30) when he cautions against "too great a readiness to translate native terminology into what is arbitrarily deemed to be the primary English equivalent". But it would be equally harmful to assume a priori that native terms can *never* match any English terms in meaning. Moreover, in suggesting that a native term for 'mother' may have two meanings, one of which corresponds to the basic (relational) meaning of the English word *mother,* I don't wish to assert that this correspondence must be absolute. What I propose is that a term such as *ngunytju* has two meanings, one of which corresponds semantically (though not pragmatically) to the meaning of the English word *mother.* (For the distinction between semantic and pragmatic equivalence see the Introduction, section 3.3.) To reject this thesis a priori would be a case of a dogmatic and unjustified application of the principle of cultural relativism.

As suggested in chapter 9, there are two crucial methodological principles which should be kept in mind: (1) If the meanings encoded in one language A (say,

Pitjantjatjara) are to be made intelligible to people from a different cultural and linguistic background B (say, English), then those meanings have to be expressed in semantic formulae constructed in simple and generally understandable words from language B. (2) If the semantic formulae constructed in simple and generally understandable words from language B (say, English) are to constitute plausible hypotheses about the native speakers' meanings encoded in language A (say, Pitjantjatjara), then those formulae must be readily translatable into language A.

For example, it is permissible to use in the English semantic formulae words such as *person, say, good, bad, mother,* or *father* if the language whose meanings the analysis is trying to represent has words for such concepts, and it is not permissible to use words such as *sex, generation, ascending, descending, moiety,* or *parent* if the language in question doesn't have words for such concepts. I am not saying that, for example, if the speakers of a language have no term for 'sex', then they have no concept of 'sex'. I am only saying that the concept of 'sex' is not sufficiently salient for that society to have merited lexicalisation and consequently it is probably less salient than concepts such as 'woman' or 'man', which *have* been lexicalised. There is no evidence that concepts such as 'woman' or 'man' are based, in the speakers' semantic system, on concepts such as 'sex'. On the contrary, the lexical evidence suggests the opposite.

Needless to say, implementing these two principles is not a simple matter. A host of methodological questions arise, which require most serious attention.

However, important and interesting as such questions are, they can, I think, be kept apart from the more basic problem of the validity of principles (1) and (2) as such. I will proceed on the assumption that, in essence, these two principles are valid—or at least that they offer a new and potentially fruitful perspective on meaning and the interpretation of cultures.

1. The Principle of 'Alternate Generations'

The importance of the principle of 'alternate generations' in social life in Aboriginal Australia has been recognised for a long time. More recently, its important role in the structure of Australian Aboriginal languages has been investigated (see, in particular, Alpher 1982; Dench 1982 and 1987; Dixon 1989; Hale 1966; Hercus and White 1973; Koch 1982; Laughren 1982; Myers 1976; Nash 1982; O'Grady and Mooney 1973; Wordick 1979; Yallop 1977).

The 'alternate generations' principle could also, I believe, be of methodological importance in cognitive anthropology and cross-cultural semantics, as a test case for different models of semantic description. Many of the major problems of kinship semantics can be easily and simply illustrated with data from the area of 'alternate generations', clarifying the analytical issues and allowing us to assess the relevance, validity, and fruitfulness of various semantic approaches.

In the words of Kenneth Hale (1966:319): "The principle of alternating generations serves to position one's kinsmen into two opposed sets of alternate generation levels". Explaining this basic statement, Hale introduces, as he says, "the less cumbersome term *harmony*", and, for reasons of convenience, I will henceforth use this term too. He goes on:

> A person will be said to be *harmonic* with respect to those of his kinsmen who belong to the same set of alternate generation levels as he; he will be said to be *disharmonic* with respect to all others of his kinsmen. The principle can be characterized in the following way: A person is harmonic with respect to members of his own generation and with respect to members of all even-numbered generations counting away from his own (e.g., his grandparents' generation, his grandchildren's generation, etc.) He is disharmonic with respect to members of all odd-numbered generations (e.g., that of his parents, that of his children, that of his great-grand-parents, etc.) (1966:319)

One way in which the principle of 'harmony' is manifested in linguistic structure consists in the existence of two pronoun sets in many Australian languages, 'harmonic' and 'disharmonic' (cf. Hale 1966; Alpher 1982; Koch 1982; Dixon 1989). The operation of such alternative pronouns is illustrated in the following example (from Lardil) offered by Hale:

> a. karan-kur   wa·ŋ-kur   ki-rri
>   where-FUT   go-FUT   you-dual:harmonic
> b. karan-kur   wa·ŋ-kur   nyi-·nki
>   where-FUT   go-FUT   you-dual:disharmonic
> 'Where will you two go?'

The first is properly addressed to two persons who belong to the same set of alternate generation levels (for example, to a man and his brother, a man and his grandfather, a man and his wife's grandfather). The second is properly addressed to two persons belonging to opposite sets of alternative generation levels (for example, to a man and his father, a man and his nephew, a man and his great-grandchild).

But what do words such as *ki-rri* and *nyi-·nki* mean? We know that they can be glossed as 'you-dual:harmonic' and 'you-dual:disharmonic', but what is the meaning behind such glosses? And this (to me) means, what do the speakers mean when they use such words?

It seems clear that terms such as 'alternating generations', 'adjacent generations', 'generation harmony', 'even-numbered generations', and 'odd-numbered generations', or 'generational moieties' (Myers 1976:426), useful as they are as an analyst's shorthand, cannot represent the native speakers' meaning. The fact that the languages in question don't even have words for concepts such as 'alternating', 'even', or 'odd' (or, for that matter, 'generation') strongly suggests, in my view, that terms of this kind don't have any psychological reality. They are useful on the level of 'hocus-pocus' but not on the level of 'God's truth' (cf. Burling 1969).

I must stress that I don't mean this as a criticism of the conventional mode of description. Labels such as 'harmony' are brief and convenient, and as technical terms, they are obviously useful. Expressions such as 'alternating generations', too, are useful as heuristic devices. But the question of meaning and psychological reality is also an important one and has to be raised.

After all, if our hypothetical teacher, or social worker, eager to understand Aborigines and their ways of thinking, asked the linguist or the anthropologist about the meaning of the harmonic and disharmonic elements and heard in reply that Aborigines have special grammatical categories for 'even-numbered generations' and 'odd-numbered generations', he or she might well give up, in despair, all attempts to understand Aboriginal people and Aboriginal culture. For what could be more puzzling, more mystifying, more exotic, and more incomprehensible? It seems to me that it is a social as well as an intellectual responsibility of the linguist, and the anthropologist, to have a more illuminating answer to offer—and a less misleading one. Surely, it is desirable not to imply to the non-linguist that Aborigines 'count' generations and assign odd-numbered ones to one grammatical category and even-numbered ones to another. And surely, it is desirable to find out what they really do have in mind when they use a disharmonic or harmonic form of one kind or another.

The solution which I have suggested (in Wierzbicka 1987c; see also chapters 3 and 9) and which still seems to me essentially correct is based on the idea that the meaning of such pronouns involves certain prototypical relations. I would suggest that a 'harmonic grouping' makes sense to the native speaker not in terms of evenly numbered generations but in terms of a relationship modelled on that between two brothers or two sisters, and a disharmonic grouping makes sense not in terms of oddly numbered generations, but in terms of a relationship modelled on that between parent and child. (I assume that in the latter case sameness of sex is less relevant than in the former.) As a first approximation, therefore, definitions along the following lines can be offered:

ki-rri

you two
I think of you like this:
you can think of each other like two men or two women who have the same
   MOTHER and FATHER think of each other

nyi-˙nki

you two
I think of you like this:
you can think of each other like a person and this person's MOTHER or FATHER
   think of each other

The fact that in some Australian languages (for example, in Dyirbal; Dixon 1989) the distinction between harmonic and disharmonic groupings seems to be restricted to dual forms provides support for the idea that the category of generational harmony is modelled on the relationship obtaining within the 'nuclear' family rather than in the community at large.

2. Simple or Simplistic?

The definitions sketched previously are, it seems to me, attractive in their great simplicity. But if we are interested in 'God's truth' about meaning and culture, and not in a hocus-pocus elegance, then simplicity can't be for us an ultimate criterion of adequacy. There are good reasons to believe that the prototypes suggested are too simple.

First, the relationship between brothers (or sisters) is too specific as a model for 'generation harmony'. In Australian Aboriginal languages people who are thought of as related 'like brothers' are called 'brothers'. Yet the 'harmonic' relationship holds not only between classificatory brothers (or sisters) but also between, say, cross-cousins, who are, terminologically and behaviourally, clearly distinguished from brothers and parallel cousins, and who are not thought of as 'brothers'.

Similarly, the 'disharmonic' relationship holds not only between a person and his or her classificatory 'mothers' and 'fathers' but also between people whose mutual relationship is conceptualised as radically different from that between parents and children. For example, in languages which distinguish, terminologically, between 'close kin' and 'distant kin', parents and children are of course treated as 'close kin'. But the harmonic forms are used with reference to distant kin just as much as they are with respect to close kin. What matters is the generation level, not closeness. If the prototypical harmonic relationship was defined simply as that between parent and child, the definition would have a very limited predictive power: it would give no indication whatsoever as to how distant relatives of different generations would be treated.

3. Toward a Solution

One way to improve the predictive power of the definitions of 'harmonic' and 'disharmonic' elements is to incorporate into them the idea of contrast. If we say, very roughly, that the relationship between two people is like that between two brothers (or sisters) and not like that between a parent and child, the idea of generation is at least hinted at. It becomes fairly clear that what is meant is not any distinction in closeness but, rather, a distinction which is related to the generation level. Still, the contrast between the brother-brother prototype and the parent-child prototype could be interpreted as one between 'same generation' and 'different generation'. To forestall this misinterpretation, an additional prototype ought, perhaps, to be introduced to the semantic representation of the harmonic relationship, along the following lines:

> two people
> I think of them like this:
> they can think of each other like two men or two women who have the same
>   MOTHER and FATHER think of each other
> or like a person and this person's MOTHER's MOTHER or FATHER's FATHER think
>   of each other
> they cannot think of each other like a person and this person's MOTHER or
>   FATHER think of each other

The idea that a contrast between two different classes of relationship is explicitly encoded in the meaning of harmonic and disharmonic forms is amply supported by linguistic, as well as ethnographic, evidence. It is not an accident that an experienced student of the phenomena under discussion such as Hale speaks of two *opposed* sets of alternate generation levels. Nor is it an accident that in a more recent study Koch (1982) prefers to speak of 'opposite generations' rather than of 'disharmonic generations'. The fact that the two sets of generations ('harmonic' and 'disharmonic') can be referred to in some Aboriginal languages by terms such as 'us-bones' and 'them-flesh' (cf. Myers 1976:426; Laughren 1982) is, I think, eloquent enough. In fact, more than enough: it seems to indicate that the native speakers' concepts of 'harmonic' and 'disharmonic' embody the components 'same' and 'different' ('not the same'), respectively. If so, then the components 'same' and 'different' should be incorporated in the semantic representations of the relevant forms. Koch (1982) is in fact moving in that direction when he substitutes the terms 'same generation' and 'opposite generation' for Hale's 'harmonic' and 'disharmonic'.

One interesting piece of evidence for the presence of the components 'same'/'not the same' comes from the area of 'switch-reference': the use of grammatical devices signalling co-reference, or otherwise, of grammatical subjects in adjacent clauses. Wilkins (1988) shows that in Arrernte (Aranda) people belonging to the same set of alternating generations are treated as 'same' subjects, whereas people belonging to the opposite sets are treated as 'different' subjects.

4. Sameness—But of What?

As a first guess we might perhaps hypothesise that what is 'the same' is not the generation but the *kind:* conceivably, two people in a harmonic relationship are thought of (by Aboriginal speakers) as people *of the same kind,* and people in a disharmonic relationship, as people who are *not of the same kind.* If we accepted this, we could define harmonic and disharmonic elements along the following lines:

A. these people
   I think of them like this:
   they are people of the same kind
   they can think of each other like two men or two women who have the same
     MOTHER and FATHER think of each other
   or like a person and this person's MOTHER'S MOTHER or FATHER'S FATHER
     think of each other

B. these people
   I think of them like this:
   they are not people of the same kind
   they cannot think of each other like two men or two women who
     have the same MOTHER and FATHER think of each other
   or like a person and this person's MOTHER'S MOTHER or FATHER'S FATHER
     think of each other

This would be sufficient to account for at least some of the data. One solution, therefore, is to stop there and to regard the meaning of harmonic and disharmonic elements as sufficiently specified.

Alternatively, one could argue that even if the idea of 'the same kind'/'not the same kind' were correct, it would not be sufficient, because it would offer no clue as to why, in what sense, a person's brothers and sisters and grandparents and grand-children should all be regarded as people 'of the same kind', whereas a person and his or her mother or father should be regarded as people who are 'not of the same kind'. After all, it would be plausible to think of a group of women, or a group of men, as composed of people 'of the same kind'. It is true that the generational prototype ('like two brothers', etc.) provides a hint as to the kind of identity which is meant. But this hint in itself is highly enigmatic and offers no possibilities for extending the contrast in question beyond the confines of kinship.

If one assumes, for these or other reasons, that my initial hypothesis is either wrong or insufficient, then three different, alternative hypotheses suggest them-selves.

First, one could attribute primary importance to the fact that the two sets con-stitute exogamous generational moieties. In support of this idea one could quote remarks such as these concerning Pintupi:

> Although the terms 'us' and 'them' are reciprocal, the categories themselves are sociocentric and every person is a member of a single category whose members act together on occasions like male initiation, death, and also in consideration of possible marriage. The prime rule for marriage is that a person must marry within his or her generation moiety—must marry someone who is one of 'us' (*nganani-tja*). Criticism of wrong marriages generally is expressed on the basis that so and so married (or tried to marry) one of 'them' (*yinyurrpa*), e.g., into the first ascending or descending generation; this was accompanied by expressions of disapproval and disgust. Informants usually did not specify that a specific 'relationship' or 'kintype' was wrong. Rather, they said, 'one should not marry *yinyurrpa*' (i.e., 'wrongness' was not expressed in kintype but moiety). Marriage to the wrong kintype in one's own generation was considered bad, but more permissible than marrying *yinyurr-pa*. (Myers 1976:456–57)

Laughren (1982:72) writes, "The social significance of this division is great since marriage can be legally contracted between elements belonging to any two sets contained in the same 'alternative generation moiety'". (See also Wafer 1982:6.) If we tried to represent the meaning of 'harmonic' and 'disharmonic' forms on the basis of marriageability, this would be analogous to the attempt to define classifica-tory kinship terms on the basis of marriage rules, rather than blood relations. (Alan Dench (p.c.) notes, however, that those grammatical constructions which mark generation harmony appear to be used predominantly in circumstances which are not related directly to marriage.)

Second, one could attribute primary importance to the fact that people who are on the same 'generation level' have an essentially symmetrical relationship (like brothers), whereas people who are on the opposite generation levels can be expected to have an asymmetrical relationship (like a parent and a child). This aspect of 'harmony' was stressed, in particular, by Tonkinson:

> Most terminology reflects the existence of generation levels, in that members of the same grouping . . . use identical reciprocal terms in most cases, which express the

openness and high degree of equality in their relationships. On the other hand, people in adjacent level groupings (all members of the first ascending and descending generations) are usually addressed by a non-identical reciprocal term, which indicates that there is a difference in status between the two people concerned. (1974:50)

Berndt and Berndt, too, strongly emphasise the equality/inequality aspect of the generation levels and link it with a difference in power structure.

> The relationship between persons belonging to different generation levels is not simply an extension or reflection of the parent-child bond. More generally it signifies difference in status and authority, if not in age, in terms of superordination-subordination. In other words, it suggests horizontal stratification on the basis of status and kinship positioning.
>
> Within a person's own generation level are to be found, to some extent at least, 'equals': brothers and sisters, cross-cousins, age-mates and so on. The generation level above him includes those with some authority over him, directly or indirectly: father, mother, father's sister, father's sister's husband, mother's brother, mother's brother's wife, perhaps mother-in-law, father-in-law and so on. Deference, and in some cases avoidance, are relevant here. (1968:88; see also Radcliffe-Brown 1930–31:428–30; and 1950:30–32)

Against this, one might cite the fact (pointed out to me by Jean Harkins) that brothers or sisters usually don't use identical reciprocal terms but use, rather, asymmetrical terms such as 'elder brother', 'younger brother (sibling)', 'elder sister', and 'younger sister (sibling)'. Moreover, the relationship between brothers is not always that of a 'high degree of equality', because older brothers can be expected to discipline, as well as protect, a younger one. If we were, nonetheless, to base our semantic formulae on the equality/inequality aspect of the phenomenon, we could formulate them along the following lines:

> these people
> I think of them like this:
> they are people of the same kind
> they can do the same things to one another
> like two men or two women who have the same MOTHER and FATHER
> or like a person and this person's MOTHER's MOTHER or FATHER's FATHER
> and not like a person and this person's MOTHER or FATHER

Third, we could attribute primary importance to the fact that people who are on the same 'generational level' can freely engage in collective activities. Laughren's (1982:72) remarks that among the Warlpiri "men's sporting teams were traditionally formed according to this division" is particularly interesting in this connection. The collective aspect of the harmonic relationship has received particular attention in an interesting recent study by Alan Dench (1987). Dench argues that in the Ngayarda languages, a suffix generally used to mark 'collective activity' has been generalised "to the marking of certain kin relationships [i.e., harmonic ones] through the recognition that collective activity is a feature of these particular relationships". He goes on to say this:

> We see then that the division into generation sets reflected in the grammar of the languages is an important principle also reflected in much social interaction within the speech community. During initiation business, this principle defines two groups who interact in a restrained manner but whose members operate as a collective. It is the perception of this contrast between open collective activity and relative restraint that reinforces the division between the two groups, rather than the abstracted principle of generation harmony. For the collective suffix to be used to mark this contrast is thus not at all surprising. In fact, the collective suffix with this kinship marking function is perhaps most often used during initiation business. Certainly, most examples I have collected from observation (rather than from text or elicitation) were gathered during initiation business and typically involved the *karnku* giving orders to the *yinyjanungu*. (1987:333–34)

Consider also the implications of statements such as the following (Hudson MS b:7): "A joking bantering relationship is acceptable with those on the same generation level (including siblings, grandparents and grandchildren) but not with those of the opposite generation level." Certainly, a statement of this kind could be interpreted in the spirit of equality and reciprocity. But it can also be interpreted in the spirit of the suggestion that siblings, grandparents, and grandchildren 'can do the same things with one another': that is, joke, play, freely cooperate in everyday activities, and so on. If we follow Dench's line of reasoning, we could propose semantic representations along the following lines:

> these people
> I think of them like this:
> they are people of the same kind
> they can do the same things with one another
> like two men or two women who have the same MOTHER and FATHER
> or like a person and this person's MOTHER's MOTHER or FATHER's FATHER
> and not like a person and this person's MOTHER or FATHER

5. Deciding Between the Alternative Analyses

If one writes about kinship in informal prose, or if one, on the contrary, invents technical terms which don't have to be verifiable by ordinary native speakers' intuitions, then one is not forced to choose between alternative analyses such as those outlined in the preceding section. But the use of a semantic metalanguage based on a simplified version of a natural language forces the analyst to be explicit. Using this framework one has to choose one of a number of clearly defined possibilities. To decide among them, we must use all the available evidence—both linguistic and ethnographic.

In the case of 'alternating generations', important evidence comes from cases which do not fit the general rule. For example, Alpher (1982) reports that in the Dalabon language spoken in south-central Arnhem Land, there are two terms which denote relatives belonging to the same generation and which, nonetheless, require disharmonic subject prefixes on the verb. The terms in question (*gom* and *birr-woyin*) denote close cross-cousins, specified as non-marriageable, who are distinguished from distant cross-cousins (*gakali*), specified as potential spouses.

The question is, why are these close cross-cousins treated as disharmonic rather than harmonic? If the contrast between harmonic and disharmonic forms really meant a contrast between two endogamous 'generational moieties', then all cross-cousins, whether distant or close, should be seen as belonging to the same set (because their potential spouses belong to the same generation). But this is not the case. If the contrast between harmonic and disharmonic forms really meant the contrast between symmetric (reciprocal) and asymmetric (non-reciprocal) relationships, then too, all cross-cousins (like brothers and sisters) should be seen as belonging to the same set. But this is not the case. If, however, the contrast between harmonic and disharmonic forms means a contrast between people who can and people who can't 'do the same things with one another', then the differential treatment of close cross-cousins and distant cross-cousins begins, it seems to me, to make sense: distant cross-cousins can marry (and can do, needless to say, many different things with one another because of this), but close cross-cousins are not mutually marriageable.

Alpher also mentions the fact that in Dalabon a group of inanimate objects (such as stones) is treated as disharmonic and that the members of an anomalous pair of humans, such as a European travelling with an Aborigine, are also treated as disharmonic. Alpher's explanation for these facts reads as follows:

> [T]he only property which dyads with *gom* or *birrwoyin* share with a pair of stones falling, or an Aborigine travelling with a European, is pure, abstract, empty salience. The principle which I believe to be involved might be called 'the empty marking of salient exceptions'. (1982:73)

I confess that, to me, Alpher's explanation doesn't make the facts much clearer or more intelligible. But the notion that the members of the group either can or cannot be expected to do the same things with one another does seem to me helpful. Close cross-cousins (unlike distant cross-cousins) can't be expected to do so; an Aborigine travelling with a European may well be viewed as unlikely to do so either, and neither would two stones be likely to be expected to engage in a joint and mutually satisfying activity ('to do the same things with one another').

Hale also noted the 'aberrant' behaviour of cross-cousins with respect to the principle of 'generational harmony':

> There is one exception to this rule. For some reason, the relationship between a person and his classificatory and actual first cross cousins (*yurwatin*) is regarded as disharmonic for the purposes of pronominal usage. This may reflect an earlier stage in Lardil history at which the marriage rule was of the Kariera type rather than the Aranda type. It is noticed that in some parts of Australia (e.g. among the Walbiri of Central Australia), the class from which a man takes his wife is treated, in certain linguistic usages, as if it were in the father's generation. If the Lardil once had the Kariera type of kinship system, first cross cousins would have been included in the

class from which a man took his wife. This explanation is to be regarded as highly
speculative. (1966:320)

Wilkins offers the following example and comment:

> [A] group of people walking along together, one of whom is a crying boy, can be
> described using either ss or ds [same-subject or different-subject] marking:
> (44) Urreye kweke artne-lape-ke, itne lhe-rlenge/lhe-mele.
>   boy   small cry-along-pci 3pl go-ds/go-ss.
>   'The little boy cried as they (excl/incl) walked along.'
> It was explained to me that the use of different-subject marking results in the
> interpretation that all other members of the group are from the same (harmonic)
> generation, but the boy is from a different (non-harmonic) generation. It is a
> cultural fact that there is a strong distinction between same and different generation
> level and that close mixing between generations, especially cross-sex, is frowned
> upon. In using different-subject marking the speaker focuses on the fact that the boy
> is not to be seen as part of the group. The inclusion principle would be used if the
> group referred to were a family, or if there were a number of people of mixed
> generation levels. (1988:165–66)

It seems to me that the formula proposed in this chapter fits all the aspects of
Wilkins' explanation: 'sameness', 'being thought of as', 'doing things together'
('close mixing'), and the 'same-sex orientation' of harmonic relationships.

6. The Possibility of a Masculine Bias

If we are to think of the harmonic relationship primarily in terms of the possibility of
'doing things together', then it is worth considering whether the prototypical harmonic pairs should not be thought of as composed of people of the same sex. The
component 'people of the same kind', if accepted, would seem to point in the same
direction. The formulae considered so far comply to some extent with that de-
sideratum, by referring to 'two brothers' or 'two sisters' rather than to 'two people
who have the same mother and father'. But the second model of the harmonic
relationship—that between grandparents and grandchildren—has been formulated
regardless of sex.

As an alternative, it may be worthwhile to consider a phrasing that would be
sex-specific:

> these people
> I think of them like this:
> they are people of the same kind
> they can do the same things with one another
> like two men or two women who have the same MOTHER and FATHER can
> or like a man and his FATHER'S FATHER or a woman and her MOTHER'S MOTHER
>   can
> and like a man and his FATHER or a woman and her MOTHER cannot

Furthermore, it is also worth considering whether it would not be justified to give the prototypical harmonic pair a masculine bias. There are perhaps reasons to think that the idea of free interaction among males (during initiation ceremonies, and perhaps during other ceremonial and religious activities, but also during profane activities such as sporting events) is more focal to the concept than the idea of free interaction among females. For the same reason, it might be more justified to oppose the relationship between a man and his brother to that between a man and his father (or perhaps his mother's brother) rather than to that between a parent and a child.

It might even appear that the phrase 'a man and his father' might be sufficient, but if we left out the phrase 'or his mother's brother', we would fail to distinguish the disharmonic relationship as such from a disharmonic-cum-agnatic one, marked in Arandic languages (see Hale 1976; Hercus and White 1973; Koch 1982). To maintain the idea of two males in a disharmonic but not necessarily agnatic relationship, it would seem preferable to provide two models (father and mother or father and mother's brother).

Of course the harmonic relationship as such is not restricted to people of the same sex in general or to males in particular. What is at issue here is merely the relevance of sex for the prototype, not the relevance of sex for the entire range of harmonic, or disharmonic, relationships.

Whether or not the prototype should be given a masculine bias is an issue which I would prefer to leave open. Among the issues which should be considered in trying to decide this point are that of the prototype of a relationship based on authority (parent:child or father/mother's brother:boy?), the relevance of sex for the grandparent-grandchild relationship, the implications of the cross-cousin usage, and also the implications of the fact that in some Australian languages the harmonic and disharmonic distinction is restricted to 'agnatic' relationships. None of these issues can be explored here. Accordingly, the two formulae given next, which do exhibit a masculine bias, are offered only for consideration. The idea that the explication should contain a reference to 'father's father' was suggested to me by Nicholas Evans (p.c.).

HARMONIC:

these people
I think of them like this:
they are people of the same kind
they can do the same things with one another
like two men who have the same MOTHER and FATHER can
or like a man and his FATHER'S FATHER can
and like a man and his FATHER cannot

DISHARMONIC:

these people
I think of them like this:
they are not people of the same kind
they cannot do the same things with one another
like two men who have the same MOTHER and FATHER can
or like a man and his FATHER'S FATHER can
and like a man and his FATHER cannot

7. Markedness

Throughout this chapter I have been talking about harmonic and disharmonic relationships as if they were both on the same level of semantic complexity. It is of course possible, and indeed likely, that one of the two contrasting forms may be unmarked. For example, the data cited in Alpher (1982) seem to suggest that in Dalabon the harmonic pronouns are unmarked, whereas the disharmonic ones carry the kind of meaning which has been suggested here for disharmonic elements in general. On the other hand, the data cited in Dench (1987) suggest that in the Ngayarda languages the harmonic verbal suffix carries the kind of meaning postulated here for harmonic elements in general, whereas the absence of the suffix constitutes the unmarked case. I must stress, therefore, that in formulating a positive meaning for both harmonic and disharmonic forms, I am not making any claims about the markedness or otherwise of any specific elements in any specific language. What I am trying to do is to provide formulae which can be assigned to various harmonic or disharmonic elements after it has been established that a particular element (as, for example, the harmonic suffix discussed by Dench) does have a positive meaning.

8. Parallels from European Languages

It seems to me that in trying to make sense of linguistic categories which at first blush appear to be exotic and incomprehensible—and the category of generational harmony is a good case in point—it is good to relate them to something comparable from familiar languages and cultures. I would suggest, therefore, that the harmonic/ disharmonic contrast can profitably be compared to the contrast between English terms of address such as *brother* and *Father* or that between *Sir* and *mate*. *Brother* and *mate*, used as terms of address, imply the same kind of equality and reciprocity that harmonic forms do in Australian languages, whereas *Father* and *Sir* (usually spelled with a capital letter) imply the kind of inequality and attitudinal asymmetry that the disharmonic forms do. In addition, the term *mate* suggests a kind of solidarity and perhaps even readiness to do the same things together as the harmonic forms do. Alan Dench (p.c.) has suggested comparing the contrast between harmonic and disharmonic pronouns to that between *tu* and *vous* in French. I find this kind of comparison very useful.

The comparison with *mate* seems instructive in other ways too. Thus, although one would address someone in English as *Father* (normally, a clergyman or a monk of high status) and, less often, as *Mother* (a nun of high status), one could never address anybody as *Parent*. Furthermore, whereas *Sir* has its feminine counterpart in *Madam*, the term *mate* is by and large restricted to males: at least prototypically, 'mateship' is a relationship between males.

The Communist terms of address such as *comrade, tovarišč* (Russian), *towarzysz* (Polish) are perhaps even clearer in their collectivist and interactional implications. Certainly, if one addresses someone as *comrade,* one implies equality and reciprocity as much as one does addressing someone as *brother.* But *comrade* implies more than that: 'comrades' are people who want to do the same things together (in the name of a common ideology). The form *brother,* whether it is used in a religious (Christian) context or in the context of a labour movement, appeals to a common condition (as sons of God, or as workers in a capitalist state). But the term *comrade* appeals to a common (collective) action. (Note especially how the phrase *X and his comrades* suggests common action rather than a common condition.)

But the English word *mate* offers perhaps the most instructive parallel to the harmonic relationship, as it can imply not only equality and reciprocity and joint activity (as in *playmate*) but also, remarkably, a readiness to engage in sexual activity with one another! This last fact throws light, I think, on the apparent anomaly of cross-cousins' being treated as disharmonic. People who are not mutually marriageable are not prospective sexual partners; that is to say, they are not prospective 'mates' in one of the senses of the word *mate* (they can't, and shouldn't, 'mate with' one another). Thus, the range of semantic possibilities of the English word *mate* seems to come remarkably close to that of harmonic relationships in Australian languages.

The comparison between the Australian harmonic and disharmonic forms, on the one hand, and the European terms of address, on the other, may seem far-fetched in view of the fact that the principle of generation harmony applies in reference as well as in address. But so do, to some extent, titles such as *brother, Father,* and *comrade.* And second, in some Australian languages (for example, in Dyirbal; cf. Dixon 1989) the harmonic/disharmonic contrast does seem to focus on the relationship between the speaker and the addressee, for the only pronouns which do make this distinction are the first-person duals ('we two').

9. Meaning Versus Knowledge

I would like to return now to the example discussed at the outset, i.e., to the Lardil dual pronouns. Dixon (1980:276) offers the following glosses:

first-person inclusive dual 'you and I'	*ŋaku-rri*	*ŋaku-ni*
first-person exclusive dual 'he and I'	*nya-rri*	*nya-anki*
second-person dual 'you two'	*ki-rri*	*nyi-inki*
third-person dual 'they two'	*pi-rri* two people in same generation level, or two levels apart, e.g., ego and brother/sister/ grandparent/grandchild	*rni-inki* two people in alternate generation levels, or three levels apart, e.g., ego and parent/child/great- grandparent/great- grandchild

(Dixon's orthography differs slightly from Hale's, cited earlier; the orthography used by the authors has been preserved.)

I do not deny that glosses of this kind, with their numerical and quasi-numerical indications such as 'alternate', 'two', or 'three', ensure a precision and conciseness that the formulae of the kind proposed here can't offer. I recognise, therefore, that glosses of the kind used by Dixon are useful, for both economic and pedagogic reasons. But they cannot be said to analyse and state the *meaning*, the concept in the speaker's mind, when a particular term is used. To explain the *meaning* of the harmonic and disharmonic pronouns, it becomes necessary to use imprecise and clumsy paraphrases of the kind proposed here. They are 'imprecise' in the sense that they don't tell the reader how, say, people five or seven generation apart would be treated. I think, however, that they have a greater chance than numerical expressions do of portraying with precision the native speakers' concept; of capturing, with precision, the psychological and cultural reality.

One could object to this on the grounds that the harmonic and disharmonic forms are in fact highly precise referentially, and yet a European unfamiliar with Aboriginal culture and presented with semantic formulae of the kind proposed in this chapter might be unable to decide whether such a relationship (i.e., one between two people five or seven generations apart) should be viewed as harmonic or disharmonic.

I believe, however, that the European's failure in this respect would have to be attributed to his or her lack of cultural, rather than semantic, competence. Similarly, the definition of the Pitjantjatjara word for 'mother', offered at the beginning of this chapter, wouldn't have much predictive power for a European unfamiliar with Aboriginal culture. It would be pointless, however, and in my view theoretically unjustified, to try to incorporate all kinds of 'useful cultural knowledge' into the definitions which seek to portray the concepts adequately. To take just one example from English, if we know that the woman A is the *wife* of the man B, it can safely be inferred from this (by anybody familiar with our culture) that A is not B's mother, sister, daughter, grandmother, granddaughter, and so on. But it would be incorrect, to say the least, to try to incorporate such information into our definition of the English word *wife*.

The line between meaning and knowledge is not always easy to draw, and both linguists and anthropologists have often expressed doubts whether it can be drawn at all (cf., for example, Haiman 1980 and Tyler 1978). I believe that although it is not easy to draw this line, it is always possible to do so, given sufficient time and effort and given an adequate theoretical framework, and I submit that such a framework is available in the 'natural language' semantics, based, ultimately, on a set of universal semantic primitives.

VI

LANGUAGE AS A MIRROR OF CULTURE AND 'NATIONAL CHARACTER'

11

Australian English

To many, it is axiomatic that language is a mirror of culture, as well as being a part of culture. To others, however, the question is much more problematic, as I found out when I gave a paper to the Sydney Linguistic Circle on linguistic differences between English and Polish, which, I argued, reflected differences between Anglo-Saxon culture and Polish culture.[1] (For a published version of the paper in question, see Wierzbicka 1985b and 1991a.)

My claims were challenged by Michael Halliday—not on empirical grounds but from a methodological standpoint. Is it justified, he asked, to link individual linguistic phenomena with non-linguistic aspects of culture directly? He acknowledged that in some cases direct links do seem to exist, but he was inclined to confine such cases to the lexicon. As far as the grammar is concerned, he was more cautious. He agreed that, for example, the rich systems of honorifics in languages such as Japanese do appear to reflect aspects of culture, but he was reluctant to accept a similar claim concerning rich systems of affectionate diminutives in Slavic languages, and on the whole he was sceptical of any search for direct correlations between language and social reality, à la Whorf. In particular, he raised the following difficulty: If one language (for example, Russian) has three genders, another (for example, French) has two, and yet another (for example, English) has none, would it be justified to try to link these differences with some extra-linguistic differences in culture? Presumably not. So at best, it is only some selected features of grammar which one might seek to correlate with something outside language. But how do we decide which linguistic phenomena can be legitimately interpreted as culturally significant outside language itself? Can it be done on a principled basis? If genders don't reflect extra-linguistic culture, what gives us the right to suggest that honorifics or diminutives do?[2]

I think that the question is interesting and worthwhile, but perhaps not quite as forbidding as Halliday seemed to suggest. After all, doesn't the same apply to the lexicon? Certainly, lexicon tends to change more quickly than grammar in response to changes in social reality. Nevertheless, lexicon, too, is subject to conservative forces, and not all lexical differences between languages reflect current differences in culture. Presumably, however, we wouldn't want to deny, on this basis, that some lexical differences are readily open to cultural interpretation.

For example, English distinguishes lexically between arms and hands, between fingers and thumbs, and between fingers and toes, whereas Polish doesn't. I am not aware of any contemporary extra-linguistic differences which could explain these lexical differences between the two languages, and perhaps no such explanation exists, on a synchronic level. But there are many lexical differences between Polish and English whose contemporary cultural significance couldn't be reasonably doubted. For example, in addition to words for Saturday and Sunday, English has a special word for weekend, which Polish doesn't have (so that Polish immigrants in English-speaking countries had to borrow the English word *weekend* to speak in Polish about weekend-related aspects of their life in those countries). Could one doubt that this has something to do with the fact that in Poland until very recently, people generally worked on Saturdays?

And a second example, this time one illustrating differences in attitudes rather than in 'objective realities': both Polish and English have pejorative words for Germans (*Jerries, Szwaby*), but only English has a pejorative word for the Japanese (*Japs*), and only Polish has several pejorative words for Russians and things Russian (*Ruscy, Kacapy, sowiecki, ruski* (Adj.)). Could anyone doubt that this reflects differences in collective historical experiences and in political outlook?

Is it 'unscientific' to claim that lexical differences such as those concerning negative words for different nationalities directly reflect culture and history? Wouldn't it rather be 'unscientific' to close our eyes to such facts?

I think that what applies to the lexicon applies also to grammar, in the broad sense of the term: it is perfectly legitimate to seek in grammar equivalents of 'Jerries' and 'Japs', and this doesn't commit us in the least to the claim that there is nothing in grammar but 'Jerries' and 'Japs', so to speak. For example, it is perfectly possible that honorifics and diminutives are like 'Jerries' and 'Japs' (as are also references to the Australian kinship systems which permeate the grammars of Australian Aboriginal languages; cf. Hale 1966), whereas genders are perhaps like 'fingers' and 'toes': a way of doing something within language for which no external cause or correlate is evident.

Clearly, the more varied and rich our linguistic evidence is, the stronger our case. If we can explain a considerable number of differences between two languages in terms of one, or of a complex of, independently posited cultural differences, then our case will be fairly strong.

Furthermore, time is clearly a relevant factor. Presumably, grammatical features inherited from earlier centuries will not reflect very recent cultural facts. Conversely, linguistic innovations which go hand in hand with historical and cultural changes will have a good claim to being a reflection and an expression of sociocultural phenomena. For this reason, Australian English, with which this chapter is primarily concerned, constitutes a particularly inviting field of study and can be regarded as an interesting test case.

Is it possible to predict which areas of language are most likely to reflect the living culture?

I would venture to suggest two general hypotheses in this regard. First, optional grammatical categories are likely to be more revealing of the on-going culture than obligatory ones. For example, affectionate diminutives are entirely optional; it is up to the speaker to use them or not. If the cultural need for expressing attitudes embodied in diminutives diminished, or ceased to be felt, the speakers could quietly and imperceptibly stop using them, without at any point having to struggle against the pressures of the system and without running the risk of being misunderstood. If, on the other hand, a grammatical distinction is obligatory (as is the contrast among the three nominal genders in Slavic languages), then it is less likely that it will be able to change quickly in response to changes in the speakers' outlook, and so it is less likely that it will be directly related to the ongoing culture.

Second, those parts of language, including grammar in the narrow sense of the term, which are related to the relationship between the speaker and the addressee are, I suggest, among those most likely to reflect the living, on-going culture. For example, distinctions embodied in the third-person personal pronouns are less likely to reflect the on-going culture than those embodied in the second-person personal pronouns. Thus, the fact that Turkish and Finnish don't have a distinction analogous to that between *he* and *she* in English doesn't seem to lend itself to convincing cultural interpretation. But distinctions in second-person pronouns do seem to mirror the culture directly and do tend to change in response to a changing cultural context. (Cf., for example, Friedrich 1966; Brown and Gilman 1960; Wierzbicka 1985b.)

Generally speaking, it is the pragmatic aspects of grammar which seem to be particularly culturally revealing. It seems reasonable to conjecture, therefore, that the pragmatic aspects of grammar would also be among those which would be most likely to change fairly quickly, in response to social and cultural change.

More specifically, among the aspects of language which would seem to be particularly revealing of social attitudes and of the style of social interaction, I would single out the following four: (1) forms of address; (2) expressive derivation; (3) illocutionary devices of different kinds, such as interjections and particles; and (4) speech act verbs.

It is remarkable that in all these areas Australian English has developed its own linguistic devices, which can be seen as uniquely suited to what is generally regarded (by people in the street as well as by serious students of Australian society) as the (Anglo-)Australian ethos and the (Anglo-)Australian style of social interaction. In what follows, I will support this claim with illustrations from each of these four areas, concentrating, however, on the first.

1. First Names

The proposition that Australian English is fond of abbreviations is a commonplace. The Australian love of abbreviations is commonly attributed to the Australian 'laziness' (according to one Australian stereotype, "an Australian is a lazy boozer"; Horne 1964:4); to the Australian 'anti-intellectualism' and distrust of all 'verbosity' (in the view of the ordinary Australian, "most of what is pumped out of the word factories is 'bullshit'"; Horne 1964:4); and to the Australian 'toughness' (in Australia, "the phlegmatic understatement will almost always command greater attention than over-statement, terseness more than volubility, the short vulgar word more than the polite polysyllable"; Baker 1959:51). But the common belief that the facts behind the truism are well known and well understood is, in my view, a fallacy. From a semantic point of view (as well as from others), Australian abbreviations fall into a number of different, though related, categories. Each of these categories embodies a distinct meaning and, I suggest, reflects a characteristic Australian attitude.

One such category comprises abbreviated forms of first names, usually ending with a consonant, such as the following:[3]

Mar	[maə]	for Mary
Marz, Mars	[ma:z]	for Mary
Mare	[mɛə]	for Mary
Marz, Mares	[mɛ:z]	for Mary
Baz	[bæz]	for Barry (or Basil)
Tez	[tʰɛz]	for Terry
Gaz	[gæz]	for Gary (or Gavin)
Caz	[kʰæz]	for Caroline (or Catherine)
Kez	[kʰɛz]	for Kerrie
Iz	[ɪz]	for Isa (or Isobel)
Muz	[mʌz]	for Murray
Shez	[ʃɛz]	for Sheridan
Shaz	[ʃæz]	for Sharon
Juz	[dʒʌz]	for Justine
Al	[æɬ]	for Alice (or Alison)
Cor	[kʰɔə]	for Cora
Laur	[lɔə]	for Laura
Ange	[æɲdʒ]	for Angela
Tash	[tʰæʃ]	for Natasha
Soph	[sʌəf]	for Sophie
Dim	[dɪm]	For Dimity
Rache	[rʌɪtʃ]	for Rachel
Man	[mæn]	for Mandy
Ness	[nɛs]	for Vanessa
Jule	[dʒuɬ]	for Julie
Julz, Jules	[dzuɬz]	for Julie
Tone	[tʰʌʊn]	for Tony

It is hard not to notice that many forms in this list end in the consonant -*z,* and also that this word-final -*z* tends to replace an -*r* of the base form. It might seem, therefore, that apart from the truncation, a simple phonological process is involved (a substitution of -*z* for an underlying -*r* in word-final position). However, the fact that forms such as *Marz, Julz,* and *Gaz* (for Gavin) are also used indicates that the word-final -*z* is in fact a suffix. This is a problem to which I will return later.

Leaving aside, however, forms such as *Marz, Julz,* or *Gaz,* one may easily form the impression that forms such as those listed are identical in status and in function with standard pan-English abbreviations such as *Bob, Sue, Pam, Kate, Tim,* or *Liz.* In fact, however, this impression is deceptive. What makes forms such as *Shaz* or *Mare* particularly interesting is that they are not standard abbreviations, in the sense that they are not used as unmarked personal designations. A person could be introduced and commonly referred to, informally, as 'Bob Brown' or 'Pam Smith', but normally, people could not be introduced or commonly referred to as 'Shaz

Jones' or 'Mare Peterson'. Forms such as *Bob* or *Pam* are informal and rather friendly, but they are not affectionate. By contrast, forms such as *Shaz* or *Mare* are affectionate, and their affectionate force stems largely from the fact that they are perceived not as standard personal designations but as fond 'distortions' of a person's 'normal' name. (See chapter 7.)

Thus, in a group of Australian schoolgirls names such as *Pam, Kate,* and *Sue* would normally be treated on a par with forms such as *Mary, Isa, Caroline, Sharon,* or *Justine,* and not on a par with forms such as *Mare* or *Marz, Caz, Shaz,* or *Juz.*

The affectionate character of forms such as *Caz* or *Shaz* is particularly clear when one considers heavy restrictions on their use in self-reference. One can say on the phone, 'Pam speaking' or 'Bob speaking', but normally one would not say, 'Caz speaking' or 'Shaz speaking'.[4] (Moreover, one could say, 'I hate Pam', but hardly 'I hate Shaz'.)

From this point of view, affectionate abbreviations such as *Caz* or *Shaz* must be seen as analogous to affectionate diminutives such as *Pammie* or *Katie* rather than to standard designations such as *Pam* or *Kate.* There is one proviso: forms homophonous with diminutives such as *Pammie* or *Katie (Debbie, Suzie, Cindy,* etc.) are often used as basic, everyday forms (and sometimes are even bestowed on children as their canonical first names). If so, then they can of course be used in self-reference, without any self-caressing connotations. Forms such as *Caz* or *Shaz* are normally not used in this way. But if the standard everyday designation doesn't have a diminutive form, for example, if a girl is normally called *Pam* or a boy *Bob,* then the speakers could not introduce themselves on the phone, or otherwise refer to themselves, seriously, as *Pammie* or *Bobby.*

Given this parallel between affectionate diminutives and affectionate abbreviations, it is all the more interesting to note that from a semantic and socio-cultural point of view the category of affectionate abbreviations differs profoundly from that of affectionate diminutives. Since the affectionate diminutives (of first names) constitute a pan-English phenomenon, whereas the affectionate abbreviations (of first names) present a characteristically (though not uniquely) Australian one, it is reasonable to infer that the latter category may embody characteristically Australian attitudes.

'Diminutive' forms of English names such as *Pammie* or *Jimmy* were discussed in chapter 7, where the following explication was proposed for them:

> *Pammie, Jimmy*
>
> I want to speak to you (or: of person X) the way people speak
>   to children whom they know well
>   and toward whom they feel something good

By contrast, the meaning of back-formations such as *Deb* or *Pen* was represented as follows:

> *Deb, Pen*
>
> I want to speak to you (or: of person X) the way people speak
>   to people whom they know well

> I don't want to speak to you the way people speak
>   to women or girls whom they know well and to children
> I feel something good toward you
> not of the kind that people feel toward children

Forms ending in *-z,* such as *Caz* or *Tez,* are very close in value to back-formations such as *Deb* or *Pen,* but they differ from them in one respect: they are not restricted to feminine names. *Deb* or *Pen* may be seen as rejecting a suffix which is felt to be childish and/or feminine. *Caz* or *Tez* can be seen as similarly anti-childish, but not as anti-feminine. This doesn't make them sound any less 'tough' than *Deb* or *Pen;* on the contrary, if anything they sound even 'tougher' or 'rougher': *Deb* and *Pen* make at least an oblique reference to femininity, whereas *Caz, Tez,* or *Gaz* make no reference to it at all. These considerations lead us to the following explication:

> *Caz, Tez*
> I want to speak to you (or: of person X) the way people speak
>   to people whom they know well
> I don't want to speak to you the way people speak to children
> I feel something good toward you
> not of the kind that one feels toward children

In what follows, I will treat back-formations such as *Deb* and forms in *-z* such as *Caz,* jointly, as 'Australian abbreviations', and I will ignore the difference pointed to previously (returning briefly to this difference later).

What I am suggesting is that Australian abbreviations such as *Caz* or *Mare* are, in effect, anti-diminutives: the speaker wishes to dissociate himself or herself emphatically from the kind of emotional attitude associated with diminutives. 'Diminutives' (such as *Pammie* or *Bobby*) imply something like tenderness; by contrast, Australian abbreviations imply a kind of affectionate 'toughness' or 'roughness'.[5] To put it differently, by using a form such as *Shaz* or *Mare,* the speaker shows that he or she wishes to avoid giving the impression that the addressee is treated as a child. By doing so, the speaker also conveys the implication that he, or she, is not a 'softie' either.

Furthermore, the speaker wishes to emphasise that he or she has a close relationship with the addressee. (As one informant put it to me, "I know a Gary. We call him Gary, but his mates call him Gazza or Gaz".) To account for this aspect of the meaning, or force, of Australian abbreviatory names, I would posit the following component:

> I don't want to speak to you the way other people do
> who don't feel toward you the way we feel toward each other

The 'anti-diminutive' intent of Australian abbreviatory names is highlighted by their form. Clearly, it is not an accident that Australian abbreviatory names are monosyllabic, and not disyllabic like most English diminutives (*Pammie, Bobby,* etc.). The notorious Australian anti-intellectualism as well as the Australian love of informality express themselves, among other ways, in a dislike for long words, making for an association between friendliness and short words, and between long words and psychological and social distance. (Extended forms such as *Gazza* will be discussed later.)

Nor is it an accident that in their canonical form Australian abbreviatory names tend to end in a consonant. Standard English abbreviatory names can end in a vowel (for example, *Sue, Joe, Flo*), but Australian abbreviatory names typically don't. Affectionate abbreviations ending in a vowel (other than those of the *Mare* type) are occasionally heard; for example, in Williamson's (1974) play "Jugglers three" one of the main characters, who is always referred to as *Graham,* is sometimes addressed affectionately as *Grah.* Informants have also reported *Fee* as an abbreviation for *Fiona* and *Dee* for *Deirdre. Sue, Di, Joe,* etc. are of course used in Australia, too, but they don't have the affectionate and solidary force of *Suze, Dize,* or *Shaz* and can be used in self-reference. It seems possible that it is this preference for abbreviated forms ending in a consonant which is responsible for the apparent substitution of a *-z* for an underlying *-r* in names such as *Baz* or *Tez* (given that Australian English doesn't have a word-final *-r*). I suggest that the reason for this preference for abbreviations ending with a consonant is to be sought in their anti-diminutive function: ideally, names of this kind should look as if they were back-formations from diminutives; that is to say, they should 'proclaim' by their very form that they have cast away the 'soppy', 'wet' diminutive suffix.

Some names of this kind are indeed back-formations from diminutives or from forms homophonous with diminutives (as when, for example, a girl whose standard name is *Debbie* is called by her close friends *Deb*). Most, however, are not. For example, *Juz* is derived from *Justine,* not from *Juzzie,* and *Caz* from *Caroline* (or *Catherine*), not from *Cazzie.* Nonetheless, names of this kind function as if they were derived from diminutives. In support of this claim I would adduce the fact that it is above all names whose final segment is homophonous with the diminutive suffix which are widely used in the 'Australian abbreviatory form'. This applies in particular to masculine names (*Barry, Terry, Murray, Gary*), in which any hint of 'soppiness' is particularly abhorrent to the Australian ear (that is to say, to the Australian ethos).

According to my observations, Australian abbreviatory names are particularly frequently used by teenagers, certainly more so than by small children. For example, I noticed that after my daughter Mary passed from primary school to high school, the frequency of the form *Mare* and *Marz* used to address her greatly increased. At the same time, her circle of friends changed from one including a *Beckie,* a *Shellie,* a *Jackie,* and a *Tammie* to one composed of a *Juz,* a *Caz,* an *Al,* an *Ez* (from Ellen), and even a *Suz* from Sachiko, a Japanese name! Moreover, her old friend Dimity, whom Mary had known almost from birth and whom she used to called *Dimmie,* became, predominantly, *Dim.* The emergence of forms such as *Suz* for *Sachiko,* or *Pabz* for *Pablo* (Tim Shopen, p.c.), indicates that the morphological processes under discussion are productive. (There may be some phonological constraints in this area; for some interesting observations on the phonology of Australian abbreviations, see Simpson (MS).)

The fact that teenagers may feel a need to display their friendships in 'tough', 'non-babyish', anti-sentimental ways is of course quite understandable. But the fact that Australian culture as a whole betrays a similar need and that Australian English caters to this need, having developed suitable linguistic devices, is far more remarkable. The combination of friendliness and anti-sentimentality has always been regarded, by all observers, as a characteristic feature of Anglo-Australians. But impressions of this kind, however strong and widely shared, are often dismissed by scholars as purely subjective and uncorroborated by intersubjectively verifiable evidence. It seems to me that linguistic facts of the kind discussed here provide such evidence.

The stereotype of 'what Australians are like' includes another crucial characteristic which, I think, is also reflected in the affectionate abbreviations. This characteristic is related to the much-commented-on ideal, and practice, of 'mateship', of solidarity shaped by common experiences and expressed in shared attitudes. It is interesting to note that Australian affectionate abbreviations tend to be used reciprocally (whenever the names of the people in a group lend themselves to such use). Drawing again on my own experience, I would like to cite here the following facts.

When she was in high school, my daughter Mary called her friend Justine *Juz* and was called by her *Muz*, and she called her friend Dimity *Dim* and was called by her *Mare*. (It is inconceivable, however, that the teachers should have addressed them as *Dim* and *Mare*, as they addressed other girls as *Pam* or *Kate*.) Similarly, my mother-in-law, Alice, often addresses her sister, Isa (a lady in her seventies), as *Iz*, and is reciprocally addressed by her as *Al*. (It must be stressed, again, that *Iz* and *Al* are not used by these ladies, or by their friends, as standard abbreviations, on a par with *Pam* or *Kate*. They are used as marked, fond 'distortions' of the 'normal' forms *Isa* and *Alice*.) Another relative, 'Auntie Cora', is often addressed by her sisters-in-law as *Cor*, and addresses them, reciprocally, as *Al* and *Iz*. And I know of one married couple in Canberra whose names are *Terry* and *Marilyn* and who regularly call one another *Tez* and *Mez*.

It seems reasonable to suppose, therefore, that the Australian affectionate abbreviations carry with them a connotation of in-groupness and of shared attitudes. If so, an appropriate component should be added to their semantic representation. This can be done, perhaps, as follows:

> speaking to you
> I feel something good toward you
> not of the kind that one feels toward children
> I think that you feel the same toward me

I should add that the expectation of shared attitudes is more important than a strict reciprocity of the linguistic usage. Affectionate abbreviatory names are used not only among friends but also in the family circle. For example, I know a family in which the parents call their daughter *Ec* (from *Eckie*, from *Erica*), whereas she calls them, naturally, *Mum* and *Dad*. And my husband, John, frequently calls his aunts Cora and Isa *Auntie Cor* and *Auntie Iz*, whereas they call him simply *John*.

The explication sketched for Australian abbreviatory names treats them as if they were primarily vocatives, forms of address, rather than referring expressions. And indeed, according to my observations, the use of such forms in reference is very limited. For example, although at one time I used to hear the two forms *Mare* and *Dim* regularly, and the forms *Al* and *Iz* fairly often, I don't recall having ever heard them used in referring. I realise, however, that to say this is not to say much, in view of the inherent mutuality which such forms imply. For example, I am told that in the circle of friends whose members frequently addressed each other as *Mare/Muz, Dim,* and *Juz,* these forms could also be used referringly (though usually not in self-reference). Thus, speaking to me, my daughter, Mary, referred to her friends Dimity and Justine as *Dimity* and *Justine,* but speaking to Dimity about Justine, or to Justine about Dimity, she did sometimes refer to them, warmly, as *Juz* and *Dim.* To account for this usage, the semantic formula proposed initially should be expanded, to include the following possibility:

> speaking to you about person X
> I feel something good toward X
> not of the kind that one feels toward children
> I think that you feel the same toward X
> (I think that we all feel like this toward each other?)

The referential use of affectionate abbreviatory forms is also illustrated in the following characteristic song, sung by the Australian comedian Barry Humphries "and a few great old mates of mine from school":

> We kicked off with a liquid lunch
> Though the frost was cruel,
> Drinking glühwein with a bunch
> of beaut young blokes from skew-ell.
> Tone and Russell, Drew and Bruce,
> Sue and Sal and Jude
> Drank vodka and tomato juice
> Then went outside and spewed. (1981:80)

Finally, I would like to comment briefly on the lengthened variants of Australian abbreviatory names, an example of which (*Gazza*) was mentioned earlier. Other examples that I have heard include *Tezza* (from *Terry*), *Bazza* (usually from *Barry*), *Dazza* (from *Darren*), *Lazza* (from *Larry*), *Muzza* (from *Murray*), *Wazza* (from *Wallace*), *Chazza* (from *Charles*), *Kezza* (from *Kerry*) and *Cazza* (from *Carol;* cf. Poynton 1984:14). As these examples show, in this category of names a final vowel is added on to a form ending with a -*z,* where -*z* tends to (though doesn't have to) be substituted for an underlying -*r.* It appears that the addition of that word-final vowel is felt as a further jocular 'distortion' and as a further sign of a 'special relationship' between the speaker and the person addressed and/or mentioned. In my judgement, this further 'distortion' is not only a stylistic device, increasing the atmosphere of informality and in-groupness, but also a semantic mechanism, introducing a further semantic component: roughly speaking, a component of congenial (and somewhat rough) good humour. This component can perhaps be represented as follows:

> speaking to you (speaking of person X)
> I feel something good
> I think that you feel the same

It is worth noting that the suffix *-za* is typically used in masculine names, and only rarely in feminine ones. But I do know of at least one girl whose name is *Kerrie* and whom her cousins call *Kezza,* and an acquaintance tells me he has a friend called *Shazza* (from *Sharon*).

The suffixes *-z* and *-za* are of particular interest as they seem to be uniquely Australian. Other affectionate abbreviations, in particular those derived by chopping off the diminutive suffix (*Debbie > Deb, Vicki > Vick, Beckie > Beck, Franny > Fran*), do seem to be used in some other regional varieties of English, although not necessarily with the same meaning, and not as widely as in Australia. For example, forms such as *Mare* for *Mary* or *Soph* for *Sophie* sound abhorrent to my non-Australian informants. But the suffixes *-za* and *-z* (as in *Gaz* for *Gavin* or as in *Julz* for *Julie*) do seem to be innovations of Australian grammar, as well of the Australian 'ethnography of speaking' (cf. Hymes 1962).

One could perhaps suggest that the emergence of the suffixes *-z* and *-za* has codified grammatically, in an unambiguous form, what would have been, otherwise, an ambiguous and somewhat opaque category. After all, when one hears forms such as *Al* or *Sal,* one can't be sure—without knowing the participants and their personal conventions—whether they are meant as fond 'distortions' or as standard personal designations, analogous to *Val* (for *Valerie*) or *Pam* (for *Pamela*). But a form such as *Gaz* or *Marz* is quite unequivocal. The existence of such unequivocal forms gives a status of a separate grammatical category to all affectionate abbreviations, including those like *Al* or *Sal,* which out of context could lend themselves to two different interpretations.[6]

I would add that just as the Australian love of abbreviations seems to reflect the Australian anti-intellectualism, 'toughness', and informality, so the Australian propensity to add with one hand what one has taken away with the other (as in forms such as *Bazza,* but also in forms such as *Tommo, Sallo,* or *Bronno,* for *Tom, Sal* and *Bron,* i.e., for abbreviated forms of *Thomas, Sally,* and *Bronwyn;* and in forms such as *mozzies* and *slippies,* for *mosquitoes* and *slippers,* to be discussed later) reflects the Australian need to express 'congenial fellowship' and good natured good humour.

Commenting on the Australian tendency to abbreviate and otherwise 'tamper with the forms of words' in a number of different ways, Baker describes it, perhaps jocularly, as a manifestation of a characteristically Australian temptation to 'distort' words, for the sake of sheer distortion.

> Such abbreviations are fairly general in all languages, but there is a special feature in Australian speech on which comment must be made. We have seen some part of this in the previous Section in such an example as *Chrissie prezzie* for a Christmas present. This can be looked on as (1) baby talk or (2) woman's talk, but in terms of

fact it extends far beyond this. True, one can feel fairly sure that a woman will be heard saying, '*Dins* will be ready in a *min*' (i.e. dinner will be ready in a minute), but it is not impossible that you will hear (as I have heard) a man referring to his main meal of the day as *din-din*, that he will say *ta* for thanks and *ta-ta* for good-bye. Since, if you listen closely, it is more than likely that you will hear the same man using such expressions as *kern oath!*, *bullsh*, *cowsh*, *frogsh*, *filmsh*, *shouse* and *touse*, it is difficult to regard such terms as other than manifestations of our lasting discontent with leaving words as they are. (1970:375)

I think, however, that there is a great deal of logic to this seemingly perverse linguistic behaviour. The urge to abbreviate names can be seen as an expression of the Australian cult of 'toughness' and the Australian dislike of articulated, intellectual, 'cultured' speech. But the urge to extend, in a new way, what has previously been shortened can be seen as an expression of the Australian need to express affection and friendliness—and to do it in a clearly 'non-sentimental' way. The suffixes -*o* and -*za* (*Sallo, Bazza*), added on to a truncated form of the name, fulfil both these needs.

Thus, both the 'chopping off' of the 'sentimental' diminutive suffix -*ie* and the introduction of the 'anti-sentimental' suffixes -*o* or -*za* constitute a parallel to the much commented on phenomenon of friendly insults. To quote one observer:

[T]he interesting thing about the Australian attitude to human relationships is the special forms it has to take to avoid coming into conflict with our basic antipathy towards the public expression of sentiment and emotion. Because we are unsentimental and cynical towards the emotions, Australians have to express their social affection in some way which is not on the face of it self-revealing. Thus, there has evolved the principle of 'rubbishing' your mates and chyacking the stranger. In an atmosphere of reciprocal banter or 'rubbishing' Australians can express mutual affection without running any risk of indecently exposing states of feeling. (Harris 1962:65–66)

A related, and striking, feature of the Anglo-Australian 'ethnography of speaking' is undoubtedly the widespread insistence on a reciprocal use of first names among people who are not intimates and who differ in social status. For example, in Australian universities undergraduates commonly address their lecturers by their first names. Journalists interviewing celebrities usually address them, and are addressed by them, by their first names. Politicians make a point of repeatedly addressing the interviewers by their first names. And perfect strangers, such as door-to-door encyclopaedia salesmen, can hardly wait for the front door to open to address the host and hostess with some phrase such as "Hello John, hello Anna. I am Max."

Presumably, this is another manifestation not only of the Australian super-egalitarianism but also of the much-commented-on cultural assumption that people are all essentially the same and can be treated on a person-to-person basis as fellow human beings. To quote Horne again (1964:35): "Since Australian friendliness often lacks knowledge of social forms and ceremonies it can sometimes seem so strange to be taken for rudeness, usually for the one reason: that most Australians are bereft of feelings of difference; they think that all people are the same, that what is good for oneself is good for anyone else. Their openness and friendship-seeking is based on this belief". (But one is also reminded of D. H. Lawrence's comment about the "aggressive familiarity" of the Australians, quoted in Pringle 1965:34.)

2. Australian 'Depreciatives'

Australian English has an interesting morphological category which, although akin to the diminutive, differs from it in a revealing way. This category could be called the 'depreciative'. A noun in the depreciative form constitutes an abbreviation of the standard noun, combined with a pseudo-diminutive suffix. Thus, the depreciative form of *present* is *prezzie*, of *mosquitoes* is *mozzies*, of *mushrooms* is *mushies,* of *barbecue* is *barbie,*of *lipstick* is *lippie,* of *sunglasses* is *sunnies,* and so on. Forms of this kind are often referred to as diminutives. In fact, however, they are not really diminutives and have a function quite different from the main function of diminutives (although it is of course a simplification to speak of diminutives as if they had only one function).

Formally, they differ from English diminutives because they are abbreviations: baby words such as *birdie, fishie,* or *doggie* add a diminutive suffix to the full form of the base word—but words such as *barbie* or *lippie* add a suffix to a truncated form of the base word. Semantically, they differ from diminutives in expressing, essentially, not endearment but convivial good humour. Their use is quite different from that of diminutives. For example, one man can easily say to another: "I always clean the car of a Sunday morning, and do a bit of pottering in the garden. Bit worried about those rhodies" (Humphries 1981:18). But one could hardly expect one Australian farmer to say to another that he is a 'bit worried about the horsies'. In Canberra, when the spring comes and the numerous local magpies become aggressive and start attacking passers-by and cyclists, one can often hear the good-humoured complaint 'those bloody maggies!', but it is inconceivable that anyone should say 'those bloody birdies!'

Forms such as *birdie* or *horsie* belong to baby-talk and are normally not used among adults, let alone among men. But forms such as *maggies, rhodies* (for *rhododendrons*), or *pozzie* (for *position*) are commonly used by Australian men. Thus, the common notion that forms such as *maggies* are 'diminutives' in the same sense in which forms such as *birdies* are diminutives is, in my view, completely wrong. The "male flavour" of many Australian abbreviations was noted by Baker (1970:375). I believe, however, that it is important to go beyond such informal observations and to sort out in a rigorous manner the different morphological categories involved, assigning to each an explicit semantic representation.

To capture and to show subtle differences in meaning in a precise and explicit way, we need a semantic metalanguage. Using the metalanguage based on a simplified and standardised version of natural language, we can portray the contrast between diminutives and 'depreciatives' along the following lines (cf. Wierzbicka 1980, 1984a, 1986b):

DIMINUTIVES (e.g., *birdie*)
I think of it as of something small
speaking about it to you I feel something good (toward you)
    of the kind that one feels toward small children

'DEPRECIATIVES' (e.g., *prezzie*)
I don't think of it as of a big thing
I think that you think of such things in the same way
speaking about it to you I feel something good

Thus, calling mosquitoes *mozzies,* the speaker is jocularly dismissing the problem; she or he does not think of mozzies as small and endearing but does not think of them as a 'big thing' either and expects the addressee to share this attitude. As I have argued (Wierzbicka 1984a and 1986b), the semantic complex explicated here reflects many characteristic features of the Australian ethos: anti-sentimentality, jocular cynicism, a tendency to knock things down to size, 'mateship', good-natured humour, love of informality, and dislike for 'long words' (Slavic or Romance diminutives are typically much longer than the base words, but Australian abbreviations are normally shorter than the base words, and Australians feel that this formal brevity is somewhat functional.)

For all these reasons, a linguistic category like the genuine diminutive would not be particularly well suited to the expressive needs of Australians. The depreciative, on the other hand, is most congenial.

The functional difference between the Australian abbreviations (misnamed 'diminutives') and the genuine pan-English diminutives was well captured in a piece which appeared in the Australian magazine *The Bulletin.* The author wrote:

> This strange Australian practice of coining diminutives by the addition of 'ie' or 'y' to hundreds, if not thousands of words is made the more incredible when we consider the fact that we are inclined to inwardly wince at the sound of grown Englishmen referring to 'Mummy' and 'Daddy'. In our own speech, from kindy on, these two words are almost totally absent. By school age we want 'Mums' and 'Dads' or we feel bubsy [babyish]. There is a need to prove we are now biggies. (Serisier 1981:72)

In view of the extreme popularity of the suffix *-ie* in Australian English, the author proposed to mark it with a special letter, for example with @, in the following way:

> [W]ashed the wool@s, ironed the hank@s and night@s, and put away the und@s. Watered the chrys@s and glad@s, made a samm@, and watched a soap@. Put on some lipp@, and rushed up to the dell@ for some soss@, then Wooll@s for some veg@s before picking up the kids from the foot@. (Serisier 1981:72)
> Translation: '[W]ashed the woollen clothes (usually sweaters), ironed the handkerchiefs and the nightdresses, and put away the underwear. Watered the chrysanthemums and gladioli, made a sandwich, and watched a soap opera. Put on some lipstick, and rushed up to the delicatessen for some sausage, then Woolworths for some vegetables before picking up the kids from the football game.'

It should be pointed out, however, that the explication of Australian depreciatives proposed can only be regarded as a rough approximation. The expression 'a
big thing' is used in it in a metaphorical sense: what is meant is of course not size in
the literal sense of the word but rather something like importance. Trying to define
away the metaphorical element of the formula in question (without introducing a
complex concept of importance), we could propose the following revised version:

> *prezzie, mozzie*
> I don't want to think much about X
> I think that you think of X like I do
> speaking about it to you I feel something good

Another, closely related, linguistic device which has developed in Australian
English and which reflects the Australian ethos is the abbreviation with the suffix *-o*,
as in *demo* (demonstration), *compo* (workers' compensation), *anthro* (anthropologist), *acco* (academic), *leso* (lesbian), or *muso* (musician). The popularity of this
suffix in Australian English is reflected in the following satirical passage:

> Thommo, a commo journo, who lived with his preggo wife from Rotto in a fibro
> in Paddo, slipped on the lino taking a dekko at the nympho next door. He missed
> out on compo, so worked for a milko, then a garbo, and took a bit part in a panto.
> His wife ran off with a muso, and Thommo got dermo and gastro. When he
> couldn't even pay his rego, he tried to shoot himself but had run out of ammo. If the
> Salvos hadn't found him and called the ambo, he could have ended up a derro on
> metho. (Serisier 1981:72)

> Translation: 'Thompson (or Thomas), a communist journalist, who lived with his
> pregnant wife from Rottnest Island in an asbestos-fibreboard house in Paddington,
> slipped on the linoleum floor taking a look at the nymphomaniac next door. He was
> ineligible for workers' compensation, so worked for a milkman, then a garbage
> collector, and took a bit part in a pantomime. His wife ran off with a musician, and
> Thompson got dermatitis and gastroenteritis. When he couldn't even pay his car
> registration, he tried to shoot himself but had run out of ammunition. If the
> Salvation Army workers hadn't found him and called the ambulance, he could have
> ended up as a derelict drinking methylated spirits.'

The force of the suffix *-o* in the words used in this passage is different from that
of the suffix *-o* in first names, such as *Johnno* or *Sallo*. The latter are affectionate,
but the former are not. As a first approximation, the meaning of the suffix *-o* in
words such as *acco* or *demo* can be represented as follows:

> I don't think of it as of something special
> I think that you think of it in the same way
> speaking about it I don't want to use long words

But again, expressions such as 'something special' are not entirely satisfactory in a
semantic metalanguage and should be reduced to some more primitive expressions.
Tentatively, this can be done as follows:

demo, Salvo, acco
I don't think of it like people think of things that they don't know about
I think you think of it like I do
speaking about it I don't want to use long words

The person who says *anthro, journo,* or *demo* rather than *anthropologist, journalist,* or *demonstration* is not trying to minimise the things he or she is talking about (as one minimises a barbecue by calling it a *barbie* or mosquitoes by calling them *mozzies*) but is just showing his or her familiarity with them. The message conveyed could be formulated, informally, as follows: 'for me, these are household concepts; I don't need big words (long words) to talk about these things'. A message of this kind would be incompatible with words familiar to everybody and referring to trivial concepts such as *mushrooms* or *mosquitoes*. For this reason, forms such as **mozzos* or **mushos* (for *mozzies* and *mushies*) are quite inconceivable. But a form such as *leso* or *muso* makes perfect sense, conveying toughness, informality, good humour, and anti-intellectualism—all quintessentially Australian values. They suit wonderfully the "markedly anti-intellectual tenor of Australian society" and the Australian "cult of informality" (Horne 1964:34).

The Australian anti-intellectualism (due in part to "the roughness of the early conditions, the need to stay alive, the comparative rarity of cultivated gentlemen"; Horne 1970:80) is often linked with the traditional Australian cult of 'toughness'. The link is illustrated in the following statement (Emerald Hill Theatre Revue, 1966, quoted in Gibbs n.d.:24): "I'm Australian through and through. I hate queers, commos, and students". The preference for "the short vulgar word" rather than for "the polite polysyllable", mentioned by Baker (1959:51), highlights the links among the cult of informality, the cult of 'tough masculinity', and the dislike of social, verbal, and intellectual graces.

I hope it has by now become clear what I meant when I spoke earlier of the cultural significance of expressive derivation. If one compares Australian 'depreciatives' (such as *mozzies*) with Slavic and Romance diminutives (such as *ptaszek,* 'birdie' in Polish) or with Japanese honorific forms of nouns and adjectives (such as *okaze,* 'respected cold' or *oakai,* 'respected red'), one can get insight into the prevailing emotional tone of a culture and into the prevailing tone of social interaction in a society. In a highly stratified 'vertical' society such as the Japanese one (cf. Nakane 1970), it is hardly surprising that the most important interpersonal attitude to be grammatically codified seems to be that of respect. In an egalitarian society of descendants of convicts and of frontiersmen, with strong pioneer traditions but also with plenty of sun and plenty of luck, such as Australia (cf. Horne 1964), it is hardly surprising that cultural ideals such as 'mateship', 'toughness', anti-sentimentality, and 'congenial fellowship' (Liberman's term; see Liberman 1982) have found their way into the grammatical system of the language (in the form of expressive nominal derivation). As for the links between rich systems of affectionate diminutives in a language such as Polish and other aspects of the corresponding culture, I must refer the reader to the study mentioned earlier (Wierzbicka 1985b; see also Wierzbicka 1991a).

Max Harris has made the following comment on the 'Australian civilisation' (quoted in Horne 1984:35): "Mateship became an attitude to human relationship, an easy readiness to strike up contact with fellow human beings in a warm and casual way. This often strikes outsiders as evidence of vulgar over-democratisation. . . . In fact the Australian has a rough but ready capacity for immediate affection, a quality which, oddly for an Anglo-Saxon breed, he shares with some of the Mediterranean peoples". I think that minute semantic analysis of the kind illustrated in this chapter helps to capture, with some precision, the differences, as well as the similarities, between the Anglo-Australian and the Mediterranean style of affection. The fact that in both cultures affectionate forms of first names are commonly used (e.g., *Baz, Bazza, Tone,* or *Mare* in Australia, and *Carmencita, Juanito,* or *Pablito* in Spanish) highlights the similarity pointed out by Harris. But the fact that the Australian forms carry an 'anti-diminutive' force, portrayed in the semantic formulae proposed in this chapter, highlights the difference between an uninhibited 'Mediterranean' display of emotions and the Australian style of friendliness, which is anti-sentimental and good-humoured rather than openly emotional.

3. Fixed Expressions

Among the most characteristic Australian expressions I would single out the following two: *no worries* and *good on you.*

No worries is an ubiquitous saying in Australian life—so much so that it has been referred to (quite justly, in my view) as 'the national motto' (King 1978:24). It is often used in response to apologies, thanks, and requests and in a number of other contexts. One part of its illocutionary force is signalled clearly by its form and can be roughly spelt out as follows:

> I want you not to worry about this

However, a doctor seeking to reassure a patient or his or her family could not say to them 'no worries', although he or she could well say, 'I don't want you to worry about this'. To predict correctly the range of the use of the expression in question, a further component has to be added: roughly, 'I don't worry about this'. The full illocutionary force can be spelt out, still roughly, as follows:

> I don't want you to feel anything bad because of this
> I don't feel anything bad because of it
> I think that we want to feel the same when we think about it
> I want you to know this:
>   one should not feel anything bad because of it

The expression *no worries* reflects some important aspects of the Australian ethos: amiability, friendliness, an expectation of shared attitudes (a proneness to easy 'mateship'), jocular toughness, good humour, and, above all, casual optimism. Its importance in Australian life is highlighted by its large family of derivatives: *no problems, no probs, no troubles, no hassles,* etc.

Horne (1964:44–45) calls Australians "cheerful and practical-minded optimists". "Suggest to an Australian that you spend some time investigating a practical problem in detail and outlining rational procedural patterns and you bore him stiff. 'She'll be right', he will say. 'We'll just give her a go.' Talking too much about what you are doing is 'bullshit'." "In the narrow shaft of clear, bright sunlight where Australians think, there is little room for the view in which we all just seem to bump around in the shadows with little understanding of what it is all about. Australians think they have life taped." Elsewhere, Horne (1970:16) links the Australian optimism with the common Australian belief that things could be changed for the better: "[E]ven during the flat decades, one of the basic promptings of Australians seemed to be that men and things could be improved. There was the sardonic humour of the absurd frontier, but there was also the optimism produced by the 'assimilation' of a significant number of the ex-convicts."

King (1978:24) writes about the Australian optimism more sharply: "No matter what else is happening around the world, in Godzone country everything is basically right. . . . The strength of this belief was affirmed for all time by the RSL Club drinker interviewed on the ABC's This Day Tonight programme in November 1976 who said 'Australia is the best bloody country in the world and I feel sorry for any poor bastard who doesn't live here'." And in Conway's (1971:256–57) words, "the Australian mind . . . is certainly deficient in the tragic view of life. . . . The point that suffering and crisis may throw some clearer light on the design of existence, that it might be the way the mindless ones are supposed to reflect and grow a little before they die—this is a proposition to which so many Australians are likely to retort: 'bloody lot of rubbish', and stalk irately away."

The same characteristically Australian propensities are reflected in the expression *good on you* (often *good on you, mate*). In many contexts, *good on you* is interchangeable with *congratulations* or with *well done*, but this is not always the case (quite apart from the stylistic differences such as the fact that *good on you* is a working-class expression). For example, if an old man or a sick man shows signs of resilience, stoicism, moral courage, or 'toughness' (say, by announcing his decision to fight his illness), it would be appropriate to say *good on you* but not *congratulations* or *well done*. Similarly, if an impecunious friend announces a decision to go on a trip around the world, despite the seemingly insurmountable difficulties that such an undertaking would involve, one might say to her, with approval, *good on you*, but not *congratulations* or *well done*. Very tentatively, I would suggest that *good on you* refers to the attitude displayed by a certain action rather than to the action itself. It refers to a set of values shared by the speaker and the addressee. Saying *good on you*, the speaker indicates that the addressee has displayed, in a conspicuous way, an attitude which the speaker assumes both she or he and the addressee admire.

The focus on the addressee's attitude rather than achievement seems clear in this example (from Arthur Wright's (1922:171) *The colt from the country,* cited in Wilkes 1978:160): " 'Good on you, mate', he said, 'We'll have a go'." Wilkes (1978:160) describes the expression *good on you* as an "expression of approval, congratulation, goodwill". The gloss is sound, but hardly sufficient as a guide to usage or as a statement of meaning. The difference between approval and congratulation is echoed in Horne's (1964:31) comment: "There is little public glorifi-cation of success in Australia. The few heroes of heroic occasions (other than those of sport) are remembered for their style rather than for their achievement. The early explorers, Anzac Day; these commemorate comradeship, gameness, exertion of the Will, suffering in silence. To be game, not to whinge—that's the thing—rather than some dull success coming from organisation and thought."

Thus, the semantic difference between the Australian expression *good on you* and the pan-English expressions *congratulations* and *well done* seems to provide striking linguistic confirmation of the view that the Australian ethos values attitudes (such as 'toughness') more than success. According to the Australian ethos, the important thing is not so much to live and to succeed as to

> . . . die hard, die game, die fighting,
> like that wild colonial boy,
> Jack Dowling, says the ballad, was his name.
> (a poem by John Manifold, quoted in Ward 1958:217)

The emergence in Australian English of the expression *good on you*, with its peculiar semantics, gives substance to the legend. It may be hard to verify whether in fact "swagman and bushranger die hard, die game, die fighting", but the fact that such attitudes are admired in Australia and that they are valued as much as or more than sheer achievement, can be verified, to some extent, by linguistic evidence.

The expression *well done!* implies, among other things, the following idea:

> I know now that you did something good
> one couldn't think: everyone could do it

The expression *congratulations!* is a bit less specific, since it can refer to 'happy events' (such as the birth of a child) as well as to 'impressive actions'. Nonetheless, in congratulating someone, we still seem to assume that the addressee has done something which caused (at least in part) the happy event. For example, if a friend completely unexpectedly received an inheritance, it would be impossible to say to him or her (without irony), *well done!*, but it would also be a little odd to say (without irony), *congratulations!*

One can portray this aspect of *congratulations* as follows:

> I know that something good happened to you
> I think that it wouldn't have happened if you hadn't done something good

But the expression *good on you* doesn't imply that something good has happened to the addressee or that the addressee has done something impressive. Rather, it implies that the addressee has shown that he or she is a kind of person who could do impressive things. Achievements can be due partly to luck (not to mention ruthless-ness, dishonesty, etc.). The expression *good on you* conveys admiration not for achievements but for the evidence that the addressee is the kind of person who could do impressive things (given the right circumstances).

According to an old Australian ballad (Wannan 1963:16), "'I'll fight but not surrender', said the Wild Colonial Boy", and one can well imagine hearing "Good on you, mate!" as a response to what the Wild Colonial Boy said. But of course neither "Well done!" nor "Congratulations!" would be appropriate.

I suggest (very tentatively) that the illocutionary force encoded in the expression *good on you* can be represented as follows:

> I now know that you can do things that other people can't do
> because of this, I think that you are the kind of person
>   that one would want people to be
> because of this, I feel something good toward you
> I say this because I want you to know what I think about it
>   and what I feel thinking about it

This explication seeks to show that in *good on you,* the stress is on people's potential, on what they *can* do, rather than on what they have done, and on the kind of person they have shown themselves to be. Whether or not something good has actually happened because of that is not specified; even if it hasn't, the attitude and the character behind it are still valued and admired.

Generally speaking, I would suggest that the set of commonly used interjections and illocutionary fixed expressions of a given language reflects in an illuminating and remarkably reliable way the 'national character' and the prevailing ethos of the users of this language. Rigorous semantic analysis of such expressions may therefore enable us to find some hard evidence to support purely impressionistic observations about such matters, often dismissed as vague and subjective.

4. Speech Act Verbs

As I have argued in detail elsewhere (see Wierzbicka 1985b and 1991a), the set of speech act verbs which a language has is usually a valuable source of insight into the culture associated with that language. For example, the fact that Australian Aboriginal languages don't have verbs corresponding to *thank* and *apologise* (cf. Harris 1980) but do have numerous verbs referring to attitudes based on kinship (such as, for example, 'demand in the name of kinship rights', Hudson MS a; or 'call someone by a kinship term'; Dixon 1989) is highly revealing. References to kinship permeate both the lexicon and the grammar of Australian languages and reflect its central role in Aboriginal culture. The absence of verbs for 'thank' and 'apologise' seems to reflect the fact that even favours given or received tend to be seen as consequences of kinship-based rights and obligations rather than as 'free' gifts from one individual to another (cf. Harris 1980).

No less telling is the fact that Japanese has no verb corresponding to *resign* (Junko Morimoto, p.c.). Apparently, from a Japanese point of view, to resign would be unilaterally and 'inconsiderately' or 'arrogantly' to terminate a contract which could be expected to last and which involves and affects another party, who could be expected to be treated with respect. The English verb *resign* reflects a culture which insists on the rights of the individual; the absence of such a verb from the Japanese lexicon reflects a different ethos, a different hierarchy of values, and a different style of social interaction.

Australian English, too, has developed a number of characteristic speech act verbs, intimately related to Anglo-Australian culture. Among such verbs, *dob in* seems to me particularly interesting.

AND (1988) defines the meaning of the expression *dob in* as "to inform upon, to incriminate". But this is not an improvement on the earlier description offered by the Supplement to OED (1933): "to betray, to inform against". The notion of 'betraying' constitutes a crucial difference between the specifically Australian concept of *dobbing* and the pan-English concept of *informing*. On the other hand, the description 'Australian slang', offered by the OED Supplement, is misleading: in Australia, *dob in* is not slang (restricted to some particular social group); it is simply part of common everyday language, a word which is in general use and which is clearly one of the key words in Australian English.

O'Grady offers the following comment in this connection (using the term *dob in*):

> Australians are noted for a deep-seated reluctance to report any fellow-citizen to anyone in a position of authority. Police, bosses, foremen, wives, etc. just do their own detecting. Anybody who 'dobs in' anybody else is a 'bastard'—in the worst sense of the word. (1965:34)

Similarly, Baker (1959:15) mentions "a totally unforgiving attitude towards 'rats', 'scabs' and betrayers in general" among the most distinctive features of the 'Australian character'. "The essence of the tradition is loyalty to one's fellows, and the strength of its appeal may be seen in the restraining power of the term 'scab' in an Australian union" (Crawford 1970:137). According to Ward (1958), quoted in Crawford (1970:135), "the combination of loyalty to one's fellows with disrespect towards superior orders [and the] enduring disrespect for authority [may be] traced back to the convicts".

All this is reflected very clearly in the key verb *dob in*. Some examples (from Wilkes 1978 and AND 1988):

> You said you'd go to the police and dob him in unless he coughed up. That's the story isn't it? (Judah Waten 1957)

> A couple of the Indonesian p.o.w's have dobbed us in. Told the Nips everything. (R. Braddon 1961)

In these two examples, *dob in* could be in principle replaced with *inform on* (though not without a significant change in meaning). In the examples which follow, however, *inform on* could hardly be used at all, since it is not used with respect to strictly personal relations (for example, family relations):

> Helen stuck on a real act and dobbed me in to Mum, screaming about how I had busted her best doll on purpose. (P. Barton 1981)

Unlike *inform on*, *dob in* is derogatory and contemptuous: *dobbing* is something a decent person cannot possibly do.

> I shut up and let Ray take all the credit. Couldn't dob him in, could I? (J. O'Grady 1973)
>
> You bitch! Go and dob me in because I gave you a bit of a shove! (Williamson 1972)
>
> But you feel such a rat to tell on her. To dob her in. (H. F. Brinsmead 1966)

The noun *dobber* is equally, or even more, contemptuous and derogatory.

> Don't look at me, you bastards! I'm no bloody dobber! (J. Powers 1973)
>
> The expression 'dobber' was one that I knew implied contempt and was apt to be applied to tale-bearers and informers. (G. A. W. Smith 1977)

One further difference between *inform on* and *dob in* is that the latter implies that the agent is definitely hurting the person spoken of, whereas the former does not necessarily imply that. In *informing*, the stress is on the transmission of (potentially damaging) information, not on interpersonal relations between the speaker and the person spoken of, but in *dobbing in*, the stress is on interpersonal relations. This semantic difference between the two verbs is reflected in a syntactic one. *Dob in* treats the victim as a direct object ('to dob someone in') and thus suggests that the agent is 'doing something to' the person dobbed in. By contrast, *inform on* treats the victim as an oblique object (one cannot 'inform someone on'); this suggests that the agent of *informing* is not necessarily 'doing something to' the person informed on.

It is interesting to note in this connection that *dob*, too, can be used with the particle *on* and that *dob on* is closer semantically to *inform on* than *dob in* is. *Inform on*, *tell on*, and *dob on* all suggest intentional transmission of damaging information without implying that serious harm has already been done, as *dob in* does. At the same time *dob on*, which appears to be used mainly by school-children, shares with *dob in* its contemptuous and derogatory character: evidently, the general Australian contempt for those who break group solidarity and who attempt to side with the authorities against fellow 'subordinates' is an important part of the Australian school ethos, as well as of the Australian ethos in general.

I will not try to propose here an explication of *dob on*, interesting as it is, focussing instead on the more basic concept *dob in*, used widely right across the whole of Australian society. (Components (a) to (f) reflect the "dobber's" attitude, and (g) and (h), the reporter's comment.)

dob in

(a) I say: person X did something bad
(b) I want you to know this
(c) I think: you will do something bad to X because of this
(d) I know: people like you can do something bad to people like X and me
(e) I know: X would think that I wouldn't say this to you

(f) I want to say this to you
(g) [if someone said something like this, people would think something bad about this person]
(h) [people would feel something bad toward this person]

It is worth noting that *dob in* also has another meaning in Australia: roughly, doing a bad turn to a 'mate' by 'volunteering' for something on his or her behalf. This meaning is related to the first one in so far as it implies saying something about a 'mate' to a person in charge, causing something bad to happen to the 'mate', and thus violating the expectation of loyalty and mutual support. The main difference between the two meanings consists in the fact that in one case, one says something bad about the mate, whereas in the other, one says something unfounded and embarrassing: namely, that he or she is willing to do something which in fact he or she is not. (For further discussion of Australian English speech act verbs, see Wierzbicka 1991a.)

5. Conclusion

Is language a mirror of culture? In many ways, it undoubtedly is, although it is not always easy to determine which aspects of the culture reflected in a given language pertain to the present and which to the past, possibly a remote past. The dangers of subjectivism and arbitrariness involved in a search for such correlations are no doubt real enough. But to abandon the search because of these dangers is, to my mind, analogous to saying, as Bloomfield did, that linguistics should stay clear of meaning because all attempts to study meaning are fraught with dangers of subjectivism and arbitrariness.

As I see it, the important thing to do is to try to sharpen our analytical tools and to develop safeguards for the study of the 'dangerous areas'. A semantic meta-language for a cross-cultural comparison of meanings seems to me, in this respect, a requirement of the first priority.

12

The Russian Language

Cultures are in some ways like living beings. They have a unity of their own, they tend to persevere in their being, and their relationship to their environment is vital. . . . These properties of a culture have their roots in the *collective identity* of the people, the living human beings who, generation after generation, find it expressed in their culture and above all, in its system of ideas and values.

(Dumont 1986:587)

1. Cultural Themes in Russian Culture and Language

I have claimed elsewhere (Wierzbicka 1990a) that nothing reflects and illuminates Russian national identity more clearly than three unique Russian concepts which keep recurring in Russian discourse and Russian literature (both 'high' and folk): *duša* ('soul'), *sud'ba* ('fate'), and *toska* ('yearning'). All three of these concepts have been studied in this book in some detail, and I am not going to repeat, or even summarise, here what has been said in the relevant chapters. Instead, I would like to point to a few fundamental semantic themes which shape the semantic universe of the Russian language. These themes are encapsulated in a particularly salient way in the concepts of *duša, sud'ba,* and *toska,* but they also manifest themselves in countless other ways. I have in mind the following interrelated themes:

(1) Emotionality—the tremendous stress on emotions and on their free expression, the high emotional temperature of Russian discourse, the wealth of linguistic devices for signalling emotions and shades of emotions.

(2) 'Irrationality' or 'non-rationality'—the opposite of the so-called scientific world view officially promulgated by the Soviet regime; the stress on limitations of logical thinking, human knowledge, and human understanding, and on the mysteriousness and unpredictability of life.

(3) Non-agentivity—the feeling that human beings are not in control of their lives and that their control over events is limited; a tendency to fatalism, resignation, submissiveness; a lack of emphasis on the individual as an autonomous agent, 'achiever', and controller of events.

(4) Moral passion—the stress on the moral dimensions of human life, on the struggle between good and evil (in others and in oneself), the tendency to extreme and absolute moral judgements.

All of these themes feature prominently both in the Russian self-image, as it emerges in Russian literature and in Russian thought, and in the writings of outside observers, scholars, travellers, and others.

1.1 Emotionality

According to the Harvard study of the Russian national character (Bauer, Inkeles, and Kluckhohn 1956:141), Russians are "expressive and emotionally alive", marked by "general expansiveness", "easily expressed feelings", and a "giving in to impulse".

On the basis of this and other similar studies, Kluckhohn (1961:611) notes that "the findings obtained by the use of a variety of psychological instruments are . . . in some respects remarkably congruent. For example, the Russians when compared with Americans and other groups stand out for their passion for affiliation, for belongingness, and for their warmth and expressiveness in human relations." Kluckhohn also cites the following proposition as one "that would gain wide acceptance": "The people are warmly human, tremendously dependent upon secure social affiliations, labile, nonrational, strong but undisciplined, needing to submit to authority."

This comment brings us to the next point.

1.2 Tendency to Passivity and Fatalism

Fedotov (1952:74) in his study of the Russian national character contrasts "the activism of the West" with "the fatalism of the East" and sees in the Eastern fatalism one of the keys to the "Russian soul".

According to Dostoevsky (1976:286), *smirenie* 'holy resignation' is the foundation of Russia's greatness, and Tolstoy (1953:879) saw an expression of the attitudes of the Russian people in the legend of the invitation to the northern tribe the Varyags, who, "at the dawn of Russian history, were invited by the Slav tribes of Russia to come and rule over them and establish order" (translator's note, Tolstoy 1929–37, v.10:429): "Come and rule over us! We joyfully promise complete obedience. All labours, all humiliations, all sacrifices we take upon ourselves; but we will not judge or decide!" The nineteenth-century Russian philosopher Vladimir Solev'ev contrasted the "West" and the "East" in terms of "energy and independence" vs. "subordination and submission" (see quote in chapter 5, section 6).

Consider also the recent remarks by the Russian poet Evgenij Evtušenko (1988:23) on the characteristically Russian concept of *priterpelost':* "I can't remember the first time I heard that profoundly Russian, tragically all-embracing word *priterpelost'* ['servile patience']. . . . The word expresses respect for patience. There is patience and tolerance worthy of respect—the patience of a woman suffering in labor, the patience of real creators at work, the patience of people under torture who will not name their friends. But there is also useless, humiliating patience." According to Evtušenko, this useless, humiliating patience (that is, *priterpelost'*) would be the death of *perestroika*.

Some scholars have sought the roots of the Russian 'submissiveness' not only in history but also in the practices of child-rearing, and in particular in swaddling (for example, Mead 1953). Erikson (1963:388) asks: "Is the Russian soul a swaddled soul?" To which he replies: "Some of the leading students of Russian character . . . definitely think so."

In support of this view, Erikson quotes, among other things, Gorky's comments on Tolstoy: "A writer, national in the truest and most complete sense, he embodied in his great soul all the defects of his nation, all the mutilations we have suffered by the ordeals of our history; his misty preachings of 'non-activity', of 'non-resistance to evil', the doctrine of passivism, all this is the unhealthy ferment of the old Russian blood, envenomed by Mongolian fatalism and almost chemically hostile to the West with its untiring creative labor, with its active and indomitable resistance to the evils of life."

1.3 Anti-rationalism

I have already quoted Kluckhohn's (1961:611) description of Russians as "nonrational". Russian thinkers have often expressed a similar view and have voiced their profound dislike of what they saw as "Western rationalism" and the Western "tyranny of reason" (cf. Samarin 1877:401–2, quoted in Walicki 1980:100). In this view, "Western European thought was everywhere infected by the incurable disease of rationalism. . . . Western Christianity was itself infected by rationalism" (Walicki 1980:103; see also chapter 1).

Usually, the Western emphasis on reason is linked with the Western emphasis on individual will and individual activity, whereas the Russian distrust of logical thinking, human knowledge, and the "tyranny of reason" is linked with the Eastern emphasis on the limitations of human will and human power. Thus, for example, Solov'ev wrote:

Having manifested the force of the human principle in free art, Greece created also a free philosophy. The content of its main philosophical ideas wasn't new: these ideas were also familiar to the East. But the basic idea—to investigate with the aid of human reason the essence of all things, for the sake of a purely theoretical interest, and that form of free philosophical reflection, which we find in Plato's dialogues and the works of Aristotle—this was something new, a direct expression of the autonomous activity of the human mind, something which either previously or subsequently never made an appearance in the East. That superhuman force to which humanity in the East subordinated itself, assumed various forms. Eastern man believed in the existence of this force, and obeyed it. But just what that force was remained a secret, a great mystery. (1966, v.4:27)

1.4 Moral Passion

Students of Russian national character repeatedly emphasise the Russian's "moral modes of expression" (Bauer, Inkeles, and Kluckhohn 1956:142), and so do many Russian thinkers, who contrast the moral orientation of the Russians with the rational orientation of the Western Europeans (cf. Walicki 1980:100–110).

The data which were studied by Bauer, Inkeles, and Kluckhohn (1956:136) show the Russians as strikingly different in this respect from the Americans. "American stress upon autonomy, social approval, and personal achievement does not often appear in the Russian protocols. Russians demand and expect moral responses (loyalty, respect, sincerity) from their group. Americans care more about just being liked. . . . Americans are appreciably more worried about their failures in achievement, lapses in approved etiquette, inability to meet social obligations. Russians are shamed more deeply by dishonesty, betrayal, and disloyalty."

Moral passions constitute of course one of the most characteristic features of Russian literature, where "the Russian preoccupation with elemental humanity" (Sapir 1924, quoted by Kluckhohn 1961:608) is very much in evidence. "In the pages of Tolstoy, Dostoevsky, Turgenev, Gorky, and Chekhov personality runs riot in its morbid moments of play with crime, in its depressions and apathies, in its generous enthusiasms and idealism."

What I want to show in this chapter is that all these themes of Russian culture and the Russian national psyche are reflected in the Russian language; or, to put it differently, that the linguistic evidence on all these points is convergent with the evidence coming from other sources and with the intuitions both of Russians themselves and of students of Russian life.

2. Emotionality

2.1 "Active" Emotions

2.1.1 English

Consider this pair of English sentences:

> a. Mary is worrying (about something).
> b. Mary is worried (about something).

Version (a) appears to suggest a mental action (Mary is 'doing something in her head'); version (b) suggests a state (Mary experiences something; she is not 'doing anything in her head').

In English, emotions are more commonly expressed by means of adjectives or pseudo-participles than by verbs:

> Mary was sad, pleased, afraid, angry, happy, disgusted, glad, etc.

Adjectives and pseudo-participles of this kind designate passive states, not active emotions to which people 'give themselves' more or less voluntarily. (I'm ignoring here any differences between adjectives and pseudo-participles, real as they may be.) By contrast, verbs of emotion imply a more active stance.

Since emotions have a cognitive basis (that is, are caused by, or related to, certain thoughts), the different conceptualisation of emotions reflected in the two patterns illustrated may be related to a different conceptualisation of thoughts.

Vendler (1967:110–11) distinguished two kinds of 'thinking' as follows:[1]

> Let us begin with *thinking*. It is clear that it is used in two basic senses. *Thinking* functions differently in
> He is thinking about Jones.
> and in
> He thinks that Jones is a rascal.
> The first "thinking" is a process, the second a state. The first sentence can be used to describe what one is doing; the second cannot. This becomes obvious when we consider that while
> He thinks that Jones is a rascal.
> might be said truthfully of someone who is sound asleep
> He is thinking about Jones.
> cannot. It shows that thinking about something is a process that goes on in time, an activity one can carry on deliberately or carefully, but this is by no means true of thinking that something is the case. If it is true that he was thinking about Jones for half an hour, then it must be true that he was thinking about Jones during all parts of that period. But even if it is true that he thought that Jones was a rascal for a year, that does not necessarily mean that he was thinking about Jones, the rascal, for any minutes of that time.

The two kinds of 'thinking' distinguished by Vendler may not correspond exactly to the different conceptualisations of emotions reflected in verbs of emotion such as *to worry* and adjectives or pseudo-participles of emotion such as *sad, pleased, afraid, angry, happy, disgusted,* and *ashamed,* but clearly there is a connection. If the sentence "He is thinking about Jones" cannot be said truthfully of someone who is asleep, neither can the sentence "He is worrying about Jones". Sentences with adjectives or pseudo-participles vary in their applicability to people who are asleep, depending on the kind of emotion. But looking at a sleeping person one would certainly be more likely to say, "He is worried" than "He is worrying".

Vendler talks of his two kinds of 'thinking' in terms of a process and a state. Clearly, a distinction between a process and a state is even more applicable in the case of the two conceptualisations of emotions: whether or not "thinking that Jones is a rascal" is a state, probably nobody would hesitate to call being *worried* or being *happy* a state. The contrast between the processual implications of verbs such as *worry* and the stative character of adjectives and pseudo-participles such as *worried* or *happy* is reflected in the ability of the former, but not the latter, to occur in the progressive aspect.

> a. She was worrying/rejoicing/grieving.
> b. *She was being sad/happy/worried.
>   (cf. She was being difficult/noisy.)

A person who is "worrying" is dwelling on certain thoughts and thus inducing certain feelings, concurrent with thoughts. "Worrying" can be said, therefore, to involve duration and to imply an inner activity. By contrast, "being worried" can be said to be passive and to be caused by external and/or past causes.

As a first approximation, then, I would propose explications along the following lines:

> a. X worried (rejoiced, grieved, etc.)   →
>   X thought something (about something)
>   X did this for some time
>   because of this, X felt something
>   X felt this when X thought this
>
> b. X was worried.   →
>   X thought something (about something)
>   because of this, X felt something

(Needless to say, these formulae are not intended as full explications.)

Both the verbal and the adjectival (participial) pattern imply that the feeling is due to the thought, but the verbal pattern implies also that the thinking is going on for some time, that a particular thought recurs throughout this time, and that the feeling is concurrent with the thinking. On the other hand, the adjectival pattern allows for the possibility that the feeling is subsequent to the thought or that it appears off and on.

I'm suggesting, then, that the verbal pattern is "voluntary" at least by implication, since it presents the feeling as concurrent with the thought, and the thought as recurring throughout a period: a person who allows the same thought to recur throughout a period can be seen as "giving in" to this thought voluntarily and as being responsible for the feeling triggered by it. (Cf. Ameka 1990.)

Probably, there is one further dimension to the contrast between the verbal and the adjectival pattern: roughly, feeling versus external manifestation of feeling. Typically, emotions designated by verbs of emotion, in contrast to those designated by adjectives of emotion, tend to be expressed in action, often externally observable action. For example, a person who *rejoices* is probably doing something because of this feeling—dancing, singing, laughing, and so on. For these reasons one might suggest that one further component should be added to the explication of such verbs:

> (X felt something)
> because of this, X was doing something

It seems safer, however, to express the dynamic character of such verbs more cautiously:

> (X felt something)
> because of this, X wanted to do something

If X wanted to do something because of this feeling (sing, laugh, cry, talk, and so on), this invites the inference that X probably did do something, but this inference is not spelt out as a certainty.

It is interesting to note that English has only a very limited number of intransitive verbs of this kind—*worry, grieve, rejoice, pine,* and a few more—and the whole category seems to be losing ground in modern English (*rejoice* being somewhat archaic and elevated, *pine* being usually used ironically, and so on).

I believe that this is not 'accidental' but reflects an important feature of Anglo-Saxon culture—a culture which tends to view behaviour described disapprovingly as 'emotional' with suspicion and embarrassment. (It is worth noting in this connection that in English intransitive emotion verbs tend to develop negative disapproving tones, for example, *sulk, fret, fume, rave.*) It is uncharacteristic of Anglo-Saxons to 'give themselves' to emotions. Their culture encourages them to be *glad* rather than to *rejoice,* to be *sad* rather than to *pine,* to be *angry* rather than to *fume* or *rage,* and so on.

2.1.2 Russian

In contrast to English, Russian is extremely rich in "active" emotion verbs. I will adduce here a selection of characteristic examples—most of them thoroughly untranslatable: *radovat'sja, toskovat', skučat', grustit', volnovat'sja, bespokoit'sja, ogorčat'sja, xandrit', unyvat', gordit'sja, užasat'sja, stydit'sja, ljubovat'sja, vosxiščat'sja, likovat', zlit'sja, gnevat'sja, trevožit'sja, vozmuščat'sja, negodovat', tomit'sja, nervničat',* and so on.

I do not claim that all these verbs have exactly the same type of semantic structure or that they all correspond exactly (in their type of semantic structure) to English verbs such as *worry* or *rejoice.* I will note, however, a number of facts which point to their active, processual, and quasi-voluntary character.

First, most (though not all) Russian emotion verbs are reflexive verbs, formed with the suffix -*sja* 'self'. This fact strengthens the impression that these verbs present the emotions in question as somehow self-induced, rather than due to external causes.

Second, many verbs of emotion—in contrast to adjectives (and adverbs, discussed later)—are able to govern the preposition *o* (*ob, obo*) 'of/about', just as verbs of thinking do. This fact supports the idea that verbs of emotion link the feeling with prolonged concurrent thinking. Some examples:

> Duša grustit o nebesax. (Esenin 1933:123)
>
> 'My soul is being sad (V.) about heaven.'

> Ne grusti tak šibko obo mne. (Esenin 1933:167)
>
> 'Don't be so sad (V.) about me.'

> *Ja grusten o tebe.
>
> 'I feel sad (Adj.) about you.'

*Mne grustno o tebe.

'I feel sad (Adv.) about you.'

Bespokojus' o tebe. (Tolstoy 1984, v.19:9)

'I worry about you.'

Ne trevož'sja obo mne. (Tolstoy 1984, v.19:10)

'Don't fear about me.'

Obo mne ne tuži. (Tolstoy 1984, v.19:3)

'Don't pine about me.'

unyvaju o tom. . . . (Tolstoy 1984, v.19:40)

'I am being downcast (V.) about that.'

Third, the active implications of Russian emotion verbs manifest themselves in the way these are used—often on a par with verbs of doing, as in the following examples from Tolstoy's diaries:

Včera nagrešil, razdražilsja o sočinenijax—pečatanii ix. (1985, v.22:203)

'Yesterday I sinned badly, I got myself all worked up (annoyed) about my works— their publication.'

Mne ne gordit'sja nado i prošedšim, da i nastojaščim, a smirit'sja, stydit'sja, sprjatat'sja—prosit' proščenie u ljudej. (1985, v.22:22)

'What I should do is not to pride myself on the past, or for that matter the present, but to humble myself, to "shame myself", to hide myself—to ask people's forgiveness.'

Vnutrennjaja rabota idet, i potomu ne tol'ko ne roptat', no radovat'sja nado. (1985, v.22:125)

'Inner work is going on, so what I should do is not to complain but to rejoice.'

Fourth, the active character of Russian verbs of emotion manifests itself, among other ways, in the fact that many of them (in the perfective form) can be used to report speech. (Cf. Iordanskaja and Mel'čuk 1981.) For example:

'Maša—zdes'?' udivilsja Ivan.

'Maša—here?' Ivan expressed his surprise.

'Ivan—zdes'!' obradovalas' Maša.

'Ivan is here!' Maša expressed her joy.

In English, too, there are some verbs which can be used to interpret human speech as manifestation of emotions: for example, *enthuse, exult, moan, thunder,* or *fume.*

'No prince has ever known the power that I have!' Nero exulted. (Ruffin 1985:44; cf. Wierzbicka 1987b:251)

Typically, however, such verbs are somewhat negative, or ironic, in their connotations, and they focus on the manner of speech as much as on the emotion itself. In Russian, verbs of emotion such as *udivit'sja* or *obradovat'sja* are used as 'pure' speech act verbs, not as manner-of-speech verbs. This, I think, is another manifestation of the cultural difference mentioned earlier: Anglo-Saxon culture tends to disapprove of uninhibited verbal outpourings of emotions, whereas Russian culture views them as one of the main functions of human speech.

Finally, it should be added that the idea of 'giving oneself' actively to an emotion is often spelt out in Russian quite explicitly, as in the following examples:

Často otdaeš'sja unynij'u, negodovaniju o tom, čto delaetsja v mire. (Tolstoy 1985, v.22:294)

'Often you give yourself over to melancholy, to indignation over what is going on in the world.'

Ne unyniju dolžny my predavat'sja pri vsjakoj vnezapnoj utrate. . . . (Gogol' 1874:567)

'We shouldn't give ourselves to melancholy whenever we suddenly lose something. . . .'

Ne otdavajsja čuvstvu dosady. . . . (Tolstoy 1984, v.19:75)

'Don't give yourself to the feeling of vexation. . . .'

In English, people normally don't talk about 'giving oneself' to a particular feeling (not in the sense of passively surrendering to it, but in the sense of actively wallowing in it), and both the idea and the practice seem alien to Anglo-Saxon culture. The marginality of verbs of emotion in the English language reflects this cultural difference.

Anthropologists often talk of 'Western' languages in general, and of English in particular, as extraordinarily focussed on emotions and extraordinarily rich in emotion terms (as a result of Western individualism and bent for introspection; cf., for example, Howell 1981; Heelas 1984; Lutz 1988). It is interesting to note, therefore, that if one compares English with Russian, it is Russian which emerges as much more focussed on emotions and much richer in both lexical and grammatical resources for differentiating emotions.

2.2 Feelings Beyond One's Control

As we have seen, Russian is richly equipped with means allowing its speakers to talk about their emotions as active and as if voluntary. We will see now that it is also richly equipped with means allowing its speakers to talk about their emotions as involuntary and beyond their control.

In speaking about people, one can take two different orientations: one can think of people as agents, or 'doers', and one can think of them as passive experiencers. In Russian, unlike most other European languages, both of these orientations play a major role. This means that the passive-experiential mode has a greater scope in Russian than it has in other Slavic languages, far greater than it has in German or French, and incomparably greater than it has in English.

In the experiential mode, the person spoken of is usually referred to in the dative case, and the predicate usually takes an 'impersonal' neuter form. One major semantic component associated with that mode is lack of control: 'not because X wants it'. (See section 3.)

In the area of emotions, too, the dative-impersonal syntax implies lack of control. The language possesses a whole category of emotion words (adverbials of a special kind) which can be used only in that type of construction and which designate, specifically, passive involuntary emotions. Frequently, these adverbials are morphologically related to verbs of 'active' emotion. For example:

> a. On   zavidoval.
>   he:Nom. envied (V. Masc.)
>
>   'He envied.'

> b. Emu   bylo   zavidno.
>   he:Dat. was (Neut.) envy (Adv.)
>
>   'He felt envious.'

Similarly:

> a. On mučilsja (skučal, stydilsja, grustil, žalel).
>
>   'He:Nom. was giving himself to torment (boredom, shame, sadness, regret/compassion).'

> b. Emu bylo mučitel'no (skučno, stydno, grustno, žalko).
>
>   'He:Dat. felt tormented (bored, ashamed, sad, regretful/compassionate).'

The active pattern suggests, as we have seen, that one has brought the feelings on oneself by persisting in thinking certain thoughts. The dative (adverbial) pattern suggests that the feeling is beyond the experiencer's control. This can be represented as follows:

> X thought something about something
> because of this, X felt something
> X couldn't not feel this

The involuntary character of the 'dative' emotions is clearly seen in the following sentences:

i, kak ni *sovestno* èto bylo emu, emu bylo *zavidno*. (Tolstoy 1953:340)

'and, although he felt guilty (Impers.) about it, he felt envious (Impers.).'

Sovestno mne očen' pered toboj, čto tebe *skverno, suetno, xlopotno,* a mne tak *prekrasno;* no *utešajus'* tem, čto èto nužno dlja moego dela. (Tolstoy 1984, v.19:23)

'I feel guilty (Impers.) before you, because you feel awful (Impers.), concerned (Impers.), anxious (Impers.), whereas I feel so wonderful (Impers.); but I console myself (Pers.) thinking that this is necessary for my work.'

The involuntary character of a feeling implied by a dative construction doesn't mean that it cannot be brought on voluntarily. One can say, for example:

> Kak vy delaete čtoby vam ne bylo skučno? (Tolstoy 1953:328)
> 'How do you do it that you don't feel bored?'

> Kak vy delaete čtoby vam bylo veselo?
> 'How do you do it that you feel merry?'

But in sentences of this kind, it is a question of intentionally doing something that would bring on, or would prevent, an 'irresistible feeling'. Once it is there, the feeling (designated by a dative construction) is seen as involuntary.

But 'adverbials of emotion' constitute only a special case of a category which is much more comprehensive than any set of emotion terms. Any adverb which can be interpreted as evaluative ('good' or 'bad') can be used in the dative-impersonal construction to imply an involuntary emotion, or, more generally, experience. The adverb itself doesn't have to imply any feeling; the construction as such does. For example:

> Emu   bylo   xorošo/prekrasno/xolodno.
> he:Dat. was (Neut.) well/marvellous/cold (Adv.)

> 'He felt well/marvellous/cold.'

English glosses for such sentences are not always easy to find because English has no general device for transforming descriptive terms into experiential ones. For example, the sentence

> Emu   bylo   trudno.
> he:Dat. was (Neut.) difficult (Adv.)

implies that the person in question experienced his situation as difficult and that the feeling was beyond his control, but this is hardly an idiomatic English gloss.

In Russian, people's feelings, and also their experience of life in general, are often described in this untranslatable way. For example:

> Pastušonku Pete
> Trudno žit' ne svete. (Esenin 1933:387)
> 'Little cowherd Petja finds his life hard to bear.'

The stuff of one's experiences—life—can be referred to either in an infinitive, as here, or in a reflexive, as follows:

> Esli by korova
> Ponimala slovo
> To žilos' by Pete
> Lučše net na svete. (Esenin 1933:387)
>
> 'If a cow could understand human words, Petja would experience his life as good.' ('couldn't be better')

What matters in the present context is that both these patterns are impersonal and that they both present people as passive experiencers of life which is beyond their control.

> Mne živetsja očen' ploxo, nas v odnu komnatu nabito četyre čeloveka. . . . (Tsvetaeva 1969:37)
>
> 'My present life is very hard for me; we are crammed four people in one room. . . .'
>
> Ej očen' tjaželo živetsja. . . . (Tsvetaeva 1972:191)
>
> 'Her present life is very hard for her. . . .'

In sentences of this kind, a person's subjective experience of life is described as either bad (difficult, troublesome, etc.) or—rarely—as good. External conditions can be mentioned, but they are not presented as a full explanation. The emphasis is not on causes and effects but on the subjective feeling. There is a difference in this respect between nominative sentences such as (a) or (b):

> a. Moja žizn' očen' ploxaja. (Tsvetaeva 1972:610)
>   'My life is very bad [difficult, poor etc.].'
>
> b. Živu durno. (Tolstoy 1985, v.22:58)
>   'I live badly [in a moral sense].'

and a dative one, such as (c):

> c. Mne živetsja očen' ploxo. (Tsvetaeva 196:37)
>   'I experience my present life as very hard.'

Sentence (a) describes the speaker's life from an objective point of view, sentence (b) can be interpreted as referring to actions (for which one is responsible), and sentence (c) has a purely internal subjective perspective—the perspective of a passive experiencer rather than an active controller of life (the reading 'I live immorally' is completely impossible). The Russian language seems to encourage and promote that perspective.

2.3 Names and Personal Relations

Russian names and their expressive derivation are discussed extensively in chapter 7. Here I would like to highlight only one or two of the most important generalisations.

I have argued that the style of interpersonal relations prevailing in a given society is epitomised in the use of names. The differences between the Russian and the English use of names give one of the best keys to the differences between the two cultures (alongside the differences between the English *soul* and the Russian *duša*).

In a recent television film about the Soviet spy Colonel Vladimir Petrov, who defected in Australia in 1954, the hero is normally called *Volodja* in Russian and *Vlad* in English. The two forms evoke two different personalities, and two different styles of social interaction.

Both forms are standard and unmarked: in Russian, it is perfectly usual to call a man whom one knows well by a short form ending in -*a* and having a soft stem (*Volodja, Mitja, Kolja,* and so on); in English, it is perfectly usual to call a man whom one knows well by a short form of his first name truncated to the first syllable and ending in a consonant (*Tom, Tim, Rod, Ed,* and so on). Clearly, *Vlad* is built on the same model as *Tom* or *Rod,* and it has the same expressive value: masculine (more so than the full name), non-sentimental, informal, familiar. I have tried to spell out the exact value of such forms as follows:

> I want to speak to you the way people speak
> to men and boys whom they know well

An unmarked Russian short form has an entirely different value. To begin with, it has no masculine connotations (other than those inherent in the full name *Vladimir*). In fact, *Volodja* feels closer in value to feminine names such as *Nadja* than the full name *Vladimir* is to the full name *Nadežda*. The fact that forms such as *Volodja* take the same case inflections as feminine names can be seen as a kind of iconic reflection of this reduced contrast in gender.

Second, Russian short forms such as *Volodja* don't have the 'anti-childish' ring of English short forms such as *Tom* or *Ed*. Although Russian children are normally showered with diminutives (e.g., *Voloden'ka* or *Katen'ka*), one doesn't graduate in Russian from *Voloden'ka* or *Katen'ka* to *Volodja* or *Katja,* the way many boys graduate in an Anglo-Saxon society from *Tommy* or *Eddie* to *Tom* or *Ed*. Since among the Russians there are no inhibitions preventing a show of affection to adults and since men are not treated differently in this respect from women, warm diminutives such as *Voloden'ka* or *Katen'ka* are not restricted to children, in the way English 'diminutives' such as *Tommy* or *Eddie* are. As a result, *Voloden'ka,* though very warm, is not particularly childish (in the way *Pammy* and *Timmy* are), and *Volodja* is not anti-childish (although it is less warm).

But although less warm than *Voloden'ka, Volodja* has still a degree of warmth, whereas English forms such as *Tom* or *Ed* are informal but (unlike *Cindy* or *Debbie*) not 'warm' at all (see chapter 7).

I have tried to reflect all these features of forms such as *Volodja* in the following semantic formula (cf. chapter 7, section 2.1.2):

> I want to speak to you the way people speak
> to people whom they know well
> and toward whom they feel something good, and to children

Another general point which was raised in the chapter on names and which I would like to highlight in the present context concerns the extraordinary proliferation of expressive categories of names in Russian. As pointed out by Brown and Ford (1964:238), "proliferation of names in intimacy accords well with a familiar semantic-psychological principle. For language communities the degree of lexical differentiation of a referent field increases with the importance of that field to the community".

When applied to Russian names and to their expressive derivation, this would seem to mean that intimate personal relations have an extraordinary importance in Russian culture. If in a particular relationship the speaker calls the addressee *Katja, Katen'ka, Katjuša, Kat'ka, Katjuxa, Katjušen'ka,* and so forth, depending on the exact shade of feeling and on the momentary state of the relationship (as perceived by the speaker), this would seem to mean that exact shades of interpersonal feelings and the vicissitudes and fluctuations of interpersonal relationships are felt to be extraordinarily important—a conclusion which seems to accord well with other evidence, both linguistic (cf., for example, the phraseology involving *duša* in chapter 1) and socio-psychological (cf., for example, Bauer, Inkeles, and Kluckhohn 1956 or Kluckhohn 1961).

The degree, and quality, of tenderness conveyed in Russian forms such as *Il'jušečka* (in *The brothers Karamazov;* Dostoevsky 1976) or *Nadjušen'ka* (in *The first circle,* Solzhenitsyn 1968c) simply cannot be conveyed in English, and neither can the rough expressive tone of a form such as *Mitjuxa* (from *Dmitrij, Mitja* plus *-uxa*).

In Tolstoy's (1953) *Anna Karenina* two types of people are contrasted, those who live 'for the belly' and those for live 'for the soul'. Tolstoy's, and his hero's, attitude toward these two types is epitomised in the contrast between the disrespectful form *Mitjuxa* and the affectionate and respectful form *Fokanyč,* a contracted form of the patronymic. The moral extremism of this categorisation is characteristically Russian, and so is its emotional intensity. The role of the expressive derivation of names in this episode is a good illustration of its general importance in Russian speech and in the Russian cultural universe.

2.4 Diminutive Adjectives

Russian is exceptionally rich in diminutives, and in Russian speech diminutives seem to be used 'all the time'. Here, I can do no more than choose one category of diminutives as an illustration. Since nominal diminutives have been discussed to some extent in the chapter on names, in the present context I will focus on the use of diminutives with adjectives, and I will have to restrict my attention to one category, based on the suffix *-en'k-*. This category of adjectives has fundamental importance in Russian speech, because of its exceptionally high frequency and exceptionally wide range of use. One has the impression that without the adjectives in *-en'kij* Russian speech wouldn't be Russian speech. (Cf. Jarintzov 1916:138.) And yet their exact expressive value is very elusive, and the role they play in speech is very hard to determine.

According to Bratus (1969:42–43), diminutive suffixes impart to the adjective various expressive emotive nuances, "from the meaning of a low degree of the quality" (as in, she claims, *xitrovatyj* 'rather cunning' from *xitryj* 'cunning') "to the expression of the emotions of love, tenderness, sympathy and delight: *rodnoj* 'dear, native'—*rodnen'kij*, *milyj* 'dear'—*milen'kij*, *čudnyj* 'marvellous'—*čudnen'kij* and contempt, hatred, disparagement and disdain: *ploxoj* 'bad'—*ploxon'kij*, *dešëvyj* 'cheap'—*dešëven'kij*, *poganyj* 'foul'—*poganen'kij*". (In Bratus' book (1969:42–43), this passage is given in the form of a table.)

Leaving aside the adjectives in *-ovatyj* (which would normally not be regarded as diminutive at all), is it true that adjectives in *-en'kij* can express such very different expressive meanings, ranging from love to hatred? If it *is* true, then it would appear that the only invariant meaning attributable to *-en'k-* is an unspecified emotion: 'I feel something (thinking about it)'. The choice between a positive and a negative interpretation (for example, between 'love' and 'hate') could then be seen as being determined partly by the base, as Bratus' examples cited earlier suggest: *milen'kij* ('dear' + Dim.) → affection, *ploxon'kij* ('bad' + Dim.) → hatred.

In fact, however, the account sketched here is difficult to maintain, in view of the fact that purely descriptive adjectives, which are inherently neither 'good' nor 'bad', usually receive a 'good' interpretation. Consider, for example, the following passage:

> Ženit'sja možno na Ksane—takaja ona tverden'kaja i sdobnen'kaja vmeste: tver-den'kaja v povedenii, sdobnen'kaja na vid. (Solzhenitsyn 1968a, v.1:303)
>
> He could marry Ksana, firm [lit. 'hard' + Dim.] and plump: firm in behavior, plump in appearance. (Solzhenitsyn 1968b:322)

It would seem that there is nothing particularly appealing about a girl's being 'hard', but the diminutive *tverden'kaja* immediately suggests something nice and attractive.

This 'niceness' and attractiveness are highlighted in sentences where the noun, too, has a diminutive suffix:

> . . . trudoljubivye svetlen'kie nemočki . . . (Solzhenitsyn 1968a, v.1:290)
>
> '. . . hard-working blond (Dim.) Germans (Fem.Dim.) . . . '

The effect is totally lost in a translation which ignores the impact of the diminutives:

> . . . hard working blond Germans . . . (Solzhenitsyn 1968b:309)

But even without a diminutive noun, a diminutive adjective can convey the same emotional appeal.

Furthermore, the form *ploxon'kij* ('bad' + Dim.), too, usually suggests a 'good feeling' (for example, tenderness, pity, or at least tolerance), as in the following passage about a baby, from one of Tsvetaeva's poems:

> Moloden'kij!
> Da rodnen'kij!
> Da ploxon'kij kakoj!
> V serebrjanom nagrudničke,
> i kol'čiki zanjatnye,
> i ničego čto xuden'kij—
> Na ličiko prijatnen'kij. (1965:363)

> 'Young-Dim.!
> And my very own-Dim.!
> And what a naughty-Dim. one!
> In a silvery bibby
> And what nice little ringlets!
> And no matter that he is thin-Dim.—
> His little face is so pleasant-Dim.'

Given this tendency of adjectives with *-en'k-* to acquire an endearing interpretation, one might be inclined to agree with the Academy grammar of Russian (AN SSSR 1960, v.1:361) which describes this suffix as "intensifying and caressing". But this description cannot be accepted as adequate either, for a number of reasons.

First, an 'intensifying' effect might be created in combination with qualitative adjectives, but it is hard to see how it could apply to relational adjectives such as 'right', 'left', or 'first', and yet these, too, take *-en'k-*. For example:

Ona razdernula xalat, da on sam uže ne deržalsja, i, snova kažetsja plača ili stonja, ottjanula svobodnyj vorot soročki—i ottuda vydvinulas' ee obrečennaja praven'ka-ja. (Solzhenitsyn 1968a, v.2:110)

She pulled off the bathrobe, which was already falling off by itself, and again, giving way to tears and wails, pulled back the loose front of her nightgown and bared her doomed breast [lit., her doomed right-Dim. (one)]. (Solzhenitsyn 1968b:457)

A 'caressing' effect might be said to apply in this particular case, but there is nothing caressing about the use of adjectives with *-en'k-* in the following examples from the same novel (*Cancer ward*):

Nazvala ona i sostav krovi, *ploxon'kij* sostav, i ROE povyšennyj. (Solzhenitsyn 1968a, v.2:135)

She mentioned her blood condition, its poor [lit., 'bad' + Dim.] composition and the increased E.S.R. (Solzhenitsyn 1968b:485)

Oleg uvidel Šulubina. Tot sidel na *ploxon'koj* uzkodosočnoj skam'e bez spinki. (Solzhenitsyn 1968a, v.2:147)

Shulubin sat on a sorry-looking [lit., 'bad' + Dim.], narrow-slatted bench without a back. (Solzhenitsyn 1968b:498)

But if these examples are not exactly 'caressing', could one at least maintain that they all imply some sort of unspecified 'good feeling'?

It seems clear that no 'good feeling' toward the object described by the adjective is necessarily implied; for example, there can hardly be any question of 'good feelings' toward the bad composition of someone's blood or toward the bad bench on which someone is sitting. Nonetheless, I would argue that a free-floating 'good feeling' is indeed implied. Frequently, this 'good feeling' can be assumed to be directed toward the person discussed. For example, the phrase about a 'bad old bench' may suggest that the person sitting on it is seen as a pitiful figure, for whom the speaker or narrator feels some pity or empathy. The translator's rendering of the word *ploxon'kaja* ('bad' + Dim.) as "sorry-looking" captures quite well the flavour of the original. Looking at the miserable old bench the narrator felt something like vague pity—presumably, not toward the bench as such but toward real or imaginary people who have to sit on it. Clearly, a similar interpretation applies to the phrase *ploxon'kij sostav krovi,* 'bad + Dim. condition of blood'.

Dlja nastojčivosti v pros'bax nužny: naivnost', cinizm, besstydstvo . . . nužno . . . prikinut'sja duračkom, ubogen'kim, niščen'kim: 'po-o-dajte, Xrista radi!' (Tsvetaeva 1969:44)

'To be persistent in requests, you must be naive, cynical, shameless, you must pretend to be a fool, a poor, threadbare little fool. "Oh ple-ease, for Jesus' sake, help me!"'

Pity or what is called in Russian *žalost'* (see chapter 4) is particularly often conveyed by adjectives with *-en'k-*. Another characteristic example:

Tot želten'kij s obostrennym nosom nesčastnyj, doedaemyj rakom legkix . . . sidel v posteli i často dyšal s poduški, so slyšnym xripom v grudi. (Solzhenitsyn 1968a, v.1:265)

The unfortunate, peak-nosed, yellowed [lit. 'yellow' + Dim.] man . . . consumed by lung cancer . . . sat in bed and breathed oxygen from the bag, an audible rattle in his chest. (Solzhenitsyn 1968b:280)

Given Russian cultural attitudes, something like warm pity, or *žalost'*, is often clearly conveyed in contexts where no misfortunes are explicitly mentioned and where a literal English translation doesn't suggest anything of the kind, for example:

V obščem sapožnik zapival. Vot šel on p'janen'kij. . . . (Solzhenitsyn 1968a, v.1:119)

It seemed the cobbler guzzled. He was walking along good and drunk [lit., 'drunk' + Dim.] one day. . . . (Solzhenitsyn 1968b:125)

In other cases, however, no free-floating pity can be detected behind the diminutive:

> Nu, čto noven'kogo? (Solzhenitsyn 1968a, v.1:259)
>
> What's new [lit., 'new' + Dim.]? (Solzhenitsyn 1968b:275)
>
> Vy by čto-nibud' veselen'koe nam šoobščili. (Solzhenitsyn 1968a, v.1:285)
>
> Why don't you tell us something cheerful [Dim.]? (Solzhenitsyn 1968b:303)

Thus, we have seen that diminutive adjectives in *-en'k-* can convey an extremely wide range of feelings: delight, attraction, pity, interest, and so on. To account for this wide range of possible interpretations, we are entitled to postulate for them no more, and no less, than an unspecified and free-floating 'good feeling', not necessarily oriented toward the person or thing described by the adjective. It can be represented as follows:

> when I think about X, I feel something good

It is possible, of course, for such a 'good feeling' to be expressed ironically, as in the following example:

> Slavnen'kaja logika! A demokratija! (Solzhenitsyn 1968a, v.1:244)
>
> How logical [Dim.]! What about democracy? (Solzhenitsyn 1968b:257)

But of course irony presupposes and exploits something 'good', which is interpreted as its opposite by virtue of the illocutionary force of the irony itself.

It should be noted that in other Slavic languages the use of diminutive adjectives is much more restricted than it is in Russian. For example, in Polish, the counterparts of English adjectives such as *new, cheerful,* or *yellow* could be used with a diminutive suffix only in reference to something delightful, not in reference to something pitiful or interesting. For example, the poet Adam Mickiewicz could describe young Polish women as "wesolutkie jak młode koteczki", 'cheerful-Dim. like young kittens' (and consequently, delightful); but one couldn't say in Polish:

> *Co nowiutkiego?
>
> 'What's new-Dim.?'
>
> *Opowiedz nam coś wesolutkiego!
>
> 'Why don't you tell us something cheerful-Dim.?'

Since the adjectives in *-en'k-* are very common in Russian prose and in Russian conversation, and since they have an extraordinarily broad scope of application, they contribute significantly to the over-all emotional colouring of Russian speech. What feeling exactly is conveyed depends on the context, but the over-all emotional temperature is high—much higher, of course, than in English, but also higher than in other Slavic languages.

3. Not Being in Control

3.1 Infinitive Constructions

3.1.1 Infinitive Constructions with Predicates of Necessity or Impossibility

Syntactic typology suggests that there are two different ways of viewing one's life, which play different roles in different languages: one can tend to view people's lives in terms of 'what I do' (an agentive orientation), and one can tend to view it in terms of 'what happens to me' (a patientive orientation). The agentive orientation, which is a special case of the causative orientation (cf. Bally 1920), means a special emphasis on action and volition ('I want', 'I do'); the patientive orientation, which is a special case of the phenomenological orientation, means a special emphasis on 'impotence' and patientivity (I cannot do anything; things happen to me).

As mentioned earlier (cf. section 2), agentivity is typically linked with nominative and nominative-like constructions, whereas 'impotence' and 'patientivity' are linked with dative and dative-like constructions.

The two poles are not on a par, in so far as agency plays an important role in all languages, whereas 'impotence' does not. But languages differ considerably in the amount of attention they pay to 'impotence'. Some tend more or less to ignore it, treating agentive sentences as a model for all, or most, sentences referring to people. In other languages, there are two major types of sentences referring to people, a nominative type, based on the agentive pattern, and a dative one, which presents people as not being in control of events.

Modern English syntax is dominated by nominative-like subject constructions, and dative-like subject constructions such as the following play a marginal role:

> it occurred to me that . . .
> it seems to me that . . .
> it is necessary/impossible for me to do it

In colloquial English, even necessity and impossibility are normally couched in the personal, nominative-like mode:

> I have to do it.
> I cannot do it.

By contrast, in Russian syntax agentive, personal, volitional sentences do not provide a general model, and nominative-like subject constructions are not similarly extended to most semantic domains. On the contrary, the role of the dative pole keyed to 'impotence' is here extremely important; and, moreover, it is constantly growing (whereas in English, any changes in this area have always gone in the opposite direction; cf. Van der Gaaf 1904 and Elmers 1981).

In English, the general expectation seems to be that one is in control of one's life, and even our limitations, and our constraints, are viewed in that perspective. In

Russian, one can also sometimes view one's limitations and constraints in this way, and one can say, for example:

> Ja   dolžen   èto   sdelat'.
> I:Nom. should   it:Acc do:Inf.

> 'I have to do it.'

> Ja   ne   mogu   èto   sdelat'.
> I:Nom. Neg. can:1SG this:Acc. do:Inf.

> 'I cannot do it.'

But next to such nominative-subject sentences Russian speech is pervaded by the much more common dative-subject constructions, where our limitations and constraints are presented in a patientive mode, formally distinct from the agentive pattern. Thus, there is a whole category of impersonal modal predicatives which refer to necessity or impossibility and which require a dative subject. In fact, the two modal meanings exemplified—'can' and 'should'—are rather exceptional in Russian in being able to be used in the personal, nominative mode. For example, necessity cannot be expressed in Russian in this way. Thus, English sentences such as "I must. I have to" cannot be rendered in Russian without first being put into a patientive perspective, which emphasises the fact that the person in question is not in control of the situation.

The category of predicates which require a dative subject includes the following: *nado*, 'it is necessary/needed'; *nužno*, 'it is necessary/required'; *neobxodimo*, 'it is necessary/indispensable'; *nel'zja*, 'one may not'; *nevozmožno*, 'one cannot'; *ne polagaetsja*, 'it is not allowed'; *sleduet*, 'one ought to'; *dolžno*, 'one has to'. For example:

> [E]xat' mne 31-go, v subbotu, neobxodimo. (Tsvetaeva 1969:34)

> 'I have to leave on the 31st, on Saturday (it's necessary; I have no choice).'

> —Berites'-ka za lopaty,—govorit Karpov.
> —Vsem nado brat'sja,—usmexajus' ja. (Okudžava 1984:77)

> '"Pick up your shovels", says Karpov.
> "Everyone should do it", I grinned.'

> Pojdem, zajdem v kontoru, esli tebe nužno. (Tolstoy 1953:282)

> 'Let's go; we'll call at the office on the way, if you need to.'

> Tebe nel'zja tak kričat'. (Tolstoy 1953:601)

> 'You must not shout like that (you are not allowed to).'

The two modes—the agentive and the patientive—are not semantically equivalent. For example, the phrase *možno li mne?* 'can I:Dat.?' tends to suggest a request for permission ('may I?'), whereas the corresponding nominative phrase *mogu li ja?* 'can I:Nom.?' is more likely to be a rhetorical question concerning one's ability ('am I able to?'). The nominative phrase *ja ne mogu* 'I:Nom cannot' suggests an impossibility generated in, or at least accepted by, the person in question; similarly, the nominative phrase *ja dolžen* 'I must' suggests a recognised and internalised necessity, whereas dative phrases such as *mne nužno, mne nado, mne neobxodimo* 'I have to' suggest a necessity imposing itself from outside.

For example, in the following sentences examples (a) and (b) refer to an internal, personal impossibility, and a nominative pattern is used, whereas the remaining examples refer to external circumstances (c) or to somebody else's will (d and e), and a dative pattern is used.

a. Mne živetsja očen' ploxo, nas v odnu komnatu nabito četyre čeloveka, i ja sovsem ne mogu pisat'. (Tsvetaeva 1969:37)

   'My present life is hard, the four of us are all crammed into one room, and I (Nom.) simply can't write.'

b. Byla by ja v Rossii, vse bylo by inače, no Rossii (zvuka) net, est' bukvy: SSSR, ne mogu že ja exat' v gluxoe, bez glasnyx, v svistjaščuju guščǔ. (Tsvetaeva 1969:62)

   'If I were in Russia, everything would be different, but Russia (the sound) is no more, there is only a set of letters: USSR [SSSR in Russian]; I can't (Nom.) travel into a vowelless wilderness, into a thicket of sibilants.'

c. Možno li mne nadejat'sja, dorogaja Anna Antonovna, ustroit'sja na èti den'gi v Prage? (Tsvetaeva 1969:41)

   'Can I (Dat.) hope, dear Anna Antonovna, to live on that money in Prague?'

d. Možno mne vas pocelovat', Sofija Nikolaevna? (Leonid Leonov, quoted in Scholz 1973:151)

   'May I (Dat.) kiss you, Sofija Nikolaevna?'

e. Možno sest' vozle vas?—sprosil on, nakonec. (Turgenev, quoted in Scholz 1973:177)

   '"May I (Dat.) sit next to you?", he asked finally.'

I am not suggesting, however, that the personal, nominative mode is semantically more complex than the impersonal, dative one. On the contrary, I believe that it is the impersonal mode which includes an additional semantic component: 'not because I want it'. Thus:

ja (Nom.) *dolžen*	=	I should do it
mne (Dat.) *dolžno* (archaic)	=	I can't think: 'if I don't want it, I will not do it' I know I should do it
mne (Dat.) *neobxodimo*	=	I can't think: 'if I don't want it, I will not do it' I know I cannot not do it
(Nom.) *ne mogu*	=	I cannot

mne (Dat.) *nevozmožno*	=	I can't think: 'if I want it, I will do it'
		I know I cannot do it
mne (Dat.) *nel'zja*	=	I can't think: 'if I want it, I will do it'
		I know I cannot do it
		I know it would be bad if I did it
mne (Dat.) *nado*	=	I can't think:
		'if I don't want it, I will not do it'
		I know it would be bad if I didn't do it

The external character of a necessity or impossibility referred to in a dative-infinitive construction is particularly clear in the case of sentences with negative pronominal expressions, such as the following (cf. Rappaport 1986; Apresjan and Iomdin 1989):

nekogda:	'I cannot because there is no time when I could (do it)'
negde:	'I cannot because there is no place where I could (do it)'
nekuda:	'I cannot because there is no place to which I could (do it)'

The use of such expressions is illustrated in the following:

Prosit' mne ne u kogo. (Tsvetaeva 1969:34)

'There is no one I could ask.'

Nikuda ne xožu, p.č. nečego nadet', a kupit' ne na čto. (Tsvetaeva 1969:36)

'I don't go out anywhere because I have nothing to wear, and no money to buy anything.'

Znaete russkoe vyraženie: nekogda o duše podumat'. (Tsvetaeva 1969:75)

'You know the Russian saying: there is no time to think about the soul.'

On ničego ne govorit, potomu čto nečego emu skazat'. (Okudžava 1984:76)

'He doesn't say anything, because there is nothing he can say.'

It is important to emphasise that sentences of this kind, which present the (dative) subject as not being in control of the circumstances, are not only possible in Russian but extremely common and that they determine to a considerable extent the characteristic flavour of Russian speech. (For example, in the three pages of Alexander Solzhenitsyn's celebrated "address to the nation" in 1990 there are about twenty such sentences, among them the very title of the address: "Kak nam obustroit' Rossiju?", 'How [should] we (Dat.) re-build (Inf.) Russia?')

3.1.2 Infinitive Constructions with No Lexical Modals

Russian also has a wealth of infinitive constructions which convey meanings related to necessity and impossibility and which include no modal words such as 'cannot', 'has to', 'should', or 'must'. Bogusławski and Karolak (1970:35) describe sentences of this kind as one of the characteristic features of the Russian language. One such construction has already been discussed (chapter 2):

> Ne byvat' Egorju na Rusi svjatoj. . . .
>
> 'Egor wasn't fated to come to holy Russia. . . .'

Another example (Solzhenitsyn welcomes the prospect of the disintegration of the Soviet Union):

> Vse uže vidjat, čto vmeste nam ne žit'!
> (Solzhenitsyn 1990:3)
>
> 'all (the world) can see now that we-Dat. [cannot; are 'fated' not to] live together [as one "Soviet Union", A.W.].'

In the present section, I will survey briefly several other constructions of this kind—some referring to helpless 'wanting', some to helpless 'wishes' or 'apprehensions', some to obligation, some to futile regrets, and some to necessity. The brief survey which follows will be divided into four sections, according to four modal meanings: 'I want', 'it would be good/bad', 'I should', and 'I have to'.

This section, and the following one (3.2) on reflexive constructions, are devoted to examples and analysis of the dozen or so distinctive syntactic constructions which express this meaning of lack of control over events. Readers who do not want to go into the detailed evidence on these constructions may want to proceed directly to section 3.3 and the following discussion of cultural attitudes reflected in syntax. (The undated examples are from Galkina-Fedoruk 1958.)

— 'I WANT'

WHAT ONE WANTS (OR MIGHT WANT) ONE CANNOT DO

Examples:

> Ni projti ni proexat'. (Chekhov)
>
> 'Impassable, by foot or otherwise.'

> Ne dognat' tebe bešenoj trojki. (Nekrasov)
>
> 'You'll not catch up with that mad troika.'

> A ved', dejstvitel'no, vinom paxnet. . . . Tol'ko vina nam ne pit'. Ono v bočke. I probka veličinoj s kulak. (Okudžava 1984:71)
>
> 'That's true, there is a smell of wine. . . . But we won't be able to drink it. It is in a barrel. And the stopper is as big as a fist.'

> Bez vsenarodnogo golosovanija—ètogo ne rešit'. (Solzhenitsyn 1990:3)
>
> 'Without a vote of all the people this [cannot] be resolved.'

Da uže vo mnogix okrainnyx respublikax centrobežnye sily tak razognany, čto ne ostanovit' ix bez nasilija i krovi—da i ne nado uderživat' takoj cenoj! (Solzhenitsyn 1990:1)

'In many republics of the periphery the centrifugal forces have such a momentum that they [cannot] be stopped without violence and bloodshed—and they should not be held in check at such a price.'

Formula:

Neg. + Infinitive$_{\text{Agentive}}$ (+ Dative$_{\text{Hum}}$)

Explication:

one can't think: 'if I want it, I will do it'
one cannot do it

Discussion:

At first sight, this construction may seem no different from the 'fated' dative-cum-infinitive (see chapter 2), and in fact out of context the second example could receive a 'fated' interpretation ('you were not fated to catch up—ever—with that carriage'). But the first example could not be given such an interpretation, and this points to a structural difference between the two constructions: the 'fated' one really does require a dative, whereas in the one presently under consideration the dative is optional. A second difference is related to the nature of the verb: in the 'fated' construction, the verb may be either agentive or non-agentive (and typically is non-agentive), whereas in the present construction the verb is normally agentive. A third difference concerns the time of the event: in the 'fated' construction the time has to be indefinite (which is often reflected in the iterative form of the verb), whereas in the present construction the time reference is quite specific, although it is usually supplied by the context (and in fact, what is meant is usually 'now').

WHAT I WANT MAY NOT HAPPEN

Examples:

Byt' pervym, vol'no odinokim!
I videt', čto bliska meta,
I slyšat' otzvukom dalekim
Udary nog i ščelk xlysta! (Brjusov)

'To be first, to be free and alone
And see the tape draw near,
And hear the distant echo
Of pounding hoof and crack of whip!'

Formula:

Infinitive + Expressive intonation

Explication:

> I want this: X will happen to me
> I know I can't think: 'if I want it, it will happen'
> because of this, I feel something

Discussion:

In this construction, the verb doesn't have to be agentive, and in fact usually it is not; there is no slot for a dative, or for any other subject or quasi-subject; and the intonation is expressive. The meaning conveyed is that of a wish, not necessarily a counter-factual wish but not necessarily a realisable one either. The expressive intonation (which appears to be an integral part of this construction) indicates that the wish is accompanied by an emotion.

— 'IT WOULD BE GOOD/BAD . . . '

PERSONAL WISH

Examples:

> Sejčas by pokurit'. . . . (Okudžava 1984:44)
> '[It would be good] to have a smoke now. . . .'
>
> Zakusit' by,—govorit Saška. (Okudžava 1984:71)
> [Some soldiers have managed to open a barrel of wine]:
> '"[It would be good if we had something] to eat with it", says Saška.'

Formula:

> Infinitive + *by* (+ I/we-Dative$_{Hum}$) + Exclamatory intonation

Explication:

> it would be good if X could happen to me (us)
> I know I can't think: 'if I want it, it will happen'

Discussion:

This construction is closely related to the preceding one, but it differs from it in two respects. First, it contains the particle *by,* which indicates that the status of the desired state of affairs is seen as purely hypothetical. Second, in the present construction there is a slot for a dative (*mne/nam* 'to me/us'), whereas in the construction without *by* the speaker cannot be mentioned explicitly. Presumably, if speakers express passionate volition, this prevents them from thinking about themselves as separate elements in the situation (cf. Langacker 1983:136), but if speakers' attitudes are more hypothetical, then they can speculate about themselves just as they can speculate about other people, possibly with the only difference being that a hypothetical wish concerning ourselves is likely to trigger an emotion, whereas a hypothetical wish concerning another person can be dispassionate. (See the next construction.)

A WISH DIRECTED AT SOMEBODY ELSE

Examples:

> Elena, tebe by v ministrax byt'! (Furmanov)
> 'Elena, you [should] be a minister!'

> Nu čto vy sidite doma? Exali by na teplye vody. . . . (Tolstoy 1953:377)
> 'Why are you sitting at home? You [should] go abroad and take the waters.'

Formula:

$$\text{Dative}_{\text{Hum}} + by + \text{Infinitive}$$

Explication:

> it would be good if X happened to person Y
> I know I can't think: 'because of this, it will happen'

Discussion:

In this construction, which can be used in a wide range of speech acts, the speaker presents a certain state of affairs as desirable, though not necessarily realisable. If the utterance concerns the addressee and if the state of affairs in question can be interpreted as realisable, then the utterance can be seen as advice, but this is not necessarily the case. The intonation may or may not be expressive, and an emotion is not part of the semantic invariant.

APPREHENSION

Examples:

> Časy kommunizma—svoe otbili.
> No betonnaja postrojka ego ešče ne ruxnula.
> I kak by nam, vmesto osvoboždenija, ne raspljuščit'sja pod ego razvalinami. (Solzenitsyn 1990:1)

> 'Communism's days are over.
> But its concrete edifice has not yet collapsed.
> And [we must be careful] not to be crushed beneath its ruins,
> instead of gaining our freedom.'

> —Poezd v tri?—sprosil nemec.—Kak by ne opozdat'. (Tolstoy 1953:652)
> '"The train leaves at 3?", asked the German. "One might miss it (I should hurry)".'

> Bezobrazno drožali ruki. 'Stakan by ne vyronit'. . . .' (Dovlatov 1983:8)
> '[My] hands were trembling horribly. "[I must be careful; I] might drop the glass. . . ."'

Formula:

$$\text{Neg.} + \text{Infinitive} + by\ (+ \text{Dative}_{\text{Hum}})$$

Explication:

> it would be bad if X happened to me
> because of this, I want to do something
> I know I can't think: 'if I don't want it, it will not happen'
> because of this, I feel something

Discussion:

In this construction, the speaker considers a hypothetical state of affairs that would be bad for him and expresses an apprehension that this bad thing might happen. In addition, as pointed out by Galkina-Fedoruk (1958:228), sentences of this kind express a desire to do something to prevent the undesirable state of affairs.

— **'I SHOULD'**

CURRENT OBLIGATION

Examples:

[M]ožet byt', mne vernut'sja, tovarišč mladšij lejtenant? (Okudžava 1984:60)
'[P]erhaps I should go back, comrade lieutenant?'

Pora idti nam s toboj. Xvatjatsja tebja. (Okudžava 1984:69)
'It's time to go for you and me. They'll start looking for you.'

Nu, barin, obedat'! (Tolstoy 1953:277)
'Well then, master, it is time to eat.'

—Zavtrakat', barin, skazal starik.
—Razve pora? Nu, zavtrakat'. (Tolstoy 1953:274)
'"It's time to eat, master", said the old man.
"Is it time already? Well then, let's eat."'

Ne "gordit'sja" nam; ne protjagivat' lapy k čužim žiznjam—a osoznat' svoj narod v provale izmoždajuščej bolezni, i molit'sja, čtoby poslal nam Bog vyzdorovet', i razum dejstvij dlja togo. (Solzhenitsyn 1990:2)

'We [should] not take pride in it; not extend our hands to other lives—but rather become aware that our people is in the depths of an enfeebling disease, and pray that God send us salvation and the wisdom of action to achieve it.'

Formula:

$$(Nu)\ \text{Infinitive}_{\text{Agentive}}\ (\text{Dative}_{\text{Hum}})$$

Explication:

>   I should do X (now)
>   I can't think: 'if I don't want it, I will not do it'
>   I will do it

Discussion:

As the preceding examples show, the bare infinitive of agentive verbs can also be used to indicate that one should do something and to prompt one (usually, oneself) to fulfil that obligation. It is difficult to see how sentences with the infinitive of obligation ('should') are distinguished from sentences with the infinitive of command (except in terms of intonation). It appears, however, that the infinitive of command is virtually incompatible with adverbial complements, especially with preposed ones, whereas the infinitive of obligation seldom if ever occurs without any complements and in fact favours preposed complements. One might add that the infinitive of obligation normally refers to the speaker and that if it refers to the addressee, the obligation seems to include the speaker as well. Frequently, utterances of this kind start with the predicative *pora*, 'It's time (to do something)', or with the particle *nu*, which prompts the speaker/addressee to action, and they convey the idea that it is time to do something, and that one should get moving. They combine, therefore, the idea of 'should' with the idea of 'let's' (or 'let me').

ONE DOESN'T KNOW WHAT ONE SHOULD DO, OR HOW

Examples:

No čto že delat? čto delat?—s otčajaniem govoril on sebe i ne naxodil otveta. (Tolstoy 1953:5)

'But what should I do? What should I do?, he was asking himself in despair and he couldn't find an answer.'

Čto mne bylo delat'? Kak podat' ej pomošč? (Pushkin 1937:68)

'What should I do? (I was asking myself.) How could I help her?'

Ne ujti li? . . . Ne podoždat' li ešče? (Dostoevsky 1957:80–81)

'Shouldn't I go away? . . . Shouldn't I wait a little longer?'

Formula:

>   Q + (Intonation of special questions) (Dative$_{Hum}$) Infinitive$_{Agentive}$

Explication:

>   I should do something
>   I can't think: 'if I don't want it, I will not do it'
>   I don't know what I should do

Discussion:

In sentences of this kind, the speaker conveys the idea that he doesn't know what he should do, or how (where 'how' includes when, where, etc.). Very frequently, questions of this kind are rhetorical and convey ideas similar to 'why should I?'. For example:

> Možet byt', vse èto xorošo; no mne-to začem zabotit'sja ob učreždenii punktov medicinskix, kotorymi ja nikogda ne polzujus'? (Tolstoy 1953:267)
>
> 'Maybe all this is good, but why should I worry about opening medical units which I will never use myself?'

— 'I HAVE TO'

PRESENT NECESSITY

Examples:

> Pust' Adja ne obižaetsja, čto ne pišu ej segodnja otdel'no, sejčas kupat' Mura, gotovit'sja k zavtrašnemu iždiveniju, myt' golovu, pisat' S. pismo—tak, do glubokoj noči. Splju ne bol'še pjati časov vot uže polgoda. (Tsvetaeva 1972:191)
>
> 'Let Adja not be offended that I'm not writing to her today separately; just now [I have] to bath Mur, get everything ready for tomorrow, wash my hair, write a letter to S.—and so on, till late into the night. For the last sixth months, I have been sleeping no more than five hours a night.'

> Nam exat'-to vsego sorok kilometrov. (Okudžava 1984:57)
>
> 'We only [have] to drive for forty kilometres.'

> Mne ved' uezžat,—govorju ja,—ty skaži, napišeš' mne? (Okudžava 1984:68)
>
> '"You know I [have] to leave now", I say, "tell me, you'll write to me?"'

> Ty ne pej mnogo, Fedoseev,—govorit Karpov,—tebe mašinu vesti. (Okudžava 1984:77)
>
> '"Don't drink too much, Fedoseev", Karpov says, "you [have] to drive."'

Formula:

$$(\text{Dative}_{\text{Hum}}) \ \text{Infinitive}_{\text{Agentive}}$$

Explication:

> X is doing/will do Y
> X can't think: 'if I don't want it, I will not do it'

Discussion:

We have seen earlier that an infinitive of agentive verbs can carry the meaning of current obligation ('I/you should do X; it is time to do X'). Sentences of the kind presently under discussion carry a similar meaning, but they imply an even lesser degree of control. The difference is, essentially, that between 'I should' and 'I have to'. Since both types have the same syntactic formula, it could be argued that they in fact form a single category. Yet I think that a good case can be made for keeping them apart.

First, 'should' sentences typically start with the urging particle *nu* (or some similar device), and they prompt to action, whereas 'have to' sentences do not have that 'prompting' quality. Second, the meaning of 'should'—and not 'have to'—is clearly encoded in interrogative dative sentences, such as:

> Čto mne delat'?
>
> 'What [should] I do?'

This suggests that at least some 'should' sentences have to be distinguished from 'have to' sentences. Third, negative dative sentences such as

> Ni projti ni proexat'.
>
> 'Impossible to pass.' (lit., 'not to pass')

clearly mean that something *cannot* be done, not that it *shouldn't* be done. This, too, shows that 'should' should be regarded as a separate grammatical meaning in Russian, not as a mere contextual variant of some unspecified modal meaning.

It is interesting to note, in this connection, the following two juxtaposed sentences, both with infinitive predicates, where the modal meaning of the two infinitives is clearly different:

> Vse uže vidjat, čto vmeste nam ne žit'.
> Tak i ne tjanut' vzaimnoe obremenenie. (Solzhenitsyn 1990:3)
>
> '[A]ll (the world) can see now that we-Dat. [can] not live together
> [as one "Soviet Union", A.W.] So we [should/must] not drag the mutual burden.'

3.2 Reflexive Constructions

INABILITY TO DO WHAT ONE WANTS

Examples:

> Ne spitsja ej v postele novoj. (Pushkin)
>
> 'She feels she can't sleep in her new bed.'

> O zdešnej žizni uže ne pišetsja, ja uže edu. (Tsvetaeva 1969:42)
>
> 'It "doesn't write itself any more" [i.e., I feel I can't write] about life here; I am already leaving.'

Formula:

Neg. Verb-3SG(Neut.)Refl. (Dative_{Hum})

Explication:

X wants to do Y
(not because X wants something to happen to something else)
because of this, X does something
X thinks something like this:
   I feel I can't do it
   I couldn't say why
   not because I don't want it

Discussion:

In this construction, a person referred to by a dative (which can be omitted in the case of the speaker) is presented as an experiencer who for some obscure psychological reason is unable to do what he or she wants to do. Most commonly, the intended activity presents no inherent difficulty and in fact consists in maintaining oneself in a certain state (for example, sitting, lying, or sleeping; cf. Apresjan and Iomdin 1989:86). The verb has to be intransitive or has to be used intransitively, and the whole difficulty is presented entirely in terms of an internal state (usually, the mood) of the experiencer and as having nothing to do with the target object, if there is one. For example:

Mne segodnja ne čitaetsja.
to-me today Neg. read-3SG-Refl.

'For some reason, I feel I cannot read today.'

*Mne segodnja ne čitaetsja knigi/knigu.
to-me today Neg. read-3SG-Refl. book-Gen/Acc.

'For some reason, I feel I cannot read a book today.'

INEXPLICABLE ABILITY TO DO SOMETHING WELL

Examples:

Pisalos' tebe?
write-3SG-Past-Refl. to-you

—Čudesno pisalos' (Veresaev)
marvellously write-3SG-Past-Refl.

'Did your writing go well?'—'Marvellously.'

Formula:

Verb_{Agentive}-3SG(Neut.)Refl. Dative_{Hum} Adv._{[well]}

Explication:

> X is doing Y
> not because X wants something to happen to something else
> X thinks something like this:
>   I feel I can do it well
>   I couldn't say why
>   it is not because I want it

Discussion:

In this construction, a person is presented as experiencing an inexplicable lack of difficulty in doing something. The agent feels that the attempted activity is going well, but pleased as he is, he cannot take credit for this because the success is not due to his efforts; rather, it is due to some inexplicable causes.

> Mne   čudesno   pisalos'.
> to-me   marvellously   write-3sg-Past-Refl.

> 'I felt my writing went marvellously well; I don't know why.'

> *Mne   čudesno   pisalos'   stat'ju.
> to-me   marvellously   write-3sg-Past-Refl. article-Acc.

> 'I felt that my writing of the article went marvellously well.'

In this case, an external goal is semantically not excluded, but it cannot be mentioned or otherwise focussed on, because the construction is concerned with the subjective aspect of the situation. This time, the reality does correspond to the desire, but what is stressed is the experiencer's feeling that there is no causal link between the two.

INVOLUNTARY MENTAL ACTS (OR PROCESSES)

Examples:

Emu xotelos' slyšat' zvuk ee golosa. (Tolstoy 1953:607)

'He (felt he) wanted to hear the sound of her voice.'

Vse novosti—pri vstreče. Teper' uže malo ostalos' xotja i samoj ne veritsja. (Tsvetaeva 1972:205)

'I'll tell you all the news when I see you. It won't be long now although it's hard to believe.'

Pomnitsja, uložila (kak sokrovišče) imenno v sunduk, no pamjat' podatliva, u menja toždestvenna soobraženiju, potomu ran'še posmotrite v knigax. (Tsvetaeva 1972:231)

'I seem to remember, I put it (like a treasure) into the trunk, but memory tells you what you want to hear; with me it's no more than imagination, so better check in the books first.'

Segodnja mne vspomnilas' Praga—sady. (Tsvetaeva 1969:75)

'Today I was reminded of Prague—of its gardens.'

Formula:

$$\text{Dative}_{\text{Hum}} \ \text{Verb}_{\text{mental}}\text{-3SG(Neut.)Refl.}$$

Explications:

Ja ne verju. = I don't believe.

Mne ne veritsja. (lit., 'It doesn't believe itself to me.') =

something in me says: I don't believe it
not because I want it
I don't want to say: I don't believe it

Ja xoču. = I want.

Mne xočetsja. (lit., 'It wants itself to me.') =

something in me says: I want it
not because I want it
I don't want to say: I want it

Ja pomnju. = I remember.

Mne pomnitsja. (lit., 'It remembers itself to me.') =

something in me says: I remember it
not because I want it
I don't want to say: I remember it

Discussion:

In English, one can contrast a conscious thought with an involuntary one or with an impression for which one doesn't take the responsibility:

a. I think/believe/recall . . .
b. It occurred to me . . .
It seemed to me . . .

But the 'dative' pattern has a very limited scope in English, and one cannot say, for example:

*It believes/doesn't believe to me. . . .

In Russian, however, the dative pattern is productive, and it is very common to speak about one's mental life in that mode, implying that mental events simply 'happen' in our minds and that we are not responsible for them.

The dative pattern appears to be semantically marked with respect to the nominative one. The nominative pattern tends to suggest responsibility, but it doesn't necessarily imply intentionality ('I think/believe, etc., because I want it'). On the other hand, the dative pattern explicitly denies responsibility: a thought, belief, or other mental state or event is presented as emerging spontaneously in our minds and we do not commit ourselves to it. For example, I may know that I am leaving soon, and I may still say, *ne veritsja*, that is, 'something in me is saying: I don't believe it'.

The most important Russian expression of this sort is the ubiquitous *xočetsja/ne xočetsja*, lit., 'it wants/doesn't want itself to me', with the extremely high frequency of 247 in Zasorina's (1977) corpus of one million words, as against a mere 41 of its closest English counterpart, the bookish and stilted *desire* (Kučera and Francis 1967). The discrepancy between these figures seems even more remarkable when one considers that *desire* has a quasi-counterpart in the Russian verb *želat'*, with the frequency of 185. (The frequencies for *xotet'* and *want* are 1295 and 573, respectively.) Admittedly, *xočetsja* can also be sometimes translated by the English expression *feel like*, but this has nothing of the intensity of *xočetsja* and is restricted syntactically to sentences about one's own actions ('X feels like doing Y'). By contrast, *xočetsja* can express a passionate, uncontrollable desire that something should happen—for example, to other people, as in the following passage:

> −A ty už dumaeš, čto on nynče sdelaet predloženie?—pribavil on, pomolčav.
> −I dumaju, i net. Tol'ko mne užasno xočetsja. (Tolstoy 1953:610)
>
> "'So you think that he will now propose to her?'", he added after a moment of silence.
> "I do and I don't. But I feel I want it awfully.'"

Semantically, therefore, *xočetja* is closer to *desire* than to *feel like*, although it is infinitely more colloquial. But English simply doesn't have an idiomatic equivalent for this concept.

As Jarintzov (1916:121) put it, *xočetsja* "conveys a vague desire for something, as if commanded by some power from without". She pointed out rightly that sentences with *xočetsja* "are amongst the numerous everyday expressions when we subconsciously acknowledge an involuntary desire, as it were. *Xočetsja ljubvi*—'one longs for love'—often comes into poems and songs".

3.3 Russian Versus English

We have seen that Russian grammar has a wealth of constructions which present reality as contrary to, or at least independent of, human desires and human will. English has very few, if any, constructions of this kind. By contrast, English grammar is extraordinarily rich in constructions which link causation with human will in a positive way. This special interest in the interplay between causation and volition is manifested in patterns such as the following (for further discussion, see Wierzbicka 1988c):

X made Y $V_{int(entional)}$-INF	(e.g., X made Y wash the dishes)
X had Y V_{int}-INF	(e.g., X had Y wash the dishes)
X had X's Z V_{int}-ed	(e.g., X had her boots mended)

X had Y $V_{non\text{-}int}$-ing	(e.g., X had Y crying)
X had Y V_{int}-ING	(e.g., X had Y staying with her)
X got Y to V_{int}-INF	(e.g., X got Y to wash the dishes)
X got Y Adj.	(e.g., X got Y furious)
X V_{int}-ed Y into doing Z	(e.g., X talked/tricked Y into doing Z)
X $V_{aspectual}$-ed Y V-ing	(e.g., X kept Y waiting)

We could also add that both the focus on causal relations and the special concern with the strategies of human interaction seem to be characteristic of English, not only in comparison with other European languages but also in a universal perspective.

It may seem foolish to try to interpret such divergencies in the light of what is known about other aspects of culture and society. But in the case of vocabulary, nobody would hesitate to seek such explanations. It is regarded as self-evident that a language would have a particularly rich vocabulary in the area of culturally important objects and concepts. As Kenneth Hale (quoted in Dixon 1980:108) puts it, "it is natural to find cultural elaboration reflected in lexical structures". I submit, however, that "cultural elaboration" is reflected not only in lexical structures but also in grammatical structures. Hale refers specifically to the area of kinship and links the "flourishing, even vibrant, elaboration of kinship nomenclature" in the Australian language Warlpiri with the important role that the "algebra of kinship" plays in Warlpiri society.

But of course kinship plays an important role not only in the lexicon of Australian Aboriginal languages but also in their grammar. (Cf., for example, Hale 1966; Dench 1982 and 1987; Heath, Merlan, and Rumsey 1982.) Generally speaking, what Hale calls areas of "cultural elaboration" and what Dixon (1980:103) calls "areas of semantic specification" don't stop at the boundary between lexicon and grammar but pervade a language as a whole. This may not apply to physical entities and features of the environment (camels, reindeer, snow, sand, rice, etc.), but I think it does apply to conceptual fields of special cultural importance. In fact, lexical elaboration of conceptual fields often seems to go hand in hand with grammatical elaboration. Kinship in Australian languages is one case in point. The perceived presence of close links between volition and causation reflected in English grammar and lexicon is another, and so is the perceived absence of such links reflected in Russian grammar and in the Russian lexicon.

As one final example, which highlights the difference between English and Russian discussed here, consider the following contrasts:

a. He succeeded.
   He failed.

b. Emu   èto   udalos'.
   he:Dat. it:Nom. succeeded-Impers.

   Emu   èto   ne   udalos'.
   he:Dat. it:Nom. Neg.   succeeded-Impers.

The English nominative construction (a) places part of the responsibility for success or failure on the person involved; the Russian dative construction (b) absolves the person involved from any responsibility whatsoever (good and bad things happen to us; they are not caused by what we do). There is no idiomatic way in Russian to convey the meaning of (a), as there is no idiomatic way in English to convey the meaning of (b). This fact epitomises the contrast in the ethnophilosophies reflected in the languages in question.

4. 'Irrationality'

4.1 'Irrationality' in Syntax

Syntactic typology of languages suggests that there are two different ways of viewing reality toward which different languages can gravitate: one can tend to view the world in terms of causes and their effects, and one tends to view it in a more subjective, impressionistic, phenomenological perspective (cf. Bally 1920).

Among European languages, Russian goes perhaps further than any other in the direction of the phenomenological tendency. Syntactically, this manifests itself in the colossal (and constantly growing) role of various so-called impersonal sentence types, which have no subject, or at least no subject in the nominative case, and whose main verb takes an 'impersonal' neuter form. As Jarintzov (1916:122) pointed out, "the impersonal form of the verbs winds its way throughout the language and presents one of the characteristic points of the Russian manner of thinking".

A number of impersonal constructions presenting people as passive and more or less impotent experiencers rather than agents was discussed in the preceding section (on 'not being in control'). In the present section, we will focus on impersonal constructions which appear to suggest that the world is a mysterious and ultimately unknowable place and that the ultimate causes of events are obscure and incomprehensible. For example:

> Ego   pereexalo   tramvaem.
> he:Acc.   ran-over   tram:Instr.
>
> 'He was run over by a tram.'
>
> Ego   ubilo   molniej.
> he:Acc.   killed(Neut.) lightning:Instr.
>
> 'He was struck down by lightning.'

In this construction, the immediate cause of the event—the lightning or the tram—is presented as if it were an 'instrument' of some unknowable force. There is no overt subject, the verb has an 'impersonal' neuter form ('impersonal' because it could never occur with a person as a subject), and the empty subject slot (cf. Mel'čuk 1974) suggests that the ultimate cause is unidentifiable and incomprehensible. "The subject is removed from the field of vision . . . as an unknown cause of the phenomenon described by the verb. . . . Precisely this search for the true cause of the phenomenon and the recognition that this cause is unknown, constitutes the basis of all impersonal sentences" (Jarintzov 1916:122).

Peškovskij (1956) points out that the same quality of "mysteriousness" is present in sentences such as

> Stučit!
> is-knocking
> 'Something is knocking (one can't understand what or why).'

which are quite different in this respect from sentences with an unidentified subject:

> Stučat!
> are-knocking
> 'Somebody is knocking.'

Galkina-Fedoruk (1958:139) notes that impersonal sentences which focus on the unknown and on the inexplicable are extremely common in folk literature and, in particular, in folk riddles.

An alternative nominative construction, which has no such implications, is of course also available:

> Ego   pereexal   tramvaj.
> him:Acc.   ran-over(Masc.)   tram(Masc.):Nom.
>
> 'A tram ran him over.'
>
> Ego   ubila   molnija.
> him:Acc.   killed(Masc.)   lightning(Fem.):Nom.
>
> 'A flash of lightning killed him.'

However, colloquial Russian speech is permeated with sentences of the former, subjectless, kind. Soviet grammarians have often shown themselves to be embarrassed by this property of Russian, as incompatible with the official 'scientific world view', and have tried to explain it away as a relic of old times. For example, the academician Vinogradov (1947:465), speaking of some of the constructions in question, asserted that "jazykovaja texnika zdes' ispol'zovala kak material otživšuju ideologiju", 'linguistic technique has used here an outlived ideology as its material'.

The irony is that constructions which breathe that "outlived ideology" not only show no signs of losing their productivity but, on the contrary, keep growing and expanding and in many areas are beginning to supplant those competitors which do not imply that events have an unknowable nature (cf. Galkina-Fedoruk 1958:148). This is in keeping with the general trend in the evolution of Russian syntax, which favours growth and expansion of 'impersonal' sentences of all kinds, especially dative-subject sentences presenting people as not being in control of events and subjectless sentences presenting events as not fully comprehensible.

Galkina-Fedoruk (1958:151) writes: "The number of impersonal sentences in the contemporary Russian language is constantly growing. This growth is to be explained not only in terms of constant development and refinement of forms of thought, and expanding means of expression, but also in terms of various grammatical processes, which, ultimately, are also shaped by the growing complexity of the content of speech. Our data show that many personal verbs are beginning to be used in an impersonal way. On the other hand, some impersonal sentences remain in the language as relics of older forms of thought".

Peškovskij (1956:345) was particularly struck by the constant growth of impersonal constructions in Russian: "We can see, then, that impersonal sentences are by no means relics . . . but, on the contrary, something which constantly grows and expands". What Peškovskij appears to have overlooked, however, is that this growth of impersonal constructions is a characteristically Russian phenomenon, and that in other European languages—for example, in German, French, and English—changes have usually occurred in the opposite direction (as pointed out by Bally 1920; cf. also Elmers 1981). This suggests that the constant growth of impersonal constructions in Russian corresponded to a quite specific orientation of the Russian semantic universe, and ultimately, of Russian culture.

To show the exact meaning of the constructions in question, I would propose for them explications along the following lines:

> Ego ubilo molniej.
>
> 'He was killed by lightning.' →
>
> something happened in that place at that time
> not because someone wanted it
> (there was a flash of lightning)
> one couldn't say why
> because of this, he was killed (he died)
>
> Stučit!
>
> 'is-knocking' →
>
> something is happening in this place
> not because someone is doing something
> one couldn't say why
> (one can hear something
> as if someone were knocking)
>
> Ego znobilo/lixoradilo/mutilo.
>
> 'him:Acc. froze/was feverish/felt sick and disturbed (V.)' →
>
> something was happening to him
> not because he wanted it
> not because someone was doing something
> one couldn't say why
> because of this, he felt cold/feverish/sick

As these explications indicate, all sentences of this kind are non-agentive: mysterious and incomprehensible events happen around us, not because someone is doing something, and they happen in us not because we want it. Agency is not viewed as mysterious: if a person does something and something happens because of that, then all seems clear; what is seen as mysterious and incomprehensible is that things happen around us, and in us, because of unknowable forces of nature.

In Russian, the scope of sentences built on an agentive personal model is more limited than it is in other European languages, much more limited than it is in English. In its wealth of 'impersonal constructions' the language reflects, and encourages, a tendency to view the world in terms of events which are largely beyond human control and human comprehension, and these events—which are seen as neither fully controllable nor fully comprehensible—are more likely to be bad for people than good. Like *sud'ba* (see chapter 2).

4.2 The 'Russian *Avos'*"

Russian is a language extraordinarily rich in particles expressing the speaker's attitudes and feelings and colouring the style of speaker-hearer interaction. (Cf., for example, Nikolaeva 1985; Rathmayr 1985; Université de Paris VII 1986.) Among European languages, the only one which can be compared with Russian in this respect appears to be German. (Cf., for example, Weydt 1969; Weydt et al. 1983; Kemme 1979; Altmann 1976.)

But among all the Russian particles there is one which the Russians themselves regard as a particularly good key to their culture and national character. It is the particle *avos'*.

According to dictionaries (for example, Axmanova et al. 1969) *avos'* means simply 'perhaps, maybe', and the related expression *na avos'* ('to do something on the basis of an *avos'* attitude') means 'on the off-chance'. But Russian, like most other European languages, has another modal expression much closer to *perhaps* and *maybe: možet byt'*, lit., 'may be'. *Avos'* is something special, not just another word for 'perhaps' (although in translations, for want of a better word, it *is* usually rendered as *perhaps*), and, in any case, there are many contexts where *perhaps* and *maybe* cannot possibly be translated into Russian as *avos'*, for example:

> Perhaps John did it?
> *Avos' Ivan èto sdelal?

To give the reader an idea of how *avos'* is used, I will first adduce two examples quoted in the Academy dictionary of Russian (AN SSSR 1957–61):

U menja golova bolit; ja vyšla na vozdux—avos' projdet. (Turgenev)

'I have a headache; I have come outside—perhaps it will pass.'

Dorogi [čerez reku] nečego bylo iskat'; ee vovse ne bylo vidno; sledovalo idti na avos': gde led deržit poka nogu, tuda i stupaj. (Grigorovič, Rybaki)

'There was no point in trying to find the path [across the river]; one couldn't see it at all; it was necessary to take pot-luck; where the ice seemed to hold you up you just kept going.'

Consider also this example from Pushkin's "Captain's daughter":

> Lučše zdes' ostanovit'sja, da preреždat', avos' buran utixnet da nebo projasnitsja: togda najdem dorogu po zvezdam. (Pushkin 1949:269–70)
>
> 'We'd better stop here and wait awhile, maybe the storm will ease and the sky will clear up; then we can find our way by the stars.'

The importance of the particle *avos'* in Russian thinking is reflected in the fact that it is at the heart of a whole derivational family of words and expressions. Thus, there is the adverbial expression *na avos'*, which means 'to act on the basis of the attitude expressed in the word *avos'*"; there is the noun *avos'*, referring to the attitude in question (the *avos'* attitude); there is the verb *avos'kat'* 'to say *avos'* habitually' (Dal' 1955[1882]:4); there is the noun *avos'ka* referring to a string bag (which might perhaps come in handy); and so on.

To appreciate the role which the *avos'* attitude plays in the Russian folk philosophy, and in the Russian self-image, consider the following characteristic examples:

> [An oncologist doesn't want to admit to herself that she has symptoms of cancer]: Sama-to dlja sebja ona probavljalas' russkim avosem: a možet byt' obojdetsja? a možet tol'ko nervnoe oščuščenie? (Solzhenitsyn 1968a, v.1:99)
>
> As for herself, she was sustained by the Russian "perhaps" [*avos'*]—perhaps it was nothing. Perhaps it was just a nervous reaction. (Solzhenitsyn 1968b:100)

> Da ponadejalsja on na russkij avos'. (Pushkin, quoted in Dal' 1955[1882])
>
> 'He puts his hopes in the Russian *avos'*.'

> [A boy of sixteen with cancer of the bone doesn't want to have his leg amputated, and a friend is trying to persuade him that it is necessary]:
> –A kakaja al'ternativa?
> –Čto?
> –Ili noga ili žizn'?
> –Da—na avos'. A možet—samo projdet'.
> –Net, Dema, na avos' mostov ne strojat. Ot avosja tol'ko avos'ka ostalas'. Rasčityvat' na takuju udaču v ramkax razumnogo nel'zja. (Solzhenitsyn 1968a, v.1:221)

> –Anyway, what's the alternative?
> –What do you mean?
> –I mean it's your leg or your life, isn't it?
> –Yes. But maybe—what if it heals by itself?
> –No, Demka, bridges can't be built on maybes [*avos'*]. Building on maybes [*avos'*] would only end in debris. You can't count on luck; you have to be guided by common sense [more literally, 'it is not rational']. (Solzhenitsyn 1968b:232)

> [Reactions to the Stalingrad victory]:
> Sperva, v poru otstuplenija, èto slovo [russkij] svjazyvalos' bol'šej čast'ju s otricatelnymi opredelenijami: rossijskoj otstalosti, nerazberixi, russkogo bezdorož'ja, russkogo avos'. . . . No, pojavivšis', nacional'noe soznanie ždalo dnja voennogo prazdnika. (Grossman 1980:463)

The word Russian once again had meaning. To begin with, during the retreat the connotations of this word were mainly negative: the hopelessness of the Russian roads, Russian backwardness, Russian confusion, Russian fatalism . . . [lit., Russian *avos'*]. But a national self-consciousness had been born—it was waiting only for a military victory. (Grossman 1985:665)

The colossal role that the *avos'* attitude plays in Russian culture is reflected in the multitude of proverbs and traditional folk sayings (often, rhymed ones) devoted to it. For example, Dal' (1955[1882]) cites the following (among many others):

Avos', nebos', da tretij kak-nibud'.

'Maybe, perhaps, and if not, somehow.'

Avos' plut, obmanet.

'*Avos'* is a trickster; it will cheat you.'

Deržis' za avos', pokol' ne sorvalos'.

'Hold on to *avos'*, for just as long as it doesn't break.'

Avos'evy goroda ne goroženy, avos'kiny deti ne roženy.

'*Avos'* (Adj.) towns have no walls; *avos'* (Adj.) children are not born.'

Kto avosničaet, tot i postničaet.

'He who lives on *avos'* (V.) has to fast.'

So what is "the Russian *avos'*"? Basically, it is an attitude which treats life as unpredictable: 'it is not worth making plans and trying to carry them out; one cannot organise one's life rationally because one cannot control life; the best one can do is to count on luck'. Explicating:

I would want this: X will happen to me
because of this, I will do Y
I cannot think: 'I know that if I do it, X will happen'
no one can think: 'I know what will happen to me'

Thus, "the Russian *avos'*" epitomises a theme which runs through the entire Russian language and Russian culture: the theme of *sud'ba,* of not being in control, of living in a world which is unknowable and which cannot be rationally controlled. If things go well for us, it is because *nam povezlo* 'we:Dat. had luck', not because we mastered our environment. Life is unpredictable and uncontrollable, and one shouldn't overestimate the powers of reason, logic, or rational action.

5. Absolute Moral Judgements

5.1 Negative Judgements

Any Anglo-Saxon reader of Russian novels must be struck by the high frequency of absolute moral judgments, especially judgements passed on people: quite often on the addressee, and not infrequently on oneself. What is particularly significant is that these words of absolute moral condemnation are often nouns. It is bad enough to say that somebody's action was *podlyj/podlaja* (Adj.) or that someone acted *podlo* (Adv.), but it is much worse, of course, to categorise a person as a *podlec* (*nomen personae*).

Yet in Russian, the word *podlec* appears to be used all the time. The closest English parallel which comes to mind is the noun *bastard,* used as a word of abuse. But *bastard* is a swear word, against whose use some taboos continue to operate. The Russian *podlec* is not a taboo word in that sense. For example, it is perfectly natural for Dostoevsky's romantic heroine Katerina Ivanovna to call Dmitrij Karamazov *podlec* (after his dishonourable behaviour toward her), but of course she could never pronounce a Russian equivalent of *bastard.*

> Ax, kakoj vy, govorit, podlec (tak i skazala)! Kakoj vy zloj, govorit, podlec! Da kak vy smeete! (Dostoevsky 1958, v.9:143)

> 'Ah, you scoundrel!'—that's what she said. 'You wicked scoundrel! How dare you!' (Dostoevsky 1974:111)

In this respect, *podlec* has its English counterpart not in *bastard* but in *scoundrel.* But *scoundrel* is a pale, literary, and somewhat archaic word in English, whereas *podlec* is a hot, colloquial, everyday word in Russian. The entirely different status of the two words is confirmed by statistical data. For example, in Zasorina's (1977) megacorpus of Russian words (based on a million running words) *podlec* occurs as many as thirty times, whereas in the corresponding American corpus (Kučera and Francis 1967) *scoundrel* occurs only twice.

Furthermore, *podlec* is not the only Russian noun conveying an absolute moral condemnation of a person: there are also *negodjaj* and *merzavec,* and these two are similarly heated, colloquial, and extremely common. In Zasorina's corpus, their frequency is comparable to that of *podlec:* for *merzavec,* the figure is twenty-five, and for *negodjaj,* it is twenty. By contrast, in English, *scoundrel* is virtually the only word of the kind. For example, *rascal* and *villain,* cited by Roget (1984) next to *scoundrel,* are even more archaic and are not used for serious moral condemnation (the current British jargon use of *villain* is not relevant here).

In fact, in the long list of words and expressions cited by Roget under 'bad man', the only ones which come anywhere near to *podlec, negodjaj,* or *merzavec* in force are the animal metaphor words *reptile* and *viper,* and, one might add, *swine.* But these already have their counterparts in Russian animal metaphor words, such as *gad, svinja,* and, above all, *skotina* (from *skot* 'cattle').

The conclusion must be that Russian has at least three widely used non-taboo nouns of absolute moral condemnation (*podlec, merzavec, negodjaj*), whereas English has only one (rather dubious) word of this kind (*scoundrel*), and the combined frequency of the three Russian words in the available data is seventy five to a million, as against two to a million on the English side. These are pretty spectacular differences.

Russian		English	
podlec	30	*scoundrel*	2
merzavec	25		
negodjaj	20		
Total	75		2

What is the exact meaning of the Russian nouns of absolute moral condemnation? The question is very difficult to answer, and Russian dictionaries provide no help in this respect. Clearly, in Russian linguistic intuition the three words are felt to be very close, because they are often used together as if they were quasi-synonyms. For example:

> Zametil, podlec!—podumal Pustjakov.—Po rože vižu, čto zametil!! A on, merzavec, kljauznik. Zavtra že doneset direktoru! (Chekhov 1950:19)
>
> 'He noticed it, the scoundrel (*podlec*)!—thought Pustjakov. I can see by his face (mug) that he noticed! He is such a pig (*merzavec*). Tomorrow he'll report me to the director!'
>
> Kakoj merzavec! Bože moj! Kakoj neslyxannyj negodjaj! (A. N. Tolstoy, quoted in AN SSSR 1957–61)
>
> 'What a scoundrel (*merzavec*)! My God! What an incredible scoundrel (*negodjaj*)!'
>
> Negodjaj, podlyj čelovek, no ved'—blogodetel'. . . . (Chekhov 1950:40)
>
> 'A scoundrel (*negodjaj*), a base man (*podlyj*)—but all the same a benefactor!'

Nonetheless, the three words do not mean exactly the same. The differences among them are highlighted by their different etymologies. *Merzavec* is etymologically related to the verb *merzit'* 'to cause disgust' and to the adjective *merzkij*, which Dal' (1955[1882]) glosses as "otvratitel'nyj" ('disgusting/repulsive'). *Podlec* suggests someone who is not so much repulsive or disgusting as dishonourable (and therefore contemptible). In this respect, *podlec* comes closer than any of the other to the English *bastard*. Like *bastard*, *podlec* is also often used on impulse, as a reaction to a single act—an unexpectedly bad and dishonourable one. If the word is given its full weight (rather than being used as an all-purpose term of abuse), it evokes the image of someone's 'falling' in the speaker's estimation from a 'normal' (expected) level to a particularly 'low' level. Dal' (1955[1882]) glosses the adjective *podlyj* as "nizkij, bezčestnyj, grjaznyj, prezrennyj", 'low/base, dishonourable, dirty, contemptible', and these are all helpful hints.

For example, Dostoevsky's heroine, Katerina Ivanovna, had at first regarded the dashing young officer Dmitrij Karamazov as an honourable man, and it is only after he degraded himself in her eyes by an apparent attempt to exploit her hopeless situation shamelessly that she lashed out at him the exclamation quoted: "*Podlec!*"

Furthermore, the words *podlec* and *podlyj* are often contrasted in Russian with the word *blagorodnyj* 'noble, lofty': if one indicates moral baseness and degradation, the other indicates moral heights, moral elevation.[2] For example:

> Krasiva byla ona tem v tu minutu, čto ona blagorodnaja, a ja podlec, čto ona v veličii svoego velikodušija i žertvy svoej za otca, a ja klop. I vot ot menja, klopa i podleca, ona vsja zavisit, vsja, vsja krugom i s dušoj i s telom. (Dostoevsky 1958, v.9:145)

> 'At that moment she was beautiful because she was noble, and I was a scoundrel; she in all the grandeur of her generosity and sacrifice for her father, and I, a bug [lit., 'bedbug']! And, scoundrel as I was, she was altogether at my mercy, body and soul.' (Dostoevsky 1974:112)

(In this last example, the speaker repeatedly applies the word *podlec* to himself, in a characteristically Russian gesture of moral breast beating.)

As for *negodjaj*, it is etymologically related to the adjective *negodnyj* and to the expression *ne goditsja*, both of which indicate that something 'is not suitable', with the further implication that 'it is good for nothing'. For example, Dal' (1955[1882]) glosses *negodnyj* as follows: "nikčemu ili nikuda nesposobnyj, durnoj, ploxoj; čelovek negodnyj, delo negodnoe, sapogi negodnye", 'incapable of anything, bad, worthless; e.g. of a man, a matter, a pair of boots'. If a person is categorised as a *negodjaj*, this suggests a deep immorality, a moral rottenness, characteristic of someone like Fedor Karamazov, of whom 'nothing good can be expected'.

One might say that the three condemnatory nouns are associated with different feelings: *merzavec* suggests something like disgust; *podlec,* something like moral indignation combined with contempt; and *negodjaj,* something like moral dismissal combined with anger.

To account for the common core of *podlec, merzavec,* and *negodjaj,* we could propose the following three components:

> (a) X is a very bad person
> (b) X can do very bad things
> (c) when I think of X, I feel something bad

To account for the differences among them, we could propose some additional component or components for each term. For *merzavec,* I would tentatively suggest the component

> I don't want to be near this person

for *podlec,* the components

> X is not like other people
> X can do bad things that other people couldn't

and for *negodjaj,* the components

> one can't think: X will do good things
> one can think: X will do bad things

These components are not motivated by the etymology (which could provide helpful clues but which could also be misleading and suggest false clues); they are motivated by the somewhat different ranges of use of the three words in question, and by the fact that their best exemplars (for example, in literature) are also different, despite possible overlaps in some cases.

5.2 Positive Judgements

Finally, it should be pointed out that Russians are as extreme and emotional in expressing moral enthusiasms as they are in expressing moral condemnations. For example, Tsvetaeva described her husband in a letter in the following words:

> On neobyčajno i blagorodno krasiv, on prekrasen vnešne i vnutrenno. . . . On blestjašče odaren, umen, blagoroden. Esli by Vy znali, kakoj èto plamennyj, velikodušnyj, glubokij junoša! (1972:23, 25)

> 'He is extraordinarily and nobly beautiful; he is beautiful externally and internally. . . . He is brilliantly talented, clever, noble. If you only knew what a fiery (nobly ardent), magnanimous, profound young man he is!'

Similarly, when Tsvetaeva (1972:191) describes her twelve-year-old daughter, Alja, she calls her not only *umnaja* 'clever' and *rebjačlivaja* 'childlike' but also *velikodušnaja* 'magnanimous' and *blagorodnaja* 'noble'. Presumably, not many Anglo-Saxons would describe their spouses or their children in similar terms. Recall also the sentence from *War and peace* which was quoted in chapter 1: "He is such a lofty, such a heavenly soul!"

The Russian lack of inhibition in expressing moral enthusiasms is reflected, to some extent, in the high frequency of adjectives such as *blagorodnyj* 'noble'—in Zasorina's (1977) data fifty-four times, as against twenty-three for *noble* in Kučera and Francis' (1967) English corpus—and above all in the extremely high frequency of the word *prekrasnyj,* which is commonly used to express moral enthusiasm.

The common expression *prekrasnyj čelovek* means literally 'a beautiful human being', and since *prekrasnyj* can also be used for things which are beautiful (or wonderful) in other respects, the high frequency of *prekrasnyj* in the moral sense is difficult to document in studies such as Zasorina's. Nonetheless the following figures are, I think, highly suggestive:

beautiful	127
krasivyj ('beautiful')	190
prekrasnyj ('beautiful' or 'morally beautiful')	130

What these data show is that the basic Russian adjective *krasivyj* is used more frequently than its English equivalent *beautiful,* and that in addition Russian has another adjective, *prekrasnyj,* which can mean either 'beautiful' or 'morally beautiful', and which has also a very high frequency.

Nonetheless, since both English and Russian also have some other adjectives which can be used to express a generalised enthusiasm for a person (for example, *ona čudesnyj čelovek,* 'she is a lovely person'), the differences between English and Russian in the area of absolute moral enthusiasm are less clear than the differences in the area of moral condemnation. There is also the added fact that English speech is generally given to understatement in expressing negative evaluation (presumably, for the purposes of social harmony) and to overstatement in expressing positive valuation of certain, usually trivial subjects—though not of serious moral virtues (presumably also for purposes of social harmony; cf. 'Lovely dress!', 'What gorgeous roses!', 'This casserole is superb!'; see Wierzbicka 1985b and 1991a)— whereas Russian speech is given to overstatement in expressing any evaluation, whether positive or negative, and, in particular, moral evaluation. This passion for absolute moral judgements echoes of course the moral, as well as emotional, orientation of the Russian *duša* (see chapter 1).

6. Conclusion

This partial attempt at characterising the Russian language as a semantic and cultural universe will no doubt strike some as foolhardy. I agree that an enterprise of this kind involves intellectual risks which are absent both from positivistic data collection and from generativist (or other) games with formal models. I believe, however, that the risks are worth taking, and that although it may have been prudent to avoid them in the period when no adequate methodology for exploring such questions was available, the failure to explore them is not something of which linguists should forever be proud. As for generativist and other formal models, it must be said that the lack of risk has a concomitant lack of any serious prospect of cultural insight.

What can't be said one should remain silent about, and what can't be investigated should not become the subject of scholarly research. But the boundaries of the realm open to serious investigation may lie further afield than mainstream modern linguistics has led us to believe. As Hymes (1961:46) points out:

> The interpretation of cognitive styles, and even acceptance of their presence, has suffered from friends, who too often have treated the problem apart from the kinds of control that are usually observed in culture-historical work, or who have given it too great an import, one that the known facts of history would seem clearly to refute. The problem must be divested of such associations, and recognised for what, in the first instance, it is: the problem of describing and interpreting an aspect of culture, one among the other aspects of culture, which can be handled empirically and historically, and which must be handled, if any historical or evolutionary theory of culture is to claim adequacy. There is precedent for linking the matter of cognitive styles to typology in the work of Sapir. The value of the link is that the typological context may impose needed rigor on the study of cognitive style, while concern with cognitive style may enhance the place of the semantic dimensions of language in typology. With a concept of cognitive styles, linked to typology, and a framework for interpretation of languages as historical products, perhaps one can be philosophically neutral, linguistically precise, yet a little adventurous too. (1961:46)

I agree that explorations of the links between language and culture in general, and language and 'national character' in particular, have in the past suffered from friends as much as (or more than) they have suffered from enemies. I believe, however, that the natural semantic metalanguage based on universal semantic primitives provides us with sharper methodological tools than those which were used by our predecessors, and that it is time that 'dangerous' but vital and irresistible problems of the kind tackled here were placed once more on the linguistic agenda.

POSTSCRIPT

National character is shaped, to a considerable extent, by a nation's history. It is, therefore, not eternal or unchangeable. It responds to changes in a nation's history, as does a nation's language, which is a mirror as well as a vehicle of both history and national character.

The extraordinary events that occurred in Russia in August 1991 have brought about a profound change in the Russian self-image as well as in Russia's international image. Unarmed Russians who resisted tanks in the streets of Moscow and Leningrad (now renamed St Petersburg) showed neither fear nor submission.

As I write this postscript in August 1991, the world is holding its breath, watching the wheel of history turn in Russia as it had two years earlier in Poland and elsewhere in Eastern Europe.

Language reflects the past as well as the present. Key lexical concepts, which both reflect and shape a nation's prevailing attitudes, can change, too, though they may not do so as quickly. For example, the concept of 'volja' (a kind of anarchic dream of absolute 'freedom'), which (according to Fedotov (1981)), was for centuries one of the key Russian concepts, has declined in the twentieth century, and the meaning of the word has changed (cf. Wierzbicka 1990d and In press d). A nation's proverbs do not change overnight, nor does its grammar, but with time these may also change.

In writing this book, I do not wish to perpetuate stereotypes against the tide of history but rather to understand both the present and the past as they are reflected in language. As the twentieth century draws to a close, some of the Russian attitudes described in this book are visibly changing. Sooner or later, changes of this kind can be expected to be reflected in language.

Polish attitudes described in this book and traced in their linguistic reflections are also changing. Traditional Polish slogans such as "Bóg, honor, i ojczyzna" ('God, honour, and motherland') are now starting to sound very much like a thing of the past. At a time when the traditional Polish goals of freedom (*wolność*) and national independence have finally become realities, and when economic concerns have become more acutely felt than political and national issues, key concepts of the past such as 'wolność', 'honor', 'ojczyzna' or 'odwaga' ('risk-taking courage') will inevitably lose some of their centrality in Polish culture. Among the graffiti that appeared on various walls in Poland in 1991, the following example in particular captured one's attention: "Bóg, handel, i ojczyzna". *Handel* basically means 'trade', but in everyday Polish it has the negative connotations of undignified profiteering and an absence of ideals. To the Polish ear (formed by what Davies (1981) calls the Polish "noble ethos") there could hardly be a greater contrast between two concepts than that between *honor* and *handel*. Thus, the graffito in question mocks the changes that Poles themselves perceive in their own outlook and attitudes. One can safely predict that the connotations of the word *handel* will also change, or that a new word will replace it in the Polish consciousness and in the Polish language.

The Romans were wont to say "tempora mutantur et nos mutamur in illis" ('times change and we change with them'). The same applies to languages: tempora mutantur, et linguae mutantur in illis.

NOTES

Introduction

1. In recounting in detail some episodes of his childhood in his *Confessions,* Rousseau says:

> Je sais bien que le lecteur n'a pas grand besoin de savoir tout cela, mais j'ai besoin, moi, de le lui dire. (1963, v.1:45)

> 'I know very well that the reader has no great need to know all this, but I, I have a need to say it.'

The principle of self-expression clearly triumphs here over the principle of communication.

2. On this particular point I agree with Chomsky (1975 or 1987).

3. In support of his idea that even concepts such as *bureaucrat* or *carburetor* could be innate, Chomsky (1987:23) suggests a parallel from immunology. Until very recently, he points out, it had been accepted that "the number of antigens is so immense, including even artifically synthesised substances that had never existed in the world, that it was considered absurd to suppose that evolution had provided an 'innate stock of antibodies'; rather, formation of antibodies must be a kind of 'learning process' in which the antigens play an 'instructive role'. But this assumption has been challenged, and is now widely assumed to be false". What Chomsky does not consider is that, unlike antibodies, concepts differ profoundly from culture to culture, and from society to society.

4. As far as I have been able to ascertain, Leibniz never spelled out the need to link the search for universal human concepts with a search for universal words. The closely related matter of the language-specific character of complex concepts was discussed at length by Locke (1959 [1690]) in his *Essay on human understanding* and was therefore within the scope of Leibniz' (1980 [1705]) counter-essay, but Leibniz chose to concentrate his discussion on other aspects of Locke's treatise.

5. It should be stressed that work on the proposed natural semantic metalanguage is far from finished. A number of tentative versions have to be experimented with before anything like the optimal version is found. Furthermore, the idea of an 'optimal' semantic metalanguage is not a straightforward one. What is optimal for one purpose is far from ideal for another. At least two different levels of an 'optimal' semantic metalanguage should be distinguished. From a purely semantic point of view, the optimal semantic metalanguage is a minimal one, one whose lexicon would contain nothing but a minimum of elements necessary for portraying semantic relations, whose syntax would contain nothing but the minimal core of grammatical constructions shared, as Humboldt (1963, v.3:16) speculated, by all languages of the world. From a practical point of view, however, a mini-language based exclusively on the 'alphabet of human thoughts' and on the mini-grammar associated with it is far from ideal, because semantic formulae couched in such a mini-language are necessarily very long and hard to read. For purposes of readability and intelligibility, less radical versions of a semantic metalanguage must often be used. (Cf. Apresjan 1980 and Wierzbicka 1988c.)

6. Truth is one of the fundamental moral ideals of Western culture, and a search for truth

is an essential part of that culture. But there are many languages which don't even have a word for 'truth' or 'true', and there are many cultures which don't attach to that idea the importance that Western culture does (cf., for example, Lutz 1987). This doesn't mean, of course, that we should be apologetic about treating the ideal of truth as our point of orientation or that we should feel obligated to dissociate ourselves from it, as for example, Lakoff and Johnson (1980) do. But we should not assume that we can rely on the concept of truth as a basic descriptive tool in investigating other languages and other cultures. On the other hand, 'good' and 'bad' do seem to be among universal human concepts (although the evidence is stronger in the case of 'good' than in the case of 'bad'; cf. Hill 1987), and so do 'think' and 'know'.

Chapter 1

1. Russian words and names throughout this book are transliterated according to the system of the *Slavic and East European Journal* (*SEEJ*). However, well-known names (Dostoevsky, Tolstoy, Chekhov, Tsvetaeva, Pushkin, etc.) are spelt in their more common form, generally as in *Encyclopaedia Brittanica*.

2. The explications proposed in the present chapter make considerable use of the word *world* and, to a lesser degree, of the word *imagine* (the latter plays a greater role in chapter 2). In earlier work (see, e.g., Wierzbicka 1980) both these concepts were regarded as semantic primitives; in more recent work, however, they have been virtually abandoned (as primitives). For this reason (among others) the explications proposed in these two chapters have to be regarded as somewhat provisional and in need of future amendments.

3. The explications proposed in this chapter and in some of the later chapters of this book include bits of fairly complex English syntax, including, for example, relative clauses and complement clauses. In recent work, I have tried to avoid such complex and language-specific syntax in the explications, trying to rely only on simple clauses (cf., e.g., Wierzbicka 1990b, and In press a, b, and c). In the present book, however, I have permitted myself the use of some complex constructions, to make the explications shorter and easier to read.

4. Limitations of space prevent me from including in the present discussion another related concept, *spirit*, whose fortunes in the Anglo-Saxon world are no doubt related to those of *soul* and *mind*. In Russian, the counterpart of *spirit* is *dux*, and if the frequency recorded in the megacorpora is any indicator at all, the two concepts, *spirit* and *dux*, appear to be equally strong in both cultures: *dux* plus Adj. *duxovnyj* and Adv. *duxovno*, 232; *spirit* plus Adj. *spiritual* and Adv. *spiritually*, 253, without including *spirits* (Zasorina 1977; Kučera and Francis 1967).

But whereas in Russian the corresponding figure for *duša* is twice as high (450), in English the figure for *soul* is three and a half times lower than that for *spirit* (73). This is consistent with the intuitive impression that in the modern Anglo-Saxon world the concept of *spirit* plays a greater role than that of *soul* (whereas in Russian culture, *duša* is even more important than *dux*).

One factor worth noting here is that in contrast to *soul*, *spirit* doesn't commit one to any metaphysical ontology of the human being: although related to soul in its nature, spirit is a free-floating element ("spiritus fiat ubi vult", 'the spirit blows where it will'), which doesn't have to be seen as a 'part' of a human being and which therefore doesn't raise the question of what happens after a person's death.

As a first approximation, I propose the following explication of this concept:

> *spirit*
> something good
> one cannot see it
> it is not part of this world
> because of it, a person can do good things

'Spirit' is invisible and immaterial, like souls, and, like souls, it doesn't belong to 'this' world, but it would be odd to say that it is 'part' of another world (what else is there, in that other world, 'the world of the spirit'?) Its ontological status is much vaguer, and it is not viewed as an entity of any kind. This may be one reason why in the secularised modern world many people feel more comfortable using the concept 'spirit' than the concept 'soul'. Like *soul, spirit* is linked with values, in a positive way, but it has a more dynamic character (in the Creed, the Holy Spirit is called 'the giver of life'): if the *soul* enables a person to *be* a good person, *spirit* enables people, it seems, to *do* good things.

Chapter 3

1. The analysis of emotion concepts proposed here shares some of the assumptions defended in Russell (1989), above all, the idea of culture-specific 'scripts' for emotions, with the components of the script being related to one another in a causal sequence. The components 'X feels something good' and 'X feels something bad' can be said to correspond, roughly, to Russell's "pancultural dimensions" of "pleasure" and "displeasure".

2. The concept 'should' used in this explication is, in my view, neither elementary nor universal. I have used it, nonetheless, in many explications of emotion concepts and moral concepts because it does appear to be a very important semantic "molecule", playing a considerable role in many cultures.

Chapter 4

1. The Polish poet and Nobel Prize winner Czesław Miłosz (1990:168) has recorded in his diary his conversation with the Russian writer Tatjana Tolstoj, in which he was commenting on compassion in her stories. Her reply: "*Žalost'*. What else is left to us, poor human beings, if not *žalost'*?"

Chapter 5

1. The components 'I think this is good' and 'I think this is bad', which are used in many explications in chapters 5 and 6, are meant to reflect the speaker's evaluation of the attitude discussed. For example, by calling somebody a *coward,* or a *reckless* or *arrogant* person, the speaker expresses a negative evaluation, whereas words such as *brave, courageous,* or *kind* convey the speaker's positive evaluation.

One could argue that evaluative terms, whether positive or negative, express the society's, not the individual's, view of certain attitudes and that the relevant components should be phrased as 'people think this is good/bad' rather than 'I think this is good/bad'. But there are (semantic) arguments on both sides. The matter requires further investigation.

2. It is worth mentioning in passing that a concept closely related to 'apatheia' is encapsulated in the Thai word *sandot* (Wipa Treerat, p.c.). In the case of the Thai word, the inspiration is Buddhist. It should be stressed that *sandot* does not belong to the 'learned' vocabulary, but to the everyday lexicon, thus illustrating the profound influence of Buddhism on everyday language. In some ways, 'sandot' is much closer to 'apatheia' than to 'smirenie', in particular in implying an absence of 'bad feelings' (suffering, sorrow, and so on) rather than an absence of 'bad feelings toward anybody'. On the other hand, it implies a passivity, which links it with 'smirenie' rather than with 'apatheia'. A precise explication of the concept of 'sandot' is beyond the scope of this chapter.

Chapter 6

1. Nearly all the explications in the present chapter include the word *and,* which is not a part of the natural semantic metalanguage based on universal semantic primitives. It is used here only for reasons of readability. The semantics of "character traits" requires further investigation, and the optimal format for their definitions remains an open question.

2. The attitudes described by Benet have also left their imprint in other areas of the Polish language. For example, as I tried to show (Wierzbicka 1987a), the tautology *co będzie to będzie* (lit., 'what will be will be') has developed in Polish a meaning somewhat different from that of its counterparts in other European languages (e.g., *que será será*). The Polish saying conveys a determination to take a risk and to close one's eyes to possible bad consequences. A similar meaning is encoded in the Polish proverbs *raz kozie śmierć* 'a goat can only die once' and *co ma wisieć nie utonie* 'what is fated to be hanged will not drown' (cf. English sayings "you only die once", "you may as well be hanged for a sheep as for a lamb"). For further discussion, see Wierzbicka 1991a; see also chapter 2.

3. These two meanings were in fact distinguished a hundred and fifty years ago by de Tocqueville (1953 [1835–40]:230). De Tocqueville also noted that *honour* in the first of these senses was not seen as a universal human value but was restricted to a certain class of people and that, consequently, the importance of this concept in a feudal society was much greater than in a democracy, such as the United States. "Honour is simply that peculiar rule founded upon a peculiar state of society, by the application of which a people or a class allot praise or blame" (p.231). "[T]he dissimilarities and inequalities of men gave rise to the notion of honour; that notion is weakened in proportion as these differences are obliterated, and with them it would disappear" (p.243).

The importance of the concept of 'honour' in European culture, and its links with the mediaeval traditions of knighthood, was also discussed with great subtlety by de Custine (1953 [1843]:13), who stressed the deep historical and cultural differences in this respect between Europe and Russia. This point is particularly relevant to the present discussion, in view of the negative Russian stereotype of the Polish 'honor' (in Russian, *gonor*).

Chapter 7

1. The distinction between palatalised and non-palatalised consonants, commonly referred to as 'soft' and 'hard' consonants, is fundamental to the Russian linguistic system. Lunt describes this distinction as follows:

There is a series of Russian consonants for which no equivalents exist in English. These consonants are *palatalized;* that is, they have both the articulation of the non-palatalized consonant plus a second, palatal articulation. The tongue arches toward the middle of the roof of the mouth. The acoustic effect is one of higher pitch, and an English speaker often has the impression that the palatalized consonant is simply a hard consonant plus *y.* Actually this 'y-quality' is simultaneous with and inseparable from the other quality. (1958:3–4)

Russian has fifteen pairs of 'hard' and 'soft' consonants:

p-p'	*b-b'*	*f-f'*	*v-v'*	*m-m'*	*t-t'*
d-d'	*n-n'*	*s-s'*	*z-z'*	*l-l'*	*r-r'*
k-k'	*g-g'*	*x-x'*			

In addition, there are three 'hard' consonants without 'soft' equivalents: *c, š,* and *ž,* and three 'soft' consonants without 'hard' equivalents: *j, č,* and *šč.* It is important to emphasise that the contrast between 'soft stems' and 'hard stems' discussed in this chapter involves only the 'paired' consonants. For example (as pointed out to me by Andrzej Bogusławski, p.c.), names with stems ending in *j,* such as *Zoja* and *Raja,* behave differently from names with stems ending in 'paired' soft consonants. For a particularly illuminating discussion of the relationship between 'hard' and 'soft' consonants in Russian, and in other Slavic languages, see Baudouin de Courtenay (1908).

2. In fact, Polish hard stem names with the suffix *-ek* fall into a number of different subclasses and don't all have exactly the same value. Some (e.g., *Janek, Jurek, Tomek, Stefek*) sound like quasi-diminutives, chosen in preference to the full names (*Jan, Jerzy, Tomasz, Stefan*); others (e.g., *Mietek, Tadek, Wojtek, Antek*) sound like quasi-augmentatives, chosen in preference to "childish", affectionate diminutives (such as *Miecio, Tadzio, Wojtuś, Antoś*). For example, one can imagine the latter group (*Mietek, Tadek,* etc.) but not the former (*Janek, Jurek,* etc.) being used among the members of a teenage street gang. The factors which determine the perceived value of different forms in *-ek* remain to be investigated; I do not think that this value is idiosyncratic and unpredictable.

3. When I was giving a talk about Polish names at Warsaw University in 1987, a middle-aged linguist said that she calls her young research assistant, of whom she is very fond, "Ewcia", and that she means nothing patronising by that form. At that point, however, the research assistant herself confessed publicly that she resents being called "Ewcia", because although she can feel the affection conveyed by that form, she doesn't like its flavour.

4. In forms such as *Dziunia* or *Niusia* the identification function can be said to be subordinated to the expressive value (as if the parents of a girl wanted to use, instead of a name, a bare diminutive suffix, or a pseudo-name such as *Baby* or *Sweetie*). Clearly, names of this kind are suited, above all, to family use. Their decline in recent decades reflects, I think, social and cultural change: there are no social milieus left where girls could be expected to live lives predominantly restricted to a closed, sheltered family setting, and not to have to interact with a wide range of people (most of them emotional strangers).

Chapter 9

1. Pitantjatjara words are spelt according to the standard orthography used by speakers of the language (as in Goddard 1988); optional diacritics for retroflex consonants are omitted.

2. Actually, *wati umari* is also an acceptable phrase, meaning 'taboo man'. *Waputju*

refers not to a literal wife's father but to a ceremonial role, which leads to the right for a man to take the other man's daughter in marriage (unlike the corresponding Walmatjari word) (Cliff Goddard, p.c.).

3. Strictly speaking, however, I don't think that the explications of the Ompela terms *piado* or *mampa* (11 and 16) require reference to the mother's younger sister or to the father's younger brother, because it would be more economical to state the equivalence 'M = MZ−' and 'F = FB−' as general interpretation rules, not as lexical facts pertaining to individual lexical items. This is further discussed in the following section.

Chapter 11

1. The literature on the links between language and culture is far too extensive to be surveyed in the present chapter. If just a few references were to be mentioned here, in symbolic recognition of the vastness of the field that this chapter is building on, I would include in this list Humboldt (1903–36), Vossler (1925), Sapir (1949), Whorf (1956), Greenberg (1957), Hoijer (1954), Hymes (1964), Levi-Strauss et al. (1953), and Geertz (1973).

2. Cf. also Sapir (1949:89–103) for a similar position, later changed, as discussed in Hymes (1983:150–58).

3. All the names given here either are known to me at first hand, being used by people whom I know personally, or were given to me by acquaintances, friends, and relatives as names which are used regularly in their own circles of acquaintances. Most of the names cited here were given to me independently by several informants.

4. I must note, however, the following advertisement, which appeared in the *Canberra Times* on December 2, 1984 (I am grateful to Alan Dench for drawing it to my attention): "Christmas gift tags, hand-made. $1.20 a packet. Ph Maz 663863 (bh)". I rang the number provided and found out that the name of the person who called herself *Maz* was in fact *Marilyn*.

5. Pringle (1965:20) says that Australians are 'rough rather than tough', and I think that in many ways this is a fair comment. Linguistic evidence of the kind discussed in the present chapter certainly points to a good deal of friendliness, good humour, and fellow-feeling, as well as anti-sentimentality in the Australian national character. But of course the Ned Kelly ideal of 'dying game' (see Wannan 1963) is one of 'toughness' rather than 'roughness'. Generally speaking, one could say that the Australian ethos requires that one should be 'tough' in the face of misfortune and 'rough' in relation to one's friends.

6. I find it very surprising that the emergence of the suffixes *-z* and *-za* is not mentioned in any of the standard works on Australian English, not even in a monograph devoted specifically to the morphology of Australian English (Dabke 1976). It is, however, mentioned by Poynton (1982, 1984, 1989). The fact that the category of hypocoristic abbreviations such as *Dim* or *Iz* is not mentioned in the literature is easier to understand, given their superficial similarity to pan-English abbreviations such as *Pam* or *Liz*. First names with the suffix *-o,* such as *Johnno* or *Sallo,* have often been commented on in the literature on Australian English, but first names with the suffixes *-z* and *-za* seem hardly to have been noted at all. A partial explanation for this discrepancy in scholarly attention may lie in the fact (if it is a fact) that the suffix *-o* (in the relevant function) is older. In fact, the use of the suffixes *-z* and *-za* seems to be increasing, whereas the use of *-o* (in first names) seems to be decreasing. These are, however, purely impressionistic observations and may be wrong.

Chapter 12

1. I am grateful to Yura Apresjan for drawing my attention to this passage.

2. In contemporary Russian, the word *blagorodnyj* is not used as widely as it used to be, but it is still in evidence, even in everyday speech. (According to Zasorina's (1977) corpus, based on one million running words, the joint frequency of *blagorodnyj* and its derivates is 105, which must be regarded as a relatively high number.)

REFERENCES

Aaron, Richard. 1955. *John Locke*. Oxford: Clarendon Press.

Adler, Lenore L., ed. 1977. *Issues in cross-cultural research*. New York Academy of Science, *Annals*, v.285.

Akoka, Abraham K. 1966. The meaning of aloha. *Mainliner* (United Airlines) 10.9.

à Kempis, Thomas. 1952 [1441]. *The imitation of Christ*. Trans. Edgar Daplyn. London: Sheed and Ward.

Alpher, Barry. 1982. Dalabon dual-subject prefixes, kinship categories, and generation skewing. In Heath, Merlan and Rumsey 1982:19–30.

Altmann, Hans. 1976. *Die Gradpartikeln im Deutschen: Untersuchungen zu ihrer Syntax, Semantik und Pragmatik*. Tübingen: Niemeyer.

Ameka, Felix. 1987. A comparative analysis of linguistic routines in two languages: English and Ewe. *Journal of Pragmatics* 11(3):299–326.

———. 1990. The grammatical packaging of experiencers in Ewe. *Australian Journal of Linguistics* (special issue on the semantics of emotions) 10(2):139–182.

AND 1988. *The Australian National Dictionary*. Ed. W. S. Ramson. Melbourne: Oxford University Press.

AN SSSR. 1950–65. *Slovar' sovremennogo literaturnogo jazyka*. Ed. V. I. Černyšev. 17 vols. Moscow: Izdatel'stvo Akademii Nauk SSSR.

———. 1957–61. *Slovar' russkogo jazyka*. 4 vols. Moscow: Gosudarstvennoe Izdatel'stvo Inostrannyx i Nacional'nyx Slovarej.

———. 1960. *Grammatika russkogo jazyka*. Moscow: Izdatel'stvo Akademii Nauk SSSR.

Andrews, Lorrin. 1974. *A dictionary of the Hawaiian language*. Rutland, Vt.: Charles E. Tuttle.

Apresjan, Jurij. 1972. Definiowanie znaczeń leksykalnych jako zagadnienie semantyki teoretycznej. In A. Wierzbicka 1972b:39–58.

———. 1974. *Leksičeskaja semantika*. Moscow: Nauka.

———. 1980. *Tipy informacii dlja poverxnostnogo semantičeskogo komponenta modeli smysl-tekst*. Vienna: Wiener Slawistischer Almanach (Sonderband 1).

———, and L. L. Iomdin. 1989. Konstrukcii tipa *negde spat'*: sintaksis, semantika, leksikografija. *Semiotika i Informatika* 29 (AN SSSR, VINITI): 34–92.

Arensburg, Conrad M., and Arthur H. Niehoff. 1975. American cultural values. In Spradley and Rynkiewich 1975:363–377.

Armstrong, Sharon L., Lila Gleitman, and Henry Gleitman. 1983. What some concepts might not be. *Cognition* 13:263–308.

Arutjunova, N. D., ed. 1988. *Pragmatika i problemy intensional'nosti*. Moscow: Akademija Nauk, Institut Jazykoznanija.

Ash. See Garton Ash, Timothy.

Aurelius. See Marcus Aurelius.

Austin, Peter K., ed. 1988. *Complex sentence constructions in Australian languages*. Amsterdam: John Benjamins.

Axmanova, Ol'ga, et al. 1969. *Russko-anglijskij slovar'*. Moscow: Sovetskaja Enciklopedija.

Baker, G. P., and P. M. S. Hacker. 1980. *Wittgenstein: understanding and meaning*. Oxford: Blackwell.

Baker, Sidney. 1959. *The drum: Australian character and slang*. Sydney: Currawong Publishing Co.

Baker, Sidney. 1970. *The Australian language*. Melbourne: Sun Books.

Bally, Charles. 1920. Impressionisme et grammaire. In *Mélanges d'histoire littéraire et de philologie offerts à M. Bernard Bouvier*. Geneva: Sonor. Microfilm, British Museum 1976:261–79.

Barnlund, Dean C. 1975. *Public and private self in Japan and the United States: communicative styles of two cultures*. Tokyo: Simul Press.

Barrett, William. 1987. *Death of the soul: from Descartes to the computer*. Oxford: Oxford University Press.

Bassani, Giorgio. 1980. *Gli occhiali d'oro*. Milan: Mondatori.

Basso, K., and H. Selby, eds. 1971. *Meaning in anthropology*. Albuquerque: University of New Mexico Press.

Bauer, Raymond, Alex Inkeles, and Clyde Kluckhohn. 1956. *How the Soviet system works*. Cambridge, Mass.: Harvard University Press.

Bendix, Reinhard. 1977. *Nation-building and citizenship: studies of our changing social order*. New enl. ed. Berkeley: University of California Press.

Benet, Sula. 1953. Courage: cumulative effects of sacrifice. In Mead and Metraux 1953:415–21.

Benson, Morton. 1967. *Dictionary of Russian personal names*. Philadelphia: University of Pennsylvania Press.

Berdyaev, Nikolai. 1947. *The Russian idea*. Trans. R. M. French. London: Centenary Press.

———. 1949. *Samopoznanie*. Paris: YMCA-Press.

Berlin, Brent, and Paul Kay. 1969. *Basic color terms: their universality and evolution*. Berkeley: University of California Press.

Berndt, Ronald M., and Catherine Berndt. 1968. *The world of the first Australians*. Sydney: Ure Smith.

Berry, J. W., S. H. Irvine, and E. B. Hunt, eds. 1988. *Indigenous cognition: functioning in cultural context*. Dordrecht: Martinus Nijhoff.

Beta, Katharina. 1988. *Die russische Seele*. Vienna: Harold.

Bettelheim, Bruno. 1983. *Freud and man's soul*. London: Hogarth Press.

Blair, D., and P. Collins, eds. 1989. *Australian English: the language of a new society*. Brisbane: University of Queensland Press.

Bloom, Alan. 1987. *The closing of the American mind: how higher education has failed democracy and impoverished the souls of today's students*. New York: Simon and Schuster.

Bloomfield, Morton. 1952. *The seven deadly sins*. Lansing: Michigan State University Press.

Blount, Ben. 1984. The language of emotions: an ontogenetic perspective. *Language Sciences* 6.1:129–56.

Boas, Franz. 1911. Introduction. *Handbook of American Indian languages*, v.1. Bureau of American Ethnology, *Bulletin* 40:5–83.

Bogusławski, Andrzej. 1966. *Semantyczne pojęcie liczebnika*. Wrocław: Ossolineum.

———. 1970. On semantic primitives and meaningfulness. In Greimas, Jakobson, and Mayenowa 1970:143–52.

———. 1978. On decision making in semantics. In Daneš and Viehweger 1978:1–107.

———. 1982. Semantic and pragmatic aspects of reference-related problems. In Daneš and Viehweger 1982:1–111.

————. 1985. De l'addressee, avec reference particulière au polonais. *Revue des Études Slaves*. Paris, LVII/3. pp.469–81.

————, and Stanisław Karolak. 1970. *Gramatyka rosyjska w ujęciu funkcjonalnym*. Warsaw: Wiedza Powszechna.

Bolshakoff, Sergius. 1977. *Russian mystics*. London: Mowbray.

Bondaletov, V. D., and E. F. Danilina. 1970. Sredstva vyraženija emocional'no-ekspressivnyx ottenkov v russkix ličnyx imenax. In Nikonov and Superanskaja 1970:194–200.

Bowler, Peter. 1987. Spiritual riches, not 'profitable' education. *The Canberra Times*, October 24, 1987.

Bratus, B. V. 1969. *The formation and expressive use of diminutives*. Cambridge: Cambridge University Press.

Brecht, Richard D., and James S. Levine, eds. 1986. *Case in Slavic*. Columbus, Ohio: Slavica.

Briggs, Jean. 1970. *Never in anger: portrait of an Eskimo family*. Cambridge, Mass.: Harvard University Press.

Bright, Jane, and William Bright. 1969. Semantic structures in Northwestern California and the Sapir-Whorf hypothesis. In Tyler 1969b:66–78.

Bright, William, ed. 1966. *Sociolinguistics*. The Hague: Mouton.

Brinton, Crane. 1959. *A history of Western morals*. London: Weidenfeld and Nicolson.

Brislin, Richard, ed. 1977. *Culture learning: concepts, applications, and research*. Honolulu: University Press of Hawaii.

————, S. Bochner, and W. J. Lonner, eds. 1975. *Cross-cultural perspectives on learning: the interface between culture and learning*. New York: Halstead Press.

Brjusov, Valerij. 1972. *Stixi*. Moscow: Sovremennik.

Brockhaus Wahrig Deutsches Wörterbuch. 1983. Ed. Gerhard Wahrig, Hildegard Krämer, and Harald Zimmerman. 6 vols. Wiesbaden: F. A. Brockhaus.

Brown, Cecil. 1985. Polysemy, overt marking, and function words. *Language Sciences* 7.2:283–332.

Brown, Roger W., and Marguerite Ford. 1964. Address in American English. In Hymes 1964:234–44.

————, and A. Gilman. 1960. The pronouns of power and solidarity. In Sebeok 1960:253–76.

Brown, S. C., ed. 1984. *Objectivity and cultural divergence*. Cambridge: Cambridge University Press. (Supplement to *Philosophy*, 1984).

Bruce, George L. 1972. *The Warsaw uprising*. London: R. Hart Davis.

Brull, Frank. 1975. A reconsideration of some translations of Sigmund Freud. *Psychotherapy: Theory, Research and Practice* 12:273–79.

Burling, Robbins. 1969. Cognition and componential analysis: God's truth or hocus-pocus? In Tyler 1969b:419–28.

————. 1970a. *Man's many voices*. New York: Holt, Rinehart and Winston.

————. 1970b. American kinship terms once more. *Journal of Anthropology* 26.1:15–24.

Buzo, Alex. 1974. The front room boys. In *Four Australian Plays*. Harmondsworth: Penguin. pp. 15–120.

Carroll, John B. 1953. *The study of language*. Cambridge, Mass.: Harvard University Press.

Chappell, Hilary. 1986a. Formal and colloquial adversity passives in standard Chinese. *Linguistics* 24(6):1025–52.

————. 1986b. The passive of bodily effect in Chinese. *Studies in Language* 19(2):271–83.

————. In press. *Analytic syntax in Standard Chinese*. Lanham, MD: United Press of America.

Chekhov, Anton. 1950. *Izbrannye proizvedenija*. 3 vols. Moscow: Gosudarstvennoe Izdatel'stvo Xudožestvennoj Literatury.

Chomsky, A. Noam. 1975. *Reflections on language*. New York: Pantheon.

———. 1987. Language in a psychological setting. *Sophia Linguistica* (Tokyo) 22:1–73.

Cieślikowski, Jerzy, ed. 1980. *Antologia poezji dziecięcej*. Wrocław: Ossolineum.

Coleman, Peter, ed. 1962. *Australian civilisation*. Melbourne: Cheshire.

Collins. 1980. *Collins German dictionary*. Ed. P. Terrell, V. Calderwood-Schnorr, W. Morris and R. Breitsprecher. Glasgow: Collins.

Comrie, Bernard, and Gerald Stone. 1977. *The Russian language since the revolution*. Oxford: Clarendon Press.

Concise Oxford dictionary of current English. 1964. 5th ed. Eds. H. W. Fowler and F. G. Fowler. Oxford: Clarendon Press.

Conklin, Harold. 1957. *Hanunóo agriculture*. Rome: Food and Agriculture Organization of the United Nations.

———. 1962. Comment [to Frake]. In Gladwin and Sturtevant 1962:89–91.

———. 1967. Lexicographic treatment of folk taxonomies. In Householder and Saporta 1967:119–41.

Conway, Ronald. 1971. *The great Australian stupor: an interpretation of the Australian way of life*. Melbourne: Sun Books.

Cooke, J. 1968. *Pronominal reference in Thai, Burmese, and Vietnamese*. Berkeley: University of California Press.

Cowan, J. 1910. *The Maoris of New Zealand*. Christchurch, N.Z.: Whitcombe and Tombs.

Crawford, R. M. 1970. *Australia*. London: Hutchinson University Library.

Crowley, Terry. 1978. *The middle Clarence dialects of Bandjalang*. Canberra: Australian Institute of Aboriginal Studies.

Cunningham, Adrian, and Deborah Tickner. 1981. Psychoanalysis and indigenous psychology. In Heelas and Lock 1981:225–45.

Curtiss, John S. 1940. *Church and state in Russia*. New York: Columbia University Press.

Dabke, Roswitha. 1976. *Morphology of Australian English*. Munich: Wilhelm Fink.

Dal', Vladimir. 1914. *Tolkovyj slovar' živogo velikorusskogo jazyka*. 4 vols. St Petersburg: T-va M.O. Vol'f. (Revised and expanded by Baudouin de Courtenay.)

———. 1955 [1882]. *Tolkovyj slovar' živogo velikorusskogo jazyka*. 4 vols. Moscow: Gosudarstvennoe Izdatel'stvo Inostrannyx i Nacional'nyx Slovarej.

D'Andrade, Roy G. 1985. Character terms and cultural models. In Dougherty 1985:321–44.

———. 1987. A folk model of the mind. In Holland and Quinn 1987:112–50.

Daneš, F., and D. Viehweger, eds. 1978. *Probleme der Satzsemantik I*. Berlin: Akademie der Wissenschaften der DDR, Zentralinstitut für Sprachwissenschaft.

———, and ———, eds. 1982. *Pragmatische komponente der Satzbedeutung*. Berlin: Akademie der Wissenschaften der DDR, Zentralinstitut für Sprachwissenschaft.

Dante Alighieri. 1980. *La divina commedia*. 3 vols. Rome: Riuniti.

Darwin, Charles. 1872. *The expression of emotions in man and animals*. London: J. Murray. Reprinted 1979, London: Julian Friedmann.

Davies, Norman. 1981. *God's playground: a history of Poland*. Oxford: Clarendon Press.

———. 1984. *Heart of Europe: a short history of Poland*. Oxford: Clarendon Press.

de Courtenay, Jan Baudouin. 1908. Zur Frage über die 'Weichheit' und 'Harte' der Sprachlaute im allgemeinen und um slavischen Sprachgebiete insbesondere. *Zbornik u slavu Vatroslava Jagića* (Berlin) 1908:583–90.

de Custine, Astolphe. 1953 [1843]. *Listy z Rosji*. Trans. Katarzyna Czermińska. London: Anneks.

Dench, Alan. 1982. Kin terms and pronouns of the Panyjima language of Northwest Australia. *Anthropological Forum* 1:109–20.

———. 1987. Kinship and collective activity in the Ngayarda languages of Western Australia. *Language in Society* 16.3:321–40.

Descartes, René. 1952. *Oeuvres et lettres*. Bruges: Gallimard. (Bibliothèque de la Pleiade).

de Tocqueville, Alexis. 1953 [1835–40]. *Democracy in America*. Trans. Henry Reeve. Ed. Phillips Bradley. New York: Alfred A. Knopf.

Devoto, Giacomo and G. C. Oli. 1977. *Dizionario della lingua italiana*. Florence: Le Monnier.

Dicks, Henry. 1952. Observations on contemporary Russian behaviour. *Human Relations* 5.2:111–75.

Dineen, Anne. 1990. *Shame/embarrassment* in English and Danish. *Australian Journal of Linguistics* (special issue on the semantics of emotions) 10(2):217–30.

Dixon, Robert M. W. 1980. *The languages of Australia*. Cambridge: Cambridge University Press.

———. 1989. The Dyirbal kinship system. *Oceania* 59.4:245–68.

Długa, M. 1930. Przyczynek do zbierania polskich form hipokorystycznych. *Język Polski* 15:83–88.

Doi, Takeo. 1974. Amae: A key concept for understanding Japanese personality structure. In Lebra and Lebra 1974:145–54.

———. 1981. *The anatomy of dependence*. Tokyo: Kodansha.

Dorner, A. 1910. Fate. In Hastings 1908–26, v.5:771–78.

Dostoevsky, Fyodor. 1951. *Crime and punishment*. Trans. David Magershack. Harmondsworth, Middlesex: Penguin Books.

———. 1957. *Prestuplenie i nakazanie*. In *Sobranie sočinenij*, v.5. Moscow: Gosudarstvennoe Izdatel'stvo Xudožestvennoj Literatury.

———. 1958. *Brat'ja Karamazovy*. In *Sobranie sočinenij*, v.9. Moscow: Gosudarstvennoe Izdatel'stvo Xudožestvennoj Literatury.

———. 1974. *The brothers Karamazov*. Trans. Constance Garnett. London: Heinemann.

———. 1976. *Brat'ja Karamazovy*. In *Polnoe sobranie sočinenii*, v.14. Leningrad: Nauka.

Dougherty, Janet W. D., ed. 1985. *Directions in cognitive anthropology*. Urbana: University of Illinois Press.

Dovlatov, Sergej. 1983. *Zapovednik*. Ann Arbor, Mich.: Ermitaž.

Duden. 1980. *Das grosse Wörterbuch der deutschen Sprache*. Ed. Günther Drosdowski. 6 vols. Mannheim: Dudenverlag.

Dumont, Louis. 1986. Are cultures living beings? German identity in interaction. *Man* 21:587–604.

Edel, May, and Abraham Edel. 1968. *Anthropology and ethics*. Cleveland, Ohio: Case Western Reserve University Press.

Eibl-Eibesfeldt, Irenäus. 1971. *Love and hate: on the natural history of basic behaviour patterns*. London: Methuen.

Ekman, Paul. 1974. Universal facial expression of emotions. In LeVine 1974:8–15.

———. 1980. *The face of man: expressions of universal emotions in a New Guinea village*. New York: Garland STMP Press.

———. 1989. The argument and evidence about universals in facial expressions of emotion. In Wagner and Manstead 1989:143–64.

———, and Wallace V. Friesen. 1975. *Unmasking the face*. Englewood Cliffs, N.J.: Prentice-Hall.

———, and H. Oster. 1979. Facial expressions of emotion. *Annual Review of Psychology* 30:527–54.

Ellis, Jane. 1986. *The Russian Orthodox church: a contemporary history.* London: Croom Helm.

Elmers, Willy. 1981. *Diachronic grammar: the history of Old and Middle English subjectless constructions.* Tübingen: Niemeyer. (Linguistische Arbeiten, 97).

Erickson, Carolly. 1976. *The medieval vision: essays in history and perception.* New York: Oxford University Press.

Erikson, Erik H. 1963. *Childhood and society.* 2nd ed. New York: W. W. Norton.

Ervin-Tripp, Susan. 1974. Sociolinguistic rules of address. In Pride and Holmes 1974:225–40.

Esenin, Sergej. 1933. *Stixotvorenija.* Moscow: Moskovskoe Tovariščestvo.

Evans, Nicholas. 1985. Kayardild. Ph.D. thesis, Australian National University.

Evtušenko, Evgenij. 1988. We humiliate ourselves. *Time* June 27, 1988:23–24. (Translated from *Literaturnaja Gazeta* no. 19, May 11, 1988).

Falski, Marian. 1976. *Elementarz.* Warsaw: Wydawnictwa Szkolne i Pedagogiczne.

Fedotov, Georgij. 1952. *Novyj grad: sbornik statej.* New York: Izdatel'stvo Imeni Čexova.

———. 1981. *Rossija i svoboda: sbornik statej.* New York: Chalidze Publications.

Fehr, Beverly, and James Russell. 1984. Concepts of emotion viewed from a prototype perspective. *Journal of Experimental Psychology: General* 113.3:464–86.

Ferguson, John. 1958. *Moral values in the ancient world.* London: Methuen and Co.

Fishman, J., ed. 1968. *Readings in the sociology of language.* The Hague: Mouton.

Fodor, Jerry A. 1975. *The language of thought.* New York: Thomas Y. Crowell.

———, M. F. Garrett, E. C. Walker, and C. H. Parkes. 1980. Against definitions. *Cognition* 8:263–67.

Fortes, Meyer. 1959. *Oedipus and Job in West African religion.* Cambridge: Cambridge University Press.

Frake, Charles. 1969. The ethnographic study of cognitive systems. In Tyler 1969b:28–41.

Frank, S. L. 1964 [1917]. *Duša čeloveka.* Paris: YMCA-Press.

Frankl, Viktor Emil. 1964. *Man's search for meaning.* Trans. I. Lasch. London: Hodder and Stoughton.

Friedrich, Paul. 1966. Structural implications of Russian pronominal usage. In Bright 1966:214–53.

Fromm, Erich. 1980 [1942]. *The fear of freedom.* London: Routledge and Kegan Paul.

Fukui, Katsuyoshi, and D. Turton, eds. 1979. *Warfare among East African herders.* Osaka: Senri. (SENRI Ethnological Studies No. 3, National Museum of Ethnology.)

Fullerton, Kemper. 1959. Calvinism and capitalism: an explanation of the Weber thesis. In Green 1959:6–20.

Gaines, Atwood. 1984. Cultural definitions, behaviour and the person in American psychiatry. In Marsella and White 1984:167–92.

Gajdar, Arkadij. 1957. *Sočinenija.* Moscow: Gosudarstvennoe Izdatel'stvo Xudožestvennoj Literatury.

Galkina-Fedoruk, E. 1958. *Bezličnye predloženija v sovremennom russkom jazyke.* Moscow: Moscow University Press.

Gal'perin, I. R. 1977. *New English-Russian dictionary.* 2nd ed. Comp. N. N. Amosova. Moscow: Russian Language Publishers.

Gallimore, Ronald, and Alan Howard. 1968a. Hawaiian life style. In Gallimore and Howard 1968b:10–16.

———, and ———, eds. 1968b. *Studies in Hawaiian community.* Honolulu: University of Hawaii. (Pacific Anthropological Records, 7).

Garton Ash, Timothy. 1983. *The Polish revolution: Solidarity 1980–82.* London: Jonathan Cape.

Gawroński, A. 1928. Wartość uczuciowa deminutywów. *Szkice językoznawcze* 1928:199–217.

Geeraerts, Dirk. 1983. Prototype theory and diachronic semantics: a case study. *Indogermanische Forschungen* 88:1–32.

Geertz, Clifford. 1971. From the native's point of view: on the nature of anthropological understanding. In Basso and Selby 1971:221–37.

Geertz, Clifford. 1973. *The interpretation of cultures: selected essays.* New York: Basic Books.

Geertz, Hildred. 1974. The vocabulary of emotion: a study of Javanese socialization processes. In LeVine 1974:249–64.

Geoghegan, W. 1971. Information processing systems in culture. In Kay 1971:3–35.

Gerber, Eleanor R. 1975. The cultural patterning of emotions in Samoa. Ph.D. thesis, University of California at San Diego.

———. 1985. Rage and obligation: Samoan emotions in conflict. In White and Kirkpatrick 1985:121–67.

Gibbs, Malcolm. No date. *The Australian character.* Sydney: Collins.

Ginzburg, Aleksandr. 1988. Skol'ko žertv u zastoja. *Russkaja mysl'* April 22, 1988:2.

Gipper, Helmut. 1976. Is there a linguistic relativity principle? In Pinxten 1976:217–28.

Gippius, Zinaida. 1971. *Živye lica.* Munich: Wilhelm Fink. (Reprint of 1925 Prague edition).

Gippius, Zinaida. 1972. *Stixotvorenija i poemy.* 2 vols. Munich: Wilhelm Fink.

Gladwin, Thomas, and William Sturtevant, eds. 1962. *Anthropology and human behavior.* Washington: Anthropological Society of Washington.

Glasnost' 1988. [Moscow, a samizdat journal.] Issue 12.

Goddard, Cliff. 1985. *A grammar of Yankunytjatjara.* Alice Springs: Institute for Aboriginal Development.

———, ed. 1988. *A basic Pitjantjatjara/Yankunytjatjara dictionary.* Alice Springs: Institute for Aboriginal Development.

———. 1989a. Issues in natural semantic metalanguage. *Quaderni di Semantica* 10(1):51–64.

———. 1989b. The goals and limits of semantic representation. *Quaderni di Semantica* 10(2):297–308.

———. 1990. The lexical semantics of "good feelings" in Yankunytjatjara. *Australian Journal of Linguistics* (special issue on the semantics of emotions) 10(2):257–92.

———. 1991. Anger in the Western Desert: semantics, culture and emotion. *Man*(n.s.) 26:602–19.

Gogol', N. V. 1873. *Polnoe sobranie sočinenij.* 4 vols. Moscow: A. I. Mamontova and K. Leont'ev.

Gordon, Robert. 1974. The aboutness of emotions. *American Philosophical Quarterly* 11.1:27–36.

———. 1978. Emotion labelling and cognition. *Journal of the Theory of Social Behaviour* 8.2:125–35.

Gorenštejn, Fridrix. 1982. S košelečkoj. *Sintaksis* 10:4–32.

Gorer, Geoffrey. 1949a. Some aspects of the psychology of the people of Great Russia. *The American Slavic and East European Review* 8.3:155–66.

———, and John Rickman. 1949b. *The people of Great Russia.* London: The Cresset Press.

Grace, George W. 1987. *The linguistic construction of reality.* London: Croom Helm.

Green, Julian. 1989. *Langage et son double.* Trans. from English by Julian Green. Paris: Seuil.

Green, Robert W., ed. 1959. *Protestantism and capitalism: the Weber thesis and its critics.* Boston: D. C. Heath.

Greenberg, Joseph. 1957. *Essays in linguistics*. New York: Wenner-Gren Foundation for Anthropological Research. (Viking Fund Publications in Anthropology, 24).

————, ed. 1966. *Language universals*. The Hague: Mouton.

————. 1980. Universals of kinship terminology: their names and the problem of their explanation. In Maquet 1980:9–32.

Greimas, A. J., Roman Jakobson, and M. R. Mayenowa, eds. 1970. *Sign, language, culture*. The Hague: Mouton. (Janua linguarum, series maior, 1).

Grossman, Vasily. 1980. *Žizn' i sud'ba*. Paris: L'Age d'Homme.

————. 1985. *Life and fate*. Trans. Robert Chandler. London: Fontana.

Guardini, Romano. 1961. *Freedom, grace, and destiny: three chapters in the interpretation of existence*. Trans. J. Murray. London: Harvill.

Guiraud-Weber, M. 1984. *Les prepositions sans nominatif en russe moderne*. Paris: Institut d'études slaves.

Haiman, John. 1980. Dictionaries and encyclopaedias. *Lingua* 50:329–57.

————. 1989. Alienation in grammar. *Studies in Language* 13(1):129–70.

Hale, Kenneth L. 1966. Kinship reflections in syntax: some Australian languages. *Word* 22:318–24.

————, Mary Laughren, and David Nash. 1983–86. Warlpiri dictionary. Unpublished drafts. Massachusetts Institute of Technology.

Halecki, Oskar. 1983. *A history of Poland*. London: Routledge and Kegan Paul.

Halle, Morris, Joan Bresnan, and George Miller, eds. 1978. *Linguistic theory and psychological reality*. Cambridge, Mass.: MIT Press.

Hare, R. M. 1961. *The language of morals*. Oxford: Oxford University Press.

Harkins, Jean. 1986. Semantics and the language learner: Warlpiri particles. *Journal of Pragmatics* 19:559–73.

————. 1988. English as a 'two-way' language in Alice Springs. M.A. thesis, Australian National University. (To be published by Queensland University Press.)

————. 1990. Shame and shyness in the Aboriginal classroom: a case for "practical semantics". *Australian Journal of Linguistics* (special issue on the semantics of emotions) 10(2):293–306.

Harnad, Stevan R., Horst D. Steklis, and Jane Lancaster, eds. 1976. *Origins and evolution of language and speech*. New York Academy of Sciences, *Annals*, v.280.

Harrap's standard French and English dictionary. 1961. Ed. Y. E. Mansion. London: George Harrap.

Harris, Max. 1962. Morals and manners. In Coleman 1962:47–67.

Harris, Stephen. 1980. *Culture and learning: tradition and education in Northeast Arnhem Land*. Darwin: Northern Territory Department of Education.

Hastings, James, ed. 1908–26. *Encyclopaedia of religion and ethics*. 13 vols. Edinburgh: T. Clark.

Hatfield, Colby R., Jr. 1986. Foci of fear in two African societies. In Scruton 1986:63–121.

Heath, Jeffrey. 1978. Linguistic approaches to Nunggubuyu ethnozoology and ethnobotany. In Hiatt 1978b:40–55.

————. 1982. Introduction to Heath, Merlan, and Rumsey 1982:1–18.

————, Francesca Merlan, and Alan Rumsey, eds. 1982. *Languages of kinship in Aboriginal Australia*. Sydney: University of Sydney Press.

Heelas, Paul. 1981. The model applied: anthropology and indigenous psychologies. In Heelas and Lock 1981:39–64.

————. 1984. Emotions across cultures: objectivity and cultural divergence. In Brown 1984:21–42.

————, and Andrew Lock, eds. 1981. *Indigenous psychologies*. London: Academic Press.

Herbert, Xavier. 1975. *Poor fellow my country.* Sydney: Collins.

Hercus, Luise A., and I. M. White. 1973. Perception of kinship structure reflected in the Adnjamathanha pronouns. *Pacific Linguistics* A36:47–72.

Herder, Johann Gottfried von. 1877–1913. *Sämtliche Werke.* Ed. Bernard Suphan. 33 vols. Berlin: Wiedemann.

Herling, Gustav. 1951. *A world apart.* Trans. J. Narek. London: Heinemann.

Herriot, James. 1986. *Dog stories.* New York: St. Martin's Press.

Hiatt, Lester R. 1978a. Classification of the emotions. In Hiatt 1978b:182–87.

———, ed. 1978b. *Australian Aboriginal concepts.* Canberra: Australian Institute of Aboriginal Studies.

Hill, Deborah. 1987. A cross-linguistic study of value-judgement terms. M. A. thesis, Australian National University.

Hoijer, Harry, ed. 1954. *Language in culture.* Chicago: Chicago University Press. (Memoirs of the American Anthropological Association, 79).

Holland, Dorothy, and Naomi Quinn, eds. 1987. *Cultural models in language and thought.* Cambridge: Cambridge University Press.

Holmer, Nils M. 1971. *Notes on the Bandjalang dialect spoken at Coraki and Bungawalbin Creek, NSW.* Canberra: Australian Institute of Aboriginal Studies.

Horne, Donald. 1964. *The lucky country.* Sydney: Angus and Robertson.

———. 1970. *The next Australia.* Sydney: Angus and Robertson.

Householder, Fred, and Sol Saporta, eds. 1967. *Problems in lexicography.* 2nd ed. The Hague: Mouton.

Howell, Signe. 1981. Rules not words. In Heelas and Lock 1981:133–43.

Hsu, Francis L. K. 1975. American core values and national character. In Spradley and Rynkiewich 1975:378–93.

———. 1985. The self in cross-cultural perspective. In Marsella, DeVos, and Hsu 1985:24–55.

Hudson, Joyce. MS a. Illocutionary verbs in Walmatjari.

———. MS b. Walmatjari kinship terms: a reflection of the social structure.

———. 1985. Selected speech act verbs in Walmatjari. In Huttar and Gregerson 1985:63–83.

Humboldt, Carl Wilhelm von. 1903–36. *Wilhelm von Humboldts Werke.* Ed. Albert Leitzmann. 17 vols. Berlin: B. Behr.

———. 1963. *Schriften zur Sprachphilosophie.* 5 vols. Stuttgart: J. G. Cotta.

Humphries, Barry. 1981. *A nice night's entertainment.* Sydney: Currency Press.

Hunn, E. 1976. Toward a perceptual model of folk biological classification. *American Ethnologist* 3:508–24.

Hunt, Earl, and Mahzarin R. Banaji. 1988. The Whorfian hypothesis revisited: a cognitive science view of linguistic and cultural effects on thought. In: Berry, Irvine and Hunt 1988:57–84.

Huttar, George, and Kenneth Gregerson, eds. 1985. *Pragmatics in non-Western perspective.* Dallas: Summer Institute of Linguistics.

Hyldgaard-Jensen, Karl, and Arne Zettersten, eds. 1988. *Symposium on lexicography III: proceedings of the Third International Symposium on Lexicography May 14–16, 1986 at the University of Copenhagen.* Tübingen: Niemeyer.

Hymes, Dell H. 1961. On typology of cognitive styles in language (with examples from Chinookan). *Anthropological Linguistics* 3.1:22–54.

———. 1962. The ethnography of speaking. In Gladwin and Sturtevant 1962:15–53. Also in Fishman 1968:99–138.

———, ed. 1964. *Language in culture and society.* New York: Harper and Row.

————. 1969. Discussion of Burling's paper. In Tyler 1969b:428–32.

————. 1983. *Essays in the history of linguistic anthropology.* Amsterdam: John Benjamins.

Iłłakowiczówna, Kazimiera. 1980. Babunia. In Cieślikowski 1980:107.

Iordanskaja, Lidija. 1974. Tentative lexicographic definitions for a group of Russian words denoting emotions. In Rozencvejg 1974, v.2:88–117. (Russian version published 1970, in *Mašinny perevod i prikladnaja lingvistika* 13:3–34).

————, and Igor Mel'čuk. 1981. On a class of Russian verbs which can introduce direct speech: constructions of the type 'Ostav'te menja!—ispugalsja bufetčik': lexical polysemy or semantic syntax? In Jacobsen and Krag 1981:51–66.

Ito, Karen L. 1985. Affective bonds: Hawaiian interrelationships of self. In White and Kirkpatrick 1985:301–27.

Izard, Carroll. 1969. *The face of emotion.* New York: Appleton-Century-Crofts.

————. 1977. *Human emotions.* New York: Plenum Press.

————, and E. S. Bartlett. 1968. Hypnotic induction of the fundamental emotions. Film, Vanderbilt University.

————, and S. Buechler. 1980. Aspects of consciousness and personality in terms of differential emotions theory. In Plutchik and Kellerman 1980:165–87.

Jackendoff, Ray. 1983. *Semantics and cognition.* Cambridge, Mass.: MIT Press.

Jacobs, Alan. 1979. Maasai inter-tribal relations: belligerent herdsmen or peaceful pastoralists? In Fukui and Turton 1979.

Jacobsen, Per, and H. L. Krag, eds. 1981. *The Slavic verb: an anthology presented to Hans Christian Sørensen.* Copenhagen: Rosenkilde and Bagger. (Københavns Universitets Slaviske Institut, Studier 9).

Jakobson, Roman, C. H. van Schooneveld, and D. S. Worth, eds. 1973. *Slavic poetics: essays in honour of Kiril Taranovsky.* The Hague: Mouton.

Jarintzov, Nadine. 1916. *The Russians and their language.* Oxford: Blackwell.

Johnson, Frank. 1985. The Western concept of self. In Marsella, DeVos, and Hsu 1985:91–138.

Johnson-Laird, P. N., and Keith Oatley. 1989. The language of emotions: an analysis of a semantic field. *Cognition and Emotion* 3:81–123.

Kane, J. F. 1967. Free will and Providence. In *New Catholic encyclopaedia* 6:94–95.

Katz, Jerrold J. 1976. A hypothesis about the uniqueness of natural language. In Harnad, Steklis, and Lancaster 1976:33–45.

Kawai, H. 1976. *Bosei shakai Nihon no byori.* [Psychopathology of contemporary Japan as a maternal society]. Tokyo: Chuo Koronsha.

Kay, Paul, ed. 1971. *Explorations in mathematical anthropology.* Cambridge, Mass.: MIT Press.

Keen, Ian. 1985. Definitions of kin. *Journal of Anthropological Research* 41.1:64–90.

Keesing, Roger. 1975. *Kin groups and social structure.* New York: Holt, Rinehart and Winston.

Kefer, Michel, and Johann van der Auwera, eds. 1991. *Meaning and grammar.* Berlin: Mouton de Gruyter.

Kemme, Hans-Martin. 1979. *Ja, denn, doch usw: die Modalpartikeln im Deutschen.* Munich: Goethe-Institut.

Kennedy, Eliza, and Tamsin Donaldson. 1982. Coming up out of the Nhaalya. *Aboriginal History* 6:5–28.

Kenny, Anthony. 1973. *The anatomy of the soul: historical essays in the philosophy of mind.* Oxford: Blackwell.

King, Jonathan. 1978. *Waltzing materialism.* Sydney: Harper and Row.

Kirkpatrick, John. 1973. *The Marquesan notion of person.* Ann Arbor: University of Michigan Press.

Kleinman, Arthur. 1977. Depression, somatisation, and the new cross-cultural psychiatry. *Social Science and Medicine* 11:3–10.

———, and Byron Good, eds. 1985. *Culture and depression: studies in the anthropology and cross-cultural psychiatry of affect and disorder.* Berkeley: University of California Press.

Kluckhohn, Clyde. 1961. *Culture and behavior.* New York: Free Press of Glencoe.

Koch, Harold. 1982. Kinship categories in Kaytej pronouns. In Heath, Merlan, and Rumsey 1982:64–71.

Kremer, Klaus, ed. 1984. *Seele: ihre Wirklichkeit, ihr Verhältnis zum Leib und menschlichen Person.* Leiden: E. J. Brill. (Studien der Problemgeschichte der antiken und mittelalterlichen Philosophie, 10).

Kučera, Henry, and Nelson Francis. 1967. *Computational analysis of present-day American English.* Providence, R.I.: Brown University Press.

Kundera, Milan. 1980. *The book of laughter and forgetting.* Trans. Michael Heim. New York: Alfred A. Knopf.

Ladd, John. 1957. *The structure of a moral code.* Cambridge, Mass.: Harvard University Press.

Lakoff, George. 1986. *Women, fire, and dangerous things.* Chicago: Chicago University Press.

———, and Mark Johnson. 1980. *Metaphors we live by.* Chicago: Chicago University Press.

Langacker, Ronald. 1983. *Foundations of cognitive grammar.* Bloomington: Indiana University Linguistics Club.

Laughren, Mary. 1982. Warlpiri kinship structure. In Heath, Merlan, and Rumsey 1982:72–85.

LDOCE. 1978. *Longman dictionary of contemporary English.* Ed. Paul Procter. London: Longman.

LDOTEL. 1984. *Longman dictionary of the English language.* Eds. Heather Gay, Brian O'Kill, Katherine Seed, Janet Whitcut. London: Longman.

Leach, Edmund R. 1961. *Rethinking anthropology.* London: Athlone.

———. 1971. More about 'Mama' and 'Papa'. In Needham 1971:75–98.

———. 1981. A poetics of power. [A review of Geertz's *Negara*]. *New Republic* 84, April 4, 1981:14.

Lebra, T. S., and W. P. Lebra, eds. 1974. *Japanese culture and behavior: selected readings.* Honolulu: East-West Center.

Lechoń, Jan. 1973. *Dziennik.* London: Polska Fundacja Kulturalna.

Le grand Robert de la langue française. 1986. 2nd ed. Ed. Alain Rey. 9 vols. Paris: Le Robert.

Leibniz, Gottfried Wilhelm. 1903. *Opuscules et fragments inédits de Leibniz.* Ed. Louis Couturat. Paris. Reprinted in 1961, Hildesheim: Georg Olms Buchhandlung.

———. 1949. *New essays concerning human understanding.* Trans. A. G. Langley. LaSalle, Ill.: The Open Court Company.

———. 1980 [1705]. *New essays concerning human understanding.* Trans. P. Remnant and J. Bennett. Cambridge: Cambridge University Press.

Lenneberg, Eric H. 1953. Cognition and ethnolinguistics. *Language* 29:463–71.

Lermontov, Mikhail. 1959. *Geroj našego vremeni.* In *Sobranie sočinenij,* v.2:365–499. Moscow: Xudožestvennaja Literatura.

Levi-Strauss, Claude, Roman Jakobson, C. F. Voegelin, and Thomas Sebeok, eds. 1953.

Results of the Conference of Anthropologists and Linguists. Bloomington: Indiana University Publications in Anthropology and Linguistics. (International Journal of American Linguistics, Memoir 8).

Levine, Nancy. 1981. Perspectives on love: morality and affect in Nyinba interpersonal relations. In Mayer 1981:106–25.

LeVine, Robert A., ed. 1974. *Culture and personality: contemporary readings.* Chicago: Aldine.

Levy, Robert. 1973. *Tahitians: mind and experience in the Society Islands.* Chicago: Chicago University Press.

———. 1974. Tahiti, sin and the question of integration between personality and sociocultural systems. In LeVine 1974:287–306.

———. 1983. Introduction: self and emotions. *Ethos* 11.3:128–34.

———. 1984. Emotion, knowing, and culture. In Shweder and LeVine 1984:214–37.

Lewis, D. K. 1970. General semantics. *Synthese* 22:18–67.

Liberman, Kenneth. 1982. Some linguistic features of congenial fellowship among the Pitjantjatjara. *International Journal of the Sociology of Language* 36:35–53.

Lindzey, Gardner. 1954. *Psychology.* Cleveland: Worth.

Lock, Margaret. 1984. Popular conceptions of mental health in Japan. In Marsella and White 1984:215–34.

Locke, John. 1959 [1690]. *An essay concerning human understanding.* Ed. A. C. Fraser. New York: Dover.

Lounsbury, Floyd. 1964. The structural analysis of kinship semantics. In Lunt 1964:1073–93.

Lowie, Robert H. 1954. *Towards understanding Germany.* Chicago: Chicago University Press.

Lunt, Horace G. 1958. *Fundamentals of Russian.* Rev. ed. New York: W. W. Norton.

———, ed. 1964. *Proceedings of the Ninth International Congress of Linguists.* The Hague: Mouton.

Lutz, Catherine. 1982. The domain of emotion words on Ifaluk. *American Ethnologist* 9.1:113–28.

———. 1983. Parental goals, ethnopsychology, and the development of emotional meaning. *Ethos* 11.4:246–62.

———. 1985a. Depression and the translation of emotional worlds. In Kleinman and Good 1985:63–100.

———. 1985b. Ethnopsychology compared to what? explaining behavior and consciousness among the Ifaluk. In White and Kirkpatrick 1985:35–79.

———. 1987. Goals, events and understanding in Ifaluk emotion theory. In Holland and Quinn 1987:290–312.

———. 1988. *Unnatural emotions.* Chicago and London: University of Chicago Press.

Lyons, John. 1977. *Semantics.* 2 vols. Cambridge: Cambridge University Press.

———. 1981. *Language, meaning and context.* Bungay, Suffolk: Fontana.

MacLeod, Robert. 1975. *The persistent problems of psychology.* Pittsburgh: Duquesne University Press.

The Macquarie Dictionary. 1981. Ed. A. Delbridge. Sydney: Macquarie Library.

Mann, Thomas. 1976. *The magic mountain.* Trans. H. T. Lowe-Porter. Harmondsworth: Penguin.

Manne, Robert. 1987. *The Petrov affair.* Sydney: Pergamon.

Maquet, Jacques, ed. 1980. *On linguistic anthropology: essays in honor of Harry Hoijer.* Malibu: Undena Publications.

Marcus Aurelius Antoninus. 1964. *Meditations.* Trans. Maxwell Staniforth. Harmondsworth: Penguin.

Marsella, Anthony, George DeVos, and Francis Hsu, eds. 1985. *Culture and self: Asian and Western perspectives.* New York: Tavistock.

———, and Geoffrey White, eds. 1984. *Cultural conceptions of mental health and therapy.* Dordrecht: Reidel.

Marshall, L. H. 1956. *The challenge of New Testament ethics.* London: Macmillan.

Mauriac, François. 1957. *Lines of life.* Trans. G. Hopkins. London: Eyre and Spottiswoode.

———, 1983 [1928]. *Destins.* Ed. C. B. Thornton-Smith. London: Methuen Educational.

Mayakovsky, Vladimir. 1958. *Polnoe sobranie sočinenij.* Moscow: Gosudarstvennoe Izdatel'stvo Xudožestvennoj Literatury.

———. 1972. *Poems.* Trans. Dorian Rottenberg. Moscow: Progress.

Mayer, Adrian, ed. 1981. *Culture and morality.* New York: Academic Press.

McIntyre, Alasdair. 1966. *A short history of ethics.* London: Routledge and Kegan Paul.

Mead, Margaret. 1954. *Coming of age in Samoa.* Melbourne: Penguin Books.

———, and Rhoda Métraux, eds. 1953. *The study of culture at a distance.* Chicago: Chicago University Press.

Mel'čuk, Igor. 1974. O sintaksičeskom nule. *Tipologia passivnyx konstrucij.* Ed. A. A. Xolodovič. Leningrad: Nauka.

———, et al. 1984. *Dictionnaire explicatif et combinatoire du français contemporain.* Montréal: Les Presses de l'Université de Montréal. (Recherches lexico-semantiques, 1).

———, and Alexander Žolkovskij. 1984. *Tolkovo-kombinatornyj slovar' sovremennogo russkogo jazyka.* Vienna: Wiener Slawistischer Almanach. (Sonderband 14).

Merriam-Webster. 1972. *The Merriam-Webster pocket dictionary of synonyms.* New York: Pocket Books.

Michnik, Adam. 1985. *Z dziejów honoru w Polsce: wypisy więzienne.* Warsaw: Nowa.

Mickiewicz, Adam. 1955. *Dzieła.* 16 vols. Warsaw: Czytelnik.

Miller, George. 1978. Semantic relations among words. In Halle, Bresnan, and Miller 1978:60–118.

Miłosz, Czesław. 1979. *Ogród nauk.* Paris: Instytut Literacki.

———. 1990. *Rok myśliwego.* Paris: Instytut Literacki.

Minamoto, R. 1969. *Giri to ninjo.* [Obligation and human feelings]. Tokyo: Chuo Koronsha.

Mischel, Theodore, ed. 1977. *The self.* Oxford: Blackwell.

Mol, Rev. Frans, M. H. M. n.d. MMA. *A dictionary of the Massai language and folklore: English-Maasai.* Nairobi: Marketing and Publishing Ltd.

Moore, T., ed. 1973. *Cognitive development and the acquisition of language.* New York: Academic Press.

Mori, J. 1977. *Nihonjin: 'kara-nashi-tamago' no jigazoh.* [The Japanese: his self-image as an 'egg without its eggshell']. Tokyo: Kodansha.

Morice, Rodney. 1977a. The language of psychiatry in a preliterate speech community: verbal repertoire as a basis for psychiatric diagnosis. M.D. thesis, University of New South Wales.

———. 1977b. Know your speech community 2: grief and depression. *Aboriginal Health Worker* 1.2:22–27.

———. 1978. Psychiatric diagnosis in a transcultural setting: the importance of lexical categories. *British Journal of Psychiatry* 132:87–95.

Mufwene, Salikoko S. 1980. 'Prototype' and 'kin-class'. *Anthropological Linguistics* 22:29–41.

————. 1983. Investigating what the words *father* and *mother* mean. *Language and Communication* 3.3:245–69.

————. 1987. The pragmatics of kinship terms in Kituba. Paper given at the International Pragmatics Conference, University of Antwerp, August 17–22, 1987.

Munn, Nancy D. 1970. *Walbiri iconography: graphic representation and cultural symbolism in a Central Australian society.* Ithaca: Cornell University Press.

Murase, Takao. 1984. Sunao: a central value in Japanese psychotherapy. In Marsella and White 1984:317–29.

Murphy, G., and L. B. Murphy, eds. 1969. *Western psychology from the Greeks to William James.* New York: Basic Books.

Mühlhäusler, Peter, and Rom Harré. 1990. *Pronouns and people—the linguistic construction of social and personal identity.* Cambridge: Blackwell.

Myers, Fred R. 1976. To have and to hold: a study of persistence and change in Pintupi social life. Ph.D. thesis, Bryn Mawr.

————. 1979. Emotions and the self. *Ethos* 7.4:343–70.

————. 1986. *Pintupi country, Pintupi self: sentiment, place and politics among Western Desert Aborigines.* Washington, D.C.: Smithsonian.

Nakane, Chie. 1970. *Japanese society.* Harmondsworth: Penguin.

Nash, David. 1982. An etymological note on Warlpiri *kurdungurlu.* In Heath, Merlan, and Rumsey 1982:141–59.

NEB. 1970. *The new English Bible.* London: Oxford University Press.

Needham, Rodney. 1971. Introduction to Needham 1971b:xiii–cxvii.

————, ed. 1971b. *Rethinking kinship and marriage.* London: Tavistock.

————. 1972. *Belief, language, and experience.* Oxford: Blackwell.

————. 1974. *Remarks and inventions: sceptical essays about kinship.* London: Tavistock.

New Catholic encyclopaedia. 1967–79. 17 vols. New York: McGraw-Hill.

Newton, Francis Noel. 1984. *Aloha and hostility in a Hawaiian-American community: the private reality of a public image.* Ann Arbor: University Microfilms International.

Nida, Eugene A., and C. R. Taber. 1969. *The theory and practice of translation.* Leiden: E. J. Brill.

Nikolaeva, Tat'jana. 1985. *Funkcji častic v vyskazyvanii.* Moscow: Nauka.

Nikonov, V. A., and A. V. Superanskaja, eds. 1970. *Anthroponimika.* Moscow: Nauka.

Nolan, P. 1967. Free will. In *New Catholic encyclopaedia* v.6:89–93.

Obrębska, A. 1929. Technika spieszczeń w dzisiejszej polszczyźnie. *Język Polski* 1929:65–71.

OED. 1933. *The Oxford English dictionary.* 12 vols. Oxford: Clarendon Press.

O'Grady, Geoffrey, and Kathleen Mooney. 1973. Nyangumarda kinship terminology. *Anthropological Linguistics* 15.1:1–23.

O'Grady, John. 1965. *Aussie English.* Sydney: Ure Smith.

Okudžava, Bulat. 1984. *Proza i poezija.* 7th ed. Frankfurt: Posev.

Orlov, Vladimir. 1965. Marina Tsvetaeva: sud'ba, xarakter, poezija. In Tsvetaeva 1965:5–54.

Osgood, Charles E., and T. A. Sebeok, eds. 1954. *Psycholinguistics: a survey of theory and research problems.* Bloomington: Indiana University Publications in Anthropology and Linguistics. (International Journal of American Linguistics, Memoir 10).

Osmond, Meredith. 1990. A lexical survey of emotion words in English. M.A. thesis, Australian National University.

Ožegov, S. I. 1972. *Slovar' russkogo jazyka.* 9th ed. Ed. N. J. Švedov. Moscow: Sovetskaja Enciklopedija.

Padučeva, Elena Viktorovna. 1985. *Vyskazyvanie i ego sootnesennost' s dejstvitel'nost'ju.* Moscow: Nauka.

Pascal, Blaise. 1963 [1667]. Sur l'esprit de geometrie. In *Oeuvres Completes.* Ed. L. Lafuma. Paris.

Pasternak, Boris. 1958. *Doctor Zhivago.* Trans. Max Hayward and Manya Harari. London: Collins and Harvill.

———. 1959. *Doktor Živago.* Paris: Mondiale.

———. 1965. *Stixotvorenija i poemy.* Moscow: Sovetskij Pisatel'.

Pawley, Andrew. 1987. Encoding events in Kalam and English. In Tomlin 1987:329–60.

Percova, N. N. 1985. *Semantika slova v lingvističeskoj koncepcii G.V. Lejbnica.* Moscow: Institut Russkogo Jazyka AN SSSR.

Peškovskij, A. M. 1956. *Russkij sintaksis v naučnom osveščenii.* Moscow: Učpedgiz.

Peters, Richard. 1956. *Hobbes.* Harmondsworth: Penguin.

Peursen, C. A. van. 1966. *Body, soul, spirit: a survey of the body-mind problem.* London: Oxford University Press.

Phillpotts, B. S. 1920. Soul (Teutonic). In Hastings 1908–26, v.11:753–55.

Pigeaud, Jackie. 1981. *La maladie de l'âme et du corps dans la tradition medico-philosophique antique.* Paris: Les Belles Lettres.

Pinxten, Rik, ed. 1976. *Universalism versus relativism in language and thought: proceedings of a colloquium on the Sapir-Whorf hypothesis.* The Hague: Mouton. (Contributions to the Sociology of Language, 11).

Pis'mo. 1988. Anonymous. Pis'mo bratu na Zapad o tom, kak my živem w Baškirii. *Russkaja mysl'* May 13, 1988.

Plato. 1970. *The dialogues of Plato.* Trans. Benjamin Jowett. Eds. R. M. Hare and D. A. Russell. 2 vols. London: Sphere Books.

Plutchik, Robert, and Henry Kellerman. 1980. *Emotion: theory, research, and experience.* Vol. 1: *Theories of emotion.* New York: Academic Press.

The pocket Oxford dictionary of current English. 1969. 5th ed. Eds. F. G. Fowler and H. W. Fowler. Oxford: Clarendon Press.

Pohlenz, Max. 1948. *Die Stoa, Geschichte einer geistigen Bewegung.* Göttingen: Vandenkoeck und Ruprecht.

Poynton, Cate. 1982. The linguistic realisation of social relations: terms of address in Australian English. In *Collected papers on normal aspects of speech and language, 52nd ANZAAS Conference (Speech and Language section).* North Ryde: Macquarie University, Speech and Language Research Centre (Occasional Papers) 1982:253–69.

———. 1984. Names as vocatives: forms and functions. *Nottingham Linguistic Circular* 13:1–34.

———. 1989. Terms of address and the semiotics of social relations. In Blair and Collins 1989.

Pride, John B., and Janet Holmes, eds. 1974. *Sociolinguistics.* Harmondsworth: Penguin.

Pringle, John Douglas. 1965. *Australian accent.* London: Chatto and Windus.

Proffer, Ellendea. 1980. *Tsvetaeva: a pictorial biography.* Ann Arbor: Ardis.

Prus, Bolesław. 1890. *Lalka.* Reprinted in *Wybór Pism* 1951:5–369. Warsaw: Książka i Wiedza.

———. 1894. *Emancypantki.* Reprinted in *Wybór Pism* 1951:371–476. Warsaw: Książka i Wiedza.

Pukui, Mary K., and Samuel H. Elbert. 1986. *Hawaiian dictionary.* Rev. enl. ed. Honolulu: University of Hawaii Press.

Pushkin, Alexander. 1937. *Kapitanskaya dočka.* London: Dent.

————. 1949. Kapitanskaja dočka. In *Polnoe sobranie sočinenij*, v.4:260–359. Moscow: Gosudarstvennoe Izdatel'stvo Xudožestvennoj Literatury.

————. 1964. *Eugene Onegin: a novel in verse*. Trans. Vladimir Nabokov. 4 vols. New York: Pantheon. (Bollinger series, 72).

————. 1981. *Evgenij Onegin: roman v stixax*. Moscow: Gosudarstvennoe Izdatel'stvo Xudožestvennoj Literatury.

Radcliffe-Brown, A. R. 1930–31. *The social organisation of Australian tribes*. Sydney: Oceania. (Oceania Monographs, 1).

————. 1950. *African systems of kinship and marriage*. London: Oxford University Press.

Radzievskaja, T. V. 1991. K èksplicitnomu opisaniju koncepta "svoboda". In *Logičeskij analiz jazyka: kul'turnye koncepty*. Moscow: Nauka.

Ramage, C. T. 1904. *Familiar quotations from French and Italian authors*. London: Routledge. Reprinted 1968, Detroit: Gale Research Co.

Rappaport, Gilbert. 1986. On the grammar of simile: case and configuration. In Brecht and Levine 1986:244–79.

Rathmayr, Renate. 1985. Les particules ont-elles une signification propre? une approche pragmatique de la question. In Université de Paris VII 1986:53–64.

Regan, C. 1967. Free will and grace. In *New Catholic encyclopaedia* v.6:93–94.

Reymont, Władysław. 1949. *Chłopi*. 4 vols. Rome: Nakładem Centralnej Składnicy Książek.

Rogers, Reginald. 1952. *A short history of ethics*. London: Macmillan.

Roget's thesaurus of English words and phrases. 1984. Rev. ed. Ed. Susan M. Lloyd. Harmondsworth: Penguin.

Rosaldo, Michelle. 1980. *Knowledge and passion: Ilongot notions of self and social life*. Cambridge: Cambridge University Press.

————. 1984. Toward an anthropology of self and feeling. In Shweder and LeVine 1984:137–57.

Rosch, Eleanor. 1975. Universals and cultural specifics in human categorisation. In Brislin, Bochner, and Lonner 1975:177–206.

Rousseau, Jean-Jacques. 1963. *Confessions*. 2 vols. Paris: Livre de Poche.

Rozencvejg, J., ed. 1974. *Machine translation and applied linguistics*. 2 vols. Frankfurt: Athenäum.

Ruffin, Bernard. 1985. *The days of the martyrs*. Huntington, In.: Our Sunday Visitor Inc.

Russell, Bertrand. 1962. *An inquiry into meaning and truth*. Harmondsworth: Penguin.

Russell, H. 1981. Second-person pronouns in Japanese. *Sophia Linguistica* (Tokyo) 8/9:116–28.

Russell, James A. 1989. Culture, scripts and children's understanding of emotion. In Saarni and Harris 1989:293–318.

Rybakov, Anatolij. 1987. Deti Arbata. *Družba narodov* 4:1–272 (pt.1), 5:67–163 (pt.2), 6:23–151 (pt.3). Moskva: Sovetskij pisatel'.

Ryle, Gilbert. 1949. *The concept of mind*. London: Hutchinson.

Saarni, Carolyn, and Paul L. Harris, eds. 1989. *Children's understanding of emotion*. Cambridge: Cambridge University Press.

Samarin, Y. 1877. *Sočinenija*. Moscow.

Sapir, Edward. 1924. Culture, genuine and spurious. *American Journal of Sociology* 29:401–29.

————. 1949. *Selected writings of Edward Sapir in language, culture and personality*. Ed. David Mandelbaum. Berkeley: University of California Press.

SAR 1971. *Slovar' Akademii Rossijskoj*. Odense: Izd-vo pri Universistete Odense. (Reprint of 2nd ed. published in St Petersburg, 1806–22.)

Scheffler, Harold. 1972. Afterword to Thomson 1972:37–52.

————. 1978. *Australian kin classification*. Cambridge: Cambridge University Press.

Schell, Jonathan. 1982. *The fate of the earth*. New York: Alfred Knopf.

Schieffelin, Edward. 1985. Anger, grief, and shame: toward a Kaluli ethnopsychology. In White and Kirkpatrick 1985:168–82.

Scholz, Friedrich. 1973. *Russian impersonal expressions used with reference to a person*. The Hague: Mouton.

Schrett, Józef. 1984. Dolina między górami. *Kultura* 1:5–18.

Scruton, David L, ed. 1986. *Sociophobics: the anthropology of fear*. Boulder, Colo.: Westview Press.

Searle, John R. 1969. *Speech acts*. Cambridge: Cambridge University Press.

————. 1979. *Expression and meaning*. Cambridge: Cambridge University Press.

Sebeok, T., ed. 1960. *Style in language*. Cambridge, Mass.: MIT Press.

Serisier, Jan. 1981. Problems with the Ocker lingo. *The Bulletin* November 24, 1981:72.

Shakespeare, William. 1872. *The complete Signet classic Shakespeare*. Ed. S. Barnet. New York: Harcourt Brace Jovanovich.

Shweder, Richard, and Edmund Bourne. 1984. Does the concept of the person vary cross-culturally? In Marsella and White 1984:97–140.

————, and Robert A LeVine, eds. 1984. *Culture theory: essays on mind, self, and emotion*. Cambridge: Cambridge University Press.

Sienkiewicz, Henryk. 1897. *Pan Michael: An historical novel of Poland, the Ukraine, and Turkey*. Trans. Jeremiah Curtin. Boston: Little, Brown.

————. 1949 [1895]. *Rodzina Połanieckich*. Warsaw: Państwowy Instytut Wydawniczy.

————. 1950 [1887]. *Pan Wołodyjowski*. Warsaw: Państwowy Instytut Wydawniczy.

Simpson, Jane. MS. Australian abbreviations. Unpublished manuscript.

SJP. 1958–69. *Słownik języka polskiego*. Ed. W. Doroszewski. 11 vols. Warsaw: Państwowe Wydawnictwo Naukowe.

Smirnickij, A. I. 1961. *Russko-Anglijskij slovar'*. Moscow: Gosudarstvennoe Izdatel'stvo Inostrannyx i Nacional'nyx Slovarej.

Smith, Charles. 1903. *Synonyms discriminated: a dictionary of synonymous words in the English language*. Ed. H. Percy Smith. Facsimile reprint, 1970, Detroit: Gale Research Co.

Smith, Hedrick. 1976. *The Russians*. London: Sphere Books.

SOED. 1964. *The shorter Oxford English dictionary*. 3rd ed. rev. Ed. C. T. Onions. 2 vols. Oxford: Clarendon Press.

Solomon, Robert C. 1984. Getting angry: the Jamesian theory of emotion in anthropology. In Shweder and LeVine 1984:238–55.

Solov'ev, Sergej. 1977. *Žizn' i tvorčeskaja evolucija Vladimira Solov'eva*. Brussels: Žizn' s Bogom.

Solov'ev, Vladimir. 1954. *Tri razgovora*. New York: Izdatel'stvo Imeni Čexova.

————. 1966–70. *Sobranie sočinenij*. 14 vols. St Petersburg: Prosveščenie/Brussels: Foyer Oriental Chrétien.

Solzhenitsyn, Aleksandr. 1968a. *Rakovyj korpus*. 2 vols. Frankfurt/Main: Posev.

————. 1968b. *The cancer ward*. Trans. Rebecca Frank. New York: Dial Press.

————. 1968c. *V kruge pervom*. London: Fontana.

————. 1971. *Krebsstation*. Trans. Christiane Auras, Agathe Jais, and Ingrid Tinzmann. Berlin: Neuwied.

————. 1979. *The first circle*. Trans. Michael Guybon. London: Collins.

————. 1986. *Krasnoe koleso*. Uzel 3, Mart semnadčatogo. Paris: YMCA-Press.

————. 1990. Kak obustroit' Rossiju.

Sorenson, E. R. 1976. *Social organisation and the facial expression of emotion*. Washington,

D.C.: National Geographic Society. (National Geographic Society Research Projects. 1968).

Spiro, Melford E. 1984. Some reflections on cultural determinism and relativism with special reference to emotion and reason. In Shweder and LeVine 1984:323–46.

Spradley, James P., and Michael A. Rynkiewich. 1975. *The Nacirema: readings on American culture*. Boston: Little, Brown.

St John of the Cross. 1979. *The collected works of St John of the Cross*. Trans. Kiernan Kavanaugh and Otillo Rodriguez. Washington, D.C.: Institute of Carmelite Studies.

Stankiewicz, Edward. 1957. The expression of affection in Russian proper names. *Slavic and East European Journal* 1:196–210.

————. 1968. *Declension and gradation of Russian substantives*. The Hague: Mouton.

Šteinfeldt, E. A. 1974. *Russian word count*. Moscow: Progress.

Stevenson, Burton. 1946. *Stevenson's book of quotations*. London: Cassell.

Stock, St. George. 1912. Fate (Greek and Roman). In Hastings 1908–26, v.5:786–90.

Stone, G. 1981. Pronominal address in Polish. *International Journal of Slavic Linguistics and Poetics* 23:55–76.

Strathern, Marilyn. 1968. Popokl: the question of morality. *Mankind* 6:553–62.

Suffrin, A. E. 1912. Fate (Jewish). In Hastings 1908–26, v.5:793–94.

Sukalenko, N. I. 1976. *Dvujazyčnye slovari i voprosy perevoda*. Kharkov: Vysšaja Škola.

Superanskaja, Aleksandra. 1969. *Struktura imeni sobstvennogo: fonologija i morfologija*. Moscow: Nauka.

————. 1970. Ličnye imena v oficial'nom i neoficial'nom upotreblenii. In Nikonov and Superanskaja 1970:180–94.

Suslova, Anna, and Aleksandra Superanskaja. 1978. *O russkix imenax*. Leningrad: Leninizdat.

Sussex, Roland, and Jerzy Zubrzycki, eds. 1985. *Polish people and culture in Australia*. Canberra: Australian National University. (Immigration Monographs, 3).

Swadesh, Morris. 1955. Towards greater accuracy in lexicostatistic dating. *International Journal of American Linguistics* 21:121–37.

Teichman, Jenny. 1974. *The mind and the soul: an introduction to the philosophy of mind*. London: Routledge and Kegan Paul.

Thomas à Kempis; see à Kempis, Thomas.

Thomson, Donald. 1972. *Kinship and behaviour in North Queensland*. Canberra: Australian Institute of Aboriginal Studies.

Thorndike, Edward, and Irving Lorge. 1963. *The teacher's word book of 30,000 words*. New York: Columbia University Teacher's College.

Tjutčev, F. 1976. *Stixotvorenija*. Moscow: Sovetskaja Rossija.

Todd, John. 1964. *Martin Luther: a biographical study*. London: Burns and Oates.

Tolstoy, Lev. 1928–37. *Tolstoy centenary edition: the works of Leo Tolstoy*. Trans. Louise Maude and Aylmer Maude. 21 vols. London: Oxford University Press.

————. 1928. *Resurrection*. Trans. Louise Maude. London: Oxford University Press.

————. 1930. *Anna Karenina*. Trans. Louise Maude and Aylmer Maude. London: Oxford University Press.

————. 1930–31. *War and peace*. Trans. Louise Maude and Aylmer Maude. 2 vols. London: Humphrey Milford.

————. 1945. *La guerre et la paix*. Trans. Henri Mongault. Paris: Gallimard.

————. 1949. *Vojna i mir*. Moscow: Gosudarstvennoe Izdatel'stvo Xudožestvennoj Literatury.

————. 1953. *Anna Karenina*. Moscow: Gosudarstvennoe Izdatel'stvo Xudožestvennoj Literatury.

————. 1978. *Detstvo, otročestvo, junost'*. (*Childhood, boyhood and youth.*) In *Sobranie sočinenij*, v.1. Moscow: Xudožestvennaja Literatura.

————. 1984. *Pis'ma*. In *Sobranie sočinenij*, v.19–20. Moscow: Xudožestvennaja Literatura.

————. 1985. *Dnevniki*. (*Diaries.*) In *Sobranie sočinenij*, v.21–22. Moscow: Xudožestvennaja Literatura.

————. No date. *Krieg und Frieden*. Trans. Ernst Strenge. Leipzig: Philipp Reclam.

Tomlin, Russell S., ed. 1987. *Coherence and grounding in discourse*. Amsterdam: John Benjamins.

Tonkinson, Robert. 1974. *The Jigalong mob: Aboriginal victors of the Desert Crusade*. Menlo Park: Cummings.

————. 1978. Semen versus spirit-child in a Western Desert culture. In Hiatt 1978b:18–92.

Torańska, Teresa. 1985. *Oni*. London: Anneks.

Treerat, Wipa. 1986. The semantics of 'I' and 'you' in Thai. Unpublished manuscript.

Trotter, Robert. 1983. Baby face. *Psychology Today* 17.8:14–21.

Tsanoff, Radoslav. 1947. *The moral ideals of our civilisation*. London: George Allen and Unwin.

Tsohatzidis, S. L., ed. 1990. *Meanings and prototypes: studies in linguistic categorization*. London: Routledge and Kegan Paul.

Tsvetaeva, Marina. 1965. *Izbrannye proizvedenija*. Ed. V. Orlov. Moscow: Sovetskij Pisatel'. (Biblioteka poeta, bol'šaja serija, 2).

————. 1969. *Pis'ma k Anne Teskovoj*. Prague: Academia.

————. 1972. *Neizdannye pis'ma*. Paris: YMCA-Press.

————. 1980. *Stixotvorenija i poemy*. 2 vols. London: Russica.

Turner, David. 1980. *Australian Aboriginal social organisation*. Canberra: Australian Institute of Aboriginal Studies.

Turner, Nigel. 1980. *Christian words*. Edinburgh: T. Clark.

Tuwim, Julian. 1955–64. *Wiersze*. 4 vols. Warsaw: Czytelnik.

Tyler, Stephen. 1969a. Context and variation in Koya kinship terminology. In Tyler 1969b: 487–503.

————, ed. 1969b. *Cognitive anthropology*. New York: Holt, Rinehart and Winston.

————. 1978. *The said and the unsaid*. New York: Academic Press.

Université de Paris VII. 1986. *Les particules énonciatives en russe contemporain*. Paris: Département de Recherches Linguistiqes (DRL), Laboratoire de Linguistique Formelle. (ATP nouvelles recherches sur le langage, Coll. ERA 6432).

Urbańczyk, S. 1968. Geneza spółgłosek ś ź ć w polskich sufiksach deminutywnych. In *Szkice z dziejów języka polskiego*, Warsaw, 1968:222–33. First pub. *Slavia* 1947–48, 28:290–99.

Ušakov, D. N., ed. 1940. *Tolkovyj slovar' russkogo jazyka*. 4 vols. Moscow: Gosudarstvennoe Izdatel'stvo Inostrannyx i Nacional'nyx Slovarej.

Van Buren, H. 1977. American ways with names. In Brislin 1977:111–30.

Van der Gaaf, W. 1904. *The transition from the impersonal to the personal construction in Middle English*. Anglistische Forschungen, 14. (Reprinted 1961, Amsterdam: Swets and Zeitlinger).

Vendler, Zeno. 1967. *Linguistics in philosophy*. Ithaca, N.Y.: Cornell University Press.

————. 1972. *Res cogitans*. Ithaca, N.Y.: Cornell University Press.

Verschueren, Jef. 1985. *What people say they do with words*. Norwood, N.J.: Ablex.

Vinogradov, Viktor. 1947. *Russkij jazyk*. Moscow: Učpedgiz.

Volek, Bronislava. 1987. *Emotive signs in language and semantic functioning of derived nouns in Russian*. Amsterdam: John Benjamins.

Voltaire, François M. Arouet de. 1769. *Dictionnaire philosophique*. Paris: Garnier.

Von Arnim, Johannes. 1964. *Stoicorum veterum fragmenta*. 4 vols. Stuttgart: B. G. Teubner.

Vossler, Karl. 1925. *Geist und Kultur in der Sprache*. Munich.

Wafer, James. 1982. *A simple introduction to Central Australian kinship systems*. Alice Springs: Institute for Aboriginal Development.

Wagatsuma, Hiroshi. 1977. Problems of language in cross-cultural research. In Adler 1977:141–50.

Wagner, H., and A. Manstead, eds. 1989. *Handbook of social psychophysiology*. New York: John Wiley.

Walicki, Andrzej. 1980. *A history of Russian thought from the Enlightenment to Marxism*. Oxford: Clarendon Press.

Wallace, Anthony, and John Atkins. 1969. The meaning of kinship terms. In Tyler 1969b:345–69.

Wallace, James D. 1978. *Virtues and vices*. Ithaca, N.Y.: Cornell University Press.

Walshe, W. Gilbert. 1912. Fate (Chinese). In Hastings 1908–26, v.5:783–85.

Wannan, Bill. 1963. *Tell' em I died game*. Melbourne: Lansdowne Press.

Ward, Russel. 1958. *The Australian legend*. Melbourne: Oxford University Press.

WDG. 1975. *Wörterbuch der deutschen Gegenwartsprache*. Eds. Ruth Klappenbach and Wolfgang Steinitz. 6 vols. Berlin: Akademie-Verlag.

Weber, Max. 1964. *The sociology of religion*. Trans. E. Fischoff. London: Methuen.

———. 1968 [1930]. *The Protestant ethic and the spirit of capitalism*. Trans. Talcott Parsons. London: Allen and Unwin.

Webster's new school and office dictionary. 1965. New York: The World Publishing Co./Crest Books.

Webster's new world dictionary. 1977. Springfield, Mass.: G. & C. Merriam.

Wędkiewicz, S. 1929. Kilka uwag o technice spieszczeń. *Język Polski* 1929:110–20.

Weydt, Harald. 1969. *Abtönungspartikel: die deutschen Modalwörter und ihre französischen Entsprechungen*. Bad Homburg: Gehlen.

———, Theo Herden, Elke Hentschel, and Dietmar Rösler, eds. 1983. *Kleine deutsche Partikellehre*. Stuttgart: Klett.

Wheeler, Marcus. 1972. *The Oxford Russian-English dictionary*. Oxford: Clarendon Press.

White, Geoffrey M. 1980. Conceptual universals in interpersonal language. *American Anthropologist* 82:759–81.

———, and John Kirkpatrick. 1985. *Person, self, and experience: exploring Pacific ethnopsychologies*. Berkeley: University of California Press.

Whorf, Benjamin Lee. 1956. *Language, thought, and reality: selected writings of Benjamin Lee Whorf*. Ed. John B. Carroll. New York: Wiley.

Wierzbicka, Anna. 1971. *Kocha—lubi—szanuje: medytacje semantyczne*. Warsaw: Wiedza Powszechna.

———. 1972a. *Semantic primitives*. Frankfurt: Athenäum.

———, ed. 1972b. *Semantyka i słownik*. Wrocław: Ossolineum.

———. 1973. The semantic structure of words for emotions. In Jakobson, van Schooneveld, and Worth 1973:499–505.

———. 1975. For the umpteenth time, kinship. *Language Sciences* 34:1–4.

———. 1980. *Lingua mentalis: the semantics of natural language*. Sydney: Academic Press.

———. 1984a. Diminutives and depreciatives. *Quaderni di Semantica* 5.1:123–30.

———. 1984b. *A small outline of the Polish language*. (Original title: *Mały portret języka polskiego—dla młodzieży w krajach anglosaskich*.) Adelaide: South Australian Department of Education.

————. 1985a. A semantic metalanguage for a cross-cultural comparison of speech acts and speech genres. *Language in Society* 14.4:491–513.

————. 1985b. Different cultures, different languages, different speech acts: Polish vs. English. *Journal of Pragmatics* 9.2:145–78.

————. 1985c. The double life of a bilingual. In Sussex and Zubrzycki 1985:187–223.

————. 1985d. *Lexicography and conceptual analysis*. Ann Arbor: Karoma.

————. 1986a. Human emotions: universal or culture-specific? *American Anthropologist* 88.3:584–94.

————. 1986b. Does language reflect culture? Evidence from Australian English. *Language and Society* 15:349–74.

————. 1986c. Metaphors linguists live by: Lakoff and Johnson contra Aristotle. *Papers in Linguistics* 19:287–313.

————. 1987a. Boys will be boys: radical semantics vs. radical pragmatics. *Language* 63.1:95–114.

————. 1987b. *English speech act verbs: a semantic dictionary*. Sydney–New York: Academic Press.

————. 1987c. Kinship semantics: lexical universals as a key to psychological reality. *Anthropological Linguistics* 29.2:131–56.

————. 1988a. L'amour, la colère, la joie, l'ennui: la sémantique des émotions dans une perspective transculturelle. *Langages* 89:97–101.

————. 1988b. The semantics and lexicography of 'natural kinds'. In Hyldgaard-Jensen and Zettersten 1988:155–82.

————. 1988c. *The semantics of grammar*. Amsterdam: John Benjamins.

————. 1989a. Semantic primitives and lexical universals. *Quaderni di Semantica* 10.1:103–21. (Round table on semantic primitives, 1).

————. 1989b. Semantic primitives: the expanding set. *Quaderni di Semantica* 10.2:309–32. (Round table on semantic primitives, 2).

————. 1989c. Prototypes in semantics and pragmatics: explicating attitudinal meanings in terms of prototypes. *Linguistics* 27:731–67.

————. 1990a. Prototypes save: on the uses and abuses of the notion of 'prototype' in linguistics and related fields. In Tsohatzidis 1990:347–71.

————. 1990b. The semantics of emotions: *fear* and its relatives in English. *Australian Journal of Linguistics* (special issue on the semantics of emotions) 10(2):359–75.

————. 1990c. *Duša* ('soul'), *toska* ('yearning'), *sud'ba* ('fate'): three key concepts in Russian language and Russian culture. In Zygmunt Saloni, ed., *Metody formalne w opisie języków słowiańskich*. Bialystok: Bialystok University Press. pp. 13–36.

————. 1990d. Antitotalitarian language in Poland: some mechanisms of linguistic self-defense. *Language in Society* 19:1–59.

————. 1991a. *Cross-cultural pragmatics: the semantics of social interaction*. Berlin: Mouton de Gruyter.

————. 1991b. Japanese key words and core cultural values. *Language in Society* 20:333–85.

————. 1991c. Lexical universals and universals of grammar. In Kefer and van der Auwera 1991:385–415.

————. In press a. Talking about emotions: semantics, culture and cognition. *Cognition and emotion* (special issue on basic emotions).

————. In press b. Cognitive domains and the structure of the lexicon. In: Susan Gelman, ed. *Domain specificity and cultural knowledge*. Cambridge, MA: Bradford Books.

————. In press c. Defining emotion concepts. *Cognitive Science*.

————. In press d. Freedom—libertas—svoboda—wolność: universal human ideals or culture-specific lexical items? In John Taylor, ed., *Language and the construal of the world*.

————. In press e. The search for universal semantic primitives. In Martin Pütz, ed. *Thirty years of linguistic evolution (a Festschrift for René Dirven)*.

————. Forthcoming. Reading human faces: a response to Ortony and Turner. *Pragmatics and Cognition*.

————, ed. 1990. *Australian Journal of Linguistics* 10(2) (special issue on the semantics of emotions) (Introduction 133–138.)

————, and Cliff Goddard, eds. Forthcoming. *Semantic and lexical universals*. Amsterdam: John Benjamins.

Wilkes, Gerald Alfred. 1978. *A dictionary of Australian colloquialisms*. Sydney: Sydney University Press.

Wilkins, David. 1986. Particles/clitics for criticism and complaint in Mparntwe Arrente (Aranda). *Journal of Pragmatics* 10:575–96.

————. 1988. Switch-reference in Mpartnwe Arrernte (Aranda): form, function, and problems of identity. In Austin 1988:141–76.

Williamson, David. 1972. *The removalists*. Sydney: Currency Press.

————. 1974. *Three plays*. Sydney: Currency Press.

Witkowski, T. 1964. *Grundbegriffe der Namenkunde*. Berlin.

Wittfogel, Karl. 1963. *Oriental despotism: a comparative study of total power*. New Haven, Conn.: Yale University Press.

Wittgenstein, Ludwig. 1953. *Philosophical investigations*. New York: Macmillan.

Wordick, F. J. F. 1979. *The Yindiibarndi language*. Canberra: Australian National University. (Pacific Linguistics, C71).

Wright, Arthur. 1922. *The colt from the country*. Sydney: NSW Bookstall.

Wyspiański, Stanisław. 1901. *Wesele*. First staged in Kraków, 1901. Reprinted in *Dramaty wybrane*. Kraków: Wydawnictwo Literackie 1972, v.1:133–321.

Yallop, Collin. 1977. *Alyawara*. Canberra: Australian Institute of Aboriginal Studies.

Zaliznjak, A. 1988. O semantike sožalenija. In Arutjunova 1988:189–213.

Zapolska, Gabriela. 1907. *Moralność pani Dulskiej*. Warsaw: Wydawnictwa Szkolne i Pedagogiczne. (Biblioteka analiz literackich, 47).

————. 1950. Żabusia. In *Pisma wybrane*, v.3:53–60. Warsaw: Książka i Wiedza.

Zarębina, M. 1954. O niektórych sposobach spieszczeń. *Język Polski* 1954:180–97.

Zasorina, L. N., ed. 1977. *Častotnyj slovar' russkogo jazyka*. Moscow: Russkij Jazyk.

Zawodny, J. K. 1978. *Nothing but honor*. Stanford: Hoover Institution Press.

Zingarelli, Nicola. 1970. *Vocabolario della lingua italiana*. 10th ed. Bologna: Zanichelli.

Zipf, George K. 1949. *Human behavior and the principle of least effort: an introduction to human ecology*. Facsimile ed. 1965. New York: Hafner.

Zwicky, Arnold M. 1974. Hey, Whatsyourname! *Chicago Linguistic Society, Papers* 10:781–801.

INDEX

N.B.: In addition to subjects and proper names, this index lists (*in italics*) words from several languages that are defined or discussed in the book. Definitions are indicated by the letter "d" following the page number. Non-English words are followed by a rough gloss for ease of reference, but this must not be taken as equivalent in meaning to the word discussed in the text. Abbreviations used include: class[ificatory], Dy[irbal], Es[kimo], exp[ressive], Fr[ench], Ge[rman], If[aluk], It[alian], Ka[yardild], La[tin], Om[pela], Pi[ntupi], Pj[Pitjantjatjara], Po[lish], Ru[ssian], suff[ix], Wa[lmatjari].